A/CN.4/SER.A/2005

YEARBOOK OF THE INTERNATIONAL LAW COMMISSION

2005

Volume I

Summary records of the meetings of the fifty-seventh session 2 May–3 June and 11 July–5 August 2005

UNITED NATIONS
New York and Geneva, 2012

NOTE

Symbols of United Nations documents are composed of capital letters combined with figures. Mention of such a symbol indicates a reference to a United Nations document.

References to the *Yearbook of the International Law Commission* are abbreviated to *Yearbook ...*, followed by the year (for example, *Yearbook ... 2004*).

The *Yearbook* for each session of the International Law Commission comprises two volumes:

Volume I: summary records of the meetings of the session;

Volume II (Part One): reports of special rapporteurs and other documents considered during the session;

Volume II (Part Two): report of the Commission to the General Assembly.

All references to these works and quotations from them relate to the final printed texts of the volumes of the Yearbook issued as United Nations publications.

*

* *

This volume contains the summary records of the meetings of the fifty-seventh session of the Commission (A/CN.4/SR.2831–A/CN.4/SR.2866), with the corrections requested by members of the Commission and such editorial changes as were considered necessary.

A/CN.4/SER.A/2005

UNITED NATIONS PUBLICATION

Sales No.: E.11.V.3
ISBN: 978-92-1-133705-1

ISSN 0082-8289

CONTENTS

	Page
Note	ii
Members of the Commission	vi
Officers	vi
Agenda	vii
Abbreviations	viii
Note concerning quotations	viii
Cases cited in the present volume	ix
Multilateral instruments cited in the present volume	xiii
Checklist of documents of the fifty-seventh session	xvii

SUMMARY RECORDS OF THE 2831st TO 2866th MEETINGS

Summary records of the first part of the fifty-seventh session, held at Geneva from 2 May to 3 June 2005

2831st meeting

Monday, 2 May 2005, at 3.10 p.m.

Opening of the session	1
Tribute to the memory of Robert Rosenstock	1
Election of officers	1
Adoption of the agenda	2
Organization of work of the session	2
Shared natural resources	2
Third report of the Special Rapporteur	2

2832nd meeting

Tuesday, 3 May 2005, at 10.05 a.m.

Shared natural resources (*continued*)	4
Third report of the Special Rapporteur (*continued*)	4
Organization of work of the session (*continued*)	11

2833rd meeting

Wednesday, 4 May 2005, at 10 a.m.

Shared natural resources (*continued*)	11
Third report of the Special Rapporteur (*continued*)	11
Organization of work of the session (*continued*)	17

2834th meeting

Friday, 6 May 2005, at 10 a.m.

Shared natural resources (*continued*)	17
Third report of the Special Rapporteur (*continued*)	17
Effects of armed conflicts on treaties	23
First report of the Special Rapporteur	23
Organization of work of the session (*continued*)	25

2835th meeting

Tuesday, 10 May 2005, at 10 a.m.

Effects of armed conflicts on treaties (*continued*)	25
First report of the Special Rapporteur (*continued*)	25
Shared natural resources (*continued*)	27
Third report of the Special Rapporteur (*continued*)	27

2836th meeting

Wednesday, 11 May 2005 at 10.15 a.m.

Shared natural resources (*continued*)	33
Third report of the Special Rapporteur (*concluded*)	33
Effects of armed conflicts on treaties (*continued*)	35
First report of the Special Rapporteur (*continued*)	35
Organization of work of the session (*continued*)	42

2837th meeting

Thursday, 12 May 2005, at 10 a.m.

Effects of armed conflicts on treaties (*continued*)	42
First report of the Special Rapporteur (*continued*)	42

2838th meeting

Friday, 13 May 2005, at 10.05 a.m.

Effects of armed conflicts on treaties (*continued*)	48
First report of the Special Rapporteur (*continued*)	48

2839th meeting

Tuesday, 17 May 2005, at 10 a.m.

Effects of armed conflicts on treaties (*continued*)	57
First report of the Special Rapporteur (*continued*)	57
Responsibility of international organizations	63
Third report of the Special Rapporteur	63

2840th meeting

Wednesday, 18 May 2005, at 10 a.m.

Effects of armed conflicts on treaties (*concluded*)	65
First report of the Special Rapporteur (*concluded*)	65
Responsibility of international organizations (*continued*)	69
Third report of the Special Rapporteur (*continued*)	69
Organization of work of the session (*continued*)	74

2841st meeting

Thursday, 19 May 2005, at 10 a.m.

Responsibility of international organizations (*continued*)	75
Third report of the Special Rapporteur (*continued*)	75

2842nd meeting

Friday, 20 May 2005, at 10.05 a.m.

Responsibility of international organizations (*continued*)	82
Third report of the Special Rapporteur (*continued*)	82
Reservations to treaties	88
Report of the Drafting Committee	88

2843rd meeting

Tuesday, 24 May 2005, at 10 a.m.

Responsibility of international organizations (*continued*)	90
Third report of the Special Rapporteur (*concluded*)	90

2844th meeting

Wednesday, 25 May 2005, at 10.05 a.m.

Responsibility of international organizations (*continued*)	97
Oral report of the Chairperson of the Working Group	97
Diplomatic protection	98
Sixth report of the Special Rapporteur	98
Statement by the Under-Secretary-General of Legal Affairs, Legal Counsel	101
Organization of work of the session (*continued*)	107

Page

2845th meeting

Friday, 27 May 2005, at 10.10 a.m.

Diplomatic protection (*continued*) 107
Sixth report of the Special Rapporteur (*continued*) 107

2846th meeting

Tuesday, 31 May 2005, at 10.05 a.m.

Diplomatic protection (*concluded*) 109
Sixth report of the Special Rapporteur (*concluded*) 109

2847th meeting

Wednesday, 1 June 2005, at 10 a.m.

Cooperation with other bodies 115
Statement of the Observer from the Inter-American Juridical Committee 115

2848th meeting

Friday, 3 June 2005, at 10.05 a.m.

Responsibility of international organizations (*concluded*) 119
Report of the Drafting Committee 119
Organization of work of the session (*continued*) 123

Summary records of the second part of the fifty-seventh session, held at Geneva from 11 July to 5 August 2005

2849th meeting

Monday, 11 July 2005, at 3 p.m.

Tribute to the memory of Qizhi He 125
Expulsion of aliens 125
Preliminary report of the Special Rapporteur 125

2850th meeting

Wednesday, 13 July 2005, at 10.05 a.m.

Cooperation with other bodies (*continued*) 128
Expulsion of aliens (*continued*) 128
Preliminary report of the Special Rapporteur (*continued*) 128

2851st meeting

Thursday, 14 July 2005, at 10 a.m.

Cooperation with other bodies (*continued*) 136
Visit by the President of the International Court of Justice 136
Expulsion of aliens (*continued*) 142
Preliminary report of the Special Rapporteur (*continued*) 142

2852nd meeting

Friday, 15 July 2005, at 10.05 a.m.

Expulsion of aliens (*concluded*) 144
Preliminary report of the Special Rapporteur (*concluded*) 144
Unilateral acts of states 152
Eighth report of the Special Rapporteur 152

2853rd meeting

Tuesday, 19 July 2005, at 10.05 a.m.

Unilateral acts of states (*continued*) 153
Eighth report of the Special Rapporteur (*continued*) 153
Cooperation with other bodies (*continued*) 156
Statement by the Observer from the Asian–African Legal Consultative Organization 156

Page

2854th meeting

Wednesday, 20 July 2005, at 10.05 a.m.

Unilateral acts of states (*continued*) 160
Eighth report of the Special Rapporteur (*continued*) 160
Reservations to treaties (*continued*) 166
Tenth report of the Special Rapporteur 166

2855th meeting

Thursday, 21 July 2005, at 10.05 a.m.

Unilateral acts of states (*continued*) 171
Eighth report of the Special Rapporteur (*concluded*) 171

2856th meeting

Friday, 22 July 2005, at 10.05 a.m.

Reservations to treaties (*continued*) 177
Tenth report of the Special Rapporteur (*continued*) 177

2857th meeting

Tuesday, 26 July 2005, at 10.05 a.m.

Reservations to treaties (*continued*) 187
Tenth report of the Special Rapporteur (*continued*) 187

2858th meeting

Wednesday, 27 July 2005, at 10.05 a.m.

Reservations to treaties (*continued*) 193
Tenth report of the Special Rapporteur (*continued*) 193

2859th meeting

Thursday, 28 July 2005, at 10.05 a.m.

Reservations to treaties (*concluded*) 204
Tenth report of the Special Rapporteur (*concluded*) 204
Unilateral acts of states (*concluded*) 208
Report of the Working Group 208
Programmes, procedures and working methods of the Commission and its documentation 208
Report of the Planning Group 208
Fragmentation of international law: difficulties arising from the diversification and expansion of international law 210

2860th meeting

Friday, 29 July 2005, at 10.05 a.m.

Cooperation with other bodies (*concluded*) 211
Visit by representatives of the Council of Europe 211
Organization of work of the session (*continued*) 217
Fragmentation of international law: difficulties arising from the diversification and expansion of international law (*continued*) 217

2861st meeting

Tuesday, 2 August 2005, at 10.05 a.m.

Draft report of the International Law Commission on the work of its fifty-seventh session 220
Chapter IV. Shared natural resources 220
Chapter V. Effects of armed conflicts on treaties 223

2862nd meeting

Tuesday, 2 August 2005, at 3.10 p.m.

Draft report of the Commission on the work of its fifty-seventh session (*continued*) 226
Chapter V. Effects of armed conflicts on treaties (*continued*) 226
Chapter VI. Responsibility of international organizations 227

	Page
2863rd meeting	
Wednesday, 3 August 2005, at 10.05 a.m.	
Shared natural resources (*concluded*)	232
Report of the Working Group	232
Draft report of the Commission on the work at its fifty-seventh session (*continued*)	234
Chapter VI. Responsibility of international organizations (*concluded*)	234
Chapter VII. Diplomatic protection	235
Chapter VIII. Expulsion of aliens	235
Chapter V. Effects of armed conflicts on treaties (*continued*)	237
Chapter IX. Unilateral acts of states	237
2864th meeting	
Wednesday, 3 August 2005, at 3.05 p.m.	
Fragmentation of international law: difficulties arising from the diversification and expansion of international law (*concluded*)	239
2865th meeting	
Thursday, 4 August 2005, at 10.05 a.m.	
Draft report of the International Law Commission on the work of its fifty-seventh session (*continued*)	240
Chapter IX. Unilateral acts of states (*concluded*)	240
Chapter X. Reservations to treaties	242
Chapter XI. Fragmentation of international law: difficulties arising from the diversification and expansion of international law	243
Chapter XII. Other decisions and conclusions of the Commission	244
Chapter I. Introduction	244
Chapter II. Summary of the work of the Commission at its fifty-seventh session	244
2866th meeting	
Friday, 5 August 2005, at 10.05 a.m.	
Draft report of the Commission on the work of its fifty-seventh session (*concluded*)	245
Chapter X. Reservations to treaties (*concluded*)	245
Chapter III. Specific issues on which comments would be of particular interest to the Commission	249
Chapter V. Effects of armed conflicts on treaties (*concluded*)	252
Closure of the session	252

MEMBERS OF THE COMMISSION

Name	*Country of nationality*
Mr. Emmanuel Akwei ADDO	Ghana
Mr. Husain AL-BAHARNA	Bahrain
Mr. Ali Mohsen Fetais AL-MARRI	Qatar
Mr. João Clemente BAENA SOARES	Brazil
Mr. Ian BROWNLIE	United Kingdom of Great Britain and Northern Ireland
Mr. Enrique CANDIOTI	Argentina
Mr. Choung Il CHEE	Republic of Korea
Mr. Pedro COMISSÁRIO AFONSO	Mozambique
Mr. Riad DAOUDI	Syrian Arab Republic
Mr. Christopher John Robert DUGARD	South Africa
Mr. Constantin ECONOMIDES	Greece
Ms. Paula ESCARAMEIA	Portugal
Mr. Salifou FOMBA	Mali
Mr. Giorgio GAJA	Italy
Mr. Zdzislaw GALICKI	Poland
Mr. Peter KABATSI	Uganda
Mr. Maurice KAMTO	Cameroon
Mr. James Lutabanzibwa KATEKA	United Republic of Tanzania
Mr. Fathi KEMICHA	Tunisia
Mr. Roman Anatolyevitch KOLODKIN	Russian Federation
Mr. Martti KOSKENNIEMI	Finland
Mr. William MANSFIELD	New Zealand
Mr. Michael MATHESON	United States of America
Mr. Teodor Viorel MELESCANU	Romania
Mr. Djamchid MOMTAZ	Islamic Republic of Iran
Mr. Bernd NIEHAUS	Costa Rica
Mr. Didier OPERTTI BADAN	Uruguay
Mr. Guillaume PAMBOU-TCHIVOUNDA	Gabon
Mr. Alain PELLET	France
Mr. Pemmaraju Sreenivasa RAO	India
Mr. Víctor RODRÍGUEZ CEDEÑO	Bolivarian Republic of Venezuela
Mr. Bernardo SEPÚLVEDA	Mexico
Ms. Hanqin XUE	China
Mr. Chusei YAMADA	Japan

OFFICERS

Chairperson: Mr. Djamchid MOMTAZ

First Vice-Chairperson: Mr. Guillaume PAMBOU-TCHIVOUNDA

Second Vice-Chairperson: Mr. Roman A. KOLODKIN

Chairperson of the Drafting Committee: Mr. William MANSFIELD

Rapporteur: Mr. Bernd NIEHAUS

Mr. Nicolas Michel, Under-Secretary-General of Legal Affairs, United Nations Legal Counsel, represented the Secretary-General. Mr. Václav Mikulka, Director of the Codification Division of the Office of Legal Affairs, acted as Secretary to the Commission and, in the absence of the United Nations Legal Counsel, represented the Secretary-General.

AGENDA

The Commission adopted the following agenda at its 2831st meeting, held on 2 May 2005:

1. Organization of work of the session.
2. Diplomatic protection.
3. Responsibility of international organizations.
4. Shared natural resources.
5. Unilateral acts of States.
6. Reservations to treaties.
7. Expulsion of aliens.
8. Effects of armed conflicts on treaties.
9. Fragmentation of international law: difficulties arising from the diversification and expansion of international law.
10. Programme, procedures and working methods of the Commission and its documentation.
11. Cooperation with other bodies.
12. Date and place of the fifty-eighth session.
13. Other business.

ABBREVIATIONS

AALCO	Asian–African Legal Consultative Organization
CAHDI	Committee of Legal Advisers on Public International Law
ESIL	European Society of International Law
GRECO	Group of States against Corruption
IAEA	International Atomic Energy Agency
ICJ	International Court of Justice
ICRC	International Committee of the Red Cross
IMF	International Monetary Fund
IOM	International Organization for Migration
MERCOSUR	Southern Common Market
NATO	North Atlantic Treaty Organization
OAS	Organization of American States
OHCHR	Office of the High Commissioner for Human Rights
PCIJ	Permanent Court of International Justice
UNCITRAL	United Nations Commission on International Trade Law
UNESCO	United Nations Educational, Scientific and Cultural Organization
UNHCR	United Nations High Commissioner for Refugees
UNICEF	United Nations Children's Fund
UNRIAA	United Nations, Reports of International Arbitral Awards
WTO	World Trade Organization
UNICEF	Fonds des Nations Unies pour l'enfance
UNITAR	Institut des Nations Unies pour la formation et la recherche

*
* *

AJIL	*American Journal of International Law*
ILM	*International Legal Materials* (Washington, D.C.)
I.C.J. Reports	ICJ, *Reports of Judgments, Advisory Opinions and Orders*
ILR	*International Law Reports*
P.C.I.J., Series A	PCIJ, *Collection of Judgments* (Nos. 1–24: up to and including 1930)
P.C.I.J., Series A/B	PCIJ, *Judgments, Orders and Advisory Opinions* (Nos. 40–80: beginning in 1931)
UNRIAA	United Nations, *Reports of International Arbitral Awards*

*
* *

In the present volume, "International Tribunal for the Former Yugoslavia" refers to the International Tribunal for the Prosecution of Persons Responsible for Serious Violations of International Humanitarian Law Committed in the Territory of the Former Yugoslavia since 1991; and "International Tribunal for Rwanda" refers to the International Criminal Tribunal for the Prosecution of Persons Responsible for Genocide and Other Serious Violations of International Humanitarian Law Committed in the Territory of Rwanda and Rwandan Citizens Responsible for Genocide and Other Such Violations Committed in the Territory of Neighbouring States between 1 January and 31 December 1994.

*
* *

NOTE CONCERNING QUOTATIONS

In quotations, words or passages in italics followed by an asterisk were not italicized in the original text.

Unless otherwise indicated, quotations from works in languages other than English have been translated by the Secretariat.

*
* *

The Internet address of the International Law Commission is **www.un.org/law/ilc/.**

CASES CITED IN THE PRESENT VOLUME

Case	*Nature and source of the decision*
Administrative Decision No. V (United States of America v. *Germany)*	*Decision of 31 October 1924, UNRIAA*, vol. VII (Sales No. 1956.V.5), p. 119.
Application of the Convention of 1902 governing the Guardianship of Infants	*(Netherlands* v. *Sweden), Judgment of 28 November 1958, I.C.J. Reports 1958*, p. 55.
Application of the Convention on the Prevention and Punishment of the Crime of Genocide	*Preliminary Objections, Judgment, I.C.J. Reports 1996*, p. 595.
Argento v. *Horn* et al.	ILR, vol. 24, p. 883.
Armed Activities on the Territory of the Congo	*(New Application: 2002) (Democratic Republic of the Congo* v. *Rwanda), Provisional Measures, Order of 10 July 2002, I.C.J. Reports 2002*, p. 219.
	(Democratic Republic of the Congo v. *Uganda), Order of 7 November 2002, I.C.J. Reports 2002*, p. 604.
Arrest Warrant	*Arrest Warrant of 11 April 2000 (Democratic Republic of the Congo v. Belgium), Judgment, I.C.J. Reports 2002*, p. 3.
Avena and Other Mexican Nationals	*Avena and Other Mexican Nationals (Mexico v. United States of America), Provisional Measures, Order of 5 February 2003, I.C.J. Reports 2003*, p.77.
	Judgment, I.C.J. Reports 2004, p. 12.
Barcelona Traction	*Barcelona Traction, Light and Power Company, Limited, Second Phase, Judgment, I.C.J. Reports 1970*, p. 3.
Belilos	*Belilos* v. *Switzerland, Judgement of 29 April 1988, Application no. 10328/83*, European Court of Human Rights, *Series A: Judgments and Decisions*, vol. 132.
Ben Tillett	*Ben Tillett Arbitration (Great Britain* v. *Belgium), Revue générale de droit international public*, vol. VI, No. 46 (1899), p. 46.
Boffolo case	UNRIAA, Vol. X (Sales No. 1960.V.4), p. 528.
Bosphorus	*Bosphorus Hava Yollari Turizm ve Ticaret Anonim Şirketi* v. *Ireland, Decision of 13 September 2001, Application no. 45036/98*, European Court of Human Rights.
Breard	*Vienna Convention on Consular Relations (Paraguay* v. *United States of America), Provisional Measures, Order of 9 April 1998, I.C.J. Reports 1998*, p. 248.
Canevaro	*(Italy* v. *Peru), Award of 3 May 1912*, Permanent Court of Arbitration, in J. B. Scott, ed., *The Hague Court Reports*, New York, Oxford University Press, 1916.
Cantoni v. *France*	*Judgement of 15 November 1996, Application no. 17862/91*, European Court of Human Rights, *Reports of Judgments and Decisions*, 1996-V, p. 1614.
Certain Criminal Proceedings in France	*(Republic of Congo* v. *France), Provisional Measure, Order of 17 June 2003, I.C.J. Reports 2003*, p. 102.
Certain Expenses of the United Nations	*(Article 17, paragraph 2, of the Charter), Advisory Opinion of 20 July 1962, I.C.J. Reports 1962*, p. 151.
Certain Norwegian Loans	*Judgment of 6 July 1957, I.C. J. Reports 1957*, p. 9.
Certain Phosphate Lands in Nauru	*(Nauru* v. *Australia), Preliminary Objections, Judgment, I.C.J. Reports 1992*, p. 240.
Certain Property	*(Liechtenstein* v. *Germany), Preliminary Objections, Judgment of 10 February 2005, I.C.J. Reports 2005*, p. 6.
Clark v. *Allen*	9 June 1947, Circuit Court of Appeals for the Ninth Circuit, 331 U.S. 503.
Clark Claim	J. B. Moore, *History and Digest of the International Arbitrations to which the United States has been a Party*, vol. III, 1898, p. 2738.
Corfu Channel	*Merits, Judgment, I.C.J. Reports 1949*, p. 4.
Costa v. *E.N.E.L.*	*Judgement of 15 July 1964, Case 6/64, Court of Justice of the European Communities, European Court Reports 1964*, p. 585.

Case	*Nature and source of the decision*
Demirel	*Meryem Demirel* v. *Stadt Schwäbisch Gmünd, Judgement of 30 September 1987, Case 12/86, European Court Reports 1987*, p. 3719.
Dorsch Consult v. *Council and Commission*	*Judgement of 28 April 1998, Case T-184/95, European Court Reports 1998-II*, p. II-670.
	Judgement of the Court (Fifth Chamber) of 5 June 2000, case C-237/98P, European Court Reports 2000, p. I-04549.
English Channel	*Case concerning the delimitation of the continental shelf between the United Kingdom of Great Britain and Northern Ireland, and the French Republic, decisions of 30 June 1977 and 14 March 1978*, UNRIAA, vol. XVIII (Sales No. E/F.80.V.7), pp. 3 and 271.
European Parliament v. *Council of the European Union*	*Judgement of 2 March 1994, Case C-316/91, Reports of Cases before the Court of Justice and the Court of First Instance 1994-3*, p. I-653.
Fisheries	*(United Kingdom* v. *Norway), Judgment of 18 December 1951, I.C.J. Reports 1951*, p. 116.
Frontier Dispute (Benin/Niger)	*Judgment, I.C.J. Reports 2005*, p. 90.
Frontier Dispute	*(Burkina Faso/Republic of Mali), Judgment, I.C.J. Reports 1986*, p. 554.
Gabčíkovo–Nagymaros Project	*(Hungary/Slovakia), Judgment, I.C.J. Reports 1997*, p. 7.
Gallina v. *Fraser*	United States, Court of Appeals, Second Circuit, Decision of 15 May 1959, ILR, vol. 31 (1960), p. 356.
International Technical Products Corporation v. *The Government of the Islamic Republic of Iran*	*Iran–United States Claims Tribunal Reports*, 1985, vol. 9, p. 18.
Interpretation of the Agreement of 25 March 1951 between the WHO and Egypt	Advisory Opinion, *I.C.J. Reports 1980*, p. 73.
Kasikili/Sedudu Island	(Botswana/Namibia), Judgment, *I.C.J Reports 1999*, p. 1045.
Kennedy v. *Trinidad and Tobago*	Communication No. 845/1999, Decision adopted on 2 November 1999, Report of the Human Rights Committee, vol. II, *Official Records of the General Assembly, Fifty-fifth Session, Supplement No. 40* (A/55/40), Annex XI, p. 258.
Krohn & Co. v. *Commission of the European Communities*	*Krohn & Co. Import-Export (GmbH & Co., KG)* v. *Commission of the European Communities*, Case 175/84, Judgment of 26 February 1986, Reports of Cases before the Court of Justice and the Court of First Instance (1986-2), p. 768.
LaGrand	*(Germany* v. *United States of America)*, Judgment, *I.C.J. Reports 2001*, p. 466.
Lake Lanoux Arbitration	*(France* v. *Spain)*, Award of 16 November 1957, UNRIAA, vol. XII (Sales No. 1963.V.3), p. 281 (French original). See also *ILR*, vol. 24, p. 101.
Land and Maritime Boundary between Cameroon and Nigeria	*(Cameroon* v. *Nigeria: Equatorial Guinea intervening)*, Judgment of 10 October 2002, *I.C.J. Reports 2002*, p. 303.
Legal Consequences of the Construction of a Wall in the Occupied Palestinian Territory	Advisory Opinion, *I.C.J. Reports 2004*, p. 136.
Legal Status of Eastern Greenland	Judgment, 1933, *P.C.I.J., Series A/B*, No. 53, p. 22.
Legality of the Threat or Use of Nuclear Weapons	Advisory Opinion, *I.C.J. Reports 1996*, p. 226.
Legality of Use of Force	*Legality of Use of Force* (*Yugoslavia* v. *Belgium*), Provisional Measures, Order of 2 June 1999, *I.C.J. Reports 1999*, p. 124. (*Yugoslavia* v. *Canada*), *ibid.*, p. 259. (*Yugoslavia* v. *France*), *ibid.*, p. 363. (*Yugoslavia* v. *Germany*), *ibid.*, p. 422. (*Yugoslavia* v. *Italy*), *ibid.*, p. 481. (*Yugoslavia* v. *Netherlands*), *ibid.*, p. 542. (*Yugoslavia* v. *Portugal*), *ibid.*, p. 656. (*Yugoslavia* v. *Spain*), *ibid.*, p. 761. (*Yugoslavia* v. *United Kingdom*), *ibid.*, p. 826. (*Yugoslavia* v. *United States of America*), *ibid.*, p. 916. (*Yugoslavia* v. *Belgium*), Order of 20 March 2002, *I.C.J. Reports 2002*, p. 192. (*Yugoslavia* v. *Canada*), *ibid.*, p. 195. (*Yugoslavia* v. *France*), *ibid.*, p. 198. (*Yugoslavia* v. *Germany*), *ibid.*, p. 201. (*Yugoslavia* v. *Italy*), *ibid.*, p. 204. (*Yugoslavia* v. *Netherlands*), *ibid.*, p. 207. (Yugoslavia v. *Portugal*), *ibid.*, p. 210. (*Yugoslavia* v. *United Kingdom*), *ibid.*, p. 213. (*Serbia and Montenegro* v. *Belgium*), Preliminary Objections, Judgment, *I.C.J. Reports 2004*, p. 279.

Case	*Nature and source of the decision*
Legality of Use of Force	(*Serbia and Montenegro* v. *Canada*), *ibid.*, p. 429. (*Serbia and Montenegro* v. *France*), *ibid.*, p. 575. (*Serbia and Montenegro* v. *Germany*), *ibid.*, p. 720. (*Serbia and Montenegro* v. *Italy*), *ibid.*, p. 865. (*Serbia and Montenegro* v. *Netherlands*), *ibid.*, p. 1011. (*Serbia and Montenegro* v. *Portugal*), *ibid.*, p. 1160. (*Serbia and Montenegro* v. *United Kingdom*), *ibid.*, p. 1307.
Legality of the Threat or Use by a State of Nuclear Weapons in Armed Conflict	Advisory Opinion, *I.C.J. Reports 1996*, p. 66.
Lockerbie	*Questions of Interpretation and Application of the 1971 Montreal Convention arising from the Aerial Incident at Lockerbie* (*Libyan Arab Jamahiriya* v. *United Kingdom*), Provisional Measures, Order of 14 April 1992, *I.C.J. Reports 1992*, p. 3.
Loizidou v. *Turkey*	Judgement of 18 December 1996, Application no. 15318/89, European Court of Human Rights, *Reports of Judgments and Decisions 1996-VI.*
Maritime Delimitation in the Black Sea	(*Romania* v. *Ukraine*), Application instituting proceedings, filed in the Registry of the Court on 16 September 2004, 2004 General List No. 132.
Masinimport v. *Scottish Mechanical Light Industries Ltd.*	*ILR*, vol. 74 (1987), p. 559.
Matthews	*Matthews* v. *the United Kingdom*, Judgement of 18 February 1999, Application No. 24833/94, Grand Chamber, European Court of Human Rights, *Reports of Judgments and Decisions, 1999-I*, p. 251.
Mavrommatis	*Mavrommatis Palestine Concessions*, Judgment No. 2, 1924, *P.C.I.J., Series A*, No. 2, p. 6.
Mergé Claim	Decision No. 55 of 10 June 1955, UNRIAA, vol. XIV (Sales No. 1965.V.4), p. 236.
Military and Paramilitary Activities in and against Nicaragua	(*Nicaragua* v. *United States of America*), Jurisdiction and Admissibility, Judgment, *I.C.J. Reports 1984*, p. 392.
MV Tampa case	*Ruddock* v. *Vadarlis*, Federal Court of Australia, 18 September 2001, ILR, vol. 131, p. 83.
North Sea Continental Shelf	Judgment, *I.C.J. Reports 1969*, p. 3.
Nottebohm	*(Liechtenstein* v. *Guatemala)*, Second Phase, Judgment of 6 April 1955, *I.C.J. Reports 1955*, p. 4.
Nuclear Tests	*(Australia* v. *France)*, Judgment of 20 December 1974, *I.C.J. Reports 1974*, p. 253. *(New Zealand* v. *France)*, *ibid.*, p. 457.
Oil Platforms	(*Islamic Republic of Iran* v. *United States of America*), Preliminary Objection, Judgment, *I.C.J. Reports 1996*, p. 803.
Prince Hans-Adam II of Liechtenstein v. *Germany*	Judgement of 27 June 2001, Application no. 42527/98, European Court of Human Rights, *Reports of Judgments and Decisions 2001-VIII.*
"Rainbow Warrior"	*Case concerning the difference between New Zealand and France concerning the interpretation or application of two agreements, concluded on 9 July 1986 between the two States and which related to the problems arising from the* Rainbow Warrior *affair*, Decision of 30 April 1990, UNRIAA, vol. XX (Sales No. E/F.93.V.3), p. 215.
Rann of Kutch case	*The Indo-Pakistan Western Boundary (Rann of Kutch)* Case (*India* v. *Pakistan*), Award of 19 February 1968, UNRIAA, vol. XVII (Sales No. E/F.80.V.2), p. 1.
Reparation for Injuries	*Reparation for Injuries Suffered in the Service of the United Nations*, Advisory Opinion, *I.C.J. Reports 1949*, p. 174.
Reservations to the Convention on Genocide	*Reservations to the Convention on the Prevention and Punishment of the Crime of Genocide*, Advisory Opinion, *I.C.J. Reports 1951*, p. 15.
Restrictions to the Death Penalty	(Arts. 4(2) and 4(4) American Convention on Human Rights), Advisory Opinion OC–3/83 of 8 September 1983, *Inter-American Court of Human Rights*, Series A, No. 3.
Slivenko	*Slivenko* v. *Latvia*, Application No. 48321/99, Decision of 9 October 2003, European Court of Human Rights, *Reports of Judgments and Decisions*, 2003-X.

Case	*Nature and source of the decision*
Tadić	*Prosecutor* v. *Duško Tadić a/k/a "Dule"*, Decision on the Defence Motion of Interlocutory Appeal on Jurisdiction, Case No. IT-94-1-AR72, 2 October 1995, International Tribunal for the Former Yugoslavia, ILM, vol. 35 (1996), p. 37. See also United Nations, *Juridical Yearbook 1995*, Part Three, p. 501.
Techt v. *Hughes*	8 June 1920, Court of Appeals of New York, 229 N.Y. 222.
Temeltasch v. *Switzerland*	Application No. 9116/80, Decision of 5 May 1982, Council of Europe, European Commission of Human Rights, *Decisions and Reports*, vol. 31, p. 120.
Temple of Preah Vihear	(*Cambodia* v. *Thailand*), Preliminary Objections, Judgment, *I.C.J. Reports 1961*, p. 17. *Temple of Preah Vihear*, Merits, Judgment, *I.C.J. Reports 1962*, p. 6.
United States Diplomatic and Consular Staff in Tehran	Judgment, *I.C.J. Reports 1980*, p. 3.
Van Gend and Loos	*NV Algemene Transport- en Expeditie Onderneming van Gend & Loos* v. *Netherlands Inland Revenue Administration*, Judgement of 5 February 1963, Case 26/62, *European Court Reports 1963*, p. 3.
"*Virginius*"	Case of the "*Virginius*", reported in J. B. Moore, *A Digest of International Law*, Washington D.C., U.S. Government Printing Office, 1906, vol. 2, p. 895.
Western Sahara	Advisory Opinion, *I.C.J. Reports 1975*, p. 12.
Yeager v. *Islamic Republic of Iran*	Case No. 10199, Award No. 324-10199-1 of 2 November 1987, *Iran–United States Claims Tribunal Reports*, 1987, vol. 17, p. 92.

MULTILATERAL INSTRUMENTS CITED IN THE PRESENT VOLUME

	Source
Pacific settlement of international disputes	
General Treaty for Renunciation of War as an Instrument of National Policy (Kellogg-Briand Pact) (Paris, 27 August 1928)	League of Nations, *Treaty Series*, vol. XCIV, No. 2137, p. 57.
European Convention for the Peaceful Settlement of Disputes (Strasbourg, 29 April 1957)	United Nations, *Treaty Series*, vol. 320, No. 4646, p. 243.
Privileges and immunities, diplomatic and consular relations, etc.	
Vienna Convention on Diplomatic Relations (Vienna, 18 April 1961)	United Nations, *Treaty Series*, vol. 500, No. 7310, p. 95.
Vienna Convention on Consular Relations (Vienna, 24 April 1963)	*Ibid.*, vol. 596, No. 8638, p. 261.
United Nations Convention on Jurisdictional Immunities of States and their Property (New York, 2 December 2004)	*Official Records of the General Assembly, Fifty-ninth Session, Supplement No. 49* (A/59/49), vol. I, Resolution 59/38.
Human rights	
Convention on the Prevention and Punishment of the Crime of Genocide (New York, 9 December 1948)	United Nations, *Treaty Series*, vol. 78, No. 1021, p. 277.
Convention for the Protection of Human Rights and Fundamental Freedoms (European Convention on Human Rights) (Rome, 4 November 1950)	*Ibid.*, vol. 213, No. 2889, p. 221.
Protocol No. 4 to the Convention of 4 November 1950 for the Protection of Human Rights and Fundamental Freedoms, securing certain rights and freedoms other than those already included in the Convention and in the first Protocol thereto (Strasbourg, 16 September 1963)	*Ibid.*, vol. 1496, No. 2889, p. 263.
Protocol No. 6 to the Convention of 4 November 1950 for the Protection of Human Rights and Fundamental Freedoms, concerning the Abolition of the Death Penalty (Strasbourg, 28 April 1983)	*Ibid.*, p. 281.
Protocol No. 7 to the Convention for the Protection of Human Rights and Fundamental Freedoms (Strasbourg, 22 November 1984)	*Ibid.*, vol. 1525, No. 2889, p. 195.
Protocol No. 12 to the Convention for the Protection of Human Rights and Fundamental Freedoms (Rome, 4 November 2000)	*Ibid.*, vol. 2465, No. 2889, p. 203.
Protocol No. 14 to the Convention for the Protection of Human Rights and Fundamental Freedoms, amending the control system of the Convention (Strasbourg, 13 May 2004)	Council of Europe, *European Treaty Series*, No. 194.
International Covenant on Civil and Political Rights (New York, 16 December 1966)	United Nations, *Treaty Series*, vol. 999, No. 14668, p. 171.
International Covenant on Economic, Social and Cultural Rights (New York, 16 December 1966)	*Ibid.*, vol. 993, No. 14531, p. 3.
American Convention on Human Rights: "Pact of San José, Costa Rica" (San José, Costa Rica, 22 November 1969)	*Ibid.*, vol. 1144, No. 17955, p. 123.
Convention on the Elimination of All Forms of Discrimination against Women (New York, 18 December 1979)	*Ibid.*, vol. 1249, No. 20378, p. 13.
Convention against Torture and Other Cruel, Inhuman or Degrading Treatment or Punishment (New York, 10 December 1984)	*Ibid.*, vol. 1465, No. 24841, p. 85.
European Convention for the prevention of torture and inhuman or degrading treatment or punishment (Strasbourg, 26 November 1987)	*Ibid.*, vol. 1561, No. 27161, p. 363.
Convention on the rights of the child (New York, 20 November 1989)	*Ibid.*, vol. 1577, No. 27531, p. 3.
Optional Protocol to the Convention on the Rights of the Child on the sale of children, child prostitution and child pornography (New York, 25 May 2000)	*Ibid.*, vol. 2171, No. 27531, p. 227.
International Convention on the Protection of the Rights of All Migrant Workers and Members of their Families (New York, 18 December 1990)	*Ibid.*, vol. 2220, No. 39481, p. 3
Framework Convention for the Protection of National Minorities (Strasbourg, 1 February 1995)	*Ibid.*, vol. 2151, No. 37548, p. 243.

	Source
Convention for the Protection of Human Rights and Dignity of the Human Being with regard to the Application of Biology and Medicine: Convention on Human Rights and Biomedicine (Oviedo, 4 April 1997)	*Ibid.*, vol. 2137, No. 37266, p. 171.
Additional Protocol to the Convention on Human Rights and Biomedicine, concerning Biomedical Research (Strasbourg, 25 January 2005)	Council of Europe, *European Treaty Series*, No. 195.
Council of Europe Convention on Action against Trafficking in Human Beings (Warsaw, 16 May 2005)	*Ibid.*, No. 197.
Refugees and stateless persons	
Convention relating to the Status of Refugees (Geneva, 28 July 1951)	United Nations, *Treaty Series*, vol. 189, No. 2545, p. 137.
Protocol relating to the Status of Refugees (New York, 31 January 1967)	*Ibid.*, vol. 606, No. 8791, p. 267.
Convention on territorial asylum (Caracas, 28 March 1954)	*Ibid.*, vol. 1438, No. 24378, p. 129.
Convention on the reduction of statelessness (New York, 30 August 1961)	*Ibid.*, vol. 989, No. 14458, p. 175.
European Convention on Nationality (Strasbourg, 6 November 1997)	*Ibid.*, vol. 2135, No. 37248, p. 213.
International trade and development	
Agreement establishing the International Fund for Agricultural Development (Rome, 13 June 1976)	United Nations, *Treaty Series*, vol. 1059, No. 16041, p. 191.
United Nations Convention on Contracts for the International Sale of Goods (Vienna, 11 April 1980)	*Ibid.*, vol. 1489, No. 25567, p. 3.
Fourth ACP-EEC Convention (Lomé, 15 December 1989)	*Ibid.*, vol. 1924, No. 32847, p. 3.
Transport and communications	
Convention on International Civil Aviation (Chicago, 7 December 1944)	United Nations, *Treaty Series*, vol. 15, No. 102, p. 295.
San Luis Protocol: Protocolo de San Luis en Materia de Responsabilidad Civil Emergentes de Accidentes de Tránsito entre los Estados Partes del Mercosur (San Luis, 25 June 1996)	R. B. Santos Belandro, *Bases Fundamentales del Derecho de la Integración y Mercosur,* Serie Documentos 1, Montevideo, Asociación de Escribanos del Uruguay, 2001, p. 399.
Navigation	
Convention between Austria-Hungary, France, Germany, Great Britain, Italy, the Netherlands, Russia, Spain and Turkey respecting the Free Navigation of the Suez Canal (Constantinople Convention) (Constantinople, 29 October 1888)	AJIL, Suppl., v. 3, p. 123.
Convention on the Intergovernmental Maritime Consultative Organization (Geneva, 6 March 1948)	United Nations, *Treaty Series*, vol. 289, No. 4214, p. 3.
Penal matters	
European Convention on Extradition (Paris, 13 December 1957)	United Nations, *Treaty Series*, vol. 359, No. 5146, p. 273.
European Convention on Mutual Assistance in Criminal Matters (Strasbourg, 20 April 1959)	*Ibid.*, vol. 472, No. 6841, p. 185.
European Convention on the suppression of terrorism (Strasbourg, 27 January 1977)	*Ibid.*, vol. 1137, No. 17828, p. 93.
Protocol amending the European Convention on the Suppression of Terrorism (Strasbourg, 15 May 2003)	Council of Europe, *European Treaty Series*, No. 190.
Inter-American Convention on extradition (Caracas, 25 February 1981)	United Nations, *Treaty Series*, vol. 1752, No. 30597, p. 190.
European Convention on the compensation of victims of violent crimes (Strasbourg, 24 November 1983)	*Ibid.*, vol. 1525, No. 26456, p. 37.
Convention on laundering, search, seizure and confiscation of the proceeds from crime (Strasbourg, 8 November 1990)	*Ibid.*, vol. 1862, No. 31704, p. 69.
Convention on the Statute of the Central American Court of Justice (Panama City, 10 December 1992)	*Ibid.*, vol. 1821, No. 31191, p. 291.
Inter-American Convention against Corruption (Caracas, 29 March 1996)	E/1996/99.

	Source
Rome Statute of the International Criminal Court (Rome, 17 July 1998)	United Nations, *Treaty Series*, vol. 2187, No. 38544, p. 3.
International Convention for the Suppression of the Financing of Terrorism (New York, 9 December 1999)	*Ibid.*, vol. 2178, No. 38349, p. 197.
Convention on cybercrime (Budapest, 23 November 2001)	*Ibid.*, vol. 2296, No. 40916, p. 167.
Additional Protocol to the Convention on cybercrime concerning the criminalization of acts of a racist and xenophobic nature committed through computer systems (Strasbourg, 28 January 2003)	*Ibid.*, vol. 2466, No. 40916, p. 205.
Agreement between the United Nations and the Royal Government of Cambodia concerning the prosecution under Cambodian law of crimes committed during the period of Democratic Kampuchea (Phnom Penh, 6 June 2003)	United Nations, *Treaty Series*, vol. 2329, No. 41723, p. 1.
United Nations Convention against Corruption (New York, 31 October 2003)	*Ibid.*, vol. 2349, No. 42146, p. 41.
Relationship Agreement between The United Nations and the International Criminal Court (New York, 4 October 2004)	*Ibid.*, vol. 2283, No. 1272, p. 195.
International Convention for the Suppression of Acts of Nuclear Terrorism (New York, 13 April 2005)	*Ibid.*, vol. 2445, No. 44004, p. 89.
Council of Europe Convention on Laundering, Search, Seizure and Confiscation of the Proceeds from Crime and on Financing of Terrorism (Warsaw, 16 May 2005)	Council of Europe, *European Treaty Series*, No. 198.
Council of Europe Convention on the Prevention of Terrorism (Warsaw, 16 May 2005)	*Ibid.*, No. 196.

Law of the sea

Geneva Conventions on the Law of the Sea (Geneva, 29 April 1958)	
Convention on the Continental Shelf	United Nations, *Treaty Series*, vol. 499, No. 7302, p. 311.
United Nations Convention on the Law of the Sea (Montego Bay, 10 December 1982)	*Ibid.*, vol. 1833, No. 31363, p. 3.
Agreement for the Implementation of the Provisions of the United Nations Convention on the Law of the Sea of 10 December 1982 relating to the Conservation and Management of Straddling Fish Stocks and Highly Migratory Fish Stocks (New York, 4 August 1995)	*Ibid.*, vol. 2167, No. 37924, p. 3.

Law applicable in armed conflict

Geneva Conventions for the protection of war victims (Geneva, 12 August 1949)	United Nations, *Treaty Series*, vol. 75, Nos. 970–973, p. 31.
Geneva Convention relative to the protection of civilian persons in time of war (Convention IV) (Geneva, 12 August 1949)	*Ibid.*, vol. 75, No. 973, p. 287.
Protocol additional to the Geneva Conventions of 12 August 1949, and relating to the protection of victims of international armed conflicts (Protocol I) (Geneva, 8 June 1977)	*Ibid.*, vol. 1125, No. 17512, p. 3.
Protocol additional to the Geneva Conventions of 12 August 1949, and relating to the protection of victims of non-international armed conflicts (Protocol II) (Geneva, 8 June 1977)	*Ibid.*, vol. 1125, No. 17513, p. 609.
Convention for the Protection of Cultural Property in the Event of Armed Conflict (The Hague, 14 May 1954)	*Ibid.*, vol. 249, No. 3511, p. 215.

Law of treaties

Vienna Convention on the Law of Treaties (Vienna, 23 May 1969)	United Nations, *Treaty Series*, vol. 1155, No. 18232, p. 331.
Vienna Convention on succession of States in respect of treaties (Vienna, 23 August 1978)	*Ibid.*, vol. 1946, No. 33356, p. 3.
Vienna Convention on the Law of Treaties between States and International Organizations or between International Organizations (Vienna, 21 March 1986)	A/CONF.129/15.

	Source
Telecommunications	
European Convention on Transfrontier Television (Strasbourg, 5 May 1989)	United Nations, *Treaty Series*, vol. 1966, No. 33611, p. 265.
Disarmament	
Treaty banning nuclear weapon tests in the atmosphere, in outer space and under water (PTBT) (Moscow, 5 August 1963)	United Nations, *Treaty Series*, vol. 480, No. 6964, p. 44.
Treaty on the Non-Proliferation of Nuclear Weapons (London, Moscow and Washington, 1 July 1968)	*Ibid.*, vol. 729, No. 10485, p. 161.
Convention on the Prohibition of Military or any Other Hostile Use of Environmental Modification Techniques (New York, 10 December 1976)	*Ibid.*, vol. 1108, No. 17119, p. 151.
Environment	
Convention on the protection of the environment (The Nordic Environmental Protection Convention) (Stockholm, 19 February 1974)	United Nations, *Treaty Series*, vol. 1092, No. 16770, p. 295.
Vienna Convention for the Protection of the Ozone Layer (Vienna, 22 March 1985)	*Ibid.*, vol. 1513, No. 26164, p. 293.
Montreal Protocol on Substances that Deplete the Ozone Layer (Montreal, 16 September 1987)	*Ibid.*, vol. 1522, No. 26369, p. 28.
Basel Convention on the control of transboundary movements of hazardous wastes and their disposal (Basel, 22 March 1989)	*Ibid.*, vol. 1673, No. 28911, p. 57.
Convention on the Protection and Use of Transboundary Watercourses and International Lakes (Helsinki, 17 March 1992)	*Ibid.*, vol. 1936, No. 33207, p. 269.
United Nations Framework Convention on Climate Change (New York, 9 May 1992)	*Ibid.*, vol. 1771, No. 30822, p. 107.
Convention on Biological Diversity (Rio de Janeiro, 5 June 1992)	*Ibid.*, vol. 1760, No. 30619, p. 79.
Convention on the Law of the Non-Navigational Uses of International Watercourses (New York, 21 May 1997)	*Official Records of the General Assembly, Fifty-first Session, Supplement No. 49* (A/51/49), vol. III, Resolution 51/229, Annex.
Miscellaneous	
Treaty between Great Britain, Russia, and The Netherlands, relative to the Russian Dutch Loan (London, 19 May 1815)	*British and Foreign State Papers 1814–1815*, vol. 2, London, James Ridgeway and Sons, 1839, p. 378.
Charter of the Organization of American States (Bogotá, 30 April 1948)	United Nations, *Treaty Series*, vol. 119, No. 1609, p. 3.
Convention (with annex) on the Settlement of Matters Arising out of the War and the Occupation (Bonn, 26 May 1952) [as amended by Schedule IV to the Protocol on the Termination of the Occupation Régime in the Federal Republic of German, signed at Paris on 23 October 1954]	*Ibid.*, vol. 332, No. 4762, p. 219.
European Convention on Establishment (Paris, 13 December 1955)	*Ibid.*, vol. 529, No. 7660, p. 141.
Treaty establishing the European Economic Community (Rome, 25 March 1957)	*Ibid.*, vol. 294, No. 4300, p. 3. See also the consolidated version of the Treaty establishing the European Community, *Official Journal*, No. C 340, 10 November 1997.
Inter-American Democratic Charter (Lima, 11 September 2001)	OEA, Official Documents, OEA/Ser.G/ CP-1.

CHECKLIST OF DOCUMENTS OF THE FIFTY-SEVENTH SESSION

Document	*Title*	*Observations and references*
A/CN.4/546	Sixth report on diplomatic protection, by Mr. John Dugard, Special Rapporteur	Reproduced in *Yearbook ... 2005*, vol. II (Part One).
A/CN.4/547	Responsibility of international organizations: comments and observations received from international organizations	*Idem.*
A/CN.4/548	Provisional agenda	Mimeographed. For agenda as adopted, see *Yearbook ... 2005*, vol. II (Part Two).
A/CN.4/549 and Add.1	Topical summary of the discussion held in the Sixth Committee of the General Assembly during its fifty-ninth session, prepared by the Secretariat	Mimeographed.
A/CN.4/550 [and Corr.1–2]	The effect of armed conflict on treaties—an examination of practice and doctrine: a memorandum prepared by the Secretariat	Mimeographed.
A/CN.4/551 and Corr.1 and Add.1	Third report on shared natural resources: transboundary groundwaters, by Mr. Chusei Yamada, Special Rapporteur	Reproduced in *Yearbook ... 2005*, vol. II (Part One).
A/CN.4/552	First report on the effects of armed conflicts on treaties, by Mr. Ian Brownlie, Special Rapporteur	*Idem.*
A/CN.4/553	Third report on responsibility of international organizations, by Mr. Giorgio Gaja, Special Rapporteur	*Idem.*
A/CN.4/554	Preliminary report on the expulsion of aliens, by Mr. Maurice Kamto	*Idem.*
A/CN.4/555 and Add.1	Shared natural resources: comments and observations received from Governments and relevant intergovernmental organizations	*Idem.*
A/CN.4/556	Responsibility of international organizations: comments and observations received from Governments and international organizations	*Idem.*
A/CN.4/557	Eighth report on unilateral acts of States, by Mr. Víctor Rodríguez Cedeño, Special Rapporteur	*Idem.*
A/CN.4/558 [and Corr.1] and Add.1 [and Corr.1]–2	Tenth report on reservations to treaties, by Mr. Alain Pellet, Special Rapporteur	*Idem.*
A/CN.4/L.665	Reservations to treaties: titles and texts of the draft guidelines adopted by the Drafting Committee on 27 May 2005	Mimeographed. See also, in the present volume, summary record of the 2842nd meeting (para. 50).
A/CN.4/L.666/Rev.1	Responsibility of international organizations: titles and texts of the draft articles adopted by the Drafting Committee on May 2005	*Idem*, summary record of the 2848th meeting (para. 1).
A/CN.4/L.667	Draft report of the International Law Commission on the work of its fifty-seventh session: chapter IV (Shared natural resources)	Mimeographed. For the adopted text, see *Official Records of the General Assembly, Sixtieth Session, Supplement No. 10* (A/60/10). The final text appears in *Yearbook ... 2005*, vol. II (Part Two).
A/CN.4/L.668	*Idem*: chapter V (Effects of armed conflicts on treaties)	*Idem.*
A/CN.4/L.669 and Add.1	*Idem*: chapter VI (Responsibility of international organizations)	*Idem.*
A/CN.4/L.670	*Idem*: chapter VII (Diplomatic protection)	*Idem.*
A/CN.4/L.671 and Add.1–2 [and Corr.1]	*Idem*: chapter X (Reservations to treaties)	*Idem.*
A/CN.4/L.672 and Add.1–2	*Idem*: chapter IX (Unilateral acts of States)	*Idem.*

Document	*Title*	*Observations and references*
A/CN.4/L.673	*Idem*: chapter I (Organization of the session)	*Idem.*
A/CN.4/L.674	*Idem*: chapter VIII (Expulsion of aliens)	*Idem.*
A/CN.4/L.675 [and Corr.1]	Programme, procedures and working methods of the Commission, and its documentation: report of the Planning Group	Mimeographed.
A/CN.4/L.676 [and Corr.1]	Report of the Study Group on fragmentation of international law: difficulties arising from the diversification and expansion of international law	*Idem.* Reproduced in *Yearbook ... 2005*, vol. II (Part Two), chap. XI, sect. C.
A/CN.4/L.677	Draft report of the International Law Commission on the work of its fifty-seventh session: chapter XI (Fragmentation of international law: difficulties arising from the diversification and expansion of international law)	Mimeographed. For the adopted text, see *Official Records of the General Assembly, Sixtieth Session, Supplement No. 10* (A/60/10). The final text appears in *Yearbook ... 2005*, vol. II (Part Two).
A/CN.4/L.678	*Idem*: chapter XII (Other decisions and conclusions of the Commission)	*Idem.*
A/CN.4/L.679	*Idem*: chapter II (Summary of the work of the Commission at its fifty-seventh session)	*Idem.*
A/CN.4/L.680	*Idem*: chapter III (Specific issues on which comments would be of particular interest to the Commission)	*Idem.*
A/CN.4/L.681 [and Corr.1]	Report of the Working Group on shared natural resources (groundwaters)	Mimeographed.
A/CN.4/SR.2831- A/CN.4/SR.2866	Provisional summary records of the 2831st to 2866th meetings	*Idem.* The final text appears in this volume.

INTERNATIONAL LAW COMMISSION

SUMMARY RECORDS OF THE FIRST PART OF THE FIFTY-SEVENTH SESSION

Held at Geneva from 2 May to 3 June 2005

2831st MEETING

Monday, 2 May 2005, at 3.10 p.m.

Acting Chairperson: Ms. Hanqin XUE

Chairperson: Mr. Djamchid MOMTAZ

Present: Mr. Addo, Mr. Brownlie, Mr. Candioti, Mr. Chee, Mr. Comissário Afonso, Mr. Daoudi, Mr. Dugard, Mr. Economides, Ms. Escarameia, Mr. Fomba, Mr. Gaja, Mr. Galicki, Mr. Kabatsi, Mr. Kamto, Mr. Kateka, Mr. Kemicha, Mr. Kolodkin, Mr. Mansfield, Mr. Matheson, Mr. Niehaus, Mr. Opertti Badan, Mr. Pambou-Tchivounda, Mr. Pellet, Mr. Sreenivasa Rao, Mr. Rodríguez Cedeño, Mr. Sepúlveda, Mr. Yamada.

Opening of the session

TRIBUTE TO THE MEMORY OF ROBERT ROSENSTOCK

1. The ACTING CHAIRPERSON declared open the fifty-seventh session of the International Law Commission. She began by informing the Commission of the death at the end of 2004 of Robert Rosenstock. Mr. Rosenstock had served the Commission with distinction for more than 10 years, from 1992 to 2003, as a member, chairperson and special rapporteur. He had taken a keen interest and actively participated in every aspect of the Commission's work, particularly the preparation of the draft articles on State responsibility, the draft statute for an international criminal court and, of course, the draft articles on the law of the non-navigational uses of international watercourses, the topic for which he had served as Special Rapporteur. He had never hesitated to express his views on the broad range of issues dealt with by the Commission, although that had not stopped him from being genuinely interested in and respectful of his colleagues' views. In his work he had made a lasting contribution to the codification and progressive development of international law, which had been so important to him. Mr. Rosenstock had been a man of character, substance and high standards. His lively contributions, sense of humour and friendship would be missed by all members of the Commission. At its first meeting during the fifty-ninth session of the General Assembly, on 4 October 2004, the Sixth Committee of the Assembly had paid a tribute to Mr. Rosenstock, who had been his country's representative to that body for many years. On behalf of the Commission, the Chairperson of the fifty-sixth session had sent a message of condolence to Mr. Rosenstock's family.

At the invitation of the Acting Chairperson, the members of the Commission observed a minute of silence in memory of their friend and colleague, Robert Rosenstock.

2. The ACTING CHAIRPERSON then gave a brief account of the discussions in the Sixth Committee on the report of the International Law Commission, the topical summary of which had been prepared by the Secretariat and issued as document A/CN.4/549 and Add.1. The first week of the Committee's consideration of the report, known as "International Law Week",[1] had given delegates an opportunity to hold high-level consultations on the topics in the Commission's current programme of work, as the Legal Advisers Meeting had been deliberately scheduled for the same week. The Commission had been represented before the Sixth Committee by the Chairperson of the fifty-sixth session and the Special Rapporteurs whose drafts had been adopted on first reading. She drew attention to the adoption by the General Assembly on 2 December 2004 of the United Nations Convention on Jurisdictional Immunities of States and Their Property, which was a significant contribution to the codification and progressive development of international law.

Election of officers

Mr. Momtaz was elected Chairperson by acclamation.

Mr. Momtaz took the Chair.

Mr. Pambou-Tchivounda was elected first Vice-Chairperson by acclamation.

Mr. Kolodkin was elected second Vice-Chairperson by acclamation.

---

[1] According to General Assembly resolution 58/77 of 9 December 2003, para. 11.

Mr. Mansfield was elected Chairperson of the Drafting Committee by acclamation.

Mr. Niehaus was elected Rapporteur by acclamation.

Adoption of the agenda (A/CN.4/548)

The agenda was adopted.

Organization of work of the session

[Agenda item 1]

3. The CHAIRPERSON drew attention to the programme of work and announced that the first Vice-Chairperson and the Chairperson of the Drafting Committee would begin holding consultations with a view to establishing their teams as soon as possible.

Shared natural resources[2] (A/CN.4/549 and Add.1, sect. B, A/CN.4/551 and Corr.1 and Add.1,[3] A/CN.4/555 and Add.1)[4]

[Agenda item 4]

THIRD REPORT OF THE SPECIAL RAPPORTEUR

4. The CHAIRPERSON invited Mr. Yamada, Special Rapporteur on shared natural resources, to introduce his third report on the topic (A/CN.4/551 and Corr.1 and Add.1).

5. Mr. YAMADA (Special Rapporteur) explained that he had prepared four informal papers[5] to supplement his third report on shared natural resources: transboundary groundwaters. The first two contained relevant excerpts from the discussions held in 2004 on his second report[6] by, respectively, the Commission[7] and the Sixth Committee (see the topical summary of the discussion held in the Sixth Committee of the General Assembly during its fifty-ninth session, prepared by the Secretariat (A/CN.4/549 and Add.1), paras. 40–74), the third was a compilation of instruments related to groundwaters and the fourth contained a selected bibliography.

6. As he felt that the approach he had taken was generally supported by the Commission and the Sixth Committee, Mr. Yamada was proposing a complete set of draft articles that took their comments into account. He had not had time to analyse the comments from Governments and intergovernmental organizations (A/CN.4/555 and Add.1), but he had attended a meeting on aquifers in the Americas organized by UNESCO, which had been attended by experts from throughout the Americas. The General Secretary of the Guaraní Aquifer System Project had given him a CD-ROM that he hoped to be able to present to the Commission soon.

7. The submission of his proposals in the form of draft articles did not prejudge their final form. He would prefer, for the moment, to concentrate on the substance of the topic. He recalled that several delegations had asked for a reference to be included in the preamble to General Assembly resolution 1803 (XVII) of 14 December 1962, on permanent sovereignty over natural resources. Given the sensitive nature of the issue, he had no difficulty with that suggestion, but would prefer to defer the drafting of the preamble to a later stage. The draft articles were contained in the annex to the report, with the article numbers that had been used in the second report[8] indicated in square brackets.

8. Draft article 1 (Scope) had not changed in substance, but the three categories of activities to be covered had been clarified. The definition of an aquifer in draft article 2 (*a*) had been reworded to eliminate the vagueness of the terms "rock formation" and "exploitable". He recalled that an aquifer consisted of two elements: an underground geological formation containing water and the extractable water it contained. The term "geological formation" was preferable to "rock formation" because such a formation could consist not only of rock but also of sand and gravel. Moreover, only the water contained in the saturated zone of the aquifer was extractable, hence his decision to avoid the term "exploitable", which might cause some confusion.

9. The definition of an aquifer system in article 2 (*b*) was also new. The phrase in square brackets had been inserted to explain that an aquifer system could consist of a series of aquifers from identical or different geological formations, although the inclusion of such an explanation was open to discussion. The new subparagraphs (*e*) and (*f*) were necessary because different rules were applicable depending on whether water resources were renewable (as in recharging aquifers, such as the Guaraní Aquifer System) or non-renewable (as in non-recharging aquifers, such as those in arid zones).

10. Draft article 3 sought to emphasize the importance of bilateral or regional arrangements concerning specific transboundary aquifer systems. Such arrangements had priority over the draft convention, as the latter was to be a framework convention. Draft article 4 was self-explanatory: according to subparagraph 1, the draft convention would take priority over the 1997 Convention on the Law of the Non-navigational Uses of International Watercourses (hereafter "1997 Watercourses Convention") in the event of a conflict between the two instruments.

11. Draft article 5 set out two fundamental, interrelated principles that could be found in most water treaties: the principle of "equitable utilization", under which a transboundary aquifer State was entitled to benefit in an equitable manner from the utilization of that aquifer, and the principle of "reasonable utilization", under which an aquifer State was required to manage the aquifer properly. Some aquifer States continued to object to the application

[2] For the history of the Commission's work on the topic, see *Yearbook ... 2004*, vol. II (Part Two), chap. VI.

[3] Reproduced in *Yearbook ... 2005*, vol. II (Part One).

[4] *Ibid.*

[5] Mimeographed; distribution limited to the members of the Commission.

[6] *Yearbook ... 2004*, vol. II (Part One), doc. A/CN.4/539 and Add.1.

[7] See *Yearbook ... 2004*, vol. I, 2797th–2799th meetings.

[8] See footnote 6 above.

of the concept of "shared" natural resources to groundwaters. The Sixth Committee had not, however, changed the title of the topic, as was clear from General Assembly resolution 59/41 of 2 December 2004, paragraph 4 (*a*). He believed that the utilization and management of a transboundary aquifer were matters for the States in whose territory the aquifer was located; there had never been any question of internationalizing transboundary aquifers. That view was shared by the experts and delegations concerned. He continued to avoid using the word "shared", but it should be noted that accepting the principle of "equitable utilization" implied recognizing the shared character of a transboundary aquifer and the absence of absolute sovereign rights over it. He had also sought to avoid the concept of "sustainable" utilization, which he felt could only be applied to truly renewable resources such as surface waters. Even in the case of recharging aquifers, "sustainable" utilization was not fully achievable, while it was impossible in the case of non-recharging aquifers, which were a non-renewable resource.

12. Draft article 6 listed factors to be taken into account in assessing the equitable and reasonable utilization of an aquifer. With regard to draft article 7, the idea of retaining a threshold of "significant harm" continued to be controversial. In his view, such a threshold was relative and took account of the fragility of resources. Another source of objections was the reference to compensation, in paragraph 3. That provision was based on an almost identical one in the 1997 Watercourses Convention, which had been proposed by the Commission in the light of State practice and adopted without any objections. Moreover, it did not constitute an obligation but was one possible means of mitigating harm. However, he was prepared to continue to debate that point.

13. Draft articles 8 and 9 dealt with the obligation to cooperate. The former recommended the establishment of joint mechanisms, a practice that was already widespread in respect of transboundary natural resources. He proposed a separate article, draft article 10, to stress the importance of monitoring in the management of transboundary aquifers. Draft articles 11 to 15 were self-explanatory. Draft article 13 was intended to solve any problems that might arise when the recharge and discharge zones of an aquifer were located in the territory of a State that received no benefits from the aquifer concerned. Such zones were vital and must therefore be protected, but a non-aquifer State could not be obliged to restrict its activities.

14. Draft articles 16 and 17 concerned activities affecting other States. He believed it was preferable to avoid setting out elaborate procedures like those in the 1997 Watercourses Convention, and to leave aquifer States to draw up such procedures themselves. Draft articles 18 to 21, on miscellaneous provisions, and 22 to 25, on final clauses, were self-explanatory. Draft article 18 was necessary because hydrogeology was still a young science and was mainly the preserve of the developed countries, whereas many aquifers were located in developing countries.

15. The future direction of his work would be guided by the comments of Commission members; he hoped to complete the draft articles for a first reading in 2006. If the Commission found it premature to move on to the drafting phase, it would be preferable to set up working groups to study certain articles in depth.

16. The CHAIRPERSON thanked the Special Rapporteur for his report and invited members of the Commission to make preliminary observations.

17. Mr. CANDIOTI asked how the discussion on the report would be organized.

18. Mr. OPERTTI BADAN said that the relationship between the general principles set out in the draft articles and any existing bilateral or regional treaty provisions should be examined in depth.

19. Mr. YAMADA suggested that the report should be considered chapter by chapter.

20. Ms. ESCARAMEIA wished to know if the Special Rapporteur was referring to parts of the report or to something else.

21. The CHAIRPERSON explained that each chapter of the report consisted of several articles of the draft convention, as grouped in the annex to the report.

22. Mr. Sreenivasa RAO proposed that articles 5, 6, 7 and 8 in part II should be considered first, as had been done in the case of the 1997 Watercourses Convention, and that the definitions should be discussed last.

23. Mr. YAMADA said that part II, on general principles, contained some key articles, and so it was possible to begin there. However, part I was just as important, as it concerned, *inter alia*, the scope of the draft convention.

24. Mr. OPERTTI BADAN pointed out that some of the points addressed in part I with regard to other conventions and international agreements, including regional and bilateral instruments, were also related, in his opinion, to the general principles.

25. Ms. XUE agreed with Mr. Rao that it would be best to concentrate on part II first. According to draft article 1, on the scope of the convention, the convention applied to three categories of activities. The activities mentioned in subparagraphs (*a*), on the utilization of transboundary aquifers and aquifer systems, and (*c*), on measures of protection, preservation and management of those aquifers and aquifer systems, were covered in part II, which dealt with general principles. However, she could not tell which part of the text covered subparagraph (*b*), on other activities that had or were likely to have an impact upon those aquifers and aquifer systems. If the Commission decided to consider the question on the basis of those three categories of activities, it would therefore be logical to begin with part II.

26. Mr. ECONOMIDES said that he was not sure whether Commission members would have enough time to share their views on the draft articles if that procedure

was followed. He thought that parts I and II of the draft were equally important and that the general principles could not be discussed until the scope of the convention had been considered. The idea of considering the draft articles on a part-by-part basis therefore seemed to him to be artificial, if not arbitrary.

27. Mr. GALICKI said that while part II appeared to constitute the core of the draft articles, it would be difficult to discuss that part before part I, which also contained some crucial points.

28. Mr. PELLET said that it would be wise to begin with part I before considering part II, and to leave the rest of the draft for later. Flexibility would be needed, and members of the Commission who wished to speak more than once should be allowed to do so.

29. Mr. DAOUDI said that the Commission should start at the beginning, as all the elements of the draft were linked.

30. Mr. YAMADA (Special Rapporteur) said that he did not mind beginning with part I or part II, and would leave the decision to the Commission.

31. Referring to the comments made by Ms. Xue, he said that the draft groundwaters convention, unlike the 1997 Watercourses Convention, provided for the regulation of "other activities", which would include, for example, the use of pesticides in agriculture, which might pollute groundwaters.

32. The CHAIRPERSON invited members of the Commission to constitute the Planning Group and Drafting Committee.

The meeting rose at 5.20 p.m.

2832nd MEETING

Tuesday, 3 May 2005, at 10.05 a.m.

Chairperson: Mr. Djamchid MOMTAZ

Present: Mr. Addo, Mr. Brownlie, Mr. Candioti, Mr. Chee, Mr. Comissário Afonso, Mr. Daoudi, Mr. Dugard, Mr. Economides, Ms. Escarameia, Mr. Fomba, Mr. Gaja, Mr. Galicki, Mr. Kabatsi, Mr. Kateka, Mr. Kemicha, Mr. Kolodkin, Mr. Mansfield, Mr. Matheson, Mr. Niehaus, Mr. Opertti Badan, Mr. Pambou-Tchivounda, Mr. Pellet, Mr. Sreenivasa Rao, Mr. Rodríguez Cedeño, Mr. Sepúlveda, Ms. Xue, Mr. Yamada.

Shared natural resources (*continued*) (A/CN.4/549 and Add.1, sect. B, A/CN.4/551 and Corr.1 and Add.1, A/CN.4/555 and Add.1)

[Agenda item 4]

THIRD REPORT OF THE SPECIAL RAPPORTEUR (*continued*)

1. The CHAIRPERSON invited the Commission to continue its consideration of the third report of the Special Rapporteur on shared natural resources (A/CN.4/551, Corr.1 and Add.1).

2. Ms. ESCARAMEIA congratulated the Special Rapporteur on his exhaustive research into the legal and scientific aspects of the topic. As general comments, she endorsed the proposed structure of the draft convention and considered part II particularly important, as general principles were fundamental. She did not agree with those who argued that bilateral or regional agreements in specific areas provided sufficient guidance: such agreements would always favour the stronger parties, a state of affairs that was totally unacceptable where environmental issues were at stake.

3. The 1997 Watercourses Convention should not be followed too slavishly. While it set out useful principles, such as equitable and sustainable utilization, the obligation not to cause significant harm and a general obligation to cooperate, the new convention covered bodies of water that raised far more sensitive issues.

4. It was her understanding that the proposed articles dealt only with those States that had an aquifer in their territory, or had some connection to an aquifer. However, third States could also play a role in the maintenance of aquifers, through charges and discharges. Accordingly, they too should be covered in the draft articles, as they clearly had an obligation to cooperate and exchange information.

5. The issue of compensation in the event of harm should also be addressed in the draft articles, rather than simply left to the operation of general rules on liability. She would also like to see the precautionary principle referred to by the Special Rapporteur in the report spelled out more strongly, in a separate article.

6. Turning to the individual draft articles, she said it would be useful to specify, perhaps in the commentary either to article 1 or to article 4, those situations in which aquifers were not covered by the present convention, being already covered by the 1997 Watercourses Convention. She also strongly endorsed the use of the term "impact", which was broader than "harm", in draft article 1, paragraph (*b*).

7. Turning to draft article 2, paragraph (*a*) (Use of terms), she agreed with the use of the expression "geological formation" rather than "rock formation", for the reasons given by the Special Rapporteur. There might be some merit in retaining the term "water-bearing", as it corresponded to the layperson's notion of an aquifer. She also endorsed the deletion of the word "exploitable". In paragraph (*b*), the bracketed phrase "[each associated

with specific geological formations]" was redundant and should be deleted. The phrase "more than two" aquifers had been corrected to read "two or more" in the text of paragraph (*b*); accordingly, paragraph 9 of the report needed to be amended in consequence.

8. Concerning the notion of an artificially rechargeable aquifer, mentioned in paragraph (*e*) and in paragraph 10 of the report, a State where an aquifer was artificially recharged should perhaps be subjected to more stringent obligations of non-pollution than a State where aquifers were recharged naturally, by rain, for example.

9. In the first sentence of draft article 3, paragraph 1, the word "encouraged" was too weak: transboundary aquifer States should be strongly urged to enter into bilateral or regional arrangements. If third States could in some way affect or be affected by aquifers, even though the aquifers were not in their territory, they should also be involved in such arrangements. She sought clarification from the Special Rapporteur on that point. Paragraph 3 also seemed to accord the draft convention a very subsidiary role by encouraging States to conclude bilateral or regional agreements without respect for the general principles set forth in the draft, an approach which, as stated by the Special Rapporteur elsewhere in the report, was unacceptable. A reference to compliance with those general principles should therefore be included in paragraph 3.

10. With respect to part II, draft article 5, paragraph 2 (*a*), she wondered how, in practice, the "sustainability" of an aquifer or aquifer system could be assessed over the long term. Several authors referred to the "economic recoverability" of an aquifer, and consideration should be given to using that concept as a criterion.

11. In draft article 6, reference might be made, perhaps in paragraph 1 (*c*), to the vital importance of water for drinking purposes. Special emphasis should be laid on that most fundamental of uses, on which the very survival of the population depended.

12. On draft article 7, paragraph 1, she continued to find the threshold of "significant" harm unacceptable, both in the general rules of liability and, *a fortiori*, in the present context. Several authors had pointed out that the precautionary principle militated against the use of the term "significant harm", and preferred to speak simply of "harm", since the impact of certain activities might take many years to become apparent. The precautionary principle was included in the International Law Association Berlin Rules on Water Resources, adopted in 2004,[1] and she firmly believed that it should also be incorporated in the convention. In paragraph 3, the possibility that a third, non-aquifer State might cause harm to an aquifer State should be foreseen and a reference to compensation should be incorporated therein.

13. Mr. MATHESON congratulated the Special Rapporteur on a valuable report that clearly defined the issues and offered carefully thought-out solutions. That work could have important benefits for the populations that depended on aquifers for basic human needs.

14. He wished to make three general points. First, the overriding consideration was that the utilization and protection of aquifers could ultimately be effectively accomplished only at the bilateral or regional level, with measures directed at specific aquifer systems and adapted to their particular conditions and to the needs of the aquifer States in question. The Commission could and should provide general principles to guide and encourage such bilateral and regional solutions, but it could not pretend to create a global solution. The States in whose territory an aquifer lay must have the flexibility to deal with their situations in the light of their own needs and conditions, and the choices they made must be respected. On the whole, that central consideration was given fair recognition in the Special Rapporteur's proposals, although sometimes the language suggested was not entirely clear. In any event, the flexibility and authority of aquifer States should not be limited beyond what was provided in the current draft.

15. Secondly, he fully supported the Special Rapporteur's emphasis on promoting the reasonable utilization and protection of aquifers. However, it was important not to impose requirements that were absolute or unrealistic or that might unduly compromise other important interests of aquifer States, including the satisfaction of their population's vital needs and the protection of other aspects of the environment. For example, States could not realistically be expected to prevent all pollution of aquifers, to halt all uses that might cause depletion or to cease all activities that might cause some degree of harm. To do so would in some cases necessitate more than was technically or economically feasible and in other cases would unduly divert public resources from other pressing requirements. A fair balance must be struck between the protection of aquifers and their use to meet human needs. By and large, the Special Rapporteur had been very attentive to those considerations, although in that regard too the language proposed was sometimes unclear. It bore repeating that requirements more categorical than those provided for in the current draft should certainly not be imposed on aquifer States.

16. Thirdly, on the ultimate form of the provisions, he was among those who believed that the Commission would attract broader support for its proposals if it were to produce non-binding principles to encourage bilateral and regional arrangements, rather than a binding convention. While he respected the Special Rapporteur's call for that question to be left in abeyance at the current stage, he believed that care should be taken not to prejudge it. The current text was drafted in the form of a binding convention, and contained terms such as "convention", "articles" and "States Parties" that identified it as an international agreement. It contained language indicating binding legal duties, such as "shall" and "obligation". To clearly indicate that the use of such terms was only provisional pending a decision on the final form, they might, for instance, be placed in square brackets. He also endorsed the Special

[1] The Berlin Rules are available on the website of the International Law Association (http://www.internationalwaterlaw.org/documents/intldocs/ILA_Berlin_Rules-2004.pdf). For the precautionary principle, see in particular article 23. See also International Law Association, *Report of the Seventy-first Conference (Berlin 2004)*, London, 2004, pp. 334–411.

Rapporteur's recommendation that the final clauses need not be considered until that matter was resolved.

17. Mr. BROWNLIE warmly congratulated the Special Rapporteur on his hard work, backed up with valuable supplementary resources in the form of papers and studies, on a subject that was of enormous importance. The draft convention was comprehensive and ambitious and, subject to specific criticisms, deserved the Commission's support. He was concerned, however, that while experts on aquifers had been called in to assist, the Commission tended to overlook general international law, which was nevertheless an important resource, highly relevant to various projects and disputes between States. In article 4, the Special Rapporteur rightly dealt with the relationship between the draft articles and other conventions and international agreements, but so far there was no mention in the draft articles of the analogous problem of the relationship between the draft articles and general international law.

18. In lectures given at the Hague Academy of International Law, Professor Richard Baxter, a prominent international lawyer and judge at the ICJ, had expressed the view that if codification was not done carefully it could actually have a negative effect, inadvertently calling into question important pieces of customary or general international law.[2] If draft article 7, on the obligation not to cause harm, was meant to fill in gaps where customary law was not clear, or did not provide redress, then he could support article 7 to that extent. He wondered, however, whether the existence of article 7 and the absence of any proviso relating to principles of general international law was a desirable state of affairs. One of the seminal decisions of the ICJ, in the *Corfu Channel* case, had established the principle that a State was responsible for harm to neighbours caused by sources of which it had—or ought to have—knowledge (p. 245 of the decision). That principle should be protected in situations where an aquifer or aquifer system was the vehicle of harm to neighbouring States and the requisite degree of knowledge existed or could be imputed to the aquifer State. Draft article 4 should accordingly be supplemented with some formulation or proviso to protect existing principles of general international law. There was no reason why such principles should not apply to aquifers, even though in the *Corfu Channel* case they had happened to apply to the territorial sea of Albania.

19. Mr. GAJA said that the Special Rapporteur was to be praised for striving to reach conclusions that were both politically acceptable and responsive to the concerns expressed by the scientific community. Although many of his proposals could hardly be criticized, the general principles set out in the draft articles might appear rather too general, providing little guidance to the States concerned. The principle of equitable and reasonable utilization had been endorsed by the 1997 Watercourses Convention, but it was somewhat vague, in view of the number of factors that needed to be considered for its application. If two or more States reached agreement on a specific transboundary aquifer, it would be difficult to say whether the agreement did or did not comply with that principle. If the application of the principle was entrusted to an international court or tribunal, the outcome would hardly be predictable. However, it would be difficult for the Commission to state more precise rules in such a complex and little-explored field.

20. The Special Rapporteur had provided the Commission with voluminous documentation, yet little of it specifically addressed issues relating to transboundary groundwaters. In 2004 States had been requested to provide information on their practice, but that request had brought to light little in the way of new materials other than bilateral and regional agreements, few of which related specifically to underground waters, while those that did covered only the provision of information and not the way the water resources should be apportioned, which was after all the crux of the issue (see A/CN.4/555 and Add.1).

21. With regard to the sovereignty that States claimed over groundwaters within their territory, the Special Rapporteur now appeared ready to concede that, although the territorial States were under a number of obligations, they "have sovereign rights over the natural resources located within their jurisdiction" (para. 19 of the report). He wondered whether it might not be wise to make that point in the draft articles themselves, in order to dispel criticism that the Commission was seeking to establish a regime whereby States had only limited sovereignty over the waters in their territory, because they had to share that sovereignty with other aquifer States. To spell out that States had sovereignty as well as obligations would at least overcome one of the obstacles to the acceptance of norms.

22. Given the definition of the scope in article 1, he agreed with Ms. Xue that the draft should make it clear to what extent, and where, activities that had or were likely to have an impact upon aquifers were regulated. As Ms. Escarameia had observed, that would also involve activities by non-aquifer States whose conduct might have an impact on aquifer States.

23. He was not entirely happy with the definitions of "recharging aquifer" and "non-recharging aquifer", which seemed unnecessary. They were based on the distinction between negligible and non-negligible contemporary water recharge, one that was not easy to make. In any case, since that distinction seemed relevant solely because different obligations were imposed under article 5, it would be preferable to differentiate less rigidly among aquifers in article 5 and to say that the issue of sustainability, and perhaps others as well, arose when there was contemporary recharge. Incidentally, the reference to sustainability did not imply that "the renewable natural resource must be kept at the level that would provide the maximum sustainable yield" (para. 21 of the report). That applied to fisheries, but not necessarily to groundwaters, which States concerned might well decide not to exploit to the limit of sustainability.

24. The future convention on the law of transboundary aquifers would not be a new Charter of the United Nations. It was therefore not appropriate to say in article 4, paragraph 1, that the provisions of the 1997 Watercourses

[2] R. R. Baxter, "*Treaties and custom*", *Collected Courses of the Hague Academy of International Law, 1970-I*, vol. 129, 1971, Leyden, Sijthoff, pp. 25–105.

Convention "apply only to the extent that they are compatible with those of the present Convention". That statement presupposed that all the States which shared an aquifer were parties to the new convention. However, all obligations under the 1997 Watercourses Convention would remain in force *vis-à-vis* any aquifer State which was a party to that Convention but not to the new instrument. In that regard, it might be useful to draw up a protocol to the 1997 Watercourses Convention.

25. Similarly, obligations arising under a regional convention towards a State that was not a party to the new instrument could not be affected. As it currently read, however, article 4, paragraph 2, might give an impression to the contrary. Perhaps a drafting change could specify that, for those States for which it became binding, the instrument was not intended to take precedence over other international agreements.

26. With regard to the question of compensation in the case of harm caused to another aquifer State, he largely concurred with Mr. Brownlie's remarks. The assertion in article 7, paragraph 3, that the State causing harm was under an obligation "where appropriate, to discuss the question of compensation" conveyed the impression that there was no obligation to provide compensation. He understood that the assumption underlying the assertion was that the harm-causing State had taken all the required measures to prevent the causing of harm. As it stood, however, the text stated that significant harm was "nevertheless" caused—in other words, caused notwithstanding the obligation to prevent the causing of harm, rather than notwithstanding compliance with that obligation. That was perhaps a drafting problem. An additional source of confusion might be that paragraph 3 also spoke of eliminating and mitigating such harm, elements that would seem to apply regardless of whether or not the obligation of prevention had been complied with. It should be made clear that the obligation to discuss, rather than to provide, compensation presupposed that the obligation of prevention had been complied with by the harm-causing State.

27. As to the method to be followed in future work on transboundary groundwaters, the best course would be to establish a working group to discuss the various provisions and reach a consensus. The text should then be referred to the plenary, which would in turn refer it to the Drafting Committee for further refinement. That process might take a few weeks, and it might be difficult to adopt the articles on first reading until 2006, but it would also give the Commission the opportunity to receive comments and information from States before finalizing the articles.

28. Mr. CHEE commended the Special Rapporteur's excellent paper. He noted, however, that it failed to address the need to set up an operational organ to enforce the terms of the convention. It was common practice to include a provision to that effect in international water treaties, an example being the Bellagio Draft Treaty, which contemplated, in article III, the establishment of a commission entrusted with enforcement and oversight responsibilities.[3]

29. Another important element that was missing was a dispute settlement procedure. International water treaties usually provided for peaceful settlement through mediation, conciliation or adjudication of the sort envisaged in Article 33 of the Charter of the United Nations. Indeed, from the Madrid Declaration on International Regulation regarding the Use of International Watercourses for Purposes other than Navigation (Madrid Declaration)[4] to the 1966 Helsinki Rules on the Uses of the Waters of International Rivers,[5] all statements of principles of law governing the utilization of international water resources had advocated recourse to the mediation and conciliation procedure. Some of those statements had made such recourse mandatory. Article XV of the Bellagio Draft Treaty also provided for the accommodation of differences to prevent the escalation of the dispute, and article XVI called for referral of the dispute to the ICJ if an agreement could not be reached.[6]

30. In view of those considerations, he was not certain that the time was ripe to produce a draft convention on the subject. In that regard he referred to an essay by a former Special Rapporteur of the Commission, Mr. McCaffrey, entitled The Law of International Watercourses: Non-Navigational Uses, in which the author concluded that, "[o]n the basis of the available evidence of [S]tate practice as well as recent codifications and the 1997 [Watercourses] Convention, it may be concluded that the law in this field has progressed only to the point that the general principles and rules governing the non-navigational uses of internationally shared surface water are applied to internationally shared groundwater resources as well";[7] thus, the law of international groundwaters could be said to be, at best, in the embryonic stages of development. In the author's view, the different characteristics and behaviour of groundwaters would seem to justify stricter standards and more stringent protection than were applicable to surface waters. The current legal regime governing surface waters, as expressed in the 1997 Watercourses Convention, might, Mr. McCaffrey concluded, "be sufficiently flexible to be capable of adaptation to the particular requirements of groundwater, but this situation should prevail only until a special regime could be tailored for international groundwater."[8]

31. Mr. ECONOMIDES said it was important to decide whether the topic under consideration involved codification, progressive development, or both. The Special Rapporteur had referred to the "scarcity of State practice and legal instruments" in the area (para. 3 of the report). Apparently, there was not yet a sufficient body of past practice to enable the Commission to engage in a codification exercise; it must therefore proceed by analogy. Clearly, the question of transboundary surface waters and groundwaters went beyond issues of national sovereignty and was a matter for international law. He agreed with

[3] R. D. Hayton and A. E. Utton, "Transboundary groundwaters: the Bellagio draft treaty", *Natural Resources Journal*, vol. 29, No. 3 (1989), pp. 663–720, at p. 684.

[4] Institute of International Law, *Annuaire de l'Institut de droit international*, Madrid session, April 1911, vol. 24 (1911), Paris, Pedone.

[5] International Law Association, *Report of the Fifty-second Conference (Helsinki 1966)*, London, 1967, pp. 484 *et seq.*

[6] Hayton and Utton, *loc. cit.* (footnote 3 above), pp. 714 and 718 respectively.

[7] Oxford University Press, 2001, p. 433.

[8] *Ibid.*

Ms. Escarameia that if the 1997 Watercourses Convention was followed too closely, the force of the present draft articles would thereby be diminished. It was therefore necessary to proceed with the topic without undue haste; the agreement of a large number of States was of the essence, and he concurred with Mr. Gaja that at the current stage it was preferable for the topic to be discussed in a working group rather than in the Drafting Committee.

32. On draft article 2 (Use of terms), Ms. Escarameia was right to point out that the bracketed phrase "each associated with specific geological formations", in paragraph (*b*), was redundant. In paragraph 9 of the report the Special Rapporteur stated that the expression had been inserted to indicate that an aquifer system could consist of aquifers not only of the same geological formations but also of different geological formations. Yet article 2, paragraph (*a*), defined an aquifer as "a permeable geological formation". That suggested that an aquifer could be associated with any geological formation, provided that it was permeable. He asked the Special Rapporteur for confirmation that that was the case. He also noted that the notion of utilization of the water had been totally eliminated from the definitions. While he agreed with the Special Rapporteur that the term "exploitable" invited controversy (para. 8), he still believed that that notion should be included in the definitions. He also wondered whether the phrase "underlain by a less permeable layer" was an integral part of the definition of "aquifer". If, as was his impression, it was not, why was it needed?

33. Lastly, he noted that, whereas the previous proposal had referred to the water contained in the aquifer, the new text used the phrase "water contained in the saturated zone of the formation". Did that mean that an aquifer was made up of several zones? What was an aquifer, strictly speaking? The text was not very clear on that point. Thus, it could be seen that the Commission was still groping its way forward, and that a number of major problems regarding the definition of "aquifer" had yet to be resolved.

34. With regard to draft article 3, all States which shared an aquifer should be encouraged to conclude bilateral and regional arrangements. As Mr. Matheson had said, that question could be regulated only at bilateral and regional levels. At the international level, indications could be given and principles elaborated that could be used in bilateral or regional negotiations. Two States which shared an aquifer could freely conclude an agreement, provided they respected the rights of others. However, article 3, paragraph 1, went too far in providing that, in some cases, such an arrangement could be entered into without the express consent of other States. The second sentence of the provision should be deleted. He was also in favour of replacing the word "encouraged", in the first sentence, by a stronger term.

35. Mr. OPERTTI BADAN noted that the topic had initially been proposed under a common heading with gas and oil and that the Commission had subsequently focused its attention on water.[9] Perhaps that was why the tendency to regard groundwater resources as shared was being diluted. He was concerned that some statements by members might reopen questions which had been regarded as settled.

36. The Special Rapporteur had left open the question whether the final text would take the form of a convention, a group of principles or recommendations, preferring instead to retain a degree of flexibility. While the Commission might eventually conclude that a number of guiding principles for the management of groundwaters would suffice, without a need for norms, it should not prejudice the question of the form that the final product would take.

37. Water in a transboundary aquifer was subject not only to the principle of the sovereignty of the territory under which it was located, but also to regulations freely agreed by partner States on its shared use for the common good, rather than for the specific benefit of one of those States. That was an area in which the Commission could provide useful guidance.

38. Mr. Sreenivasa RAO welcomed the very full and well-researched third report prepared by the Special Rapporteur and recalled that, as former chairperson of a working group of the Sixth Committee whose work had led to the adoption of the 1997 Watercourses Convention, the Special Rapporteur was well versed in every aspect of the topic which might be raised by members of the Commission.[10] It was true that the draft articles were very general in nature, replicating to a great extent the provisions of the 1997 Watercourses Convention. Some members might find that approach disappointing, but he felt that the Special Rapporteur really had no other option; a more detailed, prescriptive text could give rise to long debate and make it impossible to conclude discussions in the near future.

39. In that context, he recalled that discussion of the 1997 Watercourses Convention had continued for many years, and had included extensive debate on matters such as the threshold of significant harm, sovereignty, equitable and reasonable utilization and the obligation not to cause harm. There was a very real danger that those issues would return to haunt the Commission, which, however, would be unlikely to arrive at any definitive solution. It would therefore be pointless to reopen discussions. In his view, the term "significant harm" was in any case relatively meaningless. The adjective "significant" had been added for purely practical reasons, to prevent frivolous or politically motivated claims.

40. Turning to the specific topic of groundwaters, he recalled that there had been discussion within the Commission as to whether the draft articles on international watercourses could be considered to cover groundwaters where those waters were shared between States. The Special Rapporteur at the time, Mr. Rosenstock, had in fact proposed simply extending those draft articles, *mutatis mutandis*, to cover groundwaters.[11]

[9] See *Yearbook ... 2000*, vol. II (Part Two), chapter IX, p. 131, paragraph 726, and annex, p. 141; see also *Yearbook ... 2003*, vol. II (Part Two), pp. 15–16, paragraph 40.

[10] See the report of the Sixth Commission meeting as a Plenary Working Group (A/51/869).

[11] *Yearbook ... 1994*, vol. II (Part One), document A/CN.4/462, annex, pp. 120–121, paras. 38–39.

41. He also took note of Mr. Gaja's proposal concerning the possibility of drafting a protocol to the 1997 Watercourses Convention on the question of groundwaters, but was of the view that the matter could be resolved more simply, especially in the light of the misgivings expressed by Mr. McCaffrey in the article cited by Mr. Chee.

42. He agreed with Mr. Matheson that the Commission should show great flexibility and, so long as general principles could be arrived at based on available information and consistent with the Commission's past work, he trusted the Special Rapporteur's judgement and familiarity with the topic; if the latter had seen fit to draft articles which were fairly general in nature, he fully supported that decision. In any case, the matter required further review in a working group.

43. Mr. PELLET acknowledged the thoroughness of the third report but said that at times he would have preferred to see more detailed information on the reasoning behind the Special Rapporteur's decisions. The reader was often simply referred to previous reports or discussions, and while many of the issues at hand had already been discussed, that was not always the case. Even where the issues had been discussed, a reminder of the reasoning that had led to the choice of specific terms or language would not have gone amiss.

44. With regard to the definitions contained in draft article 2, he wondered if the term "aquifer" could still be applied if the permeable layer was not saturated, as was implied in paragraph (*a*). He also wondered why paragraph (*c*) referred to an aquifer or aquifer system, parts of which were situated "in different States" rather than the more usual formulation "in two or more States". While he welcomed the addition of paragraphs (*e*) and (*f*), especially in the light of the distinction made in draft article 5, paragraph 2, with regard to recharging and non-recharging transboundary aquifers or aquifer systems, he wondered whether the expression "contemporary water recharge" was an accepted term of art or one coined by the Special Rapporteur. In the former case the source should be indicated and in the latter case the term should be defined in the draft, or at least in the commentary.

45. Regarding the explanation of the term "geological formation" contained in paragraph 8 of the report, which covered materials other than rock, he wondered what specific materials were referred to. Such matters should be explained in the report and also in the commentary. He also wondered why, in paragraph 9 of the report, an aquifer system was described as a series of "more than two" aquifers, rather than a series of "two or more" aquifers, as in draft article 2, paragraph (*b*). Furthermore, there was no need to include the words "water-bearing" in draft article 2, paragraph (*a*), or the words "each associated with specific geological formations" in paragraph (*b*) of that article.

46. It was also highly regrettable that the comments and observations received from Governments and relevant intergovernmental organizations (A/CN.4/555 and Add.1), the paper entitled *Shared Natural Resources: Compilation of international legal instruments on groundwater resources* and other background documentation prepared by the Special Rapporteur had been distributed in English only.[12]

47. In reading the draft articles one could not but be struck by their resemblance to the 1997 Watercourses Convention. That resemblance was quite legitimate given the closely related nature of the subjects, just as it was legitimate that they should depart from the 1997 Watercourses Convention, where required by the special characteristics of aquifer systems. Thus, the Special Rapporteur's explanations for some of the departures from the text of the 1997 Watercourses Convention, while at times somewhat over-succinct, were perfectly understandable. He could accept the Special Rapporteur's preference for the term "arrangement" in draft article 3, paragraph 2, over the word "agreement" in article 3, paragraph 2, of the 1997 Watercourses Convention, and also his reasons for preferring the language chosen in draft article 5, paragraph 2, to that of article 5, paragraph 1, of the 1997 Watercourses Convention (para. 22). He also agreed with the new wording of draft article 6—which, truth be told, was an improvement on that of the 1997 Watercourses Convention. While he also welcomed the new draft article 9, paragraph 2, he felt that the reason for the inclusion of that paragraph should be more fully explained, and that it might be better located at the beginning or end of draft article 10.

48. There were a number of other instances where the language of the draft articles constituted an improvement on the 1997 Watercourses Convention, and he sincerely hoped that those improvements would be retained by the Drafting Committee and the Commission. He was thinking in particular of draft articles 10 and 18—though he had few illusions concerning the generosity of rich countries and the private sector's thirst for profit; and draft article 19, paragraph 1, on emergency situations, which was worded better than the corresponding article of the 1997 Watercourses Convention. In draft articles 16 and 17 the Special Rapporteur had quite rightly simplified the unnecessarily complicated procedures under the 1997 Watercourses Convention in favour of more flexible and realistic mechanisms for notification and consultation. However, draft article 20 on armed conflict, which simply reproduced article 29 of the 1997 Watercourses Convention, and draft article 21 on national defence or security, contributed little or nothing new and were not useful for the draft's goals; draft article 20, and probably draft article 21 as well, should not be referred to the Drafting Committee. Draft article 4 on the relation to other conventions and international agreements, pursuant to which the provisions of the draft convention prevailed in matters concerning transboundary aquifers or aquifer systems, should be placed at the end of the draft convention.

49. In the examples just mentioned, he approved of the Special Rapporteur's reasons for departing from the text of the 1997 Watercourses Convention, although he would often have welcomed a fuller explanation of those reasons. In other cases, however, the Special Rapporteur had not explained his reasons for departing from the text of that Convention. Many of the discrepancies could not

[12] The distribution of these documents was limited to the members of the Commission. Document A/CN.4/555 and Add.1 is reproduced in *Yearbook ... 2005*, vol. II (Part One).

simply be attributed to problems of translation. For example, he personally was not convinced that the wording of draft article 3 improved on the corresponding article of the 1997 Watercourses Convention, because its overly cautious wording could lead to difficulties in interpretation and implementation. Neither was he convinced that draft article 9, paragraph 3, and draft article 15 improved on article 9, paragraph 2, and article 24 respectively of the 1997 Watercourses Convention. He failed to understand why draft article 12 did not reproduce the wording of article 20 of the 1997 Watercourses Convention on the need to "individually and, where appropriate, jointly" protect and preserve ecosystems, although that wording was used elsewhere, in draft article 14. Unless the language of a draft article represented a clear improvement on that of the 1997 Watercourses Convention, the language of the latter should be retained.

50. The Special Rapporteur shared with most special rapporteurs an unfortunate tendency to seek to delay for as long as possible any decision by the Commission with regard to the final form that the draft would take. That approach was not without its drawbacks. In draft article 3, paragraph 1, draft article 5, paragraph 2 (*b*), and draft article 8, paragraph 2, aquifer States were "encouraged" to take various measures. Such language would be entirely acceptable in a soft law text, but was completely meaningless in a binding convention. Draft article 9, paragraph 2, and draft article 14 used similarly soft wordings, and also contained explanations that would be perfectly acceptable in a commentary but had no place in a convention.

51. It was therefore important that the Commission decide in plenary session whether it was attempting to draft a recommendation, guidelines or a convention, before asking the Drafting Committee to develop a final text, as the hard and soft law approaches called for very different drafting techniques. He himself was strongly in favour of drafting a convention, if only because the topic was inseparable from that of international watercourses. Perhaps the best solution, however, as suggested by Mr. Gaja, might be to propose the adoption of a protocol to the 1997 Watercourses Convention to take account of the specific characteristics of transboundary groundwaters. In any case, in order for the Drafting Committee to prepare a viable text, the Commission must decide what type of instrument it wished to draft. That issue could be further discussed in a working group.

52. He wished to make a few specific points before concluding. Firstly, draft article 4, paragraph 2 should be interpreted—like article 311, paragraph 2 of the United Nations Convention on the Law of the Sea, on which it was modelled—as giving priority to the Convention over other agreements. In fact, the whole issue of the relationship between the draft articles and other instruments needed to be studied more closely. It was difficult to see how draft article 4, paragraph 2, fitted in with draft article 3. Secondly, as the Special Rapporteur rightly pointed out in paragraph 24 of his report, natural factors and parameters needed to be taken into account; for that reason, he thought it would be better to include an express reference in draft article 6 to draft article 9, paragraph 1, and draft article 10, paragraph 1, which included indicative lists of such factors and parameters. Thirdly, draft article 9, paragraph 2, should be moved either to the beginning or to the end of draft article 10. Fourthly, given the paramount importance of applying the precautionary principle to aquifers and, in particular, non-recharging aquifers, it was very unfortunate that the Special Rapporteur had approached that principle with such caution in paragraph 33 of his report and in draft article 14, which merely "encouraged" aquifer States to take a precautionary approach. Lastly, while he was aware that it was not the Commission's practice to include the wording of final clauses in draft texts, he regretted the fact that the Special Rapporteur's draft did not envisage a clause on reservations. He believed that a majority of the members of the Sixth Committee would welcome, especially in an instrument that involved the codification of international law, provisions dealing as specifically as possible with reservations. Of course, it would be for the future negotiators of any convention or protocol to draft the details of the final clauses, but if the Commission were to propose the inclusion of final clauses in the draft articles, those clauses should contain a reference to reservations.

53. In concluding, he stressed that his main difficulties with the draft concerned its overall lack of incisiveness, particularly with regard to precautionary measures, and the problems that would arise if the Commission were to refer it to the Drafting Committee in its current form without first determining what form it should eventually take.

54. Mr. Sreenivasa RAO agreed with Mr. Pellet that the Commission needed to give clear instructions to the Drafting Committee on the form that the text was to take, but wondered if the Commission was really in a position to provide such clarity given its members' comparative ignorance of the characteristics of groundwaters and the lack of conceptual continuity in the various international arrangements in that area. There would be little point in drafting a convention based on arbitrary agreements reached by the Commission that were not supported by State practice or legal doctrine. Any convention would need to be universally acceptable to States and applicable in a wide range of local circumstances as well as sound from a scholarly viewpoint. The draft should be considered by a working group before it was sent to the Drafting Committee, so that it could be fleshed out and improved, particularly with regard to what constituted "equitable and reasonable utilization".

55. Mr. GAJA said that he had not intended to suggest replacing the draft convention with a draft protocol, but had simply meant to point out that article 4, paragraph 1, was not suitable for inclusion in a new instrument, although it could conceivably be included in a protocol to the 1997 Watercourses Convention. That was because it would be possible to apply the provisions of the 1997 Watercourses Convention to transboundary aquifers or aquifer systems "to the extent that they are compatible with those of the present Convention" only if the States parties to the first were also States parties to the second, or if the 1997 Watercourses Convention was made more flexible, by means of, for example, a protocol. While he did not think it was necessary to go that far, article 4, paragraph 1, needed to be reconsidered and redrafted. He agreed with Mr. Sreenivasa Rao that before being referred to the Drafting Committee, the draft articles should be

sent to a working group, for consideration, *inter alia*, of the final form they were meant to take.

56. Mr. MIKULKA (Secretary to the Commission) specified that document A/CN.4/555 and Add.1, referred to by Mr. Pellet, had been distributed in an unedited version in English only because the comments and observations from States and competent international organizations had been received at the last minute. As it was an official document of the Commission, it would be distributed in all official languages as soon as it had been translated. However, the paper entitled *Shared Natural Resources: Compilation of international legal instruments on groundwater resources* would remain available in English only, because there was no budget provision for translating a document of that nature.

Organization of work of the session (*continued*)

[Agenda item 1]

57. Mr. PAMBOU-TCHIVOUNDA (Chairperson of the Planning Group) announced that the Planning Group would be composed of Mr. Addo, Mr. Chee, Mr. Comissário Afonso, Mr. Daoudi, Mr. Economides, Ms. Escarameia, Mr. Fomba, Mr. Galicki, Mr. Kabatsi, Mr. Kateka, Mr. Kemicha, Mr. Kolodkin, Mr. Matheson, Mr. Niehaus, Mr. Opertti Badan, Mr. Pellet, Mr. Sepúlveda and Ms. Xue.

58. Mr. MANSFIELD (Chairperson of the Drafting Committee) announced that the Drafting Committee on the topic of reservations to treaties was currently composed of Mr. Comissário Afonso, Ms. Escarameia, Mr. Gaja, Mr. Matheson and Ms. Xue.

59. The CHAIRPERSON invited any other members wishing to join the Drafting Committee on that topic to inform Mr. Mansfield of their interest.

60. Mr. PELLET (Chairperson of the Working Group on the long-term programme of work) said that the Working Group was officially composed of Mr. Baena Soares, Mr. Galicki, Mr. Kamto, Mr. Koskenniemi and Ms. Xue, with Mr. Niehaus (member *ex officio*) as Rapporteur. However, all members of the Commission were welcome to attend the Working Group's meetings.

The meeting rose at 1 p.m.

2833rd MEETING

Wednesday, 4 May 2005, at 10 a.m.

Chairperson: Mr. Djamchid MOMTAZ

Present: Mr. Addo, Mr. Baena Soares, Mr. Brownlie, Mr. Candioti, Mr. Chee, Mr. Comissário Afonso, Mr. Daoudi, Mr. Dugard, Mr. Economides, Ms. Escarameia, Mr. Fomba, Mr. Gaja, Mr. Galicki, Mr. Kabatsi, Mr. Kateka, Mr. Kemicha, Mr. Kolodkin, Mr. Mansfield, Mr. Matheson, Mr. Niehaus, Mr. Opertti Badan, Mr. Pambou-Tchivounda, Mr. Pellet, Mr. Sreenivasa Rao, Mr. Rodríguez Cedeño, Mr. Sepúlveda, Ms. Xue, Mr. Yamada.

Shared natural resources (*continued*) (A/CN.4/549 and Add.1, sect. B, A/CN.4/551 and Corr.1 and Add.1, A/CN.4/555 and Add.1)

[Agenda item 4]

Third report of the Special Rapporteur (*continued*)

1. Mr. PAMBOU-TCHIVOUNDA thanked the Special Rapporteur for his third report on shared natural resources: transboundary groundwaters (A/CN.4/551 and Add.1). The cornerstone of the report was undoubtedly the draft articles, a text that was ambitious and carefully thought out, but also unrealistic in scope. It was ambitious owing to the very nature of the topic. Groundwaters did not reveal themselves easily to laymen, and it might prove difficult to determine where they ran and how their utilization should be organized. For lawyers, such dangers were a function of the methodology employed, yet the global approach that had been chosen meant sacrificing the specific nature of groundwaters on the larger altar of shared natural resources. It would in fact have been useful to refocus the topic, not least of all by giving it a new title, in order to avoid placing such disparate natural resources as gas, oil and water on the same footing. The use of the 1997 Convention on the Law of the Non-navigational Uses of International Watercourses as a model also tended to blur the specific characteristics of groundwaters, while the categories established in the 1997 text, though quite useful at the time, had since disappeared. That was the case, for example, with the distinction drawn between upstream and downstream States, which was central to the attribution of responsibility. That distinction must be resurrected in order to make the draft more functional.

2. As to the cautious approach taken by the Special Rapporteur, he recalled that on the previous day the members of the Commission had questioned the direction the exercise was taking and the form that the final outcome should take. Yet in his third report the Special Rapporteur himself indicated the path to be followed. In paragraph 2 he proposed "a complete set of draft articles for a convention on the law of transboundary aquifers". In paragraph 13 he stated that "[t]he draft convention [was] deemed to be a framework convention and aquifer States [were] expected to respect the basic principles stipulated therein in formulating … arrangements". States were nevertheless "authorized to depart from those principles if the special characteristics of a particular aquifer [required] certain adjustments". That was why he himself advocated the elaboration of a framework convention, the structure that best accommodated compromise, was articulated around general principles and was well adapted to the principal fields of environmental law.

3. The fact remained that excessive generality could undermine any intellectual construct, and from that standpoint the scope of the draft was sometimes unrealistic. For

example, article 1, on the scope, stated that the convention applied to the utilization of transboundary aquifers and aquifer systems without defining the term "utilization" or the "other activities" that had or were likely to have an impact on those aquifers or aquifer systems. As to measures of protection and management, they were unknown since, by definition, they came into existence only through the application of the framework convention. There was thus nothing to give the slightest indication of the scope of application or the purpose of the draft articles. However, the difference between "principal" and "incidental" utilization should be made clear, especially since utilization had to be both equitable and reasonable, concepts that were far from being construed uniformly in general international law.

4. The omission of certain institutional elements from the draft had already been mentioned by other speakers, with whom he concurred. Yet another example of the Special Rapporteur's tendency to be unrealistic was the fact that all States, whether upstream or downstream, were given equal consideration. It was therefore surprising that so little consideration was given to third States affected by the recharge and discharge of an aquifer, even though they clearly had a role to play and thus rights to defend.

5. Referring to what he termed the "mirage" of scientific and technical assistance for developing countries proposed in article 18 of the draft, he recalled the impact that similar provisions had had on such legal instruments as the United Nations Convention on the Law of the Sea. Lastly, he said that a general principle such as that of permanent sovereignty of States over natural resources should be stated elsewhere than in the preamble.

6. Mr. OPERTTI BADAN said that his comments would follow the structure proposed in the third report. Firstly, he welcomed the fact that the Special Rapporteur had not prejudged the final form the draft articles would take. He also noted with satisfaction that the Special Rapporteur had received technical assistance in drafting his report from the UNESCO International Hydrological Programme and the Japanese Ministry of Foreign Affairs.

7. Turning to the preamble, he agreed that the principle of State sovereignty over natural resources should be included in the operative portion of the text, since it was fundamental.

8. As to the scope, he was not convinced by article 1, subparagraph (*b*), unless the activities in question were carried out by the aquifer States and not by third States, in which case such activities would be regulated by general international law, particularly the law of responsibility. Subparagraph (*a*), meanwhile, could give rise to ambiguous interpretations as to which States had the right of utilization. It was explained that domestic aquifer systems were excluded from the scope of the draft articles, which applied only to transboundary aquifers. The purpose of regional agreements such as the agreement on the Guaraní aquifer was precisely to enable aquifer States to agree on the equitable and reasonable utilization of that natural resource. The encouragement to cooperate given to aquifer States was thus very useful, as was the indication that an aquifer system could consist of a series of two or more aquifers, thereby distinguishing it from transboundary aquifers and transboundary aquifer systems. However, it was not clear what would happen if States did not agree that a given aquifer was a transboundary aquifer. Such disagreement must not deprive them of their right to utilize groundwaters. The inclusion of a provision specifically recognizing that right would make the draft clearer from a legal point of view. On the other hand, it was unnecessary to redefine "transboundary", since there was a *communis opinio* on that notion, which appeared in many other international instruments.

9. As to the distinction between a recharging and non-recharging aquifer, he had serious doubts about its usefulness in legal terms, even though it might exist scientifically. In his view, the distinction was not strong enough to warrant the creation of a rule. Moreover, the notion of a rechargeable aquifer called for the introduction of the notion of sustainability.

10. With regard to bilateral and regional arrangements, it was true that if one accepted the principle of sovereignty, States could not be obliged to conclude such agreements; nevertheless, the convention should stipulate the obligation of States in whose territory a transboundary aquifer system was located to cooperate with a view to equitable and reasonable utilization of water resources. On that point there must be some flexibility. In any event, the rational use of a natural resource like groundwaters by the States that possessed it might be a good example of how the international community could promote respect for basic values without arrogating the right to regulate them as if they were universal in nature. In the case of water, it was obvious that the principle of geographical proximity and criterion of integration came into play in the use of shared natural resources. The draft convention should encourage States to cooperate in the use of such resources and to take their integration agreements into account so that understandings that facilitated greater integration of infrastructures might be reached. The MERCOSUR countries had begun work on an agreement that would be based on scientific studies currently being carried out on the Guaraní aquifer.

11. The issue of the draft convention's relationship to other international conventions and agreements might become an extremely delicate one in the future. He did not think it useful to establish an explicit link between the 1997 Watercourses Convention and the draft under consideration. Not only did the two instruments have different objects, they also dealt with different legally protected interests that were protected differently at the international level. In addition, neither of the two conventions should take precedence over the other.

12. The draft set out the principle of equitable and reasonable utilization of a transboundary aquifer or aquifer system, which had a definite impact on the conduct or behaviour of the States concerned. The objective criteria to be taken into account in that context were, firstly, surface area, and secondly, the volume of the aquifer in each State, measured in cubic metres. The latter criterion was linked both to the surface area and to the depth of the

water, which varied. Mention should also be made of conventional criteria that made it possible not only to determine surface area and volume but also to take account of the needs of certain regions that had fewer water resources. In such cases the criteria of reasonableness and equity, which related not to the quantity but to the quality of the resource's utilization, came into play.

13. The Commission should give due consideration to the question of the establishment of development plans for aquifers or aquifer systems to ensure the rational utilization of such resources. In that connection, draft article 5 suggested that a search should be made for sufficiently flexible approaches that reflected the need to balance the interests involved while addressing urgent problems and requirements. The concepts of "agreed lifespan of an aquifer or aquifer system as well as future needs of and alternative water sources for aquifer States" must likewise be taken into account.

14. In conclusion, he wished to stress a number of points. Firstly, the draft convention should be viewed as a source of encouragement for the conclusion of agreements on aquifers and aquifer systems, and not as a replacement for existing or future rules. Secondly, the Commission's objective was to formulate non-binding principles, even if the rules that aquifer States formulated themselves were binding in nature. Thirdly, general international law must be respected, both by States, when concluding regional and bilateral agreements, and by the Commission. Fourthly, it must never be forgotten that the Commission was dealing with transboundary watercourses and not international watercourses. Fifthly, the draft convention should promote the conclusion of agreements and cooperation with a view to the reasonable utilization of a transboundary aquifer by the States concerned. If that objective was not achieved, however, that did not mean that individual States should refrain from using their resources in that part of the aquifer or aquifer system located in their territory. The inclusion in the draft convention of a specific provision to that effect would avert many problems in the future. Lastly, it was the shared exploitation of resources, and not the ownership thereof, that was addressed in integration agreements dealing with natural resources.

15. Mr. KABATSI commended the Special Rapporteur on his excellent report, which was the product of extensive consultation and reflected the views of States, scholars and the bodies concerned on some rather sensitive issues such as permanent sovereignty over natural resources. The Special Rapporteur had tried to balance all the interests involved and had managed to present a complete set of draft articles which provided an excellent basis for the Commission's deliberations.

16. Like other members of the Commission, however, he feared that the Special Rapporteur's proposals were rather too general to be truly useful as part of a convention. Certain expressions and terms should be clarified, such as "negligible" in article 2, subparagraphs (*e*) and (*f*), "significant extent" in article 3, paragraph 1, "equitable and reasonable" in article 5 and "significant harm" in article 7, paragraph 1.

17. If, however, the product of the study turned out to be a framework convention providing mainly general principles governing the utilization of transboundary groundwaters, one could safely assume that bilateral and regional agreements would be sufficiently precise and detailed to provide practical guidance for the utilization, management, protection and preservation of those resources.

18. As the Special Rapporteur pointed out in paragraph 26 of his report, groundwaters constituted a "fragile natural resource". That was why any harm caused by man-made sources to such resources, on which certain communities and countries might be entirely dependent, might be extremely difficult or even impossible to reverse. Serious thought must therefore be given to the expressions used, as some common terms were perhaps more easily applicable to other resources. He was thinking in particular of the use of the term "significant" to refer to harm caused to a State through an aquifer. If such harm could be detected, the States concerned should have an obligation to intervene without waiting for the harm to become "significant", and before it became irreversible.

19. Turning to the question of permanent sovereignty over natural resources, he said he did not believe that States could be prohibited from affirming such sovereignty, especially in the absence of agreements and as long as they respected the principles of general international law. However, the importance of the issue must not be overemphasized. Accordingly, if the Commission intended to draw up provisions governing the reasonable and equitable utilization of such resources by States, the question of sovereignty must be subjected to such regulation and to bilateral and/or regional agreements for the equitable benefit of the States concerned.

20. Lastly, he agreed with the Special Rapporteur that it was not appropriate to decide on the final form the draft articles would take until the substance had more or less been agreed upon. The same was true for the preamble, which should be dealt with only after the draft articles had been agreed upon and all factors to be incorporated therein were known. In general, he welcomed the proposals contained in the third report, especially the proposed draft convention on the law of transboundary aquifers, which a working group could perhaps refine before it was referred to the Drafting Committee.

21. Mr. KEMICHA said that the Special Rapporteur had stayed as close as possible to the 1997 Watercourses Convention and departed from it when the special nature of aquifers so required. He agreed with Mr. Pellet that the main weakness of the report was the Special Rapporteur's extreme caution and, indeed, his reluctance to express a view on the future of the Commission's work on the subject. The terminology employed in phrases such as "aquifer States [...] are encouraged to enter into a bilateral or regional arrangement among themselves" in article 3, paragraph 1, or "aquifer States are encouraged to take a precautionary approach" in article 14 of the draft suggested that the Commission was considering not a draft convention that was binding on the States that signed it, but simple recommendations for States to

use as they saw fit. The fact that the Special Rapporteur wrote in paragraph 13 of the report that "[t]he draft convention is deemed to be a framework convention" did not clarify that point. He agreed with other members of the Commission who argued that the ambiguity should first be dispelled. He was convinced that the Special Rapporteur had not wanted to decide on the matter so that the Commission might do so.

22. Ms. XUE commended the Special Rapporteur for the considerable amount of work he had done and the volume of documentation compiled and also for being so receptive to the opinions of colleagues and States. She wished to start by making three general comments. Firstly, given the scarcity of fresh water and the growing demand for resources for the social and economic development of States, it was important for the Commission to take up the question of transboundary groundwaters, particularly in view of the fact that, after decades of studying the non-navigational uses of international watercourses, the Commission was technically in a better position to look further into the issue of groundwaters. However, after an exchange of views with the scientific community and States, the Commission had realized that the practical utilization of transboundary groundwaters was rather limited and that very few documents dealt specifically with the subject, a situation that complicated the Special Rapporteur's work. The very nature of underground waters—a limited, confined and fragile resource with distinct physical properties, the utilization of which might vary depending on the social and economic conditions of the country concerned—called for flexibility and greater latitude for bilateral and regional arrangements than was the case with international watercourses. However, that was not the impression given by the wording of the draft, which seemed even stricter, or less flexible, than article 3 of the 1997 Watercourses Convention. Placing emphasis on bilateral and regional arrangements did not mean that general principles should not come into play. On the contrary, they could help States negotiate and conclude agreements that the States parties concerned could accept.

23. Secondly, as pointed out by the Special Rapporteur and other members, the study should not be regarded as a mere extension of the 1997 Watercourses Convention. Given the non-renewable nature and physical character of groundwaters, their protection and preservation should be emphasized in policy considerations. The criterion of sustainability should be applied not only to water utilization, but also to protection of the ecological conditions of the aquifer or aquifer system. Consequently the third area listed under the scope of the draft, "Measures of protection, preservation and management", should be placed before the second, "Other activities", and policy objectives should be clearly formulated. Similarly, activities carried out by a third State having no aquifer in its territory, that might have an adverse impact on an aquifer of a neighbouring State, should also be taken into account.

24. Thirdly, as with surface waters, it must be conceded that mere utilization might adversely affect the resources. She agreed with the views expressed by other members that the element of harm should be assessed case by case. Senior members of the Commission would recall that, after having considered the terms "serious" or "appreciable" harm, the Commission had chosen the criterion of "significant harm" to mean harm that was more than trivial.[1] The Commission might also opt for the term "harm" without any modifier. In practice, it would not make much difference; in any event, it would not be interpreted to mean that any harm would give rise to liability or a claim for damages. The question as to what harm should be considered trivial and thus tolerable depended very much on the actual case and the relevant factors involved. It should be borne in mind, however, that the modifier did not have policy implications. In the *Corfu Channel* case, the obligation to exercise due diligence had been a determining factor in incurring the responsibility of the State to which the harm had been attributed, regardless of the degree. In the area of natural resources and the environment, however, the standard of harm could not be formulated in absolute terms because policy considerations relating to the utilization of resources were often based on a balance between the right to use and the duty to protect. If the deletion of the modifier meant that no harm whatsoever should be allowed, it might make it impossible for States even to use groundwaters.

25. Turning to a number of specific issues, she noted first that the notion of sovereign rights over natural resources as set out in paragraph 19 of the third report was a very important element that should be duly reflected in the future instrument. However, the question was not whether such sovereign rights should be absolute or not, whether or not they were limited. The key element was that the aquifer or aquifer system was transboundary, that it was thus under several national jurisdictions and that States should therefore respect each other's sovereign rights and had a duty to cooperate. For international lawyers that went without saying, and such a statement might seem unnecessary. For States, however, that was the point of departure for elaborating the legal principles that ought to guide their activities affecting the resources located in their territories.

26. Secondly, she questioned the desirability of distinguishing between recharging and non-recharging aquifers, since, as the Special Rapporteur explained in paragraph 22 of his third report, "[i]n most cases, the quantity of contemporary water recharge into an aquifer constitutes only a fraction of the main body of water therein, which has been kept there for hundreds and thousands of years". In other words, such recharge should not be given much weight when considering the sustainability of resources.

27. Thirdly, the question of compensation in draft article 7 was important, but the current wording might be problematic. The absence of agreements on activities between States did not necessarily mean that they could not reach an agreement on the settlement of damages. Besides, international liability rules could also come into play. It would therefore be preferable to use more general wording in article 7, paragraph 3.

---

[1] For discussions of the Commission on these issues see, *inter alia*, *Yearbook ... 1987*, vol., I 2001st–2011th meetings, *passim*; *Yearbook ... 1988*, vol. I, 2045th–2064th meetings, *passim*; *Yearbook ... 1990*, vol. I, 2183rd meeting, para. 6 *et seq.*, 2185th–2186th meetings, passim; and *Yearbook ... 1992*, vol. I, 2272nd meeting, para. 4 *et seq.*

28. Lastly, on the form of the draft, she agreed with the proposal that a working group should be convened to review the question in the light of current research and comments received from States. Of course the Commission might still not be able to reach an agreement on the subject, but it would in any case be premature to refer the draft to the Drafting Committee.

29. Mr. BROWNLIE noted that the general principle enunciated in the *Corfu Channel* case had been quite clear: if a State exercising territorial sovereignty had knowledge or ought to have had knowledge of a cause of harm to a neighbouring State, then the principle applied in an environmental context. If the State exercising territorial sovereignty allowed its groundwater to be a medium for chemical effluents or nuclear waste, even as the result of an accident, that should count as damage if the harmful substances eventually reached a neighbouring State.

30. Mr. MANSFIELD said that all members were aware of the huge amount of time and energy that the Special Rapporteur had devoted to the preparation of his third report and of the assistance he had received from experts from UNESCO and the Study Group of the Japanese Ministry of Foreign Affairs. The Special Rapporteur had done well to consult hydrogeologists and other experts to ensure that the Commission had the most up-to-date scientific information and that the legal norms it developed made sense at the practical level to specialists. He had also been right to present concrete formulations on a fairly complete set of issues.

31. He himself had found it particularly interesting to learn how different underground aquifers were from surface waters, not just in their behaviour but also in their vulnerability to contamination and their ability to respond to clean-up measures. Those differences might also extend to their significance for the future of mankind in a world in which fresh water was in increasingly short supply. In that regard, it might well have been reasonable to deal with groundwaters by way of a protocol to a convention on watercourses in the early 1970s, when the Commission had embarked on its work on what would become the 1997 Watercourses Convention.[2] But for those members who had had the benefit of the detailed briefings by technical experts arranged by the Special Rapporteur, it was difficult to see how that could be considered an appropriate approach at present. For the other members, it might be useful to include more information about the reasons behind particular choices and formulations and, in particular, to explain, as some had already suggested, why some formulations differed from their equivalents in the 1997 Watercourses Convention.

32. He supported the Special Rapporteur's decision to present the Commission with a complete set of formulations in the form of draft articles, without prejudice to a decision on the final form. Some members had wondered whether that was not moving too fast and whether it might not be preferable to focus on elaborating general principles before considering other matters, such as protection and management. He personally was all for taking the time and care necessary to ensure that the quality of the Commission's work did not suffer, and he was confident that the Commission was less likely to be perceived externally as moving too fast than it was as moving too slowly. Even assuming, under the most optimistic scenario, that the Commission completed a first reading in 2006, work would not be completed until midway through the next quinquennium. More importantly, it was critical for the success of the work that the Commission engage the interest of Governments and elicit their responses. Given the busy nature of life in the legal offices of most foreign ministries, such issues would be given greater attention if they were presented as a reasonably full picture that could be completed relatively quickly, rather than as isolated issues with little indication as to the final form of the work or how long it would take. The relatively complete set of draft articles gave Governments a solid and serious basis for discussion, which could only facilitate the work of the Special Rapporteur and the Commission. In that connection, he had no difficulty accepting the Special Rapporteur's recommendation to leave the decision on form until later. Doing so would affect the drafting, but it remained to be seen by how much, and it might be better to refer the question to a working group; he would support the establishment of such a body.

33. With regard to the scope of the future instrument, Mr. Mansfield was pleased that his suggestion for restructuring article 1 had met with support. However, he agreed with other members that the Commission should focus more clearly on the activities of third States that might occur outside the territories in which the aquifers were located but had an impact on them.

34. The definitions in article 2 were acceptable, although they might warrant some refining at a later stage, in particular the definitions of recharging and non-recharging aquifers, which were certainly necessary for the reasons set out in the report.

35. Article 3, on bilateral and regional arrangements, needed further discussion. He agreed that the Commission could not, in a text with a global focus, purport to prescribe how particular aquifers or aquifer systems should be managed. However, if it formulated general principles appropriately, a departure from them at the bilateral or regional level called for some justification.

36. Where the relationship with other instruments was concerned, Mr. Gaja's point regarding article 4, paragraph 1, needed to be taken into account. He welcomed the distinction made in article 5 between recharging and non-recharging aquifers. Paragraph 2 (*b*) was a helpful attempt to give meaning to the concept of reasonable use in the context of a non-recharging aquifer. He was also pleased that in article 7, paragraph 2, the Special Rapporteur had retained the phrase "have or are likely to have an impact on". As to article 7, paragraph 3, while he was aware of the vulnerability of aquifers to pollution, he was not certain that the inclusion of the qualifier "significant" would in fact prove to be "significant", but perhaps a working group could look into the issue. Lastly, the inclusion of a specific article on monitoring was important,

[2] See *Yearbook ... 1974*, vol. II (Part One), document A/9610/Rev.1, pp. 311–316, and *ibid.*, vol. II (Part Two), documents A/5409 and A/CN.4/274, pp. 37–291.

and the provisions on protection, preservation and management would be critical to the perceived value of the final outcome.

37. Mr. MATHESON, referring to part II of the draft articles, said that in his view it was essential to maintain the threshold of "significant harm", which had been adopted after careful consideration in the 1997 Watercourses Convention. As the Special Rapporteur had pointed out, the term was flexible and took account of the vulnerability of aquifers to pollution. For the same reasons, as well as for consistency's sake, the word "significantly" should be inserted in article 5, paragraph 2 (*a*), before "impair the utilization and functions of such aquifer or aquifer system". Article 7 provided that aquifer States must take "all appropriate measures to prevent the causing of significant harm to other aquifer States". That gave States adequate flexibility to take the steps that were best suited in a particular situation to prevent or mitigate harm. The same language should be used in article 5, paragraph 2 (*a*): aquifer States must be required to take all appropriate measures to avoid significant impairment to the utilization and functions of the aquifer. It would also be useful for the commentary to give some explanation of what "impairment" meant in practical terms. In addition, it had been suggested that the requirement in article 5, paragraph 2 (*a*) that States take into account the sustainability of the aquifer was too weak. There again, the Special Rapporteur had explained that a strict rule of sustainable use would not be appropriate, given the limited recharge capabilities of most aquifers. In reality, such a rule would deny aquifer States the use of the resource. It seemed to him that aquifer States must be given the flexibility to decide how to balance the objective of sustainability against the need to make use of the resources for the benefit of their populations.

38. Article 6 provided a very useful explanation of the factors to be taken into account for reasonable and equitable utilization of an aquifer. Those factors should include the degree to which an aquifer State had invested in the development and protection of the aquifer. It was not entirely clear whether subparagraph (*f*) included that consideration. The point should therefore be clarified either in the text or in the commentary.

39. He agreed that the issue of compensation, evoked in article 7, should be dealt with elsewhere. The Commission had already seen that the question of liability for transboundary harm was a complex matter that could not be reduced to a simple statement of obligation. The principles on such liability completed on first reading in 2004[3] would apply to any harm caused to other aquifer States, a fact that might be noted in the commentary. For the time being, it would be wise not to make the language on compensation more definitive or more complicated.

40. Mr. Sreenivasa RAO, referring to draft articles 5 to 7, said that it was essential to provide States with sufficient flexibility to apply those principles to their particular circumstances. However, the mechanism that the Commission was elaborating must also be tailored to fit the special characteristics of the resource in question. Two factors must be taken into consideration: the needs of States, which varied from one country to another, and requirements concerning the resources, which also differed. Those were not matters that could be objectively assessed in defining equitable and reasonable utilization. The distinction was important: equitable utilization sought to accommodate the interests of States, while reasonable utilization must be suited to the characteristics of the resource itself. As they stood, the articles did not offer immediate guidance to States. Any further clarification should be placed in the commentary, not in the text of the article, which should be left unchanged. Such an approach, which was not new, having been followed for the topic of international liability, met the concerns of members without altering the text.

41. With regard to the pace of work, it was probable that the principles defined for the 1997 Watercourses Convention could have been applied *mutatis mutandis* to groundwaters. Yet even if the Commission came to the same conclusions as in 1997, the time spent delving further into the question, notably by consulting experts, had clearly been profitable.

42. It must be borne in mind that all human interaction entailed harm. The utilization of an aquifer by one State necessarily led to a lesser utilization by another. Thus, the criterion of reasonableness was fundamental; however, it could be expressed in general terms. On the other hand, an assessment of harm made it possible to introduce the notion of prevention. That aspect must be developed within the scope of draft articles 5 and 7.

43. Draft article 7 addressed the classic doctrine of harm as a result of utilization. But as prevention had been dealt within the context of liability, a set of principles on prevention should be included. States must take all necessary precautions before utilizing a given resource, a point for which provision was made in draft article 5, paragraph 2 (*a*), pursuant to which States must refrain from "impairing" the aquifer. "Impair" did not mean "to cause harm" in the sense of article 7, but it might be considered that impairment could cause harm and that States must therefore avoid impairment through measures of prevention. If harm occurred despite prevention and reasonable utilization, the question of compensation should then be addressed, in conformity with the principle set out in article 7. The question of compensation had evolved since the 1997 Watercourses Convention. Viewing it from a broader perspective, by incorporating the notion of prevention, might lead to a set of different articles dealing with harm caused despite prevention and reasonable utilization. The working group should focus on that aspect of the question.

44. In short, the draft must ensure reasonable, equitable and sustainable utilization of resources to meet the needs not only of future generations but current ones as well, for what people could not do for themselves they could not do for others.

[3] *Yearbook ... 2004*, vol. II (Part Two), chap. VII, para. 175.

45. Mr. CHEE pointed out that article XVI of the Helsinki Rules on the Uses of the Waters of International Rivers,[4] revised in 2004 by the International Law Association at its seventy-first conference held in Berlin,[5] had spoken of "significant harm", which would appear to be appropriate. He also sought further clarification as to the meaning of the term "recharging aquifer".

46. Mr. YAMADA (Special Rapporteur) said that the shortcomings in his report were due to the fact that the draft was still preliminary; with the help of the Commission's comments, it would be improved.

47. In reply to Mr. Chee's question, he said that at an informal meeting to be held that afternoon he would be showing a highly instructive film on the Guaraní Aquifer System, which was a recharging aquifer.

48. While he had asked the members of the Commission to focus on the substance of the draft rather than the form, he had not ruled out a discussion on that point. Some delegations in the Sixth Committee had called for guidelines, but many States wanted a legally binding document (A/CN.4/549 and Add.1, paras. 73–74). If necessary, presentation in the form of a convention could easily be changed to that of guidelines. As the form and the substance were interrelated, he hoped that the working group would look into that question.

49. He was aware that some members thought that he was proceeding too quickly. However, States expected the Commission to complete its work on transboundary groundwaters fairly soon. Moreover, he had the feeling that the Commission played a less important role than it had when first established some 50 years earlier. It was therefore essential to meet the expectations of States. As Mr. Mansfield had pointed out, even if the draft was completed in first reading in 2006, many years of work still lay ahead.

Organization of work of the session (*continued*)

[Agenda item 1]

50. The CHAIRPERSON reminded members that the European Society of International Law had offered to hold a joint meeting with the Commission on the subject of the responsibility of international organizations. The Bureau would consider that proposal at its next meeting.

The meeting rose at 12.55 p.m.

---

[4] International Law Association, *Report of the Fifty-Second Conference (Helsinki 1966)*, London, 1967, pp. 477–533, at pp. 508–509.

[5] The Berlin Rules are available on the website of the International Law Association (http://www.internationalwaterlaw.org/documents/intldocs/ILA_Berlin_Rules-2004.pdf). See also International Law Association, *Report of the Seventy-First Conference (Berlin 2004)*, London, 2004, pp. 335–412.

2834th MEETING

Friday, 6 May 2005, at 10 a.m.

Chairperson: Mr. Djamchid MOMTAZ

Present: Mr. Addo, Mr. Baena Soares, Mr. Brownlie, Mr. Candioti, Mr. Chee, Mr. Comissário Afonso, Mr. Daoudi, Mr. Dugard, Mr. Economides, Ms. Escarameia, Mr. Fomba, Mr. Gaja, Mr. Galicki, Mr. Kabatsi, Mr. Kateka, Mr. Kemicha, Mr. Kolodkin, Mr. Mansfield, Mr. Matheson, Mr. Niehaus, Mr. Opertti Badan, Mr. Pambou-Tchivounda, Mr. Pellet, Mr. Sreenivasa Rao, Mr. Rodríguez Cedeño, Mr. Sepúlveda, Ms. Xue, Mr. Yamada.

Shared natural resources (*continued*) (A/CN.4/549 and Add.1, sect. B, A/CN.4/551 and Corr.1 and Add.1, A/CN.4/555 and Add.1)

[Agenda item 4]

THIRD REPORT OF THE SPECIAL RAPPORTEUR (*continued*)

1. The CHAIRPERSON invited the Commission to continue its consideration of the third report of the Special Rapporteur on shared natural resources (A/CN.4/551, Corr.1 and Add.1).

2. Mr. FOMBA said that water was a strategic resource vital to mankind's survival and development, and was rightly a concern of the General Assembly and the Commission. While the question of surface waters had been settled with the adoption of the 1997 Convention on the Law of the Non-navigational Uses of International Watercourses, international law with regard to groundwaters, regardless of whether they were connected to surface waters, had yet to be codified, or rather, progressively developed, a task not made easier by the paucity of State practice and international instruments in that area. Thorny questions therefore remained on how best to broach the subject, what kind of legal text should be proposed to States, what such a text should contain, and how to ensure that it was consistent with the 1997 Watercourses Convention and that the new instrument would be useful and effective in practice.

3. The Special Rapporteur had been well advised to seek the views of groundwater experts and, in particular, to include in the second part of his report, references to State practice and provisions from the few existing relevant international instruments. As far as regional arrangements were concerned, he would be interested to know if there were any transboundary aquifers or aquifer systems in West Africa and, if so, whether there were any programmes for cooperation in their management. He would be glad to pass on to the Special Rapporteur any useful information he could obtain in that respect from various national or regional authorities or organizations in the region.

4. While he welcomed the comprehensive scope of the draft articles contained in the report, he noted that the

Special Rapporteur, in striving for concision, had not provided sufficiently detailed explanations on some points. As to the final form that the draft would take, he agreed with those members who had criticized the Special Rapporteur's decision to present his proposals in the form of draft articles of a convention while maintaining that he did not wish to prejudge the question of their final form. However, he was less concerned than some members with the inclusion of a reference to permanent sovereignty in the preamble or elsewhere in the draft; he did not believe that there was any risk of undermining that principle even if such a reference was omitted altogether.

5. Turning to specifics, he said that while the wording of draft article 1 was acceptable as a whole, an effort should be made to further clarify the relation between transboundary aquifers and aquifer systems on the one hand and national aquifers and aquifer systems on the other, and also between aquifer States and third States. Clarification of the technical scope of the terms defined in draft article 2 would give members of the Commission a clearer understanding of the legal effect of the terms used, and thus of the content of the legal regime to be proposed. Article 3 should figure prominently in the architecture of the draft, inasmuch as it confirmed the legitimacy, legality and primacy of bilateral and regional arrangements. Draft article 4 was a step in the right direction, since it gave automatic precedence to the draft convention over the 1997 Watercourses Convention in the event of a conflict between the two and, in certain circumstances, gave it precedence over other international agreements in disputes relating to groundwaters. The principle of equitable and reasonable utilization, which was the subject of draft article 5, was already enshrined in the 1997 Watercourses Convention and other international instruments, and was even more important in relation to groundwaters by virtue of their specific nature. However, he wondered if that concept should be viewed as an absolute or relative one, whether it entailed an obligation of result or of conduct, and how the requirement that aquifer States should "not impair the utilization and functions of such aquifer or aquifer system", as mentioned in draft article 5, paragraph 2 (*a*), was to be interpreted, as it was not clear whether the aim was zero risk or some form of graduated risk or risk threshold.

6. With regard to draft article 6, he asked if there was any difference between the "natural condition of the aquifer" referred to in paragraph 1 (*a*) and the "natural factors" referred to in paragraph 24 of the report. On draft article 7, and the question whether a threshold for harm was appropriate for groundwaters, he believed that the answer depended on whether, and to what extent, the problems related to harm were posed in the same terms as in the case of surface waters. More fundamentally, the precautionary principle, according to which the lack of scientific certainty should not prevent or delay the adoption of preventive measures, was particularly important with regard to groundwaters. He noted that the Special Rapporteur accepted that scientists had good reason for favouring the application of the precautionary principle, while remaining unconvinced that the precautionary principle had yet developed as a rule of general international law (para. 33). On the question of compensation raised in draft article 7, paragraph 3, he agreed with the views expressed by the Special Rapporteur in paragraph 26 of the report.

7. With regard to draft article 13, on the protection of recharge and discharge zones, the best solution would be to try to clarify the rights and obligations of States other than aquifer States and their legal and practical links with aquifer States. Draft article 18, which dealt with scientific and technical assistance to developing States, was theoretically very important, particularly as it established a legal obligation to provide such assistance; the problem, however, was how to secure its practical application.

8. In conclusion, he agreed that the draft articles should be referred to the Drafting Committee, but only after they had been submitted to a working group for a decision on whether they should take the form of a convention, a protocol to the 1997 Watercourses Convention or a set of guidelines.

9. Mr. NIEHAUS said he agreed with the Special Rapporteur that a reference to the sensitive issue of permanent sovereignty over natural resources should be included in the preamble to the draft articles, regardless of whether it was mentioned elsewhere in the draft, in order to reflect the importance of that issue. He disagreed with those members of the Commission who felt that the draft was too weak. The Special Rapporteur had addressed a new and difficult topic with great skill and caution, in language appropriate to a framework convention. He agreed with the Special Rapporteur that a decision on the final form of the text should be taken only once the substance had been agreed upon. He also agreed with Mr. Brownlie that the text should be related more closely to the principles of general international law, in view of the crucial importance of applying those principles to the legal regulation of transboundary aquifers and aquifer systems.

10. With regard to the scope of the draft convention, he wondered if cases might not arise in which the distinction between national and transboundary aquifers or aquifer systems was not clear-cut, as when, for example, part of an aquifer lay along a border. Perhaps the draft convention should make some provision for dealing with possible disputes over the character of the water resources that were to be regulated. He wondered, moreover, if the agreement referred to in paragraph 6 of the report, which would allow States other than aquifer States to use transboundary aquifers and aquifer systems, needed to be unanimous. Although that issue was probably best dealt with in a bilateral or regional agreement rather than in a framework convention, it did illustrate the complexity and the highly technical nature of the topic.

11. Unfortunately, that complexity did not seem to be reflected in draft article 2, on the use of terms. For the sake of clarity, the list of definitions should be expanded to include more terms than the six listed. He also noted the need to amend the phrase "a series of more than two aquifers", in the third sentence of paragraph 9 of the report, to align it with the corrected wording of paragraph (*b*), namely, "a series of two or more aquifers". A stronger wording was needed in draft article 3, paragraph 1, on the entitlement of any State in whose territory an aquifer or aquifer system was located to participate in the

negotiations on a bilateral or regional arrangement, to ensure equality of opportunities to participate in those negotiations. In contrast, draft article 5, was admirably clear on the important principle of equitable and reasonable utilization. He agreed with the Special Rapporteur that the issue of liability should be dealt with in another forum. Lastly, he endorsed the suggestion to set up a working group to consider proposals for improvements to the draft articles before referring them back to the Commission for consideration.

12. Mr. GALICKI said that, thanks to the Special Rapporteur, members of the Commission had received a solid grounding in geology, hydrology and other areas of natural science of which they needed some knowledge if they were to find appropriate solutions to the legal problems relating to transboundary aquifers and aquifer systems. He fully agreed with the Special Rapporteur that a decision on the final form of the draft articles should be taken only once agreement had been reached on their substance. For the time being, at least, it was useful to be able to compare a draft in the form of a convention with existing regulations applicable to transboundary aquifers, such as the 1997 Watercourses Convention.

13. Inclusion of a reference to General Assembly resolution 1803 (XVII) seemed a good way to satisfy those States that were strongly in favour of mentioning the principle of permanent sovereignty over natural resources without actually referring to it in the operative part of the text. However, a decision on the final wording of the preamble should be postponed until a later stage. The scope of the draft convention, as formulated in draft article 1, reflected the general structure and content of the draft as a whole, but paragraph (*b*) of that article was somewhat vague; the term "other activities" was not sufficiently precise, and that lack of precision was exacerbated by the use of the term "impact" rather than the term "harm" used in draft article 7. Although the Special Rapporteur explained in paragraph 6 of his report that "[t]he term 'impact' should be construed as a wider concept than 'harm'", it was not clear to what extent the impact of "other activities" should be covered by the draft convention, especially in cases where such activities were carried out by non-aquifer States outside the territories of aquifer States. Perhaps the list of definitions of terms contained in article 2 could be extended to include terms such as "harm", "significant harm" and "impact".

14. Article 3 of the draft, entitled "Bilateral and regional arrangements", departed from the terminology of the 1997 Watercourses Convention, which referred to "agreements". That departure seemed unjustified if the "arrangements" were to rank as international legal instruments. The justification given by the Special Rapporteur in paragraph 12 of his report was not fully convincing, especially in the light of his statement in paragraph 14 that "bilateral and regional arrangements take priority, as *lex specialis*, over the draft convention".

15. The subject of article 4, the draft convention's relation to other conventions and international agreements, seemed at first glance to be a purely formal problem, yet that was far from the case. In paragraph 16 of the third report the Special Rapporteur acknowledged the possibility of dual applicability of the draft convention and the 1997 Watercourses Convention. That state of affairs might be unavoidable, as the definition of a watercourse in article 2, paragraph (*a*), of the 1997 Watercourses Convention described surface waters and groundwaters as "constituting by virtue of their physical relationship a unitary whole". The existence of two parallel legal systems, one governing transboundary aquifers and aquifer systems, and the other, watercourses, understood as including groundwaters connected with surface waters, was bound sooner or later to lead to conflict situations. It might be open to question which legal system should prevail, since the 1997 Watercourses Convention was a more comprehensive instrument, covering combined systems of surface waters and groundwaters, whereas the draft convention was limited to groundwaters located in aquifers.

16. Theoretically, there could be situations in which the physical characteristics of the waters governed by the two conventions changed: in dry seasons, certain rivers sometimes disappeared temporarily. If they were connected with underground aquifers, the aquifers could be covered for the dry half of the year by the draft convention, and for the other half, by the 1997 Watercourses Convention. To avoid such paradoxes, the relationship between the two conventions as proposed in article 4, paragraph 1, of the draft convention should be thoroughly reviewed. The discussion should take into account the proposals made, *inter alia*, on reformulation of the instrument into a draft protocol to the 1997 Watercourses Convention. Such an approach should not be seen as diminishing the new instrument's importance, and it could help create a unified, comprehensive legal system governing both surface waters and groundwaters in all their possible configurations.

17. Using such an approach, the draft articles could address specific problems concerning transboundary aquifers, while also acknowledging the general principles and applicable provisions of the 1997 Watercourses Convention. If, however, the Commission decided to have a separate convention on the law of transboundary aquifers, certain provisions could be further improved, as compared to the 1997 Convention. For instance, the phrase in article 7, paragraph 3, "to discuss the question of compensation", which was taken from article 7, paragraph 2, of the 1997 Watercourses Convention, could be reconsidered in the light of the fact that the draft convention did not, in principle, deal with matters of liability. The language of many provisions could be made stronger and more formal. Draft article 8, paragraph 2, for example, used the weak formulation "States are encouraged", and draft article 9, paragraph 2, contained the wording "States shall employ their best efforts".

18. In any case, it seemed advisable not to refer to draft articles to the Drafting Committee at the present stage, but rather to convene a working group, under the chairpersonship of the Special Rapporteur, to consider in detail the scope, substance and form of the future instrument on transboundary aquifers. He would welcome the opportunity to participate in such a group.

19. Mr. BAENA SOARES acknowledged the difficulty of breaking new ground on a technically complex and as

yet ill-defined topic. As the Special Rapporteur had indicated, while the draft articles were presented as being part of a convention, that did not prejudge their final form. He himself thought that States should be given freedom to determine the form of the text ultimately to be adopted.

20. It was essential that the principle of permanent sovereignty over natural resources, enshrined in General Assembly resolution 1803 (XVII), should figure in the draft. He did not consider that to be a sensitive question, nor did he think it should simply be mentioned in the preamble. Like other speakers, he believed that the principle should be included as a separate article in the operative part of the text in order to give it the requisite weight.

21. The Special Rapporteur was right to acknowledge the importance of bilateral and regional agreements. Agreements and negotiations in good faith constituted the most effective form of cooperation between aquifer States, which, after all, had access to the most authoritative information about the specific situation of an aquifer.

22. Mr. Opertti Badan had referred on a number of occasions to the Guaraní aquifer. The Special Rapporteur had given the Commission some general information on a four-year project being implemented with the support of the World Bank and the Organization of American States with a view to gaining a better understanding of the physical and technical characteristics of that aquifer. The Council of MERCOSUR had invited an ad hoc group to elaborate a draft agreement among member States with a view to establishing principles and criteria for the use of the Guaraní aquifer. He had had the honour of participating in that group's work, the results of which were now being considered by the Foreign Ministries of Argentina, Brazil, Paraguay and Uruguay. Three considerations had guided the group's work: permanent sovereignty over natural resources, the obligation not to cause significant harm, and conservation through rational and sustainable utilization of the aquifer (A/CN.4/549, paras. 46–47). What had emerged above all from the experience was the spirit of cooperation that would undoubtedly also prevail in other regional arrangements or agreements. That example of cooperation in the use of the Guaraní aquifer formed part of a set of initiatives of the four MERCOSUR countries to work towards economic integration.

23. The 1997 Watercourses Convention had its own specific objective and provisions. While it was entirely understandable that it should have served initially as a compass to guide those venturing into *terra incognita*, the draft under consideration catered for different conditions and circumstances. It had its own autonomous life, and the pertinence of the 1997 Convention to groundwaters was relatively tenuous. He saw little use in continuing to consider the hypothesis of dual applicability unless more technical information was provided. He also hoped that the draft would gain much wider support than the 20-odd ratifications that the 1997 Watercourses Convention had so far attracted.

24. The Special Rapporteur had made felicitous proposals in draft article 6, on factors relevant to equitable and reasonable utilization of aquifer systems. He had in mind the references to the economic and social needs of the aquifer States (para. (*b*)) and to the population dependent on the aquifer or aquifer system (para. (*c*)). With regard to utilization, he recalled the obligation not only to preserve aquifer resources for future generations, but also for the benefit of the present generation.

25. Two articles (articles 8 and 9) were devoted to modalities of cooperation. Aquifer States were left to determine the manner of their cooperation and were encouraged to exchange information. It was important to stress the need for provision of specific data that gave a better picture of the aquifer system. Without such information, it would be extremely difficult to establish plans and standards for utilization.

26. The inclusion of an article on the obligation not to cause harm (article 7) between the articles on equitable and reasonable utilization and on the obligation to cooperate was logical. He agreed with the Special Rapporteur that the threshold of "significant harm" was appropriate and should be retained; that was one of the central obligations in cooperative exercises.

27. The statement in the beginning of paragraph 33 that "[t]he objectives of the draft articles are not to protect and preserve aquifers for the sake of aquifers but to protect and preserve them so that humankind could utilize the precious water resources contained therein" should be rephrased. It might be misconstrued, particularly in its use of the word "humankind", which might be taken to imply that aquifer systems were part of the common heritage of humankind. If the concept of a common heritage of humankind was not applied to other natural resources such as oil and gas, there was no reason why it should be applied to water.

28. Lastly, he commended the Special Rapporteur on the prudent approach he had adopted. He had calculated an appropriate period for the draft to mature, one that neither precipitated nor held back the process. He had no objection to the establishment of a working group and if one was set up, he would welcome the opportunity to participate in it.

29. Mr. KOLODKIN congratulated the Special Rapporteur on his seminal report, which drew on a wide range of materials. Owing, no doubt, to his own lack of familiarity with the topic of transboundary groundwaters, he had always had some difficulty in differentiating it from that of international watercourses. Even after reading the third report, he still saw the topic as a sub-topic or extension of that of international watercourses. State practice offered precious few examples of independent regulation of aquifers, and the international legal instruments that dealt with transboundary watercourses frequently covered aquifers as well. Similarly, at the bilateral and regional levels, aquifers were governed by the same rules that applied to other transboundary watercourses. Nevertheless, the report showed that some transboundary aquifers and aquifer systems had their own specific characteristics that might necessitate special regulation differing from that of other international watercourses.

30. The draft before the Commission was largely—and, in his view, rightly—based on the 1997 Watercourses

Convention. Only one third of the 21 substantive articles were new. About the same number were to all intents and purposes borrowed from the 1997 Convention, and the remainder were largely based on it. In a number of cases the question arose whether there was any need to modify the language of the 1997 Watercourses Convention, and several of the departures made from that Convention required explanation in the commentary. It was quite natural that the two texts should largely coincide, since in many respects their subjects overlapped. A significant number of transboundary groundwaters would be regulated by the 1997 Watercourses Convention, and only a few aquifers would be governed by the new instrument; indeed, one could not rule out the possibility of disputes arising between States over which of the two applied.

31. The new instrument should, in the first place, be a legally binding instrument like the 1997 Watercourses Convention. Secondly, again like that Convention, it should be a framework convention. It must contain basic general principles with which aquifer States that were parties to the instrument must comply, whether or not pursuant to agreements concluded amongst themselves. States should be offered sufficient flexibility when concluding agreements to take due account of the specific nature of each individual aquifer or aquifer system, the particular nature of relations among the States concerned, their levels of social and economic development and the related factors to which Ms. Xue had alluded, the actual priorities for the use of aquifers at the specific time involved, and many other elements. He concurred with Mr. Matheson on the need for such flexibility. At the same time, the future instrument must also offer guidance on the conclusion of agreements *inter se*.

32. In the absence of such agreements, or in situations where not all transboundary aquifer States were parties to them, States that were not bound by the agreements had the right to act independently with respect to the aquifer, as Mr. Opertti Badan had pointed out. But that freedom, reinforced by the principle of sovereignty over natural resources located within national territory, was not and could not be absolute. Strictly speaking, it did not exist even now. In the absence of the instrument now being envisaged, there was general international law, the relevant rules of which, as Mr. Brownlie had pointed out, were applicable to the conduct of States, including in respect of transboundary aquifers. Those rules were not solely the provisions on liability for acts not prohibited by international law, but also customary rules on responsibility for internationally wrongful acts. In that connection, he saw no need for the inclusion in the draft of any provisions on its relation to general international law, although its relevance might, for instance, be confirmed in the preamble.

33. At the same time, the conduct of States that were not parties to specific agreements on aquifers must be regulated in the future instrument. That was why the provisions being formulated by the Commission must remain fairly general, like those of the 1997 Watercourses Convention. The draft submitted by the Special Rapporteur corresponded, on the whole, to the considerations he had just outlined. He would nevertheless have preferred the Commission to determine at the present juncture whether it was formulating a legally binding instrument, as he advocated, or a set of recommendations. As to the form, he would not rule out a protocol to the 1997 Watercourses Convention, although he had no objection in principle to a separate treaty.

34. Turning to specific provisions, he said he had serious doubts about draft articles 3 and 4. He agreed with Mr. Galicki that the reason for the emergence of the term "arrangements" was not clear. It could be construed as covering both legally binding arrangements, in other words, international legal instruments, and also non-binding arrangements such as political or so-called "administrative" arrangements. Or it could be construed as covering only the latter. In which sense was it used in draft article 3? If it was used in the first sense, then there was an obvious overlap between draft articles 3 and 4. If it was used in the second sense, then one wondered what was the purpose of draft article 4, which determined the relation of the draft convention with texts that were not international legal instruments. And in that case, was it right that draft article 3, paragraph 3, should give a non-international legal arrangement priority over an international treaty?

35. The second sentence in draft article 3, paragraph 1, seemed unduly detailed. If the article was retained, thought should be given to deleting that sentence. Nor was he convinced that article 311, paragraph 2, of the United Nations Convention on the Law of the Sea was a good model for article 4, paragraph 2, of the draft. That Convention, unlike the present draft, could hardly be viewed as basically a framework instrument. Paragraph 2 should refer, not to agreements compatible with the draft convention in its entirety, but to those compatible with its general principles. It might be useful to look into the advisability of replacing draft articles 3 and 4 with article 3 of the 1997 Watercourses Convention. Certainly, any departure from that text must be given full justification, which in his view was lacking at present.

36. If the distinction between recharging and non-recharging aquifers was to be retained, then the absence in draft article 5, paragraph 2 (*b*), of any reference to sustainability was justified. The applicability of that concept to recharging aquifers, especially when there was no alternative to their use, was by no means indisputable, however. Would it not be sufficient simply to retain the existing references to equitable and reasonable utilization in article 5?

37. He also favoured retaining the qualifier "significant" for the word "harm", for reasons already mentioned by others. It was not entirely clear why the title of draft article 7 omitted the term "significant", in contrast to the corresponding article of the 1997 Watercourses Convention. He did not agree with those who wanted to develop the reference in article 7, paragraph 3, to compensation, and to liability in general, since that issue was covered by the norms of general international law. The paragraph was modelled on article 7, paragraph 2, of the 1997 Watercourses Convention, which would be better left untouched.

38. Draft article 10, paragraph 1, on monitoring, was formulated in far too categorical a fashion. It was hardly possible to establish a universal obligation to agree on

harmonized standards and methodology for monitoring a transboundary aquifer or aquifer system. It would be more realistic to refer to the obligation to cooperate in monitoring matters and to exchange information. The paragraph's wording was more appropriate to agreements between aquifer States or agreements at the regional level.

39. Draft article 13, an important innovation in comparison with the 1997 Watercourses Convention, introduced the concept of detrimental impact. Yet terms like "impact" (art. 1), "significant harm" (arts. 7 *et al.*), "serious harm" (art. 19), "adverse effects" (art. 16) and "significant adverse effect" (art. 17) were also used. Some comments on or explanations of the wide variety of terms used were needed.

40. Draft article 15 was devoted to management. Unlike the corresponding article in the 1997 Watercourses Convention, however, it gave no explanation of that notion, which was used in a wide variety of senses in various international treaties. There, too, it might be worth following the example of the 1997 Watercourses Convention.

41. Paragraph 37 of the report, commenting on article 16, stated that it was based on article 11 of the 1997 Watercourses Convention. That was not entirely true, however. Article 16 set out the obligation of aquifer States themselves to assess the potential effects of their planned activities. Article 11 of the 1997 Watercourses Convention, however, spoke of exchange of information, consultation and negotiation on the possible effects of planned measures. He was not convinced that the nine articles devoted to planned measures in the 1997 Watercourses Convention should be compressed into two in the draft convention.

42. His specific comments on the articles should not be construed as in any way disparaging the draft. On the contrary, impressive progress had been made on the topic. Those who favoured discussing the draft in a working group were doubtless right, but the need for its subsequent referral to the Drafting Committee must be constantly borne in mind. Consideration of the draft on first reading at the Commission's next session seemed to him to be entirely feasible.

43. Mr. CANDIOTI commended the Special Rapporteur's excellent work and in particular his focus on the Guaraní aquifer, which was under the jurisdiction of the four MERCOSUR States. He endorsed the structure and general thrust of the draft, which served as a good basis for elaborating a set of principles on the subject. Although the decision on the form would have to be addressed at a later stage, the principles should, in his view, be formulated as normative proposals. He agreed with those members who felt that a number of provisions needed to be improved in the working group or in the Drafting Committee.

44. The principle of the sovereignty of aquifer States over their natural resources should be included in the operative part of the text, not merely in the preamble. The explicit affirmation of that principle in one of the draft articles was consistent with the legal character of the transboundary aquifer and the crucial role assigned to aquifer States in the draft. The Special Rapporteur had rightly argued that the utilization and management of a transboundary aquifer was exclusively a matter for the aquifer States and that on no account was an internationalization or universalization of such aquifers to be contemplated.

45. Turning to the individual draft articles, he endorsed the three paragraphs of article 1, on the scope of the draft. As to the order in which they were presented, he supported Ms. Xue's proposal to accord more prominence to the protection, preservation and management of aquifers in view of their fragile and vulnerable nature and the vital human needs which they must meet.

46. On draft article 2, he agreed with the new definitions of "aquifer" and "aquifer system", but was in favour of deleting the bracketed phrases in paragraphs (*a*) and (*b*). He had doubts whether the distinction made in paragraphs (*e*) and (*f*) between "recharging" and "non-recharging" aquifers was appropriate and relevant at the current stage of consideration. The Commission should postpone to a later date discussion of whether separate norms were needed as a consequence of that distinction.

47. In draft article 3, he, too, would prefer a more forceful wording of the entitlement of aquifer States to enter into bilateral or regional arrangements for the management of transboundary aquifers and the obligation of each aquifer State to respect the rights of the others. It was also right to provide, in paragraph 2, for the harmonization of such arrangements with the other principles of the draft, the consideration of the characteristics and special uses of a particular aquifer or aquifer system, and the obligation of the aquifer States to consult and negotiate in good faith.

48. The rules proposed in article 4 were appropriate, but should perhaps be relocated at the end of the draft. He also endorsed the principle of equitable and reasonable utilization as formulated in article 5, as well as the substance of the principles set out in draft articles 6 to 11.

49. He agreed with those members who had recommended the inclusion of a precautionary principle through a stronger wording than that currently found in article 14. Protection of transboundary aquifers against the risk of pollution should be a priority in all matters relating to their utilization and management.

50. Mr. CHEE noted that the issue of permanent sovereignty over natural resources would be dealt with in the preamble, in the final stages of work on the draft. In his view, States must be prepared to accept certain restrictions on their sovereignty under any treaty which they concluded.

51. On draft article 1, he noted that the reference in paragraph (*b*) to "other activities" was too vague to establish who was responsible for the impact on an aquifer or aquifer system. The word "activities" seemed merely to relate to the activities of States, whether or not parties to the convention.

52. He did not think that draft article 3 was necessary; given the large number of bilateral or regional

arrangements for managing transboundary aquifers already in existence, an additional cooperation mechanism would be superfluous. Article 3 would be more useful in regions where no such arrangements existed.

53. Draft article 4, paragraph 1, referred to the relation between the proposed draft convention and the 1997 Watercourses Convention. However, only a handful of Member States had yet ratified that Convention, which, moreover, made only one reference to groundwaters, in its article 2, paragraph (*a*), which reflected the concept of hydrological interdependence. In paragraph 16 of the third report, the Special Rapporteur admitted that the 1997 Convention's relevance to groundwaters was somewhat peripheral. Nonetheless, the 1997 Convention could perhaps serve as a framework for the current draft.

54. Draft article 5, paragraphs 1 and 2, drew heavily on article 5 of the 1997 Convention. The information contained in paragraph 22 of the report on the recharge of aquifers constituted an important contribution to the developing law on groundwaters. Draft article 7, paragraph 2, would be clearer if the word "adverse" were inserted before "impact".

55. Draft article 8 referred to the general obligation of States to "cooperate on the basis of sovereign equality, territorial integrity, mutual benefit and good faith", and reasonable utilization, and encouraged States "to establish joint mechanisms or commissions". Such mechanisms were already the basis for almost all existing transboundary water arrangements. The provisions of draft article 9 were of great importance in securing international cooperation on the protection and conservation of aquifers. Draft article 10, on monitoring, was a new and welcome proposal. He also endorsed articles 12, 13 and 14, which could be implemented if the necessary technology and information were available.

56. With regard to draft article 15, he had already suggested the establishment of a boundary commission to serve as an administrative arm of the convention. The provisions of article 8, paragraph 2, might be reproduced, as a second paragraph of article 15. Such enforcement and management bodies already existed in relations between the United States and Canada, the United States and Mexico, and between many other States.

57. Article 17 was an important provision, the subject of timely notification having already been addressed in the 1957 Lake Lanoux arbitration between France and Spain and the 1974 Convention on the protection of the environment (Nordic Environmental Protection Convention) between Denmark, Finland, Norway and Sweden. Draft article 20, however, seemed more applicable to surface water.

58. On a more general note, he said that he had not found any indication of the impact of the Bellagio Draft Treaty.[1] How the 1986 Seoul Rules on International Groundwaters[2] and the 2004 Berlin Rules on Water Resources[3] would influence the future direction of international law in that area remained to be seen. It was unfortunate that the work of Mr. McCaffrey[4] and other writers on groundwaters was still not fully appreciated. Nevertheless, the Commission should continue to work towards producing an instrument which could be signed by all States with an interest in international cooperation on aquifers and aquifer systems. He would support all efforts directed to that end.

Effects of armed conflicts on treaties (A/CN.4/552,[5] A/CN.4/550 and Corr.1–2[6])

[Agenda item 8]

First report of the Special Rapporteur

59. The CHAIRPERSON invited Mr. Brownlie to introduce his first report on the effects of armed conflicts on treaties (A/CN.4/552), and drew attention to the memorandum by the Secretariat (A/CN.4/550 and Corr.1–2), which contained a comprehensive examination of practice and doctrine concerning the question.

60. Mr. BROWNLIE (Special Rapporteur), introducing his first report on the effects of armed conflicts on treaties, said that his own conception of the subject was that it had a clear centre of gravity: the draft constituted a package of articles that it had been difficult to break down into parts, since it formed a cohesive whole.

61. The first goal of the draft was to clarify the legal position. The second was to promote and enhance the security of legal relations between States. Therefore, the underlying agenda was to limit the occasions on which it might be said that the incidence of armed conflict had an effect on treaty relations. That had a bearing on the ambit of the concept of armed conflict. The third goal was to increase access to and utilization of State practice on the subject. Given the subject matter, the method adopted had been to provide a set of articles, without prejudice to the final form which the draft might take. In any event, because of the need to clarify the legal position, some expository drafting had been necessary.

62. Writers on the subject usually stressed the uncertainty attending the sources, but that concern might be exaggerated. The subject was dominated by the doctrine, whereas practice was thin on the ground. Any available practice had been brought into play, but much of it was more than 60 years old. That did not necessarily invalidate it: it was not necessarily the case that policy perspectives on the effects of armed conflict had changed qualitatively since 1920. As he saw it, the key change in the inter-war period had been the gradual shift towards pragmatism and away from the view that the incidence of armed conflict was beyond the realm of law and more or less non-justiciable. That being said, there was an obvious

[1] See Hayton and Utton, *loc. cit.* (2832nd meeting, footnote 3).

[2] International Law Association, *Report of the Sixty-Second Conference (Seoul 1986)* London, 1987 ("Committee on International Water Recourse Law, Report of the Committee", p. 8).

[3] See 2832nd meeting, footnote 1.

[4] See, in particular, the seventh report of Mr. McCaffrey on the law of the non-navigational uses of international watercourses, *Yearbook ... 1991*, vol. II (Part One), document A/CN.4/436, paras. 17–49.

[5] Reproduced in *Yearbook ... 2005*, vol. II (Part One).

[6] Mimeographed; available on the Commission website.

need for access to more evidence of practice, and especially recent practice.

63. The draft articles had a provisional character and a practical purpose: to generate an input of information and opinions from Governments. The need for evidence of State practice was clear enough, but the process of collecting practice and opinion would be more effective if Governments were presented with a package of draft articles that was more or less comprehensive.

64. The draft articles were intended to be compatible with the 1969 Vienna Convention on the Law of Treaties. There was a general assumption that the subject matter under examination formed a province of the law of treaties, rather than a development of the law relating to the use of force. As members would recall, article 73 of the 1969 Vienna Convention expressly excluded the subject of the effects of an outbreak of hostilities.

65. The next problem was the treatment of the concept of an armed conflict. When the topic had first been proposed as an addition to the agenda, justifiable concerns had been expressed that it would lead to a general academic exposition of the question. The Special Rapporteur therefore hoped that the Commission would be satisfied with a working definition, to be applied contextually, as opposed to an attempt at a complex codification, an approach which would be an unnecessary distraction.

66. The Secretariat memorandum to which he had referred in his report as a resource had not influenced his general approach to the subject, which had been fully developed before the memorandum had appeared. The memorandum had been crafted as a learned and substantial monograph, whereas his report was built around an axis of draft articles.

67. The subject had already shown its practical relevance in the area of the peaceful settlement of disputes. Just recently, the legal issues presented in the first report had figured prominently in the proceedings of the Eritrea–Ethiopia Claims Commission in The Hague. Thus, the first report had already been of use to judicial bodies.

68. The introduction to the substantive part of the report began with a brief exposition of the conceptual background underlying the various concepts which appeared in the doctrine regarding the effects of armed conflicts on treaties. There were four basic rationales: according to the first, largely outdated, rationale, war was the polar opposite of peace and involved a complete rupture of relations and a return to anarchy; it therefore followed that all treaties were annulled without exception and that right of abrogation arose from the occurrence of war regardless of the original intention of the parties. The second rationale, which to some extent was a modification of the first, held that the test was compatibility with the purposes of the war or the state of hostilities, and was also expressed in the form that treaties remained in force subject to the necessities of war.

69. The third rationale stated that the criterion was the intention of the parties at the time they had concluded the treaty. The fourth, which represented a separate strand in the doctrine, was related to the datum that since 1919, and especially since the appearance of the Charter of the United Nations, States no longer possessed a general competence to resort to the use of force, except in case of legitimate defence and it therefore followed that the use of force should not be recognized as a general solvent of treaty obligations. The Special Rapporteur believed that the third rationale was the most workable and the most representative of the existing framework of international law; there would be no useful purpose in endeavouring to examine all the rationales at great length.

70. Turning to the text of the draft articles themselves, he said that the language of draft article 1 on the scope of the convention followed the provisions of article 1 of the 1969 Vienna Convention on the Law of Treaties. Draft article 2 on use of terms defined the terms "treaty" and "armed conflict" in its paragraphs (*a*) and (*b*) respectively. The definition of "treaty" followed the definition set out in the 1969 Vienna Convention and the definition of "armed conflict" was based on the formulation adopted by the Institute of International Law in its resolution of 28 August 1985 (hereinafter referred to as "resolution II/1985").[7] The latter, while not totally comprehensive, was reasonably so and he felt that it was preferable to adopt a contextual approach and to deal with "armed operations which by their nature or extent are likely to affect the operation of treaties between States parties to the armed conflict or between States parties to the armed conflict and third States" (art. 2 (*b*)). Accordingly, despite discussion in the literature on the effects of war and the ambit of armed conflict, he had deliberately worded draft article 2, paragraph (*b*), to stress the contextual approach. The Commission might wish to address the question of whether or not to attempt a general codification of armed conflict as a first general principle, although he hoped it would choose not to do so.

71. The second general question of policy would be to decide whether or not armed conflict also included internal conflicts. His own preference would be to exclude non-international armed conflict and to focus on international armed conflicts, which inherently interrupted treaty relations between States. Of course, as noted in the report (para. 17), there was a point of view according to which internal armed conflicts could involve external elements and thereby "affect the operation of treaties as much as, if not more than international armed conflicts". The Commission might wish to express its views, possibly in the commentary, on whether internal armed conflicts should be included. The wording of draft article 2, paragraph (*b*), left that question unresolved, but given situations such as those in the former Yugoslavia or, more recently, in the Democratic Republic of the Congo, where a national Government had chosen to incorporate irregular units in its command structure, the Commission might wish to take a policy decision on the issue of including non-international conflicts. He remained of the opinion, however, that the purpose of the draft articles was to reinforce, rather than weaken, the legal security of relations between States.

72. Draft article 3, on *ipso facto* termination or suspension, replicated article 2 of resolution II/1985 of the Institute of International Law and, given the wording of

[7] Institute of International Law, *Yearbook*, vol. 61, part II (session of Helsinki 1985), Paris, Pedone, 1986, pp. 278–282.

subsequent articles, in particular draft article 4, might, strictly speaking, not be necessary. It did however seem important to emphasize that the older position, according to which armed conflict automatically abrogated treaty-based relations, had been replaced by a more contemporary view according to which the mere outbreak of armed conflict, whether declared war or not, did not *ipso facto* terminate or suspend treaties in force between parties to the conflict. If the Commission so desired, he would not be opposed to the deletion of draft article 3.

73. Draft article 4, on the indicia of susceptibility to termination or suspension of treaties in case of an armed conflict, was a key provision; paragraph 2 (*b*) in particular highlighted the contextual character of the operation. Modern doctrine in general seemed to highlight the intention of the parties, although French-language commentators often adopted an approach which seemed to be an amalgam between the old and newer positions. According to the doctrine of *caducité*, the effect of war was to terminate treaty relations, though with some important exceptions based upon intention or inferences of intention. The Special Rapporteur felt that it was inherently contradictory to say that armed conflict was qualitatively incompatible with treaty relations and was therefore non-justiciable while at the same time saying that there could be exceptions to that rule, the test being the object and purpose of the treaty. In the final analysis, however, both approaches seemed to highlight the notion of intention, and therefore draft article 4 sought to universalize the test of intention, with regard both to the nature of the treaty itself and to the nature and extent of the armed conflict in question.

74. The remaining draft articles contained more specialized ancillary provisions. Draft article 5 dealt with the effect of express provisions on the operation of treaties and reflected the situation whereby treaties expressly applicable to situations of armed conflict remained operative in case of an armed conflict (para. 1) and the outbreak of an armed conflict did not affect the competence of the parties to the armed conflict to conclude treaties (para. 2). There were in fact well-known examples of the belligerents in an armed conflict concluding agreements between themselves during that armed conflict, and the principles enunciated in draft article 5 were supported by the relevant literature.

75. Draft article 6 dealt with the issue of treaties relating to the occasion for resort to armed conflict. Although some authorities held the opinion that in cases in which an armed conflict was caused by differences as to the meaning or status of a treaty, the treaty could be presumed to be annulled, the more contemporary view was that such a situation did not necessarily mean that the treaty in question would no longer be in force. In fact, the practice of States confirmed that, when a process of peaceful settlement was commenced, the existing treaty obligations which had led to the conflict remained applicable. The *Rann of Kutch* Case (*India* v. *Pakistan*) and the awards of the Eritrea–Ethiopia Boundary Commission[8] were examples of situations where the provisions of agreements, the interpretation of which had given rise to conflict, had been observed in achieving a final settlement.

[8] Letter dated 15 April 2002, addressed to the Chair of the Security Council by the Secretary-General (S/2002/423). See also *ILM*, vol. 41, No. 5 (September 2002), p. 1057.

76. Finally, as a preliminary introduction to draft article 7 on the operation of treaties on the basis of necessary implication from their object and purpose, namely, treaties which would continue in operation during an armed conflict, he noted that paragraph 2 included an indicative list of some such treaties. In compiling that list he had also referred to the memorandum prepared by the Secretariat on the effect of armed conflict on treaties (A/CN.4/550), which had been most helpful. The list was not exhaustive and inclusion of a type of treaty in the list should not be taken as an endorsement on the part of the Special Rapporteur. His basic criterion in compiling the list had been whether the treaties in question were candidates for consideration by the Commission.

Organization of work of the session (*continued*)

[Agenda item 1]

77. Mr. MANSFIELD (Chairperson of the Drafting Committee) announced that in its final composition the Drafting Committee on the topic of reservations to treaties would consist of Mr. Comissário Afonso, Mr. Daoudi, Ms. Escarameia, Mr. Fomba, Mr. Gaja, Mr. Galicki, Mr. Kemicha, Mr. Kolodkin, Mr. Matheson, Ms. Xue and the Special Rapporteur, Mr. Pellet.

The meeting rose at 1.05 p.m.

2835th MEETING

Tuesday, 10 May 2005, at 10 a.m.

Chairperson: Mr. Djamchid MOMTAZ

Present: Mr. Addo, Mr. Baena Soares, Mr. Brownlie, Mr. Candioti, Mr. Chee, Mr. Comissário Afonso, Mr. Daoudi, Mr. Dugard, Mr. Economides, Ms. Escarameia, Mr. Fomba, Mr. Gaja, Mr. Galicki, Mr. Kabatsi, Mr. Kateka, Mr. Kemicha, Mr. Kolodkin, Mr. Koskenniemi, Mr. Mansfield, Mr. Matheson, Mr. Niehaus, Mr. Pambou-Tchivounda, Mr. Pellet, Mr. Sreenivasa Rao, Mr. Rodríguez Cedeño, Mr. Sepúlveda, Ms. Xue, Mr. Yamada.

Effects of armed conflicts on treaties (*continued*) (A/CN.4/552 and A/CN.4/550 and Corr.1–2)

[Agenda item 8]

First report of the Special Rapporteur (*continued*)

1. The CHAIRPERSON invited the Special Rapporteur to continue with the introduction of his first report on the effects of armed conflicts on treaties (A/CN.4/552).

2. Mr. BROWNLIE (Special Rapporteur) said that draft article 7, which was closely linked to draft articles 3 and 4, set out a legal position that was widely recognized in the

doctrine and reflected in State practice. It listed the 11 categories of treaties whose object and purpose involved the necessary implication that they continued in operation. The list was largely indicative, and the Commission might find that some of the treaties could be omitted. In particular, the inclusion of treaties for the protection of human rights and treaties relating to the protection of the environment might be controversial.

3. With regard to the former, it should be recalled that the topic under consideration did not relate directly to the law of treaties but to certain provisions of general international law dealing with the question of whether the occurrence of an armed conflict in itself prevented the operation of a treaty. The draft articles he had presented did not provide an answer to that question, as they were limited to setting out a principle, that of the intention of the parties. Moreover, he was not entirely convinced by the reasoning followed in the memorandum by the Secretariat (A/CN.4/550), which consisted of drawing an analogy between the non-derogability of the provisions of human rights treaties and *jus cogens* norms, and then linking the criterion of derogability with the effects of armed conflicts. Nevertheless, treaties for the protection of human rights should be included in the list if treaties of friendship, commerce and navigation and bilateral investment treaties were included.

4. With regard to treaties relating to the protection of the environment, he said that, as the law in that area was not unified but fragmented, there was no single position on the effects of an armed conflict on that category of treaty. In its advisory opinion of 8 July 1996 on the legality of the threat or use of nuclear weapons, the ICJ had been careful to avoid making a general statement on that point. It could thus be concluded that there was no real *opinio juris* on the subject.

5. Obviously, articles 1 to 7 constituted the essence of the draft he had submitted, while draft articles 8 to 14 simply dealt with the legal consequences resulting therefrom. One issue that was not dealt with was the peaceful settlement of disputes, but in his view that issue should be set aside until the Commission had completed its consideration of the essential points and reflected further on the nature of the study it was conducting on the effects of armed conflicts on treaties. Moreover, shocking as it might seem, he did not think it was essential to include that issue in a standard-setting text. In any case, everyone knew that under the 1969 Vienna Convention it was usual to give States the option to attach a dispute settlement plan to a treaty if they so wished.

6. Draft article 8 was a statement of the obvious in that it dealt with an issue that commonly arose when an armed conflict resulted in the termination or suspension of a treaty, namely, the mode of suspension or termination. The article was not absolutely essential, but it did seem sensible and useful to include it in the draft. The same was true of draft article 9, on the resumption of suspended treaties, the comment on which was fairly succinct. The idea was that States should clarify their positions and remove ambiguities from their post-conflict relations.

7. Draft article 10 was controversial and reflected an entirely different approach from that taken by the Institute of International Law in its resolution II/1985.[1] In his opinion, the draft under consideration did not tackle the question of the legality of any threat or use of force, although that did not mean that the question was completely ignored. It was precisely because the subject was controversial that he had included the relevant provisions of the resolution of the Institute of International Law in the commentary.

8. Draft article 11 was not strictly necessary, but was nonetheless useful in an expository draft, and he had drawn attention in that connection to article 75 of the 1969 Vienna Convention. Draft article 12 was also not strictly necessary, but had a pragmatic purpose. Draft article 13 was a technical consequence of the preceding articles. Given the links between the subject of the report and other well-established aspects of treaty law, it seemed necessary to point out that the draft articles were without prejudice to the termination or suspension of treaties as a consequence of the agreement of the parties, a material breach, supervening impossibility of performance, or a fundamental change in circumstances. Such a reservation was of course a statement of the obvious, but it was still useful. Lastly, draft article 14 was not really necessary either, but reflected the widespread practice of reviving "pre-war" treaties that had been suspended or terminated as a result of an armed conflict.

9. Mr. GAJA commended the Special Rapporteur for the speed with which he had produced his first report on the effects of armed conflicts on treaties and for the clarity of his arguments. The Special Rapporteur had a clear sense of the direction he would like the study to take, and it would be tempting, in the light of such conviction, to allow him a free hand. However, the Commission had a duty to view his approach with a critical eye, a task made particularly difficult by the lack of information on how the solutions proposed by the Special Rapporteur to the problems identified actually related to practice. In fact, the Special Rapporteur did not systematically analyse practice, but was content to make a some references to it, noting in paragraph 43 that "[i]t is probable that much of the practice of States takes the form of observations to the effect that the existence and nature of a general principle is the subject of doctrinal controversy", and in paragraph 44 that it was generally recognized that municipal decisions were "not of great assistance". A thorough analysis of practice would make the Special Rapporteur's work and, ultimately, the Commission's draft articles more persuasive and would also encourage States to produce examples of possibly divergent practices, which would give the Commission a fuller picture of the situation. It was true that the report was to some extent supplemented by the memorandum on the subject by the Secretariat, but the latter had been prepared separately and was of a preliminary nature. It was certainly useful in that it suggested solutions to some problems and highlighted some examples of practice, but it was no replacement for the analysis to be undertaken by the Special Rapporteur and then by the Commission.

[1] See 2834th meeting, footnote 7.

10. In the examination of practice and the analysis of problems a clear distinction ought to be drawn between the effects of armed conflicts on treaty relations between the parties to a conflict and the effects of armed conflicts, such as civil conflicts, on third States. He drew attention in that connection to the reference in the study by the Secretariat to the suspension by the United States of America of its Peace Corps programmes in cases of armed conflict, either because the United States was directly involved or, more often, because a civil war was taking place (A/CN.4/550, para. 101, footnote 349). However, while practice might differ depending on whether a State was directly involved in the conflict or not, the Special Rapporteur seemed to think that the same principle was applicable in every case. The rules set out in the 1969 Vienna Convention might offer sufficient justification for suspending the operation of a treaty, but that was not the only possible conclusion to be drawn, and the relevant practice should be considered further.

11. With regard to the key idea on which the Special Rapporteur's report was based, namely, that armed conflicts *per se* did not affect the operation of a treaty unless that was the intention of the parties, he noted that several instances of practice to which both the report and the Secretariat memorandum referred appeared to suggest the opposite—that armed conflicts did lead to the automatic suspension of various categories of treaty relations, in full or in part. While he was willing to concede that on grounds of principle there was an argument against such automatic effects of conflicts, he was not persuaded that the available evidence of practice could be ignored in order to posit an idea that, while undoubtedly original and interesting, did not provide a sound basis for discussion. Moreover, the criterion of intention, as contemplated in draft articles 4, 6 and 9, was rather elusive. Although the 1969 Vienna Convention did refer to intention in a number of its articles, it did not say how a State's intention was to be ascertained. Contrary to the proposed draft articles 4 and 9, articles 31 and 32 of the 1969 Vienna Convention dealt with the interpretation of treaties, not with the determination of intention, so they were not really helpful for the purposes of the Commission's study. Moreover, it would have to be determined whether the intention referred to was the actual intention or the presumed intention of a State; if the latter, perhaps different wording was necessary. If it was a question of the interpretation of a treaty, it would be sufficient to include a proviso to the effect that the general criterion would be applied only if the treaty did not provide otherwise. Draft article 7 as it stood should be reconsidered, and an attempt should be made to draw a more broadly applicable principle from it.

12. Commenting on specific draft articles as proposed by the Special Rapporteur, he said that draft article 1 should not limit the scope of the articles to treaties between States, but should also cover those involving international organizations, and should refer to the 1986 Vienna Convention on the Law of Treaties between States and International Organizations or between International Organizations. The definition in draft article 2 (*b*) of an armed conflict as armed operations which by their nature or extent were likely to affect the operation of treaties was somewhat circular, as the reply to the question of whether or not a treaty would be affected by a conflict was given in the following article. The wording of that provision should perhaps be reconsidered. He agreed with the Special Rapporteur's suggestion in paragraph 28 that the phrase "*ipso facto*" in draft article 3 should be replaced by the word "necessarily". Lastly, he proposed that in draft article 5, paragraph 2, and perhaps also in draft article 14, the word "competence" should be replaced by the word "capacity", to reflect the terminology of the 1986 Vienna Convention. In conclusion, he expressed the hope that the Special Rapporteur would develop more fully the ideas that he would like the Commission to eventually endorse.

Shared natural resources (*continued*) (A/CN.4/549 and Add.1, sect. B, A/CN.4/551 and Add.1 and Corr.1, A/CN.4/555 and Add.1)

[Agenda item 4]

Third report of the Special Rapporteur (*continued*)

13. Mr. SEPÚLVEDA said that the wealth of documentation that the Special Rapporteur had compiled and reviewed showed that it was possible to formulate draft articles on transboundary groundwaters even if State practice in that area was minimal. There were also a great many multilateral, regional and bilateral agreements that set out principles that could form the basis of the study of the topic.

14. The first point deserving of attention was the nature and scope of the draft articles. The Commission might consider drafting a convention on the law of transboundary aquifer systems, but by its very nature such an instrument would be universal in character. The subject at hand did not lend itself to such treatment, however, since not all States possessed transboundary aquifer systems. Consequently there did not seem to be much point in elaborating a protocol to the 1997 Watercourses Convention. A framework convention setting out principles to facilitate the conclusion of bilateral or regional agreements would be more appropriate.

15. A second point related to the political powers and legal entitlements of States over the transboundary aquifer systems located in their territory. It had been said that such hydrological resources were the property of the State concerned, which exercised exclusive sovereignty over them in accordance with General Assembly resolution 1803 (XVII). Yet to recognize sovereign, absolute and unlimited entitlements in respect of every aquifer State would be to void the draft articles, which were aimed at conferring rights and imposing duties on the States concerned, since such entitlements would not facilitate the equitable sharing of resources among all aquifer States and went against the idea that States should utilize the aquifer in a sustainable and reasonable manner.

16. He assumed that the idea of "sovereign rights" of States over the natural resources located within their jurisdiction, referred to in paragraph 19 of the report, had not appeared by chance but reproduced similar wording used in the United Nations Convention on the Law of the Sea to define the powers of a coastal State over its exclusive economic zone, which were not absolute property rights but had to accommodate certain rights of third States. It

thus seemed reasonable to consider simultaneously that aquifer States exercised sovereign rights over the transboundary aquifer or aquifer system located in their territory and that the international community must impose certain duties on them to ensure that they used those groundwaters responsibly. However, he did not see why reference was made to "territorial integrity" in article 8, on the general obligation to cooperate, and he requested clarification on that point, which was not explained in the commentary.

17. In the context of the obligation not to cause harm, it was necessary not only to discuss the question of compensation, as indicated in article 7, paragraph 3, but also to determine whether the significant harm resulted from a wrongful act, in which case the responsibility of the State concerned was incurred. On the other hand, if the damage was caused by acts not prohibited by international law, then it was the State's liability that came into play. Reparation for harm was part and parcel of the obligation not to cause harm. The draft articles should in fact contain provisions outlining the nature, origin and target of the harm.

18. Water quality should be included among the factors relevant to equitable and reasonable utilization in draft article 6. The concept had been taken into account in various legal instruments, including the Agreement on Great Lakes Water Quality, signed by Canada and the United States of America in 1978,[2] and the Convention on the Protection and Use of Transboundary Watercourses and International Lakes, concluded at Helsinki in 1992, which defined transboundary impact. That idea could be interpolated into article 1, subparagraph (*b*) of the draft, which stated that the convention applied to other activities that had or were likely to have an impact upon aquifers and aquifer systems. That was why one of the criteria for equitable and reasonable utilization should be preservation of the quality of groundwaters.

19. Lastly, he thought it might be useful to include in the draft articles a provision similar to article 33 of the 1997 Watercourses Convention, which contemplated a mechanism for the settlement of disputes concerning the interpretation or application of the Convention.

20. Mr. COMISSÁRIO AFONSO said that he agreed with the Special Rapporteur on the need for an explicit reference to General Assembly resolution 1803 (XVII) on permanent sovereignty over natural resources; like other members of the Commission, however, he believed that the reference should be incorporated in the body of the draft. It was obvious that territorial sovereignty was exercised over underground resources, including aquifers, and insofar as the draft convention dealt with transboundary groundwaters, the exercise of such sovereign rights must be understood to go hand in hand with the obligation to cooperate.

21. He had no objection to draft article 1 in its present form but wondered whether the relationship between the draft convention and the 1997 Watercourses Convention could be made clearer by highlighting their differences and complementarities. The Commission could go further in certain areas or even travel a different road. It could, for example, bring the natural interrelationship that already existed between surface waters and groundwaters into the legal sphere in a more global and integrated manner. Mr. Galicki had rightly drawn the Commission's attention to the conflict that might arise between the 1997 Watercourses Convention and the draft under consideration. In addition, the Special Rapporteur had noted that the term "impact" should be construed as a broader concept than "harm". It would be useful to specify in the draft or the commentary the actual scope of the concept, which was more precisely defined in such legal instruments as the 2002 Tripartite Interim Agreement between the Republic of Mozambique, the Republic of South Africa and the Kingdom of Swaziland for co-operation on the protection and sustainable utilization of the water resources of the Incomati and Maputo watercourses and the 1998 Agreement on cooperation for the protection and sustainable use of the waters of the Spanish–Portuguese hydrographic basins.[3]

22. With regard to draft article 2, he said that the explanation offered in paragraph 8 of the report appeared to imply that the term "water-bearing" in subparagraph (*a*) of the draft article was not necessary. The definition of an aquifer in the Bellagio Draft Treaty was shorter and more concise.[4] In addition, he wondered how the "negligible" or "non-negligible" amount of water recharge mentioned in subparagraphs (*e*) and (*f*) was to be measured.

23. In article 3, States were encouraged to enter into bilateral and regional arrangements, but for those members who wanted the Commission to adopt a legally binding instrument, the language of the article was too weak. It could doubtless be improved in order to commit States, where necessary, to negotiate and conclude such arrangements.

24. Article 4 dealt with the relation to other conventions and international agreements, and he agreed that the draft should also mention the relation to the applicable principles and rules of customary or general international law, as Mr. Brownlie and Mr. Niehaus had proposed. In fact, the draft would be stronger if it contained a body of fundamental principles to guide States in their activities and relations in the areas covered by the draft convention. While some of the principles were already in the text, others, including the precautionary principle and the "polluter pays" principle, for example, were not.

25. He welcomed the Special Rapporteur's decision to include in draft article 5 the principles of equitable utilization and reasonable utilization, which in his view made that article one of the most important in the text. It emphasized the need to strike a balance between the sovereign right of a State over its natural resources and the interests not only of other States but also of present and future generations. It was in that provision, and not in the preamble or draft article 8, that the question of sovereignty should be dealt with, and it should be made clear that the two

[2] Signed at Ottawa on 22 November 1978 (*United States Treaties and Other International Agreements, 1978–1979*, vol. 30, part 2, Washington D.C., United States Government Printing Office, 1980, p. 1383).

[3] United Nations, *Treaty Series*, vol. 2099, No. 36496, p. 275.

[4] Hayton and Utton, *loc. cit.*

above-mentioned principles must take precedence over the sovereign equality and territorial integrity of States.

26. With regard to draft article 7, on the obligation not to cause harm, he agreed with the idea of retaining the threshold of "significant harm" already established in article 7, paragraph 1, of the 1997 Watercourses Convention and in many other international instruments. At the same time, it was hard to see what legal consequences could be derived from draft article 7, paragraph 3, which stipulated that, in the event of significant harm, "States [...] shall [...] take all appropriate measures [...] to discuss the question of compensation". It was unfortunate that the draft contained no rules for the settlement of disputes. Two States that shared an aquifer, one of which was open to discussions while the other was not, would find the draft article unhelpful. He was firmly convinced that on that particular point the Commission should take a different course from that of the 1997 Watercourses Convention.

27. Lastly, he supported the idea of setting up a working group to consider the draft in greater detail before referring it to the Drafting Committee.

28. Mr. RODRÍGUEZ CEDEÑO commended the Special Rapporteur for the significant work he had done on a topic that was both legally and technically complex. He wished to start by making four general comments. First, the topic was difficult and not very well known. Aquifers and aquifer systems were extremely diverse in form and size, as well as in the volume and quality of their waters. Second, State practice was not extensive, and close attention should be paid to various ongoing bilateral or regional negotiations aimed at regulating the use of aquifer systems. Third, the main purpose of the draft articles was to encourage and help States that shared an aquifer system to manage that resource in the best possible manner. The bilateral and regional, rather than global, perspective adopted in the draft was thus the best suited to its purpose. Fourth, the Special Rapporteur had obviously produced the draft with a view to having the final result be a convention, but the Commission would have to decide whether it would be an independent convention, a framework agreement or a protocol to the 1997 Watercourses Convention. In his view, the most appropriate form would be an independent framework convention, but the matter should be considered by the working group that was to be established, an initiative that he fully supported. In any event, the draft should retain ties not only to the 1997 Watercourses Convention, which must be its main source of inspiration, but also to existing bilateral and regional agreements and related instruments. Obviously, the views of States on the subject would be a decisive factor.

29. Turning to more specific points, he said that the preamble should be drafted later, but that it must contain a specific reference to General Assembly resolution 1803 (XVII), the content of which should be reflected in a clear and comprehensive manner. Draft article 2, on use of terms, was in his view acceptable, although he had some reservations about the definitions of recharging and non-recharging aquifer. Draft article 3, on bilateral and regional arrangements, should be considered in conjunction with draft article 8, on the general obligation to cooperate. The obligations of conduct in question should be stated more clearly and more precisely. For example, the weakness of the term "encouraged", which appeared in paragraph 1 of article 3 and paragraph 2 of article 8, had been pointed out. The Drafting Committee should therefore review the wording of the articles without elaborating a binding or unduly rigid rule. Since the legal obligations of States would not be modified by the draft, it would be preferable to speak not of "arrangements" but of "agreements", as in articles 3 and 4 of the 1997 Watercourses Convention. Draft article 7, on the obligation not to cause harm, was acceptable. The obligation it placed on States, namely to discuss the question of compensation, was quite important. Turning to draft articles 8 and 9, he said that the obligation to cooperate was one of the foundations of the draft. It was a clear rule, binding upon States, even though the manner of cooperation could be flexible, as was evident from draft article 8, paragraph 2. The influence of article 8 of the 1997 Watercourses Convention was entirely appropriate there. The same could be said of the obligation to exchange data and information regularly, wording that was modelled on article 9 of the Convention. Lastly, draft article 18, on scientific and technical assistance to developing States, was of fundamental importance, since aquifers were a vital resource for the international community. The word "States" should simply be replaced by "countries".

30. Mr. ECONOMIDES noted that the issue of aquifers had more to do with the progressive development of international law than its codification. The Commission was attempting to deal with the topic by analogy, following the model provided by the provisions of the 1997 Watercourses Convention; he wondered, however, if that was in fact the appropriate model. The law of international watercourses was dominated by the striking contrast between the interests of the upstream and downstream countries, the former generally able to pollute a watercourse or modify its flow, the latter usually the victims. It was not at all obvious that the same difference existed in relation to aquifers, in particular those that were not linked to surface waters. Another difference was the high degree of vulnerability of aquifers relative to rivers, which necessitated the establishment of a regime affording greater protection. Moreover, aquifer waters, while not "international", were nevertheless "transboundary" waters, and that made them subject to international law, so that they had an international character after all. Lastly, with regard to the final form of the draft, he said it would be wise to adopt the approach taken by Mr. Sreenivasa Rao the previous year with regard to the draft articles on international liability in the case of loss from transboundary harm arising out of hazardous activities,[5] which was simply to develop draft principles for first reading, with the option of developing those principles into a set of binding rules at second reading if States greeted them favourably.

31. Turning to the draft articles themselves, he said that he supported the Special Rapporteur's suggestion that the preamble be drafted at a later date. Draft article 1, subparagraph (*b*), posed a problem, as he wondered what

[5] "Second report on the legal regime for the allocation of loss in case of transboundary harm arising out of hazardous activities" in *Yearbook ... 2004*, vol. II (Part One), document A/CN.4/540. See also the draft principles and commentaries thereto, adopted on first reading by the Commission, *ibid.*, vol. II (Part Two), chap. VII, sect. C, paras. 175–176.

apparently negative "other activities" were contemplated there; the commentary did not provide sufficient explanation. The definition of the term "aquifer" in draft article 2 was not clear enough. It should contain two elements: first, any geological formation, provided that it was permeable and, second, the water contained therein, provided that it could be exploited for a useful purpose. Draft article 3 should be greatly simplified. Only the first six lines would be retained and the paragraph would end after "particular project, programme or use"; the rest of the paragraph, which would be too difficult to apply, would be included in the commentary. He also felt that a much stronger term than "encouraged" should be used. Draft article 4 should be placed at the end of the text, and the bilateral and regional arrangements referred to in draft article 3 should be more clearly excluded from paragraph 2. Turning to draft article 5, he said the notion of "equitable" could be dangerous if not precisely defined, at least in the commentary. In draft article 7 the adjective "significant" should be deleted for reasons already mentioned relating to the vulnerability of aquifers. Paragraph 2 of draft article 8, on joint mechanisms or commissions, should be greatly strengthened and, once again, the term "encouraged" was too weak. Mr. Chee's suggestion that aquifer States should provide for appropriate dispute settlement mechanisms should be retained. He strongly supported draft article 10 on monitoring and, like other Commission members, sought further explanation of the principle of prevention contemplated in draft article 14. He well understood Mr. Pambou-Tchivounda's concern with regard to draft article 18: the provisions on scientific and technical assistance to developing States should be drafted in a more realistic manner.

32. Lastly, with regard to next steps, he saw no need for haste; the draft should be considered as a whole, article by article, in a working group before it was submitted to the Drafting Committee.

33. Mr. DAOUDI said that the Special Rapporteur's third report called for a number of general comments. First, while he did not wish to question the Commission's decision to deal, as a first step, only with aquifers under the topic of shared natural resources, the draft convention as submitted would seem to indicate that every natural resource or category of resources would require a separate instrument. If that was the case, not only would it be inconsistent with the Commission's mandate as stated, but it immediately posed the problem of how to align the current draft with any future drafts dealing with shared natural resources.

34. Second, State practice relating to the use and management of shared aquifers was not yet at a stage where it would be possible to identify standards that would be acceptable to all States concerned. It seemed, then, that the Commission was taking the opposite approach to the one it had taken in codifying the law of watercourses by seeking to establish an international regime without the benefit of any conventional regimes that reflected State practice. That might explain why the Special Rapporteur had based his text to such an extent on the 1997 Watercourses Convention and, in draft article 3, paragraph 3, had taken the unusual step of suggesting that bilateral and regional arrangements should take precedence over the draft convention.

35. Third, the exclusive sovereignty of a riparian State, which in the current context meant an aquifer State, over water resources shared among several States, had always been contested because any such claim of sovereignty would be tantamount to denying the rights of the other States to the equitable and reasonable utilization of those resources. The notion of sovereignty was not in fact mentioned in the 1997 Watercourses Convention. In any case, it was essential to exclude from the draft any reference to the General Assembly resolution 1803 (XVII) on permanent sovereignty over natural resources.

36. Fourth, the distinction drawn in draft article 5 between recharging and non-recharging aquifers, while conjunctural, remained fundamental. Nevertheless, since aquifer waters were not inexhaustible, other criteria besides equitable and reasonable utilization must be considered, in particular the surface area of the territory, population density and level of development.

37. Fifth, the obligation not to cause significant harm was essential, but given that aquifer waters did not recharge or did so only slightly and were therefore susceptible to pollution, it would be more appropriate to refer to harm without being restrictive and to develop the issue of compensation further, as suggested by Mr. Brownlie and others.

38. For all those reasons, it would be preferable to submit the draft to a working group which could consider it in the light of all the points raised during the discussion.

39. Ms. ESCARAMEIA said that draft articles 12 and 13 should also deal with third States, namely States where recharge or discharge zones were located, and create rights and obligations for any State that could affect or be affected by aquifers. The Special Rapporteur said that it would be difficult to place any obligation on States that did not benefit from aquifers. That was a contractualistic, synallagmatic view and would be tantamount to not placing any obligations on third States not to pollute, even though some of them, such as discharge States, could benefit greatly from an aquifer that was not situated in their territory.

40. Turning to draft article 14 on prevention, reduction and control of pollution, she said that she would not repeat her concerns about the use of the adjective "significant" to qualify harm; however, she regretted that the particular vulnerability of groundwaters to pollution was not reflected in the draft article. States were simply "encouraged to take a precautionary approach", which meant absolutely nothing. The precautionary principle should be included in the draft articles, since the effects of certain activities were little known, difficult to detect and often long-lasting. It was therefore encouraging to note that Mr. Pellet had stated that if there was an instrument where that principle ought to be enshrined, it was undoubtedly the draft articles on transboundary groundwaters. The Special Rapporteur claimed that the precautionary principle had not yet developed as a rule of general international law without, however, explaining why. Yet, that principle

had been enshrined in numerous instruments, both binding and non-binding, in particular in Principle 15 of the Rio Declaration.[6]

41. Turning to draft article 16, she said that the expression "as far as practicable", which was very weak, should be deleted and replaced with "as far as possible". Draft article 17, on planned activities, should be more specific. The 1997 Watercourses Convention, for example, devoted nine articles to such activities; the provision should therefore be developed further. She agreed with the inclusion of draft article 19, on emergency situations, and suggested that a draft article providing for the establishment of a dispute settlement mechanism should be included with a view to protecting the weakest negotiators and maintaining a balance among negotiating States.

42. The final form of the draft articles should be a binding convention rather than a protocol to the 1997 Watercourses Convention, which dealt with very different issues and had still not entered into force.

43. Mr. MANSFIELD, commenting on part III of the draft convention, asked how draft article 12 would apply, if at all, to non-recharging aquifers. Turning to draft article 13 and paragraph 33 of the report, he acknowledged that it would certainly be desirable to seek the cooperation of third States to prevent pollution from entering the recharge or discharge zones of an aquifer system where those zones were located in the territory of the third State; he wondered whether it was really the case that they had no legal obligations in that regard. As Mr. Brownlie had pointed out, in a situation where third States knew or ought to have known that their territory was being used to cause harm to adjoining aquifer States, general international law would apply. The working group might need to consider whether it would be desirable to spell that out or at least refer to it in draft article 13. Since aquifers were much more vulnerable to pollution than watercourses and prevention was therefore imperative, the order of the articles might need to be reconsidered. The relevance of the precautionary principle likewise needed to be further highlighted.

44. Draft article 15 as it stood might inhibit sensible management because it gave the impression that if three or four States shared an aquifer, then each must establish a management plan. Only if one of them requested consultation would they be required to enter into consultations that might lead to a joint management mechanism. That was surely not a situation to be encouraged. It would be preferable to propose that aquifer States should enter into consultations with a view to agreeing on a management plan and perhaps a management mechanism. It could then be stipulated that in the absence of agreement on a joint management plan the aquifer States should establish and publish their own management plans, but it should also be made clear that those plans should comply with the principles reflected in the draft convention and take into account the interests of the other aquifer States, as provided for in draft article 17.

45. Draft articles 16 and 17 would both benefit from further examination by the working group. In the light of international law and practice it would seem unthinkable and certainly unacceptable that an aquifer State could have grounds for believing that a planned activity in its territory might have adverse effects on a transboundary aquifer and yet not carry out a proper environmental impact assessment. In that regard draft article 17, paragraph 1, seemed deficient to the extent that it might imply that the information to be supplied to the other aquifer States about an activity that might adversely affect them needed to include an environmental impact assessment only if one had been conducted.

46. In the last sentence of paragraph 37 the Special Rapporteur had made the point that nothing prevented planned activities from being carried out without the consent of the affected States, but that in such a situation liability might arise. There was surely a case for making it clear that while an aquifer State might not have to obtain the consent of the other aquifer States for its planned activities, general international law precluded it from carrying out activities in its territory which it knew or ought to have known would cause harm to other aquifer States.

47. Mr. ADDO said that the topic that the Special Rapporteur had considered in his third report was of particular importance, as the solution to the world's water crisis might well lie hidden below the Earth's surface. Aquifers, which could extend for thousands of miles, contained enough water to satisfy all of humanity's needs for many decades. Like watercourses, they could be shared by several States, yet little was known about transboundary aquifers. The Special Rapporteur's draft articles thus filled a vacuum. As Governments were often reluctant to admit that other countries shared the aquifers they relied on for drinking water and irrigation, transboundary aquifers were a potential source of conflict, especially in arid regions, where fierce competition for water resources might well intensify in the future because of population growth and climate change. Noting that the draft articles did not contain any provision on dispute settlement or conflict resolution, he asked the Special Rapporteur whether he intended to include such a provision in the text or whether he did not consider that aspect important. He himself did not think that any reference to the permanent sovereignty of States over their natural resources was appropriate: if transboundary aquifers were supposed to be a shared natural resource, then no aquifer State could claim to have permanent sovereignty over them.

48. Mr. KATEKA noted that the draft articles were based mainly on the 1997 Watercourses Convention. As a number of members had pointed out, that instrument continued to be controversial, in particular with regard to the role of previous agreements and certain aspects of equitable and reasonable utilization. The Commission should be careful not to replicate those controversial provisions in the current draft.

49. It had been observed that there was not much State practice in the area of transboundary aquifers. He thus appreciated the compilation of bilateral and regional agreements on the subject which the Special Rapporteur had included in his third report.

[6] Report of the United Nations Conference on Environment and Development, Rio de Janeiro, 3–14 June 1992 (United Nations publication, Sales No.: E.93.I.8 and corrigenda), vol. I: Resolutions Adopted by the Conference, Resolution 1, annex I.

50. The Special Rapporteur had not wanted to prejudge the final form the draft articles would take. He personally supported the adoption of a binding instrument. If that was to be the case, however, the instrument would need to include dispute settlement provisions.

51. The concept of the permanent sovereignty of States over their natural resources should be incorporated in the main body of the text and not be relegated to the preamble.

52. On certain issues, the Special Rapporteur had been too cautious. For example, in article 3, paragraph 1, he referred to bilateral and regional "arrangements", as opposed to "agreements". Yet the compilation of instruments contained binding bilateral and regional agreements, some of which had already entered into force.

53. Article 3, paragraph 3, on bilateral and regional arrangements taking priority as *lex specialis*, and article 4, paragraph 1, which gave precedence to the draft articles over the 1997 Watercourses Convention, should be examined closely by a working group. There was also a need to look at article 2, subparagraphs (*e*) and (*f*), on the terms "non-negligible" and "negligible", more carefully. The same applied to "significant harm" in article 7. The threshold for groundwaters should be lower, owing to their more sensitive nature.

54. In paragraph 33 of the report, the Special Rapporteur remarked that the draft articles in part III "should not be construed as environmental protection provisions" and that the objective was not to protect and preserve aquifers for their own sake, but to do so to allow humankind to utilize the precious water resources contained therein. That view implied an encroachment on the sovereign rights of aquifer States. In the same paragraph, while noting that scientists strongly favoured the application of the precautionary principle, the Special Rapporteur argued that that principle had not yet developed as a rule of general international law. If that was true, progressive development of international law might well be called for. In fact, the precautionary principle was already included in many international instruments, which he enumerated, and thus could certainly be incorporated in the draft articles.

55. In conclusion, he expressed the hope that the Commission would be able to complete a first reading of the draft articles on transboundary groundwaters by the end of the quinquennium and said that a working group should be set up to focus on them.

56. Mr. MATHESON said that he had already argued that the threshold of significant harm must be kept. For the same reasons, the words "an impact" in article 1 (*b*) should be changed to "a significant impact". That would avoid the impression that important agricultural and industrial activities having only a negligible impact on aquifers would nevertheless be subject to the restrictions set out in the articles.

57. With regard to article 3, he did not agree with those members who believed that instead of being "encouraged" to enter into bilateral and regional arrangements, States should be "required" to do so, because in certain situations it might not be necessary or feasible to negotiate an arrangement. That would be the case, for example, if there were no plans to exploit the aquifer or if an armed conflict broke out between aquifer States. The most the Commission should do, then, was to encourage States to conclude such arrangements. It was also not entirely clear whether article 3, paragraph 3, would apply to arrangements that had already been concluded by States for the utilization and protection of transboundary aquifers. In his view, those arrangements should not be renegotiated because they had been entered into in good faith based on the particular circumstances of the aquifer in question. The matter could be clarified by adding that the articles did not affect aquifers that were already the subject of arrangements among the aquifer States concerned. It would also be useful to confirm, either in the text or in the commentary, that if arrangements among aquifer States had not yet been concluded, any aquifer State could still use the aquifer in question and conduct other activities in its territory that might affect it, provided that it did so in a manner consistent with the principles set out in part II of the draft articles.

58. Turning to article 12, he said that the proposed language on the protection of ecosystems might be too categorical, given the state of knowledge on aquifers and their effects on ecosystems. It would be preferable to require States to endeavour to take all appropriate measures to meet the objectives set out in article 12, rather than imposing an absolute obligation to achieve them.

59. With regard to article 14, he agreed with the Special Rapporteur's conclusion that the precautionary principle had not yet developed as a rule of international law. The proposed language was a sensible way of indicating that States should make every effort to anticipate possible pollution risks and to act in a timely way to deal with them.

60. While he agreed that States should be encouraged to provide various forms of assistance to developing States for the protection and management of their aquifer systems, the current language of article 18 on that question appeared to impose an obligation on all States that they might not be in a position to meet. The text should therefore be revised.

61. Lastly, on article 21, he said that no State should be required to provide information vital to its national defence or security. In his view, that provision should apply also to industrial secrets and intellectual property, as in article 14 of the draft articles on prevention of transboundary harm from hazardous activities.[7]

62. He concluded by endorsing the proposal to establish a working group to discuss all those matters at greater length.

63. The CHAIRPERSON said that the wide-ranging discussion on the report of the Special Rapporteur, in which most members of the Commission had taken part, testified to the importance attached to the topic of shared natural resources. He drew the Commission's attention to the report of the High-level Panel of Eminent Persons

[7] *Yearbook ... 2001*, vol. II (Part Two) and corrigendum, chap. V, sect. E, p. 148, para. 98.

on Threats, Challenges and Change, of which Mr. Baena Soares had been a member, entitled "A more secure world: our shared responsibility"; chapter IV of the report addressed the subject of conflict between and within States.[8] It established a link between armed conflicts and the question of shared natural resources, and it referred in paragraph 93 to the role of the International Law Commission in developing rules for the use of transboundary resources such as water, oil and gas.

The meeting rose at 1 p.m.

2836th MEETING

Wednesday, 11 May 2005 at 10.15 a.m.

Chairperson: Mr. Djamchid MOMTAZ

Present: Mr. Addo, Mr. Baena Soares, Mr. Brownlie, Mr. Candioti, Mr. Chee, Mr. Comissário Afonso, Mr. Daoudi, Mr. Dugard, Mr. Economides, Ms. Escarameia, Mr. Fomba, Mr. Gaja, Mr. Galicki, Mr. Kabatsi, Mr. Kateka, Mr. Kemicha, Mr. Kolodkin, Mr. Koskenniemi, Mr. Mansfield, Mr. Matheson, Mr. Niehaus, Mr. Pambou-Tchivounda, Mr. Pellet, Mr. Sreenivasa Rao, Mr. Rodríguez Cedeño, Mr. Sepúlveda, Ms. Xue, Mr. Yamada.

Shared natural resources (*continued*) (A/CN.4/549 and Add.1, sect. B, A/CN.4/551 and Corr.1 and Add.1, A/CN.4/555 and Add.1)

[Agenda item 4]

THIRD REPORT OF THE SPECIAL RAPPORTEUR (*concluded*)

1. The CHAIRPERSON invited the Special Rapporteur to sum up the debate on his third report on shared natural resources: transboundary groundwaters (A/CN.4/551 and Corr.1 and Add.1).

2. Mr. YAMADA (Special Rapporteur) expressed his sincere gratitude to all those members who had offered valuable comments on his third report, comments which he had carefully noted and would take into account in his future work. Given the number of members who had taken the floor, it would be difficult to cover all the points raised in his summary, and he begged the Commission's indulgence if he failed to do so.

3. Some members had wondered whether the sub-topic of transboundary groundwaters was ripe for codification. He felt, however, that in recommending the topic of shared natural resources to the General Assembly in 2000 on the basis of the syllabus prepared by Mr. Rosenstock, which had focused exclusively on groundwaters and such other single geological structures as oil and gas,[1] the Commission had taken the position that the topic was in fact ready for codification. It was true that he himself had initially felt there was a scarcity of State practice and existing norms on groundwaters, and he expressed regret that his repeated statements to that effect in his successive reports might have contributed to creating an erroneous impression that there was not sufficient evidence for codification.

4. Groundwaters represented 97 per cent of the freshwater resources available on the planet. Global estimated dependency on groundwaters, which had already been more than 50 per cent for drinking water, 40 per cent for industry and 20 per cent for irrigation at the time of preparation of his first report,[2] had greatly increased and many areas of the world were currently faced with problems of over-exploitation and pollution of aquifers. Groundwater experts and administrators were making every effort to cope with that situation; however, most such cooperative efforts in Africa, the Americas and Europe had taken place since the year 2000. Furthermore, most of the books, articles and instruments relevant to groundwaters had been written since 1998. Although the titles did not necessarily mention groundwaters, the instruments in *Shared Natural Resources: Compilation of international legal instruments on groundwater resources*, distributed by the Secretariat, all contained specific references to groundwaters, and those formulated after 1998 focused principally on groundwaters. There were therefore numerous examples of State practice, arrangements and agreements which had emerged in recent years on the basis of which the Commission could pursue its work.

5. Mr. Brownlie had referred to the lectures given by Professor Richard Baxter on "Treaties and Custom" at the Hague Academy of International Law in 1970, in which Baxter had affirmed that antiquity was not necessarily a relevant criterion in determining the existence of a rule of customary international law,[3] citing the ICJ decision in the *North Sea Continental Shelf* case, according to which the passage of only a short period of time did not stand in the way of the creation of a new rule of customary law. Professor Baxter had concluded that a treaty which purported to be wholly declaratory of customary international law was an extremely rare phenomenon and none of the so-called "codification treaties" drawn up under the auspices of the Commission was of that character.[4]

6. It was therefore perfectly appropriate for the Commission to proceed towards the progressive development and codification of the law on groundwaters, in accordance with its mandate from the General Assembly. Groundwaters would be one of the major topics of discussion at the Fourth World Water Forum, to take place in Mexico in 2006. Groundwater experts and administrators had high expectations of the Commission, which must keep up with the rapid pace of developments and respond to current needs, or see its usefulness and credibility called into question.

7. The issue of the relationship of general international law to the draft instrument had also been raised; he agreed with Mr. Kolodkin that it was a rule of international law that general international law would have parallel application

---

[8] A/59/565 and Corr.1.

[1] See *Yearbook ... 2000*, vol. II (Part Two), annex, p. 135.

[2] *Yearbook ... 2003*, vol. II (Part One), document A/CN.4/533 and Add.1.

[3] Baxter, *loc. cit.* (2832nd meeting, footnote 2), pp. 41–47.

[4] *Ibid.*, p. 42.

with any instrument drafted by the Commission. He recognized, however, that there were precedents for specific references to general international law in previous instruments formulated by the Commission, such as the fifth preambular paragraph of the United Nations Convention on Jurisdictional Immunities of States and their Property, similar preambular paragraphs in the 1961 Vienna Convention on Diplomatic Relations and the 1963 Vienna Convention on Consular Relations and article 56 of the draft articles on responsibility of States for internationally wrongful acts.[5] If the Commission wished to add a similar reference stating that the rules of customary international law continued to govern matters not regulated by the present Convention, he would have no objection to such an addition.

8. There had also been comments with regard to the inclusion of the issue of sovereignty over natural resources; several members felt that the issue should be raised in an article rather than in the preamble, whereas two members thought it would be preferable not to include the issue at all. He had originally included it in the preamble, given the precedents in the 1997 Watercourses Convention, the 1985 Vienna Convention for the Protection of the Ozone Layer, the 1992 United Nations Framework Convention on Climate Change and the 1992 Convention on Biological Diversity. He had since discovered, however, that the United Nations Convention on the Law of the Sea contained a specific article (art. 193) on sovereignty. He would therefore study that matter further before taking a decision.

9. It had been suggested by some members that there should be broader provisions concerning third States; currently only draft article 13, paragraph 3, which dealt with a non–aquifer State in whose territory either a recharge or discharge zone was located, mentioned third States, and did not impose any obligation on those States. He had felt that that was the most that could be done with regard to third States. It was very probable that only aquifer States would become parties to the convention; most States which had no transboundary aquifers would not become parties, in which case articles 34 to 38 of section 4 of the 1969 Vienna Convention on the Law of Treaties would apply. The Commission could create neither obligations nor rights for third States without their consent; if it wished non-aquifer States to accede to the convention, it would have to offer them incentives to do so, and he seriously doubted whether aquifer States would be prepared to offer such incentives to third States. Such an attempt might likewise have grave consequences: he wondered how the Commission could justify requiring non-aquifer States to bear some obligation for the preservation of the transboundary aquifers of other States. If the justification was that transboundary aquifers were so important for humankind, he wondered why domestic aquifers would not likewise be subject to the same criterion. If domestic aquifers were also included, then the Commission would be coming very close to asserting that those aquifers were the common heritage of mankind.

10. On draft article 7, some members favoured retaining the threshold of "significant" harm, whereas others opposed it. In response to Ms. Xue's comment on draft article 7, he noted that the article did not deal with the question of the responsibility of a State; in the case of State responsibility, an internationally wrongful act had been committed that entailed the responsibility of the State, and any damage caused by that wrongful act must be fully compensated. The activities foreseen in draft article 7, however, were not prohibited by international law and were essential for human survival. Even if such activities had some adverse effect on other States, that effect must be tolerated to a certain degree; that was why the Commission had established a threshold for such tolerance. Not to allow such a level of tolerance would be tantamount to prohibiting any utilization of aquifers. Draft article 7 referred to the typical case of international liability arising out of acts not prohibited by international law. Paragraph 1 dealt with the obligation to prevent the causing of significant harm and paragraph 3 dealt with the eventuality of significant harm being caused in spite of the fulfilment of the obligation of prevention contained in paragraph 1. Even where all appropriate measures and due diligence had been observed, transboundary harm could nevertheless occur because the risks attendant to such activities could not be entirely eliminated; nevertheless, no internationally wrongful act would have been committed.

11. The Special Rapporteur had not succeeded in dissuading the Commission from discussing the final form of the product to be adopted. He had simply wished to avoid a somewhat theological debate. He fully realized that the substance and the form of the instrument were interrelated and that the Commission would have to make a choice sooner or later.

12. As to the relationship of the current topic with possible future work on other natural resources within the broader framework of the topic of shared natural resources, he reiterated that the syllabus prepared by Mr. Rosenstock had provided the basis for the topic and that it had been generally understood that it would cover at least groundwaters, oil and gas (see paragraph 3 above). His mandate was, however, to take a step-by-step approach and to concentrate on groundwaters for the time being. He did not know whether or when the Commission would proceed to deal with oil and gas. There were, however, many similarities between groundwaters, oil and gas; many measures relating to groundwaters would have implications for oil and gas. Conversely, current State practice and norms relating to oil and gas had implications for the Commission's work on groundwaters. Due attention should be given to that matter before consideration of the draft articles on second reading was completed.

13. Turning to more specific suggestions and questions relating to various draft articles, he acknowledged that his report had shortcomings, including insufficient explanations of his reasoning. He had also deliberately used a variety of terms such as "harm", "impact" and "adverse effects", in an effort to express similar but somewhat different concepts. He would try to provide more detailed explanations in the form of commentaries, and stressed his willingness to modify his position on the basis of the wishes of the Commission.

[5] *Yearbook ... 2001*, vol. II (Part Two) and corrigendum, pp. 30 and 141, paras. 76–77.

14. Some members had expressed doubts about draft article 1, paragraph (*b*), covering “other activities”. That was a new element not found in the 1997 Watercourses Convention, and in that connection he referred members to figure 3 in his first report,[6] which illustrated activities other than mere utilization of the aquifer which caused pollution; those activities included the use of agricultural chemicals, dumping of waste, municipal sewage treatment and underground storage. It was essential to regulate such activities for the proper management of aquifers and the issue was in fact being addressed by groundwater experts and administrators.

15. It had been asked whether the definition of “aquifer” in draft article 2, paragraph (*a*), needed to contain the phrase “underlain by a less permeable layer”. The answer was in the affirmative: without such a layer, a geological formation could not function as a reservoir of water. He would try to include appropriate illustrations to clarify the definition. As for the need to define recharging and non-recharging aquifers in draft article 2, paragraphs (*e*) and (*f*), that would depend on whether the Commission formulated different rules for renewable and non-renewable water resources. With regard to a question on the term “contemporary” water recharge, he was not sure whether the problem related to the English term “contemporary” or to a discrepancy between the English and French texts. One example of an artificial recharge installation was to be found in the Franco–Swiss Genevese Aquifer.[7]

16. On draft article 3, concerning bilateral and regional arrangements, he noted that the most contentious point during the negotiation of the 1997 Watercourses Convention had been the treatment of existing agreements on watercourses. There did not, however, seem to be many such agreements relating to groundwaters, and he had decided not to include the relevant paragraph from the 1997 Watercourses Convention. Although it had been suggested that the term “arrangement” should be replaced by “agreement”, it was his view that the former term better reflected the current state of affairs. In addition, it had been suggested that language such as “aquifer States are encouraged” [to enter into a bilateral or regional arrangement] was rather weak; his own view was that such language was in fact much stronger than the wording “may”, contained in the 1997 Watercourses Convention. It had also been suggested that draft article 6, paragraph 1 (*c*) should emphasize the use of water for drinking; in his view, however, it would be more appropriate to incorporate that idea in draft article 11. He would give further thought to that proposal.

17. With regard to comments on the absence of provisions for the administrative organization of transboundary groundwaters, he noted that there was a long history of international cooperation concerning international rivers; indeed, international river commissions had been the precursors of international organizations. In the case of groundwaters, however, only the Franco–Swiss Genevese Aquifer Commission could be considered to be a fully functioning international organization. Although various cooperative organizational arrangements were emerging, they were as yet loose entities; that was why he had included draft article 8, paragraph 2, which recommended the establishment of joint mechanisms or commissions.

18. Many members had suggested the inclusion of a provision on settlement of disputes similar to article 33 of the 1997 Watercourses Convention. While he had no objection to that proposal, he had not replicated that article because he considered it to be simply an ornament with no practical utility, since it did not provide for compulsory jurisdiction. Any dispute would be more properly settled in the context of the bilateral and regional arrangements which governed the relations between the parties to the dispute. In his view, the only important provision of article 33 was the requirement for mandatory submission of the dispute to impartial fact-finding, contained in its paragraph 3; accordingly, he had included that concept in draft article 17, paragraph 2, on resolution of a disagreement on the effect of planned activities.

19. Many members had said that part IV, on activities affecting other States, was too simple in comparison with part III, on planned measures, of the 1997 Watercourses Convention. He simply did not believe that evidence existed of customary rules for such detailed procedural provisions concerning groundwaters; however, he was ready to consider any improvements which might be suggested.

20. Many members had also argued for and against the inclusion of the precautionary principle. While some legally binding instruments incorporated that principle, he did not believe that such provisions were declaratory of customary international law or constitutive of new customary international law. In any event, the precautionary principle or approach was an abstract concept and the Commission would have to define which measures must be implemented for the management of aquifers in accordance with that concept. He would continue to seek an appropriate formulation and would appreciate any guidance provided by the Commission.

21. It seemed to be the general view that a working group on the issue of transboundary groundwaters should be established. He hoped that such a group could meet towards the end of the first part of the current session and again early in the second part of the session. He would try to produce a working paper for the working group and would contact members to ascertain their counter-proposals for draft articles.

Effects of armed conflicts on treaties (*continued*) (A/CN.4/552 and A/CN.4/550 and Corr.1–2)

[Agenda item 8]

First report of the Special Rapporteur (*continued*)

22. Mr. BROWNLIE (Special Rapporteur) said he had the impression that at the previous meeting Mr. Gaja had implied, albeit perhaps unintentionally, that his presentation of existing State practice was inadequate. He wished

[6] See footnote 2 above.

[7] The replenishing station is provided for in article 3 of the Convention on the Protection, Utilisation, Recharge and Monitoring of the Franco–Swiss Genevese Aquifer, see *Yearbook ... 2004*, vol. II (Part One), second report of the Special Rapporteur, document A/CN.4/539 and Add.1, annex IV, sect. C, pp. 271–272; para. 13.

to point out that his report had been prepared, not "early", as alleged, but during the time available to him having regard to his other professional commitments. He had personally and thoroughly researched current State practice, using his own extensive international law collection accumulated over 50 years of practice, as well as the resources of All Souls College, Oxford. Paragraphs 66 to 107 of his report contained numerous, well-documented references to State practice on practically every page. It was to be hoped that such professionally damaging statements would not be made in the future.

23. That being said, he was grateful to Mr. Gaja and other members of the Commission for their comments on matters of law, to which he would respond, as was appropriate, in his concluding statement.

24. Mr. GAJA said he regretted any misunderstanding that might have been caused by his comments. His reference to the early submission of the Special Rapporteur's report had been intended as a compliment, and he had certainly not meant to imply that the Special Rapporteur had not adequately researched the topic of existing State practice. Mr. Brownlie had been working on the question for many years, he had prompted the Commission to take up the topic, and it was perfectly natural that he had been appointed Special Rapporteur. He had simply wished to give it as his view that the Special Rapporteur could have entered into a fuller discussion of the correspondence between existing State practice and the proposed draft articles. He hoped that the apparent misconception about his comments would not mar what he regarded as a very pleasant and fruitful working relationship with the Special Rapporteur that extended back over many years.

25. Mr. ECONOMIDES said that, given the complex and sensitive nature of the topic of the effects of armed conflicts on treaties, the Commission should begin with a general discussion on how it should approach the subject, on the principles on which it should base its decisions and on an appropriate structure. The Commission should take every opportunity to undertake useful and constructive work on behalf of States and the international community at large, and the topic under consideration provided just such an opportunity, giving it a chance to argue the case against armed conflicts and for the continuing applicability of international treaties.

26. He agreed with the conclusion drawn in the memorandum by the Secretariat (A/CN.4/550 and Corr.1–2) that there were advantages to trying to make treaties resistant to armed conflict (para. 163). He felt that the Special Rapporteur had paid insufficient attention in his report to the Charter of the United Nations, Article 2 of which required all Members to settle their international disputes by peaceful means and to refrain from the threat or use of force against the territorial integrity or political independence of any State, or in any other manner inconsistent with the purposes of the United Nations. The principle of the prohibition of the threat or use of force was the cornerstone of United Nations efforts to maintain international peace and security, and must not be ignored in the draft text.

27. The text should take as its starting point the objective fact that acts of aggression were illegal: in particular, the aggressor State should not be placed on an equal footing with a State exercising its right of individual or collective self-defence. In that connection, he believed that the text should draw on articles 7 and 9 of resolution II/1985 of the Institute of International Law on the effects of armed conflicts on treaties.[8] The Institute had wisely drawn a distinction between a State acting in self-defence and an aggressor State, stipulating that: "A State exercising its rights of individual or collective self-defence in accordance with the Charter of the United Nations is entitled to suspend in whole or in part the operation of a treaty incompatible with the exercise of that right, subject to any consequences resulting from a later determination by the Security Council of that State as an aggressor" (art. 7). The last phrase of that article, from "subject to any consequences" onwards, could be deleted, however, as the Security Council should know at any given time whether a State had committed an act of aggression. Indeed, under Article 51 of the Charter, self-defence was a temporary measure available until the Security Council had "taken measures necessary to maintain international peace and security", and the Security Council was expressly given responsibility for taking "at any time such action as it [deemed] necessary in order to maintain or restore international peace and security".

28. In article 9 of its resolution II/1985, the Institute of International Law stipulated that: "A State committing aggression within the meaning of the Charter of the United Nations and resolution 3314 (XXIX) of the General Assembly of the United Nations shall not terminate or suspend the operation of a treaty if the effect would be to benefit that State." The last phrase of that article, from "if the effect" onwards, should be either reworded or deleted in the text to be produced by the Commission.

29. The draft should be constructed on the basis of those two provisions, which, unfortunately, the Special Rapporteur had not seen fit to include.

30. Draft article 4, as proposed by the Special Rapporteur, made the intention of the parties to a treaty at the time it was concluded the prime criterion for terminating or suspending the treaty in cases of armed conflict. On that question he endorsed the comments made by Mr. Gaja at the previous meeting. Although that criterion had been given priority between the two world wars—for instance, in the work of Professor Constantin Eustathiades, an eminent Greek expert on the law of war and a former member of the Commission—it had lost most of its significance since the entry into force of the Charter of the United Nations, except in certain types of treaty such as those relating to international humanitarian law, and was no longer to be found in international treaties.

31. One of the first provisions to be discussed by the Commission should be the one currently contained in draft article 3 (*b*), according to which the outbreak of an armed conflict did not *ipso facto* terminate or suspend the operation of treaties as between one or more parties to the armed conflict and a third State. It should also be

[8] See 2834th meeting, footnote 7.

stipulated that the outbreak of an armed conflict did not *ipso facto* terminate treaties as between the parties to the armed conflict. However, the suspension of the operation of treaties as between the parties to an armed conflict should be dealt with separately, on the basis of the two articles from resolution II/1985 of the Institute of International Law to which he had already referred (para. 27 above).

32. It was also imperative that the draft should expressly stipulate that all treaties specifically related to armed conflict and international humanitarian law in the broad sense of those terms must be applicable, for humanitarian reasons, to the armed conflicts covered by the draft. The same applied to military agreements (*pacta bellica*) concluded in the course of the conflict.

33. The draft should include a provision similar to the one provided by the Special Rapporteur in draft article 7, listing all the treaties that could not be suspended by a State exercising its right of self-defence. As a minimum, the following types of treaties should be included in such a list: treaties establishing or regulating a permanent regime or status; treaties for the protection of human rights; treaties relating to diplomatic and consular immunity; treaties relating to the protection of the environment; law-making treaties; and treaties relating to the settlement of disputes. A provision should also be included to ensure that the suspension of the operation of those treaties was lifted as soon as possible after the end of a conflict.

34. Lastly, the Commission should consider including in the draft a provision similar to article 8 of the resolution of the Institute of International Law, which read:

> A State complying with a resolution by the Security Council of the United Nations concerning action with respect to threats to the peace, breaches of the peace or acts of aggression shall either terminate or suspend the operation of a treaty which would be incompatible with such resolution.

Such a provision would strengthen the United Nations system of collective security.

35. Mr. PELLET said it was unfortunate that the very useful memorandum by the Secretariat (A/CN.4/550 and Corr.1–2) concentrated largely on the English-language literature on practice and doctrine in relation to the effects of armed conflict on treaties; in this respect, he was grateful to the Special Rapporteur for taking a rather broader view of the literature. Unusually for a first report, the report before the Commission was hardly a "preliminary" report in that it presented a complete set of draft articles. The advantage of presenting the report in that way was that it would stimulate discussion and enable members and States to see at the outset what the Special Rapporteur had in mind. The disadvantage was that readers found themselves confined to a single perspective, often without access to the facts that would allow them to make a considered judgement of their own, although the Special Rapporteur did provide some background information in his commentary to some of the draft articles, particularly draft article 4. In the circumstances, he thought it would be premature to enter into detailed discussions on the individual draft articles, each of which, except for draft article 5, raised important problems. For that reason, he did not think it would be appropriate to consider referring the draft articles to the Drafting Committee at the current stage. Moreover, as the Special Rapporteur himself acknowledged in paragraph 13 of the report, the draft articles could be expected to attract comment from Governments and elicit information on State practice, which would enable the Commission to pursue its mission of clarifying the law.

36. He wished to make five general remarks. The first was that, in reading the report, he had often felt frustrated at the recurring claim that a point was "obvious" when he would personally have appreciated more information to allow him to draw his own conclusions. For example, paragraph 5 presented four very different rationales for the legal regime. The first of those rationales, according to which war by its very nature entailed the annulment of all treaties, could be dismissed out of hand, as it simply did not reflect reality. Of the other three rationales, only the third found favour with the Special Rapporteur: that of the intention of the parties at the time they concluded the treaty. That was also the only rationale whose validity was defended in the commentary to draft article 4 (paras. 29–35). The remaining two rationales were summarily dismissed because "the thinking [was] relatively unsophisticated and incoherent" and "the generalizations involved [tended] to be pre-legal and full of ambiguity" (para. 6). However, he personally found nothing absurd about the test of "compatibility with the purposes of the war or the state of hostilities" (para. 5 (*b*)). Indeed, that criterion was reflected in a number of the draft articles proposed by the Special Rapporteur. Moreover, he was strongly inclined to agree with Mr. Economides that the principle of the prohibition of the use of armed force, which had been rejected out of hand without really being discussed by the Special Rapporteur, could play a very important role in the draft text.

37. He was similarly surprised by the categorical rejection, in paragraph 40 of the report, of what the Special Rapporteur called the "extrajuridical thesis". Nor was he sure that the Special Rapporteur had correctly interpreted what he himself had written on that subject. It was obvious that war was not, in itself, a juridical phenomenon, in that it was not deliberately intended to produce legal effects, but it was equally obvious that it did produce such effects. That was the difference between a juridical act, which was intended to have legal effects, and a juridical event, which was an event that produced unintended legal effects. Unlike the Special Rapporteur, he saw no "major contradictions" in that distinction, and the very purpose of dealing with the topic seemed to him to be to determine the legal effects on treaties in force of events that took the form of armed conflicts and were by their very nature extrajuridical.

38. Nor could he see why it should be "evident" that the principle of intention would determine all the legal incidents of a treaty (para. 48). Of course, intention, or perhaps rather consent to be bound, was the basic principle governing the law of treaties—the principle of *pacta sunt servanda*, as referred to in article 26 of the 1969 Vienna Convention (para. 47). However, the grounds for the invalidity of treaties set out in articles 46 to 53 of the 1969 Vienna Convention were not all related

to consent or intention. Moreover, it was at least possible to draw an analogy between armed conflicts and the "supervening impossibility of performance" of a treaty (1969 Vienna Convention, art. 61) or a "fundamental change of circumstances" (art. 62). Although the Secretariat had addressed that central issue in its memorandum, the Special Rapporteur had taken no position on it in his report.

39. One must also raise the question, as did the memorandum by the Secretariat, how circumstances precluding wrongfulness, particularly *force majeure* (A/CN.4/550, paras. 127–135), were related to the topic under consideration. The law of responsibility and the law of treaties were two distinct sets of rules whose complex interrelationship had been highlighted, *inter alia*, by the "*Rainbow Warrior*" arbitration and the ICJ judgment in the *Gabčíkovo–Nagymaros Project* case. The existence of the two sets of rules was perhaps the reason why the Special Rapporteur, in paragraph 10 of his report, indicated that the approach taken in the law of treaties was the only one suited to the topic. A detailed explanation of that point in the report would not, however, have been superfluous. Even if one posited, on academic, theoretical grounds, a separation between the two sets of rules, that must not prevent the Commission from investigating the relationship between the topic and the law of responsibility, at the very least as a means of shedding some useful light on the subject.

40. His final cause for perplexity in relation to the report derived from paragraph 50, which indicated that the distinction between relations between the parties to an armed conflict and relations with, or between, third States was "obviously" significant, but only within the framework of the criterion of intention. In the absence of any explanation, he had to admit to not really understanding the reasoning behind that affirmation. It seemed to him that the distinction between parties to a conflict and third parties was important in terms both of the nature of the treaty and of the nature of the conflict.

41. Lest his position should be misconstrued, he stressed that he was not fundamentally hostile to the criterion of intention, but the other theories should not be discarded out of hand without being given serious consideration. Intention was not the sole criterion, and the Special Rapporteur himself seemed fundamentally to take that view, since draft article 7 was based not on the intention of the parties but on the object and purpose of the various types of treaties cited.

42. That led to his second general remark, concerning the criterion of intention, which was so central to the draft. He had no strong feelings as to whether it should indeed be central, but he firmly believed that no criterion should be applied to the exclusion of all others. He was troubled by the way the criterion of intention was used in the draft. In paragraph 47 of the report, the Special Rapporteur stated that the principle of intention promoted legal security. That was by no means obvious, for two reasons. First, it was far from easy to determine the intention of the parties to a treaty. Secondly, the reason for that difficulty was that in general, the parties had no intention at all: they simply did not envisage the possibility that armed conflict might break out, whether among themselves, among third parties, or in one of their territories, in the case of a domestic conflict.

43. It might of course happen that States had some idea that armed conflict was a possibility. That was obviously the case with treaties expressly applicable in case of an armed conflict, mentioned in draft article 7, paragraph 2 (*a*), and with the treaties mentioned in draft article 5, paragraph 1. Aside from the situations described in those two provisions, however, States did not generally have any intentions whatsoever regarding the possible effects on their treaty relations of an outbreak of armed conflict. In most cases, they concluded treaties on the assumption that they would remain at peace. Accordingly, their intentions were less relevant than the object and purpose of the treaty they had concluded. One might consider that the object and purpose of the treaty reflected their implicit intentions, but that was a fairly artificial intellectual construct and it would be more comprehensible and clearer to say plainly that in the absence of express intention, it was the object and purpose of the treaty that constituted the general guidance.

44. In draft article 4, paragraph 2, and draft article 9, paragraph 2, the Special Rapporteur suggested that for the purpose of determining the susceptibility of a treaty to termination or suspension in case of an armed conflict, or to resumption if it had already been suspended, the intention of the parties to a treaty should be determined in accordance with articles 31 and 32 of the 1969 Vienna Convention on interpretation of treaties, on the one hand, and with the nature and extent of the armed conflict, on the other hand. Those were two very different criteria, however, and the second, namely, the nature and extent of the armed conflict, had nothing to do with the intention of the parties. It seemed strange to use articles 31 and 32 of the 1969 Vienna Convention to determine the intention of parties to a treaty. On the contrary, in the case of article 31 it was the intention of the parties as reflected in the object and purpose of the treaty, and in the case of article 32 the *travaux préparatoires*, that made it possible to interpret the treaty. Referring to articles 31 and 32 amounted to circular reasoning: in order to determine the intention of the parties, one must base oneself on the intention of the parties.

45. His third general remark was on the scope of the draft articles, but went beyond consideration of draft article 1, entitled "Scope", which merely reproduced the title of the topic and gave no clear indication as to what the scope might actually be. The first problem was whether the draft applied solely to treaties that had already entered into force, or also to those signed but not yet in force. If the latter was the case, then a distinction should be made between contracting States within the meaning of article 2, paragraph 1 (*f*), of the 1969 Vienna Convention, and those that were not contracting States. Those issues should be dealt with in the draft.

46. A related problem was whether the draft covered capacity to conclude a treaty. Draft article 5, paragraph 2, seemed to indicate that that was the case, even if the indication was given in a very strange place: he could not see how paragraph 2 followed from or related to paragraph 1.

The issue of whether war had an impact on the capacity of States to conclude treaties should be covered in the draft.

47. Another problem relating to the scope concerned the very definition of armed conflict. In principle he favoured a broad definition, like the one proposed in draft article 2 (*b*). It should be expressly stated, however, that the draft articles covered both domestic and international conflicts, a view that the Special Rapporteur—who had noted that the distinction between the two was not always clear-cut—seemed to share, even though he had not incorporated such wording in the draft. Furthermore, he himself was not sure that the effects of domestic and international armed conflicts were necessarily the same in all cases, and he regretted the apparent absence of any subsequent reference to the distinction.

48. In paragraph 16, the Special Rapporteur stated that the definition of armed conflict included blockade, even in the absence of armed actions. It was difficult to reconcile that approach with the express mention made of armed operations in draft article 2 (*b*). That mention seemed, moreover, to leave some ambiguity as to whether situations infinitely more important in the contemporary world than blockade were covered by the draft. He was thinking in particular of the Arab–Israeli conflict. States, and not solely those that were directly involved, needed to know whether the draft articles applied to armed conflicts of that type.

49. The final problem with regard to the scope was the absence of answers to a number of very fundamental questions. Draft article 10, entitled "Legality of the conduct of the parties", indicated that the incidence—for which the French translation, "la conséquence", should be plural, not singular—of the termination or suspension of a treaty "shall not be affected by the legality of the conduct of the parties to the armed conflict according either to the principles of general international law"—presumably both *jus in bello* and *jus ad bellum*—"or the provisions of the Charter of the United Nations". It was hard, in the year 2005, not to ask whether the legality of the conduct of the parties did not play a role, and most probably a fundamental role, in the fate of the treaties concerned. It was precisely because of the thorny nature of the problem that, in 1963, the Commission had decided not to take the topic up.[9] The draft would be much more useful and interesting if it dealt with such thorny issues. In that respect he fully concurred with Mr. Economides: in 2005, one could hardly behave as if the law of war had undergone absolutely no changes. The issue of legality of conduct should be one of the key elements of the draft and must not simply be swept under the carpet by the use of a "without prejudice" clause in draft article 11. In any event it would be useful to know what States had to say about those questions, and an express request to that effect should be included in chapter III of the Commission's report, in which it listed specific issues on which comments would be of particular interest to it.

50. Another omission concerned treaties concluded by international organizations. Integration treaties, whether for the European Union or MERCOSUR, could not be entirely ignored.

51. His fourth general remark was that the draft failed to distinguish sufficiently between a variety of situations whose legal effects were very different. It would, for example, have been useful to make a distinction between international armed conflicts and domestic ones; between States parties to an international armed conflict and third—more specifically, neutral—States; between States that were parties to a treaty and those that were not but were parties to the conflict; between States parties and contracting States that had not ratified the treaty; between situations when a treaty was terminated owing to an armed conflict and those when its application was simply suspended; between the effects of an armed conflict on the provisions of a treaty that had already been executed, or were being executed, and those that had not been executed; and between the effects of an armed conflict on substantive provisions, on the one hand, and on final clauses or procedural provisions, on the other.

52. His final general remark was that treaties tended to be regarded in the draft as an integral whole. A more nuanced approach should be taken. From the memorandum of the Secretariat, especially paragraphs 153 *et seq.*, one could see that, especially in the case of complex treaties, not all the provisions were subjected to the same effects in the event of armed conflict. In a single treaty, some provisions might be suspended, while others were irremediably terminated and others again continued to be applied in full. He was thinking, *mutatis mutandis*, of the 1980 ICJ judgment in the *United States Diplomatic and Consular Staff in Tehran* case, in which the Court had clearly stressed the special character of the dispute settlement clauses in the event of a substantial breach of the treaty. That obviously raised the delicate issue of the separability of treaty provisions, but it was an issue central to the topic and one mentioned in the Secretariat memorandum (paras. 153–157).

53. One might go further: was the fundamental issue that of the effects of armed conflict on a treaty as a whole, on its distinct provisions, or on the obligations and rights flowing from the treaty? Article 63 of the 1969 Vienna Convention, entitled "Severance of diplomatic or consular relations", stipulated that severance "does not affect the legal relations established [...] by the treaty". It was noteworthy that it was the "legal relations" that were not affected, not the treaty itself or its provisions. While he was not familiar with the genesis of that provision, he was quite sure that every word in it had been carefully weighed. The Commission would therefore do well to think carefully about the effects of armed conflicts on treaties: was it the treaty itself, its provisions individually and separately or, as he suspected was the case, the obligations flowing from the treaty that were affected? In some cases an armed conflict might suspend the obligations imposed by the treaty. Articles 57 and 65 of the 1969 Vienna Convention set forth procedures for the suspension of a treaty, procedures that were hardly compatible with armed conflict situations. The problem did not arise if one acknowledged that it was not the treaty or its provisions whose application was suspended, but rather the obligations arising from those provisions or, to

[9] See *Yearbook ... 1963*, vol. II, document A/5509, p. 189, para. 14.

use the language of article 63 of the 1969 Vienna Convention, the legal relations established between the parties to a treaty. If the issue was indeed the effects on obligations arising from a treaty, that seemed to shed a special light on the topic, which could then no longer be envisaged solely from the standpoint of the law of treaties: a substantial element of the law of responsibility was also involved. That issue needed to be given serious consideration.

54. In concluding, he thanked the Special Rapporteur for having submitted a thought-provoking report which, nevertheless, left some important issues in the dark. The problems that the Special Rapporteur had raised, and some that he had not, must now be discussed thoroughly. Judging from paragraph 13 of the report, that was the objective that the Special Rapporteur had set himself. In any event, problems of principle stood in the way of adopting a package of draft articles at the present stage.

55. Mr. DUGARD congratulated the Special Rapporteur on his first report. It was an admirable achievement to have submitted a complete set of draft articles, thereby enabling the Commission to have a full picture right from the outset, rather than having to wait for new articles to be submitted each year. The report was thoroughly researched and clearly presented, and he agreed with the general approach adopted, in particular with regard to the use of force.

56. He had two suggestions to make on the draft as a whole. The first had to do with the relevance of municipal court decisions. Such decisions were a source of international law, albeit a subsidiary one. In some branches of international law they were of little assistance, whereas in others they were very important, for example for the development of customary international law in respect of restrictive immunity for acts *jure gestionis* in the field of sovereign immunity. The Special Rapporteur took the view that the law governing the effect of armed conflicts on treaties fell within the category of international law which was not influenced by municipal court decisions. In paragraphs 20, 44 and 105 of the report he stressed that he did not find such decisions to be of much assistance, that they were a problematic source and that they generally depended on the explicit guidance of the executive. He disagreed with that approach. Municipal courts had frequently considered the effect of armed conflicts on treaties. It was true that those decisions were not consistent, but the development of the law relating to the restrictive approach to sovereign immunity showed the same inconsistency, as did other forms of State practice, in particular Government statements. Whereas countries such as the United Kingdom and the former Soviet Union had resisted the changes in other municipal court jurisdictions and had preferred to retain the absolute approach, other jurisdictions had taken the restrictive approach. In his opinion, municipal court decisions provided helpful evidence of State practice—of the intention of parties in respect of certain kinds of treaty and the effect of the nature of a treaty on that treaty's survival. The importance of such decisions was borne out by the Secretariat memorandum (A/CN.4/550 and Corr.1–2), which referred to a number of cases, such as the *Techt* v. *Hughes* and *Clark* v. *Allen* cases in the United States (para. 11) and also cited decisions on extradition treaties, such as those in the *Gallina* v. *Fraser* (footnote 233) and *Argento* v. *Horn et al.* (footnote 9) cases, which had recently been followed by the South African courts. The memorandum also contained references to Italian, Greek and a host of other municipal court decisions. Indeed, the Special Rapporteur himself referred to municipal court decisions, citing Whiteman's *Digest of International Law* at great length (paragraph 78 of the report) and *Masinimport* v. *Scottish Mechanical Light Industries Ltd.* (para. 105). He urged the Special Rapporteur to reconsider his view that municipal court decisions were of little assistance.

57. His second suggestion related to the need to include some reference to the nature of a treaty. The Special Rapporteur regarded the intention of the parties as the key to the question of which treaties were to survive an armed conflict; he did, however, cite a number of authors who argued that the nature of the treaty should be considered. In paragraph 33 of the report, for example, Lord McNair was quoted as saying that "the nature of the treaty is clearly the best evidence of the intention of the parties"; a similar point was made by Fitzmaurice (para. 34). The Special Rapporteur also cited Hurst (para. 32), according to whom "[t]he cases that present difficulties are where the treaty provides no clear indication of the intentions of the parties, and where that intention must be presumed from the nature of the treaty or from the concomitant circumstances". It was therefore strange that the Special Rapporteur declined to include a reference to the nature of the treaty in his draft. In Mr. Dugard's own view, articles 4 and 9 should refer not only to the nature of the armed conflict, but also to the nature of the treaty as evidence of the intention of the parties. That would be more helpful than a reference to articles 31 and 32 of the 1969 Vienna Convention, and in that connection he associated himself with the comments made by Mr. Gaja and Mr. Pellet.

58. It was odd that the Special Rapporteur did, in fact, stress in draft article 7, paragraph 1, that the object and purpose of the treaty must be taken into account. Was that not much the same as stressing the importance of the nature of the treaty? After all, the object and purpose of the treaty were part of the nature of the treaty. It would therefore be more appropriate to refer to the nature of the treaty. In paragraph 62, the Special Rapporteur seemed to accept that position, because he wrote that "a major aspect of the treatment in the literature is the indication of categories of treaties in order to identify types of treaty which are in principle not susceptible to suspension or termination in case of armed conflict". The Special Rapporteur's position was therefore ambivalent. It was worth noting that article 3 of resolution II/1985 of the Institute of International Law also referred to the "nature or purpose" of the treaty.

59. On the articles themselves, his first comment related to article 2 (*b*) and the definition which the Special Rapporteur had taken from the Institute of International Law. There was now a widely accepted definition of armed conflict which was not that of the Institute, and he referred in that connection to the decision in the *Tadić* case of the Appeals Chamber of the International Criminal Tribunal for the Former Yugoslavia, in which the Court had found that "an armed conflict exists whenever there is a resort to armed force between States or protracted armed violence

between governmental authorities and organized armed groups or between such groups within a State" (para. 70 of the decision). While that definition took no account of the treaty element considered in the Institute of International Law's definition, it was now the definition of armed conflict most frequently cited, particularly in international criminal law, and the Commission could not ignore it.

60. He was pleased that the Special Rapporteur had drawn attention to the problem of military occupation unaccompanied by protracted armed violence or armed operations. As Mr. Pellet had rightly pointed out, that was an important question in the context of the Middle East. However, he would not have expected the Special Rapporteur to go into the complexities of the Middle East conflict, an approach that would certainly lead to additional difficulties.

61. With regard to article 3, he had no objection to using the word "necessarily", but hoped that it was not used simply to avoid the Latin term "*ipso facto*". The Commission should not be hostile in principle to Latin expressions.

62. Article 4 should include a reference to the nature of the treaty in a new subparagraph 2 (*c*); the reference to the Vienna Convention on the Law of Treaties in subparagraph 2 (*a*) should perhaps be deleted.

63. On draft article 7, the long list of types of treaty which the Special Rapporteur had provided simply confirmed his own view that account should be taken of the nature of the treaty. The Secretariat memorandum had referred to a number of additional types of treaty, for example extradition agreements, and there was a host of municipal court decisions on the subject. Other categories should also be included; for instance, in its resolution II/1985 the Institute of International Law had referred to treaties establishing international organizations (art. 6). It was not clear from the report whether that category was covered by the Special Rapporteur's reference to multilateral treaties.

64. His comments on article 4 applied equally to draft article 9. He had no difficulties with draft articles 10 to 14. On article 11, the Commission should perhaps in due course pay greater attention to the effect of Security Council resolutions and of Article 103 of the Charter of the United Nations on treaties, even if that went beyond the scope of its current mandate.

65. He was not quite sure how to interpret paragraph 13 of the report. He did not think that the Special Rapporteur was suggesting that the Commission should approve all the draft articles as they stood and forward them to States for comments: the Commission had a responsibility to consider the articles before they were transmitted to States, and the response of States was not always very helpful, particularly if the Commission had not itself digested the principles. In his view, the Commission should at least consider referring some of the draft articles, perhaps articles 1 to 3, to the Drafting Committee at the present session. The Special Rapporteur could then reconsider the other provisions, with or without the benefit of a working group.

66. Mr. PELLET, referring to the Arab–Israeli conflict, said he had emphatically not proposed that the Commission should examine that issue in detail. He had simply argued that the draft should indicate whether or not it was applicable in such a case. In his view, the Special Rapporteur was too cautious and abstract with regard to that conflict. Special rapporteurs should not be afraid to address specific situations in their reports.

67. As to paragraph 13, the mere fact that the draft was not referred to the Drafting Committee did not mean that States could not comment on it. In the first place, all relevant ministries received copies of the Special Rapporteurs' reports; secondly, it was common practice for the report of the Commission to reproduce the articles discussed in footnotes.

68. Mr. PAMBOU-TCHIVOUNDA said he was wholly dissatisfied with the report on the effects of armed conflicts on treaties, which could have provided the Special Rapporteur with an opportunity to elaborate on the law of treaties, as regulated in the 1969 and 1986 Vienna Conventions. The definition of a treaty was already established, and he was not certain that it was needed in the current draft. Draft article 4, with its references to articles 31 and 32 of the 1969 Vienna Convention, was also well established, though it probably had a place in the draft, because the Special Rapporteur had based his argument on the notion of the intention of the parties. He wondered, however, whether the provisions on the interpretation of treaties were the best way of tackling the question. Article 6 left open questions concerning the regime of nullity, and, indeed, concerning the very purpose of the draft.

69. With regard to the method, the basic issues did not clearly emerge from the report, so that it was not apparent why the Commission had chosen to take up the topic, or whether it had been right to do so. The whole subject had been diluted by the Special Rapporteur's failure properly to develop his approach to the topic.

70. The very notion of "effects" had not been explained, although it was the key to the subject, regardless of whether a restrictive or a broad approach was taken. Since recourse to war was prohibited by international law—unless one agreed with the line taken in article 10, which he did not—except in the cases of authorization by the Security Council and self-defence, the question was whether the violation of said prohibition by a State which resorted to war entailed consequences—as distinct from "effects"—for that State, by virtue of its breach of an obligation under general international law. In that context, the subject should have established a link with the law of State responsibility, not just with the law of treaties. The notion of "effect" could then have been clarified by linking it with the notion of "consequence".

71. Even if the Commission focused solely on the effects dealt with by the Special Rapporteur, namely, the suspension or termination of a treaty, there was every reason to ask what consequences such suspension or termination might have either for the parties themselves, owing to their commitments under the treaty, or *vis-à-vis* third, neutral, parties. All those questions were left open in the report. It would have been useful for the Commission to

have received more information on those matters. He was dismayed not to have found replies to those preliminary considerations in the report, which failed to provide either a method, an approach, a definition of the subject or a discussion of the issues.

Organization of work of the session (*continued*)*

[Agenda item 1]

72. The CHAIRPERSON said that if he heard no objection he would take it that the Commission wished to establish a Working Group on Transboundary Groundwaters.

It was so decided.

73. The CHAIRPERSON invited members who wished to participate in the Working Group to inform the Special Rapporteur on the topic of their interest.

74. He announced that it had also been proposed to hold a joint meeting of the Commission and the European Society of International Law on 27 May 2005 at 3 p.m., on the subject of the responsibility of international organizations. More than 100 members of the Society, including its president, Judge Simma, proposed to attend. Preliminary arrangements had already been made for that important event. If he heard no objection he would take it that the Commission agreed to the holding of that meeting.

It was so agreed.

The meeting rose at 12.45 p.m.

2837th MEETING

Thursday, 12 May 2005, at 10 a.m.

Chairperson: Mr. Djamchid MOMTAZ

Present: Mr. Addo, Mr. Baena Soares, Mr. Brownlie, Mr. Candioti, Mr. Chee, Mr. Comissário Afonso, Mr. Daoudi, Mr. Dugard, Mr. Economides, Ms. Escarameia, Mr. Fomba, Mr. Gaja, Mr. Galicki, Mr. Kabatsi, Mr. Kateka, Mr. Kemicha, Mr. Kolodkin, Mr. Koskenniemi, Mr. Mansfield, Mr. Matheson, Mr. Niehaus, Mr. Pambou-Tchivounda, Mr. Pellet, Mr. Sreenivasa Rao, Mr. Rodríguez Cedeño, Mr. Sepúlveda, Ms. Xue, Mr. Yamada.

Effects of armed conflicts on treaties (*continued*) (A/CN.4/552 and A/CN.4/550 and Corr.1–2)

[Agenda item 8]

First report of the Special Rapporteur (*continued*)

1. Mr. KOSKENNIEMI commended the Special Rapporteur for preparing a comprehensive set of draft articles which gave an overview of the topic and placed the articles in the public domain so as to elicit practical comments from Governments.

2. Like Mr. Gaja, he had initially been surprised at the peremptory tone of some of the Special Rapporteur's statements. In the introduction, after introducing four theories without explaining where they came from, the Special Rapporteur declared, in paragraph 6, that they were not of great assistance. Later, in paragraph 20, he said that the decisions of municipal courts were "not of much value". In paragraph 64, he spoke of "the available material, which is substantial", but gave no further details. However, the most striking statement was the one in paragraph 16, where he said: "There can be no doubt that the work of the Commission will be much delayed if a high level of sophistication is sought." The Special Rapporteur was clearly relying on his readers' willingness to take him on faith. He had undoubtedly rendered a great service to the Commission by submitting such a clear and forceful draft, but the Commission needed to decide if it was fully acceptable before sending it to the Drafting Committee.

3. It was unfortunate that whenever it approached a new topic the Commission did not give greater consideration to the overall direction of its work. It might ask, for example, what alternative solutions there were to the question of the effects of armed conflicts on treaties, what the repercussions of such alternatives might be in specific situations, such as the Israeli–Palestinian conflict, and what issues were at stake. All those points deserved to be discussed; otherwise the work of codification was in danger of being reduced to the drafting of a collective work on the law of treaties. That comment was not a criticism of the Special Rapporteur but was directed at the Commission's general methods of work.

4. The main problem was that an armed conflict was such a major, overwhelming event that when one occurred, the fate of treaties was of secondary importance. It was unlikely that those willing to breach the prohibition of the use of force would be impressed by a few rules on treaties. Moreover, against a background of death and destruction, formalism was out of place. The Commission needed to be both realistic and very sensitive if it expected compliance with the rules under consideration.

5. He had initially thought, like most members who had spoken before him, that the concept of "intention" was as general as the concepts of "reasonableness" or "equity", and that it was not a very useful one for jurists whose task was to determine what would become of a given treaty. On reflection, however, he thought that the reference to the fiction of intention actually made it possible, by introducing some flexibility, to take the context of a given situation into account and, consequently, to preserve the realism and effectiveness that had been mentioned.

6. According to draft article 4, paragraph 2 (*b*), draft article 5 and draft article 7, paragraph 1, intention was to be determined on the basis of the nature of the armed conflict, the express provisions of the treaty, and the object and purpose of the treaty. A list of examples of treaties that should remain in force was given in draft article 7, paragraph 2. That was the most important provision, as it provided the basis for any hypothesis about intention.

* Resumed from the 2834th meeting.

However, it was unclear why some treaties were on the list and others were not. An explanation was needed. In seeking one, three elements could be considered: the interests at stake, specific real-life cases and the historical development of doctrine. Clearly, a more thorough discussion of the direction the study should take would be useful.

7. He wished to make some specific suggestions: he first wished to know how the question of the use of force, which arose in connection with draft articles 10 and 11, could possibly be avoided. In paragraph 122, the Special Rapporteur said that it was not dealt with because illegality could not be determined, but that was not always true, which made it no different from other auto-interpretative rules. He agreed with the distinction drawn by Mr. Pellet between the effects of international armed conflicts and those of internal armed conflicts. The interests at stake were indeed quite different and, in the case of internal conflicts, the key issue was treaties involving third States. As Mr. Pellet had suggested, the possibility of partially terminating or suspending treaties in certain situations should be considered. In that respect, too, closer attention should be paid to the specific context in each case.

8. Mr. PELLET said that, in the first place, he certainly did not claim to have been the first to draw a distinction between the effects of internal conflicts and those of international conflicts; that distinction was in fact mentioned in the report, and he agreed with it. In the second place, he was not really sure there was much point in delving further into the "historical/doctrinal" aspect of the question. He did agree, however, that a casuistic approach must be followed in order to give due weight to the actual context in which problems arose and had been solved.

9. Mr. CHEE asked how treaties, which were international instruments, could be related to internal affairs.

10. Mr. PELLET replied that internal events could obviously have an impact on international instruments. Moreover, in keeping with what had been expressly stated when the topic had been adopted, the report itself said that the Commission would consider internal as well as international conflicts (paras. 17–18).

11. Mr. BROWNLIE (Special Rapporteur) said that he had distinguished four theories in paragraph 5 of his report only after going through a wealth of literature on the topic. One of the *raisons d'être* of a special rapporteur, it seemed to him, was precisely to save the Commission time by attempting to synthesize existing writings on the topic. Although the questions raised by the topic under consideration might not have been resolved, they certainly had not been ignored. That said, producing a synthesis did lead one to state generalities. He agreed that context was important, but one of the problems that arose was the wide range of armed conflicts, which predated by far the contemporary problem of foreign interference that turned some internal conflicts into semi-international conflicts. The range of conflicts itself affected the context, making it more difficult to legislate for every case. The references to the concepts of intention, object and purpose were therefore generalities, but it was very difficult to move from the general to the particular.

12. Mr. MATHESON agreed with the Special Rapporteur's desire to encourage continuity of treaty obligations in cases of armed conflict where there was no real need to suspend or terminate them. Also, where treaty obligations did not continue, the presumption should be that they had been temporarily suspended rather than terminated. Such a complex topic should not, however, be reduced to categorical general rules. The effect of a conflict on treaties would depend more on the provisions of the treaty concerned and on the specific circumstances than on general rules. It would be better to set out the considerations that States needed to take into account rather than lay down definitive rules that they must always follow.

13. With regard to draft article 1, he wondered whether the draft articles as a whole should not also cover treaties to which international organizations were parties. With regard to the definitions, and particularly to draft article 2, subparagraph (*b*), he said that, while it was true that it was not the Commission's task to redefine the concept of armed conflict, it might be useful to simplify the proposed text, which as it stood might not apply to situations that fell outside the ordinary definition of armed conflict, such as acts of terrorism.

14. He agreed with the idea in draft article 3 that the outbreak of an armed conflict did not necessarily terminate or suspend treaties. As drafted, however, the article applied only to the operation of treaties between parties to the conflict or between those parties and a third State. The article could perhaps be applied to treaties between third States or between States and international organizations. It might suffice simply to say that the outbreak of an armed conflict did not necessarily terminate or suspend the operation of any treaty.

15. With regard to draft article 4, he shared the concerns expressed by Mr. Gaja and Mr. Pellet. When the intention of the parties could be ascertained from the text or from the negotiating record, it should be carried out. However, the intention was not usually expressed clearly, and so it was necessary to consider other factors, including the object and purpose of the treaty, the nature of the specific provisions in question and the particular circumstances of the conflict. It would therefore be preferable to acknowledge that fact directly in draft article 4 rather than to assume that the parties always had an intention that needed only to be discovered or that could be presumed.

16. Although the provisions of draft article 5 appeared obvious and superfluous, it would be desirable, for the sake of clarity, to retain them. There was also another important point to be made about the treaties and rules that were expressly applicable in cases of armed conflict. As the ICJ had pointed out in its advisory opinion on the *Legality of the Threat or Use by a State of Nuclear Weapons*, certain human rights and environmental principles did not cease to apply in times of armed conflict, but their application was determined by the applicable *lex specialis*, namely, the law governing the conduct of hostilities.

17. Draft article 6 did not need to be included, as its provisions could be reflected in the commentary on draft article 3.

18. Draft article 7 was the most problematic and most complex of the draft articles, and even the Special Rapporteur was not sure it was necessary. He personally had serious doubts as to whether it was possible or desirable to attempt to designate categories of treaties whose object and purpose involved the necessary implication that they continued in operation during an armed conflict. First, treaties did not fall into neat categories. Second, some provisions of a treaty might by their very nature be subject to suspension during an armed conflict, while other provisions might not. Third, even with respect to particular types of provisions, the language of a treaty and the intention of the parties might well differ from one treaty to another. Fourth, State practice was not very consistent and provided no clear-cut answers as to whether a category of treaties could be suspended or terminated. There were gradations in the applicability of different categories of treaties. Fifth, any attempt to categorize treaties in such a way could lead to such a prolonged and contentious debate that it might not be possible to reach consensus in the Commission or among States. In short, it would be better to list the factors that might lead towards one conclusion or another, such as the degree to which the treaty provisions in question interfered with the requirements of armed conflict, the particular circumstances of conflicts that might lead to one outcome or another, and the importance of continuity when such fundamental values as the protection of human rights were involved. Moreover, State practice and the decisions of international tribunals could be summarized in the commentary.

19. With regard to the categories of treaties listed in paragraph 2 of draft article 7, he thought that the first one, in subparagraph (*a*), was unnecessary, as the matter was already covered by draft article 5. The second category, in subparagraph (*b*), was somewhat ambiguous. For example, it raised the question of which rights and obligations were "permanent" and which were tantamount to a "regime" or "status". Furthermore, some provisions of treaties of that type might be incompatible with the obligations and rights of States under the law of armed conflict and might need to be temporarily suspended for that reason. The third category, in subparagraph (*c*), was a good example of treaties that contained provisions that ordinarily could and should continue during an armed conflict, such as those relating to the personal status and property rights of foreign nationals, while others might need to be suspended in certain circumstances, such as those relating to the regulation of navigation and commerce between the States parties to a conflict. The sources cited by the Special Rapporteur seemed to focus on specific types of provisions rather than on the treaties as a whole. In the memorandum by the Secretariat, such treaties were considered as not having a high likelihood of applicability (A/CN.4/550, paras. 70–75).

20. Treaties for the protection of human rights belonging to the fourth category, in subparagraph (*d*), were among those that would probably continue to apply. However, the ICJ had made it clear that human rights must be applied in accordance with the law of armed conflict.

21. In contrast, the presumption of continuity was not high in the case of treaties belonging to the fifth category, in subparagraph (*e*). The memorandum by the Secretariat suggested that some environmental principles would generally apply in times of armed conflict, while others would not (paras. 58–63). There did not seem to be a general presumption of continuity for all treaties related to the protection of the environment.

22. With regard to treaties in the sixth category, in subparagraph (*f*), the scholarly opinion cited by the Special Rapporteur showed that the operation of such treaties could be partially suspended, subject to revival on the restoration of peace. State practice in that area was contradictory, and he had serious doubts as to whether there could be a general presumption of continuity for treaties related to international watercourses and related installations and works, given that it might be imperative in wartime to prevent or restrict air and sea traffic to or from an enemy State.

23. With regard to multilateral law-making treaties, in subparagraph (*g*), both the Special Rapporteur and the Secretariat (paras. 47–51) considered that there was a reasonable basis for continuity, though both recognized that State practice was not entirely consistent and that there were many examples of suspension or partial application of such treaties in wartime. It was, moreover, difficult to determine what constituted a "law-making" treaty, since all treaties created law.

24. To sum up, he said that it would be far more useful to identify the factors that would indicate continuity or the lack thereof and to supplement that exercise with an analysis of State practice in various areas.

25. With regard to draft article 9, he agreed that the Commission should favour the resumption of suspended treaties when the reasons for the suspension no longer applied. If draft article 4 was changed to reflect factors other than intention, draft article 9 would need to be revised accordingly.

26. As far as draft article 10 was concerned, it was incorrect to say that the incidence of termination or suspension of a treaty was not affected by the legality of the conduct of the parties. Where a State was exercising legitimate self-defence or complying with decisions taken by the Security Council under Chapter VII of the Charter of United Nations, the result might be, in some circumstances, the suspension of treaty provisions. That point could be made in the form of a savings clause or in the commentary, but for the time being the Commission should not attempt to define the scope of self-defence or the authority of the Security Council.

27. Lastly, he supported the reiteration in draft article 13 of the rules of the 1969 Vienna Convention, which might be triggered in appropriate circumstances by the outbreak of an armed conflict. In general, the Commission should analyse State practice more closely before drawing conclusions. It should therefore encourage Governments to provide more information on their practice and their views on the topic before it formulated definite rules.

28. Ms. ESCARAMEIA thanked the Special Rapporteur for his clear and comprehensive report and the Secretariat for its memorandum, an excellent compilation

of sources that ought to be published. She had found it difficult to comment on the report owing to the comprehensive scope of the topic, the Special Rapporteur's vast knowledge of it and his innovative approach of submitting a complete draft to test the general reaction of the Commission and of States. However, the report erred by omitting certain distinctions, thereby oversimplifying the situations contemplated. For example, distinctions should have been drawn between: the effects of armed conflicts on the parties to the conflict and the effects on third States; situations involving the suspension, termination or continuation of treaties during armed conflict; the effects of international and internal conflicts, both of which must be covered; the effects on different provisions of the same treaty; rights of an aggressor State and those of a State acting in self-defence or in compliance with a Security Council resolution on the use of force, as had been done in articles 7 to 9 of resolution II/1985 adopted by the Institute of International Law.[1]

29. The relationship of the draft to the law of treaties, the law of war and the law of State responsibility was also problematic. She did not fully understand the Special Rapporteur's reasons for situating the draft articles in the context of the law of treaties rather than the law of war—that had not been the Commission's intention in article 73 of the 1969 Vienna Convention—unless he was simply reaffirming the old-fashioned theory that war was nothing more than a situation of total anarchy. Yet the legality of a war and the position of the party in question mattered. In the context of the law of treaties, consideration must be given to the relationship between the draft articles and the provisions of the 1969 Vienna Convention, in particular those on supervening impossibility of performance (art. 61), fundamental change of circumstances (art. 62), and even severance of diplomatic or consular relations (art. 63) and perhaps termination or suspension as a consequence of breach of a treaty (art. 60). Reference was made to those provisions in draft article 13, but more detail was needed.

30. She also had difficulties with the Special Rapporteur's choice of the criterion of the intention of the parties, which in most cases amounted to the presumed intention of the parties, a vague and subjective notion. For example, she wondered why a State conducting an illegal war of aggression would be allowed to terminate a treaty and benefit therefrom. Such a situation could arise if the Commission adopted the criterion of the intention of the parties. Some members felt that that criterion, which was stated in draft article 4, was further developed in draft article 7, which considered the object and purpose of treaties. In her opinion, however, articles 4 and 7 dealt with quite different criteria. Article 7 actually set as criteria the nature of the treaty and the type of conflict, and provided a list of categories of treaties that would continue to apply during armed conflicts. If any general criterion ought to prevail, it would probably be the notion that, in principle, the provisions of treaties would continue to apply depending on their viability, taking into account the existence of an armed conflict and the party's position regarding the legality of the conflict.

[1] See 2834th meeting, footnote 7.

31. She preferred the definition of armed conflict used in the *Tadić* case to the one contained in draft article 2, subparagraph (*b*), because the former more easily encompassed all problems stemming from civil wars as well as international wars, thereby avoiding difficulties involved in distinguishing between those two types of conflicts. The definition should be preceded by the words "For the purposes of this Convention" in order to avoid discussions of the definition of armed conflict; there should also be a reference to situations of occupation, even if the occupation met with no armed resistance, as stipulated in article 18 of the 1954 Convention for the Protection of Cultural Property in the Event of Armed Conflict.

32. Draft article 4 posed problems not only insofar as the criterion of the intention of the parties was concerned but also with regard to any general criterion such as the nature or object and purpose of a treaty. A treaty's susceptibility to termination or suspension would depend on the armed conflict in question and many other circumstances, such as the legality of the party's position or the treaty provisions at stake.

33. Draft article 6, on treaties relating to the occasion for resort to armed conflict, likewise seemed to depend on many particular circumstances, and more explanation and examples would be welcome.

34. The status of the treaties listed in article 7 would also seem to vary depending on the circumstances, with the exception of treaties that were expressly applicable. However, certain treaties must always apply: the intention of the parties could not prevail over *jus cogens*, several non-derogable human rights treaties or certain general provisions relating to environmental protection.

35. The best solution would be to establish a working group. Some non-controversial articles, however, such as articles 1 to 3, 5 and 13, could be submitted to the Drafting Committee immediately.

36. The CHAIRPERSON, speaking in his personal capacity, noted that the decision of the International Tribunal for the Former Yugoslavia in the *Tadić* case contained a definition of internal armed conflict that was nearly identical to the definition contained in article 8 of the Rome Statute of the International Criminal Court. He preferred the definition proposed by the Special Rapporteur, which was sufficiently broad to encompass both internal and international conflicts.

37. Mr. DUGARD said that there ought to be some mention of the development of international criminal law. He asked the Special Rapporteur whether he intended to enter into the debate on the legality of the use of force, which would oblige the Commission to undertake a definition of aggression, or whether he preferred not to address that question.

38. Mr. BROWNLIE (Special Rapporteur) said that he had tried to carry out his mandate as Special Rapporteur. Draft article 10 should be viewed as a kind of intellectual provocation, which had indeed been successful. He had no intention of avoiding any kind of debate. The list in

article 7 had been submitted to stimulate discussion by the Commission.

39. Ms. ESCARAMEIA thanked the Chairperson for his intervention regarding the definition of armed conflicts but said that she supported the broader definition of *Tadić*'s Appeal Chamber of 1995 (para. 70), which covered both internal and international conflicts.

40. Mr. PELLET said he was surprised that the Special Rapporteur claimed not to be taking a position on the inclusion of civil wars in the current topic, since in paragraph 17 of his report he indicated that the definition of armed conflict and the report itself covered both internal and international conflicts. That seemed to him to be very important, if only because the distinction between the two types of conflicts was often blurred. Furthermore, the Commission could not avoid dealing with the issue of the legality of armed conflicts, although that did not mean that it had to undertake to define what was legal or what constituted aggression. It simply had to consider what effects aggression would have on treaties.

41. Mr. BROWNLIE (Special Rapporteur) recalled that recent doctrine, including the report by the Institute of International Law, drew an important distinction between internal and international conflicts.

42. Mr. Sreenivasa RAO said that he agreed with many of the views expressed by the Special Rapporteur in his first report, in particular the view that the Commission must not engage in a futile and time-consuming attempt to produce a general definition of the term "armed conflict". There were situations in the contemporary world in which it was impossible to distinguish clearly what constituted an armed conflict from what did not. That was a debate that the Commission could do without, and draft article 2 was a step in the right direction, even if the proposed definitions could certainly be refined and developed. The threshold set—the nature and extent of the conflict—was not the only possibility and should be more fully explained in the commentary. Furthermore, the distinction made in terms of the treaty relationship between the parties to the conflict on one hand and between those parties and third States on the other was very important and should be retained. Some members of the Commission, including Mr. Gaja and Mr. Pellet, had suggested that the draft articles should also cover the relationship between the parties to a conflict and international organizations. While he could see the merits of that proposal, he would be reluctant to accept it because such relationships were always treated separately, both in the law of treaties and in the law of State responsibility, not to mention the fact that including that aspect would delay completion of the work on the topic.

43. There was also a need to analyse the types of effects of armed conflicts that would be dealt with in the draft articles. Many had been identified in the Secretariat memorandum, and Mr. Pellet had likewise mentioned several. It would also be useful to state at the outset that the draft articles applied only to treaties in force at the time of the armed conflict and to distinguish between the termination or suspension of treaties as a result of an armed conflict and what might be called "impossibility of performance".

44. Another question that required the Commission's attention was whether an armed conflict could automatically serve as a ground for the termination or suspension of a treaty or whether additional criteria relating to a fundamental change of circumstances, as provided for in the 1969 Vienna Convention, was necessary. The extent to which State responsibility or liability would be incurred if a treaty was terminated or suspended as a direct result of an armed conflict should also be addressed.

45. Some members of the Commission had suggested that if a third party, such as the Security Council, determined that one of the parties in an armed conflict had engaged in the unlawful use of force, then the other party was automatically considered to have lawfully exercised its right to self-defence. In such a scenario, the responsibility of the offending State would be incurred not only for the wrongful use of force but also for the termination or suspension of any treaties in force. In the real world, however, it was difficult to pass judgment on the legality of conflicts, and the Security Council rarely made any such pronouncements. He wondered how one could evaluate claims of State responsibility in such grey areas. It might be useful to elaborate other provisions to cover the situations mentioned by Mr. Economides and Mr. Pellet.

46. The list of categories of treaties in draft article 7 was fairly standard. He supported the inclusion of treaties relating to the protection and preservation of the environment. As to whether internal armed conflicts ought to be included in the draft, he agreed with the Special Rapporteur and other members that they should, but believed that the effects of international and internal conflicts should be clarified.

47. Turning to the central theme of the draft articles, he wondered what criteria should be used to decide which treaties would be presumed to survive an armed conflict: the intention of the parties, the object and purpose of the treaty, or the nature of the treaty itself. There should not, however, be any presumption of automatic termination or suspension in the event of an armed conflict. It was also clear that in the context of the negotiation of treaties, whether bilateral or multilateral, the parties rarely included provisions indicating their intention regarding the operation of the treaty in the event of an armed conflict. Accordingly, a combination of approaches or hypotheses, as suggested by Mr. Pellet and other members of the Commission, seemed advisable.

48. Having concluded his general remarks, he requested clarification on draft article 6 (Treaties relating to the occasion for resort to armed conflict), which seemed to imply that even when the substance of a treaty was in dispute and an armed conflict was a direct result of that dispute, the treaty was presumed not to be terminated unless the contrary intention of the parties was clearly established. The very existence of an armed conflict indicated that at least one of the parties did not agree with the substance of the treaty or its continued applicability. Under those circumstances it might be impossible to obtain the agreement of both parties to the conflict unless the dispute involved only the interpretation of the treaty and not its validity. The parties could disagree on the continuance of a treaty or of some of its provisions due to a change in

circumstances because the historical circumstances that had justified the conclusion of the treaty were no longer valid or because the treaty had been concluded under duress, for example in the context of occupation or colonial domination. Armed conflict could result from those situations, and the entire treaty or parts thereof would have to be renegotiated. The Commission must decide how to address such situations in the draft articles.

49. He hoped that the Commission would move forward in its work, preferably within the context of a working group, with a view to adopting a draft instrument on first reading at its next session.

50. Mr. KOLODKIN thanked the Special Rapporteur for having submitted a complete set of draft articles at the outset, which was unusual and most useful. He also thanked the Secretariat for its very useful memorandum, which had provided him with much additional background on the topic at hand.

51. He suggested that it might be preferable not to deal with issues relating to the lawful or unlawful use of force in the draft articles. That would be possible if the Commission took the approach that armed conflict directly and automatically had effects on international treaties. In that case, knowing which of the parties to the conflict had violated international law by using force and which had acted lawfully in exercising its right to self-defence would be of no importance. It would appear, however, that the Special Rapporteur had taken another approach. According to draft article 3, the outbreak of an armed conflict did not *ipso facto* terminate or suspend the operation of a treaty, which meant that it did not automatically have an effect on the treaty. If that was the case, then the status of the treaty depended also on the subsequently declared intentions of the parties to the treaty, who were often parties to the conflict. Obviously, it would then be legally possible for the State which had unlawfully used force and the State which had exercised its right of self-defence to find themselves in the same situation and enjoying the same rights with regard to the treaty that bound them. However tempted the Commission might be to exclude the effects of the legality of the use of force on treaties from its consideration of the topic, it could not do so unless, of course, it based its discussions solely on the rule of the automatic effects of armed conflicts on treaties. Yet that rule could not be included in the draft articles in that, at least as an absolute concept, it no longer existed. In that connection he drew attention to articles 7 to 9 of resolution II/1985 on that subject adopted by the Institute of International Law.

52. One might wonder, however, whether it was possible to totally reject the existence, even if only in a few specific cases, of direct automatic effects of conflicts on treaties. Although he had no firm opinion on that issue, he tended to believe that in certain cases it was nevertheless possible to say that an armed conflict would, by its very nature, automatically suspend, at the very least, the operation of an international treaty. That might happen in the case of a demarcation treaty or a treaty establishing a political union, or even just certain provisions of a treaty. In that regard, he recalled the conclusions drawn in paragraphs 162 and 163 of the Secretariat memorandum, which merited consideration.

53. Although draft article 3 did not state that it was an armed conflict *per se* but the outbreak thereof that did not *ipso facto* lead to the termination or suspension of the operation of treaties, he could not accept that formulation as a general rule. While such a position might be deduced from doctrine and judicial decisions, even though the latter were extremely diverse, it was not borne out by practice in the area of peace treaties between States. In any case, he would prefer that, as the Special Rapporteur had suggested in paragraph 28 of his report, if the Commission wished to retain the introductory part of draft article 3, the expression "*ipso facto*" should be replaced by the word "necessarily".

54. As had already been noted, the draft articles did not distinguish between situations in which both parties to a conflict were also parties to a treaty, and situations involving a treaty to which a State involved in a conflict and a third State were both parties. There were, however, objective reasons for making such a distinction. Political relations and, in particular, treaty relations between parties to a conflict could not as a rule be the same as the relations between a State that was involved in a conflict and a State that was not party to that conflict. In the former case one generally referred to temporarily hostile relations, whereas in the latter case relations could continue to be entirely normal, and could even go as far as to constitute an alliance. Naturally, the effects of an armed conflict could be identical in both those situations, as for example when the object of a treaty disappeared as the result of a conflict, or when for other reasons it became impossible for a treaty to operate between the parties to a conflict and also between a party to the conflict and a third State. However, that did not justify failing to make a distinction between those two situations as a general rule. He agreed with Mr. Gaja that the effects of armed conflicts on treaties between a party to a conflict and a third party could be considered in the context of the provisions of the 1969 Vienna Convention, in particular articles 61 and 62.

55. The effects of a non-international armed conflict on international treaties could likewise be considered in the context of the provisions of the 1969 Vienna Convention. He was not convinced that the effects of such armed conflicts should be considered in the context of the current topic. In any case, those effects could not be identical for objective reasons. An international armed conflict directly and inevitably affected the relations between the States parties to the treaty who were also parties to the conflict. Although, as had been stated, the distinction between international and non-international armed conflicts had become blurred, that was true above all with regard to the observance of humanitarian principles and international humanitarian and human rights law in the context of such conflicts.

56. If the draft articles under consideration must contain a definition of the notion of "armed conflict" it should be the one put forward by the Special Rapporteur, who in paragraph 21 of his report described his definition as contextual. Without wishing to go into detail, he wondered whether it was really necessary to define armed conflict. Many universal treaties that used the term "armed conflict" did not define it.

57. He wished to associate himself with those members of the Commission who had expressed doubts about basing the susceptibility to termination or suspension of a treaty in case of an armed conflict on the criterion of the intention of the parties to a treaty at the moment the treaty was concluded (draft art. 4). It would be more appropriate to refer to the object and purpose of the treaty or to its nature or substance. The Commission must consider the issue of whether to deal with the effects of conflicts on treaties in general or the effects of a conflict on specific provisions of a treaty or even the effects of a conflict on a treaty as a whole and/or on certain of its provisions. The Commission would also have to consider the issue from the point of view of the separability of treaty provisions. In that connection he commended the Secretariat memorandum and drew attention in particular to chapter VI of that document, which dealt with the relationship of the topic to other legal doctrines.

58. He considered the draft articles to be primarily expository in nature. It would not be appropriate at the current stage to refer all or even some of the draft articles to the Drafting Committee. The objective of the report and of the comments by Commission members which would be reproduced in the Commission's report was to elicit interest and reactions from States. The questions which members might put to Governments and, of course, the latter's responses would have a great influence on the Commission's future work on the topic.

59. The CHAIRPERSON, returning to the issue of the legality of the use of force, said that draft article 10 did not really deal with that question. He wondered whether that article did not in fact tend to favour the belligerent State, which might be tempted to resort to the use of force in order to void a treaty it was having difficulty applying.

60. Mr. BROWNLIE (Special Rapporteur) said that the wording of draft article 10 was somewhat provocative but nevertheless should be kept within certain limits. He believed it would be possible to find a middle ground between the current text and the position of members who would like the Commission to codify the legitimate use of force. As Mr. Kolodkin and others had pointed out, the issue of legitimate self-defence must be addressed, possibly in a specific provision.

61. Mr. DAOUDI said the issue of the aggressor State remained unresolved.

62. Mr. ECONOMIDES said the central issue was whether the Commission should deal with that question without taking into account the new situation introduced by the Charter of the United Nations or whether it should in fact deal with the Charter. The international community would never understand why the Commission might choose to disregard the Charter. An aggressor State and a State acting in self-defence could not be placed on the same footing. The Commission had an obligation to differentiate between the two, the issue being to define what the consequences of that distinction should be. He believed that an aggressor State should not have the right to suspend any treaty whatsoever, whereas a State acting in self-defence had the right to suspend only treaties whose provisions were not compatible with its exercise of the right of self-defence.

63. Mr. GAJA wondered if the question raised by Mr. Kolodkin and others as to whether an armed conflict would affect certain provisions of a treaty more than the treaty as a whole had not already been dealt with in draft article 8, in the light of the reference contained therein to articles 42 to 45 of the 1969 Vienna Convention.

64. Mr. BROWNLIE (Special Rapporteur) said that that was indeed the case. The issue of the separability of the provisions of a treaty, which had been examined at greater length in the Secretariat memorandum, should surely be included in the draft articles in some form or another.

The meeting rose at 12.50 p.m.

2838th MEETING

Friday, 13 May 2005, at 10.05 a.m.

Chairperson: Mr. Djamchid MOMTAZ

Present: Mr. Addo, Mr. Baena Soares, Mr. Brownlie, Mr. Candioti, Mr. Chee, Mr. Comissário Afonso, Mr. Daoudi, Mr. Dugard, Mr. Economides, Ms. Escarameia, Mr. Fomba, Mr. Gaja, Mr. Galicki, Mr. Kabatsi, Mr. Kateka, Mr. Kemicha, Mr. Kolodkin, Mr. Koskenniemi, Mr. Mansfield, Mr. Matheson, Mr. Niehaus, Mr. Pambou-Tchivounda, Mr. Pellet, Mr. Sreenivasa Rao, Mr. Rodríguez Cedeño, Mr. Sepúlveda, Ms. Xue, Mr. Yamada.

Effects of armed conflicts on treaties (*continued*) (A/CN.4/552 and A/CN.4/550 and Corr.1–2)

[Agenda item 8]

First report of the Special Rapporteur (*continued*)

1. Mr. FOMBA congratulated the Special Rapporteur on his excellent report (A/CN.4/552), which was an intellectual *tour de force*, and expressed appreciation to the Secretariat for its useful memorandum (A/CN.4/550 and Corr.1–2).

2. Referring first to the report's conceptual framework and the approach to the subject, he said that the terms "armed conflicts", "treaties" and "effects" posed semantic and conceptual problems with regard to their definition, classification, consequences and scope *ratione personae, materiae, temporis* and *loci*. Following on from that, and more fundamentally, was the question of the link with positive international law and/or the prospects for the progressive development of law in respect of each of those elements.

3. With regard to the term "armed conflict", the questions that arose included whether it had a universally established and recognized definition; how positive

international law currently stood on the matter; what relation there was between "armed conflict" and related terms such as "war", "state of war", "hostilities" and "armed operations"; whether the terms could be systematized; and what the significance was of the distinction between "international armed conflict" and "internal armed conflict" in the light of the nature of contemporary armed conflict, and the forms it took.

4. As to the term "treaty", although there was no real problem of definition, it might prove difficult to elaborate a clear and generally accepted classification. He also noted that the 1969 Vienna Convention did not contain any definition of the term "effects".

5. It might also be asked whether the focus was on the "juridical" or "extrajuridical"—i.e. practical—effects of armed conflicts on treaties, or on both. It should be borne in mind that armed conflicts were not "juridical acts", but "juridical events".

6. In respect of the scope *ratione personae*, the question arose whether the effects were confined to the belligerent States that were parties to the treaty or whether other States were also concerned. As to the scope *ratione materiae*, it needed to be asked whether the effect of the armed conflict concerned the treaty as a whole, certain provisions or only the obligations arising therefrom.

7. On the link between "armed conflict" and "treaty", Mr. Fomba agreed with the emphasis placed by Rousseau on the incompatibility between the two and the need to nuance their scope, and also with his conclusion that the situation was a complex one which was difficult to categorize by using general formulations (paragraph 37 of the report). That being said, an effort must still be made to find some such formulations, difficult though that enterprise might be.

8. He had a number of comments on specific paragraphs in the report. On paragraphs 4 to 10, the Special Rapporteur had been right to review the conceptual background of the draft, even if the priority given to the criterion of intention was debatable. It would, however, be useful to study all the rationales, not only from a strictly legal perspective, but also from a logical, practical and functional point of view. The statement made in paragraph 6 might then be qualified.

9. With regard to paragraph 10, whereas the Special Rapporteur was in favour of dealing with the topic in the framework of the law of treaties, he personally thought that it would be just as appropriate and sensible to consider possible links with other subjects, such as the law of responsibility. As to the approach, he agreed on the whole with the Special Rapporteur's comments in paragraphs 12 and 13.

10. Turning to the articles themselves, and first to article 2, paragraph (*b*), he agreed with the Special Rapporteur that the Commission would be much delayed if a high level of sophistication was sought (para. 16). In that connection, he recalled the difficulties posed by a strictly legal definition of the notion of aggression, and in particular the definition of crime of aggression in international criminal law.[1] That said, there was broad agreement as to what the notion of armed conflict basically covered in international law, even though not all aspects of the question were sufficiently clear to some. The Commission should therefore confine itself to those points that seemed to command consensus, with regard to doctrine and treaty practice, particularly that stemming from the law of armed conflicts. In his view, the Commission should adopt the broadest possible definition, one that included both international and internal armed conflicts, while remaining open to the possibility of taking other situations, such as the Israeli–Palestinian conflict, into account. Notwithstanding the questions it raised, the definition proposed in article 2, paragraph (*b*), was nevertheless a good starting point for discussion.

11. The Special Rapporteur was right to observe that contemporary armed conflicts had "blurred the distinction between international and internal armed conflicts" (para. 17). It was worth considering what were the significance and implications of the current tendency to link the two categories from the point of view not only of their actual scope but also of their legal regime. It was an interesting thought that "[i]nternal armed conflicts could affect the operation of treaties as much as, if not more than international armed conflicts" (para. 17). The Special Rapporteur had been right not to address the question of the legality of the use or threat of force in the definition. That vital legal principle, which was at the basis of the draft, should be taken up elsewhere.

12. Article 3 was important, and he endorsed the point made in paragraph 28 that, although it was not unproblematic, it was a useful and logical beginning which laid a foundation. By and large, its current wording seemed to be on the right track. But he did not see any fundamental difference between the terms "*ipso facto*" and "necessarily"; indeed, he preferred the former, since it denoted the necessary consequence inferred from an event.

13. With regard to article 4, the Special Rapporteur favoured the criterion of intention, but any attempt at decryption of the criterion of intention entailed reference to other criteria which were contained in other notions. That was a subtle way of relating ideas which at first glance seemed discrete. Whereas the criteria defined in the 1969 Vienna Convention were relatively clear, the criterion of the nature and extent of an armed conflict was not self-evident.

14. He concurred with the Special Rapporteur's preliminary positions set out in paragraph 45 and agreed that it was "more logical, and more coherent, to formulate a general principle based upon the intention of the parties in respect of all types of treaty" (para. 46). The explanation in paragraph 47 was acceptable, provided that the approach was as broad as possible.

15. On article 6, he supported the Special Rapporteur's conclusion in paragraph 61 that the supposition that a treaty forming an element in a dispute was a nullity,

[1] See *Yearbook ... 1995*, vol. II (Part Two), chap. II, Draft Code of Crimes against the Peace and Security of Mankind, pp. 20–22, paras. 60–73; and *Yearbook ... 1996*, vol. II (Part Two), article 16 and commentary, pp. 42–43.

simply because it formed part of the "causes" of an armed conflict, was unacceptable.

16. He agreed with the Special Rapporteur that the content of draft article 7 was, on a strict view, superfluous and that the criterion of intention was, in principle, of general application (para. 62), but nevertheless thought that such a provision was useful, given the importance of the criterion of the object and purpose, not only in the overall mechanism of the 1969 Vienna Convention, but also for an analysis of the concept of intention. He did not have a firm view on whether the list in article 7, paragraph 2, was necessary and, if so, what the chances were that the Commission could reach a broad consensus on which categories of treaty should be included therein. Another possibility would be to deal with the matter in the commentary, citing as illustrations only those categories of treaty which seemed least likely to cause problems.

17. With regard to draft article 10, the point was not to address the substantive question of the legality of the threat or use of force or the mechanism for identifying and applying rules of general international law, but rather to decide what consequences the legal or illegal nature of the conduct of the parties to the conflict would have for the exercise of the right to terminate or suspend the treaty. Clearly, the State that exercised the right of self-defence could not be placed on the same footing as the State that committed an act of aggression. The current text of article 10 was far from satisfactory, whereas articles 7 to 9 of resolution II/1985 of the Institute of International Law were a good basis for discussion.[2]

18. As to the working method to be adopted, in view of the arguments put forward by a number of members, it seemed sensible to establish a working group to consider the draft as a whole in order to find areas of consensus before referring it to the Drafting Committee. He doubted the wisdom of sending individual articles to the Drafting Committee at the current stage.

19. Mr. BROWNLIE (Special Rapporteur) agreed that it would be very premature to refer any of the articles to the Drafting Committee. His aim was to obtain the comments of members and subsequently those of Governments. In the light of the very helpful debate in the Commission and the responses awaited from the Sixth Committee and Governments, he would then produce a second report, at which stage the Commission could set up a working group or start to refer articles to the Drafting Committee. He saw no point in establishing a working group at the present time. It would be better to move more slowly and use his first, expository report as a way of collecting views of Governments and filling lacunae on recent practice. In that regard, he had to say that he did not find the section on practice in the Secretariat memorandum, which was excellent in most respects, to be cogent or useful.

20. Mr. KABATSI said that the Special Rapporteur deserved the thanks of all members of the Commission for producing, at short notice, not only a first report mapping out the entire spectrum of the topic but also a full set of draft articles. He also welcomed the Secretariat's useful and instructive memorandum. He noted the Special Rapporteur's intention to attract comments, especially from Governments, to assist the Commission in pursuing its task of codification and progressive development of a complex and problematic area of international law. Indeed, the Special Rapporteur's plan was already bearing fruit, to judge by the lively discussion and useful suggestions made for improving the draft. While the subject was fraught with uncertainties and contradictions, it was undoubtedly an important one.

21. He endorsed the Special Rapporteur's proposed approach, which linked the consequences of armed conflicts on treaties to the intention of the parties to the treaties, as agreed before the hostilities began, on whether the obligations undertaken would continue to be honoured, be it in whole or in part, temporarily or permanently. He agreed with the approach of adhering closely to the logic of the 1969 Vienna Convention. The Commission was in a better position to take up the topic than it had been in 1966, when it had been more concerned about the completion of the work on the Convention itself.[3] There was no longer any danger of muddying the waters of the treaties project by delving into the uncertainties and complications of the effects of armed conflicts on treaties.

22. There seemed to be near unanimity that the intention of the parties was the most important criterion in determining the susceptibility to termination or suspension of a treaty in case of an armed conflict, although factors such as the nature and object of the treaty and the nature and extent of the armed conflict must be taken into account. Even questions relating to the nature, purpose and object of the treaty, however, were linked to the intention of the parties in designing and entering into that treaty, and therefore strengthened the case for considering intention to be the most important criterion. In spite of attempts to categorize treaties according to their degree of likelihood of applicability, such as that attempted in the memorandum by the Secretariat (chap. III), the intention of the parties remained the most important determinant.

23. Problems arose, however, when that intention was not expressly stated in the treaty itself and had to be inferred. Even in cases which might seem obvious, such as the implementation of humanitarian law treaties, issues like the impossibility of performance due to armed conflict could still arise, at least temporarily. He agreed with Mr. Matheson that even in the situation presented in draft article 7, one could not be completely categorical. Each situation must be dealt with in a flexible manner as events presented themselves for each particular armed conflict, with the understanding that the outbreak of armed conflict did not *ipso facto* terminate or suspend the operation of treaties as between the parties and even as between them and third States, albeit with certain exceptions.

24. As suggested by the Special Rapporteur and other members of the Commission, the definition of a state of war should include situations where, although there were no armed operations under way, the belligerents were poised for war and the effect was the same; a blockade

[2] See 2834th meeting, footnote 7.

[3] See *Yearbook ... 1966*, vol. II, document A/6309/Rev.1, Part Two, chap. II, p. 192, para. 29.

was an example of one such situation. The effects of international and internal conflicts on treaties, which could be significantly different, and the notion of separability, where certain treaty obligations might survive the outbreak of armed conflict, required further study.

25. It would likewise be difficult to avoid treating at some level the provisions of the Charter of the United Nations relating to the legitimacy of armed conflicts and the consequences thereof on treaties. The treatment of that issue needed to be strengthened, taking into account the position adopted by the Institute of International Law in its resolution II/1985. That subject involved important policy issues.

26. As to how the Commission should proceed in considering the draft articles, his own view was that since there appeared to be little disagreement on the principles underlying certain draft articles, those articles could be referred to the Drafting Committee, thereby enabling the Commission to make rapid progress. He nevertheless understood and supported the position adopted by the Special Rapporteur on that question.

27. Mr. KEMICHA thanked the Special Rapporteur for an excellent first report, and also the Secretariat for its memorandum on the topic. Such documents would be most welcome with regard to all the items on the Commission's agenda.

28. The first report had provoked fertile discussion, raising fundamental issues which the Special Rapporteur, with the assistance of the Commission, would have to address. One such issue was the Special Rapporteur's decision to categorize the problem of the effects of armed conflicts on treaties as a part of the law of treaties, rather than as a part of the law relating to armed conflict. He associated himself with those members who had raised points concerning the legality of the use of force, the distinction between aggressor and victim and the implications of internal conflicts with regard to their effect on treaties. The Special Rapporteur must take those issues into account, as well as the relevant provisions of the Institute of International Law's resolution II/1985, without however straying into the realm of the law of armed conflicts. That exercise, while fraught with hazards, was essential to the success of the project. Although the Special Rapporteur had raised those issues in passing in his comments on draft article 2, they had not been reflected in the texts of the draft articles.

29. The other fundamental question was the excessive and exclusive weight given by the Special Rapporteur to the intention of the parties in the text of draft article 4. Like other members of the Commission, he felt it would be extremely difficult to determine "the intention of the parties at the time the treaty was concluded" as provided for in draft article 4, paragraph 1. That implied rather Machiavellian intentions on the part of States when negotiating treaties, although he could not deny that that might sometimes be the case.

30. Advocates of the criterion of intention had to qualify that criterion with presumptions regarding the nature, object and purpose of the treaties in question, as the Special Rapporteur had done in draft article 7, which referred to "treaties the object and purpose of which involve the necessary implication that they continue in operation during an armed conflict". In paragraph 63 of the report he described such treaties as "exceptions to the general principle, based upon the object and purpose of the treaty". Draft article 4 should be reformulated in order to encompass all such criteria and better reflect the current situation and State practice.

31. Turning to the list of 11 categories of treaties "the object and purpose of which involve the necessary implication that they continue in operation during an armed conflict", contained in draft article 7, paragraph 2, he recalled Mr. Matheson's comment on the risks and limitations of such a list, even though the Special Rapporteur had stated that the list was not exhaustive. Rather than establishing a list, which inevitably posed problems, the criteria mentioned should be incorporated into a new draft article 4.

32. Ms. XUE said that the topic of the effects of armed conflicts on treaties should be considered in the broad context of treaty law. She recalled that during negotiation of the 1969 Vienna Convention three relevant areas, namely, State succession in respect of treaties, State responsibility for breach of international treaty obligations, and the effects of armed conflicts on treaties, had been deliberately excluded.[4] Complete sets of legal rules and principles had since been codified and developed with regard to the first two areas. Although the remaining area, the effects of armed conflicts on treaties, was perhaps the most complicated, much could be learned from the discussions on the previous two topics, as the current topic was in many respects linked with the 1969 and 1986 Vienna Conventions, the 1978 Vienna Convention on succession of States in respect of treaties and the draft articles on responsibility of States for internationally wrongful acts.[5]

33. In codifying and developing the international treaty regime, the Commission must deal with treaty relations both in time of peace and in time of war. Those two terms were currently perceived to be relative, and there was no longer a clear-cut distinction between the law of peace and the law of war; treaty provisions therefore inevitably affected each other. For example, if an armed conflict resulted in a change of State or dissolution of a State, succession rules would apply in relation to treaties. However, if the result was a change of Government, it was not clear whether the rule of continuity, succession rules, *mutatis mutandis* or the rule of fundamental change of circumstances under article 62 of the 1969 Vienna Convention would apply. Practice pointed in differing directions, and she questioned whether the Commission could, or should, attempt to make those rules coherent.

34. Moreover, having prescribed the legal consequences of a serious breach of international obligations in the regime of State responsibility, the Commission should perhaps also examine the new conventional rules on international crimes under the current topic if they

[4] *Ibid.*, paras. 29–31.

[5] *Yearbook ... 2001*, vol. II (Part Two) and corrigendum, pp. 26–143, paras. 76–77.

also covered acts which occurred during armed conflicts, because the question whether those conventions did or did not remain operative during armed conflicts would determine whether the State concerned would be held responsible for its acts under international law. The Special Rapporteur had made a few references to the provisions of the 1969 Vienna Convention in some of the draft articles, and further study of their applicability could well be necessary.

35. Further study of that issue might also help clarify the scope and ascertain the content of the draft articles. The Commission's objective should be to ensure treaty relations in accordance with the principles of free consent, good faith and the *pacta sunt servanda* rule in the event of an armed conflict; to clarify the rights and obligations of the States parties to the armed conflict as well as their relations with third parties, in the interests of the security and stability of international relations; and to determine the legal consequences arising out of the interruption of treaty relations as a result of armed conflict. It should be noted at the outset that some of the questions raised by members regarding, for example, whether the issue of use of force should be dealt with in the draft to some extent depended on what objectives the Commission was pursuing in endeavouring to progressively develop and codify that area of international law.

36. She welcomed the Special Rapporteur's timely submission of a comprehensive set of draft articles with a view to provoking discussion and reactions from Governments, and agreed that at the present stage the Commission should continue to discuss policy issues and that it would be premature to refer any of the articles to the Drafting Committee. The Commission should bear in mind that the topic was constantly evolving, not only because the nature of modern armed conflicts had changed greatly, in particular since the Second World War, but also because the content and regimes of international law had undergone tremendous changes which had a direct bearing on various aspects of State life, even in time of armed conflicts, whether internal or external. The Commission should bear those factors in mind when considering State practice.

37. She had found the introduction to the report very useful, and welcomed the succinct and straightforward summary of the four rationales underlying current doctrine. She regretted, however, that the Special Rapporteur had not fully explained his reasons for preferring the third rationale, namely, the criterion of the intention of the parties at the time they concluded the treaty. She wondered what empirical basis there was for the various doctrinal positions adopted, and why, after taking into account the many exceptions to each rationale, they did not appear to differ dramatically, so that the results would not necessarily differ, whichever of the four rationales was applied. That issue should be explored in greater depth.

38. Turning to the draft articles themselves, she wondered why draft article 1 did not include treaties with international organizations. There were obvious reasons to include them; for example, treaties on the privileges and immunities of international organizations should apply in armed conflicts where United Nations personnel and peacekeeping missions were involved. The draft article should make it clear that the relevant treaties between the belligerents and international organizations should continue to apply during armed conflicts. There was no need for a separate set of articles dealing with treaties involving international organizations.

39. Draft article 2, subparagraph (*b*), defined the term "armed conflict" and she could understand why the Special Rapporteur had suggested that internal armed conflicts should also be included. Although recent large-scale internal armed conflicts had led to serious human disasters as well as interruptions of normal international relations, including treaty relations, she noted that in internal armed conflicts it was often the interests of the third party, whether or not a neutral party, which were at stake. By referring simply to "a conflict" in subparagraph (*b*), rather than "international conflict", the term used in the text of resolution II/1985 of the Institute of International Law, the Special Rapporteur had broadened the scope of the term "armed conflict". As a result, at the domestic level, any military operation launched against rebel forces or even criminal organizations could affect treaty relations in areas such as trade, border controls, customs cooperation and narcotics control. She doubted whether the Commission wished to see such activities included. Although a perfect definition of armed conflict might not be possible, the current language of the draft article needed to be tightened. She also expressed concern that in including the concept of "blockade", even in the absence of armed actions between the parties, in his report (para. 16), the Special Rapporteur was again defining armed conflict too broadly.

40. Furthermore, determination of the continuing validity of existing treaties during armed conflicts would have a direct bearing on the issue of State responsibility, because if the State party to the armed conflict breached its treaty obligations, it would be held responsible under international law. In a domestic setting, however, the principle of abrogation should perhaps prevail, subject to certain exceptions. Her initial comment was that the effects of domestic armed conflicts on treaties should be given separate treatment.

41. She agreed with the principle laid down in draft article 3 on *ipso facto* termination or suspension but reiterated that treaties with international organizations should be included. It was a long-recognized principle of international law, reinforced by modern State practice, that treaties were not necessarily suspended or terminated in time of armed conflict. Unless otherwise indicated, States would consider it to be in their best interests to maintain existing treaty relations, which was in accordance with the general proposition on the criterion of intention and was a good policy basis for discussion of the effects of armed conflicts on treaties. That principle should therefore be clearly stated in the draft article.

42. On draft article 4, she agreed that in principle the intention of the parties should prevail in deciding whether a treaty was still applicable during and after armed conflicts, but felt that the current draft could be improved in some respects. In determining the intention of the parties, the nature and object of the treaty and its provisions were also relevant. They should be determined at the time of

the conclusion of the treaty, and in addition, subsequent actions taken in application of the treaty, including those taken after the outbreak of the conflict, should be considered. The element of intention, if related to the nature and extent of the armed conflict in question, should not be limited to the intention at the time the treaty was concluded. That was particularly true when determining whether the parties intended to terminate or suspend the treaty in the event of armed conflict. In practice, during armed conflict States did not express their intention regarding the application of existing treaties. That had to be presumed from relevant factors such as: the context in which the treaty was applied; the terms of the treaty; the particular circumstances of the armed conflict; and the treaty practice of the individual parties. The current drafting left too much room for subjective interpretation and would be difficult to apply.

43. Two points in draft article 5 required some explanation. First, she could not see what purpose was served by the word "lawful" in paragraph 1; if it meant that the parties should comply with existing treaty rules to formulate a new treaty or that the treaty should be governed by international law, it was redundant. Secondly, with regard to the capacity of parties to the armed conflict to conclude treaties, some rules, such as rules under international conventions on humanitarian law, were considered to be peremptory norms of international law. States parties could not opt out of their legal obligations by means of bilateral agreements. She wondered whether the Special Rapporteur intended to address that issue. In the contemporary practice of international law, the capacity of States to conclude treaties in times of armed conflict was seldom challenged, but the content of such treaties could be examined in the light of human rights law, humanitarian law and international criminal law.

44. If draft article 6 was meant to cover cases in which States resorted to armed conflict to resolve a territorial dispute and supported their territorial claims with differing interpretations of a treaty on the status of the territory concerned, she doubted whether the article was really necessary, since the principle applicable was the peaceful settlement of international disputes, rather than the maintenance of stable treaty relations.

45. The Special Rapporteur should explain the relationship between draft article 7 and draft article 3. If the outbreak of an armed conflict did not *ipso facto* terminate or suspend the operation of treaties, as stated in draft article 3, she saw no useful purpose in attempting an exhaustive categorization of treaties according to the likelihood of their being applicable in cases of armed conflict. Moreover, for the purposes of the draft articles, it was the nature of treaties that needed to be examined, rather than their categorization by subject matter. The Commission might like to consider taking an approach similar to the one taken during its consideration of State responsibility with regard to the nature or hierarchy of international rules.

46. Draft article 8, on the mode of suspension or termination, should be considered together with draft article 13 on the cases of termination or suspension. The relationship between the two was not clear, and the special circumstances of an armed conflict might make it impossible for the parties to follow the same procedure for suspending or terminating a treaty as in time of peace.

47. The idea of linking the resumption of the operation of a treaty that had been suspended to the intention of the parties at the time the treaty had been concluded, as expressed in draft article 9, paragraph 1, was problematic for the reasons she had already discussed in relation to draft article 4.

48. With regard to the issue of the legality of the use of force, she believed there was room to improve articles 10 and 11 of the draft in the light of article 7 of resolution II/1985 of the Institute of International Law on the effects of armed conflicts on treaties. The Special Rapporteur's comment in paragraph 122 of his report that "[i]n the absence of an authoritative basis for a determination of an illegality, the unilateral assertion of illegality would be self-serving and inimical to stability of relations" was a very strong argument, but the actual wording of draft article 10 gave the impression that the legality of the conduct of the parties to the armed conflict had nothing to do with treaty relations. Such an interpretation would be contrary to the fundamental principles of international law. In addition, draft article 11 addressed only Security Council decisions taken in accordance with the provisions of Chapter VII of the Charter of the United Nations, whereas other action taken by the United Nations to maintain international peace and security, such as the adoption by the General Assembly of resolution 377 (V) of 3 November 1950 on "Uniting for peace", might also affect treaty relations.

49. Mr. MANSFIELD said that the Special Rapporteur's first report was presented in such a way as to require the Commission to confront directly the essential policy choices involved in the complex subject of the effects of armed conflicts on treaties. He commended the Special Rapporteur for producing a full set of draft articles, a course which not only provided a comprehensive overview but would also be of practical value to the legal offices of ministries of foreign affairs around the world as they began to consider the topic.

50. One point that emerged very clearly both from the report and from the Secretariat's memorandum on the subject was that the codification of the topic would bring considerable benefits by helping to remove the significant uncertainties that stemmed largely from the practice of another era. Both the report and the memorandum were quite open about the underlying policy objective, which was to seek, in the interests of promoting the security of legal relations between States, to limit the cases in which armed conflict had an effect on treaties. While he could only support that objective, he was inclined to think that, in articulating the basis for it, more could have been made of the prohibition of the use of force by the Charter of the United Nations, and that earlier doctrine and practice should be reviewed in the light of the Charter. Such an approach would not in any way undermine the Special Rapporteur's view, which he shared, that the topic was properly located within the law of treaties.

51. The Special Rapporteur had basically incorporated the aforementioned policy objective into draft articles 3 and 4, in combination with draft article 7, by coupling the general proposition that armed conflict did not *ipso facto* terminate or suspend treaties with the central idea that any effect it had on them depended on the intention of the parties, and that if their intention was not clear, some assumptions could be made about their intention on the basis of the object and purpose of the treaty concerned and the category to which the treaty belonged.

52. He was less concerned than some previous speakers about whether further material relating to past practice, including municipal court decisions, would be needed to convince Governments to accept codification of the law on the basis of such propositions. His main concern was how useful the draft articles would be in practice. In particular, he wondered if they would be relevant to the kind of armed conflicts that arose in the contemporary era. Both the report of the Secretariat and the memorandum made the point that the distinction between international and internal armed conflicts had become blurred, and it was clear that whatever text the Commission adopted must be relevant to "untidy" conflicts that could not be neatly categorized as international or internal. Even if that did not mean that the Commission should attempt to produce a definitive definition of the term "armed conflict", or that the effects of the various forms of conflict on treaties would be uniform, he did think there was further work to do on the definition contained in draft article 2 (*b*). In that connection, he agreed with previous speakers who had emphasized that the effects of armed conflict might well be different in respect of States that were parties to the conflict and those that were not. He saw no reason why treaties to which international organizations were parties should be excluded from the scope.

53. Another question that sprang to mind when considering the usefulness of the draft articles in practice was whether they helped to distinguish treaties that would be affected by armed conflict from those that would not. That question, in turn, raised an issue that had been commented on by many speakers in the debate, that of determining the intentions of the parties. Whether or not it was in order to establish some fictional intent, he had serious doubts about the usefulness of using categories of treaties as a means of determining which treaty-based legal obligations would survive an armed conflict. Even if agreement could be reached on such categories, they might not be of much practical help, given the staggering range and diversity of treaties and the diversity and complexity of provisions within treaties of the same general type. Perhaps it would be more useful to identify the factors that might be relevant to whether a treaty or a particular treaty provision remained applicable, as suggested by Mr. Matheson, or to discuss the substantive interests involved in the applicability or non-applicability of treaty provisions, as suggested by Mr. Koskenniemi. In any event, if the outcome of the Commission's work on the topic was to be relevant and practical, it would be necessary to conduct some form of policy analysis, perhaps with the help of the Secretariat, and to test the results of such an analysis against State practice, particularly recent State practice. A policy analysis would provide some assurance that the Commission was not oversimplifying matters or ignoring significant issues.

54. It was important to make it clear that, as the Special Rapporteur had confirmed, draft article 8 was intended to cover the case of partial suspension or termination. There was also a need to acknowledge the possibility of suspending or terminating treaty provisions that were inconsistent with the exercise of legitimate self-defence. In that connection, he had to admit that he was rather uncomfortable with article 10 as currently drafted.

55. Mr. BROWNLIE (Special Rapporteur) stressed that the categories of treaties listed in draft article 7, paragraph 2, reflected the literature on the subject, although he was personally responsible for the inclusion of human rights treaties, since they were actually an extension of the protection of individuals provided by bilateral treaties of friendship, commerce and navigation. Although the Commission might well decide to discard the methodology of categorizing treaties, as it could study the object and purpose of treaties without categorizing them, he believed it should perhaps pay special attention to at least one or two of the categories listed. For example, the categories in subparagraphs (*b*) and (*c*) were based on a considerable amount of State practice and had long been recognized in relation to the effects of war on treaties, and the experience of municipal courts was closely related to treaties of friendship, commerce and navigation.

56. Mr. Sreenivasa RAO said it would not be helpful to dispense with the categories of treaty altogether. Rather, some way should be found to indicate that the list of categories was illustrative only.

57. Mr. KOSKENNIEMI agreed with Mr. Sreenivasa Rao that the categories should not be dispensed with altogether. Not only did the categories reflect the literature, as Mr. Brownlie had pointed out, but they were also included in the literature for good reason, and the rationale for their inclusion should therefore be explained. However, the Commission was not facing an either/or situation: it did not have to choose between including categories or providing criteria. The two approaches could be combined. The Commission might like to note that there were some categories which, for good reason, had become so well established that they could be listed as such, while also acknowledging the criteria that had led to the identification of those categories.

58. Mr. MANSFIELD said he had not suggested that categories should be discarded altogether. It was simply that he did not believe the Commission would be able to reach agreement on categories until a proper policy analysis had been carried out to establish the reasoning behind the categorization. To do that, a representative sample of treaties should be studied, in order to identify the treaties or treaty provisions that deserved to survive and group them together in categories on the basis of their commonalities.

59. Mr. CHEE said that the issue seemed to be whether to expand the categories of treaty. The Special Rapporteur had made a good start with draft article 7, paragraph 2,

on the basis of which the Commission could pursue its analysis.

60. Ms. XUE said that, while the approach taken by the Special Rapporteur in draft article 7 was very useful, the Commission should look hard at the categories of treaty listed therein, in order to bring out the underlying policy considerations. Draft article 3 indicated that the outbreak of an armed conflict did not terminate or suspend the operation of treaties, whereas draft article 7 said that the incidence of an armed conflict would not as such inhibit the operation of certain treaties. She sought further clarification of what distinction the Special Rapporteur had had in mind in drafting article 7.

61. In that regard, some aspects of the policy considerations underlying the rules on State responsibility were worth examining. While a categorization based on subject matter might be questionable, that did not mean that other types of categorization could not be attempted. There seemed to be general agreement that some areas were of particular relevance, but it would be very difficult to agree on which specific areas, elements or principles were to be singled out. At any event the Commission was not yet in a position to decide whether to incorporate a categorization of treaties into the text of the draft articles. It first needed to decide what objectives it had in mind in developing the draft articles.

62. Mr. ECONOMIDES said that before the Commission considered the categories or lists of agreements that should be envisaged in the draft, one question of capital importance had to be resolved, namely, what party would have the right to seek the termination or suspension of treaties. Could an aggressor State do so? In modern practice, everyone agreed that an act of aggression, which was an unlawful act, could not produce legal effects. To give an aggressor State the right to suspend or terminate certain treaties would be to abet it in an unlawful act. The draft articles on State responsibility had been aimed precisely at doing everything possible to put an end to wrongful acts. For the Commission now to make rules that would assist a State in perpetrating a wrongful act would be contrary to general international law. He could not condone the elaboration of any list that helped an aggressor State; however, one that helped a State in the exercise of legitimate self-defence would be acceptable.

63. Mr. MATHESON explained that it had not been his intention simply to dismiss the relevance of the way State practice had affected various kinds of treaties and treaty provisions: that, obviously, was quite important. He merely objected to making the continuity of treaty obligations turn upon whether a particular treaty fell within one or another category in a relatively arbitrary list. Obviously, specific treaties within a particular category varied among themselves, their provisions varied, circumstances varied, and all of that had to be taken into account. He was confident that, as the Commission discussed the matter further, it would be able to find some way of taking into account past practice regarding different kinds of treaty provisions that did not result in a rigid structure based on categorization but instead focused on the underlying factors and policies.

64. Mr. BROWNLIE (Special Rapporteur) said it should have been made much clearer in his commentary on draft article 7 that the effect of the categories was simply to create a rebuttable presumption. The categories were a series of weak legal presumptions constituting evidence of the object and purpose of certain types of treaty to the effect that they survived a war. Moreover, it was not just at the outset of a war or the conclusion of a treaty that certain problems were identified as legal issues: clearing up the legal detritus of a major armed conflict was a process that often took many years.

65. Mr. NIEHAUS said that while some members had criticized the Special Rapporteur for failing to explore the topic in sufficient depth and for adopting an overly cautious or abstract approach, in his view precisely the opposite was true. The Special Rapporteur had presented a stimulating report that invited analysis and discussion, which, after all, was the chief purpose of a first report. He had clearly outlined the long-standing uncertainty in the treatment of the topic in the literature. That was why the Commission must remain cautious and proceed slowly in its work. He agreed with Mr. Economides that, in view of the difficult and sensitive nature of the material, the Commission should begin with a general discussion aimed at clarifying major principles and problems.

66. The first general point he wished to make concerned the essential role played by the intention of the parties in determining the effects of armed conflict on a treaty. In draft articles 4, 6 and 9, the Special Rapporteur referred frequently to intention. Owing to the difficulty of establishing intention, however, he himself would have liked to see a better explanation of how that concept should be construed, based not only on articles 31 and 32 of the 1969 Vienna Convention but also on the relevant literature.

67. Draft article 4, paragraph 2 (*b*), adduced the "nature and extent of the armed conflict" as a factor determining the intention of the parties. Even though there was support for that approach in the literature, Mr. Niehaus had difficulty in understanding the relation between intention and the nature of the conflict. Could the Commission accept that the nature and extent of an armed conflict should determine the intention of the parties, an intention that had existed at the time the treaty had been concluded and thus predated the conflict? Was it not the real intention, rather than a presumed intention, that the Commission was seeking to determine? To what extent could intention be clearly expressed before the outbreak of an armed conflict? What if there had been no intention in that regard? Mr. Gaja had already pointed to the difficulty of identifying intention. In his own view, the whole subject required fuller consideration and analysis.

68. Another matter that needed to be better explained was the distinction between international and internal conflicts. Although modern-day doctrine tended to equate the two, especially because of the presence of external factors in so-called "civil wars", he did not think it was correct to do so. The effects and consequences of the two types of conflict were different. Hence the need for a broader definition of "armed conflict". It was also necessary to distinguish between a party that engaged in armed

conflict in breach of international law and one that did so in self-defence in accordance with the provisions of the Charter of the United Nations. In addition, the situation of third parties had to be made clear. The terms "continuity", "suspension" and "termination" had not been defined and should be better explained, not only in relation to the treaty as a whole, but also in relation to individual and separate parts or provisions thereof.

69. He wished to end by expressing the hope that all the comments made on the first report would be of use to the Special Rapporteur when he came to produce his second report. As the Special Rapporteur had stressed, the set of draft articles was expository in nature, and accordingly, the time was not ripe for referring any of them to the Drafting Committee. The Commission must continue to enrich the topic by its contributions, with a view to eliciting reactions from States.

70. Mr. KATEKA noted that the Special Rapporteur had shown an operational preference for draft articles, without prejudice to the final form the instrument would take, and wished to defer consideration of peaceful settlement of disputes until the end of the work on the topic. That seemed a wise approach, given its difficult nature.

71. None of the draft articles included a provision like that to be found in article 6 of resolution II/1985 of the Institute of International Law, which stated that a treaty establishing an international organization was not affected by the existence of an armed conflict between any of its parties. He would like to know the reason for that omission, since the effects of armed conflict could extend to an international organization. An obvious example was the United Nations involvement in military action in parts of the former Yugoslavia.

72. The definition of armed conflict in draft article 2 (*b*) had triggered controversy, some members wishing it to be restricted to international armed conflicts, while others believed that it should also cover internal conflicts. He supported the latter approach. Since the end of the Second World War, there had been more internal than international conflicts and they had in fact killed more people. Paragraphs 146 and 147 of the Secretariat memorandum stated that "any complete study of the effects of armed conflict on treaties [could] not ignore domestic hostilities", which could and did affect international treaties. Elements of the definitions of armed conflict used in the *Tadić* case, in article 8, paragraph 2 (*f*), of the Rome Statute of the International Criminal Court ("… armed conflicts that take place in the territory of a State when there is protracted armed conflict between governmental authorities and organized armed groups or between such groups") and in the commentary to article 2, paragraph 1, of the 1949 Geneva Convention for the Amelioration of the Condition of the Wounded and Sick in Armed Forces in the Field ("[a]ny difference arising between two States and leading to the intervention of armed forces …")[6] could be used to improve the definition of armed conflict in draft article 2 (*b*).

73. A related matter was that of non-State actors involved in conflicts. In introducing his report, the Special Rapporteur had referred to irregular units and militias that were incorporated into the structure of regular armies. Another question was whether the term "armed conflict" should include the fight against terrorist organizations.

74. The Special Rapporteur had indicated, both in paragraph 23 of his report and in his oral presentation, that the legality of the use or threat of force was not directly addressed and that draft article 10 was intended to cover it. That seemed to be a fair approach. Any attempt to develop the question could lead the Commission to a dead end, as might an attempt to address situations of belligerent occupation such as the Israel/Palestine situation, as proposed by some members. It would do better to focus on the law of treaties rather than on the law of war.

75. Draft article 3 should be abbreviated so as to make it correspond more closely to the wording of article 2 of resolution II/1985 of the Institute of International Law. Draft article 4 laid emphasis on intention. One member of the Commission had described intention as a fiction, and another had suggested that it should be combined with the nature of the treaty. The Secretariat memorandum proposed a combination of intention and compatibility with policy during armed conflict (para. 11). In paragraph 29 of his report, the Special Rapporteur stated that intention was "supplemented by a series of presumptions related to the object and purpose of treaties". Yet in reality, the Commission could not avoid giving prominence to the intention of the parties in matters relating to the termination or suspension of the treaty.

76. Draft article 7, paragraph 2, categorized treaties according to type. That was of some help, but it also created controversy. He himself supported the inclusion of treaties on the environment, whereas the Special Rapporteur thought the subject too fragmented. Paragraph 160 of the Secretariat memorandum referred to treaties governing intergovernmental debt. In his view, the Special Rapporteur had been right to exclude that category of treaties from the draft. On the other hand, he supported the case for the continuity of treaties regarding non-derogable human rights, conventions on diplomatic and consular relations and those relating to the peaceful settlement of disputes. Thus, some of the categories in article 7 should be reviewed, or else consigned to the commentary.

77. In conclusion, while he had initially supported those who had called for the creation of a working group to consider the draft articles, he would be pleased to defer to the Special Rapporteur's preference for the matter first to be referred to States for their comments. He also supported those who wished to refer some of the draft articles to the Drafting Committee. His suspicion was that those opposed to such a course were fearful lest such early submission should set a precedent. Since the Special Rapporteur himself was not in favour of that course of action, it would be best to await the second report before referring any texts to the Drafting Committee.

78. Mr. BROWNLIE (Special Rapporteur) said he was not opposed to the creation of a working group at a later stage; he hoped, however, that the impressions of

[6] *Geneva Convention for the Amelioration of the Condition of the Wounded and Sick in Armed Forces in the Field*, J. Pictet (ed.), 1952, Geneva, International Committee of the Red Cross, p. 32.

Governments and the Sixth Committee could be gathered before such a course was taken.

The meeting rose at 1 p.m.

2839th MEETING

Tuesday, 17 May 2005, at 10 a.m.

Chairperson: Mr. Djamchid MOMTAZ

Present: Mr. Addo, Mr. Baena Soares, Mr. Brownlie, Mr. Candioti, Mr. Chee, Mr. Comissário Afonso, Mr. Daoudi, Mr. Dugard, Mr. Economides, Ms. Escarameia, Mr. Fomba, Mr. Gaja, Mr. Galicki, Mr. Kabatsi, Mr. Kateka, Mr. Kolodkin, Mr. Koskenniemi, Mr. Mansfield, Mr. Matheson, Mr. Niehaus, Mr. Pambou-Tchivounda, Mr. Sreenivasa Rao, Mr. Rodríguez Cedeño, Mr. Yamada.

Effects of armed conflicts on treaties (*continued*) (A/CN.4/552 and A/CN.4/550 and Corr.1–2)

[Agenda item 8]

First report of the Special Rapporteur (*continued*)

1. Mr. YAMADA noted first that, as draft articles 1 and 2 indicated, the study seemed to cover every kind of treaty. However, some treaties governing the rules of warfare or engagement, such as the Hague and Geneva Conventions, although negotiated and technically valid in time of peace, became operative only in time of armed conflict. Those treaties did not fall under the categories of treaties described in draft article 7, paragraph 1, because they were not operative in peacetime and therefore could not logically "continue in operation during an armed conflict". When they became operative they were applied equally to the forces of belligerents, regardless of whether the States were aggressors or were fighting in self-defence or under the authorization of the United Nations Security Council. That category of treaties should be excluded from the scope from the outset, although in reality it was difficult to define such a category or separate it from others.

2. While he recognized that State practice before the Second World War had not lost its importance or effect, he nevertheless felt that the prohibition of the use of force by the Charter of the United Nations had influenced the rights and duties of States in the area under consideration, and he hoped that recent practice, notably in Asia, the Middle East and Africa, would be studied.

3. Draft article 10, as he read it, disregarded the legality of the conduct of the parties. Under the rules of warfare, the legality of an armed conflict should not be taken into account, but he doubted that that was the case where the termination or suspension of other categories of treaties was concerned, for that would be contrary to the rules of the 1969 Vienna Convention. Of course that instrument did not deal with armed conflicts but differentiated between defaulting States and others and stipulated, in article 60, article 61, paragraph 2, and article 62, paragraph 2 (*b*), that defaulting States were not entitled to terminate or suspend treaties.

4. Like many members of the Commission, he thought that the intention of the parties at the time the treaty had been concluded, to which draft article 4 referred, might not have existed in many cases or would at least be very difficult to prove even if it had. The determination of such intention in accordance with draft article 4, paragraph 2, might thus be subjective. It might be necessary to distinguish between termination and suspension. The 1969 Vienna Convention grouped them together because it dealt with elements that justified termination or suspension, whereas the Commission was dealing with the effects of conflicts on treaties. In that context suspension was more relevant. For example, Japan had not terminated most of its treaties during the war, nor had it taken formal action to suspend them and later revoke that suspension: what it had done amounted to a *de facto* suspension of their operation. If the Special Rapporteur's position was that the outbreak of an armed conflict did not by itself terminate or suspend the operation of treaties and that procedures to that end had to be taken, he had no objection to it as a statement of principle, but he wondered whether it conformed to State practice; due attention would also have to be given to the partial suspension of treaties.

5. It might also be necessary to distinguish between bilateral and multilateral treaties. As normative multilateral treaties were playing an increasing role, more information on practice in that area would have to be collected. Moreover, given the increased importance given to private persons and entities in international relations and the many treaties which dealt with their rights, the Commission would also have to consider how those rights were affected by armed conflicts.

6. He wished to address two specific points: first, he assumed that in paragraph 67 the Special Rapporteur was referring to the Treaty banning nuclear weapon tests in the atmosphere, in outer space and under water, or Partial Test Ban Treaty (PTBT), and he agreed with the conclusion of the General Counsel of the United States Department of Defense, but not necessarily with his reasoning. That instrument was a disarmament agreement, which constituted a specific category of treaties whose object and purpose, which were to minimize the risk of and avoid armed conflicts, were lost if an armed conflict occurred, so that even though such treaties were not terminated, their operation became impossible, in the manner described in article 61 of the 1969 Vienna Convention.

7. Secondly, noting that the Special Rapporteur referred in draft article 7, paragraph 2 (*f*), to treaties relating to international watercourses and related installations and facilities and, in paragraph 97 of his report, cited article 29 of the 1997 Convention on the Law of the Non-navigational Uses of International Watercourses, he drew attention to article 20 of his own draft, which dealt with the protection of aquifers, related installations, facilities and other works in time of armed conflict (A/CN.4/551,

para. 42); he hoped that the Special Rapporteur would include groundwaters in his draft article 7.

8. Mr. CHEE said that the Special Rapporteur seemed to think that intention was the only criterion that seemed to be of any relevance in determining whether or not a treaty survived a war; however, the compatibility test was also fairly well accepted in case law. In the *Techt* v. *Hughes* case, for example, Judge Cardozo had said that "provisions compatible with a state of hostilities, unless expressly terminated, [would] be enforced", and that treaties lost their efficacy in war only if their execution was incompatible with war. That ruling seemed to be in line with the view of the Special Rapporteur, for whom the intention of the parties governed the effects of war on treaties, although he did not reject the compatibility test; that showed that the compatibility test was also accepted in other cases. In that connection, it might be relevant to refer to the observation on the effects of war on treaties made by Jost Delbrück, who said that current legal doctrine appeared to be better characterized as a pragmatic approach, with a view not only to the intent of the belligerent parties but also to those of the international community, the basic idea being "to minimize the disruptive effects of war in the sphere of treaty law without overlooking the fact that in some areas of political and social relations between States, the continuing effectiveness of treaties [was] incompatible with a state of war".[1] In other words, it was in the interest of the international community to minimize the effects of war in order to preserve the international legal order.

9. Draft article 1 did not specify whether "armed conflicts" were international or internal; it should be recalled that in the modern age, armed conflicts frequently took the form of a proxy war aided and directed by foreign powers, the classic case being the Spanish Civil War in the 1930s, with more recent examples having been witnessed in Asia and Africa. The two 1977 Protocols additional to the Geneva Conventions (Protocol additional to the Geneva Conventions of 12 August 1949, and relating to the protection of victims of international armed conflicts (Protocol I) and Protocol additional to the Geneva Conventions of 12 August 1949 and relating to the protection of victims of non-international armed conflicts (Protocol II)) distinguished between international and internal conflicts, and it might be relevant to look into the reasons for that distinction. In draft article 2 the Special Rapporteur offered a definition of the notion of "armed conflict" to reflect the evolution of the traditional conception of war. He cited a number of authors in support of the proposition which he posited in draft article 3, including Herbert W. Briggs,[2] according to whom the mere outbreak of armed conflict did not *ipso facto* terminate or suspend treaties in force, the intention of the parties being decisive. He was not sure he agreed with the Special Rapporteur's assertion in paragraph 44 of the report that "municipal decisions are 'not of great assistance'", and he drew attention to the *Techt* v. *Hughes* case on the effects of war on treaties decided by the Court of Appeals of New York. Noting that Richard Rank, in his article "Modern war and the validity of treaties",[3] had also referred to decisions by United States courts, he stressed that international law was implemented and enforced by States. Draft article 5, meanwhile, stipulated that even during an armed conflict the belligerent parties needed some rules that would enable them to continue that conflict.

10. Although not exhaustive, the list of categories of treaties which continued to operate during an armed conflict, set out in draft article 7, would be very useful for the Commission's deliberations. With regard to paragraph 2 (*c*), he said that in its judgment of 6 November 2003 in the *Oil Platforms* case, the ICJ had ruled that the 1955 Treaty of Amity, Economic Relations and Consular Rights between the United States of America and Iran had been in operation notwithstanding the hostilities between the two parties and had considered in detail potential breaches of the treaty.[4] The 1976 Convention on the prohibition of Military or any Other Hostile Use of Environmental Modification Techniques was a good example of a treaty relating to the protection of the environment that continued in operation during an armed conflict (para. 2 (*e*)).

11. He wondered whether it was not really the "presumed" intention that was meant in draft article 9, paragraph 1, because it was difficult to imagine that the parties to a treaty, in particular a friendship, commerce and navigation treaty, would have contemplated what might happen to such an instrument in two opposite situations, namely in time of peace and in time of war, unless they had expressly agreed to do so.

12. He expressed support for draft article 10, on the legality of the conduct of the parties, and the commentary thereon and said that, according to W. E. Hall, "international law had [...] no alternative but to accept war, independently of the justice of its origin, as a relation which the parties to it might set up if they chose, and to busy itself only with regulating the effects of the relation".[5] As Professor Brierly had observed in 1932, that was an admission that international lawyers had failed to establish a distinction between the legal and illegal use of force.[6] However, with the adoption of the General Treaty for Renunciation of War as an Instrument of National Policy (Kellogg–Briand Pact) in 1928, war had been condemned as a means of solving international disputes, and the contracting parties had renounced war as an instrument of their national policy. Moreover, given that Article 2, paragraph 4, of the Charter of the United Nations prohibited the use of force, the legality of the use of force, with the exception of self-defence, had to be decided by the Security Council. In that connection it should be noted that even acts of reprisal were prohibited under the 1970 Declaration on Principles of International Law concerning Friendly Relations and Co-operation among States in accordance with the Charter of the United Nations.[7]

[1] War, effect on treaties", in R. Bernhardt (ed.), *Encyclopedia of Public International Law*, vol. 4, Amsterdam, Elsevier, 2000, p. 1369.

[2] H. W. Briggs (ed.), *The Law of Nations*, 2nd ed., New York, Appleton-Century-Crofts, 1952, p. 938.

[3] *Cornell Law Quarterly*, vol. 38 (1952–1953), pp. 321–355.

[4] Signed at Tehran on 15 August 1955 (United Nations, *Treaty Series*, vol. 284, No. 4132, p. 93).

[5] W. E. Hall, *A Treatise on International Law*, 8th ed., Oxford, Clarendon Press, 1924, p. 82.

[6] J. L. Brierly, "International law and resort to armed force", *Cambridge Law Journal*, vol. 4 (1930–1932), p. 308.

[7] General Assembly resolution 2625 (XXV) of 24 October 1970, annex.

13. Lastly, he endorsed draft articles 8, 11, 12, 13 and 17, including the reference to the relevant provisions of the Charter.

14. Mr. GALICKI said that the first report on the effects of armed conflicts on treaties and the proposed draft articles should be viewed as a warm-up exercise that gave the Commission an opportunity to consider the various issues in greater depth. Given the introductory nature of the draft articles, they should not be sent to the Drafting Committee at the current stage; it would be preferable to establish a working group to discuss, analyse and complete the proposed text.

15. With regard to draft article 2, he said that the proposed definition of armed conflict, which included both international and non-international conflicts, was broader than that suggested by the Institute of International Law in its resolution II/1985.[8] Although such an approach was acceptable in principle, in practice it might create problems in determining whether specific situations qualified as armed conflicts within the meaning of the draft articles. For example, in December 1981 the Polish authorities had declared martial law, which under internal law was tantamount to proclaiming a state of war; perhaps that situation could be treated as an armed conflict within the meaning of the draft articles. At first glance, that did not seem to be the case, but the fact that the United States had then unilaterally suspended the operation of binding aviation agreements with Poland might be regarded as an effect of an internal armed conflict. The situation became even more complicated in the light of article 9 (*b*) of the 1944 Convention on International Civil Aviation, which provided that "[e]ach contracting State reserve[d] the right, in exceptional circumstances or during a period of emergency, or in the interest of public safety, and with immediate effect, temporarily to restrict or prohibit flying over the whole or any part of its territory". Consequently, restrictions introduced by the Polish authorities in connection with the proclamation of a state of war, including temporary restrictions on access to Polish airspace, could hardly be considered to be a legal justification for the suspension by the United States of a binding international treaty. If the Commission decided to extend the scope of the draft articles to include armed conflict of a non-international nature, a more detailed definition of internal armed conflicts would be needed, specifying the extent to which such conflicts were covered by the draft articles.

16. Another type of problem arose in connection with draft article 3, which categorically announced that "[t]he outbreak of an armed conflict [did] not *ipso facto* terminate or suspend the operation of treaties". The Special Rapporteur himself felt that such wording was too rigid, because in paragraph 28 of his report he proposed replacing "*ipso facto*" by "necessarily". While he fully agreed with that proposal, it would then become necessary to explain that in certain exceptional circumstances treaties could be terminated *ipso facto* following the outbreak of a military conflict. No one would contend, for example, that the Ribbentrop–Molotov Pact had not been terminated with the outbreak of the German–Soviet conflict in 1941.[9]

17. Turning to draft article 7, he suggested that the Commission should verify whether the list of treaties continuing in operation during an armed conflict was exhaustive. To complete it, the Commission could refer to the Secretariat memorandum (A/CN.4/550 and Corr.1–2), and some categories of treaty, such as "multilateral law-making treaties", would have to be explained more clearly.

18. The Special Rapporteur had acknowledged that the question of possible separability of the provisions of treaties for the purpose of assessing the effects of armed conflicts on them had not been sufficiently developed in the draft articles or in the report. Clearly, that shortcoming should be addressed without delay.

19. Like some other members of the Commission, he doubted whether it was necessary to introduce into the draft articles more detailed provisions concerning the legality of armed conflicts. The Commission should avoid politicizing its work or entering areas in which other international bodies had competence. Accordingly, the wording proposed by the Special Rapporteur for draft article 10 seemed most suitable.

20. The CHAIRPERSON, speaking in his capacity as a member of the Commission, said that Mr. Galicki's example of measures taken by the United States following the proclamation by Poland of a state of emergency prompted him to make two observations. First, he wondered whether those measures had been justified by the existence of an international conflict or whether they were countermeasures taken because of the violation of human rights treaties. Second, he pointed out that the threshold above which "domestic unrest" could be termed an "internal armed conflict" remained controversial. However, in view of the definition proposed by the Special Rapporteur in draft article 2, it could hardly be said that the example cited had involved an internal armed conflict.

21. Mr. COMISSÁRIO AFONSO thanked the Special Rapporteur for his first report, which dealt with a complex issue, and expressed agreement with his idea of proposing draft articles as "prophylactic measures" (para. 12). Commenting on the draft articles, he said that, with regard to the use of terms in draft article 2, a definition of the term "treaty" was unnecessary, since it was already defined in at least three Vienna Conventions. On the other hand, a clear and precise definition of the term "armed conflict" was needed. The one offered by the Special Rapporteur suited the Commission's purposes perfectly.

22. Draft article 3, which was limited to a reaffirmation of an established principle of international law, should be regarded as the point of departure of the subject under consideration. Draft article 4 was problematic, to say the least. The Special Rapporteur's doctrinal exposition was interesting, but the way in which those ideas were reflected in the draft articles was less persuasive. Since a process of codification was at issue, it was important to be as clear as possible. The expression "indicia of susceptibility" was likely to cause problems of interpretation; it should probably be defined in draft article 2. In order to determine the intention of the parties to a treaty, draft article 4 referred to articles 31 and 32 of the 1969 Vienna Convention. In

[8] See meeting 2834, footnote 7.

[9] Non-aggression Pact between Germany and the Union of Soviet Socialist Republics, signed at Moscow on 23 August 1939, *British and Foreign State Papers 1939*, vol. 143 (1951), p. 503.

its commentary to article 31, which set out what could be called the "golden rule" of the interpretation of treaties, the Commission had said that the starting point in interpretation was the elucidation of the meaning of the text, not an investigation into the intentions of the parties. Accordingly, the intentions of the parties to a treaty should be derived mainly from the text of the treaty itself and, if need be, from the preparatory work (1969 Vienna Convention, art. 32). The question, however, was how the intention of the parties relating to the treaty in general could help determine their intention with regard to its susceptibility to termination or suspension. He therefore wondered whether the function of articles 31 and 32 of the 1969 Vienna Convention was compatible with the function the Special Rapporteur wanted to assign to draft article 4. That matter needed to be clarified. Rather than formulating an abstract principle, it might be preferable to find a more objective criterion that was linked mainly to the treaty itself and not solely to the intention of the parties or the nature and extent of the armed conflict.

23. Mr. Comissário Afonso agreed with Mr. Fomba that draft article 7 was not superfluous. On the contrary, for those who favoured neither the principle of intention nor the *principe de caducité*, compatibility with the object and purpose of the treaty might be the most useful, albeit not the sole, criterion. It would have the additional advantage of being connected to the Vienna regime in general and to each treaty in particular. Moreover, in an era when the use of force was prohibited, the nature and extent of armed conflict should not be allowed to determine the life and death of a treaty. The Secretariat study showed that the Second World War had had little effect on treaties. More recently, during the apartheid period, South Africa had been at war with most of its neighbours, yet the treaties it had concluded with them had remained in force. The Secretariat study used the criterion of likelihood of applicability. The treaties in chapter III, sections A and B, of that document, namely treaties exhibiting a very high or a moderately high likelihood of applicability, could fit well into draft article 7, paragraph 2. It was also important to refer to *jus cogens* in the draft articles. Another model that could be used was the one proposed by Daillier and Pellet, which classified treaties in four categories, depending on the effects that armed conflict might have on them.[10] The advantage of that model was that it was both comprehensive and simple. The best solution for draft article 7 would probably be to combine several models and create a single text that was best suited to the Commission's work. In closing, he said that he subscribed to the position of Mr. Economides on the use of force (Charter of the United Nations, Art. 2, para. 4).

24. Mr. ADDO noted that, in introducing the topic, which was a particularly difficult one, the Special Rapporteur had said that he was focusing on international armed conflicts. He himself did not agree with those members of the Commission who had argued that internal armed conflicts should be included in the study, because there were fundamental differences between international and internal conflicts. The inclusion of internal conflicts might lead the Commission into a quagmire. Moreover, the definition proposed in draft article 2 did not fit a situation of internal conflict.

25. Draft article 3 could be taken to be *lex lata* because it reaffirmed an established principle of international law according to which the outbreak of an armed conflict did not *ipso facto* terminate or suspend treaties in force. That provision was a logical beginning for the study and an important source of clarification.

26. Under draft article 4, whether a treaty was terminated or suspended was determined in accordance with the intention of the parties at the time the treaty was concluded. The problem there was that it was not always easy to ascertain what those intentions were. According to Sir Gerald Fitzmaurice, the question of the survival of a treaty must be decided in each case on the basis of the nature of the treaty and the intention of the parties regarding it.[11] In his own view, either of those criteria would yield the same results because the nature of the treaty was clearly the best evidence of the intention of the parties.

27. He assumed that the list of treaties presented in draft article 7 was not exhaustive: for example, it did not include treaties governing intergovernmental debt. However, it was a well-established principle that an armed conflict between parties to a treaty of that type had no effect on the treaty. To cite one example, Great Britain had continued loan payments to Russia during the Crimean War, thus honouring an 1815 treaty that expressly provided for continued payments in case of war (Treaty between Great Britain, Russia, and The Netherlands, relative to the Russian Dutch Loan).

28. In closing, he said that, since the draft articles were in the public domain, it was to be hoped that Governments would forward their comments and information on State practice to the Commission, as that would greatly facilitate work on the topic.

29. Mr. CANDIOTI said that the effects of armed conflict on treaties could be studied from a historical perspective, since the way armed conflict was characterized under international law had changed radically in the past century and the legitimacy of the use of force under international law had been severely curtailed by the Charter of the United Nations. The Commission should accordingly take up the question of whether the use of force was lawful or unlawful without getting into a detailed examination of such issues as aggression, self-defence and the application of Chapter VII of the Charter.

30. The Special Rapporteur had thus been right to place the topic in the context of the law of treaties, thereby dispelling some of the ambiguity that had characterized the Commission's previous position. The sources of law he had consulted and the Secretariat memorandum tracing the historical evolution of the topic provided interesting food for thought, but that documentation should be used with discretion. Adequate information on the current or recent practice of States and possibly of international organizations should be assembled and the opinions

[10] P. Daillier and A. Pellet, *Droit international public (Nguyen Quoc Dinh)*, 7th ed., Paris, Librairie générale de droit et de jurisprudence, 2002, pp. 309–310, para. 200.

[11] G. Fitzmaurice, "The juridical clauses of the peace treaties", *Recueil des cours, 1948-II*, Paris, Librairie du Recueil Sirey, vol. 73, pp. 308–312.

of States and organizations should be sought on how to approach the codification and progressive development of the law in that area. He endorsed the Special Rapporteur's proposal to send out a questionnaire for that purpose.

31. Turning to the draft articles, he said that, like other members of the Commission, he believed that draft article 1 should also cover treaties to which international organizations were parties. The same applied to draft article 2 where the definitions of "treaty" and "armed conflict" were concerned. The latter definition, which seemed sufficiently detailed and appropriate at first glance, should also take into account armed conflicts in which international organizations were involved. In addition, article 2 or the commentary thereto should specify what effects were contemplated by the draft. They were obviously legal effects, but the draft did not indicate clearly enough all the effects of armed conflict on treaties. The concepts of applicability, validity, derogation, termination, suspension, extinction, modification and separability referred to in the report must at some point be duly analysed and classified.

32. Draft article 3 set out the draft's fundamental principle, namely the continuity of treaties in the event of armed conflict, but provisions on exceptions to that principle should be included: for example, the right of a State that was exercising its right of self-defence or complying with a decision of the Security Council under Chapter VII of the Charter to suspend the application of certain treaties. Another exception to the principle, mentioned in draft article 4, paragraph 2, was the intention of the parties at the time the treaty was concluded, which was to be determined in accordance with "the provisions of articles 31 and 32 of the 1969 Vienna Convention" and "the nature and extent of the armed conflict in question".

33. He endorsed the comments made by the Special Rapporteur in paragraph 47 of his report on the need to maintain an appropriate relation with the law of treaties and the provisions of the 1969 Vienna Convention, the importance of legal security and the application of the principle of *pacta sunt servanda*. He also agreed with the statement in paragraph 49 that "the reliance upon the principle of intention [was] without prejudice to the termination or suspension of treaties as a consequence of: (*a*) the agreement of the parties; or (*b*) a material breach; or (*c*) supervening impossibility of performance; or (*d*) a fundamental change of circumstances", all of which was expressly stated in draft article 13. The explanations provided in draft articles 5 and 6 were useful in that they were consistent with the basic principle established in draft article 3.

34. Draft article 7 had provoked intensive debate. The categories of treaty that must necessarily continue in operation owing to their object and purpose were given extensive coverage, both in the Special Rapporteur's commentary and in the Secretariat memorandum. In that connection he agreed with Mr. Matheson and others that unduly rigid or general categories should not be established. Given the wide range of matters that treaties could deal with, and the possibility that a single treaty might contain provisions that differed in nature and content, some of which might be affected by an armed conflict and others not—in short, the diversity of international treaty law as it was manifested in reality—it would be better not to formulate categories that were too absolute. Since the basic, general and universal principle was that of the continuity of operation of treaties in the event of armed conflict, it seemed superfluous to specify exactly what types of treaties continued in operation. In addition, whereas draft article 4 attributed a decisive role to the intention of the parties, deemed to be indicative of the susceptibility of a treaty to termination or suspension, in draft article 7 it was the object and purpose of the treaty that necessarily implied that the treaty should continue in operation. That should be made clear both conceptually and linguistically, since the two criteria, though not incompatible, were not synonymous.

35. With regard to draft article 8, he pointed out that articles 42–45 of the 1969 Vienna Convention dealt less with the modalities or forms of suspension and termination than with the conditions for the continuance in force or termination of treaties. It should be made clear whether the decision of a State party to a treaty, defined in accordance with draft article 2, paragraph 1, to suspend, abrogate or continue the operation of the treaty, in whole or in part in the event of armed conflict, had to be notified in writing.

36. Draft article 9, on the resumption of suspended treaties, was in line with the general principle of continuity of treaties and the principle of *pacta sunt servanda*. It might perhaps include a provision stipulating that in case of doubt as to whether a treaty had been suspended or abrogated as a consequence of an armed conflict, it would be assumed to have been suspended unless the parties had agreed otherwise. Draft article 10 could be improved and supplemented by a provision derived from article 9 of resolution II/1985 of the Institute of International Law.

37. Lastly, he endorsed draft articles 11–14 and expressed his agreement with the suggestion that in future reports further consideration should be given to the consequences of the distinction between international and internal conflicts, the effects of armed conflict on treaties for the parties and for third States and for both belligerent and non-belligerent parties, the effects of suspension and termination, and the separability of treaties.

38. Mr. DAOUDI said that the effects of armed conflict on treaties remained a difficult topic of international law. State practice regarding the way such effects were viewed had greatly evolved, since the hypothesis that treaties were suspended or terminated by war had given way to the realization that war did not *ipso facto* put an end to treaties between the parties to an armed conflict. Resolution II/1985 of the Institute of International Law and the report of the Special Rapporteur reflected that evolution.

39. The Special Rapporteur took the intention of States parties to a treaty at the time of its conclusion to be the operative criterion for determining whether the treaty continued to produce effects in the relations between the parties during an armed conflict in which they were involved. Although that criterion was corroborated by legal theory and certain precedents in case law, it could not in itself explain situations in which treaties were suspended during armed conflict. At the time a treaty was

concluded the parties did not necessarily foresee the outbreak of hostilities. Consequently, when such a situation was not anticipated, the Special Rapporteur's proposal to refer to articles 31 and 32 of the 1969 Vienna Convention to determine the intention of the parties was not very helpful. It was essential to take account of other criteria, such as the object and purpose of the treaty and the nature and duration of the conflict, and he therefore believed that it was necessary to redraft articles 4 and 9.

40. Although the prohibition in the Charter of the United Nations of the use of force meant that international armed conflicts were occurring less frequently, internal armed conflicts were in fact proliferating. There was thus every reason to expand the definition of armed conflict to include internal armed conflict. The meaning of the term "third States" in draft article 2, subparagraph (*b*), should also be made clear. It might refer to a State that, without being the ally of one of the belligerents, expressed politically motivated support for that State by suspending the operation of commercial agreements with that State's adversary without declaring war or taking part in the hostilities. Such had been the case with the Syrian Arab Republic which, following the outbreak of hostilities between Iraq and the Islamic Republic of Iran in 1980, had closed its borders with Iraq, thereby prohibiting the passage of persons and goods for the entire duration of the hostilities. The term might also mean a neutral State; paragraph 118 of the Secretariat memorandum referred to the decision of the United States, a neutral country that was not participating in the armed conflict between Eritrea and Ethiopia, to suspend the operation of an agreement relating to the Peace Corps programme in Eritrea in 1998[12] and in Ethiopia in 1999.[13] Clarification of the term "third State" would thus make it possible to differentiate between the effects of armed conflict on treaties and cases of international responsibility incurred through failure to implement a treaty.

41. Some members of the Commission regretted that the Special Rapporteur had omitted from the draft a reference to the Arab–Israeli conflict and its effect on treaties, yet there were virtually no treaty relations between the Arab States and Israel. The sole existing agreements between the antagonists were the General Armistice Agreements concluded under United Nations auspices at the end of the first Arab–Israeli war in 1948[14] and the 1974 disengagement of forces agreement concluded between the Syrian Arab Republic and Israel after the 1973 war.[15] The other applicable international conventions were part of international humanitarian law, such as the fourth Geneva Convention of 12 August 1949, and were applicable solely during periods of armed conflict. Thus there were no instances of suspension or abrogation of treaties in the context of that conflict. It would be more interesting to study agreements concluded between the antagonists, particularly the Palestine Liberation Organization and Israel, during the peace process launched in Madrid in 1991, which would remain in force as long as neither of the parties involved formally announced its decision to terminate them.

42. Given that belligerents had the option of concluding such agreements, draft article 5, paragraph 2, ought to refer to "capacity" and not "competence" to conclude treaties.

43. Draft article 7, which the Special Rapporteur called superfluous, referred to the objective criterion of the object and purpose of treaties, and not to the subjective criterion of the intention of the parties, in determining which treaties would continue in operation during an armed conflict. That to him was proof positive that the criterion of intention was inadequate to the purpose. As to the non-exhaustive list of treaties that were meant to be applied during an armed conflict, some of them seemed to fall into more than one category. The 1961 Vienna Convention on Diplomatic Relations and the 1963 Vienna Convention on Consular Relations to which draft article 7, paragraphs 2 (*j*) and 2 (*k*) alluded, were also multilateral law-making treaties, mentioned in paragraph 2 (*g*), and treaties expressly applicable in case of an armed conflict, cited in paragraph 2 (*a*), given the content of their provisions. As for the other categories of treaties, such as those relating to international watercourses, State practice was not necessarily unanimous where their operation during an armed conflict was concerned. Indeed, the Special Rapporteur himself felt that the arguments in favour of their inclusion were not conclusive. If a classification of treaties was really called for in the draft articles, it should be structured differently.

44. Draft article 10, which the Special Rapporteur called provocative, said nothing about the legality of the use of force and its subsequent effects on treaties and, consequently, about the distinction between an aggressor State and a State exercising its right to self-defence. The Commission ought to follow the approach taken by the Institute of International Law and build on articles 7–9 of the Institute's resolution II/1985. He could accept the principle of the separability of treaty provisions from the standpoint of their operation during an armed conflict, since that was entirely consistent with State practice.

45. Lastly, he thought it was too early to refer the draft articles even to a working group, much less to the Drafting Committee.

46. The CHAIRPERSON said that he was not in favour of making a distinction between non-belligerence and neutrality, even though certain States did so. The distinction, in his opinion, undermined the principle of equal treatment of belligerents. He also wondered, when two ex-belligerents were no longer actively engaged in hostilities, whether it was possible to speak of a state of war. In that connection he recalled the practice followed by the Security Council in the 1950s during the conflict between Israel and Egypt, when it had considered that,

[12] Agreement between the United States of America and Eritrea, effected by exchange of notes, signed at Asmara May 20, 1994, *Treaties and Other International Acts Series*, No. 12103, Washington D.C., United States Government Printing Office.

[13] Exchange of notes constituting an agreement relating to the Peace Corps Program (Addis Abeba, 23 May 1962), United Nations, *Treaty Series*, vol. 456, No. 6563, p. 293.

[14] General Armistice Agreement between Israel and Eygpt (Rhodes, 24 February 1949), United Nations, *Treaty Series*, vol. 42, No. 654, p. 251; General Armistice Agreement between Israel and Lebanon (Ras En Naqoura, 23 March 1949), ibid., No. 655, p. 287; General Armistice Agreement between Israel and Jordan (Rhodes, 3 April 1949), *ibid.*, No. 656, p. 303; General Armistice Agreement between Israel and Syria (Hill 332, near Mahanayim, 20 July 1949), *ibid.*, No. 657, p. 327.

[15] Signed at Geneva on 31 May 1974, S/11302/Add.1.

in the absence of active hostilities, the 1888 Convention between Austria-Hungary, France, Germany, Great Britain, Italy, the Netherlands, Russia, Spain and Turkey respecting the Free Navigation of the Suez Canal (Constantinople Convention) was applicable.

Responsibility of international organizations[16] (A/CN.4/549 and Add.1, sect. A, A/CN.4/547[17] and A/CN.4/553,[18] A/CN.4/556,[19] A/CN.4/L.666/Rev.1)

[Agenda item 3]

Third report of the Special Rapporteur

47. The CHAIRPERSON invited the Special Rapporteur to introduce his third report on responsibility of international organizations (A/CN.4/553).

48. Mr. GAJA (Special Rapporteur) said that his third report addressed two sets of issues which concerned, respectively, the objective element of internationally wrongful acts of an international organization and the responsibility of an international organization in connection with the act of a State or of another organization. Those issues corresponded to a large extent to those covered in part One, chapters III and IV, of the articles on responsibility of States for internationally wrongful acts.[20] The topics might at first seem different and might eventually lead to two different chapters, but they were not totally unrelated. There were also some issues that were specifically relevant to international organizations. His next report would deal with two further sets of issues. The first concerned circumstances precluding wrongfulness, and in that connection Governments and international organizations had been asked to comment on the state of necessity; the second concerned the responsibility that States or international organizations might incur for the internationally wrongful act of an international organization of which they were members.

49. He regretted that his third report gave the impression of being highly theoretical: it did so because available practice was very limited on the issues considered. He had tried to take into account all the practice that had been available and hoped that in the future there would be more. Several international organizations were taking a growing interest in the Commission's work on responsibility of international organizations and some had sent written comments and expressed their views, which was useful.

50. Several States had also made comments on subjects that the Commission had already discussed and on those currently under consideration, and those comments would be duly taken into account. Some comments, for example from the European Union and the German Government, were included in the document entitled "Comments and observations received from Governments and international organizations" (A/CN.4/556), which for the time being was available only in English. Unfortunately, some interesting comments, particularly those made by Interpol, had not been taken into account in the report because they had reached the Special Rapporteur too late.

51. In the case of most of the issues discussed, there was little reason to depart from the content and wording of the draft articles on responsibility of States for internationally wrongful acts. Questions relating to the existence of a breach of an international obligation, the need for an obligation to exist at the time the act occurred, the extension of the breach in time and a breach consisting of a composite act did not vary according to the subject of international law that committed the breach. That remark applied also to wrongful acts caused through omissions, notwithstanding the doubts that had been raised in that regard by the General Counsel of the IMF (see paragraph 8 of the report). Whenever an international organization had an obligation to do something, it breached that obligation if it did not engage in the required conduct.

52. A question that had been raised concerning the objective element was particularly relevant to the European Union: the Legal Service of the European Commission had expressed criticism of the rules of attribution adopted by the Commission in 2004, maintaining that when a member State engaged in conduct in an area of exclusive competence of the European Union or in implementation of binding acts of the European Union, it was acting almost as an agent of that organization.[21] That view, which was not a new one, had been endorsed by a WTO panel. The International Law Commission's position, on the other hand, was that conduct of State organs was always attributable to the State and not to the organization of which the State was a member, unless the organ was placed at the organization's disposal.

53. Without reverting to questions of attribution, there could be explanations of an organization's responsibility that did not derogate from the rules of attribution although that might not be totally obvious, and something might have to be said in the commentary about it. For instance, treaties like the WTO agreements might imply that the European Union was under an obligation to prevent certain conduct by its member States; if that was the case, while attention might be focused on the conduct of the member State, the breach really lay in the organization's failure to prevent that conduct, a view that was consistent with traditional rules of attribution. Another possible explanation was that the international organization's obligation was to achieve a certain result, irrespective of the entity that engaged in the conduct required for that purpose. For example, under agreements concluded with non-member States, the European Union might undertake an obligation not to levy import duty on a certain product. That result could be achieved only with the cooperation of member States which, as the German Government had

[16] For the draft articles and the related commentary adopted on first reading by the Commission, see *Yearbook ... 2004*, vol. II (Part Two), chap. V, sect. C, pp. 46 *et seq.*

[17] Reproduced in *Yearbook ... 2005*, vol. II (Part One).

[18] *Ibid.*

[19] *Ibid.*

[20] *Yearbook ... 2001*, vol. II (Part Two) and corrigendum, pp. 26–27.

[21] See *Official Records of the General Assembly, Fifty-ninth Session, Sixth Committee*, 21st meeting (A/C.6/59/SR.21), paras. 17–18. See also P. J. Kuijper and E. Paasivirta, "Further exploring international responsibility: the European Community and the ILC's project on responsibility of international organizations", in *International Organizations Law Review*, vol. 1, No. 1 (2004), pp. 111–138, at p. 127 *et seq.*

stressed in its recent comments (see A/CN.4/556), were not bound under international law to non-member contracting States, but were under an internal obligation to contribute to the fulfilment of treaties. The existence of that internal obligation explained why the European Union could accept under treaties with non-member States certain obligations whose implementation was left to member States. In the event of a breach it was the responsibility of the organization and not of its member States that was incurred.

54. The phrase in draft article 8 that read "an act of that organization is not in conformity with what is required of it by that obligation" was not a very apt description of all the instances he had referred to, but the matter could be taken care of in the commentary; moreover, the phrase fully corresponded to article 12 of the draft articles on State responsibility.

55. Concerning the objective element, he said that the only specific provision that should be added to the text of the draft articles on State responsibility for internationally wrongful acts related to the rules of the organization. The legal nature of those rules—whether or not they were part of international law—was a controversial question. It did have practical importance, because even if one considered that the rules of the organization were special rules that prevailed over general international law, it must be acknowledged that they did not cover all questions relating to responsibility of the organization. It was therefore important to determine whether the international law of responsibility provided a backdrop that filled any gaps in the existing special rules. In draft article 8, paragraph 2, he proposed saying that the preceding paragraph should also apply "in principle" to the breach of an obligation set by a rule of the organization, because some organizations had achieved such a degree of integration that they could be considered to have given rise not to a special regime of international law but to a body of law that was separate from international law. Moreover, there were some issues relating to the responsibility of international organizations for which the rules the Commission was elaborating might not be applicable, and the words "in principle" left the door open to certain exceptions.

56. In his written comments made in April 2005, the General Counsel of the IMF had stated that when an international organization acted pursuant to its charter, it would not be subject to responsibility under general international principles, but its responsibility would be determined under its own charter (see A/CN.4/556). In other words, international law did not come into play because everything was covered by the rules of the organization. For his part, he found it difficult to say that an international organization that acted in conformity with its own rules could never be seen as breaching one of its obligations under general international law or a treaty binding it. The question was not whether the latter rules were rules of *jus cogens*, since there might well be no conflict between the rules of the organization and a particular rule of general international law.

57. Apart from draft article 8, paragraph 2, the wording of draft articles 8–11 reproduced articles 12–15 of the draft articles on State responsibility, simply replacing the word "State" with "international organization". Some members had feared that the Commission was relying excessively on that text, but there was no valid reason for distinguishing between the position of States and that of international organizations in that context.

58. The same observation applied to the second set of issues dealt with in his third report, namely the responsibility of an international organization in connection with the act of a State or another organization. Draft articles 12–15 reproduced verbatim articles 16–19 of the draft articles on State responsibility, except for the replacement of the word "State" by "international organization" and for the references to cases when an international organization was aided or assisted, directed, controlled or coerced.

59. Some cases did not appear to fall into any of the categories considered. For example, an international organization might prompt its members to take conduct that might be lawful or not for those members but implied the circumvention by the organization of one of its obligations. The member State was then used by the organization in a way similar to the way Venetian warships used to use unmanned barges loaded with explosives to attack the enemy fleet. It stood to reason that an international organization could not escape responsibility by acting through one of its member States.

60. The term "control" in draft article 13 had sometimes been understood as covering also what had been termed "normative control". Draft article 13 related to a different issue, however, because it was based on the assumption that the act in question was unlawful for the State as well. For the purpose of circumventing one of its obligations an organization might use a binding decision that might or might not leave discretion to the member State, or it might recommend or authorize a certain act. If the position of the member State varied depending on the situation, from the standpoint of the organization, the distinction was not necessarily important, as some representatives in the Sixth Committee had pointed out. What was important was that at the organization's prompting the conduct in question actually took place and that the organization's obligation was circumvented. To avoid any misunderstanding, he wished to emphasize that the organization might incur responsibility if the authorized conduct enabled it to circumvent one of its obligations, but it would not be responsible for all the wrongful conduct that a member State might commit when availing itself of the recommendation or authorization. He had tried to express the conclusions of that analysis in draft article 16, but he realized that the text might not be sufficiently clear or, more fundamentally, that the approach he had taken might be held to be incorrect. He hoped in any event that his efforts would be considered useful.

The meeting rose at 1 p.m.

2840th MEETING

Wednesday, 18 May 2005, at 10 a.m.

Chairperson: Mr. Djamchid MOMTAZ

Present: Mr. Addo, Mr. Baena Soares, Mr. Brownlie, Mr. Candioti, Mr. Chee, Mr. Comissário Afonso, Mr. Daoudi, Mr. Dugard, Mr. Economides, Ms. Escarameia, Mr. Fomba, Mr. Gaja, Mr. Galicki, Mr. Kabatsi, Mr. Kateka, Mr. Kolodkin, Mr. Koskenniemi, Mr. Mansfield, Mr. Matheson, Mr. Niehaus, Mr. Pambou-Tchivounda, Mr. Pellet, Mr. Sreenivasa Rao, Mr. Rodríguez Cedeño, Mr. Yamada.

Effects of armed conflicts on treaties (*concluded*) (A/CN.4/552 and A/CN.4/550 and Corr.1–2)

[Agenda item 8]

FIRST REPORT OF THE SPECIAL RAPPORTEUR (*concluded*)

1. Mr. BROWNLIE (Special Rapporteur), summing up the discussion on the item, began by reiterating that the overall goals of his first report (A/CN.4/552) had been, first, to clarify the legal position on armed conflict and its effect on treaties; second, to promote the security of legal relations between States; and, third, to increase access to and utilization of State practice.

2. The method used had been to provide a complete package of formulations, without prejudice to the final form, on the working assumption that a set of draft articles was the best way forward, given the nature of the subject matter. The use of draft articles should not, however, lead to the assumption that he had been rushing to judgment. It had simply seemed to be a useful vehicle for presenting a comprehensive scheme. It had not been intended to produce a definitive and dogmatic set of solutions. The normative form was accompanied by elements of open-mindedness and left issues open for the formation of collective opinion. Some of the articles were expository in character, and that in itself was a strong reason for not yet resorting to the Drafting Committee. The draft articles clearly had a provisional character and a practical purpose, namely, to elicit information and opinions from Governments. The need for evidence of State practice was clear enough, but practice and opinion could be collected more effectively if Governments were presented with a relatively comprehensive package of draft articles.

3. On sources, he acknowledged that more reference to doctrine was called for. Because he had been writing a report, rather than a learned article, he had not recorded all the work done, for example his consultation of Spanish-language sources. He would welcome assistance from members with the literatures with whose language he was not familiar. Mr. Economides had drawn attention to the work of the famous Greek scholar of international law, Professor Constantin Eustathiades, and Mr. Kolodkin had referred to items from the Russian literature, but the German and Polish classics—for instance, the work of Ludwik Ehrlich—remained unplumbed.

4. Turning to the subject of municipal court decisions, he noted that the laconic style he had adopted for the report had apparently led to a misunderstanding. He had taken the view, not that municipal cases were of no value, but that they tended to be contradictory. In seeking evidence of international law, one had to distinguish between those municipal decisions in which the court actually adverted to public international law as applicable law and those in which the court was approaching legal problems from the standpoint of domestic law exclusively. The Codification Division had now produced a collection of municipal decisions as a background document for the exclusive use of the Commission.

5. More examples of State practice, especially recent practice, were clearly needed. Such material called for careful evaluation, however, to see whether the specific point of law of interest to the Commission was actually addressed. The decisions of international tribunals also required careful assessment. Often, when analysed carefully, they proved not to be very helpful. For example, in the legal relations between the Islamic Republic of Iran and the United States, whether before the Iran–United States Claims Tribunal or the ICJ, it was generally agreed that the 1955 Treaty of Amity, Economic Relations and Consular Rights between the United States of America and Iran was still in force,[1] and that the real issue hinged on its interpretation and application. While the way the two States behaved before international tribunals was of interest, the decisions in the relevant cases, such as the *Oil Platforms* case, were not very helpful. As to the *Military and Paramilitary Activities in and against Nicaragua* case, astonishing as it might seem, the fact of the matter was that Nicaragua and the United States had never been at war and had maintained diplomatic relations throughout the period, so that the precise point of law that the Commission was looking for had never arisen.

6. On the question of scope, a number of members had adverted to the need to include treaties with organizations. His own assumption had been that there were enough problems to solve already; he was not certain that the question fell within the Commission's mandate; and he was also concerned about possible overlaps with the work of other Special Rapporteurs. Despite those doubts, he would not seek to oppose the general opinion. No doubt the issue would be included in any questionnaire that might be addressed to Governments.

7. The question of the relation of the draft articles to other areas of international law needed to be seen as a general question. The specific problem in each case was the need to avoid grafting other subjects onto the draft without good cause. One specific instance was the legality of the use of force. Unnecessary excursions into the legal position on that point, to which he would revert in due course, had to be avoided. A second case was the proviso in article 13 that the draft was without prejudice to

[1] Treaty of Amity, Economic Relations and Consular Rights between the United States of America and Iran (Tehran, 15 August 1955), United Nations, *Treaty Series*, vol. 284, No. 4132, p. 93.

the termination or suspension of treaties as a consequence of the four events or situations enumerated. He continued to believe that that proviso was sufficient. Admittedly, there was some overlap, but he did not see that this mattered. There were many situations in both municipal and international law in which a single subject lent itself to multiple classifications. In addition, if the Commission began trying to encroach upon certain areas of the ordinary law of treaties, serious problems of compatibility with the 1969 Vienna Convention would arise.

8. A third case was that of *jus cogens*. He wondered if it was desirable to embark upon the codification of *jus cogens* as a by-product of the work on the topic. While a proviso might be included on that point, he did not think that would be a very advisable or elegant solution. In addition, one would have to identify which principles of *jus cogens* were involved.

9. A fourth question concerned the relevance of principles of State responsibility. They certainly stood in the background to the law of treaties, but they were not really part of the present project. In the general context of relations to other areas of the law, the policy aims should be the avoidance of confusion and unjustifiable distraction from the Commission's main purposes.

10. A number of members had suggested that the separability of treaty provisions should be given a clearer profile. Article 44 of the 1969 Vienna Convention was expressly concerned with that subject, which at present was merely alluded to in draft article 8. It might ultimately be made part of a provision on the consequences of the incidence of armed conflict.

11. On the central question of intention, which related primarily to draft articles 4, 7 and 9, members had indicated major concerns and referred to the familiar problems of proof. It was his own intention to produce a much fuller examination of those problems in a second report. There was a clear need for fuller treatment of intention, but a sense of proportion was also needed. No member had proposed replacing intention by some other criterion. Mr. Pellet had stated that he was not hostile to the principle of intention as such, and Mr. Koskenniemi had described intention as an elusive or vague criterion, but had then relented somewhat and declared himself less critical of intent, because it left room for contextual elements and flexibility. Mr. Pellet and others had seen the object and purpose of the treaty as a better guide than the criterion of intention *per se*. Mr. Dugard had suggested that articles 4 and 9 should include a reference to the nature of the treaty. He would take all those views carefully into account in any future draft. There was, however, no simple answer to the problem of proving intention. In the first place, the concept of intention would not go away: for better or worse, it was the basis of international agreements, the law of contract, the law of trusts and the interpretation and application of legislation. It was often a construct, but it provided the necessary force field within which decision makers could design solutions, as in the *Gabčíkovo-Nagymaros Project* case.

12. Secondly, as Mr. Pambou-Tchivounda had pointed out, the elements of intention relating to draft article 4 were complex. Obviously, the nature and extent of the conflict in question were necessary criteria, because the application of the criterion of intention was not an abstract process, but contextual. Everyone seemed to agree on that, and it was difficult to go along with those members who insisted that the nature of the armed conflict had nothing to do with intention.

13. The function of article 7 had elicited a variety of views. Some had considered that the use of a presumption was very problematic. Others, including Mr. Fomba and Mr. Comissário Afonso, considered the criterion of object and purpose, as deployed in article 7, to be a useful tool.

14. Turning to individual articles, he said that draft article 1, on scope, had attracted two types of comments: first, that it should refer to treaties with organizations, and secondly, that it should include treaties that had not yet entered into force. He had no problem with the latter suggestion and had already addressed the former point.

15. In the commentary to draft article 2 (paragraphs 17 and 18 of his report), he had suggested that the Commission should decide whether to include non-international armed conflicts, and the great majority of members had favoured such inclusion. Draft article 2 as presently worded did not refer to that distinction, as Mr. Pellet had pointed out. Mr. Matheson had expressed the opinion that the Commission should not attempt to redefine the concept of armed conflict and favoured a simpler statement to the effect that the articles applied to armed conflict, whether or not there was a declaration of war.

16. He himself was not a very warm supporter of draft article 3, as could be seen from paragraph 28 of his report. In any event, it was proposed that the locution "*ipso facto*" be replaced by "necessarily". Ultimately, draft article 3, with improved wording, should probably be retained. A number of members considered it to be the point of departure of the whole draft. Mr. Kateka had supported it but thought it should be shortened, and Mr. Candioti had pointed out that it stated the basic principle of continuity.

17. On draft article 4, two points should be stressed. First, the relation between draft articles 3 and 4 required more explanation: there might be a good case for amalgamating the two. Secondly, draft article 4 needed to be developed further, with particular reference to the effects of termination or suspension, a point made by Mr. Pambou-Tchivounda.

18. Draft article 5, on express provisions on the operation of treaties, had been uncontroversial. It was complementary to draft article 3. Mr. Matheson had pointed out that it should be included for the sake of clarity. Ms. Xue had questioned the use of the word "lawful" in relation to agreements between States that were already in a situation of armed conflict. There were, however, interesting situations when States were at war yet made special agreements that purported to modify the application of the law of war. He had included the term "lawful" in an attempt to cover such situations, but he now felt that that attempt had not been very successful. In a future draft he would

elaborate the commentary to draft article 5 to explain the nature of the problem addressed.

19. Draft article 6 concerned treaties relating to the occasion for resort to armed conflict. In principle, it was complementary to the principle of continuity formulated in draft article 3. It had, however, proved to be problematic. Its history was quite simple: in the course of his research he had learned that certain authorities, including Hall and, more recently, Briggs, held that in all cases in which war was caused by differences as to the meaning of a treaty, the treaty must be taken to be annulled. He himself found it unreasonable that a treaty which stood in the background to an armed conflict and which was later the subject of some legal process should be assumed to be annulled. In retrospect, however, he felt that draft article 6 was redundant in view of the earlier provisions in the draft. He had included it as a way of removing detritus from the past, but as Mr. Matheson and Ms. Xue had pointed out, it was not needed. Mr. Sreenivasa Rao had said that draft article 6 was confusing: the effects of the armed conflict could occur at several levels. He acknowledged that further research was needed on the subject in general and that the commentary should be replaced with more apposite material. Neither of the two decisions referred to in paragraph 61 of the report truly illustrated the principle with which he was concerned. More relevant was a decision not cited, namely, the decision of *the Eritrea–Ethiopia Boundary Commission* regarding the delimitation of the border, dated 13 April 2002.[2]

20. In principle, draft article 7, which had attracted a great deal of comment, was a corollary of draft article 4, but that connection was not properly spelled out in the commentary. The content was intended to be tentative and expository. Moreover, taking a strict view, the draft article was superfluous as the principle of intention had already been put in place in draft article 4. However, as was pointed out in paragraph 62 of his report, a major aspect of the treatment in the literature was the indication of categories of treaty in order to identify types of treaty which were in principle not susceptible to suspension or termination in case of armed conflict. Draft article 7 was thus not an invention: many of the categories therein were a familiar feature of the existing literature.

21. The response to draft article 7 had been very varied: some members had accorded it some sceptical acceptance, others wanted new categories of treaties to be included—for example, Mr. Addo had suggested the inclusion of treaties governing intergovernmental debt. Some, like Mr. Pellet, thought the draft article was not based on intention. Mr. Koskenniemi had thought the list worthwhile but had made the logical point that if one knew what the intention was, no list was needed at all. Mr. Matheson had thought that identifying whole categories of treaties was problematic, and Ms. Escarameia had emphasized the contextual aspect of the operation of draft article 7 but had not been hostile to the article. On a rough count, there seemed to be about 11 supporters and 3 critics of draft article 7.

22. In conclusion, on draft article 7: it was, in the first place, expository in character and thus provisional; secondly, it was intended only to create a rebuttable presumption; and lastly, several categories of treaties were to be distinguished, as they had a firm base in State practice—treaties creating a permanent regime (paras. 68–71); treaties of friendship, commerce and navigation (paras. 77–79); and multilateral law-making treaties (paras. 101–104). Mr. Matheson had pointed out that it was difficult to define the latter category, but a number of decision makers, including in municipal decisions, took the view that such treaties were not automatically affected by armed conflict.

23. Draft article 8 was unproblematic, and draft article 9 was ancillary to the purposes of article 4. Draft article 10, which dealt with the legality of the conduct of the parties, was probably the most provocative provision of all. The provision had attracted justified criticism, and stood in need of amendment. In his view, it should take the form of a proviso in general terms, referring to the right of individual or collective self-defence. He was still a little uneasy about that proposal, however, because if States reserved the right of individual or collective self-defence, it did not automatically follow that the States concerned could use that reservation as a basis for suspending or terminating treaties, unless there was some sort of legal causal connection which necessitated suspension or termination. The Commission had not yet taken such problems into account.

24. The proviso contained in draft article 11 was necessary, although it might be combined with the proviso in article 10 concerning the Charter of the United Nations. Draft article 12 had not attracted any criticism. Draft article 13 seemed to enjoy general support; he had suggested that the Commission should await the response of States to that provision. Draft article 14 was included for the sake of clarity and to complete the picture.

25. A few further issues of principle and policy remained. The first concerned what might be called the applicable *lex specialis*. Mr. Matheson had drawn attention to the need clearly to state, preferably in the articles themselves, the principle enunciated by the ICJ in its advisory opinion in the *Legality of the Threat or Use of Nuclear Weapons* case, in which it had found that certain human rights and environmental principles did not cease in time of armed conflict, but that their application was determined by "the applicable *lex specialis*, namely, the law applicable in armed conflict which is designed to regulate the conduct of hostilities" (para. 25 of the advisory opinion).

26. The second general issue of principle was the role of third parties, and especially the relations of third parties *inter se*. Article 3 raised the question whether the same concept should apply to the operation of treaties between one third party and another, a problem adverted to by Mr. Matheson. Mr. Gaja, too, had indicated that the issue called for further examination. The distinction between third party relations and relations between the parties to the conflict was significant, but only in the framework of the criterion of intention, which would govern relations between belligerents and neutrals. That point applied both to article 3 and to article 4, but, as Mr. Gaja had proposed,

[2] The text of the decision is annexed to the "Letter dated 15 April 2002 from the Secretary-General to the President of the Security Council" (S/2002/423).

the practice should be reviewed to see whether different solutions were possible. Mr. Pellet had also pressed for more emphasis on the question.

27. The last issue concerned the distinction between bilateral and multilateral treaties, which was discussed in paragraphs 51 and 52 of the report. That question had not elicited much comment or discussion. The principle of intention appeared to provide the general criterion, and there seemed to be no good case for seeking to design special criteria for the two categories. As might be expected, it was the particular context that mattered.

28. In sum, there seemed to be considerable interest in the subject and a general feeling of optimism in the Commission. The discussions had attracted contributions from 24 speakers and the Chairperson, and he was very grateful to members for their helpful comments.

29. As to the way forward, his own preference would be to prepare a second report in January 2006 in the light of the debate during the current session and, he hoped, the comments of Governments. A working group would be of limited utility at the present early stage.

30. Mr. PELLET pointed out that he, along with Mr. Koskenniemi and a number of other members, had not expressed a view on individual articles, because he believed that it was first necessary to explore questions of principle in greater depth. That did not imply that he endorsed the articles. There was only one article which he could support; all the others posed problems for him. He hoped that the second report would dissect the problems and not simply rehash the contents of the first, and that it would not again include a complete set of draft articles. The time had come to proceed slowly, step by step and problem by problem.

31. Ms. ESCARAMEIA asked whether the Special Rapporteur intended to draft the questionnaire for States without assistance, or whether a working group should be established for that purpose.

32. Mr. ECONOMIDES said that the Commission's task was one of codification and progressive development. Codification required it to focus on existing customary rules and possibly on other elements, such as doctrine and, in particular, practice. In the current case, however, the Special Rapporteur had not attempted to undertake a codification on the basis of existing customary law governing the effects of armed conflicts on treaties. Everyone agreed that the Charter of the United Nations was customary law and constituted *jus cogens*. The Charter pointed to three conclusions not reflected in the Special Rapporteur's report: first, that international armed conflicts were *ipso facto* illegal; secondly, that aggression was prohibited; and thirdly, that the State which exercised its right of self-defence had the sympathy of the international community as a whole and must be assisted in every way possible, *inter alia*, by the Security Council. Draft article 10 referred instead to the general law on legality; but that legality did not exist, and the Commission must bring out the obligations which stemmed from the Charter. The Special Rapporteur's plan to deal with the problem by including a proviso or a reference to the right of collective security would not suit the purpose. Instead, the Commission must proceed as it had in article 41 of the draft articles on responsibility of States for internationally wrongful acts, which contained specific obligations in the form of substantive rules, and the sole relevant rule in the current case was that a distinction must be drawn between the aggressor State and the State that exercised its right of self-defence.[3] The Commission must adopt the distinction made by the Institute of International Law in its resolution II/1985,[4] attempting to improve upon it as much as possible. Otherwise, it would give the impression that it was out of step with the times.

33. Mr. PAMBOU-TCHIVOUNDA supported Ms. Escarameia's suggestion that a working group should be established to draft a questionnaire. He would be pleased to take part in the work of such a group. He welcomed the comments by Mr. Economides, especially with regard to the need to have recourse to the resolution of the Institute of International Law. However, it must be borne in mind that the Institute had been engaged in what might be termed "doctrinal codification", whereas the Commission dealt with positive law. It must therefore not appear to be merely repeating the Institute's ideas, but must put the resolution of the Institute of International Law to good use.

34. Mr. BROWNLIE (Special Rapporteur) said he had been working on the assumption that at some point a questionnaire would be prepared to elicit the views of Governments in an organized way, rather than waiting for their more spontaneous reactions, if any. While he was open-minded on how that was to be done, the idea of having a working group for that sole purpose seemed to him to be top-heavy. Obviously, some sensible mechanism was needed. Perhaps the task of preparing a questionnaire could be carried out in the second part of the current session.

35. On the comment by Mr. Pambou-Tchivounda, for the Commission to seek to codify the law relating to the use of force would be the worst possible approach, because that was not part of the Commission's mandate, and it would also cause serious confusion by giving the impression that the Commission thought that those principles were not well settled. That was why a proviso relating to Article 51 of the Charter was the obvious way of dealing with the problem. Some other issues were involved, such as the relationship between the exercise of the right of self-defence and the treaty relations in question, which was a problem of causation.

36. Mr. ECONOMIDES said that he had never called for a codification of the law on the use of force or even for an attempt to analyse or reproduce it. The point he had made was that the Commission was under an obligation to identify the consequences of the illegal character of an international armed conflict for the suspension or termination of treaties. Did the aggressor State have the right, having unleashed a war of aggression, to suspend

[3] *Yearbook ... 2001*, vol. II (Part Two) and corrigendum, pp. 113–114.

[4] See 2834th meeting, footnote 7.

or terminate any international treaty which was not to its liking? In his view, the answer was a categorical "no", and the Institute of International Law thought so too. Did the State that exercised its right of self-defence have the right to suspend or terminate certain treaties which were incompatible with the exercise of the right of self-defence? The answer was a categorical "yes". That was the difference.

37. Mr. PAMBOU-TCHIVOUNDA said he had simply wanted to stress the difference between doctrinal codification, which was a task for academics, and the codification of positive law, which was a task for the Commission. In some areas, the two exercises could borrow from each other. The Special Rapporteur had quite misunderstood the point he was making, which was that the Commission should build on the resolution II/1985 of the Institute of International Law.

38. Mr. DUGARD said he tended to agree with the Special Rapporteur on the relationship between the draft articles and the use of force. However, there were clearly differences of opinion on the subject. Mr. Economides had forcefully drawn attention to another perspective, one which required consideration at an early stage of the Commission's work. It might be helpful to establish a working group to discuss the issue; otherwise, there was a danger that the Special Rapporteur might prepare a second set of draft articles in which he simply repeated the position he had adopted in his first report. As the Commission's agenda for its current session was not as full as it was likely to be in 2006, it might be useful to resolve the issue at the current session in a working group.

39. Mr. CHEE said that there were differences between the provisions of the Charter and State practice with regard to the exercise of the use of force. Pursuant to Article 51 of the Charter, force could be used, pending a Security Council decision. Thus the question whether an action was legal or illegal was currently decided by the Security Council. In using the wording "all measures as appropriate", Security Council resolutions seemed to go beyond what the Charter prescribed. The whole concept of the use of force should be examined.

40. Mr. BROWNLIE (Special Rapporteur) said he was somewhat surprised at Mr. Dugard's assumption that his second report would simply repeat the drafting of article 10. He had made it clear on a number of occasions that article 10 had been meant to elicit comments, as indeed it had. It was highly unlikely that he would leave the provision unchanged. Indeed, he had recently stated that he would amend it. Moreover, he had made a point of including in his report the three relevant articles of resolution II/1985 of the Institute of International Law (para. 123). Having been a member of that body for nearly 30 years, he was well aware of its activities, and he was entirely happy to use its material.

41. The CHAIRPERSON pointed out that the Special Rapporteur had full latitude to prepare the questionnaire to be addressed to States, and that the Secretariat was at his disposal to assist him in that task.

Responsibility of international organizations (*continued*) (A/CN.4/549 and Add.1, sect. A, A/CN.4/547, A/CN.4/553, A/CN.4/556, A/CN.4/L.666/Rev.1)

[Agenda item 3]

Third report of the Special Rapporteur (*continued*)

42. Mr. PELLET said the Special Rapporteur had once again submitted a dense and comprehensive report which, although at times somewhat allusive, was both thought-provoking and, overall, persuasive. Nevertheless, he wished to raise one important point on which he disagreed with the Special Rapporteur before entering into a discussion of the draft articles themselves and the reasoning which underlay them.

43. He did not agree with the Special Rapporteur's wording of draft article 8, paragraph 2. Paragraph 1 stated that "[t]here [was] a breach of an international obligation by an international organization when an act of that international organization [was] not in conformity with what was required of it by that obligation, regardless of its origin and character". Paragraph 2 stated that paragraph 1 also applied "in principle" to the breach of an obligation set by a rule of the organization. He did not understand why the Special Rapporteur had chosen to include the words "in principle". In the first place, he did not find it satisfactory from a functional point of view. The draft articles should enlighten States and international organizations concerning ways in which international responsibility might arise for them. The words "in principle" alerted them to the existence of a problem, but provided no explanation of what the problem was or of how they should deal with it.

44. That problem had been illustrated by the Special Rapporteur in the first sentence of paragraph 22 of his comments: if an organization failed to apply its own rules, on which States could count, then its responsibility was incurred, unless there were special rules which were unique to the organization, in which case member States, though not third States, would not be able to rely on a wrongful act. But that exception was covered by paragraph 23 of the report, in which the Special Rapporteur announced his intention of submitting a draft covering the case of special rules concerning specific treatment of breaches of obligations, including with regard to the question of the existence of a breach. He did not know if any concrete cases of such a circumstance had yet arisen, but he felt it was certainly a wise precaution on the part of the Special Rapporteur to provide for such a possibility. It should be mentioned somewhere that, like the draft articles on the responsibility of States for internationally wrongful acts, the present draft articles were residual in character.

45. If that was in fact the situation referred to by the words "in principle", they were superfluous, since the matter could be dealt with in the future general clause to be drafted; otherwise, every draft article would have to state that the rules would apply "in principle" unless there were special rules which took precedence over the general rules.

46. However, that was not the only meaning that the Special Rapporteur seemed to attribute to the words "in principle", to judge from the last sentence of paragraph 22 of his report, according to which "the wording of the paragraph should be flexible enough to allow exceptions with regard to those organizations whose rules [could] no longer be regarded as part of international law". He feared that was a reference to international integration organizations, in particular the European Union. That was confirmed by the Special Rapporteur's reference in paragraph 21 to the *Costa* v. *E.N.E.L.* case, in which the Court of Justice of the European Communities had stated that "the EEC Treaty has created its own legal system" (p. 593), overlooking the fact that in an earlier judgment it had found that the European Community legal system was a new legal system of international law, grounded in a treaty, which formed the basis for its existence (*Van Gend and Loos*, p. 12). That would continue to be the case if the European Constitution, which was also a treaty, entered into force. Theoretical discussions on such systems, although important, would not help settle the problem that concerned him.

47. For the purposes of article 8, a distinction must be made between the existence of a breach of an international obligation *vis-à-vis* the member States of an organization and *vis-à-vis* third States. Regardless of the nature of the rules of the organization or of the organization itself, third States were obviously not bound by those rules; and if they were entitled to count on those rules being respected, it was on the basis of a commitment made by the organization to them, whether in a treaty, in a deliberate unilateral act, or by estoppel, but certainly not because the rules of the organization had any particular value *vis-à-vis* third States; they were *res inter alios acta*.

48. In the case of member States of the organization, the nature of the internal rules of the organization was again of little consequence, but for other reasons. Either the principle stated in draft article 8, paragraph 2, applied without exceptions, in which case the "in principle" was superfluous, or the internal rules in question did not apply because the relations between the organization and its member States were governed by special rules, a case which would be covered by the "without prejudice" clause envisaged by the Special Rapporteur for submission at a later date and which made the words "in principle" not only superfluous but also ambiguous.

49. It would be a mistake for the Commission to attempt to preserve the specificity of the internal rules of the European Union in its draft articles. Of course, Community law existed and constituted a legal system, as did those of all other international organizations; it obviously exhibited many original features as compared to general international law. It was, however, the latter that the Commission was mandated to progressively develop and codify. The relations between the European Union and non-member States, like those of other international organizations, were subject to the rules of general international law, which was flexible enough to allow such organizations to organize their relationship with their member States as they wished. The draft articles must treat the European Union and similar organizations like any other international organization, on the understanding that such organizations must be allowed to regulate questions involving responsibility in their internal law as they wished.

50. The problems posed by the inclusion of the words "in principle" in draft article 8, paragraph 2, had seemed important enough to dwell upon at some length. His remaining comments had less to do with the wording of the draft articles themselves than with the Special Rapporteur's reasoning, as explained in his comments. He hoped the Special Rapporteur would take his remarks into account when drafting his commentary to the articles.

51. He did not reproach the Special Rapporteur for his decision to use the 2001 articles on the responsibility of States for internationally wrongful acts as a starting point, departing from the text of those articles as necessary. That approach had its advantages, not least the fact that the Commission would not have to have to start again from square one in drafting the present articles. At times, however, the Special Rapporteur underestimated the differences between his own topic and the topic of the responsibility of States. For example, in paragraphs 8 and 9 of his report, the Special Rapporteur stated that, as in the case of States, difficulties with compliance by international organizations with their international obligations might be due to the political decision-making process. There was, however, a significant difference: in the case of international organizations, the persons or organs involved in the political decision-making process were themselves subjects of international law—in most cases, States—and not subjects of internal law. Although it might conceivably be possible to transpose the reasoning behind the articles on the responsibility of States, it was not enough simply to say that the problem was the same, even if the end result was the same.

52. Likewise, it was perhaps not necessary to specify in the draft articles that an international organization was responsible at the international level for compliance with the obligations it had assumed even where it met such obligations through the intermediary of its member States, as was pointed out by the Special Rapporteur in paragraph 15 of his report. There again, however, it must be borne in mind that the context was very different from that of the articles on the responsibility of States, because the actors responsible for compliance with the obligation were themselves subjects of international law.

53. The Special Rapporteur had a regrettable tendency to put off consideration of certain problems. In paragraph 14 of his report, for example, the Special Rapporteur cited the judgment of the Court of Justice of the European Communities in the *European Parliament* v. *Council of the European Union* case, which had found that the European Community and its member States were jointly liable to the ACP States for the fulfilment of every obligation arising from the commitments undertaken in the Fourth ACP–EEC Lomé Convention of 15 December 1989 (pp. I-661–I-662 of the judgement). In paragraph 15 of his report, the Special Rapporteur said that such cases did not need to be taken into account in the draft articles; no doubt because he felt that they could be addressed when dealing with the issue of implementation of responsibility. Although it was certainly at that level

that the principle of joint responsibility entered into play, in the case of joint responsibility the wrongful act could be jointly attributed to both categories of subjects of international law, namely, the European Community or other international organizations and States. It might have been preferable to deal with that issue at the level of the attribution of the act to both subjects of international law in order to draw the appropriate conclusions when discussing the issue of implementation of responsibility.

54. He agreed with the spirit of draft article 16, which enunciated two points of principle, namely, that an international organization incurred international responsibility if it obliged a member State or States to commit, by an action or omission, an internationally wrongful act, and that it might incur responsibility if it recommended or authorized the commission of such an act—although the draft article did not explain how it might incur responsibility in the latter case. He nevertheless had some reservations with regard to the text of the draft article, as well as a real concern with one aspect of the Special Rapporteur's reasoning.

55. With regard to paragraph 1, subparagraph (*b*), he wondered if it was really necessary for the act to have been committed for the responsibility of the international organization to be incurred. That seemed to be the opinion of the Special Rapporteur, although he provided no explanation of the matter in paragraph 36 of his report, but he himself felt that such a conclusion was far from obvious. In fact, he wondered whether the requirement that a wrongful act had to have been committed might prejudge the sensitive question whether a State would incur responsibility merely by adopting a law contrary to international law. The question whether the mere adoption of such a law constituted an internationally wrongful act or whether the law had to have been applied remained a moot point. In its commentary to article 4 of the articles on the responsibility of States,[5] the Commission had merely cited judgements of the PCIJ and the ICJ, which found that a State incurred responsibility on the basis of its laws. Those precedents, cited, *inter alia*, in footnote 108 to the report of the Commission on its fifty-third session,[6] seemed to show that the mere adoption of such a law sufficed for a State to incur responsibility. Likewise, in paragraph 2 of its commentary to article 12 of the articles on State responsibility, the Commission had expressly stated that the mere passage of a law could result in a breach of international law, thereby entailing the State's responsibility.[7]

56. He agreed that the mere enactment of a law allowing an internationally wrongful act, even if not implemented, was sufficient to entail a State's responsibility. Otherwise, a State would be able to use the existence of such a law as a deterrent, with formidable effect. The same should hold true for an international organization if it adopted a decision which would oblige its member States to commit an internationally wrongful act, if only because prevention was better than cure. For those reasons, draft article 16, paragraph 1 (*b*), should be closely examined by the Drafting Committee.

57. A different problem arose in paragraph 2 (*b*) of draft article 16, pursuant to which an international organization incurred international responsibility if it authorized or recommended a member State to commit an internationally wrongful act and the act in question was committed. In that case, a wrongful act did not ensue merely by virtue of the fact that the international organization authorized or recommended it. The State retained its freedom to choose whether to implement the resolution, and only if it did so would an internationally wrongful act be committed. That being said, if one accepted, like the Special Rapporteur, that the international organization nonetheless incurred responsibility, that posed at least two very thorny legal problems which were not resolved by the Special Rapporteur. The first was the question of the moment at which the international organization incurred responsibility. Was it at the date of adoption of the resolution or at the date of commission of the wrongful act by the member State? It was clearly an example of a composite act within the meaning of article 15 of the draft articles on State responsibility, but unfortunately the articles adopted by the Commission in 2001 were much less clear on that point than the "Ago draft" adopted on first reading in 1996.[8] The Special Rapporteur and the Drafting Committee should consider that problem with reference not only to the draft articles of 2001 but above all to the "Ago draft", which covered all contingencies.

58. The second problem posed by the solution adopted—rightly, in his view—by the Special Rapporteur in paragraph 2 (*b*) of article 16 was the question of how the responsibility of the organization and of the member State or States were combined. Would responsibility be joint, joint and several, shared, or parallel? He agreed with the Special Rapporteur's statement, in paragraph 41 of the report, that the responsibility of the organization would depend on the extent to which it was involved in the act. But how was that "extent" to be determined? That again raised the question of the difficulties involved in the decision-making process in international organizations, to which he had already alluded. The Special Rapporteur, in paragraph 43, recommended that the issue of the degree of responsibility should be examined at a later stage, perhaps when dealing with implementation of responsibility. He himself was of the opinion however, that it would be better for the Commission to tackle that problem forthwith.

59. Before returning to draft article 16, paragraph 1, he had a comment with regard to paragraph 2 (*a*) of that same article. That provision, which stated that an international organization incurred international responsibility if it authorized or recommended an internationally wrongful act only if the act fulfilled an interest of the same organization, was illustrated, in paragraph 40 of the report, by an example which he did not find persuasive. If an international organization recommended or authorized a member State to commit an act which was a breach of international general law, and the organization had no authority to release the State from its obligations under international law, then the organization was complicit in

[5] *Yearbook ... 2001*, vol. II (Part Two) and corrigendum, pp. 40–42.

[6] *Ibid.*, p. 40.

[7] *Ibid.*, pp. 54–55.

[8] *Yearbook ... 1996*, vol. II (Part Two), chap. II, sect. D, p. 58 *et seq.*

that wrongful act, although the extent of its complicity was difficult to determine. The example given by the Special Rapporteur in paragraph 40 of the report seemed to confirm that position.[9] The Sanctions Committee had the authority to release a Member State from its obligations under the Charter of the United Nations if it was acting in accordance with chapter VII of the Charter, but only on condition that such an act did not breach an obligation arising from a peremptory norm of international law (*jus cogens*). Even if the export of freon to Iraq had constituted an internationally wrongful act in spite of the authorization by the Sanctions Committee, the fact remained that the act had been committed thanks to, perhaps at the instigation of, the Organization, which bore some degree of responsibility for the act, even if the act did not directly fulfil its interests.

60. For those reasons he believed that the Drafting Committee should simply delete draft article 16, paragraph 2 (*b*), although it could be explained in the commentary that a situation might arise where an international organization which had authorized or recommended an internationally wrongful act might not incur responsibility, if any convincing examples of such a scenario could be found. However, he had not found any such examples and he did not find the Special Rapporteur's own example convincing. In any case, even if any such examples could be found, the rule enunciated in draft article 16, paragraph 2 (*b*) was too general and absolute to be included in the draft.

61. In paragraph 31 of his report, the Special Rapporteur stated that if the conduct mandated by a binding decision of the organization necessarily implied the commission of a wrongful act, the organization's responsibility would "*également*" ("also") be involved. Responsibility would thus be shared, to an extent that remained to be determined, between the organization and the State or States implementing such a decision, even though States might have no choice, under the rules of the organization, but to implement it. However, at the same time, States might have another international obligation that would be violated by the implementation of the decision. It was not clear that there was necessarily a sharing of responsibility as implied by the use of the word "*également*". However, what was clear was that if a State could choose to fulfil its obligations towards the international organization or to commit or not commit an internationally wrongful act, it was ultimately the State that decided. That the State alone was responsible for breaches of its international obligations could be inferred from draft article 16, paragraph 2, and from the decision of the *European Court of Human Rights in Matthews* v. *the United Kingdom*, in which the United Kingdom had been found to have fulfilled its obligations towards the European Community in a manner that violated the European Convention on Human Rights when it could have chosen to fulfil them in a manner that did not violate the Convention. However, when an international organization forced one of its members to breach international law, the organization alone should be held responsible, and that was the conclusion that should be drawn from the *Krohn & Co.* v. *Commission of the European Communities* and *Dorsch Consult* v. *Council and Commission* cases cited in paragraph 34 of the report, although the Special Rapporteur was right to point out that the decisions in those cases concerned matters of jurisdiction.

62. When a State had an obligation towards an international organization that conflicted with an obligation under international law, the State had to decide which obligation it would fulfil. Consequently, the State incurred responsibility through its decision not to fulfil the other obligation. In such a case, he did not think that the State and the international organization could be said to be "*également*" responsible; they were responsible separately for different reasons, as the international organization might have forced the State to act in a manner contrary to its obligations under general international law, while the State was responsible as a result of having complied with its obligations towards the organization.

63. Moreover, the idea of the State and the international organization sharing responsibility appeared to be incompatible with the current trend towards deeper regional integration, not only in Europe but also in Latin America and Africa. In the light of that trend, to confront States with the dilemma of choosing between their obligations towards an organization and their obligations under international law was to put them in an intolerable position. It would be better to encourage the organizations themselves to comply with general international law and oblige them to assume responsibility for their own actions.

64. Of course, such reasoning led to the usual objection: if organizations, not States, were held responsible, international courts might well find themselves unable to make a ruling. That was indeed a possibility, given that the international courts—wrongly in his opinion—did not currently have jurisdiction over violations committed by international organizations. For that reason, few such cases reached the courts. However, the substantive issues related to responsibility should not be confused with problems related to the jurisdiction of international courts.

65. In sum, he did not object to draft article 16, paragraph 1 (*a*), but felt that it did not go far enough. If the Special Rapporteur thought that the responsibility of international organizations did not exclude State responsibility, he should say so plainly, giving his reasoning, and the relationship between the two kinds of responsibility should be clarified. In his view, the Commission should decide, as a matter of principle, that in cases where an international organization forced States to act in breach of international law, the organization bore sole responsibility.

66. Mr. YAMADA said that, as a matter of form, it would be advisable to group the seven draft articles on the topic that had already been provisionally adopted by the Commission,[10] under chapter headings, as had been done in the case of the draft articles on responsibility of States for internationally wrongful acts. Similarly, draft articles 8 to 11 on the responsibility of international

[9] The provision of freon gas to Iraq was authorized by the Security Council Sanctions Committee under Security Council resolution 661 (1990) of 6 August 1990, as amended by resolution 687 (1991) of 3 April 1991. For the exporting State, this provision was a violation of the Montreal Protocol on Substances that Deplete the Ozone Layer. See also United Nations, *Juridical Yearbook 1994* (Sales No.: 00.V.8), pp. 500–501.

[10] See the 2839th meeting, footnote 16.

organizations should be grouped under the heading "Breach of an international obligation on the part of an international organization" and draft articles 12 to 16 under the heading "Responsibility of an international organization in connection with the act of a State or another organization". The use of chapter headings would not only help the reader but would also help emphasize that draft article 7 dealt with the attribution of conduct, not the attribution of responsibility. According to that article, which was based on article 11 of the draft articles on responsibility of States,[11] "[c]onduct which is not attributable to an international organization under the preceding draft articles shall nevertheless be considered an act of that international organization under international law if and to the extent that the organization acknowledges and adopts the conduct in question as its own". The problem with that provision was that, while it was possible for an international organization to shift attribution of conduct from the wrongdoing State or international organization, it was not possible to shift responsibility from the wrongdoer without the express consent of third States or international organizations adversely affected by the wrongful act: responsibility remained with the original wrongdoer. Unfortunately, that problem had not been resolved by the Special Rapporteur in his third report, though it could still be addressed by including a reference to draft article 7 in draft article 15.

67. On the question of the rules of the organization in connection with a breach of an international obligation, he agreed with the Special Rapporteur that some rules of international organizations constituted a part of international law and that breaches of such rules must be covered in the draft articles. However, he still had a problem with draft article 8, paragraph 2. He understood that the Special Rapporteur was trying to limit the scope of the rules of the organization by inserting the words "in principle", but more precise wording was required. Moreover, draft article 8, paragraph 2, as currently formulated, might imply that the breach of an obligation set by a rule of the organization was different from the breach of an international obligation mentioned in paragraph 1 of the same article. However, the Drafting Committee should be able to clarify that point.

68. He also had a problem with draft article 15, another of the articles modelled on the corresponding article of the articles on responsibility of States. According to draft article 15, articles 12 to 14 were without prejudice to the international responsibility of States or international organizations. That accorded with draft article 12, according to which an international organization which aided or assisted a State or another international organization in the commission of an internationally wrongful act was internationally responsible for the aid or assistance provided, while the original wrongdoer remained responsible for the act in question. However, draft articles 13 and 14 assumed that both the international organization and the original wrongdoer were responsible for the act in question. If that was the case, he wondered how responsibility was to be apportioned between them. That problem required further study.

[11] *Yearbook ... 2001*, vol. II (Part Two) and corrigendum, p. 52.

69. The draft articles on the responsibility of international organizations also applied to the international responsibility of a State for the internationally wrongful act of an international organization, as stipulated in draft article 1, paragraph 2. The fact that the State's responsibility arose as a result of its membership of an organization was a crucial point, and he looked forward to receiving draft articles or a preliminary view dealing with that aspect of the topic.

70. Mr. KOLODKIN said he agreed with the Special Rapporteur that some of the draft articles already adopted should be reviewed before first reading, taking into account the comments received from Governments and international organizations, particularly with regard to the attribution of conduct to international organizations and the rules of such organizations. With regard to draft article 3, on general principles, the Special Rapporteur had raised the question whether a wrongful act of an international organization could consist not only of an action but also of an omission. In theory, the answer was in the affirmative, but that was not clear from the example given in paragraph 10 of the report of a wrongful act by omission—the failure by the United Nations to prevent the genocide in Rwanda. That example raised the question of whether the responsibility to provide protection was already established as an international obligation and whether a breach of any such obligation entailed the international responsibility of the United Nations, and, possibly, of its Member States. Moreover, it was not clear what the position was with regard to the international responsibility of members of the Security Council who vetoed a resolution that might have averted the genocide. It was one thing to carry out a political evaluation of the failure to prevent the genocide in Rwanda; it was quite another to attribute international responsibility to the United Nations for its failure to act.

71. With regard to the question of whether the draft articles should cover such organizations as the European Community, he believed that a special exception or protective reservation for such organizations should be included in the draft articles, especially since Community law was unlike the internal rules of international organizations in the traditional sense and since the Community resembled an international organization less and less as it became more integrated.

72. With regard to the rules of the organization, it was quite clear from article 4, paragraph 4, of the draft articles that many such rules belonged to the sphere of international law. There was no hard and fast distinction between the rules of the organization and international law. Moreover, he believed that the term "rules of the organization" did not refer to all the rules or individual decisions adopted by international organizations, but only to those relating to the internal functioning of the organization. He did not think that the example given in paragraph 20 of the report was a very useful one; the Security Council resolution considered by the ICJ in the *Lockerbie* case could not be seen as a rule of the organization.

73. With regard to draft articles 8 to 11, he agreed with the Special Rapporteur that they should, *mutatis mutandis*, replicate the corresponding draft articles on responsibility of States. It should be noted, however, that the

wording of draft article 8, paragraph 2, did not fully reflect the idea expressed in paragraph 22 of the report that the scope of the draft articles should include breaches of obligations under the rules of the organization to the extent that those rules had retained the character of rules of international law.

74. Turning to the chapter of the report on the responsibility of an international organization in connection with the act of a State or another organization, he said that draft article 12 on help or assistance in the commission of an internationally wrongful act could, like draft articles 8 to 11, be sent to the Drafting Committee. However, draft articles 13, 14 and 16, which touched on the fundamental distinction between States and international organizations, should not just reproduce the corresponding articles on responsibility of States. An international organization, in contrast to States, could oblige other international organizations to commit certain acts and coerce them into acting in a certain way by adopting decisions that were binding in relation to them. An international organization could therefore have normative control over the activities of other subjects of international law. States did not have that possibility, except within their own territory. The Commission faced the problem of defining the effects of the binding decisions of an international organization in the context of international responsibility, a problem that was compounded by the fact that international organizations had members who took part in the adoption of decisions within the organization. The adoption of the binding decisions mentioned in draft article 16, paragraph 1 (*a*), could in many cases be considered a form of coercion. If it was possible to talk about "normative control", it was also possible to talk about "normative coercion" (para. 35 of the report). In fact, he believed that the decisions adopted by the Security Council under Chapter VII of the Charter could be considered a coercive measure. If the coercive measures covered by draft article 14 referred to measures other than binding decisions adopted by international organizations, that point should be made clearly.

75. Another issue was whether the adoption by an international organization of a binding decision was conduct attributable to the organization itself, rather than to its members. If the answer was in the affirmative, the organization would bear responsibility not, or not only, for the conduct of its members but also for its own conduct, as expressed in the relevant decision. The example given in paragraph 34 of the report demonstrated that in the case of *Krohn & Co.* v. *Commission of the European Communities* the Court of Justice of the European Communities had found that the unlawful conduct was to be attributed to the Commission of the European Communities because such conduct could have taken place only as a result of the adoption of the relevant decision. He wondered if a binding decision by an organization could be considered as conduct giving rise to the attribution of responsibility to that organization.

76. Similarly, with regard to draft article 13, on the direction and control exercised over the commission of an internationally wrongful act, he wondered if the adoption of a binding decision by an international organization could be considered as a form of direction and control. In paragraph 35 of the report, the Special Rapporteur spoke of the concept of control being extended to encompass normative control if it directed and controlled the member State in the commission of a wrongful act. That seemed to suggest that draft articles 13 and 16 overlapped to some extent.

77. The chapter of the report on the responsibility of an international organization in connection with the act of a State or another organization raised questions about the responsibility of member States of international organizations, particularly with regard to the adoption of decisions contrary to international law, and the implementation of such decisions, whether or not the individual member had voted for them. It was not clear whether the responsibility of States for the decisions of organizations of which they were members belonged to the field of State responsibility or of the responsibility of international organizations.

78. Lastly, he agreed with the application of the criteria of the member State's liberty to act or use discretion in implementing the binding decisions of an international organization, as mentioned in paragraphs 30 and 32 of the report and discussed by the delegations of France and the Russian Federation in the Sixth Committee.[12]

Organization of work of the session (*continued*)*

[Agenda item 1]

79. The CHAIRPERSON announced that, following consultations, it had been agreed that the working group established to discuss the topic of shared natural resources would be composed of Mr. Candioti (Chairperson of the Working Group), Mr. Comissário Afonso, Mr. Daoudi, Ms. Escarameia, Mr. Fomba, Mr. Gaja, Mr. Galicki, Mr. Kabatsi, Mr. Mansfield, Mr. Matheson, Mr. Opertti Badan, Mr. Sreenivaso Rao, Mr. Sepúlveda, Ms. Xue, Mr. Yamada (Special Rapporteur), and Mr. Niehaus (Rapporteur, *ex officio*).

The meeting rose at 12.55 p.m.

2841st MEETING

Thursday, 19 May 2005, at 10 a.m.

Chairperson: Mr. Djamchid MOMTAZ

Present: Mr. Addo, Mr. Baena Soares, Mr. Brownlie, Mr. Candioti, Mr. Chee, Mr. Comissário Afonso, Mr. Daoudi, Mr. Dugard, Mr. Economides, Ms. Escarameia, Mr. Fomba, Mr. Gaja, Mr. Galicki, Mr. Kabatsi, Mr. Kateka, Mr. Kolodkin, Mr. Koskenniemi, Mr. Mansfield, Mr. Matheson, Mr. Niehaus, Mr. Pambou-Tchivounda, Mr. Pellet, Mr. Sreenivasa Rao, Mr. Rodríguez Cedeño, Mr. Yamada.

---

* Resumed from the 2836th meeting.

[12] See *Official Records of the General Assembly, Fifty-ninth Session, Sixth Committee*, 22nd meeting (A/C.6/59/SR.22), para. 13; and 23rd meeting (A/C.6/59/SR.23), paras. 22–23, respectively.

Responsibility of international organizations (*continued*) (A/CN.4/549 and Add.1, sect. A, A/CN.4/547, A/CN.4/553, A/CN.4/556, A/CN.4/L.666/Rev.1)

[Agenda item 3]

Third report of the Special Rapporteur (*continued*)

1. Mr. MATHESON said that the first set of articles in the report (arts. 8–11) was a reasonable adaptation of the corresponding articles on State responsibility for internationally wrongful acts.[1] He agreed in particular with the Special Rapporteur that a wrongful act of an international organization could consist of either an act or an omission and that both possibilities should be covered by the draft articles. However, he was not convinced by the example given in paragraph 10 of the report, which suggested that the United Nations might be held responsible for failing to prevent the genocide in Rwanda. Although he believed that the Security Council should have authorized the use of force under Chapter VII of the Charter of the United Nations, he doubted whether the Security Council had a legal obligation to do so or that it could be held legally responsible for not doing so. It might be preferable to refer in the commentary to examples that did not involve the Security Council's discretionary powers under Chapter VII of the Charter. In any event, draft articles 8–11 could be sent to the Drafting Committee.

2. With regard to the second set of articles (arts. 12–15), on the responsibility of an international organization in connection with the act of a State or another organization, he agreed in principle with the Special Rapporteur's proposals. An international organization could indeed be held responsible for aiding or assisting, directing, controlling or coercing another organization or a State in the commission of an internationally wrongful act, although one might ask how the principle applied in specific cases: it was not certain, for example, that the imposition by an international financial organization of strict conditions for a loan constituted coercion, as suggested in paragraph 28 of the report.

3. With regard to draft articles 13 and 14, according to which an international organization was responsible only if the act of the State would be internationally wrongful if committed by the organization, he wondered how that provision would apply to acts that could be committed by a State but not by an international organization, such as the imposition of national economic sanctions or the failure to prosecute, under domestic law, individuals who had committed certain types of crime. He would appreciate some clarification on that point by the Special Rapporteur. Having said that, he was in favour of sending draft articles 13–15 to the Drafting Committee.

4. The most problematic article was without a doubt draft article 16 on decisions, recommendations and authorizations addressed to member States and international organizations, since it went further than the corresponding articles on State responsibility. Paragraph 1, which stipulated that an international organization incurred international responsibility if it adopted a decision binding a member State or international organization to commit an act that would be internationally wrongful if taken by the former organization directly, was acceptable. It should be made clear, however, either in the article itself or in the commentary, that responsibility was not incurred if the State concerned was in a position to comply with the decision in a manner that did not constitute an internationally wrongful act. He did nevertheless have doubts about paragraph 2, according to which an international organization incurred responsibility if it authorized or recommended an internationally wrongful act, although he agreed that such an authorization or recommendation might, in certain circumstances, fall within the scope of the conduct covered by articles 12–14, on aid or assistance, direction and control, and coercion. That point could, if necessary, be clarified in the text or commentary. However, it would be going too far to claim that authorizations and recommendations made by an international organization entailed the organization's international responsibility in other cases, since, as the report indicated, States were not obliged to act upon such decisions and were, after all, best placed to judge whether it was possible to do so in a lawful manner. In his opinion, it was questionable whether the international organization was automatically responsible in such cases.

5. He agreed that the wording of article 16, paragraph 2 (*a*) was designed to limit the reach of that provision, but he doubted that the proposed criterion was suitable. It would, in fact, be very difficult to judge whether a particular act "fulfils an interest of the same organization". It was probably extremely rare for an organization to authorize or recommend any action if it did not believe that doing so was in its own interest. He was also concerned that if international organizations incurred responsibility for an authorization or recommendation in circumstances other than those set out in draft articles 12–14, they might be unduly inhibited in carrying out one of their essential roles, which was to give advice and authorization. It would be questionable to impose on an organization the burden of judging whether its recommendations could be lawfully implemented in all cases and to hold it responsible if a State acted unlawfully in carrying out such recommendations. The paragraph should therefore be reconsidered.

6. Paragraph 3 of draft article 16 should also be reworded or explained, as it was unclear whether an international organization could be held responsible for requiring a State to commit an act that did not breach the international obligations of that State. Draft article 16 raised substantive issues that needed to be resolved before it was referred to the Drafting Committee.

7. Lastly, he wished to raise a question that was not directly dealt with in the draft articles but was mentioned in the body of the report (para. 19), and on which the Commission had sought the views of States in 2004: namely, whether the Commission should consider, under the current topic, breaches by an international organization of its obligations towards its member States (see A/CN.4/556). He did not believe it should, as such matters were governed by the agreements establishing the organization, the rules and decisions adopted pursuant to those agreements and the practice of the organization

[1] See 2838th meeting, footnote 5.

and its members. It would therefore be difficult to draft general rules applicable to all organizations; moreover, no set of generic rules should override the obligations imposed or decisions taken by the competent organs of the organization. For example, if the General Assembly took a decision on the allocation of responsibility between the United Nations and its Member States with respect to peacekeeping operations, or if the Security Council took a decision under Chapter VII of the Charter on the allocation of responsibility between a Member State and the Organization, such decisions ought not to be called into question on the basis of the general provisions of the draft articles. Accordingly, the Commission should in due course consider adopting an article making it clear that the draft articles did not govern the relations between an organization and its member States. At the very least, it should be specified that the articles did not override the decisions or practice of organizations. He suggested that the Commission begin to think about that question and encourage States to express their views on it.

8. Mr. PELLET said that he found Mr. Matheson's comments very interesting and agreed with most of them, particularly those concerning article 16, paragraph 1. However, he was not convinced by his last remark, notwithstanding the merits of the arguments put forward. It was essential that the draft articles should cover the responsibilities of international organizations towards their member States. To delete that aspect from the study outright would render the exercise meaningless.

9. Mr. MATHESON suggested that it might be better to defer the debate on that point; in any case, the draft articles did cover the relations between organizations and third States, which could be important for organizations that did not have universal membership.

10. Mr. BROWNLIE agreed with Mr. Pellet that the topic would lose much of its interest if the Commission decided not to deal with the crucial question of the occasional attempts by States to evade their responsibility by hiding behind an international organization.

11. Mr. GAJA (Special Rapporteur) pointed out that an aspect of the relations between international organizations and their member States was addressed in article 8, paragraph 2, and in the commentary. It was not consideration of that aspect of the topic that had been deferred but consideration of the responsibility of member States for an internationally wrongful act of an organization. For the time being, the Commission should deal with the responsibility of an international organization towards its members or towards other States or other international organizations.

12. Mr. ECONOMIDES agreed with Mr. Pellet's position. International organizations could certainly be responsible with respect to third States, but they also incurred responsibility for acts committed by their member States, unless there was a special regime governing responsibility in the relations between the organization concerned and its member States. A general clause should therefore be included at the end of the draft articles to specify that the articles were not applicable when a special regime governing responsibility was already in place.

13. Mr. Sreenivasa RAO said that the methodology adopted by the Special Rapporteur, which consisted of following the general pattern of the articles on State responsibility, had allowed the Commission to make progress in its work. However, as the Special Rapporteur himself had recognized, the reports and debates on the topic had been highly theoretical, and it was difficult for Commission members who had not taken part in the tumultuous debates on State responsibility to analyse the draft articles in depth or in a critical manner. Leaving that problem aside, he was not entirely comfortable with the basic thrust of the draft articles. There were 200 to 300 international organizations around the world that had been established by international treaties or other instruments of international law, and their members consisted not only of States but also of other entities. Their constituent instruments and mandates differed widely, as did their decision-making procedures. Most international organizations made recommendations and set standards, leaving their member States to implement them according to their means and particular circumstances. It was well known that the recommendations of international organizations had played a more important role in the implementation of international law than their binding decisions. Furthermore, in many international organizations, and particularly in financial institutions, policies were decided by member States but their implementation was left to the organization. The activities of international organizations were mainly governed by the rules of the organization, generally defined as their constituent instruments, resolutions, decisions and established practice. It was open to question whether in determining the legal basis for the conduct of the organization it was possible to rely solely on the rules of the organization without taking into account the collective responsibility of the member States who set the organization's overall policy.

14. It would also be desirable to look more closely at the role of the recommendations or authorizations provided by an organization to its member States for the pursuit of conduct that might later be considered as wrongful in establishing responsibility. In the area of State responsibility, there was little difference between recommendations and authorizations, inasmuch as States had some leeway in acting upon them. However, the responsibility of international organizations might be slightly greater in the case of an authorization. Those matters were more important for determining the remedies needed as a consequence of responsibility than for establishing the responsibility of international organizations and their member States.

15. The diversity of international organizations and their mandates made it necessary for the Commission to take a more nuanced approach to the attribution of responsibility to an international organization. Discussions had already revealed certain differences, depending on whether the subject was the work of the United Nations or the situation of the European Union. The situation would be equally different in the case of the IMF or the World Bank. For example, according to paragraph 28 of the report, "an international organization could incur responsibility for assisting a State, through financial support or otherwise, in a project that would entail an infringement of the human rights of certain individuals". That example and others required further study before the Commission

could conclude that the organization concerned had incurred responsibility. One important consideration for establishing responsibility was whether or not the international organization was aware of the circumstances in which the internationally wrongful act had been committed. Another important consideration was whether the member State that received aid or assistance had any choice but to accept the aid and the constraints attached to it. It should also be determined whether several options were available to the State concerned and whether some of them were consistent with its international obligations, including those related to human rights.

16. As far as the decisions of the United Nations Security Council or NATO were concerned, they were undoubtedly mandatory and binding on their member States and could to some extent be considered as orders, but they were always taken on the basis of a set procedure. Accordingly, member States that approved the decisions taken under such a procedure could not subsequently claim that those decisions had been forced on them and that they were therefore absolved of any responsibility for following or implementing them. In every case responsibility was shared jointly and severally by the organization and all its member States. After all, an international organization was the sum of its members. Similarly, it was not easy to directly attribute responsibility to the United Nations for not preventing the genocide in Rwanda, since any action that had to be taken by the Organization could only be taken in accordance with the applicable decision-making procedure. Member States and, in particular, the permanent members of the Security Council played an indispensable role in that procedure and thus incurred responsibility. He agreed with Mr. Kolodkin that the mere fact that the Secretary-General had recognized that the United Nations could have played a role was not sufficient to establish the Organization's responsibility.

17. There were few examples of practice relating to the responsibility of an international organization that deliberately and willingly assisted or aided, directed and controlled, or coerced another organization or State in the commission of an internationally wrongful act, as the Special Rapporteur himself admitted. Perhaps the European Community and its institutions, which were in many respects *sui generis*, should be given special treatment. The responsibility of the United Nations in the case of wrongful acts committed by peacekeeping forces operating under its general direction and control should also probably be treated separately, in the light of the relevant status-of-forces agreements between the United Nations and troop-contributing Member States.

18. Subject to those general comments, he had no particular objections to the basic thrust of the draft articles presented in the third report, but he did think that they would have to be revised, or formulated or organized differently in the light of further comments by the various specialized international organizations and remarks by Commission members.

19. He did hope that the words "origin and character" in article 8, paragraph 1, would be explained in the commentary and that they would cover not only acts but also omissions. Although he had no particular problem with the use of the phrase "in principle" in article 8, paragraph 2, he thought that the comments made by Mr. Pellet and Mr. Yamada should be considered before the paragraph was finalized.

20. Draft article 16 was particularly complicated; although Mr. Pellet had put forward some interesting arguments, recommending that paragraph 1 (*b*) should be redrafted and paragraph 2 (*b*) deleted altogether, and even wondering whether the issue dealt with in paragraph 2 should not be treated in the same way as a breach consisting of a composite act, he did not fully share those views (see paragraphs 4–6 above). As he understood it, draft article 16 meant that a mere decision by the organization was not sufficient to have the act in question considered as completed unless it had been committed by the State or by the other organization concerned. In the case of a composite act, in which the breach might involve a series of events, the first event in the series was in itself a complete act for the purpose of establishing responsibility, whereas the case contemplated in draft article 16 could be considered as an incomplete act in that it had been conceived and prepared but not actually committed. He concluded by expressing the hope that international organizations would help the Special Rapporteur by sharing their observations with him and providing him with information on their practice.

21. Mr. BROWNLIE said that the Commission had not yet addressed the issue of risk creation and the fact that the amounts an organization might have to pay out in damages were not necessarily budgeted for. For example, it was virtually certain that the budget of organizations that developed and launched space vehicles did not make provision for any damage those vehicles might cause. That raised the preliminary question of whether an international organization was a risk-creating body, acknowledged that it was such a body, and was legally and practically prepared to pay out large sums of money in cases of harm. If an organization was not a risk-creating body, its member States would be responsible on a residual basis. That issue should be studied closely, given the scale of compensation that would have to be paid in cases of dereliction of duty by peacekeeping forces.

22. Mr. ECONOMIDES said that Mr. Sreenivasa Rao's argument that States that approved a decision of an international organization could not then be absolved of any responsibility incurred in respect of that organization ran contrary to all law governing international organizations. Clearly, the acts of international organizations were autonomous acts that were not considered to be agreements between the States members of the decision-making body. In theory, then, the question of responsibility might arise even in respect of the States members of the organization. If that argument was accepted, it would no longer be possible to talk of responsibility in respect of any States that had not taken part in the vote but had suffered harm as a result of an internationally wrongful act.

23. Mr. GAJA (Special Rapporteur), responding to members' comments, said that the issue of the responsibility of the States members of an international organization would be addressed in his fourth report. It was not the subsidiary responsibility of member States that should

be considered at present, since the rules governing the responsibility of international organizations must first be established before the relations between them and their member States could be considered.

24. Mr. Sreenivasa RAO said that the responsibility of international organizations and State responsibility were two sides of the same coin. That being said, some of the statements cited in the report claiming that organizations and not States were solely responsible in certain cases were debatable.

25. With regard to the comment made by Mr. Economides, he said that he had never suggested that an organization did not incur a share of responsibility as an organization. He had simply been making a distinction between States that could not be absolved of responsibility for decisions that the organization had taken at their prompting and that they had encouraged and implemented, and States that had disagreed with those decisions, voting against them or abstaining in the vote on them. However, as an organization was the sum of the States that composed it, the responsibility of its member States was also implied by acts of the organization as such, even if those States disagreed with the decision in question. The problem was therefore clearly one of the responsibility of international organizations. Like the Special Rapporteur, he believed that the decision-making procedure and the involvement of member States therein did nothing to diminish the solemn nature of the obligations contracted by an organization as such.

26. Mr. BROWNLIE clarified his earlier comments, saying that it must be acknowledged that some organizations had not been intended to take on certain risks. That was a preliminary problem that needed to be considered regardless of the order in which the various aspects of the topic were tackled. The purposes and budgets of some organizations did not allow them to make provisions for delictual responsibility. In a way, the problem was one of the status of international organizations.

27. Mr. GAJA (Special Rapporteur) asked whether Mr. Brownlie meant that an international organization might be exonerated from any responsibility for a breach of an international obligation by reason of its status.

28. Mr. BROWNLIE said that he was not trying to promote lawlessness, but the Commission was in danger of treating international organizations as if they were just another kind of legal person, even though some of them might have a special quality. In his opinion, there was an intimate link between the nature of an organization and any residual responsibility of member States for risks actually created through that organization, even though its founders had probably never considered making any budgetary provision for responsibility. In short, he thought that the status of some international organizations did not allow them to assume responsibility for significant harm even when they caused it.

29. Mr. MANSFIELD said that it was necessary to proceed on the basis of the agreed definition of international organizations and scope of the draft articles. Such an approach was quite valid from a methodological standpoint, even if it subsequently proved necessary to face up to reality.

30. Mr. KATEKA drew attention to the genocide in Rwanda, which was discussed in paragraph 10 of the report and which had been mentioned by various members, and said that it would be unfortunate if the Commission gave the impression, in its commentary, that it was dealing with abstractions when events of that type had actually taken place. Even if it did not express an opinion on the responsibility of international organizations in such cases, the Commission should not appear to be downplaying the fact that serious crimes could be committed without the intervention of the organization concerned, whether by omission or for any other reason, or to be suggesting that it found that situation normal.

31. Mr. CHEE said that an international organization consisted of individual States, and it was thus quite possible for it to be responsible for a crime that had actually been committed by individuals, or for it to commit delictual acts in the name of a State.

32. Mr. Sreenivasa RAO said that he fully agreed with the point made by Mr. Kateka and was glad that he had raised it. It was not at all a question of exonerating the United Nations from moral responsibility for its failure to intervene during the genocide in Rwanda and thus for having been incapable of fulfilling the mission for which the Organization had been created. Allowing the genocide to take place was a particularly serious failure for an organization that aimed, among other things, to promote and defend human rights. It was simply a question of making a distinction between the moral and legal issues involved.

33. Mr. MATHESON, clarifying his previous statement, said that the Security Council should have taken more forceful action in Rwanda but was under no legal obligation to do so, even though it might be morally responsible.

34. Mr. KOSKENNIEMI said that the two sets of issues considered in the report—the objective element, consisting of the breach of an international obligation, and the breach of an obligation in a context where several actors were involved—had many aspects on which there were few differences of opinion. With regard to the first set of issues, addressed in draft articles 8–11, he said that he had no objection to taking the draft articles on State responsibility as a model, as the similarities between the two topics were self-evident. His only reservation concerned the words "in principle" in draft article 8, paragraph 2, which should be deleted. Paragraphs 18–22 of the report, however, posed a problem. It was not the Commission's task to make judgments on the nature of the rules of an organization. What mattered was the relationship between those rules, regardless of their nature, and the responsibility of the organization under general international law; that question was clearly closely linked to the interaction between *lex specialis* and *lex generalis*. Most of the major international organizations had special rules to deal with a breach of an internal rule, and it was clear that such rules ought to take precedence over the general rules that the Commission was drafting, but that certainly did not mean that general law was set aside. It should

therefore not be implied that special rules constituted a self-contained or entirely separate regime. The Commission should reject Mr. Matheson's proposal to include a general article specifying that the draft articles did not cover the relations between an organization and its member States. Apart from the fact that it would considerably diminish the usefulness of the exercise, as Mr. Pellet had pointed out, such an article would be genuinely dangerous, as it would forcefully reintroduce the notion of the self-contained regime.

35. With regard to the second set of issues and the three situations identified in the draft articles by the Special Rapporteur—those in which the organization provided aid or assistance (art. 12), exercised direction and control (art. 13) or exercised coercion (art. 14)—he agreed with the idea of taking as the criterion for the attribution of responsibility the fact that the organization acted with full knowledge of the facts. However, it was unnecessary to add that the act would be internationally wrongful if committed by the organization. To do so revealed an unconscious analogy with a type of thinking more appropriate to criminal law, which could place too great an emphasis on conduct.

36. He welcomed the fact that the Special Rapporteur intended to look more closely in his fourth report at the relations between the various actors who might incur responsibility.

37. With regard to draft article 16, he endorsed paragraph 1, under which an international organization incurred responsibility if it adopted a binding decision that was implemented by means of a wrongful act by a member State or international organization, but he disagreed with the idea in paragraph 2 that the responsibility of the organization should be treated differently if the entity committing the wrongful act acted either on its recommendation or with its authorization. While it was true that conduct was not the basis for responsibility, it was not appropriate to exonerate the organization in such cases. Organizations had to be taken seriously, and they should be held responsible if they authorized or recommended wrongful acts. Unlike Mr. Matheson, he was not afraid that doing so might prevent organizations from adopting clear-cut positions or taking clear decisions.

38. In his view, all the draft articles could be sent to the Drafting Committee.

39. Mr. DUGARD acknowledged that the Special Rapporteur had a very difficult task, largely because he had to consider the practice of very different international organizations. However, it was unfortunate that he had relied so heavily on the jurisprudence of the European Union, to the detriment of other, less integrated organizations such as the African Union or the Organization of American States, and it was to be hoped that he would redress the balance in his next report.

40. It was quite appropriate to model the draft articles on those on the responsibility of States for internationally wrongful acts, the provisions of which could often be transposed in full into the articles on the responsibility of international organizations. He therefore agreed with the Special Rapporteur's viewpoint on the responsibility of an organization for omissions and disagreed with that of the General Counsel of the IMF on the same subject. In the same way that a State could not hide behind its internal law, an organization could not invoke its internal rules to avoid its international responsibilities. Accordingly, it might be useful to include a provision based on article 3 of the draft articles on the responsibility of States for internationally wrongful acts, according to which the characterization of an act of a State as internationally wrongful was governed by international law and was not affected by the characterization of the same act as lawful by internal law.[2]

41. With regard to the very disturbing example given in paragraph 10 of the report, he agreed with Mr. Kateka that an international organization could not be absolved of all responsibility for failing to intervene in situations like the genocide in Rwanda. It was clearly morally responsible; the question was whether it was legally responsible. He agreed with draft article 8, paragraph 2, but, like Mr. Pellet, who had already said all that needed to be said on the subject, he would prefer to delete the words "in principle". Draft articles 8–11 could be sent to the Drafting Committee, as could draft articles 12–15, which were based on the equivalent articles on State responsibility.

42. With regard to draft article 16, he thought that international organizations should be held responsible for decisions they had taken or acts they had authorized. As the Special Rapporteur had pointed out, paragraph 1 (*b*) was necessary because a wrongful act must have been committed as well as a decision taken. With regard to State responsibility, if a State adopted legislation that violated international law, no internationally wrongful act was committed until effect was given to that legislation. That was the case with the highly controversial Cuban Liberty and Democratic Solidarity Act, or Helms–Burton Act, which allowed United States courts to punish companies that invested in property that had been nationalized in Cuba. The Act had been adopted by the United States Congress but had not been put into effect;[3] the United States could not be held responsible until some effect was given to the Act. In the same way, an international organization could not be held responsible until some effect was given to its decisions. He was therefore in favour of retaining draft article 16, paragraph 1 (*b*). Draft article 16, paragraph 2, referred to the power of international organizations to make recommendations; that was particularly relevant to the United Nations, which issued more authorizations and recommendations than binding decisions. When an international organization acted by way of a recommendation, it often found itself in an area of doubtful legality. For instance, the United Nations could recommend that a State should intervene in order to secure human rights in a particular area and might recommend for that purpose that it should violate a treaty, such as an aviation agreement. That type of situation arose frequently, and the jury was out on whether such recommendations were lawful, given that they certainly did not have the same weight as decisions taken by the Security Council under Article 103

[2] *Yearbook ... 2001*, vol. II (Part Two) and corrigendum, pp. 36–38.

[3] "Cuban Liberty and Democratic Solidarity (LIBERTAD) Act" (Helms-Burton Act), *ILM*, vol. XXXV, No. 2 (March 1996), p. 359.

of the Charter of the United Nations. The General Assembly and, to some extent, the Security Council, frequently engaged in such "unlawful" conduct, and it would be wrong to try to discourage them from doing so. At the same time, it would be wrong to hold States alone responsible for actions taken in pursuance of such recommendations, as that might discourage States from acting upon them in the future. In such circumstances, then, international organizations ought to be held responsible and States should have secondary or residual responsibility.

43. Lastly, with regard to draft article 16, paragraph 2 (*a*), he tended to agree with Mr. Matheson that it was difficult to imagine a situation in which an international organization would adopt a recommendation that ran counter to its own interests. A trade embargo recommended by the General Assembly might result in a violation of treaty obligations yet still clearly further the general interests of the United Nations in maintaining international peace and security, promoting human rights or protecting the environment. The paragraph might therefore be considered superfluous, although it was not quite clear whether the Special Rapporteur's intention had been to require that the act committed by the organization should be *intra vires*; that would not be the correct approach in any case, and did not necessarily follow from the paragraph in question. Particular attention should therefore be paid to that phrase. Nevertheless, he was in favour of sending draft article 16 to the Drafting Committee, together with the rest of the draft articles submitted by the Special Rapporteur.

44. Ms. ESCARAMEIA observed that the Special Rapporteur dealt with two issues, namely the breach of an international obligation by an international organization and the responsibility of an international organization in connection with the act of a member State or another international organization. She agreed with Mr. Yamada that it would be useful to draft two separate documents, modelled on the reports on State responsibility. Three issues arose in connection with the breach of international law by an international organization, as covered in draft articles 8–11, and State responsibility, as covered in draft articles 12–15: (*a*) the first concerned omissions and due legal process; (*b*) the second concerned the European Union, when the implementation of treaties it had concluded with third States was left to its member States, as was often the case; and (*c*) the third concerned the rules of the organization—an issue that was closely linked to the European Union issue and that had given rise to some confusion, which the Special Rapporteur would no doubt be able to dispel. With regard to the first issue, the Special Rapporteur believed that, despite the objections raised by some international organizations, the internal procedures of a State were the same as those of an international organization, and there was therefore no need to make any distinction between them. There was a need for further reflection on that question, since, in a normal international organization, States were not organs of the organization; moreover, in a domestic setting, States often had more power over their organs than an international organization had over its member States. States should not be allowed to evade their responsibility by shifting it to an international organization. States were also subject to international law and could not be allowed to breach their obligations and allow an international organization to take responsibility in their stead.

45. With regard to the European Union and the implementation of treaties by its member States, the most appropriate working hypothesis would be to consider member States as necessary organs at the permanent disposal of the European Union for the purpose of implementing treaties. The European Union could not in any case avoid that, or fully control its member States. Perhaps a special article should be devoted to regional integration organizations. In any case, draft article 4, paragraphs 1 and 3, which had already been provisionally adopted by the Commission in 2004,[4] should apply, as they dealt with the organs of an organization that were implementing the organization's policy or assuming its obligations. To establish the parallel, an article stipulating that draft article 4 was applicable to regional integration organizations should be included.

46. The discussions to determine whether the rules of an organization fell under internal or international law or some other type of law seemed closely bound up with European law, but she could not bring herself to consider the enormous body of Community law as "rules of the organization" and even doubted whether it would fit the definition in article 2, paragraph 1 (j), of the 1986 Vienna Convention. The European Union did not constitute a good example of what draft article 8, paragraph 2, was probably trying to say. Although other opinions had already been expressed on that question, it seemed to her that whenever an organization had an obligation towards a third State, that obligation was governed by international law, not by the rules of the organization, unless those rules were so important that the organization had lost control of the way in which its international obligations were met; she would appreciate some clarification on that point from the Special Rapporteur. She also had a problem with the phrase "in principle" in draft article 8, paragraph 2, and thought that the paragraph should be redrafted or even deleted.

47. With regard to the responsibility of an international organization in connection with the act of a State or another organization, she still did not see why the title of draft article 13 should speak of "direction and control exercised over the commission of an internationally wrongful act" rather than "direction or control", as either one or the other would suffice. Thus, in the example given by the Special Rapporteur in paragraph 28 of his report, the fact that neither NATO nor the United Nations had exercised both direction and control of the international security force in Kosovo (KFOR) at the same time did not mean that neither of them bore responsibility. Similarly, it should be specified whether responsibility arose at the time of the act of direction or control or at the time of the commission of the unlawful act, and whether the unlawful act really had to have been committed; she did not think it did.

48. Perhaps draft article 15, the "without prejudice" clause, should not refer to draft article 14, on coercion,

[4] See 2839th meeting, footnote 16.

but should consider other types of responsibility, such as joint, separate, proportional or residual responsibility.

49. Turning to draft article 16, she said that decisions, recommendations and authorizations were not the same thing—decisions were more binding—and that distinctions should probably be made between them. Paragraph 1 seemed to duplicate draft article 13, which dealt with the same situation, though it did not require that the act should be committed. For responsibility to be incurred, it seemed sufficient for a decision that was binding on a State to be taken, even if no act was committed. As for paragraph 2, an international organization should be held responsible for authorizing or recommending the commission of an unlawful act, even if the act did not directly further its interests, as the organization was in some ways the co-author of the act. Like many other members of the Commission, she could not accept the current wording; as anything could be in the organization's interest, it should at least be specified that the interest in question was a direct interest. Generally speaking, international organizations should be held responsible for what they did. In conclusion, she was in favour of sending all the draft articles to the Drafting Committee.

50. Mr. MANSFIELD agreed with the general approach to the topic taken by the Special Rapporteur, particularly the idea of following the articles on State responsibility where there was no reason to depart from them. On the general issue of omissions, discussed in paragraphs 8–10 of the report, he agreed with the Special Rapporteur's analysis that, where an international organization had an obligation to act under international law, it could not excuse its failure to act by pointing to difficulties in the decision-making process, since States, too, sometimes faced comparable difficulties in their legislative and other bodies. He also thought that it was unnecessary to list in the draft articles the different types of obligations discussed in paragraphs 13 and 14 of the report. As to the question of whether the rules of an international organization were part of international law, the answer was surely yes, even though that was not the case for certain rules in certain organizations; however, that did not necessarily mean that the issue needed to be addressed directly in the draft articles. Besides the fact that it seemed superfluous, as the Special Rapporteur noted in paragraph 22, to say that the breach of an international obligation might concern an obligation set by the rules of the organization, draft article 8, paragraph 1, actually referred only to the breach of an international obligation by an international organization. If an obligation arising under the rules of the organization was not a rule of international law, it was not covered. That raised the question of whether paragraph 2 of the draft article was necessary and whether the issue could be dealt with in the commentary; if not, paragraph 2 should be redrafted to clarify the meaning. In any case, since he, like others, had a real problem with the inclusion of the phrase "in principle", he would prefer to have the paragraph deleted.

51. With regard to the question of the responsibility of an international organization for aiding, directing, controlling or coercing a State or another international organization in the commission of an internationally wrongful act (draft articles 12–15), the Special Rapporteur had clearly shown that in those complex areas the nature of the decision taken by the international organization, in terms of whether it was binding on member States or whether the latter had room for manoeuvring to avoid breaching an international obligation, was decisive. In many cases, the criterion set out in paragraph 31, namely whether the organization's decision was not only binding but also actually required the commission of the wrongful act, seemed to be the key. However, that criterion would be difficult to apply in some circumstances and in any event did not solve one potentially serious problem to which the Special Rapporteur had drawn attention, which was a situation where an international organization that was bound by a particular obligation used its power to compel member States that were not bound by that obligation to allow it to circumvent that obligation. The arguments put forward for including draft article 16 in order to deal with such a situation were persuasive (paras. 32–33 of the report), but the current wording of the draft article was not entirely satisfactory. If, as Mr. Pellet had suggested, paragraph 1 (*b*) was omitted, draft article 13 would become redundant, as draft article 16 would have the same effect as that article, though without the additional requirement that the organization concerned must have acted with knowledge of the circumstances of the internationally wrongful act.

52. The case dealt with in draft article 16, paragraph 2, was generally more complex, but the requirement set out in subparagraph (*b*), that responsibility arose only when the act was committed, seemed even more difficult to justify in that situation. If responsibility was to be incurred, it was because the international organization was seeking to circumvent its obligation by authorizing, although not compelling, a member State to commit the act in question. In the case in point, it was hard to see why the responsibility of the international organization should be dependent on whether or not the member State exercised its discretion and committed the act. Subparagraph (*a*), on the other hand, was necessary, even though it should perhaps be redrafted. There was certainly an advantage in making it apparent in the draft articles that international organizations needed to be aware that their member States might have wide-ranging international obligations and that the organization should be careful not to encourage, or require, them to act in contravention of those or other related obligations.

53. He hoped that the Special Rapporteur would clarify the thinking that had led him to draft the article in its current form, and he wondered whether it might not be necessary to seek the assistance of the legal counsel of an international organization in order to consider the different ways in which the article might be redrafted.

The meeting rose at 12.48 p.m.

2842nd MEETING

Friday, 20 May 2005, at 10.05 a.m.

Chairperson: Mr. Djamchid MOMTAZ

Later: Mr. Guillaume PAMBOU-TCHIVOUNDA

Present: Mr. Addo, Mr. Al-Marri, Mr. Baena Soares, Mr. Candioti, Mr. Chee, Mr. Comissário Afonso, Mr. Dugard, Mr. Economides, Ms. Escarameia, Mr. Fomba, Mr. Gaja, Mr. Galicki, Mr. Kabatsi, Mr. Kateka, Mr. Kolodkin, Mr. Mansfield, Mr. Niehaus, Mr. Pellet, Mr. Sreenivasa Rao, Mr. Rodríguez Cedeño, Mr. Yamada.

Responsibility of international organizations (*continued*) (A/CN.4/549 and Add.1, sect. A, A/CN.4/547, A/CN.4/553, A/CN.4/556, A/CN.4/L.666/Rev.1)

[Agenda item 3]

THIRD REPORT OF THE SPECIAL RAPPORTEUR (*continued*)

1. Mr. ECONOMIDES said he agreed with the general approach taken by the Special Rapporteur in basing his third report on the articles on responsibility of States for internationally wrongful acts,[1] which the draft articles on the responsibility of international organizations should follow as closely as possible.

2. With regard to the question raised by the General Counsel of the IMF in paragraph 8 of the report, whether the organization could be held responsible for not taking action if its non-action was the result of the lawful exercise of their powers by its member States, he fully agreed with the Special Rapporteur that omissions were clearly wrongful when an international organization was required to take some positive action and failed to do so. On the question whether the United Nations could be held responsible if, in a case of armed aggression, the Security Council did not take the measures necessary to maintain international peace and security, in accordance with Article 51 of the Charter of the United Nations, he believed that even if the Security Council was prevented from acting as a result of the exercise of its veto by a permanent member, the United Nations would still be responsible towards the State or States that were the victims of the armed aggression, as the right of veto did not constitute a circumstance that precluded wrongfulness within the meaning of chapter V of the articles on responsibility of States and under general international law. In that connection, he endorsed the spirit of Mr. Kateka's comments on the example of the genocide in Rwanda given in paragraph 10 of the report (see the 2841st meeting, above, para. 30).

3. The Commission should study more closely whether responsibility arising as a result of a binding decision of an organization, especially a regional integration organization such as the European Community, lay exclusively with the organization rather than with the members required to implement it. He found the view expressed by the European Union in paragraph 12 of the report reasonable and legally sound. In the case of an obligation to implement a binding decision of the organization, the State's action should be directly attributed to the organization by means of a special provision on attribution of responsibility, which could be added to draft article 4.

4. With regard to rules of the organization, he fully agreed with the comments made by Mr. Pellet (see the 2840th meeting, above, paras. 42–52). Such rules, whether or not they dealt with the internal workings of the organization, were automatically part of international law as they were dependent on the international treaty constituting the organization. He did not believe that rules of the organization, including those of the European Union, could be considered as not being part of international law: there was as yet no intermediate law between international law and the internal law of States, at least as traditionally understood.

5. Draft article 8, paragraph 2, with the words "in principle", would be hard to accept. In his view, the words "regardless of its origin and character", in paragraph 1 of that article, covered all international obligations, including those flowing from the rules of the organization. In the current state of the law, draft article 8, paragraph 2, was therefore redundant and should be deleted.

6. He noted that draft article 15, on the effect of the preceding articles, did not appear to be identical to article 19 of the draft articles on the responsibility of States for internationally wrongful acts, which had a wider scope.[2]

7. He agreed with the Special Rapporteur that the draft articles already provisionally adopted should be reviewed before the end of the first reading. In that context, draft article 16, paragraph 1, on unlawful binding decisions, should be addressed within the framework of draft article 4, on the general rule on attribution of conduct to an international organization. In draft article 16, paragraph 2, a distinction should be made between an authorization that implied a competence of the organization and a recommendation that left the State some choice in the matter, if not complete freedom of action. In the case of an authorization, the international organization and the State taking action should incur shared responsibility, whereas, in the case of a recommendation, the State committing the act should incur principal, if not sole, responsibility.

8. In conclusion, he considered that all the draft articles under consideration, with the exception of article 8, paragraph 2, which should be deleted, and draft article 16, which needed further work, could be referred to the Drafting Committee.

9. Mr. FOMBA said that the key issue in approaching the responsibility of international organizations was to decide how to interpret the relations between States and international organizations in their capacity as primary and secondary subjects of international law. At the heart of that issue lay the question of the link between international

---

[1] *Yearbook ... 2001*, vol. II (Part Two) and corrigendum, para. 76.

[2] *Ibid.*, p. 27.

legal personality and the international responsibility to which such personality gave rise. While the responsibility of States for internationally wrongful acts had already been elucidated by the Commission, the very concepts of the "international organization" and its "responsibility" were still controversial subjects in legal doctrine, and practice shed little light on them. It was therefore essential to carry out a comprehensive, in-depth comparison of States and international organizations in order to determine the characteristics of the latter. The first step was to establish whether the international organization had its own legal personality and its own will, and, if so, how they differed from those of its member States. In that connection, he drew attention to the 1995 resolution of the Institute of International Law on the legal consequences for member States of the non-fulfilment by international organizations of their obligations toward third parties, article 1 of which stated that the resolution dealt with issues arising in the case of "an international organization possessing an international legal personality distinct from that of its members".[3] The next step was to identify the various possible instrumental consequences of the responsibility of international organizations. The possibilities could be categorized according to whether they concerned the international organization itself, the international organization and its members, the international organization and third States, the international organization and other international organizations, member States alone, member States and third States, or member States and other international organizations. Such an analysis revealed the existence of two broad categories of responsibility: exclusive responsibility and "shared" responsibility. In that connection, it should be noted that related terms such as "joint", "joint and several" or "solidary" derived from national legal systems needed to be used with care in the context of international law, as had been pointed out by the Special Rapporteur on State responsibility, Mr. Crawford, in his second report.[4] Once the theoretical framework had been established, the practice of international organizations and States should be studied, to see if it was necessary or possible to propose new legal rules on the subject. At that point, and on the basis of the Special Rapporteur's proposals, the Commission would be in a position to ensure that the draft articles were both relevant and appropriate.

10. He agreed with the suggestion in paragraph 1 of the report that the draft articles that had already been provisionally adopted in 2003 and 2004 should be reconsidered by the Commission before the end of the first reading in the light of comments made by States and international organizations, especially as there was little in the way of practice or new material to guide the Commission. He also agreed that the draft articles should follow the general pattern of the articles on responsibility of States for internationally wrongful acts—an approach which did not exclude replicating those articles *mutatis mutandis*.

11. He commended the Special Rapporteur's approach to the question of a breach of an international obligation on the part of an international organization, which involved taking the articles on responsibility of States as the starting point, examining them to see if and how they could be adjusted to be applicable to international organizations, and then analysing the questions raised, including wrongful acts consisting of an omission, difficulties with compliance due to the political decision-making process, and breaches of obligations by international organizations under a rule of general international law. He was especially interested in the last point, for which the Special Rapporteur had given as an example in paragraph 10 of his report the failure of the United Nations to prevent the genocide in Rwanda. While a member of the Commission of Experts established pursuant to Security Council resolution 935 (1994) of 1 July 1994, with a view to examining violations of international humanitarian law committed in Rwanda, he had been approached informally by Rwandans and Burundians with questions about the responsibility of France and the United Nations. He had drawn their attention to the obligation of the Contracting Parties to the Convention on the Prevention and Punishment of the Crime of Genocide to prevent genocide (art. I), the possibility of calling on the competent organs of the United Nations to take such action under the Charter of the United Nations as they considered appropriate for the prevention of acts of genocide (art. VIII), and the obligation to submit disputes relating to the interpretation, application or fulfilment of the Convention, including those relating to the responsibility of a State for genocide, to the ICJ at the request of any of the parties to the dispute (art. IX). He had concluded that, if all the necessary conditions were met, some form of legal proceedings could be envisaged.

12. With regard to organizations such as the European Union that were empowered to conclude with non-member States treaties whose implementation was left to authorities of member States, two types of rules governed such organizations. One consisted of primary law (*droit primaire*), which was part of traditional international law, and the other of secondary law (*droit dérivé*), which was not, as it was based on the primacy of Community law over members' internal law and took immediate effect in members' domestic legal systems. It was not clear whether, and if so, to what extent, the attribution of conduct and responsibility should be the same for the two types of rules.

13. On the question of the definition and legal nature of the rules of the organization, he agreed with the Special Rapporteur that a distinction needed to be made between rules that had the character of rules of international law and those of which that was no longer true, and that the draft articles should also include a proviso for the existence of special rules, or perhaps a general final provision.

14. On the whole, the Special Rapporteur set out those substantive questions very ably, even though his arguments were not always clear to the reader. He himself had as yet reached no fixed conclusions on the main points of contention.

15. Draft articles 8 to 11 followed closely the articles on responsibility of the State and posed no particular problem, except for draft article 8, paragraph 2, which dealt

[3] See *Yearbook of the Institute of International Law*, vol. 66-II (1996), p. 444, at p. 445.

[4] *Yearbook ... 1999*, vol. II (Part One), document A/CN.4/498 and Add.1–4, pp. 45–46, para. 161 (*a*).

with a matter that did not arise in the case of States. The paragraph raised two questions: the first was whether it was necessary to take a formal position regarding the nature of a rule of the organization as compared to international law; the second was whether a breach of an obligation set by a rule of the organization should be treated in the same way as a breach of an international obligation. The retention of the qualifier "in principle" would suggest that the two types of rule and the obligation arising thereunder were considered as being on an equal footing. He therefore saw three options: if the two types of obligation were regarded as equal in terms of their nature, regime and treatment, the words "in principle" should simply be deleted; or, if that assumption was not made, the whole of paragraph 2 should be deleted; or else those two options could be combined, accepting that there was no need to deal separately with an obligation set by a rule of the organization and explaining in the commentary that such an obligation was already covered by the phrase "regardless of its origin and character" in paragraph 1. While he had no clear preference for any one of those options, he tended to think it would be better to retain a reworded paragraph 2, or else, if that posed insurmountable difficulties, to rely on an explanation in the commentary, in which case paragraph 2 could be deleted.

16. With regard to the responsibility of an international organization in connection with the act of a State or another organization, he agreed with the idea of applying the scheme devised for States to international organizations (para. 26). He also agreed that a distinction should be made between cases involving binding decisions and those involving authorizations or recommendations, as discussed in paragraph 30 *et seq.* On the question of the amount of assistance and the ensuing degree of responsibility (para. 43), he agreed that the degree of responsibility concerned the content of responsibility but not its existence, and that the question should be examined at a later stage. He also agreed that, in addition to the four draft articles 12 to 15 corresponding to articles 16 to 19 on State responsibility, a further article was needed to cover cases in which responsibility of an international organization was involved because it would otherwise circumvent an international obligation by requesting member States to take a certain conduct which the organization would be forbidden to take directly.

17. He had no particular problem with draft articles 12 to 15. Draft article 16, however, had elicited many comments, and appeared to need further consideration. While there seemed to be general agreement on the distinction between binding decisions, on the one hand, and recommendations and authorizations, on the other, there appeared to be none on the general mechanism to be proposed for formulating and implementing the responsibility of the international organization in respect of those two categories of acts. For example, it was not entirely clear if the international organization should bear exclusive responsibility, or whether it should be shared by the organization and its members, and there was no agreement on the very concept of the wrongful act. The case cited by Mr. Pellet could be taken by way of illustration: did the fact that a State had adopted legislation contrary to international law suffice for it to incur responsibility, or must the law enter into force and actually be applied? (See the 2840th meeting, above, paras. 54–56.)

18. The specific options available to the Commission were either not to refer draft article 16 to the Drafting Committee, or to request the Special Rapporteur to revise the draft article on the basis of the discussion or to set up a working group to elucidate the substantive issues concerning that article. Subject to the Special Rapporteur's approval, his own preference was for the third option. However, draft articles 8 to 11 and 12 to 15 could be referred to the Drafting Committee.

19. The CHAIRPERSON, speaking as a member of the Commission, said that a number of speakers had raised an issue that troubled him, namely, the obligations of the Security Council regarding threats to the peace, breaches of the peace and acts of aggression. The Charter did not define any of those three situations, but the practice of the Security Council in recent decades revealed that it had very broad discretionary powers to identify them. For the Security Council to have obligations in such situations, there had to be a specific rule. In the absence of a definition, did the obligation exist? If not, could one say that the Security Council bore responsibility for failure to discharge its duties, and that that omission entailed the responsibility of the United Nations?

20. Mr. PAMBOU-TCHIVOUNDA said that the Chairperson was not alone in being troubled by that issue. In view of the lack of definitions of the three broad concepts mentioned, he wondered whether the bringing of a dispute before the ICJ might shed some light on the matter.

21. The CHAIRPERSON noted that Mr. Pambou-Tchivounda had raised another troubling issue, namely, jurisdictional control by the ICJ over the acts of the Security Council.

22. Mr. CHEE recalled that on 14 December 1974 the General Assembly had adopted resolution 3314 (XXIX), "Definition of Aggression". That definition, however, had never been put to effective use. The best course of action was for States and the Security Council to treat cases on a case-by-case basis.

23. Mr. GAJA (Special Rapporteur) said that the question was whether an international organization such as the United Nations might be under an obligation, and whether the failure to comply with this obligation would cause it to incur responsibility. The fact that the rules of an organization did not provide the means for complying with an obligation was not decisive. The Commission had not yet dealt with circumstances precluding wrongfulness; that subject would be addressed at its next session. However, he found it hard to imagine that an organization could invoke its own rules in order to justify a breach. The Commission was not really concerned with the internal machinery of the United Nations or with the question whether, under Articles 39 *et seq.*, the Security Council had an obligation to respond to an act of aggression. The Commission was working on the basis of the hypothesis that the organization had an obligation, and while there

might be difficulties with compliance, the mere fact of the existence of rules that did not facilitate compliance was not relevant to the discussion at the present stage.

24. Mr. ECONOMIDES endorsed the Special Rapporteur's remarks. The Security Council was an organ of the United Nations and, like all such organs, was bound by its constituent instrument. The Charter was an international treaty, and the primary responsibility of the Security Council was thus to respect the obligations set out therein. If those obligations were breached, the United Nations must incur responsibility for any act of omission.

25. Turning to the question raised by the Chairperson, he said that while the pivotal terms in the Charter were not defined, one crucial element was that aggression must always take the form of armed aggression. There was also the General Assembly resolution 3314 (XXIX) with the extremely useful Definition of Aggression. The characteristics of armed conflict were thus fairly well known. The characteristics of self-defence were also well known, since it was the diametrical opposite of aggression. The only thing that remained unresolved was what constituted a threat to the peace, a concept that had recently been extended, generally in the right direction, by the practice of the Security Council. Collective security had become such a crucial issue of international law that he had once proposed that the Commission should look into the law of collective security. That proposal had not been taken up, however.[5] In any event the Charter already provided enough material to enable individual situations to be dealt with on a case-by-case basis, as Mr. Chee had pointed out.

26. Mr. GALICKI said the problem raised by the Chairperson was highlighted in draft article 10, paragraph 3, on the breach of an international obligation requiring an international organization to prevent a given event. The Charter placed an obligation on the Security Council to take measures that would prevent an event that constituted a threat to the peace from occurring. Theoretically that was a very simple matter, but there was no binding definition or description in the Charter of the concept of a threat to the peace. In practice, the Security Council itself had first to establish whether a situation could be so described. If it found that there was a threat to the peace, it then had an obligation to react. It was not clear, however, to what extent the Security Council had an obligation actually to establish the existence of a threat to the peace. Was that connected to its primary obligation to react to a threat to peace, or was it a separate obligation not directly assigned to it? The provisions of the Charter were not exhaustive and did not specify how the Security Council should operate. In situations where the Security Council had failed to react, other solutions had been sought, as in the case of General Assembly resolution 377 (V) of 3 November 1950, on "Uniting for peace". The Commission should consider to what extent an organization was bound by an international obligation when the description of the obligation was not exhaustive or did not clearly indicate that it should react. The case covered by draft article 10, paragraph 3, of an obligation to prevent an event from occurring, needed to be given particular consideration, since the legal basis for that obligation of prevention remained obscure, especially as it applied to the Security Council.

27. The CHAIRPERSON, speaking as a member of the Commission, said that while the Security Council had primary responsibility for the maintenance of international peace and security, it had sometimes decided that identifying a given State as an aggressor would not facilitate the discharge of that primary responsibility, and might indeed be counterproductive.

28. Mr. PELLET said that the somewhat emotive question raised by the Chairperson had reduced the discussion to the rather narrow question whether the Security Council could trigger the responsibility of the United Nations, given that the concepts of aggression and threat to the peace were not clearly defined. A much more interesting general issue was what happened when there was no general agreement as to the scope of international obligations. The Commission's work both on State responsibility and on the responsibility of international organizations showed that there were indeed such international obligations but it did not pinpoint the circumstances in which a breach of those obligations occurred. That determination had to be made on a case-by-case basis.

29. Could a problem of that type be brought before the ICJ? That certainly could and should happen, although States rarely seized the Court of such matters. It was also possible for an organization to request an advisory opinion. In the latter case, the Court might well say that given the lack of precision surrounding the concept of aggression, it was not in a position to rule on the matter. Such a finding was not very laudable, but had already been made, for example in the *Legality of Use of Force* cases, and, in the context of an advisory opinion, seemed not unreasonable. On the other hand, it was also perfectly feasible for a contentious case to be brought before the Court. Bosnia and Herzegovina had envisaged bringing a case against the United Kingdom for having failed to veto the resolution imposing an arms embargo on the States that had emerged from the former Yugoslavia. If it had done so, the Court would have had to address the question of whether it was the United Nations that bore responsibility, or its Members, particularly those that could have prevented the adoption of the resolution by using their veto. As counsel to Bosnia and Herzegovina, he had dissuaded it from engaging in a fascinating academic exercise which, nevertheless, had seemed unlikely to lead to any practical results. In such a situation, however, the Court would not be able to shirk its duties and would have to reply on the basis of the circumstances of the case.

30. What form would that response take? Surely not an abstract definition of aggression, but rather, a finding that in the specific instance, the organization had or had not failed to discharge its duties, either by omission or by commission. It seemed clear that as the Security Council was an organ of an international organization, it did not really represent a special case. Other than for the intellectual pleasure some derived from berating the Security Council, there seemed little to be gained from discussing

[5] See *Yearbook ... 1999*, vol. I, 2575th meeting, p. 56, para. 3, and 2610th meeting, p. 313, para. 61.

whether obligations existed in the absence of rules. What was more interesting was what happened when a rule was vague. General Assembly resolution 3314 (XXIX) did not give an operational definition of aggression and in any case amounted to nothing in that it concluded by saying that the Security Council could characterize aggression as it saw fit.

31. On the substance of the Chairperson's question, he had the feeling that the Security Council probably had an obligation of conduct, although Article 24 of the Charter was quite vague, speaking of the "discharge" of duties (para. 2). One might thus conclude that the primary responsibility of the Security Council was to fulfil its duty. The word "duty", however, as distinct from "obligation", had connotations that were less legal than political. Could one say that the Security Council had an "obligation" to act in the legal sense of the term, even in a situation that was obviously one of aggression? Articles 41 and 42 of the Charter were couched in very soft legal language, providing that the Security Council "may decide", "should" it consider … . The Security Council's discretionary powers thus seemed fairly broad from the legal standpoint. He therefore doubted whether one could say that the Security Council had a legal obligation to act with respect to threats to the peace, breaches of the peace or acts of aggression. However, he had no doubt whatsoever that it had a political responsibility to do so. The *travaux préparatoires* for the Charter clearly showed that the five permanent members, especially the United States and the Soviet Union, had sought to retain the possibility of preventing the Security Council from acting and had considered that there was no legal obligation in such situations. Thus, before involving itself with the definition of aggression and threats to and breaches of the peace, the Commission had first to establish whether the Security Council had an obligation to act, something he was very far from ready to concede.

32. With regard to Rwanda, he was of the view that the responsibility of the United Nations was incurred to a certain degree, which had to be determined, along with that of the responsibility of certain States, in particular Belgium and France, but not because of the Security Council's failure to act—after all, it was under no absolute obligation to do so. In any case, it was not clear whether there had been a threat to the peace, strictly speaking, in Rwanda. Nonetheless, responsibility was incurred for other reasons, which had to do more with the hasty withdrawal of the small peacekeeping force and other similar actions.

33. Mr. Sreenivasa RAO said that the Special Rapporteur's approach was to develop the topic within limited confines that could not be extended to include other issues, regardless of how urgent, important or tempting they might be. That said, he agreed with Mr. Pellet that the Security Council was a political organ, and General Assembly resolution 3314 (XXIX), on Definition of Aggression, was only an aid, even though some had argued that it should be more than that. The Security Council could find that an act of aggression had taken place, or it could remain silent if it saw fit. Thus, the parties could be forced, by use of the veto, not to resort to armed force, but to use persuasion and other means to deal with an act of aggression. Use of the veto did not mean that a particular crisis could simply be ignored, but that there was no consensus in the Security Council to deal with it by armed force, and that any State which decided to take unilateral action did so at its own risk.

34. Mr. CHEE said that Mr. Pellet appeared to be claiming that the Security Council operated in isolation; however, Articles 24 and 25 of the Charter made it clear that it could not simply do as it liked. Article 24, paragraph 2, limited its power. The Commission should not condemn acts of omission by the Security Council: under Article 24, paragraph 1, Member States agreed that in carrying out its duties the Security Council acted on their behalf; and under Article 25 they agreed to carry out its decisions.

35. With regard to Mr. Galicki's remark on the question of a threat to the peace, he recalled that the draft code of crimes against the peace and security of mankind, as adopted on first reading, had contained the crime of "the threat of aggression".[6] On second reading, that crime had been eliminated, supposedly because the concept was too vague,[7] although it had to be said that there was nothing vague about a situation in which 700,000 troops were massed on a country's borders and thousands of pieces of artillery were pointed in its direction. In the fourth edition of his International Law, Malcolm Shaw made the point that modern technology had evolved to a stage at which threats to the peace were visible and easy to identify.[8]

36. Mr. ECONOMIDES said that the Special Rapporteur had more or less settled the problem by saying that omissions were illegal when the international organization was bound to act but failed to do so. That applied to all international organizations, including the United Nations. If an obligation existed and was not complied with, the omission was illegal and the organization was responsible.

37. On Mr. Pellet's comments he said that in his view "duty" and "obligation" were synonymous. Even if one accepted—which he did not—that "duty" had a connotation slightly weaker than that of "obligation", duty denoted an obligation. He could not accept the proposition that "duty" was a political term with no legal connotation. Although the Charter conferred discretionary powers on the Security Council in many areas, a number of its provisions required it to take immediate action, for example with regard to the right of self-defence, in connection with which the Security Council was clearly and unambiguously required to take measures necessary to maintain international peace and security. Thus, in certain cases the Security Council had considerable leeway, whereas in others it must decide in a manner specified. He therefore disagreed with the assertion that the Charter did

[6] See *Yearbook … 1991*, vol. II (Part Two), chap. IV, p. 96, article 16. For the first version of the text, see *Yearbook … 1989*, vol. II (Part Two), chap. II, p. 68, article 13.

[7] See *Yearbook … 1995*, vol. II (Part Two), p. 22, para. 74; *ibid.*, vol. I, 2380th–2382nd meetings, pp. 10–26, *passim*. For the draft articles and related commentary adopted by the Commission, see *Yearbook … 1996*, vol. II (Part Two), para. 50, pp. 17–56.

[8] M. Shaw, *International Law*, 4th ed., Cambridge University Press, 1997.

not lay down legal obligations which must be carried out by the organs responsible for those obligations.

38. Mr. MANSFIELD said that the debate seemed to have strayed from the point. He had not heard anyone argue that a clear obligation under international law for an international organization to take a certain course of action could be disregarded. In other words, omission could entail responsibility, and difficulties in the decision-making process were no excuse for failing to take action. That was the essential point, and it applied to all international organizations, including the Security Council. However, it was not the Commission's task to discuss whether there was a clear obligation under international law for all organizations to take action in every conceivable circumstance. As far as the Security Council and indeed any other international organization were concerned, that would hinge largely on the specific case and an interpretation of the facts as they related to the role of the body in question. In the case of the Security Council, that involved consideration of its important political responsibilities. The general proposition was thus clear, and although it was doubtless interesting to discuss the question with regard to particular international organizations, such a course would not get the Commission very far.

39. Mr. PELLET said he was surprised at the categorical positions taken by some members, particularly Mr. Economides. The Security Council clearly had obligations, which should be considered in the light of the means at its disposal. The permanent members of the Security Council had a right of veto, and it was not reasonable to interpret its legal obligations without taking that fact into account. Mr. Economides had peremptorily asserted that there was at least one case in which the Security Council had an obligation to act, but he had chosen the worst possible example, namely Article 51, pursuant to which States had a right of self-defence "until the Security Council has taken measures necessary to maintain international peace and security". Article 51 thus clearly provided for the case in which the Security Council did not take action, and he did not see how it could be said that the provision was proof that the Security Council was required to act. In fact, the last sentence of Article 51 gave the Security Council broad discretionary powers, because it provided that measures taken by Members in the exercise of the right of self-defence must be immediately reported to the Security Council, which was authorized "to take at any time such action as it deems necessary in order to maintain or restore international peace and security".

40. With regard to a comment by Mr. Chee and the more general problem of Article 24, on a number of occasions the ICJ had noted that the Security Council had only primary responsibility and had not excluded the possibility of action being taken by other bodies, in particular the General Assembly. *A contrario*, he concluded that the failure of the Security Council to take action did not automatically entail its legal responsibility, irrespective of the circumstances. He was not sure that the notion of primary responsibility was a legal one, but in any case, the Organization had a global responsibility. If the aim was for the Organization to incur responsibility, then the Commission must decide whether the General Assembly was bound to step in when the Security Council did not fulfil its primary obligation: otherwise, the word "primary" was meaningless. Although he did not have any particular affection for the Security Council, it was an easy target for those given to righteous indignation; unfortunately international relations were more complicated than that.

Mr. Pambou-Tchivounda (Vice-Chairperson) took the Chair.

41. Mr. KABATSI commended the Special Rapporteur's third report, which enabled the Commission to continue making significant and rapid progress on the topic. Articles 8 to 11 had been closely modelled on four similar provisions in the draft articles on responsibility of States for internationally wrongful acts, an approach he fully supported. There was no need to reinvent the wheel if the available wheel did the job. Those articles were ready for referral to the Drafting Committee.

42. The Special Rapporteur was correct in saying that the wrongful act of an international organization might consist in an action or in an omission, that omissions were wrongful when an international organization was required to take some positive action and failed to do so (paragraph 8 of the report), and that internal constraints on an international organization which might result in a breach of its international obligations should not absolve it from responsibility for the breach. As had been pointed out by a number of members, States might sometimes try to evade responsibility by shifting their obligations to international organizations which they had put in place for that purpose. It would be unfortunate if those organizations were allowed to shirk their responsibility by claiming that they had been unable to comply with their international obligations owing to difficulties in their internal decision-making process. Such dangerous gaps should not be allowed to exist even as a matter of positive international public policy. As to the question posed by the General Counsel of the IMF and cited in paragraph 8 of the report, as to whether an organization would be responsible for not taking action, if that non-action was the result of the lawful exercise of their powers by its member States, the answer was an emphatic yes.

43. Given that the Organization had been formed on the basis of a determination to save succeeding generations from the scourge of war, which had brought untold sorrow to mankind, and that its universal membership at its making had reaffirmed its faith in the dignity and worth of the human person, there could hardly be any question that the United Nations was obliged, as a rule of general international law and where the evidence was available, to prevent genocide. The Convention on the Prevention and Punishment of the Crime of Genocide had not introduced that obligation, but had codified it as a rule of general international law that had already existed as such. The failure to stop the genocide in Rwanda could not be attributed to ignorance of the fact that it had been happening. As recent events in Rwanda and the Balkans had shown, omissions could be as bad as, if not worse than, acts of commission in terms of negative consequences. For that reason, he would have favoured inclusion of the

word "omission", as an extension of "act", in article 8 paragraph 1, but for the fact that the corresponding provision in the draft articles on State responsibility did not do so. He hoped that the commentary to the article would expand on that issue. He also supported the deletion of the words "in principle" in article 8, paragraph 2.

44. Draft articles 12 to 16 presented no problems and could also be referred to the Drafting Committee, which should be able to take into account all the comments made on article 16 and bring it more closely into line with article 13.

45. Mr. CHEE, referring to wrongful omissions on the part of an international organization and of a State, said that an international organization, while a subject of international law, did not operate on the same plane as a State in relation to international law, as had been noted by the ICJ in the 1949 *Reparation for Injuries* case. Further clarification was needed of the meaning of the words "in principle", in draft article 8, paragraph 2. Draft articles 9 to 11 posed no problems. Draft articles 12 and 13 dealt respectively with the cases of an international organization which aided or assisted in the commission of an internationally wrongful act or which exercised direction and control over the commission of an internationally wrongful act. However, there seemed to be little State practice in that area. The position adopted by the Special Rapporteur with regard to those articles in paragraphs 27 and 28 of his report was not sufficiently substantiated by footnotes. He nevertheless supported the two draft articles, which covered events that were likely to arise in the future. However, there seemed to be no need for the proviso in draft article 15.

46. Turning to draft article 16, paragraph 2, he agreed that member States of an international organization were prone to act on the basis of authorizations and recommendations from that international organization. State practice in that regard should not therefore be ignored. Also relevant was the 1962 advisory opinion of the ICJ in the *Certain Expenses of the United Nations* case.

47. As to the failure of the Security Council to act to prevent the genocide in Rwanda, interesting parallels could be drawn between that situation and the situation in Kosovo and the Balkans, where NATO had intervened to prevent further conflict or a spread of the conflict. What conclusions were to be drawn from a comparison of those two situations remained a moot point.

48. In conclusion, he recommended that all the draft articles with the exception of draft article 16, paragraph 2, should be referred to the Drafting Committee.

49. The CHAIRPERSON invited members wishing to participate in the work of the Drafting Committee on the topic of responsibility of international organizations to inform the Chairperson of the Drafting Committee of their intention.

Reservations to treaties[9] (A/CN.4/549 and Add.1, sect. D, A/CN.4/558 [and Corr.1] and Add.1 [and Corr.1]–2,[10] and A/CN.4/L.665)

[Agenda item 6]

Report of the Drafting Committee

50. The CHAIRPERSON invited the Chairperson of the Drafting Committee to introduce the first report of the Committee for the current session, on the topic of reservations to treaties (A/CN.4/L.665).

51. Mr. MANSFIELD (Chairperson of the Drafting Committee) presented the report of the Drafting Committee on the topic. The Committee had held two meetings on the topic, on 9 and 10 May 2005, at which it had considered two draft guidelines referred to it by the Commission during its fifty-sixth session. The two draft guidelines dealt with the definition of objections. Draft guideline 2.6.1 dealt with the definition of objections *per se* and draft guideline 2.6.2 dealt with a specific category of objections, namely those to the late formulation of reservations or to the widening of the scope of reservations.

52. The new text of draft guideline 2.6.1 read:

"*Definition of objections to reservations*

'Objection' means a unilateral statement, however phrased or named, made by a State or an international organization in response to a reservation to a treaty formulated by another State or international organization, whereby the former State or organization purports to exclude or to modify the legal effects of the reservation, or to exclude the application of the treaty as a whole, in relations with the reserving State or organization."

53. The new text of draft guideline 2.6.2 read:

"*Definition of objections to the late formulation or widening of the scope of a reservation*

'Objection' may also mean a unilateral statement whereby a State or an international organization opposes the late formulation of a reservation or the widening of the scope of a reservation."

54. Draft guideline 2.6.1 had first been introduced by the Special Rapporteur in his eighth report in 2003.[11] Other versions of the guideline had been proposed by the Special Rapporteur in his ninth report in 2004,[12] and in the report of the Commission on its fifty-sixth session, taking into account the views expressed in plenary session.[13] The Drafting Committee had worked on the latest version of the guideline, which had appeared in paragraph 293 (*e*) of the Commission's report.

[9] For the text of the draft guidelines provisionally adopted so far by the Commission, see *Yearbook ... 2004*, vol. II (Part Two), para. 294.

[10] Reproduced in *Yearbook ... 2005*, vol. II (Part One).

[11] *Yearbook ... 2003*, vol. II (Part One), document A/CN.4/535 and Add.1.

[12] *Yearbook ... 2004*, vol. II (Part One), document A/CN.4/544.

[13] *Ibid.*, vol. II (Part Two), chap. IX, sect. B, paras. 275–293.

55. The Drafting Committee had discussed at length whether the definition of objections should focus on the effects of objections, as did the text proposed by the Special Rapporteur, or whether an objection should constitute a factual statement whereby the objecting State or international organization indicated that it did not accept the reservation or considered it unlawful. Various arguments had been put forward in support of or in opposition to those two approaches. It had been pointed out that a strictly factual definition would be incomplete or would risk including mere political declarations which were not intended to be "objections" producing legal effects; some members had thought that such a definition would be tautological. The Drafting Committee had tried to combine the two approaches in a single definition but it had become obvious that such a definition would be excessively long and impractical.

56. The Committee had finally agreed that the words "exclude or modify" were key elements of any objection purporting to produce legal effects and that, without necessarily listing all the possible effects of an objection, the definition based on them should include a very general description of such effects. That description followed the one found in article 20, paragraph 4 (*b*), and article 21, paragraph 3, of the 1969 Vienna Convention. Such a definition should include the possible exclusion of the application of the treaty as a whole, reflecting article 21, paragraph 3, of the 1969 Vienna Convention.

57. The Committee had also thought that the definition should not be overly elaborate, since future draft guidelines would deal with other aspects of objections. The current wording closely followed the wording of the draft guideline proposed in 2004. The term "formulated" had been retained as more appropriate than the term "made", in view of the fact that under the Vienna Convention a reservation was deemed to be "formulated" until no objection had been made. The French term "*auteur de la réserve*" had been rendered in English as "the reserving State or organization". The definition did not affect the ability of States to make statements or comments about reservations on political grounds, a point that would be developed in the commentary. The commentary would likewise make it clear that the definition was without prejudice to the validity or legal effects of objections. Draft guideline 1.6 (Scope of definitions) was of particular relevance in that context.

58. Draft guideline 2.6.2 followed closely the original drafting as proposed by the Special Rapporteur. The Committee had contemplated modifying the wording to align it with that of draft guideline 2.6.1 by using the words "purports to oppose" rather than "opposes", but had abandoned that idea, realizing that the two draft guidelines covered different cases. The purpose of draft guideline 2.6.2 was to underline the fact that the term "objection" might also be used in relation to opposition to late formulation of a reservation or to the widening of the scope of a reservation.

59. The Drafting Committee had agreed that a more appropriate placement for draft guideline 2.6.2, which was currently placed immediately after draft guideline 2.6.1, would be between guidelines 2.3.2 (Acceptance of late formulation of a reservation) and 2.3.3 (Objection to late formulation of a reservation). The current numbering had, however, been retained, in order not to upset an already complex numbering of the draft guidelines, on the understanding that on second reading it should be placed in the section dealing with late formulation of reservations.

60. The Drafting Committee recommended to the Commission the adoption of the two draft guidelines.

61. Mr. Sreenivasa RAO said that the question of the definition of objections to reservations was important, because States had been known to make declarations that were subsequently construed as objections by the depositary, as had happened in the case of India's declaration relating to the constituent instrument of the International Maritime Organization. He would have preferred to see objections purporting to exclude the application of the treaty as a whole treated separately from objections purporting to exclude or to modify the legal effects of the reservation. However, the Drafting Committee had chosen to deal with both in the same guideline, and he was willing to live with that decision.

62. The CHAIRPERSON said that if he heard no objection he would take it that the Commission wished to adopt the titles and texts of draft guidelines 2.6.1 and 2.6.2 as contained in document A/CN.4/L.665.

It was so agreed.

Guidelines 2.6.1 and 2.6.2 were adopted.

63. Mr. PELLET (Special Rapporteur) welcomed the adoption of guidelines 2.6.1 and 2.6.2, which had necessitated two years of hard work. Responding to Mr. Sreenivasa Rao's remarks, he noted that India's difficulties regarding the constituent instrument of the International Maritime Organization had concerned reservations, not objections. That said, it was true that differences of opinion could arise between States and depositary bodies or international jurisdictions as to the nature of submissions made by States. One need only think of the *Belilos* v. *Switzerland* case of 29 April 1988, in which the European Court of Human Rights had found that what purported to be a declaration in fact constituted a reservation. Hence the importance of the two guidelines.

64. He also recalled that in his eighth report he had expressed his intention of first proposing a general definition, before moving on to specific definitions of the various types of objections, including the refusal by a State to be bound by a treaty with the State making the reservation.[14] Like Mr. Sreenivasa Rao, he would have preferred a separate treatment of objections purporting to exclude or to modify the legal effects of the reservation and of those purporting to exclude the application of the treaty as a whole. However, he could accept the text of guideline 2.6.1 as formulated by the Drafting Committee.

The meeting rose at 12.55 p.m.

---

[14] *Yearbook ... 2003*, vol. II (Part One), document A/CN.4/535 and Add.1, paras. 98–106.

2843rd MEETING

Tuesday, 24 May 2005, at 10 a.m.

Chairperson: Mr. Djamchid MOMTAZ

Present: Mr. Addo, Mr. Al-Baharna, Mr. Al-Marri, Mr. Baena Soares, Mr. Candioti, Mr. Chee, Mr. Comissário Afonso, Mr. Dugard, Mr. Economides, Ms. Escarameia, Mr. Fomba, Mr. Gaja, Mr. Galicki, Mr. Kabatsi, Mr. Kateka, Mr. Kolodkin, Mr. Koskenniemi, Mr. Mansfield, Mr. Niehaus, Mr. Pambou-Tchivounda, Mr. Pellet, Mr. Sreenivasa Rao, Mr. Rodríguez Cedeño, Ms. Xue, Mr. Yamada.

Responsibility of international organizations (*continued*) (A/CN.4/549 and Add.1, sect. A, A/CN.4/547, A/CN.4/553, A/CN.4/556, A/CN.4/L.666/Rev.1)

[Agenda item 3]

THIRD REPORT OF THE SPECIAL RAPPORTEUR (*concluded*)

1. Mr. RODRÍGUEZ CEDEÑO endorsed the idea of basing the draft articles on the articles on responsibility of States for internationally wrongful acts,[1] although he thought it was necessary to be very careful in doing so. The fact that there were different types of international organizations—cooperation, financial and regional integration organizations—raised questions about the nature and scope of the recommendations or decisions adopted by their organs. Those differences were important, not only in theory but also in terms of their practical effects. The international law of international organizations did not constitute a single body of legal rules, as each organization had its own rules, even though some general principles were common to all organizations. Consequently, the obligations stemming from the acts of organizations were not all of the same nature. Some were best-endeavour obligations, others were obligations to produce specific results; some took the form of recommendations or authorizations, others of decisions that were binding on member States. The nature of the obligation was thus fundamental to determining whether an act was attributable to an international organization. A distinction should therefore be made between an organization's rules and its acts, even though it was not easy to define the obligation in either case, as had become apparent during the discussion on the powers of the Security Council. In that connection, he recalled that under Article 24 of the Charter of the United Nations the Security Council had primary responsibility for the maintenance of international peace and security. Under Chapter VII of the Charter, it could, where there was a threat to peace, recommend that Member States should take certain measures, or call on them to do so. That was an important point, as the Security Council could commit an internationally wrongful act by omission, with the result that the United Nations would incur responsibility.

2. It should not be forgotten that the legal personality of an international organization was different from that of the States that constituted it; that point had a bearing on the determination of the responsibility of the organization *per se* and, where necessary, the residual responsibility of its member States. The definition of an international organization adopted by the Commission in 2003 was quite clear in that regard.[2] An organization had the capacity to act, to acquire rights and to incur obligations, and it could thus incur responsibility. It would therefore be solely responsible, under the conditions set out in the draft articles, for the commission of an internationally wrongful act. The responsibility of member States was a far more complex question, however.

3. Turning to the draft articles proposed by the Special Rapporteur, he said that the principle, set out in draft article 8, of the existence of a breach of an international obligation by an international organization, regardless of the origin and character of the breach, could also apply to non-treaty obligations such as unilateral obligations entered into by the organization by means of a unilateral act or a resolution. That raised questions about acts taken by the secretary-general of an organization within the scope of his or her powers, given that organs of the same organization that were made up of member States had different powers. One example of that was the authorization given by the Secretary-General of the United Nations in connection with Operation Turquoise.[3]

4. The issue of the internationally wrongful act of an organization in connection with an act attributable to it did not appear to raise any great difficulties. However, the situation was less clear when an omission was involved. The Rwandan genocide, cited in paragraph 10 of the report, was an interesting example of such a situation, although he did not entirely share the view that the decision-making process could be the source of an omission that might give rise to an internationally wrongful act. An organization might find itself unable to act because of disagreement among its members, in which case it did not necessarily incur responsibility. A distinction should be drawn between the structure of organizations composed of sovereign States and the structure of States themselves, which were made up of separate branches of government. It was true, as stipulated in article 4 of the articles on State responsibility, that the State could incur responsibility for an internationally wrongful act committed by any of its organs, regardless of whether they were decentralized, regional, federal or other organs.[4] It was accepted that an international organization could be responsible for an internationally wrongful act, but it was more difficult to accept that it might be responsible for an omission.

5. As to the question of whether the rules of the organization were part of international law or not, the diversity of international organizations had again to be taken into account. Such rules often concerned the functioning of the organization or established a special legal regime that was not necessarily part of international law. That point should

---

[1] See 2838th meeting, footnote 5.

[2] See *Yearbook ... 2003*, vol. II (Part Two), chap. IV, sect.C.1, para. 53, draft article 2.

[3] See Security Council resolution 929 (1994) of 22 June 1994.

[4] *Yearbook ... 2001*, vol. II (Part Two) and corrigendum, pp. 40–42.

always be borne in mind. The overall wording of the draft articles was acceptable since it covered all possibilities.

6. Draft article 9, as it stood, was also acceptable.

7. The chapter on the responsibility of an international organization in connection with the act of a State or another organization dealt with a complex and sensitive issue that needed to be considered carefully. Draft article 13 presented no problems. With regard to draft article 16, if an international organization adopted a decision that clearly bound a member State to commit an internationally wrongful act, it incurred responsibility if, according to paragraph 1 (*b*), "the act in question is committed". The authorization of an act raised a different question that had to be taken into account in establishing responsibility. In the absence of a binding decision—in other words, when the member State had some room to manoeuvre—the act would not be attributable to the organization, which would therefore not incur responsibility, as the *Bosphorus* case, mentioned in paragraph 32 of the report, made clear. Paragraph 2 should therefore be reworded to clarify that, in the case of an authorization by an organ of the organization, responsibility was in principle transferred to a member State acting of its own volition.

8. In conclusion, he said that the draft articles as a whole could be sent to the Drafting Committee and that a working group should be set up to consider the points on which there was no general agreement.

9. Ms. XUE said that at first sight there might appear to be some similarity between the responsibility of international organizations and that of States with regard to a breach of an international obligation and responsibility in connection with the act of another subject of international law. However, the report raised a number of fundamental questions about international organizations, since the latter differed greatly from sovereign States in their ability to fulfil an international obligation. The differences between them were due not only to the decision-making process involved, but also to the fact that members of international organizations were also subjects of international law. The capacity of international organizations to fulfil an international obligation was affected, if not dictated, by their member States. In most cases, the obligations of international organizations were general and limited, and often implemented indirectly through their member States. Whereas domestic process had no effect on State responsibility at the international level, the internal process of international organizations did have an effect at the international level. In theory, draft articles 8–12 presented few problems; the rules of State responsibility could be applied, by analogy, to international organizations. However, a closer examination of those draft articles raised a number of issues.

10. On the question of whether an omission by an international organization constituted a breach of an international obligation, she believed that the Special Rapporteur had not paid sufficient attention to the response of the General Counsel of the IMF, which was mentioned in paragraph 8 of the report. The example given in paragraph 10 of the report, on the inability of the United Nations to prevent genocide in Rwanda, might seem appropriate from a human rights standpoint, but was not convincing as an example of a breach of an international obligation, as it was not the United Nations that had failed to act but its Member States. The Special Rapporteur was right to point out that it was difficult to determine what constituted an omission. In the case of the prevention of genocide, for instance, even the definition of an act was not obvious: she wondered whether condemnation by the Secretary-General of the United Nations, the adoption of a resolution condemning the genocide, the imposition of sanctions or the deployment of military forces to stop the killing could be defined as acts. In light of such problems, she would prefer to reserve her position on the inclusion of the concept of "omissions" in the draft articles.

11. Moreover, she found paragraphs 11–13 of the report a bit confusing. The quotation from the European Union in paragraph 12 set out the notion of special rules of attribution of conduct and the notion of special rules of responsibility. The former referred to the attribution of conduct in the implementation of an obligation of the European Union, and the latter determined who bore responsibility for an action carried out at the international level. It might be necessary to make a distinction within the organization between the attribution of conduct and the attribution of responsibility in order to determine whether international responsibility lay with the organization or with its member States; however, as far as the draft articles were concerned, such a distinction was unnecessary insofar as the acts that should be considered as acts of the organization were specified in the organization's constituent instrument, regardless of who actually performed them. In considering the responsibility of member States, it might be necessary to consider the internal rules of attribution of conduct of international organizations; conceptually, however, they should still be distinguished from the rules of attribution under the international responsibility regime.

12. It was difficult to say whether obligations arising under the rules of the organization were part of international law or not. Some rules of international organizations, such as decisions taken by the Security Council under Chapter VII of the Charter of the United Nations, clearly imposed international obligations; others, such as internal rules on how to implement treaty obligations, might have some effect on determining international obligations; still others, such as staff regulations, were purely internal administrative rules without any external legal effects. The question was how to define the term "rules of the organization". Perhaps the Special Rapporteur could indicate in the commentary the extent to which obligations imposed by the rules of the organization should be regarded as obligations under international law. The current wording of article 8, paragraph 2, did not adequately address the complexity of the issue.

13. With regard to responsibility in connection with the act of another subject of international law, she noted that the Special Rapporteur was faced with a lack of international practice in the cases contemplated in draft articles 12–16. In theory, such situations were possible but, as the report showed, it was difficult to find empirical support for them at the moment. A large part of that chapter of the report was devoted to the relations between an international organization and its members. She also doubted

whether the direction and control implied by "normative control" (para. 35 of the report) were the same as the direction and control referred to in article 17 of the articles on State responsibility.[5] For one thing, such relations were determined by the constituent instrument established by member States. Moreover, the legal personality of international organizations was a fiction, as their power was exercised primarily through their member States. In short, while one could argue that an international organization was capable of committing an internationally wrongful act, it was difficult to imagine that one might knowingly require member States to commit a certain act in order to "achieve indirectly what was directly prohibited" (para. 36 of the report). Given that an international organization was a subject of international law, it functioned under both the rules of the organization and international law. The requirement of knowledge of circumstances of the wrongfulness of the act was also relevant, since without it there was no circumventing of obligations. In other words, if an international organization requested its members to perform an action that it believed to be in conformity with international law but that eventually turned out to be a wrongful act, the international responsibility of the organization and its members should be determined by the rules of the organization and by the relevant primary rules of international law. As a matter of law, draft article 13 was not necessary.

14. The general content of draft article 16 had a direct bearing on the relations between an organization and its member States, since the extent of the binding force of an international organization's decision on its members dictated the extent of the organization's responsibility. In that respect, the element of interest should not be deemed a decisive factor in determining the responsibility of the organization. The example given in paragraph 40 of the report should therefore be reconsidered. While it was true that the Montreal Protocol on Substances that Deplete the Ozone Layer prohibited the supply of freon gas, it was clear that the Security Council Committee established by resolution 661 (1990) concerning the situation between Iraq and Kuwait should not have authorized the supply of the gas to Iraq. Whether or not the United Nations had any interest in the deal did not preclude the wrongfulness of its authorization. Useful as it was, draft article 16 should not be included in that part of the report. As the responsibility of international organizations was different from State responsibility, it should be determined by special rules governing the relations between international organizations and their members in connection with a wrongful act under international law. Decisions, recommendations and authorizations were normal acts of international organizations. The question that constantly arose was how member States implemented them and how responsibility for the acts committed should be allocated between the organization and its members. Given the importance of that issue, she proposed that it should be treated separately as a special legal issue.

15. Mr. DUGARD, returning to the issue of the possible responsibility of the United Nations for human catastrophes such as the genocide in Rwanda, said he was puzzled by Ms. Xue's argument that in such circumstances only Member States could be held responsible for an omission, and not the United Nations itself. He could understand how, in cases like the one in Srebrenica, where the failure of the peacekeeping forces could clearly be attributed to the Netherlands, the State could be held responsible for what had taken place, as could the United Nations itself. However, the situation in Rwanda was different in that there had been no State present on the ground to which fault could be attributed. If there was fault, it lay with the United Nations for failing to act. In such circumstances, a State could not be expected to act unilaterally, since the Charter of the United Nations prohibited unilateral action. Consequently, in his view, an international organization as such must incur responsibility for its mistakes.

16. Mr. FOMBA said that he would appreciate it if Ms. Xue could clarify her comment that genocide was an inappropriate example because it ought to be dealt with by a rights-based approach that differed from the approach under international law. If that was so, he wished to know what the difference was between human rights and international law and whether or not the Convention on the Prevention and Punishment of the Crime of Genocide was part of international law.

17. Ms. XUE said she was afraid that there had been a misunderstanding. Her intention in citing the Special Rapporteur's example of the genocide in Rwanda had been to point out that it did not illustrate how an omission could be considered a wrongful act on the part of an international organization. She had not meant to say that the United Nations should not be held responsible for its failure to act in Rwanda. In fact, it was not the United Nations and its Member States that had failed to act effectively, but the international community as a whole. The United Nations could not be accused of failing to act when its Member States had been so reluctant to take action.

18. Human rights were certainly a major concern for every State and for the international community as a whole, but that did not mean that responsibility could automatically be attributed to an international organization. The difficulty lay in the concept of omission; it was therefore necessary to consider what actually constituted responsibility. The consequences and long-term effects of accusing the United Nations of not intervening in Rwanda, in terms of obtaining reparation or ensuring that the same thing did not happen again, would need to be considered. It was not a question of saying that the Organization should not have intervened, but of determining whether there was a link with the questions of legal responsibility and omission on which the Commission had to take a position.

19. The CHAIRPERSON, speaking as a member of the Commission, said that it was too vague to talk of the responsibility of States Members of the United Nations for failing to react to the genocide in Rwanda without specifying how they ought to have reacted. Everyone knew that the Charter of the United Nations prohibited the use of force: the question was what obligation States did have.

20. Ms. XUE said that if the Commission took the very same approach as it had taken to State responsibility, it

[5] *Ibid.*, pp. 67–69.

would see that the issue at hand was the complex one of the primary rules for international organizations. The fact was that, even in a situation as serious as the genocide in Rwanda, it was very difficult to say that the United Nations bore responsibility.

21. Mr. DUGARD agreed that the issue was a very difficult one but he did not think it could be sidestepped by saying that the international community as a whole was responsible, as the international community did not have legal personality. If an international legal entity was to be held responsible for the events in Rwanda, it must be the United Nations, and compensation might be considered as a form of reparation.

22. Mr. ECONOMIDES said that Ms. Xue had made a distinction between a wrongful action and a wrongful omission, and had said that she found it difficult to accept the idea of the responsibility of an international organization for an omission. Where responsibility was concerned, however, both actions and omissions were universally taken into account, regardless of whether the case concerned States or international organizations. Moreover, the responsibility of the organization was in no way diminished by the fact that an omission on the part of the organization was due to the inability of member States to take a decision or to take a decision in time. One might ask whether the organization had any recourse against the States that had prevented the decision from being taken, but that issue would be addressed towards the end of the Commission's consideration of the draft articles, as had been the case with the articles on the responsibility of States for internationally wrongful acts.

23. Mr. KABATSI said that there were definitely cases where an international organization was expected to do something. The Rwandan genocide, however, was a complex case, especially as the United Nations had already been present on the ground, with forces authorized by the Security Council that had been withdrawn as soon as the genocide began: that was a clear example of an act of omission.

24. Mr. CHEE said that, firstly, the question facing the Commission concerned the attribution of responsibility to an organization or to its member States. As the President of the ICJ had affirmed, a crime was not committed by a State but by individuals. The question of attribution should therefore be considered separately from the question of the crime itself. Secondly, the Security Council had not intervened in Rwanda, yet had done so in Kosovo: the reasons for those different reactions needed to be considered.

25. The CHAIRPERSON, speaking as a member of the Commission, agreed that only the responsibility of individuals, and not the criminal responsibility of States, was addressed in the Rome Statute of the International Criminal Court. However, it was responsibility in general that was being addressed in the topic under consideration, and questions were being raised specifically about the civil responsibility of States.

26. Mr. Sreenivasa RAO said that, with hindsight, paragraph 10 appeared to be the most important one in the Special Rapporteur's report. That had probably not been his intention, for if it had, he would have provided more facts. The various reactions to the paragraph had been, understandably, very emotional, but it was not in fact unusual for the Security Council to act when it wished to do so and not to act when it did not wish to do so. In citing the case of Rwanda, the Special Rapporteur assumed, firstly, that general international law required States and other entities to prevent genocide "in the same way" as the Convention on the Prevention and Punishment of the Crime of Genocide. He wondered what precisely was meant by "in the same way". The Special Rapporteur's second assumption was that the United Nations had been in a position to prevent genocide. However, it was one thing to be in a position to prevent genocide and quite another to be able to prevent it. Everyone agreed that there had been a moral failure and that, given what had happened in other countries, the United Nations had applied a double standard. However, it was easier to talk about the inability of the United Nations to act as quickly as it should have than it was to talk about its legal responsibility. For many members it was going too far to say that "failure to act would have represented a breach of an international obligation". Moreover, while the debate was undoubtedly useful, most of it went far beyond the scope of the Commission's mandate.

27. Mr. KOLODKIN said that in his earlier statements he had accepted the idea that an international organization could be held legally responsible in cases of omission, but he had also said that the case cited in paragraph 10 of the report was not the best example to illustrate that point. The debate on that question was very interesting but had not changed his mind. In order to determine if an international organization had any responsibility whatsoever, it was necessary to begin by considering its constituent instruments, then its rules, and then any agreement concluded by it. If an obligation to act in a certain way was identified, the organization would be responsible for failing to act. In the case of Rwanda, the United Nations had no clearly expressed obligation to act in a certain way in that kind of situation. As others had stressed, the Security Council had full discretion in that respect, in keeping with the vision of the framers of the Charter. That discretion must be maintained if the United Nations was to retain the possibility of deciding on the best line of conduct to take in any situation of vital importance to the international community. In that respect, he agreed with the proposal by the High-level Panel on Threats, Challenges and Change to define the criteria to be met if the Security Council and the United Nations as a whole should be required to intervene, particularly in order to prevent a humanitarian disaster.[6]

28. Mr. GAJA (Special Rapporteur) assured members that he had no intention of involving the Commission in the project to reform the United Nations, which was being undertaken by other perfectly competent bodies. Draft article 8 mainly concerned agreements concluded by an international organization, and in paragraph 10 of his report he had simply intended to give an example of a breach of an obligation under general international law

[6] *A More Secure World: Our Shared Responsibility*, A/59/565 and Corr.1, part two, chap. IX, sect. B, para. 207.

consisting in an omission. Nevertheless, he disagreed with the idea that only States had an obligation to prevent genocide. In any event, it was not the task of the Commission to resolve that question.

29. Mr. PELLET said that it was too facile to dismiss the problem by criticizing paragraph 10 of the Special Rapporteur's report, especially by attributing responsibility to the international community as a whole, which would only ensure that no one was held responsible. It was also too facile to say that international organizations were responsible when they acted but not when they did not act. As Mr. Kolodkin had said, the only real problem lay in determining whether an organization did or did not have an obligation to act. If it did, it was obvious that it was responsible for failing to act. Moreover, the question was resolved in draft article 3. Matters would be made infinitely more complicated by taking highly emotionally charged examples that posed problems that were more human, moral or political in nature than legal. Besides Rwanda, the case of Srebrenica could be cited, but the prime example was the withdrawal of the emergency international United Nations Force from Sinai just before the second Israeli–Arab war. One could say that the aggressor was Israel or Egypt, or even the Secretary-General, since he had ordered the withdrawal. The question of responsibility had to be addressed; he therefore called on the Commission to stop discussing such cases and to restrict itself to the technical aspects of the subject.

30. Mr. AL-MARRI said that, unlike some of his colleagues, he thought that when responsibility could not be attributed to a State or to individuals, the United Nations would be the international organization most likely to bear responsibility. Criminal acts could not go unpunished, regardless of who was responsible for them; he therefore agreed with Mr. Dugard that it was possible to establish responsibility in the case of Rwanda.

31. Mr. DUGARD observed that Mr. Pellet, after making the point that the withdrawal of United Nations peacekeepers from Sinai was the prime example of the responsibility of international organizations, had then suggested that such "emotional" problems should be avoided in order to focus on technical aspects. He personally believed that the Commission, even though it was more of a technical than a political body, should bear such important issues in mind when dealing with the kind of problem before it.

32. Ms. XUE said that on an emotional level she agreed with Mr. Kabatsi; from a technical viewpoint, however, she had to point out that when peacekeeping forces withdrew from a territory on the eve of a massacre, it was because they had received the order to do so. Thus it was not a question of whether the United Nations had committed an act of omission, but of whether its decision to withdraw its troops had been unlawful or not, which was a question of interpretation. Moreover, the situation with regard to omissions was extremely complex, since it was necessary to consider cases in which the problem fell within the competence of several international organizations, none of which actually took any action. In the case of Rwanda, for example, the United Nations was not solely responsible, since many other international organizations could also be held responsible for not intervening. When it came to maintaining international peace and security, obviously the United Nations and, in particular, the Security Council had primarily responsibility. However, under Article 51 of the Charter, regional organizations and the States concerned were also responsible, as they could exercise their right to self-defence. Furthermore, the mandates of international organizations often overlapped, so that it was very difficult to find a case in which it could be stated unambiguously that a given organization ought to have acted.

33. Mr. CHEE said that it was very difficult to challenge the decisions taken by the Security Council under the Charter of the United Nations, since under Article 24 Member States conferred on the Security Council primary responsibility for taking action and agreed that the Security Council acted on their behalf. Moreover, Article 25 stipulated that the Members of the United Nations agreed to accept and carry out the decisions of the Security Council in accordance with the Charter. Thus it was not easy to determine whether the Security Council was right or wrong, whether it should intervene or not and what type of intervention Member States could request. Such problems posed a real dilemma with regard to what the Security Council should or should not do, for in cases of omission the question arose as to whether the Council was prepared to be held responsible for the United Nations. Perhaps omissions and actions should be analysed in the light of the due diligence standard set out in general international law, thereby avoiding the requirement under the Charter of the United Nations that the Charter should have priority. The Repertory of Practice of United Nations Organs and the Repertoire of the Practice of the Security Council could be consulted for that purpose. However, he doubted that they would be of much help, and he thought the best solution was still to consider omission in terms of the due diligence standard set out in general international law; on that basis it would be possible to decide if the Security Council was responsible or not.

34. Mr. PELLET said that it might be possible, by taking small examples of problems amenable to practical solutions, to deduce general rules that would be applicable even to extremely sensitive cases in which, in his view, the law did not really have a fundamental role to play. The law could not solve every problem, as it tended to apply to mundane cases rather than to dramatic ones.

35. He recalled that the Commission had already debated the issue of responsibility for action or failure to act by peacekeeping forces in 2004 and that it had been pointed out then that such forces, which could undoubtedly be considered an organ of the organization, were in a double bind.[7] Problems that were specific to responsibility for the action or failure to act of such forces should be dealt with separately from the topic under consideration. As Chairperson of the Working Group on the Long-Term Programme of Work, he wondered if the Commission ought not to consider a proposal on that particular type of responsibility, which was a topic in its own right. Every time examples were sought to illustrate it, the emotional problems referred to earlier surfaced and, since peacekeepers were still subject to their national chain

[7] *Yearbook ... 2004*, vol. I, 2800th–2802nd meetings, *passim*.

of command, specific individual problems arose regarding the attribution of responsibility. As peacekeeping forces were never a good example with which to illustrate the topic under consideration, Commission members should reach a "gentlemen's agreement" to take up the issue in the Commission's long-term programme of work so as not to interfere with the topic dealt with by the Special Rapporteur.

36. The CHAIRPERSON said that he had not intended to start a debate on emotional issues, but had simply wished to draw attention to the question of the obligation of United Nations organs, especially the Security Council, to act in a number of specific cases. Mr. Kolodkin had referred to the proposal by the High-level Panel on Threats, Challenges and Change to the effect that, in the specific case of genocide, the Security Council should adopt a "normative" resolution spelling out the conditions under which the Security Council should act and establishing a set of criteria for making action an obligation.[8]

37. Mr. PAMBOU-TCHIVOUNDA said that the two issues into which the topic had been split—the breach of an international obligation by an international organization and the responsibility of an international organization in connection with the act of a State or another organization—were closely linked, as the approach to them was logically and chronologically interdependent in their illustration and application of the general rule on the attribution of an internationally wrongful act to an international organization. However, it was unfortunate that, in endeavouring to lay the foundations for the international responsibility of the international organization, the Commission had tended to overlook the essential point, namely, what constituted a breach of an international obligation, rather than whether such a breach existed. If the Commission agreed to follow the approach suggested by the Special Rapporteur in paragraph 5 of his report and included, either after draft article 4 or after draft article 8, a draft article adapting article 13 of the articles on State responsibility to international organizations, the result, in terms of the organization and adaptation of normative texts, would be to unify the two parts of the report.

38. The Commission should, by means of a draft article, give full effect to the case law in the *Demirel* case. The Commission would thereby accord the phenomenon of regional integration, which was rooted in contemporary international realities, its rightful place as a phenomenon that generated specific, consistent and valuable practice and, as such, practice that was suitable for codification, particularly as it yielded jurisprudence of an indisputably international nature. Although in the draft articles on responsibility of States for internationally wrongful acts the Commission had chosen to overlook the normative development of the distinction between an international regional-integration organization and an international cooperation organization, it ought to give due consideration in the draft articles it was currently preparing to international regional-integration organizations. No one could say whether the joint involvement of the European Union and the African Union, or of the United Nations and NATO, in the current situation in Darfur could be assessed by the same measure should either of them breach the obligations they had assumed under special arrangements or under their constituent instruments or their own specific rules. In Darfur it was the result that mattered.

39. Accordingly, the breach of an obligation to achieve a certain result should, as indicated, in paragraph 15 of the report, be considered as implying a possible exception to the general principles set out in draft article 3. The Commission should carefully define the concept of the "best endeavours" obligation as the specific basis for the international responsibility of international regional-integration organizations, coupled with the responsibility of their member States. In raising the question in paragraph 16 of the report of whether obligations under the rules of the organization pertained to international law, the Special Rapporteur was pushing against an open door, for no purpose was served by questioning the legal nature of the rules of the international organization, regardless of whether they stemmed from a treaty or an instrument governed by international law or from a subject of international law other than the State. Since the Commission had defined the concept of the rules of the organization in draft article 4, it was difficult to see who might demand an explanation from the ICJ as to why it had not listed the rules of the World Health Organization in its advisory opinion of 20 December 1980.

40. The question of the status of the rules of the organization in the international order had already been settled, so that it would be sufficient to say, if necessary, that the rules of the international organization were an integral part of the international legal order. In any event, draft article 8, paragraph 2, should be deleted. He recommended sending draft article 8, without paragraph 2, and draft articles 12–15 to the Drafting Committee. Draft article 16 would benefit from being reviewed in the light of international practice.

41. Mr. GAJA (Special Rapporteur), summing up the debate, said that he agreed that it was a good idea to divide the draft articles on the responsibility of international organizations into chapters. Once the substantive articles had been drafted, it would be useful to introduce chapter headings corresponding to the divisions made in the articles on the responsibility of States for internationally wrongful acts. However, as some members had expressed reservations about the wisdom of that choice, the Drafting Committee should discuss it. The idea of a final provision referring to the existence of special rules, including those contained in the rules of the organization, could be mentioned in the commentary, although it seemed premature to try to draft the text of such a provision immediately. Concerning the relations between the rules of the organization and other rules of international law, the former would certainly not prevail over the rules governing the relations between the organization and non-member States. Thus it could not be said that the rules of the organization generally prevailed over other rules of international law.

[8] A/59/565, para. 203; see also paras. 207 and 256.

42. The debate had inevitably touched on some questions that were connected with those dealt with in his third report but that were not of immediate concern to the Commission. He admitted that he had perhaps contributed to that situation by citing, in paragraph 12 of his report, the position of the Legal Service of the European Commission on attribution of conduct. He had included that reference to introduce some alternative explanations of the responsibility of the European Union for the conduct of its member States, because it had been argued that the conduct of member States should be attributed to the organization when they acted in areas in which the European Union was considered to have exclusive competence, and also when they implemented Community legislation. There was no need to reopen the debate on that issue, as the Commission had adopted draft articles that were in line with the basic principles expressed in article 4 of the articles on State responsibility to the effect that the conduct of an organ of the State was attributed to the State in question.

43. Various questions raised in the debate concerned the responsibility of member States in relation to the responsibility of an international organization, which would be the subject of his next report. The responsibility of States was not otherwise covered by the draft articles currently before the Commission, but by the articles on State responsibility. The concern that States should not be exonerated from their responsibility when an international organization was held responsible had already been expressed in the commentary adopted in 2004, in which it was stated that: "attribution of a certain conduct to an international organization does not imply that the same conduct cannot be attributed to a State".[9] Similarly, with regard to the attribution of responsibility, draft article 15 and draft article 16, paragraph 3, were consistent with the idea that the question of State responsibility was not prejudiced.

44. The scope of the draft articles as defined in article 1, paragraph 2, did not cover cases in which a State and an international organization could both be held responsible, concurrently or otherwise, for an internationally wrongful act. A question arose as to the relationship between the responsibility of an international organization that assisted a State or another international organization in the commission of an internationally wrongful act and the responsibility of the State or organization that actually committed the wrongful act. That question would have to be answered in the same way as would the case of a State that assisted another State in the commission of an internationally wrongful act, but that question had not been addressed in the articles on State responsibility. His third report, and particularly draft article 16, dealt with situations in which an international organization incurred international responsibility for conduct attributed to one of its member States. That article did not necessarily imply that the member State concerned would also be held responsible. That was made clear in draft article 16, paragraph 3, which specified that when the State was not acting in breach of an international obligation, it could not be held responsible. However, if the member State was bound by an international obligation and committed an internationally wrongful act, it would also be held responsible. He saw no reason for exonerating a member State that had committed an internationally wrongful act simply because an international organization had asked it to do so or because it had acted under the direction or control of that organization. The only situation in which the State concerned would not be held responsible was one in which such direction or control amounted to coercion.

45. Most members of the Commission had agreed to send draft articles 9–15 to the Drafting Committee, and some had been prepared to send draft article 8, paragraph 1, as well. For that reason, his comments would deal primarily with the most innovative and controversial provisions: draft article 8, paragraph 2, and draft article 16.

46. Most members of the Commission were in favour of retaining draft article 8, paragraph 2, although several had criticized the use of the words "in principle". He was not sure that the solution would be to delete those words from the text of the draft article while explaining in the commentary that there might be exceptions. Nor was he sure that there should be no mention at all of possible exceptions on the grounds that the rules of the organization were necessarily part of international law. The main problem that would arise if that approach was adopted would be that European Union law would be considered as part of international law even though many commentators, as well as the 25 countries concerned, held the opposite view. If the Commission held that Community law was part of international law, it would be out of step with recent developments in international law. Most commentators saw Community law not as *lex specialis*, which would suppose that it was of the same nature as international law, but as a self-contained regime. He was not in favour of including a general clause exempting the European Union from the scope of the draft articles. In many respects, the European Union functioned like other international organizations, particularly in its relations with third States. Moreover, the same scenario could be repeated in the future with other regional organizations of economic integration. If the words "in principle" were to be replaced, he personally would prefer wording that excluded the rules of regional organizations that had given rise to a form of integration entailing a system of law that could no longer be regarded as part of international law. Another solution would be to delete article 8, paragraph 2, altogether and to ignore the whole question of the nature of the rules of the organization. While that was a possible option, the whole chapter would be weakened and would make little contribution to clarifying questions that were important to international organizations.

47. He noted that the principle underlying draft article 16 had been generally well accepted. One objection had been that draft articles 13 and 16 might overlap. However, if draft article 13 was taken as referring not only to the actual control exercised by an organization over its member States but also to normative control in the form of recommendations and authorizations, that risk would exist only in cases where the State breached one of its obligations, since draft article 13 presupposed that the State acting under the control of the international organization

[9] *Yearbook ... 2004*, vol. II (Part Two), chap. V, sect. C.2, para. 72, commentary on the attribution of conduct to an international organization, para. 4.

committed a wrongful act. In any event, there would be no drawback in considering an international organization to be responsible under both draft article 13 and draft article 16.

48. Turning to article 16, paragraph 2, which had aroused most of the criticism, he reiterated that the reason for including that provision was to address cases in which an international organization used a recommendation or authorization directed at a member State to circumvent one of its own obligations. He hoped that some consensus could be reached on ways of restricting the responsibility of the organization to a limited number of cases, including those in which its authorization or recommendation had made a significant contribution to the conduct constituting an internationally wrongful act. It would still have to be decided whether a distinction needed to be made between authorizations and recommendations on the grounds that one category had a greater impact on unlawful conduct than the other.

49. In conclusion, he noted that it was generally accepted that draft articles 9–15 could be sent to the Drafting Committee, while draft articles 8 and 16 should be considered by a working group in order to resolve the outstanding problems.

50. Mr. PELLET said that he really must stress one point that seemed to him fundamental and on which he disagreed profoundly with the Special Rapporteur. No one was claiming that Community law was part of international law—it was a self-contained legal order, as were the rules of every international organization. However, unlike internal rules, Community law was derived from international law, which provided the basis for it. He was categorically opposed to including in the draft articles a specific exception for economic integration organizations since, just as States could not hide behind domestic law to justify a breach of an international obligation, organizations could not fall back on their internal rules to evade international law. The proposal to exclude economic integration organizations would be tantamount to according them the status of super-States, which was unacceptable.

51. Mr. GAJA (Special Rapporteur) replied that he had never suggested that Community law could justify non-compliance with an international obligation. The question was whether the rules of an organization were necessarily an integral part of international law and thus whether a breach of one of those rules amounted to a breach of international law.

52. The CHAIRPERSON said that, if he heard no objection, he would take it that the Commission wished to send draft articles 9–15 to the Drafting Committee and draft articles 8 and 16 to an open-ended working group.

It was so decided.

The meeting rose at 1.05 p.m.

2844th MEETING

Wednesday, 25 May 2005, at 10.05 a.m.

Chairperson: Mr. Djamchid MOMTAZ

Present: Mr. Addo, Mr. Al-Baharna, Mr. Al-Marri, Mr. Baena Soares, Mr. Chee, Mr. Comissário Afonso, Mr. Dugard, Mr. Economides, Ms. Escarameia, Mr. Fomba, Mr. Gaja, Mr. Galicki, Mr. Kabatsi, Mr. Kateka, Mr. Kolodkin, Mr. Koskenniemi, Mr. Mansfield, Mr. Matheson, Mr. Pellet, Mr. Sreenivasa Rao, Mr. Rodríguez Cedeño, Ms. Xue, Mr. Yamada.

Responsibility of international organizations (*continued*) (A/CN.4/549 and Add.1, sect. A, A/CN.4/547, A/CN.4/553, A/CN.4/556, A/CN.4/L.666/Rev.1)

[Agenda item 3]

Oral report of the Chairperson of the Working Group

1. Mr. GAJA (Special Rapporteur) said that the Open-ended Working Group established to discuss some controversial aspects of draft articles 8 and 16 had met the previous afternoon and, after thorough discussion, had agreed to recommend that revised versions of those two draft articles should be referred to the Drafting Committee. The commentary would reflect the main differences of opinion expressed during the debate in the plenary and in the Working Group.

2. Draft article 8, paragraph 1, remained unchanged. Paragraph 2 had been revised to read: "The preceding paragraph also applies to the breach of an obligation under international law set by a rule of the organization."

3. The Working Group had considered that it would be useful to point out that obligations under international law were also set by rules of the organization; in the absence of special rules the general rules on international responsibility currently being drafted would therefore also apply to breaches of those obligations. The question whether all the rules of the organization imposed obligations under international law had not been fully settled by the revised text. The Working Group had felt that the matter should be resolved at a later stage, taking into account the comments of Governments and international organizations.

4. Paragraph 3 of draft article 16 remained unchanged. Paragraphs 1 and 2 had been revised to read:

> "1. An international organization incurs international responsibility if it adopts a decision binding a member State or international organization to commit an act that would be internationally wrongful for the former organization.
>
> 2. An international organization incurs international responsibility if:

(*a*) it recommends or authorizes a member State or international organization to commit an act that would be internationally wrongful for the former organization; and

(*b*) that State or organization relies on the recommendation or authorization for the commission of the wrongful act."

5. The Working Group had been of the view that a sharper distinction should be made between the case in which an international organization made a decision binding member States to engage in conduct designed to circumvent an obligation of the organization, on the one hand, and, on the other, the case of a recommendation or authorization to engage in that conduct.

6. Thus, paragraph 1 was categorical on the organization's responsibility in the first case, that of a binding decision, whereas paragraph 2 gave weight to the context and introduced the criterion of reliance on the part of the member State on the organization's recommendation or authorization. In the latter case, responsibility arose only when the act was committed, a requirement which had not been stated in paragraph 1. He noted that there had not been unanimity within the Working Group on this point.

7. The CHAIRPERSON said that if he heard no objection, he would take it that the Commission wished to refer the revised versions of draft articles 8 and 16 to the Drafting Committee.

It was so agreed.

Diplomatic protection[1] (A/CN.4/549 and Add.1, sect. F and A/CN.4/546[2])

[Agenda item 2]

Sixth report of the Special Rapporteur

8. The CHAIRPERSON invited the Special Rapporteur to introduce his sixth report on diplomatic protection (A/CN.4/546).

9. Mr. DUGARD (Special Rapporteur), introducing his sixth report, concerning the clean hands doctrine, said that while no one could deny the importance of that doctrine in international law, the question before the Commission was whether it was sufficiently closely linked to the topic of diplomatic protection to warrant its inclusion in the draft articles on the topic. His conclusion, indicated in his sixth report (para. 18), was that the clean hands doctrine did not obviously belong to the field of diplomatic protection and that it should therefore not be included in the draft articles.

10. It had been argued that the clean hands doctrine should be included in the draft articles because it was invoked in the context of diplomatic protection in order to preclude a State from exercising diplomatic protection if the national it was seeking to protect had suffered injury as a result of his own wrongful conduct.

11. Three main arguments were adduced in support of that position (para. 3 of the report). First, it was contended that the doctrine did not belong to the realm of inter-State disputes, i.e. those involving direct injury by one State to another rather than injury to a national. Second, it was suggested that if the individual seeking diplomatic protection had himself violated the domestic law of the respondent State or international law, then the State of nationality could not protect him. Third, it was contended that in a number of cases the clean hands doctrine had been applied in respect of diplomatic protection.

12. With regard to the first argument, the ICJ provided no real guidance because none of its decisions asserted that the doctrine belonged to the realm of a State claim either for direct or for indirect injury. The fact was, however, that the clean hands doctrine had most frequently been raised in the context of inter-State claims for direct injury. Several such cases were cited in paragraph 5 of his sixth report. In none of those cases had the Court dismissed the relevance of the clean hands argument; it had instead always found that the doctrine was inapplicable for some unrelated reason. In its advisory proceedings on the *Legal Consequences of the Construction of a Wall in the Occupied Palestinian Territory*, in which Israel had contended that Palestine bore the blame for the construction of the wall because of its responsibility for acts of violence against Israel, the Court had found that argument to be not pertinent on the ground that it was giving an advisory opinion, not a judgment in contentious proceedings (paras. 63–64 of the judgment). In the *Oil Platforms* case, the United States had raised the clean hands doctrine against the Islamic Republic of Iran, while the latter had argued that the clean hands doctrine applied to diplomatic protection only. The Court had dismissed the argument of the United States on the facts, but had not commented on the argument of the Islamic Republic of Iran that the clean hands doctrine applied to diplomatic protection only.

13. In the *LaGrand* (paras. 61–63 of the judgment) and *Avena and other Mexican Nationals* (para. 45 of the judgment) cases, where the United States had objected to Germany's and Mexico's own treatment of aliens in criminal proceedings, the Court had not found that argument relevant. In the *Gabčíkovo–Nagymaros Project* case, the Court had held that both parties had unclean hands but that that did not affect the legal situation (para. 133). In the *Arrest Warrant* case, an inter-State case with undertones of diplomatic protection, Belgium had claimed that the Democratic Republic of the Congo had unclean hands in that its Minister for Foreign Affairs had incited sections of the community to commit genocide. The Court had made no comment, but in her dissenting opinion Judge *ad hoc* Van den Wyngaert had found that the Democratic Republic of Congo had not come to the Court with clean hands (para. 35). That case could be seen as akin to a case involving diplomatic protection in that the Democratic Republic of the Congo had been seeking to protect its Minister, who was at the same time its national. The conduct of the individual, however culpable, was deemed to be irrelevant by the Court (paras. 55–71). In

[1] For the text of draft articles 1–19 and the related commentary adopted on first reading by the Commission at its fifty-sixth session, see *Yearbook ... 2004*, vol. II (Part Two), chap. IV, sect. C, pp. 18 *et seq.*

[2] Reproduced in *Yearbook ... 2005*, vol. II (Part One).

the *Military and Paramilitary Activities in and against Nicaragua* case, the United States had argued that Nicaragua had unclean hands (paras. 89–98 of the judgment). The Court had not pronounced on that matter, although Judge Schwebel, in his dissenting opinion, had held that Nicaragua had unclean hands in an inter-State dispute (para. 268). In the *Legality of the Use of Force* cases, several respondents had argued that the Federal Republic of Yugoslavia did not have clean hands; however, the Court had found that it did not have jurisdiction so had not ruled on the matter.

14. That brief survey of the jurisprudence of the ICJ showed that the argument of clean hands was frequently raised in inter-State claims involving direct injury to a State. In no case had the Court relied on or upheld that doctrine, but in no case had it stated or suggested that the argument was inapplicable in inter-State claims and that it applied only to cases of diplomatic protection.

15. Turning to the argument that the clean hands doctrine applied to diplomatic protection claims only, and that the State of nationality could not protect a national who had himself committed a wrongful act in the host State, he noted that the State of nationality would seldom protect one of its nationals who had behaved improperly or illegally in a foreign State, because in most circumstances no internationally wrongful act would have been committed. If a national committed an act of fraud and was imprisoned after a fair trial, there was no violation of international law and the State of nationality would not exercise diplomatic protection; in that sense it was true that the clean hands doctrine served to preclude diplomatic protection. If, however, the foreign national was imprisoned for fraud and was tortured or denied a fair trial, then an internationally wrongful act had been committed and the national's own misconduct became irrelevant: the respondent State could not invoke the foreign national's fraudulent act as a defence in a claim based on torture.

16. In the *LaGrand* and *Avena* cases, for example, the foreign nationals had committed atrocious crimes but their misconduct had not been raised by the United States to defend itself against the charges of failure to grant them consular access. Once a State took up a claim of its national in relation to a violation of international law, the claim became that of the State, in accordance with the Vattelian fiction introduced in the *Mavrommatis* case, and the misconduct of the national ceased to be relevant; only the misconduct of the plaintiff State itself might then become relevant.

17. Relatively few cases were cited of applicability of the clean hands doctrine in the context of diplomatic protection, and, upon analysis, they did not support the case for its inclusion. In the *Ben Tillett* case, where Belgium had deported a British labour union activist, the arbitration tribunal had found that Belgium had acted correctly (see paragraph 12 of the report). The issue of whether Mr. Tillett had clean hands had not been raised. In the "*Virginius*" case, cited in paragraph 13 of the report, Spain had acknowledged that it had committed an internationally wrongful act in executing United States and United Kingdom nationals and had paid compensation to those States; the fact that those nationals had been supporting rebels was deemed to be irrelevant. Although some writers nevertheless maintained that the clean hands doctrine belonged in the context of diplomatic protection, they offered no authority to support their views, and many writers, such as Salmon and Rousseau, were highly sceptical about the doctrine.

18. During consideration of the Special Rapporteur's sixth report by the Sixth Committee of the General Assembly at its fifty-ninth session, most delegations had made no comment whatsoever with regard to the clean hands doctrine and those that had commented had agreed that the clean hands doctrine should not be included in the draft articles on diplomatic protection (A/CN.4/549, paras. 127 and 128). Only one delegation, that of Nepal, had made a statement that might be construed as favouring inclusion of the doctrine.[3]

19. In conclusion he said that, while the issue of whether to include a provision on the clean hands doctrine in the draft articles on diplomatic protection was undoubtedly an important one which had warranted a full response, after considering it carefully he had concluded that the doctrine had no place in the draft articles on diplomatic protection.

20. Mr. ADDO said that, having considered the arguments for and against the applicability of the clean hands doctrine to the topic of diplomatic protection set forth in the report of the Special Rapporteur, he agreed that there were not sufficient grounds for inclusion of that doctrine in the draft articles. Although arguments based on the clean hands doctrine had been regularly raised in inter-State cases before the ICJ, none of those arguments had been upheld. Inclusion of a provision relating to the doctrine in the draft articles would not be an exercise in codification, nor could it be justified as an exercise in the progressive development of international law.

21. Mr. PELLET said he seemed to have detected a note of irritation in the Special Rapporteur's presentation of his sixth report. The Special Rapporteur evidently saw the production of the report as a needless imposition. He himself did not think that was the case, and he thanked the Special Rapporteur for providing a firm response to the question on which he had insisted at the previous session, namely, whether the absence of clean hands might constitute grounds for inadmissibility of a claim to exercise diplomatic protection, as might a failure to exhaust local remedies or the absence of nationality of the protecting State. Having read the Special Rapporteur's sixth report, he was ready to concede that he had been wrong in thinking that clean hands might constitute a requirement for the exercise of diplomatic protection. Although there were differences of opinion in the literature and the practice of the ICJ was not entirely conclusive, the Special Rapporteur's analysis of the *Ben Tillett*, *Clark* v. *Allen* and "*Virginius*" cases (paras. 11–15) was persuasive, and showed that the advocates of the clean hands doctrine put forward no decisive reasons for their thesis, which thus belonged to the realm of the progressive development rather than the codification of international law.

[3] *Official Records of the General Assembly, Fifty-ninth Session, Sixth Committee*, 24th meeting (A/C.6/59/SR.24), para. 44.

22. He was not, however, entirely convinced by either of the two arguments put forward in paragraphs 8 and 9 of the report, although, taken together, they did justify the Special Rapporteur's decision not to contribute to the progressive development of international law in that regard. On the first argument, he was not convinced that the Special Rapporteur was correct in asserting in paragraph 8 that once a dispute had assumed the character of a dispute between States, the previous conduct of the individual involved was no longer of any importance. That by no means went without saying. While he would not presume, at the current stage, to question the sanctity of the fiction on which the *Mavrommatis* principle was based, the Commission should not make that principle say more than it actually did. While it was true that it resulted in a sort of "transubstantiation" of the injury initially caused to an individual by an internationally wrongful act of a State, the factor triggering diplomatic protection nevertheless remained, and there was nothing intrinsically incongruous in considering that the individual's having clean hands could constitute a precondition for the exercise of diplomatic protection, just as the exhaustion of domestic remedies was a requirement incumbent on the individual, not on the State exercising diplomatic protection.

23. The second argument put forward by the Special Rapporteur, relying on the *LaGrand* and *Avena* cases, was that if the individual committed an unlawful act in the host State and was tried and punished in accordance with due process of law, no internationally wrongful act occurred and the clean hands doctrine was irrelevant. Such a conception of the clean hands doctrine was far too vague. The Special Rapporteur took into account only cases of individuals with unclean hands under the domestic law of the State whose responsibility was invoked, without considering the relationship between the illegal act committed by the individual and the internationally wrongful act of the State. The Special Rapporteur's reasoning might be tenable in the cases cited, but did not represent the primary consideration behind the clean hands doctrine. In determining whether an individual's conduct was in some way related to diplomatic protection, it was necessary to ascertain whether the individual enjoying diplomatic protection had himself been responsible either for a breach of the rule of international law which he accused the State of breaching, or at least whether the breach of which he was accused was directly related to the internationally wrongful act of which the State was accused.

24. For example, in the *LaGrand* case, if the individual concerned had refused any form of communication with the United States judicial authorities, or had concealed his German nationality from them, the question would have arisen whether the requirement of clean hands would be grounds for inadmissibility of a claim to exercise diplomatic protection by Germany, not with respect to the murder committed by that individual, which was completely unrelated to the alleged internationally wrongful act, but with respect to the refusal to communicate with the judicial authorities or the concealment of his German nationality, since the individual would, through his unclean hands, have put himself in a position in which he was not entitled to the protection afforded by the 1963 Vienna Convention.

25. To take another example, if a transnational corporation concealed some of its profits and was expropriated without compensation, the question of unclean hands would arise because the company's attitude was directly related to the internationally wrongful act. However, although the Special Rapporteur implied otherwise, it was not enough for the individual simply to have breached the internal law of a State which had itself caused an injury to the individual by committing an internationally wrongful act unrelated to the original breach. Those two hypothetical cases illustrated that the examples chosen by the Special Rapporteur were ill-chosen. However, he acknowledged that the consequence of the illegal conduct was generally not to prevent the exercise of diplomatic protection, but rather to blot out the internationally wrongful act: either the exercise of protection by the State became impossible, as in his hypothetical case based on *LaGrand*, or else some other circumstance ruled out any wrongful act.

26. In other words, although he was prepared to go along with the position proposed by the Special Rapporteur, it was not for the oversimplistic reasons given by the Special Rapporteur in paragraphs 8 and 9 of his report, but for two other reasons. First, he was convinced that there were no true precedents to the contrary, so that if the clean hands doctrine was elevated to the status of a precondition for the exercise of diplomatic protection, the Commission would not be engaged in the codification of international law but in its progressive development. Second, it would not be helpful, in the case of what he considered to be the "true" clean hands doctrine, to stipulate in advance that the State of nationality could not exercise protection; it would be sufficient, as the Special Rapporteur said in paragraph 16, to state that the clean hands doctrine "would more appropriately be raised at the merits stage as it relate[d] to the attenuation or exoneration of responsibility".

27. He continued to disagree with another aspect of the report, though that disagreement did not concern diplomatic protection as such but rather the general framework of inter-State claims for direct harm caused to a State by the wrongful act of another State. In that respect, he found the Special Rapporteur's arguments in paragraphs 5 to 7 and 18 regrettably ambiguous. His own view, which was reflected in the introduction to the report, was that the clean hands doctrine had no effect on the admissibility of an inter-State claim, but that it might have an effect on the possibility of exercising diplomatic protection. The Special Rapporteur's arguments had persuaded him that he had been mistaken on the second point. However, on that second point, the Special Rapporteur's argument was rather weak, as it took an ambiguous assertion as its starting point. The Special Rapporteur stated in paragraph 5 of the report that it might—why "might"?—be correct that the clean hands doctrine did not apply to disputes involving inter-State relations, but then argued that it was in that area that the clean hands doctrine was most appropriate, as that was the area in which it was most frequently invoked. The examples cited by the Special Rapporteur were something of a hotchpotch: for example, he cited, *inter alia*, the *LaGrand* and *Avena* cases not only in support of the non-applicability of the clean hands doctrine to disputes involving inter-State relations but also in support of its

non-applicability in the context of diplomatic protection. He could not have it both ways. Moreover, one thing that all the examples showed was that the clean hands doctrine concerned the merits of a case, not its admissibility; either the State invoking the clean hands doctrine had itself argued the case on the basis of the merits, as in the *Gabčíkovo–Nagymaros Project* case, or the Court had ruled that the doctrine applied only to the consideration of the merits. The clean hands doctrine, which was derived directly from the principle of good faith, therefore applied not to the admissibility of international claims but to their merits, exactly as in cases of diplomatic protection.

28. That said, he wished again to thank the Special Rapporteur for his willingness to engage in a debate he had regarded as futile from the outset. That discussion had enabled an important question to be clarified. He wished to stress once again his regret at the very premature transmission of the draft articles on diplomatic protection to the General Assembly on first reading. Although those articles were on the whole acceptable to him, despite their timidity—especially in relation to the *Mavrommatis* principle—the draft did not deal with diplomatic protection in general, despite its title, but rather with only one aspect of it, namely, the conditions for the exercise of diplomatic protection. States were given no guidance on questions such as who could exercise such protection, how it should be exercised and the consequences of its exercise. For example, there was no discussion of the effect of the exercise of diplomatic protection on other international proceedings open to injured individuals. The "without prejudice" clause in article 17 raised the question but, by definition, did not resolve it. Nor was the question of how to evaluate harm in cases involving the exercise of diplomatic protection addressed. According to the Vattelian fiction, harm should be evaluated on the basis of the injury suffered by the State, but in fact it was the injury suffered by the protected individual that was the basis for assessing compensation. It would not have been amiss to discuss that point in the report and to spell it out in the draft.

29. Another question that had not been addressed was the fact that, under article 2 of the draft articles, only a State had the right to exercise diplomatic protection, while an individual had no actual right to be compensated, even if the State responsible discharged its obligations in terms of compensation. The question of the justification for that rule should surely have been raised, with a view to abrogating or attenuating it in the context of the progressive development of international law. Such a rule was hard to countenance in the twenty-first century, and the failure to deal with that fundamental question was a major gap in the draft articles.

30. Those omissions were particularly regrettable in view of the Special Rapporteur's usual concern for the protection of the rights of individuals. The debate on the clean hands doctrine was really of secondary importance in the context of the draft articles as a whole, but the Special Rapporteur had at least discussed it: it was highly regrettable that the Special Rapporteur had not been as open to discussion on other more fundamental aspects of the topic that he had raised some two years previously.

31. Mr. GAJA recalled that although the clean hands doctrine had been discussed in the *Barcelona Traction* case, the ICJ had not addressed the question, basing its decision on other considerations. He personally had never been convinced that the clean hands doctrine should apply in the case of diplomatic protection, since to deny the possibility of diplomatic protection on that basis would in practice exonerate a State from its responsibility for a breach of an international obligation relating to the treatment of aliens. Paragraph 16 of the report seemed to go too far in suggesting that there might be some exoneration from the consequences of responsibility.

32. Mr. DUGARD (Special Rapporteur) said he wished to dispel one misapprehension. Mr. Pellet had claimed to detect a certain annoyance on his part at having been obliged to prepare a report on the clean hands doctrine. That was not the case: he had found the whole exercise important and useful, and he was indebted to Mr. Pellet for having insisted that the matter be considered.

33. Mr. ECONOMIDES said that no conclusions could be drawn on the clean hands doctrine from the *LaGrand* and *Avena* cases, since the doctrine did not apply to consular assistance, which was provided to individuals in prison who almost all, by definition, had unclean hands. The key point with regard to diplomatic protection was that it was the State exercising such protection that decided on the amount of compensation, while individuals had no say in the matter. For example, when certain Greek assets had been nationalized, the decision had been a political one and the owners of the assets had often been very inadequately compensated for the injury suffered. For the moment, such matters were dealt with under States' domestic law, while international law remained at the stage of the *Mavrommatis* fiction, and individuals were still not fully protected. That question should perhaps be considered at a later stage.

34. Mr. MATHESON said he agreed with the Special Rapporteur's recommendation that the Commission should not take up the clean hands doctrine in the context of the draft articles on diplomatic protection. As mentioned in the report, the question of clean hands had been raised many times in the context of claims for direct State injury, but remained unresolved and was, in any case, outside the scope of diplomatic protection. As for the cases that were within the scope of diplomatic protection, the report showed that there was not enough practice to support codification, and he did not believe that the Commission should to go beyond codification at the present juncture.

Statement by the Under-Secretary-General of Legal Affairs, Legal Counsel

35. The CHAIRPERSON invited Mr. Nicolas Michel, Under-Secretary-General of Legal Affairs, Legal Counsel, to brief the Commission on the latest legal developments in the United Nations.

36. Mr. MICHEL (Under-Secretary-General of Legal Affairs, Legal Counsel) said that it was an honour to address the International Law Commission for the first time as Legal Counsel and to provide an overview

of events and activities related to its work. The General Assembly, in its resolution 59/41 of 2 December 2004, had expressed its appreciation to the Commission for the work accomplished at its fifty-sixth session, in particular for the completion of the first reading of draft articles on diplomatic protection and of the draft principles on the allocation of loss in the case of transboundary harm arising out of hazardous activities. It had also endorsed the Commission's decision to include in its agenda the topics "Expulsion of aliens" and "Effects of armed conflicts on treaties" and had renewed its invitation to Governments to provide information on the draft articles and commentary on diplomatic protection and on the draft principles on allocation of loss in the case of transboundary harm arising out of hazardous activities. To that end, the Secretary-General had transmitted *notes verbales* to Governments and the Secretariat would submit the comments received to the Commission before the second reading of the draft articles.

37. In the same resolution, the General Assembly encouraged the Commission to continue taking cost-saving measures; he was therefore sure that the General Assembly would appreciate the Commission's decision to shorten the second part of its current session by one week. The Secretariat was in the process of preparing the budget for 2006–2007 and would make every effort to ensure that due provision was made for the Commission's future programme, in line with the approach outlined in paragraph 735 of the report on the work of its fifty-second session.[4] He was sure that the Commission, for its part, would decide on any appropriate cost-saving measures it could take at its next session.

38. In its resolution 59/38, the General Assembly had adopted the United Nations Convention on Jurisdictional Immunities of States and their Property, the draft articles of which had been prepared by the Commission in 1991.[5] Many of those articles had remained unchanged in the final version after long and difficult negotiations in the Sixth Committee, showing that the Convention struck a fine balance between the different viewpoints of States. The Convention, which had been opened for signature on 17 January 2005, had already been signed by Austria, Belgium, Morocco and Portugal. It would remain open for signature until 17 January 2007, and would enter into force following the deposit of the thirtieth instrument of ratification.

39. On 13 April 2005, the General Assembly had adopted by consensus, in its resolution 59/290, the International Convention for the Suppression of Acts of Nuclear Terrorism, which was a significant addition to the 12 existing conventions relating to terrorism. The Convention encouraged States to collaborate closely and required them to extradite or prosecute criminals according to the *aut dedere aut judicare* principle, which the Commission had included in its long-term programme of work. The adoption of the Convention demonstrated how the General Assembly could make an effective contribution to the development of international legal norms even in the most politically sensitive fields. Member States would now be focusing on the drafting of another important legal instrument, namely, a comprehensive convention on international terrorism. *In his report In Larger Freedom: Towards Development, Security and Human Rights for All*, the Secretary-General had urged world leaders to do their utmost to ensure that the convention was adopted at the sixtieth session of the General Assembly.[6]

40. An international convention against the reproductive cloning of human beings had been on the agenda of the Sixth Committee since 2001, and had been the source of much contention among Member States. The Sixth Committee had considered a compromise proposal for negotiating an international instrument other than a convention, and on 8 March 2005 the General Assembly, in its resolution 59/280, had adopted the United Nations Declaration on Human Cloning. The Declaration called on Member States to prohibit all forms of human cloning inasmuch as they were incompatible with human dignity and the protection of human life. The General Assembly had thus concluded its consideration of the topic.

41. Turning to developments in the field of international criminal jurisdiction, he said that by resolution 58/318 of 13 September 2004, the General Assembly had approved the Relationship Agreement between the United Nations and the International Criminal Court which had been approved by the Assembly of States Parties to the Rome Statute of the International Criminal Court on 7 September 2004. The Secretary-General and the President of the Court had then proceeded to sign the Agreement on 4 October 2004. It had entered into force that same day. Under the Agreement, the United Nations undertook to cooperate with the Court with due regard to its responsibilities and competence under the Charter and subject to its rules. At the request of the Court or the Prosecutor, the United Nations could provide information and documents relevant to the work of the Court. It could also agree to provide the Court with other forms of cooperation and assistance. The Relationship Agreement anticipated the conclusion of supplementary arrangements to implement its terms. On the basis of such arrangements, the United Nations had already rendered extensive logistical assistance to the Prosecutor, particularly in connection with his investigations in the Democratic Republic of the Congo. It had also provided access to information and documentation and facilitated the interviewing of witnesses.

42. Concerning the Khmer Rouge trials, work had continued over the past year to put in place the necessary arrangements for the entry into force of the Agreement between the United Nations and the Royal Government of Cambodia concerning the prosecution under Cambodian Law of crimes committed during the period of Democratic Kampuchea. In December 2004, a third planning mission had visited Phnom Penh to complete work on identifying the probable requirements of the Extraordinary Chambers and their related institutions in terms of personnel, equipment, furniture and supplies. It had proved possible to reach agreement with the Government of Cambodia on a complete budget and staffing table as well as to establish the basic outlines of the two ancillary arrangements

[4] *Yearbook ... 2000*, vol. II (Part Two), p. 132.

[5] *Yearbook ... 1991*, vol. II (Part Two), pp. 12–62.

[6] A/59/2005.

provided for in the Agreement, on security and on utilities, facilities and services.

43. On 28 March 2005 the Secretary-General had convened a pledging conference with a view to seeking the US$43 million needed to fund the assistance that the United Nations was committed to provide under the Agreement. He had received sufficient contributions and pledges to meet the Organization's obligations for nearly the whole of the Extraordinary Chambers' expected three-year lifespan. On 28 April 2005 the Secretary-General had notified the Cambodian Government that the United Nations had complied with the legal requirements for entry into force of the Agreement. The Agreement had accordingly entered into force the following day, Cambodia having already provided its corresponding notification on 16 November 2004. Steps were being taken to appoint key international personnel with a view to their early deployment to Phnom Penh. The Legal Counsel would shortly send a letter to all States inviting them to suggest individuals whom the Secretary-General might nominate for appointment as international judges, international prosecutor, international investigating judge or judges of the Pre-Trial Chamber.

44. The tenth anniversary of the entry into force of the United Nations Convention on the Law of the Sea had been celebrated in 2004. The year 2005 marked the tenth anniversary of the adoption of the Agreement for the Implementation of the Provisions of the United Nations Convention on the Law of Sea of 10 December 1982 relating to the Conservation and Management of Straddling Fish Stocks and Highly Migratory Fish Stocks. There were now almost 150 parties to the Convention and over 50 parties to the Fish Stocks Agreement.

45. Three important issues would hold centre stage in the next few years: first, international fisheries and how to deal with illegal fishing, destructive fishing practices and the depletion of fish stocks in many parts of the world; second, the conservation and sustainable use of marine biological resources beyond national jurisdiction; and third, the development of a regular process for global reporting and assessment of the state of the marine environment, including its social and economic dimensions. Aspects of the first issue would be discussed at the sixth meeting of the Open-ended informal consultative process on oceans and the law of the sea in June 2005. In addition, pursuant to article 36 of the Fish Stocks Agreement, the General Assembly had requested the Secretary-General to convene a review conference in the first part of 2006 in order to assess the effectiveness of the Agreement in securing the conservation and management of straddling fish stocks and highly migratory fish stocks.

46. With respect to marine biological resources, the General Assembly had established an Ad Hoc Open-ended Informal Working Group to study issues relating to the conservation and sustainable use of marine biological diversity beyond areas of national jurisdiction, including the past and present activities of the United Nations and other relevant international organizations. In the light of its work on the fragmentation of international law, the Commission might be particularly interested in that issue, since it would require compiling and reconciling a diverse body of law in different sectors so as to create new law consistent with the general principles contained in the Convention.

47. With regard to UNCITRAL, he noted that 2005 marked two important anniversaries: the twenty-fifth anniversary of the adoption of the United Nations Convention on Contracts for the International Sale of Goods and the twentieth anniversary of the adoption of the UNCITRAL Model Law on International Commercial Arbitration.[7] Conferences were being organized in various parts of the world to celebrate the anniversaries and to discuss the experience of courts and arbitral tribunals with those texts. In March 2005, two conferences dedicated to those anniversaries had been held in Vienna. The main topic on the UNCITRAL agenda at its thirty-eighth session, to take place in Vienna in July 2005, was the finalization of a draft convention on the use of electronic communications in international contracts. The draft convention reaffirmed the principle of functional equivalence between paper documents and electronic communications, as well as between electronic authentification methods and handwritten signatures. It established uniform rules for substantive contractual issues where needed to ensure the effectiveness of electronic communications. It was hoped that the draft convention would facilitate the use of electronic communications exchanged in connection with contracts covered by other international instruments, some of which presently created legal obstacles to electronic commerce.

48. Among the activities undertaken by the Treaty Section to promote greater participation in treaties, treaty events had been organized to coincide with the high-level segment of the General Assembly. In September 2004, in the context of the treaty signature and deposit ceremony, Focus 2004: Treaties on the Protection of Civilians had resulted in 101 treaty actions by 34 States. Focus 2005: Responding to Global Challenges was scheduled to be held from 14 to 16 September 2005 during the high-level summit of the sixtieth session of the General Assembly. As a lead-up to Focus 2005, a high-level panel of experts was planned for 9 June 2005 on the theme *Terrorism: A Challenge to Civilized Society*. Treaty events since—and including—the United Nations Millennium Summit had resulted in 927 treaty actions.[8]

49. Turning to information on other activities that might be of interest to the Commission, he said that an important part of the mandate of the Office of Legal Affairs was to organize courses and seminars, prepare publications and keep numerous websites on international law constantly updated. The Codification Division, in cooperation with the United Nations Institute for Training and Research (UNITAR), continued to organize courses and seminars for young professionals, government officials and teachers of international law, in particular from developing countries. The courses were held in The Hague concurrently

[7] *Official Records of the General Assembly, Fortieth Session, Supplement No. 17* (A/40/17), "Report of the United Nations Commission on International Trade Law on the work of its eighteenth session", annex I, p. 81.

[8] The list of the events, publications and reports published parallel to the treaty ceremonies is available in English and in French on the website of the United Nations Treaty Collection (http://treaties.un.org/).

with The Hague Academy courses so as to enable participants to benefit from the latter. Another component of the programme was the organization of regional courses, which had been facilitated in recent years through cost-saving measures taken by the International Fellowship Programme and through contributions from States, particularly those that had agreed to host such events. Negotiations were currently under way with a view to organizing, in cooperation with UNITAR, a course in Thailand for countries of South-East Asia. The International Law Seminar organized in conjunction with the Commission's own session would be held from 11 to 29 July 2005, bringing together 24 participants.

50. The Division for Ocean Affairs and the Law of the Sea had organized two training courses for developing countries on the very topical issue of the establishment of the outer limits of the continental shelf. The first course had been held in Fiji for developing countries of the South Pacific and East Asia. The second course had taken place in Sri Lanka for countries in the Indian Ocean region. Similar courses were planned for December 2005 in Ghana, for the West African region and for Latin American and Caribbean countries in early 2006. The courses covered both scientific and legal aspects of implementation of article 76 of the United Nations Convention on the Law of the Sea. Courses on treaty law and practice were likewise offered twice a year at United Nations Headquarters. Regional seminars had been organized in 2004 for the Caribbean Community (CARICOM) and in Viet Nam for over 100 participants from ministries of various countries.

51. With regard to publications, the volume of the *United Nations Juridical Yearbook* for 1998 would be issued in October 2005, while the volumes for 1999, 2000 and 2001 had already been edited and were in the process of publication. A number of volumes of the *Yearbook of the International Law Commission*, spanning the years 1993 to 2000, had been published in Arabic, Chinese, English, French and Russian. The Commission had already received the most recent publications prepared by the Codification Division, particularly the English version of the second edition of *International Instruments related to the Prevention and Suppression of International Terrorism*, with the French soon to be issued; Volume XXIII of the Reports of International Arbitral Awards; and the sixth edition of *The Work of the International Law Commission* in English, French and Spanish. The other language versions were still being translated. The Division for Ocean Affairs and the Law of the Sea was completing work on a new publication on the settlement of disputes, entitled *Digest of International Cases of the Law of the Sea*. In order to assist States in preparing their submissions to the Commission on the Limits of the Continental Shelf, the Division had drafted a manual on the preparation of submissions. The Treaty Section had prepared thematic publications giving an overview of treaties of particular relevance to events held concurrently with the General Assembly.

52. The Information Technology Project undertaken by the Office of Legal Affairs involved the conversion of several United Nations legal publications into electronic format with a view to making them available on the Internet. Various volumes of the *Repertory of Practice of United Nations Organs* were already available on the Internet, organized by study. Work had also been undertaken on the *Yearbook of the International Law Commission*, both the English and French versions of which had been converted into electronic format in their entirety. Work had progressed on the conversion into electronic format of the *United Nations Juridical Yearbook* and some other publications. The Office of Legal Affairs also maintained a number of websites covering the areas for which it was responsible, which, it was to be hoped, provided information useful to Commission members in their work. The Legal Counsel was pleased to announce that the Secretariat intended to hold presentations on using the electronic version of the *Yearbook of the International Law Commission*.

53. Having completed the formal part of his statement, and since he was meeting the Commission for the first time in his capacity as Legal Counsel, he wished to conclude by sharing some of his personal views on the major challenges facing international law. First, his experience of the past few months prompted him to mention the complex debate on the nature and role of international law. International law was a set of binding rules, not simply a set of political commitments. It must be seen as a decisive factor in international relations and not as simply one among many instruments determining international relations, to be taken up when useful and ignored when at variance with national interests.

54. The second challenge was ensuring respect for the rule of law, which should be seen as a priority by States and international organizations, particularly the United Nations, in their activities aimed at achieving a more just and more peaceful international community. He was thinking in particular of the rule of law within the international community as a whole, and in that connection he recalled the package of reforms contained in the report of the Secretary-General entitled *In Larger Freedom: Towards Development, Security and Human Rights for All*,[9] and the Secretary-General's report of August 2004 on "the rule of law and transitional justice in conflict and post-conflict societies".[10]

55. The third challenge was to achieve effective implementation of international law, something that required particular attention to be paid to the international and domestic machinery for its implementation. In that connection, parliaments had an essential role to play through the adoption of legislation for implementing the international obligations of States. The United Nations could and should make special efforts to provide States with appropriate assistance when they requested it. Domestic courts must also play a role in that field.

56. The CHAIRPERSON thanked the Legal Counsel for his valuable report on legal developments in the United Nations over the past year, and invited members to make comments and put questions.

[9] See footnote 6 above.

[10] S/2004/616.

57. Mr. GALICKI said it was a source of great satisfaction for all international lawyers that, after protracted negotiations, the International Convention for the Suppression of Acts of Nuclear Terrorism had recently been adopted. The Secretary-General had urged States to continue their efforts to complete the work on another long-standing task, namely, a comprehensive convention on international terrorism. The obstacles to the completion of that task were well known, but the issue was an important one because other, regional, bodies dealing with international terrorism, such as the Council of Europe, could not go forward with their work while the work of the Ad Hoc Committee on International Terrorism remained incomplete. He would accordingly like to know the Legal Counsel's views as to the likelihood of finalizing the work on the comprehensive convention on international terrorism.

58. Ms. ESCARAMEIA noted that the Legal Counsel had not mentioned the report of the High-level Panel on Threats, Challenges and Change.[11] Some subjects covered in that report, for example terrorism and the responsibility to protect, related to international law. She asked how the negotiations between States were progressing and whether it was intended that the Sixth Committee might become involved in future work in that area. She would also welcome further information on the presentations to be held on using the electronic version of the *Yearbook of the International Law Commission*.

59. Mr. Sreenivasa RAO said that one highly important issue mentioned by the Legal Counsel was the elaboration of a comprehensive convention on international terrorism. In the aftermath of the events of 11 September 2001, considerable progress had been made, and only three provisions had been left in abeyance because of lack of agreement on article 18 and on the article concerning the convention's relations with other instruments.[12]

60. Article 18 raised fundamental issues such as humanitarian law, the role of the military and the role of armed forces in occupied territories. Other conventions concluded on terrorism under United Nations auspices had sought to avoid clear-cut positions or the resolution of issues that should be dealt with in a broader political context. The formulas currently proposed did not take account of that requirement. However, the successful conclusion of the negotiations on the International Convention for the Suppression of Acts of Nuclear Terrorism in a spirit of good will and common sense seemed to augur well for completion of the work on the draft comprehensive convention on international terrorism,[13] and he would like to hear the Legal Counsel's views on the prospects for a successful outcome.

[11] See 2835th meeting, footnote 8.

[12] See, on this subject, *Official Records of the General Assembly, Fifty-seventh Session, Supplement No. 37* (A/57/37), annexes I–III, and annex IV for the texts related to article 18. For the rest of the work on the draft general convention, see the reports of the special Committee created by General Assembly resolution 51/210 of 17 December 1996 at the fifty-eighth, fifty-ninth and sixtieth sessions of the General Assembly (A/58/37, A/59/37, A/60/37).

[13] *Ibid., Sixtieth Session, Supplement No. 37* (A/60/37), chaps. II–III, annex I, paras. 24–29 and annex II, sect. A.

61. Mr. KOSKENNIEMI said that the Study Group on fragmentation of international law would finalize its work in 2006,[14] in all probability in the form of a comprehensive report on the question, together with guidelines or recommendations. During the years in which the Commission had dealt with the subject, considerable uncertainty had persisted as to its content. As the topical summary of the discussion of the Commission's work held in the Sixth Committee (A/CN.4/549 and Add.1) showed, delegations were not always sure where the work was heading. The suggestion had been made in the Study Group as well as at the fifty-ninth session of the General Assembly that the results of the Study Group's work should be disseminated as widely as possible, and a more specific proposal had been made that the Office of Legal Affairs should organize a panel discussion or seminar on the issue in 2006, perhaps in the Sixth Committee to explain the content of the topic to delegations in an informal setting. He asked whether the Office of Legal Affairs would be willing to help to organize such an event.

62. Mr. PELLET said it was fitting to pay tribute to the Secretariat in the Legal Counsel's presence for the services it rendered not only in ensuring the smooth functioning of the Commission, but also in advancing the development of international law in general. He noted the Secretariat's excellent studies on such questions as liability, the effect of armed conflict on treaties and the responsibility to protect in the context of natural disasters, all of which had been highly useful to the Commission. International legal experts were also most grateful to the Office of Legal Affairs and the Codification Division for their publications, such as the *Reports of International Arbitral Awards*, which were of constant usefulness. It was, however, unfortunate that the older volumes seemed to be out of print, and he asked whether they could be re-issued. It was also absolutely essential to make the *Repertory of Practice of United Nations Organs* available for online access, and he greatly hoped that that project would be continued and completed for the benefit of researchers and practitioners of international law. While he was pleased that the Office of Legal Affairs had been placing an increasing number of documents on the Internet, that did not mean that printed publications could be dispensed with. It was most regrettable that the volumes of the *Yearbook of the International Law Commission* were published so late; in particular, the enormous delay in the publication of Volume II (Part One), containing the reports of the Special Rapporteurs, was becoming totally unacceptable.

63. As he had pointed out at the previous session, it was also totally unacceptable that, while the members of the Commission had free online access to the United Nations *Treaty Series*, researchers and doctoral students should have to pay for access to an international public service. He urged the Legal Counsel to reconsider a decision that had been taken without giving any thought to its implications. Law was not just a commodity.

64. As Special Rapporteur on the topic of reservations to treaties, he hoped that in 2006 a joint seminar could be convened involving the Commission and the human

[14] See *Yearbook ... 2004*, vol. II (Part Two), chap. X, para. 302.

rights treaty monitoring bodies and that some financially acceptable arrangement could be found for carrying out an exercise that would be beneficial in the areas both of general international law and of international human rights law.

65. Mr. MANSFIELD noted that the Legal Counsel had made reference to an Ad Hoc Open-ended Informal Working Group to study issues relating to the conservation and sustainable use of marine biological diversity beyond areas of national jurisdiction, which might be of interest to the Commission because of the importance of coordinating different areas of law and the relevance for fragmentation, noting that that might involve the harmonization of different elements in international law. He asked the Legal Counsel to expand upon those remarks and also to comment on progress made in coordinating the work of the various international bodies with responsibility for oceans. Such activities had not been properly coordinated in the past, because they operated in different areas, over some of which the Secretary-General himself did not have authority. The Legal Office in the Division for Ocean Affairs and the Law of the Sea had a key role to play, but a high level of coordination was needed, and he wondered whether the Legal Counsel could play a personal part in that effort.

66. Mr. MICHEL (Under-Secretary-General of Legal Affairs, Legal Counsel) thanked members of the Commission for their positive comments and welcomed the opportunity to discuss areas in which progress could be made.

67. He shared the Commission's satisfaction with the outcome of negotiations on the International Convention for the Suppression of Acts of Nuclear Terrorism; the lessons to be learned might be useful in bringing work on the draft comprehensive convention to a successful conclusion. It was, however, important to avoid false analogies, because there were major differences between the two instruments with regard both to the subject and to the political context. The successful conclusion of work on the Nuclear Terrorism Convention was attributable to a number of reasons: the quality of the work done, especially by the coordinator; universal agreement about extent of the danger; and also, perhaps, the unvoiced desire on the part of many delegations to prove that the Organization's ordinary legislative mechanisms were able to function. Indeed, the Sixth Committee and its subsidiary bodies had achieved results on a politically sensitive matter, thereby illustrating the General Assembly's role and responsibility in that area. The Security Council had recently adopted provisions which had been perceived by the Sixth Committee and its subsidiary bodies, as well as by the General Assembly, as an expression of very wide-ranging legislative activity.

68. Similar considerations applied to the draft comprehensive convention, but only to a certain extent. In adopting the International Convention for the Suppression of Acts of Nuclear Terrorism, the participants had shown that the process was no longer completely deadlocked, and had disproved the conventional wisdom that no progress could be made until certain urgent political questions were resolved. Thus, some momentum had begun to develop, although that did not mean that there were grounds for undue optimism with regard to the draft comprehensive convention. There were still substantial obstacles concerning the substance and in connection with the general climate of the negotiations. It was unfortunate that the political discussion had sometimes focused on problems that were not really relevant. Mr. Sreenivasa Rao had drawn attention to the obstacles that still had to be overcome. It was to be hoped that at the High-level Plenary Meeting in September 2005, Heads of State would show the political will needed to make headway on the draft. Meanwhile, the Office of Legal Affairs would do its utmost to encourage that outcome. The oral report presented by the coordinator of negotiations, Mr. Díaz Paniagua, had provided a useful account of the state of negotiations and outstanding issues and was included in the report of the Ad Hoc Committee.[15] Both conventions were instruments of criminal law whose aim was to prohibit, prevent and punish certain conduct by establishing rules of criminal law, not to produce a general political condemnation of terrorism. He shared the eagerness of the Commission to see the work completed during the sixtieth session of the General Assembly.

69. With regard to Ms. Escarameia's comments on the work of the High-level Panel on Threats, Challenges and Change, he said that the main points regarding follow-up by the Secretariat were contained in the report of the Secretary-General, *In Larger Freedom: Towards Development, Security and Human Rights for All*;[16] it was now for the General Assembly to take up that work in accordance with the working method established by the President of the General Assembly, so that various questions could be addressed in greater depth before the debate in the General Assembly itself. Thus, by following the work of the General Assembly, it would be possible to see which questions raised in the report of the High-level Panel and reflected in the report of the Secretary-General had subsequently been debated in the General Assembly. With specific regard to terrorism in that context, he had nothing to add to what he had already said about the work in the Sixth Committee or the Ad Hoc Committee on Terrorism.

70. Indirect reference had been made to the proposal to adopt guidelines on the use of force. While he did not wish to prejudge the final outcome of the current discussions on the matter, the general perception seemed to be that it was not at all certain that such guidelines would be adopted. Those discussions were helping to clarify the concept of "responsibility to protect". Until now, the question had been posed in such a politically sensitive context that the reactions had been based to a large extent either on instinctively positive or instinctively negative perceptions; a rational, in-depth discussion of the concepts at issue would be most welcome, if only to prevent the idea from taking hold that the concept of responsibility to protect would automatically result in the recognition of a new criterion for legality of the use of force, additional to those set forth in the Charter of the United Nations.

71. A presentation on access to the electronic versions of the *Yearbook of the International Law Commission* and documentation sources would be held the following week.

[15] See footnote 13 above.

[16] See footnote 6 above.

72. As to Mr. Koskenniemi's remarks, it was his experience that seminars held at Headquarters involving academics, United Nations officials and representatives of non-governmental organizations were an excellent way of reflecting on problems that merited the attention of the international community. Thus, he was open to Mr. Koskenniemi's proposal and was prepared to consider with him how it could be given concrete form. Resourcefulness and a search for potential partners should make it possible to find funding for those activities. He would not wish to see financial issues place undue constraints on progress in the field of international law, and he would make that issue a focal point of his future activities. If the rule of law was really a priority for the international community, then it required a corresponding financial commitment.

73. He thanked Mr. Pellet for his kind words addressed to the Secretariat. He was proud of the quality of its work. With regard to the question of reprinting old volumes, he hoped that, with the introduction of new information technologies, documents that had been out of print could be made available on websites. He shared Mr. Pellet's concern about the lateness of publications. He was trying to find a solution to the question of Internet access, although he was cautious about the outcome, since he had no personal control over the matter. He took note of the proposal for a joint seminar involving the Commission and human rights treaty monitoring bodies and was grateful for all such suggestions.

74. On the question raised by Mr. Mansfield on fragmentation, he said that was an area with which he was as yet unfamiliar. He had noted with interest that colleagues closely involved in that area had stressed the importance of the law of the sea in the context of the subject of fragmentation. In recent months, he had learned that the resources earmarked for coordination were manifestly insufficient. Every effort must be made to obtain such funding, but increased attention should also be given to coordinating the resources currently available, and not only in the area of the law of the sea. Every year, two meetings of legal experts were held, one for United Nations funds, programmes and departments and another for the various entities of the system. The Office of Legal Affairs at Headquarters must work to improve all such coordination efforts. He had no illusions at the current stage: the system was complicated and cumbersome, and the various entities had their own rules, but much could be achieved on the basis of good faith. He had been reminded of the issue of fragmentation during the presentation of a report in New York by the Chairperson of the Study Group, who had noted that institutional fragmentation had not been addressed.[17] Thus, the question remained at the centre of attention. If, for understandable reasons, the Study Group could not take up the question, ways must be found of overcoming the most important obstacles in that area. While he was not very optimistic as to the short-term results, in the longer run, the problem could not be disregarded: the credibility and effectiveness of the system were at stake.

[17] See *Official Records of the General Assembly, Fifty-eighth Session, Sixth Committee, 20th meeting* (A/C.6./58/SR.20), statement of Mr. Candioti, Chairperson of the Commission, paras. 5–8.

75. The CHAIRPERSON thanked the Legal Counsel for his comments and clarifications.

Organization of work of the session (*continued*)*

[Agenda item 1]

76. Mr. MANSFIELD (Chairperson of the Drafting Committee) announced that the Drafting Committee on responsibility of international organizations would be composed of Mr. Comissário Afonso, Mr. Chee, Ms. Escarameia, Mr. Economides, Mr. Gaja (Special Rapporteur), Mr. Kolodkin, Mr. Matheson, Mr. Sreenivasa Rao, Ms. Xue, Mr. Yamada, and Mr. Niehaus (Rapporteur, *ex officio*).

The meeting rose at 1 p.m.

2845th MEETING

Friday, 27 May 2005, at 10.10 a.m.

Chairperson: Mr. Djamchid MOMTAZ

Present: Mr. Addo, Mr. Al-Baharna, Mr. Al-Marri, Mr. Baena Soares, Mr. Brownlie, Mr. Candioti, Mr. Chee, Mr. Comissário Afonso, Mr. Dugard, Mr. Economides, Ms. Escarameia, Mr. Fomba, Mr. Gaja, Mr. Galicki, Mr. Kabatsi, Mr. Kateka, Mr. Kolodkin, Mr. Mansfield, Mr. Matheson, Mr. Pambou-Tchivounda, Mr. Pellet, Mr. Sreenivasa Rao, Mr. Rodríguez Cedeño, Ms. Xue, Mr. Yamada.

Diplomatic protection (*continued*) (A/CN.4/549 and Add.1, sect. F and A/CN.4/546)

[Agenda item 2]

Sixth report of the Special Rapporteur (*continued*)

1. Mr. AL-BAHARNA commended the Special Rapporteur and recalled that his report had been submitted in response to a request from the Commission to consider the advisability of including a provision reflecting the clean hands doctrine in the draft articles. He agreed with the Special Rapporteur's findings that such an inclusion would be unwarranted and noted that the debates on that doctrine in the Sixth Committee had reached a similar conclusion. In the *LaGrand* and *Avena* cases, to which reference had been made in the report, the plaintiff States, whose nationals had been tried and sentenced in accordance with due process of law for the serious crimes they had committed under the domestic law of the respondent State, had based their claims on the wrongful conduct of the respondent State in respect of the crimes committed. In both cases the Court had refuted the arguments of the United States and rejected the applicability of the

* Resumed from the 2840th meeting.

clean hands doctrine to the claims raised by Germany and Mexico respectively.

2. Although the Special Rapporteur had concluded that it would be injudicious to include the clean hands doctrine in the draft articles, it was open to question whether there might not be cases in which it might serve to preclude the exercise of diplomatic protection. If that was so, an article to fill that gap might be required. The Special Rapporteur seemed to admit that possibility in paragraph 8 of his report, when he stated that "[i]f an alien [was] guilty of some wrongdoing in a foreign State and [was] as a consequence deprived of his liberty or property... by that State it [was] unlikely that his national State [would] intervene to protect him". Moreover, in the third sentence of that paragraph the Special Rapporteur added, "In this sense the clean hands doctrine serves to preclude diplomatic protection". The Commission should therefore look into the question of the inadmissibility of a plea in the light of the clean hands principle.

3. Mr. Sreenivasa RAO, echoing the words of Sir Gerald Fitzmaurice quoted in paragraph 2 of the Special Rapporteur's report, to wit, "He who comes to equity for relief must come with clean hands", said that, generally speaking, a person could not complain of the wrongful consequences of an act if they stemmed from another act of which the complainant was the author. The application of the principle of good faith, as Mr. Pellet had termed it, might yield different results in different situations and did not necessarily deny the complainant the right to seek a suitable remedy, even if the complainant's own illegal conduct had elicited the wrongful response.

4. For example, a State that had engaged in a wrongful act prompting a disproportionate response might be entitled to lodge a complaint. Alternatively, a party adversely affected by wrongful conduct was entitled to complain even it was found that the party had itself contributed to such conduct through its own negligence. In that case, due account should be taken of its share of responsibility, although the latter would not automatically constitute grounds for denying the claim itself.

5. The Special Rapporteur, with his customary thoroughness, had surveyed the most recent case law on the matter and had concluded in paragraph 6 of his report that the cases in question "make it difficult to sustain the argument that the clean hands doctrine does not apply to disputes involving direct inter-State relations". He had reached that conclusion principally because the ICJ had not expressly voiced any negative view of States' claims, but had simply considered that they did not justify a denial by the Court of its jurisdiction on the basis of the clean hands doctrine, which they had invoked in one form or another.

6. While the Special Rapporteur might be right on that point, it was more important to consider whether the Commission really needed to debate the issue. He was inclined to believe that, like the Court, it did not need to pronounce on the question, since the issues at stake were not central to the topic under consideration. On the other hand, it was necessary to decide whether or not to include a provision on the clean hands doctrine in the draft articles. In the chapter of his report on the cases of application of the clean hands doctrine to diplomatic protection, the Special Rapporteur put forward the convincing argument that, unlike cases involving direct inter-State claims, the doctrine in question had rarely been relied upon in the context of diplomatic protection. Furthermore, writers who had expressed support for the application of the doctrine in that context had done so without sufficient legal authority. The Special Rapporteur was therefore right to conclude that the insertion of such a provision was unnecessary, for it would not constitute an exercise in codification or the progressive development of law. If, as the Special Rapporteur had usefully pointed out in paragraph 16 of the report, the doctrine was applicable to claims relating to diplomatic protection, it would be more appropriate to raise it at the merits stage. However, on the questions of attenuation or exoneration of responsibility, which were also mentioned in that paragraph, Mr. Gaja had correctly observed that the admission of wrongdoing by the plaintiff State should have the appropriate consequences when determining remedies, but must not lead to exoneration.

7. Since opinions within the Commission were divided about the advisability of using the opportunity afforded by the debate on the clean hands doctrine to engage in the progressive development of the law on diplomatic protection, as advocated by Mr. Pellet, it would be helpful if the Special Rapporteur could provide some guidance in the matter.

8. Mr. BROWNLIE said that while he approved of the general conclusions reached by the Special Rapporteur, the question of the clean hands doctrine ought possibly to be analysed in a different manner. In opining that, on the whole, the clean hands doctrine was not part of either positive international law or *lex lata*, the Special Rapporteur had, perhaps, overestimated the strength of some evidence and attached too much importance to the status of that doctrine in the sources of international law, since contrary to what was stated in paragraph 6, the clean hands doctrine had not been "frequently raised" by States; it had been raised only from time to time, very briefly, as a preliminary objection and always by the same States. Curiously, the report did not mention the *Certain Phosphate Lands in Nauru* case, in which Australia had invoked that doctrine. It could not, therefore, be said that the courts had ever had to consider the clean hands doctrine very seriously, despite the impression given in paragraph 6.

9. While the importance of the clean hands doctrine being part of *lex lata* was debatable, the Special Rapporteur's conclusion, which he endorsed, did not preclude the Commission from adopting some version of the doctrine as a form of progressive development of the law. The key question turned on the precise definition of the clean hands doctrine because in reality the same term covered several different legal positions, which did not make the task any easier. It was often hard to determine on what account States were invoking the doctrine in a particular case. In some cases, it would certainly be part of the merits, if evidence eventually supported the alleged facts. It would then be of significance to discover whether the courts had ever joined the issue of clean hands to the merits, on the grounds that it was not exclusively a preliminary objection. In other cases, the doctrine was invoked by way of

prejudice and presented as a form of international public policy. Each case therefore called for contextual analysis and careful characterization.

10. A distinction could therefore be drawn between two qualitatively different situations: first, where the alleged illegality would, in principle, form part of the merits and thus would not fall within the Commission's mandate to deal with diplomatic protection; and secondly, where it was invoked as a principle of international public policy which constituted a bar to the admissibility of a claim, in which case the admissibility in question did not fall under the rubric of diplomatic protection. It was an international public policy point that could, of course, be raised *ex parte* by a respondent State, but it was not a form of diplomatic protection.

11. Since the Special Rapporteur had concluded that the issue should not be covered in the draft articles, the Sixth Committee should be provided with an explanation of why the Commission had decided to omit the clean hands doctrine. Another possibility would be to provide for a reservation referring to general international law, simply stating that the draft articles were without prejudice to the application of general international law to questions of admissibility in other situations. Very broad wording along those lines would satisfy those who thought that the Commission's position on the clean hands doctrine was too neat and tidy.

12. Mr. YAMADA said that he accepted the Special Rapporteur's conclusion but agreed with Mr. Pellet that the logic employed in paragraph 9 was a little odd, as the penultimate sentence seemed to imply that the seriousness of the crimes committed by the nationals in question was a factor that determined whether their hands were clean or not. However, in order to ascertain whether the nationals to be protected had clean hands, it was necessary to establish the existence of a causal link between the act or omission of the national in question and the internationally wrongful act committed by the host State. For example, in the *LaGrand* case, the heinous nature of the crimes committed by the foreign nationals was irrelevant; what counted was whether they had contributed to the failure of the United States authorities to notify the German consular authorities, in other words whether they had misled the United States authorities by hiding their German nationality, or whether they had requested that the German consular authorities not be contacted and had thus been instrumental in preventing the United States authorities from complying with an international obligation.

13. He accepted that there was no evidence establishing that the clean hands principle was the cause of the inadmissibility of a claim. However, as the principle was certainly relevant to the merits of the case, the rule concerning contribution to the injury, termed "contributory negligence" or "comparative fault" in national legal systems and set forth in draft article 39 on State responsibility for internationally wrongful acts, was applicable.[1]

14. Mr. KABATSI said that he fully agreed with the Special Rapporteur's conclusion that it was unnecessary to incorporate a provision on the clean hands doctrine in the draft articles on diplomatic protection.

15. Mr. CANDIOTI endorsed the Special Rapporteur's findings and Mr. Yamada's comment about the applicability of the draft article 39 on State responsibility, especially in an overall context. On second reading, it might be possible to consider a broad provision along the lines suggested by Mr. Brownlie, such as a reference to nonspecific provisions on the application of general international law, especially the law of responsibility.

The meeting rose at 10.48 a.m.

2846th MEETING

Tuesday, 31 May 2005, at 10.05 a.m.

Chairperson: Mr. Djamchid MOMTAZ

Present: Mr. Addo, Mr. Al-Baharna, Mr. Brownlie, Mr. Candioti, Mr. Chee, Mr. Comissário Afonso, Mr. Dugard, Mr. Economides, Ms. Escarameia, Mr. Fomba, Mr. Galicki, Mr. Kateka, Mr. Kolodkin, Mr. Koskenniemi, Mr. Mansfield, Mr. Matheson, Mr. Pambou-Tchivounda, Mr. Pellet, Mr. Sreenivasa Rao, Mr. Rodríguez Cedeño, Ms. Xue, Mr. Yamada.

Diplomatic protection (*concluded*) (A/CN.4/549 and Add.1, sect. F and A/CN.4/546)

[Agenda item 2]

SIXTH REPORT OF THE SPECIAL RAPPORTEUR (*concluded*)

1. The CHAIRPERSON invited the Special Rapporteur to sum up the debate on his sixth report on diplomatic protection (A/CN.4/546).

2. Mr. DUGARD (Special Rapporteur) said that the Commission's consideration of his sixth report had been a worthwhile exercise. The clean hands doctrine was an important principle of international law which should be taken into account whenever there was evidence that an applicant State had not acted in good faith and that it had come to court with unclean hands. It should be distinguished from the *tu quoque* argument, which allowed a respondent State to assert that the applicant State had also violated a rule of international law, and should instead be confined to cases in which the applicant State had acted improperly in bringing a case to court.

3. He thanked Mr. Pellet for having raised the issue and for having agreed, after consideration, that the doctrine did not, at least principally, belong to the realm of diplomatic protection and therefore did not warrant inclusion in the draft articles.

4. Although no other speaker had contended or even suggested that the clean hands doctrine should be included in

[1] *Yearbook ... 2001*, vol. II (Part Two) and corrigendum, pp. 109–110.

the draft articles on diplomatic protection, some members had referred to its place in the international legal order in general, and in international litigation in particular.

5. A number of points in his report had been the subject of fair criticism. For Mr. Gaja and Mr. Sreenivasa Rao, the suggestion in paragraph 16 that the clean hands doctrine might lead to exoneration at the merits stage went too far. Mr. Pellet and Mr. Yamada had argued that the reference in paragraph 9 to the *LaGrand* and *Avena* cases failed to analyse properly their relevance to the conduct of the United States. Mr. Brownlie had contended that paragraph 6 gave too much credit to the importance of the clean hands doctrine, and he was of course right: courts had never really had to give it serious consideration. Mr. Brownlie had also rightly drawn attention to the failure of the report to take up the *Certain Phosphate Lands in Nauru* case or to examine whether the clean hands doctrine had ever been joined to the merits. He personally had never come across such a case of joinder.

6. A number of useful suggestions had also been made. For example, Mr. Brownlie had proposed that a clause be inserted on second reading to the effect that the articles on diplomatic protection were without prejudice to general international law. In the course of his helpful comments, Mr. Pellet had raised two fundamental issues which related, not to the clean hands doctrine, but to the draft articles on diplomatic protection, and he would now consider those issues at some length.

7. First, Mr. Pellet had expressed reservations about the *Mavrommatis* principle, according to which an injury to an individual was an injury to a State; second, he had again raised the question whether it might be appropriate to examine the consequences of diplomatic protection in the draft articles. As the Commission's agenda at its next session was likely to be very full, and as there was general agreement that the draft articles on diplomatic protection must be completed by the end of the quinquennium, it would be wise to consider those two issues immediately, if only in a preliminary manner.

8. Mr. Pellet had correctly noted that the *Mavrommatis* principle was a fiction—something that he himself had repeatedly acknowledged. That had serious implications for the individual. One implication was that, because the claim was seen to be that of the State and not of the individual, it was generally accepted that it had discretion as to whether to bring a claim for diplomatic protection. In his first report, he had tried to persuade the Commission to make it obligatory for States to exercise diplomatic protection where a norm of *jus cogens* had been violated in respect of the individual;[1] however, the Commission had rejected his proposal on the ground that that would have meant engaging in progressive development. Another implication was that the State had discretion as to whether to pay out money which it received by way of compensation as a result of the exercise of diplomatic protection.

9. The *Mavrommatis* principle was of course inconsistent and flawed. For example, how did the Commission explain the principle of continuous nationality? Why must the injured individual be a national of the claimant State both at the time of injury and at the time of presentation of the claim? If the injury was to the State, then surely the time of injury would be the crucial one, yet that was not the case. Then there was the question of the assessment of damages: if the injury was to the State, why should the damage suffered by the individual be taken into consideration? And why should the individual be required to exhaust local remedies if it was the State's claim? Yet, notwithstanding its flaws, the *Mavrommatis* principle was the basis of customary international law on the subject of diplomatic protection, and the Commission had sought to codify, rather than progressively develop, the principles of diplomatic protection. The Commission could not now abandon the *Mavrommatis* principle and construct a completely new institution which recognized the individual as the real claimant. Many members had criticized the draft articles for being too cautious and conservative and for failing to take account of the fact that the individual was the real claimant, but to discard *Mavrommatis* would be to discard principles of customary international law which had been in existence for more than a century.

10. Secondly, Mr. Pellet had suggested that the draft articles should include a consideration of the consequences of diplomatic protection. Mr. Sreenivasa Rao had also sought guidance on the subject. His response to those comments was that the draft articles focused on two issues: the nationality of claims and the exhaustion of local remedies. That was the accepted scope of diplomatic protection, and the approach which most textbooks adopted. Indeed, he was heartened to find that Mr. Daillier and Mr. Pellet themselves adopted that approach in the seventh edition of their *Droit international* public.[2] The Sixth Committee also favoured that approach. Almost all speakers in the Sixth Committee had expressed the wish to see the draft articles completed by 2006, and there was general agreement on limiting their scope to nationality of claims and exhaustion of local remedies (A/CN.4/549/Add.1, para. 2). That was also what the draft articles on responsibility of States for internationally wrongful acts had contemplated. Article 44 of those draft articles dealt fleetingly with nationality of claims and exhaustion of local remedies and it had been made clear in the commentary that those matters would be taken up in the supplementary draft articles on diplomatic protection.[3]

11. A second reason why the Commission should not consider the consequences of diplomatic protection was that they were already covered in the draft articles on responsibility of States. The State responsibility project had initially included an examination of diplomatic protection, and the first Special Rapporteur on State responsibility, Mr. García Amador, had indeed dealt with diplomatic protection as an aspect of that topic.[4] Later, Mr. Ago had focused attention on secondary rules and moved away from diplomatic protection, but had not

[1] *Yearbook ... 2000*, vol. II (Part One), document A/CN.4/506 and Add.1, pp. 225–226, paras. 87–93.

[2] Daillier and Pellet, *op. cit.* (2839th session, footnote 10), p. 809, para. 495.

[3] *Yearbook ...2001*, vol. II (Part Two) and corrigendum, p. 121, especially footnotes 683 and 687.

[4] *Yearbook ... 1956*, vol. II, document A/CN.4/96, chaps. VI–VII, pp. 199–209, paras. 134–191.

excluded diplomatic protection completely.[5] The draft articles on State responsibility adopted on first reading had contained a provision on diplomatic protection and exhaustion of local remedies.[6] The draft articles adopted on second reading also included a provision on the subject in article 44, which, interestingly enough, assumed that the consequences of diplomatic protection were covered by the draft articles on State responsibility; and it was clearly stated that the two issues which would be dealt with in the draft articles on diplomatic protection were simply an elaboration of nationality of claims and exhaustion of local remedies. In other words, with one exception to which he would revert, everything relating to the consequences of diplomatic protection was already dealt with in the draft articles on responsibility of States, in particular, in articles 30, 31, 32 and 36 (with paragraphs (16) to (34) of the commentary to article 36 focusing exclusively on claims arising out of diplomatic protection); and in articles 37 and 39 (as confirmed in the debate by Mr. Sreenivasa Rao, Mr. Yamada and Mr. Candioti, all of whom had suggested that the clean hands doctrine should be addressed in terms of that article, which made it abundantly clear that it was concerned with reparation arising out of claims based on diplomatic protection). Even articles 40 and 41 were applicable to diplomatic protection. Article 40, on serious breaches of obligations under peremptory norms, would obviously include, for example, the torture of an alien. In other words, many of the draft articles on responsibility of States were directly applicable to diplomatic protection and relied on the jurisprudence on the subject.[7] Thus, he did not see the need to deal with the question of consequences any further.

12. There was, however, one issue which was not dealt with, and to which Mr. Pellet had referred in passing, namely, the question whether a State was under an obligation to pay over to an injured individual money which it had received by way of compensation for a claim based on diplomatic protection. While he agreed that that was an important issue, he noted that it would be strange, albeit possible, to address only one issue pertaining to consequences in draft articles devoted to nationality of claims and exhaustion of local remedies. The Commission was faced with two options. The first would be simply to codify existing law. In doing so, it would confirm what many members regarded as a retrogressive rule, namely, that the State was not obliged to transfer money to the injured person. That was a consequence of the *Mavrommatis* principle: since the claim was that of the State, the State could retain any money it received and was not obliged to pay it over to the individual. The authorities were clear on the subject. In *Administrative Decision V (United States of America* v. *Germany)*, Umpire Parker had stated that in exercising control the nation was "governed not only by the interest of the particular claimant but by the larger interests of the whole people of the nation"; and that "even if payment is made to the espousing nation in pursuance of an award, it has complete control over the fund so paid to and held by it" (p. 152 of the decision). The English cases, too, were clear: according to Ian Brownlie, it was the view of the English courts and the United States Court of Claims that when a claim was presented and compensation was paid over, the State was not a trustee or agent for the nationals with respect to whom the claim had been made.[8] United States law was equally unambiguous: the *Restatement of the Law, Third, The Foreign Relations Law of the United States* stated that the money received from a foreign Government as a result of an international award, or in settlement, belonged to the United States.[9] Damrosch, Henkin, Pugh, Schachter and Smit stated in their *International Law: Cases and Materials* that "[t]he entire reparation [was] paid to the claimant State and disbursed to its national claimants at its discretion".[10] Thus, the present view was clearly that, just as the State had discretion on the question whether to exercise diplomatic protection, it had discretion as to whether to pay over to the injured individual money which it had received by way of compensation in a claim involving diplomatic protection.

13. The other option was to engage in progressive development and enunciate a new rule whereby the State was obliged to pay over to the injured individual money that it had received by way of compensation. He did not think that the Commission would want to choose that option. In the light of its decision not to compel States to exercise diplomatic protection on behalf of an individual, the Commission would presumably not want to engage in progressive development in respect of the payment of monetary compensation received by the State. Generally speaking, he did not detect a willingness on the part of the Commission to progressively develop the law in the face of existing authority, and that was what it would have to do under that option. In practice, he suspected that most States did pay over money received by way of compensation, but at the same time they stressed that they were under no obligation to do so, particularly in the case of lump sum payments. Injured individuals often received much less than their entitlement. He did not think the Commission would be wise, at the current stage, either to try to codify what many regarded as an unfortunate principle, or to attempt to progressively develop a new principle that would be unacceptable to States. In his view, it would be best to leave the draft articles as they currently stood, focusing solely on diplomatic protection in the sense of nationality of claims and exhaustion of local remedies. The consequences of diplomatic protection should be left to the draft articles on State responsibility, and the Commission should leave untouched the question whether the State was obliged to pay over to the injured individual money it had received by way of compensation, just as it

[5] *Yearbook ... 1969*, vol. II, document A/CN.4/217 and Add.1, pp. 126–127, paras. 1–6, and *Yearbook ... 1970*, vol. II, document A/CN.4/233, pp. 177–179, paras. 1–11.

[6] *Yearbook ... 1996*, vol. II (Part Two), article 22, p. 60. For the commentary to article 22, see *Yearbook ... 1977*, vol. II (Part Two), pp. 30–50.

[7] For the draft articles and related commentary adopted by the Commission on second reading, *Yearbook ... 2001*, vol. II (Part Two) and commentary, paras. 76–77, pp. 26–143.

[8] "... when a claim is presented and compensation is paid over, the state is not a trustee or agent for the nationals with respect to whom the claim was made", I. Brownlie, *Principles of Public International Law*, 5th ed., Oxford University Press, 1998, p. 597.

[9] The American Law Institute, *Restatement of the Law Third: The Foreign Relations Law of the United States*, vol. 2, St. Paul (Minnesota), American Law Institute Publishers, 1987, p. 348, para. 902 *l*.

[10] L. F. Damrosch *et al.*, *International Law: Cases and Materials*, 4th ed., St. Paul (Minnesota), West Group, 2001, p. 803.

had done in respect of the rule that a State had absolute discretion as to whether to bring a claim by way of diplomatic protection—a matter it had left open in the hope that things might change. In recent years national courts had begun to address the question whether States were constitutionally obligated to exercise diplomatic protection. There had been a number of important decisions in that regard, and it might be said that a rule of customary international law was in the process of emerging; thus the Commission had acted properly in not obstructing its development. In the same way, the question of the payment of money by the State of nationality to the injured party should be left untouched so as to allow customary international law to develop in that area.

14. Mr. BROWNLIE said he found the Special Rapporteur's proposals to be generally sensible and workable; he would, however, like to address the issue of the paying over of compensation by a Government to the individual whose interests had been directly involved in the claim which had given rise to the payment of compensation. The Special Rapporteur had focused on the duty of a Government to pay over that compensation but had not analysed the issue of the position of the individual, and specifically, the general question of the degree of control that an individual, who might well be a corporation or other legal person, should have in respect of an international claim: in other words, the extent to which an individual or legal person could require a Government to make a claim in the first place.

15. That issue was being discussed in the context of the progressive development of international law but, as so often, the question was how to achieve that progressive development. One element was the actual enforcement of legal standards. The individual or corporation concerned, on the basis of its particular economic interests, might take the view that the best course of action would be not to present the claim; alternatively, the interest concerned might try to insist that a claim be made which lacked merit and was unconnected to any real enforcement of legal standards. The question was thus the extent to which individuals and corporations should be able to insist on particular determinations by Governments in those matters. He wondered if the general results of an analysis of such situations would in fact contribute to progressive development; he suspected that the result would be rather mixed.

16. The former European Commission of Human Rights and the European Court of Human Rights had very early on rightly taken the view that claims made on behalf of individuals pursuant to the European Convention on Human Rights were in fact matters involving the public order of Europe. Although there was a question of *locus standi*, aspects other than a claim by the individual entered into play. The underlying logic of that view had been that even if an individual chose not to pursue a claim, as had in fact occurred on a number of occasions, the issue at hand still involved the public order of Europe and the claim would go forward even though the private interests had been removed because the individual had chosen not to pursue the claim. The progressive view in the context of the European Convention on Human Rights had therefore been not to allow an individual to waive his right to pursue a claim, because the ultimate objective was the effective enforcement of standards. Accordingly, the question of what was progressive in that context must include an assessment of the extent to which individuals and corporations should have control over what Governments did in that respect. That was not a simple question and it was not confined to the end question of what should happen to compensation paid once it had been handed over by the respondent State.

17. Mr. ECONOMIDES agreed with Mr. Brownlie. There were two main issues: the first was whether the State which was exercising diplomatic protection on behalf of one of its nationals, at the final phase of the awarding of compensation, required the consent of the individual concerned when accepting the sum negotiated with the respondent State. He recalled that in the past the Greek Government had, in the exercise of diplomatic protection, negotiated compensation agreements on behalf of Greek nationals whose property had been appropriated in certain Eastern European countries; without first seeking the consent of its nationals it had accepted and distributed to the individuals concerned a lump sum that had been wholly incommensurate with the value of their property. In such cases it was assumed that the State intervened to protect the interests of its nationals, who were the victims, not to secure any benefit for itself. It was therefore logical for the State to ask for the consent of the individual before agreeing to any compensation, thereby securing adequate protection for the interests of the individual, as was currently provided for neither in the draft articles on responsibility of States nor in those on diplomatic protection.

18. A second issue was whether a State had the right to keep all or part of any compensation awarded. There was State practice in that regard: the Greek Government, for example, always distributed all compensation awarded, less costs, to the injured individuals. All such examples of State practice should have been examined with a view to possibly developing rules based thereon. Although he agreed with the Special Rapporteur that those were sensitive and difficult questions which should not be dealt with in undue haste, the Commission should not exclude the possibility of dealing with them in the future. The Commission would be wrong to try to give the impression that all possible problems had been settled when some important aspects of the topic had still to be adequately addressed.

19. Mr. PELLET said that although the Special Rapporteur had maintained his position with regard to the draft articles, he himself remained unconvinced with regard to some issues. He had raised many of those issues on numerous occasions over the past few years, and he continued, for example, to have serious doubts about the Commission's cautious and conservative approach with regard to the *Mavrommatis* principle. He had always been of the view that the Commission's topic was not the conditions for the exercise of diplomatic protection, but diplomatic protection itself, yet the Commission had dealt only with the former.

20. With regard to the *Mavrommatis* fiction, he had bowed to what appeared to be the majority view in the Commission. Consequently, in the absence of any

criticism on the part of States—which seemed unlikely, given that States tended to be even more conservative than the Commission—the draft articles would remain as currently drafted because they tended to endorse States' own approach to the topic. It should be borne in mind, however, that it was not the Commission's task to make States happy but rather to ensure the progressive development and codification of international law. It was thus regrettable that the Commission had chosen to opt for an easy solution that would meet with the approval of States.

21. The *Mavrommatis* fiction had two facets: a State exercised diplomatic protection in exercise of its own right, and also to assert its right to ensure respect for international law in the person of its national. He agreed with the first principle, that diplomatic protection was a right of the State, in the sense that it would be irresponsible or dangerous to propose a general principle of an obligation of a State to exercise diplomatic protection. The State had full discretionary power to decide whether or not to pursue a claim of diplomatic protection on the basis of general policy considerations and the general interest, which was not always the same as the interest of the individual concerned. The Commission could have discussed the question of the limits within which a State could decide whether or not to exercise diplomatic protection, but unfortunately it had chosen not to do so.

22. The second principle was far more questionable and constituted the real fiction in the *Mavrommatis* principle. The State's right to ensure respect for international law in the person of its national was an outdated concept. The *Mavrommatis* principle dated back to 1924, when the fundamental purpose of diplomatic protection had been to guarantee the monopoly of States as subjects of international law. A situation had arisen in which some capital-exporting States of the North with investments in Latin America and elsewhere had felt the need to protect the interests of their nationals. The solution had been the emergence of diplomatic protection, whereby States exercised their own right to ensure respect for international law in the person of their national, and the countries of the South had been required to provide compensation for any injury.

23. However, it seemed unacceptable, 80 years later, to adhere to a fiction which had been created in response to that specific historical context. Individuals were now recognized as subjects of international law; only a total reactionary could refuse to recognize that individuals had some degree of international legal personality. Individuals had direct remedies available to them in areas such as human rights and investments, and diplomatic protection should serve only as a safety net where no direct remedy for individuals was available. In such cases, it was absolutely essential that States should retain the right to exercise diplomatic protection, but there was no need to maintain the fiction. It would be infinitely simpler to say that a State could choose whether or not to act on behalf of its national, and that would be a far better reflection of present-day needs. The Commission had missed an opportunity to offer States that choice, while also making it clear that when a State chose to exercise that right, it was acting on behalf of its national and not in order to ensure respect for international law in the person of that individual.

24. As to the Special Rapporteur's implied assertion that the Commission had completed its task, he did not agree; the Commission had codified the conditions for the exercise of diplomatic protection but not the consequences of such exercise. The Special Rapporteur had given three reasons for that omission: the need to complete the draft articles by the end of the quinquennium; the fact that the consequences of diplomatic protection were already covered in the draft articles on responsibility of States; and his view that to attempt to codify the remaining point would be to confirm a retrogressive rule.

25. The first argument was simply not credible: if the task of the Commission was to codify international law, it must take the time needed to do so even if that task proved difficult. There would have been ample time at the present session to deal not only with the clean hands doctrine, but also with the other, more fundamental, problems he had raised.

26. As for the argument that the consequences of diplomatic protection were already covered in the draft articles on responsibility of States, that went without saying. The purpose of diplomatic protection was to ensure that the consequences of the responsibility of States were drawn. The consequence of diplomatic protection was to trigger the responsibility of the State. The commentary to those draft articles cited examples of direct injury to a State and, by means of the Vattelian fiction, of indirect injury to a State in the person of one of its nationals. Those draft articles did not, however, deal with the special consequences attached to the exercise of diplomatic protection and did not distinguish between responsibility arising from direct injury caused to a State by another State and that arising from indirect injury to a State in the person of one of its nationals. In codifying diplomatic protection the Commission might reasonably be expected to deal with the specific consequences of such indirect injury. If it was really enough simply to say that the draft articles on responsibility of States already dealt with the consequences of diplomatic protection, why should the same argument not be used, for example, with regard to the exhaustion of local remedies, which was dealt with in article 44 (*b*)? Yet the Special Rapporteur had quite rightly addressed that matter at length in his draft articles. Moreover, the reference to article 39 was particularly perplexing, as in his opinion that article basically referred to the question of clean hands, about which he would, however, say no more.

27. The Special Rapporteur had himself conceded that one important question was missing from his draft articles, namely, the question of restitution of compensation to the individual where diplomatic protection was exercised. The Special Rapporteur noted that in most cases the State was under no obligation to pay over that compensation to the injured individual, and took the view that if the Commission attempted to codify the issue of payment of compensation to the individual, it would have to endorse a retrogressive rule. However, the Commission's mandate was not limited to the codification of international law; had it had the courage to discard the *Mavrommatis* fiction, it would not be faced with the present dilemma.

28. There were of course intermediate solutions, as indicated by Mr. Economides and others. Nonetheless, the Commission was undoubtedly setting an unfortunate precedent in declining to deal with such an allegedly thorny topic. The Commission should say to States that their position of absolute sovereignty of action was no longer appropriate in the new international context and propose that that position be either abandoned or modified.

29. The third argument put forward by the Special Rapporteur for not addressing the consequences of the exercise of diplomatic protection was that the paying over of compensation to individuals was an isolated problem and that the other consequences had been addressed in the draft articles on responsibility of States. However, while some of the consequences were touched on, many other problems had not been dealt with. For instance, did the exercise of diplomatic protection prevent the individual from taking further action? Were individuals bound to accept the compensation agreed by the State, or could they pursue their claims on the grounds that the State had not properly exercised diplomatic protection and that they had not received redress for the injury suffered? What were the consequences of the successful exercise of diplomatic protection for an individual's right of appeal? What method was to be used for calculating the amount of compensation? Should compensation be based on the harm suffered by the individual, as was the current practice, or on the harm suffered by the State, which would be in line with the *Mavrommatis* fiction? Was the individual bound by an agreement reached by the State on its own behalf? All those questions should be dealt with in the draft.

30. In sum, while he appreciated the Special Rapporteur's openness to discussion, he regretted his and the Commission's inflexibility with regard to the consequences of the exercise of diplomatic protection, which posed a number of serious problems of practical importance to States.

31. Mr. Sreenivasa RAO commended the Special Rapporteur's balanced and scholarly summary of the debate. Nonetheless, a number of issues related to the broader subject of diplomatic protection, notably the issue of the interests of the individual, merited further discussion. While he believed strongly that the State's discretion in the matter should not be circumscribed by an obligation to sponsor claims by individuals in every individual case, he would be willing to support any proposal by the Special Rapporteur to encourage States to ensure that, where appropriate, any compensation received was passed on to the individual concerned. He did not see any contradiction between leaving the State with the discretion to exercise diplomatic protection and ensuring that appropriate and equitable compensation was paid to the individual. While the Special Rapporteur had correctly sensed that some members of the Commission were not in favour of the progressive development of international law in respect of diplomatic protection, he personally would keep an open mind, should the Special Rapporteur judge it appropriate to move in that direction with regard to the payment of compensation to individuals.

32. Mr. ECONOMIDES said that one way of attenuating the effects of the exercise of diplomatic protection would be to include, during the second reading of the draft articles, a final clause to the effect that, where a right of individual recourse for compensation existed under a human rights convention, such recourse would take precedence over diplomatic protection. Individuals could then pursue their case as they saw fit and would receive any compensation due. Diplomatic protection was in any case a cumbersome political procedure: even when all the conditions for exercising it were met, a Government would often not pursue the matter beyond the initial *démarche*. The inclusion of a final clause would obviate the need to consider the question whether the individual must consent to the exercise of diplomatic protection.

33. Mr. PELLET said that a "without prejudice" clause had already been adopted at the fifty-sixth session, in draft article 17, although that article could perhaps be amended to stipulate that the draft articles were without prejudice to the specific consequences of the exercise of diplomatic protection. He had always been puzzled by what precisely constituted "diplomatic protection". According to the *Mavrommatis* principle, diplomatic protection could be exercised either through judicial or through diplomatic channels. In his view, even informal approaches to States responsible for an internationally wrongful act were a form of diplomatic protection; diplomatic protection procedures were far more flexible than court procedures, and certainly need not be cumbersome, as Mr. Economides claimed. The failure to specify the procedures or minimum formalities for the exercise of diplomatic protection was yet another serious gap in the draft articles.

34. The CHAIRPERSON, speaking as a member of the Commission, said that Mr. Economides had made the distinction between undertaking the diplomatic protection procedure, which might or might not have an immediate effect, and judicial proceedings, which were much more protracted and costly.

35. Mr. BROWNLIE said that scholarly discourses on the status of the individual in international law were not very instructive; the Commission should pay less attention to abstractions and more to the real world. Individuals were sounding boards for group interests; indeed, in the past, the United Kingdom Parliament had been a sounding board for the interests of white settlers in Kenya, used as a way of validating the mistreatment of other individuals. It was deplorably unrealistic to talk about "individuals" in the abstract, when in the real world diplomatic protection involved the manipulation of individuals in pursuit of certain interests. Even if the Commission decided at some time in the future to consider the separate question of what were the practical consequences of the legal status of the individual in international law, it would not necessarily be contributing to the progressive development of international law: merely talking about the legal status of the individual was not in itself "progressive", but simply revealed a total lack of realism and knowledge of history.

36. Mr. ECONOMIDES, responding to Mr. Pellet's comments, said that of course every diplomatic protection procedure was initiated by a diplomatic *démarche*, such as summoning a country's ambassador to the foreign ministry. That action drew the attention of the Government to a given case; the Government then decided

whether to exercise diplomatic protection. Negotiations at the diplomatic level were the next step, and judicial remedies were available after the negotiations had been completed. However, an initial *démarche* did not in itself constitute the exercise of diplomatic protection; if the Government took the matter no further, diplomatic protection was not exercised.

37. Mr. PELLET said he took it that Mr. Economides was saying that a step taken before the exhaustion of domestic remedies did not constitute diplomatic protection, but he himself continued to believe that a *démarche* taken after that point, even informally, fell within the ambit of the topic.

38. He took issue with Mr. Brownlie for suggesting that the speakers in the debate were out of touch with reality: in fact, they had a wealth of practical experience between them. Moreover, everyone was well aware that the word "individuals" was a convenient way to refer to private individuals in general. He had himself always preferred to avoid taking examples from the field of human rights, in the belief that examples from the field of investment—the origin of diplomatic protection, after all—were more illuminating.

39. Mr. DUGARD (Special Rapporteur) said he suspected that many of the points raised in the debate would be raised again in the coming year by States and academics. He was grateful to members of the Commission for their suggestions, particularly on how to deal with the question of the payment of compensation to the injured individual. It had been a great pleasure to hear Mr. Pellet speak on behalf of the "*droits-de-l'hommiste*" school, to which he normally disclaimed any allegiance.

The meeting rose at 11.30 a.m.

2847th MEETING

Wednesday, 1 June 2005, at 10 a.m.

Chairperson: Mr. Djamchid MOMTAZ

Present: Mr. Addo, Mr. Al-Baharna, Mr. Brownlie, Mr. Candioti, Mr. Chee, Mr. Comissário Afonso, Mr. Dugard, Mr. Economides, Ms. Escarameia, Mr. Fomba, Mr. Gaja, Mr. Galicki, Mr. Kolodkin, Mr. Koskenniemi, Mr. Mansfield, Mr. Matheson, Mr. Pambou-Tchivounda, Mr. Pellet, Mr. Sreenivasa Rao, Mr. Rodríguez Cedeño, Ms. Xue, Mr. Yamada.

Cooperation with other bodies

[Agenda item 11]

Statement of the Observer from the Inter-American Juridical Committee

1. The CHAIRPERSON invited Ms. Villalta Vizcarra, Observer from the Inter-American Juridical Committee, to describe the Committee's activities.

2. Ms. VILLALTA VIZCARRA (Observer from the Inter-American Juridical Committee) retraced the history of the Inter-American Juridical Committee since its establishment in Rio de Janeiro in 1906, described its principal objectives and operating procedures and then elaborated on the topics on its agenda. The first was legal aspects of compliance within the States with decisions of international courts or tribunals or other international organs with jurisdictional functions. While States acknowledged that international decisions had a binding character, most did not possess the necessary internal mechanisms for implementing them. At the request of the General Assembly of the OAS, the Committee had drawn up a questionnaire which it had transmitted to the legal advisers of the foreign ministries of OAS member States, *inter alia*, on the following subjects: international tribunals or other comparable international bodies to whose jurisdiction the State was subject under treaties or other international instruments; constitutional and legislative provisions and administrative practices that mandated, permitted or facilitated the application of the decisions concerned; decisions, sentences and other international rulings handed down in disputes to which the State was a party, accompanied, where possible, by a summary of the main provisions; the form in which such decisions were applied, including legal texts adopted exclusively for that purpose (such as laws, decrees and administrative decisions); and, where appropriate, legal grounds for non-application. Responses had already been gathered from 11 member States and the Committee would submit its report on the matter in 2006.

3. Under the second topic on the agenda, legal aspects of inter-American security, the Committee was considering the rules applicable to OAS action in the area of international peace and security, taking into account, as the General Assembly of OAS had requested in its resolution AG/RES 2042 (XXXIV-O/04), the Declaration on Security in the Americas adopted at the Special Conference on Security held in Mexico City in October 2003 and the multidimensional nature (political, economic, social and cultural) of the issue. The Committee had concluded that the Declaration on Security in the Americas was a tangible expression of the political will of the States members of OAS to give impetus to the progressive development of international law.

4. The third topic, one of interest also to the Commission, related to the inter-American specialized conferences on private international law, which were devoted to the progressive development of international law. For the Seventh Conference the Committee, which contributed to the preparatory work for the conferences, had considered the question of the applicable law and competency of international jurisdiction in respect of non-contractual civil liability. It had concluded that favourable conditions existed for elaborating a model law or convention on non-contractual civil liability with respect to traffic accidents, based on the San Luis Protocol relating to civil responsibility resulting from traffic accidents between the States Parties of MERCOSUR, which applied to all States members of MERCOSUR, and with respect to products and transboundary environmental damage. The Seventh Inter-American Specialized Conference would also consider the issue of electronic commerce.

5. The fourth topic was legal aspects of the interdependence between democracy and economic and social development, which had been studied in the light of article 1 of the Inter-American Democratic Charter, which stated in part that "Democracy is essential for the social, political, and economic development of the peoples of the Americas." The Committee was considering the action to be taken in the event of a breach of the legal constitutional order but also measures required for economic and social development, taking account, *inter alia*, of the recommendations of the High-Level Meeting on Poverty, Equity, and Social Inclusion held from 8–10 October 2003 at Isla de Margarita (Bolivarian Republic of Venezuela), contained in the Declaration of Margarita; the Monterrey Consensus;[1] the Declarations and Plans of Action issued at the Summits of the Americas; and the objectives contained in the United Nations Millennium Declaration.[2]

6. In the context of a fifth topic, entitled "Joint efforts of the Americas in the struggle against corruption and impunity", and at the request of the General Assembly of OAS, the Inter-American Juridical Committee had conducted a study on the legal effects of giving safe haven in regional or extraregional countries to public officials and persons accused of crimes of corruption after having exercised political power, and on cases in which appealing to the principle of dual nationality could be considered a fraud or abuse of the law, corruption being viewed as an aspect of transnational organized crime. OAS had likewise requested the Committee to take account, at its annual session, of the following texts: the Inter-American Convention against Corruption, especially concerning legal aid and cooperation; the United Nations Convention against Corruption, in particular concerning international cooperation and the principle that corruption was an extraditable offence; the General Assembly resolution on efforts to combat corruption (AG/RES. 2022 (XXXIV-O/04)); international jurisprudence on "effective nationality or genuine link", especially the rulings of the ICJ in the *Nottebohm* case and the sentence of the Permanent Court of Arbitration at The Hague in the *Canevaro* case. The study was also based on the draft articles on diplomatic protection elaborated by the Commission, particularly draft articles 1 and 7,[3] which stipulated that a State had the right to determine the nationality of persons and, in the case of multiple nationality, to take into account the predominant nationality, a term also used by the Italian–United States Conciliation Commission in the *Mergé Claim*, which might be considered to be the point of departure for the development of existing customary rules.

7. Forum shopping or fraud occurred when a person who had dual nationality exploited his or her option to be governed by legislation that was more favourable than that which normally would apply. In determining the effective nationality of individuals in such cases, account was taken of the nationality that they had always used in their social, family and professional relations, as had been done in the *Nottebohm* case and the *Canevaro* claim. International law had been progressively developed in that area, so that when a claimant State demanded the extradition of a person accused of corruption who was a national of a requested State, it was the predominant nationality that was taken into account—in other words, the nationality that the person had had when he or she had committed the acts in question. The Inter-American Juridical Committee had concluded that principles on dominant nationality and the need for an effective link to determine nationality had been established within the framework of diplomatic protection as set forth by international law. It considered, however, that certain conclusions derived from diplomatic protection could be applied in the sphere of extradition, even if they did not necessarily reflect the current state of international law. Thus in the event of a conflict of nationality, if the nationality of the claimant State was the dominant or predominant nationality or represented a genuine and effective link, extradition must not be denied solely on the grounds of nationality. When nationality was acquired or invoked for the purpose of fraud or abuse of rights, extradition could not be refused solely on the grounds of nationality. The legal effect of those conclusions would be to prevent: impunity where crimes of corruption were involved; the undermining of the general objectives of international criminal justice and judicial cooperation among States; any attempt to subvert the primacy of law in international relations; and any harm to the interests of States requesting extradition. The Committee considered that those conclusions could make a contribution to the progressive development of international law and promote the achievement of objectives and the strengthening of international justice.

8. The Committee's agenda also included preparations for the commemoration of its centennial and the organization for that purpose of five meetings under the theme of "The Inter-American Juridical Committee: a Century of Contributions to International Law", which would address the main contributions made by the inter-American system in the fields of private international law, the maintenance of international peace and security, international jurisdiction and international economic law.

9. The Committee also intended to re-examine the inter-American conventions on private international law. It had suggested, among other things, that during the Seventh Inter-American Specialized Conference on that subject, a committee should be established to study the reasons for the decline in the number of convention ratifications and the number of States participating in the conferences, and for the failure to apply the model laws.

10. Since its previous session the Committee had contacted the Justice Studies Center of the Americas with a view to establishing cooperation in the field of the administration of justice in the Americas and, ultimately, to developing general principles of judicial ethics in order to facilitate access to justice.

11. Other services included a course on international law that the Committee had organized annually since 1974. In 2005 the course would be held from 1 to 26 August, and its main topic would be the contribution of international organizations to current international law". Every two years the Committee met with the legal advisers of

[1] Report of the International Conference on Financing for Development, Monterrey (Mexico), 18–22 March 2002 (United Nations publication, Sales No.: E.02.II.A.7), chap. I, resolution I.

[2] General Assembly resolution 55/2 of 8 September 2000.

[3] See *Yearbook ... 2004*, vol. II (Part Two), chap. IV, sect. C.1, p. 18, para. 59.

the foreign ministries of OAS member States, and at the most recent meeting, in August 2003, the following issues had been considered: hemispheric security; mechanisms for rectifying and preventing grave and recurrent violations of international humanitarian law and international human rights law and the role of the International Criminal Court in that regard; the inter-American legal agenda; and legal aspects of the implementation of decisions of international tribunals or other international bodies having jurisdictional functions. Lastly, the Committee issued annual reports, which could be consulted on the OAS website (www.oas.org).

12. Mr. ECONOMIDES said he was pleased to hear that the Inter-American Juridical Committee was tackling important issues of international law, some of which were also being addressed by the Commission. He was thinking in particular of the work that the Committee was doing on enforcement of decisions of international tribunals and the legal aspects of inter-American security, the results of which he awaited with great interest.

13. He believed that cooperation between the Commission and the Inter-American Juridical Committee should go beyond a simple exchange of information to include, among other things, more active support for Commission projects. For example, the draft articles on State responsibility, which had occupied the Commission for over 50 years, had been completed in 2001, but their final form remained an open issue, since the General Assembly had decided to take a position on that question in 2007. In the area of highly legal issues like that of State responsibility, it would be useful for all international law bodies to take a more responsible stance by giving in-depth consideration to the Commission drafts and, where appropriate, expressing an opinion as to the final form they should take. Regional legal bodies were best placed to explain the issues involved to the States of their region. He was convinced that if the Inter-American Juridical Committee had taken a stance on the draft articles on State responsibility, more American States would have supported its objectives, and that would have accelerated the adoption of the instrument. The current President of the Committee, Mr. Sacasa, had participated in the preparation of the draft articles while he had been a member of the Commission, and he undoubtedly had his own views on the subject.

14. Mr. RODRÍGUEZ CEDEÑO endorsed the comments of Mr. Economides and called for more active cooperation between the Commission and the Inter-American Juridical Committee. Among the elements of the Committee's interesting programme of work he drew attention to the study on the relationship between democracy and economic and social development, which could not fail to strengthen the Inter-American Democratic Charter, adopted by OAS in 2001. Another important subject was the enforcement of decisions taken by international courts. He had no doubt that the Committee's recommendations in that regard would be extremely valuable to the States of the region, which had had to adapt their legislation following the adoption of the Rome Statute of the International Criminal Court. With regard to corruption, he asked how the Committee's work would tie in with the two inter-American instruments that already existed on that subject.

15. Mr. MATHESON said that he was particularly interested in the subject of the enforcement of decisions of international courts because there was currently a controversy in the United States as to how to ensure that state Governments, as opposed to the federal authorities, complied with binding decisions of the ICJ. He asked whether the Inter-American Juridical Committee had considered the question of the enforcement of decisions of international courts in a federal system.

16. Mr. PAMBOU-TCHIVOUNDA commended the great vitality of the Inter-American Juridical Committee, which he saw as a genuine laboratory for preparing the political action of OAS. The Committee was also the reflection of inter-American regionalism in the legal sphere, which was not new and which had made an important contribution to the question of diplomatic protection in particular. Regionalism served as a framework for promoting the elaboration of rules of law at the global level. In that sense, it acted as an intermediary, bringing certain aims to universal prominence.

17. Inter-American regionalism could be viewed from a continental perspective, since OAS brought together all the States of the continent, but also from a transcontinental perspective, as embodied in such entities as the International Organisation of La Francophonie, of which a number of States in the Americas were members. The transcontinental perspective provided an additional impetus that in no way contradicted the continental dimension.

18. The Inter-American Juridical Committee was interested in the question of security in a regional context. Yet according to the latest thinking, security was no longer just a state of non-war, but also implied such elements as democracy, living standards and so forth. Thus the question was also related to the interdependence of democracy and socio-economic development, which had been talked about ever since the major international financial organizations such as the World Bank and the IMF had realized that structural adjustment plans, which instead of leading to development had exacerbated extreme poverty, were a failure. It was now a known fact that there could be no development without democracy, and efforts were focused above all on promoting democratization. He was pleased to learn that the Inter-American Juridical Committee was dealing with that issue, and he looked forward to seeing how it would tackle it and what suggestions it would make.

19. Mr. CHEE asked Ms. Villalta Vizcarra whether, with regard to the *Canevaro* case, to which she had referred in her statement, the Inter-American Juridical Committee was in a position to assist the Peruvian Government in extraditing Fujimori, who had also been implicated in a corruption case.

20. He also enquired how the Inter-American Juridical Committee's work on the definition of security tied in with Article 51 of the Charter of the United Nations, which concerned self-defence and armed attack.

21. Lastly, citing the example of the European Union, which had gradually developed a system of Community law, he asked why, given the close ties that existed among

Latin American countries, the jurists of those countries had not created the conditions necessary for the emergence of a body of Latin American law.

22. Mr. CANDIOTI, associating himself with the remarks made by Mr. Economides, called for increased cooperation between the Inter-American Juridical Committee and the International Law Commission. It would be particularly useful for the Committee to consider the work of the Commission and then convey to the Commission its comments and reactions. He noted with satisfaction that the Inter-American Juridical Committee did not hesitate to tackle topical issues, such as international and regional security, the interdependence of democracy and economic and social development, and the fight against corruption. He was also pleased that the Committee took account of the work of the Commission, particularly in the areas of diplomatic protection and nationality.

23. He was particularly interested in the conclusions that the Committee might reach in its study of the trend towards non-ratification of international legal instruments by States. He also wondered whether the Committee's documents were accessible online, as were the documents of the Commission.

24. Ms. ESCARAMEIA asked Ms. Villalta Vizcarra how the States of the region reacted to the work of the Inter-American Juridical Committee. She also wished to know what relations the Committee had with bodies in other parts of the world, such as the Council of Europe and the International Law Institute, and whether those relations consisted solely of information exchanges or whether they led to joint activities. She supported the suggestion by Mr. Economides that closer relations between the Committee and the Commission should be promoted.

25. The CHAIRPERSON, speaking in his capacity as member of the Commission, said that he wished to know what role the Inter-American Juridical Committee played in harmonizing the legislation of OAS member States, particularly in the areas of pardon, statutory limitation on crimes, and amnesty.

26. Ms. VILLALTA VIZCARRA (Observer from the Inter-American Juridical Committee), replying to Commission members' questions, said that the Committee was trying to clarify the concept of the legal aspects of inter-American security in the light of the conclusions contained in the Declaration on Security in the Americas, adopted by the Special Conference on Security held in 2003 in Mexico City. The Committee was studying in particular the possibility of reforming the OAS Charter in order to incorporate the question of the multidimensional nature of security, which was currently lacking.

27. With regard to the enforcement of the decisions of international courts, the Inter-American Juridical Committee considered reports submitted to it by OAS member States. That question raised a problem of harmonization, because some legal systems in the Americas were based on common law and others on Roman law. Thus, in some States the enforcement of decisions was a matter for the executive branch, whereas in others the legislative and judicial branches were also involved. Accordingly, the Committee had to receive and consider all State reports before formulating recommendations and determining, in collaboration with the international courts, the best way of enforcing their decisions. She added that the Statute of the Central American Court of Justice stipulated that that Court's decisions were to be enforced in the same manner as those of domestic courts.

28. The Inter-American Juridical Committee believed that it would be useful to enhance cooperation between the various organizations working on the question of State responsibility, given the complementarity of regional systems with the universal system. In the three regions of the Americas, namely North America, South America and the Caribbean, one of the Committee's tasks was to improve the harmonization of legal systems. In that connection, she pointed out that the 11 jurists who made up the Committee came from all those regions. Currently the Committee was working to develop a framework anti-terrorism law.

29. The task of the rapporteur on democracy and socio-economic development was primarily to coordinate the literature on the topic. The Inter-American Juridical Committee had played an active part in the drafting of the Inter-American Democratic Charter, adopted in 2001 in Peru, and it was studying the possibility of giving that text binding force. Nicaragua had been the first State to request enforcement of the Charter as a preventive measure, and OAS had sent a mission to that country to study that issue.

30. In the area of corruption and impunity, the Inter-American Juridical Committee was currently endeavouring to improve the Inter-American Convention on extradition. It was also considering ways of promoting mutual legal assistance in criminal matters and legal cooperation, particularly with regard to transnational crime. OAS had also asked the Committee to take up the question of corruption and to produce a form for requests for mutual legal assistance. A Committee mechanism monitored implementation of the Inter-American Convention against Corruption (MESICIC). Another of the Committee's study topics was combating international organized crime.

31. While most of the decisions by the Inter-American Court of Human Rights had been accepted by the States members of OAS that had recognized the Court's competence, those States were experiencing practical problems in enforcing those decisions. Accordingly, the Committee provided them with guidance in that regard.

32. Concerning relations with other bodies and organizations, she said that the Inter-American Juridical Committee had working relations with a variety of entities, in particular universities, and that it would like to conclude a cooperation convention with the Justice Studies Center of the Americas on the administration of justice.

33. Replying to the question raised by the Chairperson, she said that the Committee sought to coordinate the legislation of the countries of the region in the three areas to which he had referred. It also addressed problems that might arise for those Latin American States that had abolished the death penalty and wished to reintroduce it, given

the ban on that punishment in the American Convention on Human Rights, as well as questions raised by the incompatibility of the ban on life imprisonment, which was established in the constitutions of some States, with the Rome Statute of the International Criminal Court.

34. In closing, she said that the Inter-American Juridical Committee's annual report, Statute and Rules of Procedure, as well as information on the courses on international law that the Committee organized, could be consulted on the OAS website (www.oas.org).

The meeting rose at 11.50 a.m.

2848th MEETING

Friday, 3 June 2005, at 10.05 a.m.

Chairperson: Mr. Djamchid MOMTAZ

Present: Mr. Addo, Mr. Al-Baharna, Mr. Brownlie, Mr. Candioti, Mr. Chee, Mr. Comissário Afonso, Mr. Dugard, Mr. Economides, Ms. Escarameia, Mr. Fomba, Mr. Gaja, Mr. Galicki, Mr. Kolodkin, Mr. Mansfield, Mr. Matheson, Mr. Pambou-Tchivounda, Mr. Sreenivasa Rao, Mr. Rodríguez Cedeño, Mr. Yamada.

Responsibility of international organizations (*concluded*)* (A/CN.4/549 and Add.1, sect. A, A/CN.4/547, A/CN.4/553, A/CN.4/556, A/CN.4/L.666/Rev.1)

[Agenda item 3]

Report of the Drafting Committee

1. Mr. MANSFIELD (Chairperson of the Drafting Committee), introducing the titles and texts of the draft articles adopted by the Drafting Committee on 27 May 2005, as contained in document A/CN.4/L.666/Rev.1, said that the Drafting Committee had held four meetings on the topic, on 25, 26 and 27 May 2005. The Drafting Committee had considered draft articles 8 to 16 referred to it by the Commission in plenary at its present session, and had also considered and was recommending a structure for the draft articles so far adopted. He would first introduce the draft articles, before going on to explain the structure.

2. The titles and texts of the draft articles read:

Part One

THE INTERNATIONALLY WRONGFUL ACT OF AN INTERNATIONAL ORGANIZATION

Chapter I

INTRODUCTION

[Articles 1, 2 and 3[1]]

Chapter II

ATTRIBUTION OF CONDUCT TO AN INTERNATIONAL ORGANIZATION

[Articles 4, 5, 6 and 7[2]]

Chapter III

BREACH OF AN INTERNATIONAL OBLIGATION

Article 8

Existence of a breach of an international obligation

1. There is a breach of an international obligation by an international organization when an act of that international organization is not in conformity with what is required of it by that obligation, regardless of its origin and character.

2. Paragraph 1 also applies to the breach of an obligation under international law established by a rule of the international organization.

Article 9

International obligation in force for an international organization

An act of an international organization does not constitute a breach of an international obligation unless the international organization is bound by the obligation in question at the time the act occurs.

Article 10

Extension in time of the breach of an international obligation

1. The breach of an international obligation by an act of an international organization not having a continuing character occurs at the moment when the act is performed, even if its effects continue.

2. The breach of an international obligation by an act of an international organization having a continuing character extends over the entire period during which the act continues and remains not in conformity with the international obligation.

3. The breach of an international obligation requiring an international organization to prevent a given event occurs when the event occurs and extends over the entire period during which the event continues and remains not in conformity with that obligation.

Article 11

Breach consisting of a composite act

1. The breach of an international obligation by an international organization through a series of actions and omissions defined in aggregate as wrongful, occurs when the action or omission occurs which, taken with the other actions or omissions, is sufficient to constitute the wrongful act.

2. In such a case, the breach extends over the entire period starting with the first of the actions or omissions of the series and lasts for as long as these actions or omissions are repeated and remain not in conformity with the international obligation.

---

* Resumed from the 2844th meeting.

[1] For the text of these draft articles and the commentaries thereto, provisionally adopted by the Commission, see *Yearbook ... 2003*, vol. II (Part Two), chap. IV, sect. C.2, para. 54.

[2] For the text of these draft articles and the commentaries thereto, provisionally adopted by the Commission, see *Yearbook ... 2004*, vol. II (Part Two), chap. V, sect. C.2, para. 72.

Chapter IV

RESPONSIBILITY OF AN INTERNATIONAL ORGANIZATION IN CONNECTION WITH THE ACT OF A STATE OR ANOTHER INTERNATIONAL ORGANIZATION

Article 12

Aid or assistance in the commission of an internationally wrongful act

An international organization which aids or assists a State or another international organization in the commission of an internationally wrongful act by the State or the latter organization is internationally responsible for doing so if:

(*a*) That organization does so with knowledge of the circumstances of the internationally wrongful act; and

(*b*) The act would be internationally wrongful if committed by that organization.

Article 13

Direction and control exercised over the commission of an internationally wrongful act

An international organization which directs and controls a State or another international organization in the commission of an internationally wrongful act by the State or the latter organization is internationally responsible for that act if:

(*a*) That organization does so with knowledge of the circumstances of the internationally wrongful act; and

(*b*) The act would be internationally wrongful if committed by that organization.

Article 14

Coercion of a State or another international organization

An international organization which coerces a State or another international organization to commit an act is internationally responsible for that act if:

(*a*) The act would, but for the coercion, be an internationally wrongful act of the coerced State or international organization; and

(*b*) The coercing international organization does so with knowledge of the circumstances of the act.

Article 15 [16] [3]

Decisions, recommendations and authorizations addressed to member States and international organizations

1. An international organization incurs international responsibility if it adopts a decision binding a member State or international organization to commit an act that would be internationally wrongful if committed by the former organization and would circumvent an international obligation of the former organization.

2. An international organization incurs international responsibility if:

(*a*) It authorizes a member State or international organization to commit an act that would be internationally wrongful if committed by the former organization and would circumvent an international obligation of the former organization, or recommends that a member State or international organization commit such an act; and

(*b*) That State or international organization commits the act in question in reliance on that authorization or recommendation.

3. Paragraphs 1 and 2 apply whether or not the act in question is internationally wrongful for the member State or international organization to which the decision, authorization or recommendation is directed.

Article 16 [15] [4]

Effect of this chapter

This chapter is without prejudice to the international responsibility of the State or international organization which commits the act in question, or of any other State or international organization.

3. Mr. MANSFIELD (Chairperson of the Drafting Committee), introducing the report of the Drafting Committee, said that draft articles 8 to 15, as proposed by the Special Rapporteur, corresponded to draft articles 12 to 19 in chapters III and IV of the draft articles on responsibility of States for internationally wrongful acts.[5] As noted by the Special Rapporteur, the issues involved in the breach of an international obligation on the part of an international organization and in responsibility of an international organization in connection with an act of a State or another international organization were for the most part identical to those in State responsibility and there was no reason for the Commission to take a different approach. The Special Rapporteur had identified two issues which were specific to international organizations and needed to be addressed in draft article 8, paragraph 2, and draft article 16. The plenary had agreed with the Special Rapporteur that to the extent that the issues were the same the corresponding articles on responsibility of States should be retained with only minimal changes; that approach was necessary to avoid conflicting interpretations in the future. The two exceptions which had led to a substantial debate in plenary session had been referred to a Working Group and the texts proposed by that Group for draft article 18, paragraph 2, and draft article 16 had also been discussed by the Drafting Committee.

4. Draft article 8 corresponded to draft article 12 on responsibility of States, dealing with the existence of a breach of an international obligation; in paragraph 1 the word "State" had been replaced with "international organization". The paragraph provided that there was a breach of an international obligation by an international organization when an act of that organization was not in conformity with what was required of it by that obligation, regardless of its origin and character. The paragraph had been acceptable to the plenary and the Drafting Committee had made no changes to the text.

5. Paragraph 2 had led to considerable discussions in plenary on whether such a paragraph was needed. The Working Group established by the Commission in plenary session had recommended retention of the paragraph and proposed a text for it, which had been accepted by the plenary and referred to the Drafting Committee, which had debated it extensively. Some members had reserved their position on it but the Drafting Committee had finally agreed to propose the present text for paragraph 2, which was very little changed from that recommended by the Working Group.

[3] The square bracket refers to the corresponding article in the third report of the Special Rapporteur (A/CN.4/553).

[4] *Ibid.*

[5] *Yearbook ... 2001*, vol. II (Part Two) and corrigendum, p. 26, para. 76.

6. The difficulty identified by some members of the Drafting Committee with regard to paragraph 2 was that in their view it did not add anything to what was already said in paragraph 1 but instead created an unnecessary ambiguity about the nature of the rules of an international organization. The paragraph stated that some rules of the organization might give rise to international responsibility without providing any criteria or indications as to which rules had that potential. For other members the difficulty was in identifying the law that applied in the context of paragraph 2; for example, it was unclear whether it was the rules of the organization that gave their breach the character of an internationally wrongful act or whether it was general international law that provided that violation of certain rules of the organization was internationally wrongful. Furthermore, in their view it was uncertain which law applied in terms of determining the consequences of such an internationally wrongful act—again, whether it was general international law or the rules of the organization. Concern had also been expressed that the uncertainty in paragraph 2 could lead international organizations to themselves select which rules of the organization fell within the scope of paragraph 2, a situation which was not desirable.

7. The majority of the Drafting Committee was of the view that paragraph 2, although broadly covered by paragraph 1, added value to the latter by specifically stating that the breach of certain rules of the organization could be an internationally wrongful act. Paragraph 2 flagged an important point in the context of the responsibility of international organizations and although the matter could have been addressed in the commentary to paragraph 1, it was deemed useful to highlight it in the text of the article itself. The commentary to the draft article would explain the reasons for the inclusion of the provision and make it clear that it was not attempting to make a definitive statement about which rules of the organization were international law.

8. In terms of drafting, the Drafting Committee had agreed that the words "in principle" did not provide the clarity necessary for a normative text. It had also decided that instead of referring to an "international obligation", as used in paragraph 1 and other draft articles, the construct "breach of obligation under international law" would be used. That was intended to highlight the point that the obligation referred to was one that arose under international law; the commentary would explain that that construct meant the same as "international obligation".

9. The title of draft article 8 was the same as the title of draft article 12 on responsibility of States.

10. Draft articles 9 to 14 were identical to articles 13 to 18 on responsibility of States; they had not posed any problem in plenary and the Drafting Committee had recommended only minimal changes.

11. Draft article 15 corresponded to draft article 16 as proposed by the Special Rapporteur. The draft article was new and had no equivalent in the articles on responsibility of States; it dealt with incidents in which an international organization used decisions, recommendations and authorizations directed at its members to evade its own obligations. The draft article had been extensively debated in plenary and in the Drafting Committee. The Working Group established by the Commission had introduced a revised text for the draft article which the Drafting Committee had taken as the basis for its work.

12. While draft articles 12 to 14 dealt with attribution of responsibility to an international organization for the conduct of any State or international organization, draft article 15 dealt with that responsibility in connection with the conduct of a State or international organization that was a member of the international organization in question. The difficulty with drafting that article had been the lack of empirical reference; while the possibility of such incidents theoretically existed, there were no clear examples in practice to assist in formulating the draft article. The other difficulty had been with the broad category of decisions, recommendations and authorizations, which encompassed a wide range of statements and utterances made in and by international organizations and their various organs which had different normative and authoritative values as well as different purposes. Moreover, the steps taken at the stage of compliance or implementation could be of significant relevance in the context of the draft article.

13. The Drafting Committee, following the approach taken by the Working Group, had made a distinction between "binding" decisions and "non-binding" acts. Non-binding acts included, but were not limited to, recommendations and authorizations. Such acts could be made under other titles, but it was the non-binding character of the acts and the fact that they directed the membership toward certain behaviour which counted.

14. Draft article 15, paragraph 1, was based on the text proposed by the Working Group and dealt with binding decisions of international organizations. The Working Group had suggested a text that would provide for responsibility of an international organization if the organization adopted a decision binding a member State or organization to commit an act that would be internationally wrongful for the former organization. The Drafting Committee had seen difficulties with the latter part of the paragraph, specifying that the act must be one that would have been wrongful if committed by the organization itself. In practice, international organizations adopted binding decisions to enable their membership to do certain things that they themselves could not do: for example, they might adopt a binding decision requiring a State or an international organization to investigate and prosecute war crimes or crimes against humanity, as the organization itself did not have such capacity. The purpose of the paragraph had been to address situations in which the organization used decisions that were binding on its members to circumvent an international obligation of its own. The Drafting Committee had accordingly added to the latter part of the paragraph the notion of circumvention of the obligation by the international organization. As now drafted, the paragraph referred to a binding decision to commit an act that would not only be wrongful if committed by the international organization but would also circumvent an international obligation of that organization. The commentary would further clarify the meaning of the notion of an act that

would be internationally wrongful if committed by the international organization itself.

15. Paragraph 1 of draft article 15 did not require the commission of the act in question. That was a matter that had been extensively discussed in plenary session. The Special Rapporteur's proposal had required the commission of the act as a precondition for entailing responsibility, but the Working Group's recommendation did not include that requirement, and that was the basis on which the provision had been referred to the Drafting Committee. The logic underlying that approach had been that the adoption of a binding decision of that nature should suffice to entail the responsibility of the organization. It had been considered that, in that situation, responsibility stemmed from the decision to place members in that quandary, rather than being dependent upon whether members carried out the act concerned. In addition, if the commission of the act were to be a requirement for wrongfulness, a potentially injured State or international organization might not have the opportunity to request preventive measures before the act was committed.

16. Draft article 15, paragraph 2, dealt with non-binding resolutions, which were referred to as recommendations and authorizations. Paragraph 2 was identical to paragraph 1 with one exception: the act in question must have been committed, a requirement that was contained in subparagraph (*b*). The logic was that the member State or international organization was not compelled to comply with the recommendation or authorization. The responsibility of the international organization therefore arose only if the member State or international organization not only committed the act but did so in reliance on that recommendation or authorization. The purpose was to signify the crucial role played by such a recommendation or authorization.

17. Some members of the Drafting Committee had been concerned that, in view of the large number of non-binding resolutions adopted by international organizations, some safeguards must be put in place to preclude the possibility that responsibility might arise for the organization where member States or international organizations abused a non-binding resolution or used it unreasonably. The paragraph was not intended to cover situations such as one in which an outdated recommendation or authorization had been relied upon for the commission of an act. Nor did it include situations in which a member State or international organization relied on a recommendation or authorization in a context in which it had not been intended to apply or when the circumstances had changed substantially since the adoption of the recommendation or authorization. Reliance on the authorization or recommendation in such situations would be unreasonable. The notions of "reasonableness" and "good faith" were both relevant in the application of that paragraph, and the commentary would elaborate on those issues.

18. During the consideration of draft article 15, paragraphs 1 and 2, questions had been raised as to whether they overlapped with draft articles 13 and 14, which dealt with direction and control and coercion in the commission of a wrongful act. The point was whether taking binding decisions or making recommendations or authorizations could fall within the scope of any of the other articles. It had been agreed that an overlap was possible, at least with draft articles 12 and 13, whereas an overlap with draft article 14 was more uncertain, because coercion, at least in the context of State responsibility, was intended to be more factual and have the character of *force majeure*. It was unlikely that even binding decisions of an international organization would necessarily meet that high threshold. Those were matters that would have to be determined in the context of specific cases. However, the Drafting Committee had seen no particular problem with overlap between those articles and article 15, paragraphs 1 and 2.

19. Draft article 15, paragraph 3, provided further clarification with respect to paragraphs 1 and 2 and was based on the text proposed by the Special Rapporteur, with some drafting adjustments. It provided that the responsibility of the international organization in question was incurred under paragraphs 1 and 2 even if the act in question was not wrongful for the member State or organization to which the decision, recommendation or authorization was addressed.

20. Draft article 15 was entitled "Decisions, recommendations and authorizations addressed to member States and international organizations".

21. Draft article 16 had been proposed by the Special Rapporteur as draft article 15, and had been based on article 19 of the draft on responsibility of States, with slight changes. The discussions in plenary session had indicated support for the draft article, with some questions as to whether its application should be limited to draft articles 12 to 14, as the Special Rapporteur had proposed in his third report (A/CN.4/553), given that paragraph 3 of the Special Rapporteur's draft article 16 had contained a specific "without prejudice" clause that also covered responsibility. The Drafting Committee had preferred draft article 16 to take the form of a general "without prejudice" clause. According to the text, the responsibility of the State or international organization that had committed the wrongful act with aid and assistance, under direction and control or subject to coercion of the international organization remained intact, whether the responsibility arose under the provisions of the draft articles or under any other rule of international law. The draft article did not affect the responsibility of any other State or international organization.

22. The difference between article 19 of the draft on responsibility of States and draft article 16 was the scope of the "without prejudice" clause. In article 19, international responsibility was preserved with regard to any other provisions of the articles on State responsibility. In the present draft article, the "without prejudice" clause was more general, preserving the international responsibility that might be established not only in accordance with the draft articles but also under any other rule of international law. It had been necessary to use broad language because the provisions on State responsibility were also relevant to the attribution of responsibility to a State.

23. The draft article was now placed after draft article 15 and the opening clause had been replaced with

the words "This chapter is without prejudice ...". That change had been made because the Drafting Committee had agreed that the draft article was relevant not only to draft articles 12 to 14 but also to draft article 15, all of which were now placed in a single chapter. The title of the draft article had also been changed and was now identical to that of draft article 19 on responsibility of States.

24. Having introduced draft articles 8 to 16, he drew members' attention to the structure that the Drafting Committee proposed for the articles so far adopted by the Commission. Some members had suggested in plenary session that it would be helpful to divide the draft articles into parts and chapters. That had also been the view of the Drafting Committee, which therefore proposed that draft articles 1 to 16 be divided into four chapters. There again, it had followed the structure of the articles on responsibility of States to the extent that that was relevant to the draft articles on responsibility of international organizations. Draft articles 1 to 16 belonged to what had been referred to as Part One in the articles on responsibility of States, defining the general conditions necessary for responsibility to arise. The title for Part One for the draft on responsibility of international organizations was the same as that for responsibility of States, with one necessary adaptation, namely, replacing the words "a State" with "an international organization".

25. Chapter I comprised draft articles 1 to 3. Chapter I of the draft on responsibility of States had been entitled "General principles". In the context of the current topic, those rules were set forth in draft article 3. Draft articles 1 and 2 dealt not with general principles but with the scope and use of terms. For that reason, the Drafting Committee had decided to entitle Chapter I "Introduction".

26. Chapter II comprised draft articles 4 to 7. As in the draft on responsibility of States, they defined the conditions under which conduct was attributable. The Drafting Committee therefore recommended retaining the same title as in those articles, with one necessary adjustment to the title of chapter II, which read "Attribution of conduct to an international organization".

27. Chapter III comprised draft articles 8 to 11 and, again as in the case of responsibility of States, spelled out in general terms the conditions under which a conduct amounted to a breach of an international obligation. The Drafting Committee had therefore retained the same title, which read "Breach of an international obligation".

28. Chapter IV comprised draft articles 12 to 16 and dealt, as in the case of responsibility of States, with certain exceptional cases where an international organization might be responsible for the conduct of a State or another international organization. The title of the chapter was the same as in the case of responsibility of States, with appropriate adjustment, and read "Responsibility of an international organization in connection with the act of a State or another international organization".

29. The CHAIRPERSON invited the Commission to adopt the titles and texts of draft articles 8 to 16 submitted by the Drafting Committee.

The titles and texts of draft articles 8 to 16 were adopted.

30. The CHAIRPERSON said that if he heard no objection, he would take it that the Commission wished to adopt the report of the Drafting Committee on responsibility of international organizations as a whole, together with the chapter structure proposed by the Drafting Committee for draft articles 1 to 16 of Part One.

It was so decided.

Organization of work of the session (*continued*)*

[Agenda item 1]

31. The CHAIRPERSON announced that the Commission had received an invitation from the Secretary-General of the Asian–African Legal Consultative Organization to be represented at its forty-fourth session, to be held in Nairobi from 27 June to 1 July 2005. He was willing to represent the Commission on that occasion.

It was so agreed.

32. The CHAIRPERSON announced that the Commission had received an invitation from the Director of the Secretariat of the Assembly of States Parties to the Rome Statute of the International Criminal Court to be represented at the Assembly's fourth session, to be held at The Hague from 28 November to 3 December 2005. Mr. Dugard had expressed his willingness to represent the Commission on that occasion.

It was so agreed.

33. The CHAIRPERSON announced that the Commission had concluded the first part of its fifty-seventh session.

The meeting rose at 10.50 a.m.

---

* Resumed from the 2844th meeting.

SUMMARY RECORDS OF THE SECOND PART OF THE FIFTY-SEVENTH SESSION

Held at Geneva from 11 July to 5 August 2005

2849th MEETING

Monday, 11 July 2005, at 3 p.m.

Chairperson: Mr. Djamchid MOMTAZ

Present: Mr. Addo, Mr. Brownlie, Mr. Candioti, Mr. Chee, Mr. Comissário Afonso, Mr. Daoudi, Mr. Dugard, Mr. Economides, Ms. Escarameia, Mr. Fomba, Mr. Gaja, Mr. Galicki, Mr. Kamto, Mr. Kateka, Mr. Kemicha, Mr. Kolodkin, Mr. Koskenniemi, Mr. Mansfield, Mr. Matheson, Mr. Pambou-Tchivounda, Mr. Sreenivasa Rao, Mr. Rodríguez Cedeño, Mr. Sepúlveda, Ms. Xue, Mr. Yamada.

Tribute to the memory of Qizhi He

1. The CHAIRPERSON said that the Secretariat had been informed of the death of Mr. Qizhi He, who had been a member of the International Law Commission from 1994 to 2001. Legal Counsel of the Ministry of Foreign Affairs of China and professor of international law at the University of Beijing, Mr. Qizhi He had also been a member of several learned societies and the author of a large number of articles and works on international law, notably space law. The members of the Commission would remember him as an amiable colleague always ready to offer advice, the fruit of his long and rich experience as an eminent theoretician and practitioner of international law. His death was an immense loss for international law and for those who had known him personally.

At the invitation of the Chairperson, the members of the Commission observed a minute of silence in tribute to the memory of Mr. Qizhi He.

Expulsion of aliens (A/CN.4/554)[1]

[Agenda item 7]

Preliminary report of the Special Rapporteur

2. The CHAIRPERSON invited Mr. Kamto, the Special Rapporteur, to introduce his preliminary report on the expulsion of aliens (A/CN.4/554).

3. Mr. KAMTO (Special Rapporteur) said that the Commission had been wise in deciding specifically to address the expulsion of aliens. The question was a very old one that was closely linked to the organization of human societies into States and yet was more topical than ever in that it highlighted the paradox between a world that was technically and economically globalized while also highly compartmentalized by barriers of political sovereignty that acted like a filter on immigration. It was also a topic that raised real questions of international law and, owing to the vast practice to which it had given rise on every continent, lent itself to codification. National or regional practice did not exist solely in a few regions or large States, as was often the case: the expulsion of aliens affected all regions of the world, and all countries had national legislation on the subject from which general principles of law applicable in the international legal order could be derived. As it was also a phenomenon involving human rights, a number of its aspects were dealt with in the many international conventions that existed in the field of human rights.

4. He had not wanted to start drawing up draft articles immediately as he thought that a preliminary report stage was needed to give the Commission some idea of his thinking on the subject and the methodological questions to which it gave rise, thus allowing him to receive any guidance or indications that might be forthcoming as to the best way to proceed. The preliminary report thus aimed to give an overview of the topic, pinpointing legal problems and methodological difficulties associated with their consideration. In the report, he had outlined the notion of the expulsion of aliens and reviewed the right to expel in international law: that right was an inherent right of State sovereignty that had never been called into question. The grounds for expulsion could vary, although they were not all admissible under international law, because the expulsion of an alien challenged protected rights, in particular fundamental human rights, the violation of which entailed legal consequences under international law.

---

[1] Reproduced in *Yearbook ... 2005*, vol. II (Part One).

5. The report also contained a draft workplan in annex I, which provided an outline of his future reports on the topic. The draft was open to discussion, but if it was approved by the Commission, he intended to address in the first report, which he proposed to submit to the Commission in 2006, the general rules governing the expulsion of aliens, in particular the scope of the future draft articles. Needless to say, he was receptive to any proposals aimed at improving the workplan and would be grateful for any additional bibliographical information that members of the Commission might wish to add to the partial bibliography in annex II.

6. A question had arisen with regard to terminology: whether it was proper to speak of the "expulsion" of aliens, a term which, as a review of comparative legislation on the subject made clear, referred to a phenomenon that was much more limited than that of the "removal" of aliens. He had retained the term "expulsion", at least provisionally, but the term should be taken in its broadest sense. Similarly, a decision would have to be taken on whether to address the expulsion of categories of persons other than aliens. It would be up to the Commission to determine which term was appropriate, but it seemed to him that "aliens" covered all categories of persons concerned.

7. More fundamentally, methodological questions had also arisen on subjects on which he sought guidance from the Commission. For example, he was not sure how to deal with existing treaty rules on the issue. Should they be incorporated in the future draft articles so as to achieve as exhaustive a legal regime as possible, or should the draft articles be restricted to the formulation of basic principles to bridge any gaps in international law? He favoured the elaboration of an entire legal regime on the subject, even if treaty law might offer elements that could be incorporated in the future draft articles, given that some of the rules in question were to be found in comparative national legislation and in international case law, particularly that of regional human rights courts, but he was, of course, open to suggestions from Commission members and looked forward to any direction they might wish to give him.

8. Mr. GAJA commended the Special Rapporteur for producing a readable and useful report. The main question raised by the Special Rapporteur concerned the scope of the study on expulsion. That was problematic because of the connections between the expulsion and the admission of aliens. It was not clear whether the Commission could usefully contribute to the regulation of such a politically sensitive matter as immigration control. It therefore seemed preferable to limit the scope to those measures that concerned resident aliens, although aliens who had stayed irregularly for a certain length of time might also be included in the study.

9. He agreed with the Special Rapporteur when he advocated a wide definition of expulsion. The definition given in paragraph 13 could, however, be taken as implying that expulsion consisted solely in a formal measure aimed at turning an individual out of a territory. It would be useful for the definition to take into account situations in which aliens were forced to leave the territory without being officially ordered to do so, and he drew attention in that connection to the definition of expulsion given by the Iran–United States Claims Tribunal in 1985 (*International Technical Products Corporation* v. *The Government of the Islamic Republic of Iran*, p. 18).

10. The Special Rapporteur proposed that the Commission should focus on admissible grounds for expulsion. For example, the Convention relating to the Status of Refugees set as a precondition that "national security or public order" should be endangered (art. 32). However, since the expelling State had broad discretionary powers, it would be difficult for a supervising body to come to a conclusion that was different from that of the State concerned.

11. Further questions concerning the lawfulness of an expulsion should be considered. They could be grouped into four categories. Firstly, a decision on expulsion must be in accordance with the law, as expressly stipulated in a number of international instruments. One question that arose in that context was whether the expulsion could be used as a disguised form of extradition. Secondly, a decision on expulsion must be consistent with the principle of non-discrimination. Thirdly, the State's interest in expelling must be weighed against the individual's right to private and family life. Fourthly, there was the question of the risk to which the expulsion decision exposed the expelled person. For example, the Convention against Torture and Other Cruel, Inhuman or Degrading Treatment or Punishment provided that a State must not expel a person to another State where there were substantial grounds for believing that he would be in danger of being subjected to torture. Procedural guarantees, especially remedies that could prevent expulsion, needed to be specifically considered. Respect for human rights was particularly at risk in cases of collective expulsion.

12. Mr. PAMBOU-TCHIVOUNDA thanked the Special Rapporteur for his lucid report and commended him for having accurately identified the questions raised by the topic. He was grateful to Mr. Gaja for having endeavoured to bring together all the questions relating to grounds for expulsion. Other questions remained, such as whether the form to be taken by the draft articles should be a regime or a set of basic principles. Since the report was a preliminary report, some aspects had not yet fallen into place, and the Special Rapporteur had been wise to leave it to the Commission to help in reorganizing the study of the topic.

13. He himself had concluded that expulsion could be analysed as a juridical event but also as a unilateral act, since the State decided it at its own discretion. His second question related to the status of an expellable alien. Aliens did not all have the same standing; their situation differed according to whether their status was recognized by the receiving State or enshrined by customs and mores, or even by conventions. Accordingly, all aliens were not "expellable" to the same degree.

14. As to grounds for expulsion, it was obvious that competence to expel was a matter of national sovereignty, but the lawfulness of such a decision had also to be considered. The decision could be viewed from the standpoint of both national law and international law. That raised the question of whether the right to expel was enforceable,

and the Commission ought to consider whether expulsion measures were enforceable under international law. Lastly, he wondered about the relationship between the two States involved or, in some cases, between a State and an international organization. That relationship naturally brought into play the institution of diplomatic protection, which might be seen as a component of the expulsion regime or, more appropriately, as an obstacle to the capacity to expel.

15. Mr. DUGARD requested clarification of the delimitation of the project. He had the impression that the Special Rapporteur intended to deal with cases of aliens expelled by unfair procedures, and not with large-scale population expulsions. He was thinking in particular of Palestinians expelled from Palestine at the birth of the State of Israel and then again after the 1967 war, the expulsion of Greek Cypriots from Turkish-occupied Northern Cyprus and the large-scale population removals that had followed the dissolution of Yugoslavia. It was sometimes difficult to define the status of the individual, but the persons who had been expelled in all those cases had not had the nationality of the State that had expelled them and might accordingly be classified as aliens. He had no fixed views on the scope of the project but thought that the question of large-scale expulsions warranted inclusion, despite the difficulties that might raise.

16. Ms. ESCARAMEIA said that the preliminary report by the Special Rapporteur raised questions of fundamental importance, in particular how to reconcile the sovereign right of a State to expel with the requirements of international law, primarily human rights law.

17. The scope of the topic should be very broad and include situations in which armed conflict led to the forced exit of populations as well as the expulsion of illegal workers or illegal aliens. On the other hand, the non-admission of or refusal to admit aliens should not be part of the topic. It would be preferable to use the term "expulsion", which was a technical term, rather than "removal", which was more ambiguous.

18. The definition in paragraph 13 seemed too narrow: expulsion was described there as a legal act, but it might be merely an administrative act. She thought expulsion should be defined as any act by which a State compelled an individual or group of individuals of a different nationality to leave its territory. Great care should be taken in dealing with collective expulsions, since, contrary to what was often said, such expulsions were not accepted in international law. Any decision to expel should be taken in respect of an individual and not of a group. The issue certainly merited consideration, but the practice must not be considered to be authorized.

19. On the question of methodology, she agreed with the Special Rapporteur that the Commission should produce draft articles forming a complete regime, not just a subsidiary regime.

20. With regard to the draft workplan, it would be better to reverse the order of sections A ("Expulsion and related concepts") and B ("Definitions"), or even to merge the two, as the issues were closely linked. Under "General principles" the Commission should not study a right inherent in State sovereignty only as a customary rule: doctrine, international case law and treaties must also be scrutinized. She would in fact like to know if there were any examples of "higher interests of the State" other than public order and State security. Lastly, with regard to "collective expulsion" or the "right to return to the territory of the expelling State", she thought it would be better to speak of a possible collective expulsion or right to return, since the question was highly debatable.

21. Mr. KOSKENNIEMI said that the approach followed by the Special Rapporteur in drafting a workplan reflected a more general problem which the Commission had been dealing with for a long time: determining what ought to be done first when taking up a new topic. Following the Commission's tradition, the Special Rapporteur had started by defining the scope of the topic and the basic concepts and before bringing in existing customary and treaty rules on the matter. Far from suggesting that those issues were unimportant, he thought that some issues should be considered before the Commission took up the conceptual aspects of scope and definition. They concerned the interests involved and the values affected by the expulsion of aliens. It would seem useful to have a general overview on the problem in the contemporary world. It would in fact be very difficult to foresee the significance of legislative intervention in that field without figuring out in advance what the problems were and who the people, groups, entities and States were whose interests were at stake. As currently drafted, the workplan was too far removed from real problems. The Commission's task was not to write a textbook on the issue, but rather to draft rules.

22. In paragraph 5 of the report the Special Rapporteur stated that "[t]he key problem in this area is how to reconcile the right to expel, which seems inherent in State sovereignty, with the demands of international law and, in particular, the fundamental rules of human rights law". To some extent that was a natural way to address the issue, but he was concerned by the tendency to try to balance opposing values as being equally important and *a priori* valid. Some of the problems the Commission had encountered in considering other topics lay in that conceptual approach, which had the disadvantage of leading to excessive generalities.

23. Paragraphs 14–16 of the report seemed to presume that there was an absolute right to expel. That seemed questionable, both in legal terms and on a practical level. In some situations a State might be justified in expelling aliens, but that was no reason to affirm the existence of such a right categorically. Naturally, the same could be said of the rights of the individual: there was no reason to say that every individual had the right to reside in a given territory. He therefore called on the Special Rapporteur to move quickly from generalities to practical suggestions as to the procedures to apply to expulsion.

24. The CHAIRPERSON, speaking as a member of the Commission, said that he was wondering about the scope of the topic and, in particular, whether the Special Rapporteur intended to look into the question of the deportation of persons living in occupied territories in times of

armed conflict. He recalled that when the Security Council had raised that issue, it had spoken of deportation, not expulsion.

The meeting rose at 4.35 p.m.

2850th MEETING

Wednesday, 13 July 2005, at 10.05 a.m.

Chairperson: Mr. Djamchid MOMTAZ

Present: Mr. Addo, Mr. Brownlie, Mr. Candioti, Mr. Chee, Mr. Comissário Afonso, Mr. Daoudi, Mr. Dugard, Mr. Economides, Ms. Escarameia, Mr. Fomba, Mr. Gaja, Mr. Galicki, Mr. Kabatsi, Mr. Kamto, Mr. Kateka, Mr. Kemicha, Mr. Kolodkin, Mr. Koskenniemi, Mr. Mansfield, Mr. Matheson, Mr. Pambou-Tchivounda, Mr. Sreenivasa Rao, Mr. Rodríguez Cedeño, Mr. Sepúlveda, Ms. Xue, Mr. Yamada.

Cooperation with other bodies (*continued*)*

[Agenda item 11]

1. The CHAIRPERSON said members would recall that on 27 May 2005 the Commission had held a joint meeting with the European Society of International Law (ESIL) as part of the Research Forum on International Law which ESIL had held in Geneva. He had just received a letter from Judge Bruno Simma, President of ESIL, thanking the members of the Commission for agreeing to hold the joint meeting, and in particular expressing appreciation to Mr. Gaja, the Special Rapporteur on the responsibility of international organizations, for addressing the Forum on the subject. According to Judge Simma, the participants had considered the meeting to be a highlight of the Forum, and he had been particularly pleased at the reaction of the young students of international law to Mr. Gaja's remarks.

Expulsion of aliens (*continued*) (A/CN.4/554)

[Agenda item 7]

PRELIMINARY REPORT OF THE SPECIAL RAPPORTEUR (*continued*)

2. Mr. BROWNLIE said that the topic of expulsion of aliens was proving much more difficult than had been expected, but was also one of considerable importance. He commended the qualities of the Special Rapporteur's well-researched and comprehensive preliminary report. One difficulty was that the accepted term "expulsion" was merely descriptive. The complexity of the topic became apparent when the question of the causes of action arose. If a person was the victim of an unlawful expulsion, what bases of claim were recognized in international law? One version might be breaches of the normal principles of State responsibility, and in particular what was still referred to in arbitrations as the international minimum standard, which included denial of justice, a concept which, at least in United States sources, was often quite broad. Thus, first there were causes of action in terms of general international law. Secondly, there were numerous bilateral treaties setting what appeared to be rigorous standards for the treatment of aliens and their investments, such as treaties of friendship, commerce and navigation and bilateral investment treaties. Thirdly, claims would probably be available under specific human rights treaties. Fourthly, in extreme cases, expulsions would involve international crimes and perhaps even genocide or crimes against humanity. Lastly, there could be breaches of what was almost certainly a general principle of non-discrimination in international law, a principle which went beyond treaties.

3. The main difficulties, to which the Special Rapporteur had himself referred, concerned the scope of the topic. In paragraph 30 of the report, Mr. Kamto sought members' views on whether the study should include existing treaty restrictions on expulsion. His own view was that it should, for practical reasons: at least in certain, possibly special circumstances, a pattern of treaty provisions might provide evidence of principles of general international law.

4. The Special Rapporteur seemed to favour including a study of cases of lawful expulsion. That would entail a lengthy catalogue of institutions, including extradition and deportation as part of a punishment. While a catalogue of cases of lawful expulsion might be useful, he did not think it was central to the Commission's concerns.

5. Another problem, to which other speakers had already alluded, was what might be called collateral breaches of general international law. If groups of people, including vulnerable persons such as pregnant women or the elderly, were left at remote frontier posts without any assistance available on the other side, then the modalities of the expulsion would themselves constitute breaches of international law even if the expulsion as such was not contrary to international law. The same applied to the principle of discrimination; an expulsion might be lawful on its face, but in fact involve discrimination. There were analogous examples in the law of expropriation, where a legal expropriation was deemed to be illegal if there was proof of discrimination, for example on racial grounds. However, those were secondary questions, and he was not sure that they added much to the subject under consideration.

6. In his view, the real centre of gravity of the subject was not expulsion and refusal of entry, but the control which a State had over its territory. He was very positivist about the importance of States and, while he was aware that it was politically incorrect to say so, maintained that the human rights system still did not provide primary care and attention. Many of the worst patterns of inhumanity stemmed from the collapse of States. A functioning State with boundaries which were properly supervised was thus, in his conservative view, one of the more simple foundations for the protection of human rights. It was when States collapsed that trouble started. Therefore, the basis of any study should be the concept that the State had not only the right but also the duty to control its territory and to maintain law and order. That had to be borne in

---

* Resumed from the 2847th meeting.

mind as the background to what the Commission might choose to call "expulsion of aliens".

7. "Expulsion" was not a very good descriptive term because it covered an enormous variety of situations, including illegal presence, informal migrants and even unlicensed foreign traders. In Ghana, for example, it had once been common for foreign traders to enter the country across open borders. When they had become sufficiently numerous, their presence had become a matter of contention with the local traders and the Government had expelled them. Those persons were what he would call informal migrants: people who were not immediately expelled or controlled, but tolerated, although they had never been given permission to be present or granted a proper status. Yet another situation was when the territorial sovereign modified its legislation, for example on the licensing of traders, and people who had hitherto been tolerated, or even lawful visitors, might find that their presence had become unlawful and that they were subject to removal.

8. References had been made in the debate to issues of self-determination and statehood, such as the position of the Palestinians. While it was not his intention to play down the expulsion of minorities, forced secession and similar problems, he was not convinced that they were part of the Commission's mandate. Similarly, he would be surprised if the Commission were to decide to define aliens. It would be too ambitious to go into the question of nationality, and he doubted that the Sixth Committee expected the Commission to do so.

9. There was also the question of whether a right of residence existed. Leaving aside the technicalities of nationality law, it had been common, not least in major peace treaties, to grant a status to persons resident or domiciled. Did the right of residence or domicile granted to an alien place limitations on his expulsion? He was leaving aside the question of whether in many cases long-standing residents would in any event have effective nationality in the State concerned.

10. He had a few specific criticisms of statements made in the report. In paragraph 16, he could not follow the assertion that "[t]he State resorting to expulsion is bound to invoke the grounds used to justify it". He was not certain whether, in the absence of a dispute or of another State or institution raising issues, the territorial sovereign had an original duty to invoke grounds of justification. Paragraph 16 tended to contradict some of the general statements of principle in paragraph 15.

11. Paragraph 24 spoke of "collective expulsion", a term which he did not regard as being very precise, as it usually involved other conditions, which were not specified. Was the removal of 100 unlicensed traders more lawful or more unlawful than removing 5? The term should either be spelled out more clearly or else avoided. Paragraph 26 referred to the possibility of States protecting their nationals by providing diplomatic protection. He had no objection to the statements made on that subject, but did not think that diplomatic protection fell within the scope of the present topic. In paragraph 30, the Special Rapporteur expressed his preference for presenting "as exhaustive a legal regime as possible, founded on general principles forming the legal basis for the expulsion of aliens under international law". While he did not want to quarrel with that principle, he had his doubts about what such an exhaustive legal regime would entail.

12. Lastly, there was the question of the subject matter. Mr. Koskenniemi had said that, when approaching a topic, the Commission should seek to analyse the interests involved. The difficulty was that in the present case, a wide range of very varied and specialized interests was involved, including migrant workers, illegal immigrants, international criminals and fugitive offenders. Thus, it was difficult to go beyond an analysis which simply accepted that the policy basis of the subject was the lawful control which a State had over its territory, and that that lawful control was an important element in public order and in that State's ability to discharge its obligations under international law, including human rights standards.

13. Mr. ADDO said that the term "expulsion" was commonly used to describe that exercise of State power which secured the removal of an alien from the territory of a State, either voluntarily, under threat of forcible removal, or forcibly. The sovereign right of States to expel aliens was generally recognized in international law. It did not matter whether the alien was only on a temporary visit or had settled down for professional business or other purposes. While a State had wide discretion in exercising that right, such discretion was not absolute. Customary international law required that a State must not abuse its right by acting arbitrarily in taking its decision. It must also act reasonably in the manner in which it effected the expulsion. Each State could use its own criteria for determining the grounds for expulsion of an alien. The State of nationality of an expelled alien could assert the right to enquire into the reasons for the expulsion. It had been ruled in a number of cases that States must give convincing reasons for expelling an alien. For example, in the *Boffolo* case (1903), which concerned an Italian expelled from the Bolivarian Republic of Venezuela, the Mixed Claims Commission (Italy–Venezuela) had held that States possessed a general right of expulsion, but that it could be resorted to only in extreme circumstances and accomplished in a manner least injurious to the person affected. In addition, the reasons for the expulsion must be stated before an international tribunal when the occasion demanded. Many municipal systems provided that the authorities of a country could deport aliens without stating reasons. The position under customary international law was therefore somewhat confused and uncertain.

14. As far as treaty law was concerned, article 13 of the International Covenant on Civil and Political Rights provided that:

> [a]n alien lawfully in the territory of a State Party to the [...] Covenant may be expelled therefrom only in pursuance of a decision reached in accordance with law and shall, except where compelling reasons of national security otherwise require, be allowed to submit the reasons against his expulsion and to have his case reviewed by, and be represented for the purpose before, the competent authority or a person or persons especially designated by the competent authority.

15. Expulsion should not entail hardship, violence or unnecessary harm to the expelled alien. Compulsory

detention of an alien under an expulsion order must be avoided, except in cases where the alien refused to leave or tried to escape from the control of the State authorities. The alien must normally be given a reasonable time to settle his personal affairs before leaving the country and be allowed to choose the country to which he might apply for admission. In *Yeager* v. *Islamic Republic of Iran*, the Iran–United States Claims Tribunal had awarded compensation to an American expelled from Iran who had been given only 30 minutes to pack a few personal belongings without advance notice, on the basis that customary international law recognized that a State must give the foreigner to be expelled sufficient time to wind up his affairs.

16. To sum up, the function of expulsion was to protect the essential interests of the State and to preserve public order. The power of expulsion must not be abused. If its aim and purpose were to be fulfilled, the power must be exercised in good faith and not for some ulterior motive, such as genocide, confiscation of property or as unlawful reprisal.

17. The function of expulsion, together with the requirement of good faith, involved the subsidiary point that expulsion had to be justified. The expelling State must show reasonable cause, although in determining whether its interests were adversely affected or whether there was a threat to public health and order, international law allowed that State a fairly wide margin of appreciation. The principle of good faith and the requirement of justification demanded that due consideration be given to the interests of the individual, including his basic human rights, his personal interests including family and other connections with the State of residence, his property interests and other legitimate expectations, all of which must be weighed against the competing demands of public order.

18. General international law imposed as a precondition to the validity of an order of expulsion that it be issued in accordance with the law. That rule entailed the further requirement that there should be an effective remedy available permitting an unlawful exercise of discretion to be challenged. The expulsion itself must be carried out in accordance with the general standards of international law for the treatment of aliens, due regard being given to the dignity of the individual and his basic rights as a human being.

19. Mr. MANSFIELD said that the preliminary report was a useful overview, leaving no doubt as to the complexity of the subject but also as to the potential for a significant contribution by the Commission. As the Special Rapporteur had pointed out in paragraph 5, the right to exclude foreign goods or people had long been seen as inherent in State sovereignty. Yet while in recent times States had been moving steadily to reduce restrictions on the entry of foreign goods, there had been no similar movement with respect to the entry of foreign nationals. The reasons were complex, but it was a reality that was unlikely to change in the foreseeable future. What had changed was the state of international law with regard to the rights of individuals, and any treatment of the topic must take those developments fully into account.

20. The Special Rapporteur drew attention to the fact that the topic was plagued with definitional problems closely linked to the issue of the scope of the Commission's work. One of the difficulties in that regard was that national laws did not deal with the issues that concerned the Commission under headings such as "expulsion of aliens". Many of the legitimate actions resulting in the transfer of a foreign national out of the jurisdiction of the receiving State were taken under laws on immigration or temporary entry for business or tourist purposes. Less legitimate actions might be taken under broad-ranging powers, pursuant to innocuously titled legislation or without any legislative basis at all. He therefore agreed with those who had suggested that the Commission must ensure that whatever definitions it used, they encompassed situations where persons were not legally or administratively compelled to leave but in practice had no option to remain.

21. He also thought it would be necessary to cover the removal of foreign nationals who had entered illegally or whose presence had become illegal, in addition to removal of foreigners who were lawfully in the country. In many jurisdictions, persons might have entered legally but their continued presence might have become illegal because they had exceeded the period for which they were given entry or had broken a condition of their entry permit. Like those who entered illegally, they did not perhaps have a right to remain, but they were not without procedural rights, particularly that their removal should be in accordance with the law. That right must surely also involve some ability to seek review of the decision while still in the country.

22. On the other hand, he was inclined to agree with those who had responded in the negative to the Special Rapporteur's question as to whether the Commission should attempt to deal with issues relating to the refusal of admission or prevention of entry. Leaving aside situations when there was dispute as to whether persons had or had not entered the territory of a State, refusal to admit persons or prevention of their entry certainly seemed to lie at the margins of the topic and would be likely to complicate the work unduly. All those considerations led to the point that in order to settle on a work plan, the problems or issues that the Commission was attempting to address must be identified in broad terms.

23. Lastly, he did not yet have a firm view concerning the question posed in paragraph 30 of the report, relating to existing treaty rules on the issue, but was inclined to think that the aim of the Commission's work should be a comprehensive text with references, as appropriate, to other relevant conventions.

24. Mr. RODRÍGUEZ CEDEÑO said that consideration of the topic was justified, first of all, by the large number of persons, now totalling over 100 million, who had left behind their countries of origin, and second, by the conservative attitude of States in immigration matters. The Special Rapporteur had asked some important questions, including how to delimit the scope of the topic and what definitions to establish. On the first question, the Special Rapporteur had raised related issues, such as extradition, asylum, refuge, *refoulement* and deportation,

which needed thorough consideration so as to distinguish them from the specific issue of expulsion of aliens.

25. On definitions, the term "alien" was quite broad, encompassing different categories and groups of persons living in the territory of a State other than their own and covered by differing legal regimes. For example, political asylum-seekers were governed, at any rate in the inter-American context, by the Convention on territorial asylum adopted at Caracas in 1954. Refugees subjected to forced displacement were covered by the 1951 Convention relating to the Status of Refugees and the 1967 Protocol relating to the Status of Refugees. Migrant workers were another category of persons that were displaced, not forcibly, but in order to seek better living conditions, and their rights were protected in the 1990 International Convention on the Protection of the Rights of All Migrant Workers and Members of their Families. The term "alien" had to cover all those categories of non-nationals, including stateless persons, who were protected by the domestic legislation of States on aliens or refugees and by existing international regulations.

26. The Special Rapporteur rightly excluded internally displaced persons, who fell within the scope of the topic only when, having crossed a border, they became asylum-seekers. That brought in a principle closely related to expulsion, namely, *non-refoulement*, a fundamental principle in international legislation on refugees, particularly with respect to asylum-seekers, who could not arbitrarily be returned to their country of origin without their requests for asylum having been heard. Thus, the domestic legislation of States and international regulations for the protection of specific categories of non-nationals—a much more appropriate term than "aliens"—must be taken into account when considering the very broad concept of "alien".

27. Concerning the term "expulsion", the State clearly had a right to regulate entry into its territory and, conversely, to expel non-nationals. However, expulsion must not be arbitrary: it must be reasoned and expressed or transmitted through an administrative act so as to enable the person concerned to appeal against any allegedly arbitrary measures taken by the State. The Special Rapporteur and Mr. Pambou-Tchivounda had rightly noted that expulsion was a unilateral act of the State. However, it was very different from the unilateral acts being studied in the context of another, eponymous, topic. He himself saw it as being more closely related to the international responsibility of the State for wrongful acts or for breach of its domestic regulations, and to diplomatic protection.

28. The work plan submitted by the Special Rapporteur in annex I to his report covered the salient points that would have to be addressed as part of the Commission's consideration of a difficult and complex subject. He hoped that the Special Rapporteur would examine some domestic legislation, not only on aliens in general but also specifically on migrant workers, refugees and asylum-seekers, and also look at the case law of the regional courts, for example the Inter-American Court of Human Rights, which was no doubt relevant to the issue of treatment of aliens.

29. Mr. KOLODKIN noted that in paragraph 6 of his report, the Special Rapporteur stated that the essence of a preliminary report was to present the topic, to formulate issues and to suggest approaches rather than to offer final solutions. In his view, the report had fully achieved those aims.

30. One could only agree with the Special Rapporteur that the right to expulsion was an inalienable and sovereign right of States, although after reading paragraphs 14 to 16 of the report, one got the impression that the right had not evolved since the nineteenth century. In paragraph 16, the Special Rapporteur correctly pointed out that the right to expel was not an absolute right of the State; among the factors restricting the exercise of that right, a State had to show grounds for resorting to expulsion. Chapter III of the report was thus devoted to an analysis of the grounds for expulsion, and in paragraph 20 the Special Rapporteur pointed out that "the question to be answered is which of the many grounds for expelling aliens are admissible under international law, or *a contrario*, which are prohibited". Subsequently, in chapter IV, the Special Rapporteur addressed rights related to expulsion, stating, *inter alia*, that "[t]he exercise of the right to expel brings into play the rights of the aliens being expelled and those of their State of origin" (para. 21).

31. The grounds for expulsion and the question whether they were internationally lawful were undoubtedly important, but in his opinion the problem should be viewed from a slightly different angle. It was a matter, not of whether the grounds for expulsion were lawful, but rather of how the right of the State to expel, and the interests protected by the exercise of that right, were related to, or perhaps conflicted with, the rights of expelled persons and their interests. The right of the State to expel was not a thing of value in and of itself, although the State sovereignty from which the right flowed was itself a thing of value. It was necessary, and it was protected under international law, because it in turn was a means for defending the interests of the society in the territory of that State, of preserving law and order and the security of the State and its citizens. In other words, it was a means of defending human rights and, as Mr. Brownlie had pointed out, it was both a right and a duty of the State.

32. Such rights and interests associated with expulsion had to be correlated with the rights of expelled persons such as the rights to privacy and family life, to humane and just treatment and not to be subjected to torture, not only by the State that expelled them but also by that to which they were expelled. Those were simply some of the rights of individuals that must clearly be taken into account. It was precisely the problem of balancing such rights, obligations and interests that was paramount, especially for jurists considering the matter. In that regard he referred to the practice of the European Court of Human Rights when considering expulsion cases. In its 2003 decision in the *Slivenko* case, the Court had stated that its task consisted "in ascertaining whether the impugned measures struck a fair balance between the relevant interests, namely the individual's rights protected by the Convention on the one hand and the [interests of Latvian society] on the other" (para. 113 of the decision). It had reiterated that "no right of an alien to enter or reside in a particular country [was]

as such guaranteed by the Convention"; that it was for States "to maintain public order, in particular by exercising their right, as a matter of well-established international law and subject to their treaty obligations, to control the entry and residence of aliens" (para. 115 of the decision). The Court had been propounding that approach to expulsion cases for many years.

33. Accordingly, it was not only or primarily the grounds for expulsion that limited the sovereign right of States, acknowledged in international law, to expel aliens: rather, it was the right of the individual, protected by international law. The Commission's task in considering the topic was to establish a normative balance between those important rights.

34. In paragraph 22, the Special Rapporteur pointed out that "the lawfulness of an expulsion [depended] on two factors: conformity with the expulsion procedures in force in the expelling State and respect for fundamental human rights". In paragraph 23, he noted that the requirement concerning respect for procedures provided for by law could be considered an obligation under general international law. In paragraph 27, however, he remarked that the responsibility of the expelling State could arise from injury suffered by the persons expelled improperly (rules of procedure) or on grounds contrary to the rules of international law (substantive rules). In other words, the Special Rapporteur reverted to the hypothesis that expulsion procedures were provided for only under domestic law, while the material rights of the expelled person were protected by international law. That hypothesis should be rectified and brought into line with paragraph 23, for contemporary international law did to some extent consolidate the right of the individual to equitable expulsion procedures and the duty of States to provide for such procedures: witness Protocol No. 7 to the Convention for the Protection of Human Rights and Fundamental Freedoms.

35. In considering the topic, key concepts such as "expulsion" and "alien" had to be defined. In defining "expulsion", a number of similar concepts mentioned in paragraph 8 had to be considered so that a distinction could be drawn. In that regard he cited a number of terms used in Russian legislation that had no equivalent in other legal systems. He agreed with the Special Rapporteur that for the purposes of the topic, the term "expulsion" should be retained but interpreted broadly. On the other hand, the definition proposed in paragraph 13 needed further consideration. The reference to a "legal" act by which a State compelled an individual to leave its territory raised certain doubts, and what categories of individuals were concerned needed to be clarified. In the definition of "expulsion" they were nationals of another State, but in paragraph 7 the term "alien" was described as covering not only nationals of a State other than the expelling State, but also stateless persons. Why, then, did the definition of "expulsion" refer solely to foreign nationals?

36. Questions had been raised as to whether the Special Rapporteur intended to study expulsion from occupied territories and, in general, in times of armed conflict. Those questions, in his view, fell within the sphere of international humanitarian law and should not be taken up under the current topic. If the Commission's final product were to take the form of a set of draft articles, then an article could be incorporated to the effect that the articles were without prejudice to the duties of States under international humanitarian law in respect of civilian populations.

37. In response to a number of questions raised by the Special Rapporteur in paragraph 30 of his report, he would say that a set of draft articles on the topic would be of interest only if they were comprehensive, albeit not exhaustive, in nature. He found it difficult to see how the work could be limited to bridging certain gaps in international treaty law, since in his view it could scarcely be said that there was any reasonably well developed universal conventional regime in the field at present. He likewise concurred with the Special Rapporteur's suggestion in paragraph 29 that an analysis of regional practice, including court decisions and treaties, was essential for future consideration of the topic.

38. Mr. PAMBOU-TCHIVOUNDA said that Mr. Kolodkin had talked of expulsion to another State. That raised the question of whether expulsion always occurred on a State-to-State basis, or whether third States or transit States might sometimes be involved. If so, did the transit State have any rights? Was its consent required? Could it oppose the expulsion proceedings?

39. Mr. FOMBA commended the Special Rapporteur's clear, concise but informative preliminary report. The freedom of movement of persons and the expulsion of aliens were major concerns for peoples and States, as abuses in the conduct of States were commonplace. To cite only the example of his own country, every day at least one Malian citizen was forcibly expelled from French territory, and he had once had to protest in his official capacity about the inhumane treatment of a compatriot deportee on a flight from France to Mali. Such incidents were legion, and gave the impression that a State could get away with anything in the name of sovereignty in an area on which international law was silent. The preliminary report provided an opportunity to refute the mistaken notion that there was a legal vacuum, to call States to order and to guarantee individuals and groups of individuals their fundamental rights.

40. The report provided a good introduction to the central issue, namely, how to reconcile the right to expulsion inherent in sovereignty with the requirements of international law and to interpret them from the standpoint of *lex lata* and *lex ferenda*. The objectives and general approach described in paragraph 6 seemed to be heading along the right lines. Paragraphs 7 to 13 raised the problem of how to define the concept of expulsion, but for the time being the Special Rapporteur merely sought the Commission's advice on the methodology, rather than on the substance. While he endorsed the idea of clarifying the concept of expulsion in a subsequent report, the provisional definition given in paragraph 13 seemed a good basis for discussion.

41. On the question, raised in the last sentence of that paragraph, "whether a distinction should be made between the legal act of expulsion and the expelled person's physical crossing of the border or leaving the territory" concerned, he wished to make a few general comments. At

first sight there seemed to be a logical connection between the basic concept of the expulsion of aliens and related factors such as nationality, territory, borders, the right of entry, residence and settlement which argued in favour of its definition as both a legal act and a legal event, particularly when a distinction between *de jure* and *de facto* expulsion was recognized. There were many different types of situations: in some cases, even when the expulsion was based on a court decision, the enforcement of the decision could give rise to unlawful acts; in other cases, as in time of war or raids on lawfully or unlawfully resident aliens, there was no legal basis and such acts were totally arbitrary. He agreed with the Special Rapporteur that the right to expel aliens fell within the realm of international law (para. 16), the question being to what extent.

42. The report clearly defined the grounds for expulsion in paragraphs 17 to 20, and he agreed that "[t]he question to be answered [was] which of the many grounds for expulsion were admissible under international law, or *a contrario*, which [were] prohibited" (para. 20). He endorsed the reservation regarding the absolute nature of the prohibition on collective expulsion (para. 24); and agreed that it was worthwhile to examine all the legal consequences of expulsion within the context of the responsibility of the expelling State and the ensuing compensation due for the injury suffered by victims (para. 27).

43. Broadly speaking, he endorsed the Special Rapporteur's methodological approach. He noticed, however, that no reference was made in paragraph 28 to specific legal regimes such as those of the European Community and other regional and subregional regimes, based on new concepts of nationality, territory and frontiers that might call for a different approach to the question.

44. On the two questions raised by the Special Rapporteur in paragraph 30, his response to the first question was that while existing treaty rules on the expulsion of aliens could be taken up in the future draft articles, any legal gaps should also be bridged. The reason for that was that the rules in question were far from clear to everyone, even at ministry level, as was borne out by the reaction in his own country to some articles he had written in the national press on the subject of the mass expulsion of Malian citizens from France.

45. As for the second question, namely, whether the draft articles should be restricted to the formulation of basic principles relative to the expulsion of aliens or propose an entire legal regime, he was in favour of the latter course, for at least two reasons. First, experience showed that a simple body of general principles was seldom very useful. Second, the Commission's work must be as effective and thorough as possible. It must produce a text that would help prevent or handle disputes involving the expulsion of aliens in the best way possible. In concluding, he said that the draft work plan proposed by the Special Rapporteur was a good basis for the future work of the Commission.

46. Mr. GALICKI said that the new topic was an interesting one, both intrinsically and in the combination of factors it embraced. On the one hand, it was a well-established subject in traditional international law, based on the principle of the exclusive sovereign prerogatives of States; on the other, it reflected contemporary trends in international law influenced by relatively new ideas of the international protection of human rights. Those contradictory trends made the Special Rapporteur's task all the more challenging. It should also be borne in mind that the expulsion of aliens was still used as a means of retaliation in relations between States, often being applied to a special category of aliens, namely, those with diplomatic status.

47. The report gave a clear picture of how the Special Rapporteur intended to approach the topic and contained a useful—albeit "partial"—bibliography (annex II). In general he found the approach outlined acceptable; nonetheless, he had identified some problems. First, he would not be in favour of a very broad definition of expulsion that embraced some of the related concepts listed in the draft work plan (annex I). In the light of recent practice, the Commission should keep the expulsion of aliens separate from those related concepts, which were based on different factual and legal grounds, in its thorny task of codification.

48. Secondly, not enough emphasis had been placed on the human rights aspect of the expulsion of aliens. For example, article 13 of the International Covenant on Civil and Political Rights, which laid down the requirements for the expulsion of aliens, had merely been referred to in a footnote. Similarly, although there was also a footnote reference to article 4 of Protocol No. 4 to the Convention for the Protection of Human Rights and Fundamental Freedoms, which prohibited the collective expulsion of aliens, no mention was made, in the list of international documents, of Protocol No. 7 to the same Convention, whose article 1 contained procedural safeguards relating to expulsion of aliens that went further than those contained in the two aforementioned instruments. It was also worth noting that article 3 of the 1955 European Convention on Establishment provided that nationals of any Contracting Party lawfully residing in the territory of another Party could be expelled only if they endangered national security or offended against *ordre public* or morality. Lastly, it should be recalled that special international regulations governed the excessive use of the expulsion of aliens by States in situations of emergency, such as those connected with the fight against terrorism. Particularly noteworthy was Guideline XII of the Guidelines of the Committee of Ministers of the Council of Europe on human rights and the fight against terrorism adopted in 2002.[1] In conclusion, he expressed his appreciation of the preliminary report and draft work plan, which would provide a good basis for further work on the topic.

49. The CHAIRPERSON, speaking as a member of the Commission, sought clarification regarding Mr. Galicki's comment about States resorting to expulsion by way of retaliation in their relations with other States. Such action was prohibited under the provisions relating to countermeasures contained in chapter II of part three of the draft

[1] Adopted by the Committee of Ministers on 11 July 2002, at the 804th Meeting of the Ministers' Deputies, document CM/Del/Dec(2002)804, appendix 3; annexed to the "Letter dated 1 August 2002 from the Permanent Representative of Luxembourg to the United Nations addressed to the Secretary-General" (A/57/313).

articles on the responsibility of States for internationally wrongful acts adopted in 2001.[2]

50. Mr. GALICKI said that his comment about expulsion being used as a means of retaliation did not of course imply his endorsement of that procedure. He was merely giving an example of current practice. Moreover, the fact that the matter had been considered by the Commission several years previously did not mean that it could not be raised again in connection with the topic under discussion.

51. Mr. MATHESON commended the Special Rapporteur's very interesting and useful introduction to a topic of considerable importance on which the Commission should be able to make a significant contribution. At that early juncture, he could do no more than comment briefly on the scope of the topic and the issues to be covered.

52. First, he agreed with Ms. Escarameia and Mr. Mansfield that the issue of refusal to admit aliens should not be dealt with. Denial of admission was a much less onerous action than expulsion and involved quite different questions of law and policy. The Commission should not allow itself to be diverted from the serious issues relating to expulsion in an attempt to investigate the whole complex area of immigration law.

53. Second, the provisional definition of expulsion given in paragraph 13 of the report was understandably very broad, but might cover situations that did not fall within the scope of the topic. For instance, it could be interpreted as covering transfers of aliens to the authorities of another Government for law enforcement purposes. Such transfers involved an entirely different set of issues, norms and policy considerations, many of which would presumably be dealt with when the Commission turned to the new topic "Obligation to extradite or prosecute (*aut dedere aut judicare*)".[3] For the sake of simplicity, they should be excluded from the scope of the current topic. Moreover, as Mr. Galicki had pointed out, the definition embraced foreign diplomatic personnel, who were already adequately covered by the separate body of law and conventions on diplomatic privileges and immunities.

54. Third, a distinction must be drawn between aliens who were lawfully present in a country and those who were not. The right of a State to expel persons not lawfully present in its territory was an integral component of that State's right to deny admission or set conditions for it. Any alien who entered a country illegally, or who violated the conditions of his entry, was liable to expulsion on those grounds alone. That distinction between aliens lawfully and not lawfully present was clearly recognized both in State practice and in international agreements such as the Convention relating to the Status of Refugees (art. 32) and the International Covenant on Civil and Political Rights (art. 13). If it were decided that it was desirable for the Commission to deal with the removal of persons who were not lawfully present, perhaps for the purpose of addressing such questions as due process and humane treatment, it would at least be necessary to acknowledge that States had the right of expulsion without the need for further justification.

55. Fourth, the Commission could not begin to deal with the question of legitimate grounds for exclusion of aliens lawfully present in a country without a comprehensive study of State practice. Thus, it was gratifying to learn that the Secretariat would be conducting just such a study. While he suspected that it might prove difficult to find a coherent pattern of admissible and inadmissible grounds for exclusion, it was important for the Commission to base its work on a thorough grasp of that practice.

56. Lastly, while it was understandable that the Special Rapporteur should wish to produce as exhaustive a legal regime as possible, the Commission should not attempt to revert to—still less change—all the rules and principles it had already elaborated on State responsibility, diplomatic protection and liability. Instead, it should first focus on the basic question of States' rights and duties with respect to expulsion, leaving a decision on whether to examine the consequences of breaches of those duties for a later stage.

57. Ms. XUE said that the expulsion of aliens was a rather complicated issue because States followed a wide variety of procedures for preventing foreign nationals from entering or staying in their territory. Yet national restrictions on the movement of people had international political, economic and social repercussions. In an era of globalization it would therefore be helpful to identify some general rules of international law in order to protect States' interests and individuals' rights. The Special Rapporteur's preliminary report provided an extremely useful analysis of the issue.

58. Regarding the general approach to the topic, she agreed with the Special Rapporteur that it would be wise to formulate a whole set of general principles of international law forming the legal basis for the expulsion of aliens, since the matter was for the most part governed by national laws and existing treaty law in that area was fragmented, covering only certain categories of persons. Of course, existing treaty regimes should remain intact as *lex specialis* within a general legal framework. In general, the methodology proposed by the Special Rapporteur was acceptable.

59. Turning to the draft work plan and the scope of the topic, she drew attention to the key importance of the notion of "aliens" or "non-nationals". Hence, mass expulsions of the sort referred to in paragraph 10 of the report, such as the case of the Palestinians, should be excluded from the scope of the draft articles, not only because they were politically sensitive and legally inappropriate in that they concerned territorial claims and occupied territory, but also because it was disputable whether those people had been expelled from a foreign territory and, indeed, whether they were aliens. There was no need for a separate definition of each kind of expulsion, but it might be necessary to clarify the term "alien" by specifying that it referred to two kinds of foreign nationals: those who stayed or lived in a foreign country, either legally or illegally, and those who were denied entry before they physically set foot in the country concerned. Similarly, it would

[2] *Yearbook ... 2001*, vol. II (Part Two) and corrigendum, pp. 116–138.

[3] See *Yearbook ... 2004*, vol. II (Part Two), chap. XI, sect. A.1, para. 362, and annex.

be necessary to decide whether the physical crossing of the expelling State's border by the person expelled was a constituent of the concept of expulsion or whether it was a consequence thereof. In her view, a broader concept should be adopted, because aliens prevented from entering the territory of the State concerned while they were still on the high seas or on board an aeroplane might nonetheless be regarded as expelled aliens.

60. While every State had the sovereign right to expel aliens from its territory on any grounds it deemed appropriate, that right was subject to certain limitations under international law. Referring to the three principles outlined in part 1, chapter II, section B of the draft work plan (annex I of the report), she said it was questionable whether the Commission should address the principle of the non-expulsion of nationals, since the right of nationals to leave and return to their home country belonged to a different area of the law. The principle of not expelling stateless persons was sound, because such expulsion might result in unbearable hardship for those persons. She wondered, however, if the principle should still apply if the stateless person to be returned to a State of which he or she was a permanent resident had illegally entered the expelling State.

61. On the second principle, the fundamental rights and dignity of aliens must be respected throughout the expulsion process. National laws tended to neglect that question, and unfair treatment of aliens and abuses of their human rights were matters to which neither the authorities nor the public of expelling countries paid sufficient attention. It was to be hoped that the Special Rapporteur would pay due regard to the practical aspects of that problem.

62. On the third principle, she sought clarification of the term "collective expulsion", which, to judge from paragraph 24 and footnote 34, appeared to refer to expulsions on grounds of nationality or race. Although such expulsions should certainly be prohibited, situations could nonetheless arise in which States might find it necessary to expel a boatload of people collectively in order to curb illegal immigration. In such circumstances, once exceptions were allowed the consequences could be serious. Migrant workers should be treated separately, and the relevant international treaty should apply.

63. Grounds for expulsion were primarily determined by national laws. From the international standpoint, maintenance of public or political order and national security could be regarded as absolute grounds for denying an alien the right to enter or stay in the country. Rather than considering whether there were still higher interests of States, the Commission should perhaps consider what factors could not serve as grounds for expulsion. While everyone agreed that no one should be expelled on grounds of nationality, the position was much more complicated when it came to religious belief, sexual behaviour or an alien's physical or mental state. For instance, when a foreigner from a region affected by an epidemic of a serious disease was refused entry temporarily for reasons of public health, denial of entry on those grounds might be hard on the person concerned, but was perfectly legitimate. Even in such circumstances, however, the right to denial of entry under international law was not absolute.

64. Lastly, with regard to part 3 of the draft work plan, in view of their vulnerable status, respect for aliens' individual rights and dignity was especially important. Where it was found that a person who had been resident in the expelling State for a long time had been expelled groundlessly, that person should enjoy the right of return and might, in some instances, be entitled to State compensation for personal injury and material damages. The draft articles should therefore make specific provision for such compensation. The provisions on State responsibility and diplomatic protection were also relevant and should apply in the context of the expulsion of aliens.

65. Mr. ECONOMIDES agreed with the content of the concept of "expulsion" as set out in paragraphs 12 and 13 of the report. That notion had to be broad enough to cover all procedures for the removal of foreigners from the territory of the State exercising the right of expulsion, irrespective of whether they were legally resident. Only *refoulement* at the border should be excluded from the scope of the study.

66. While every State had the right to expel aliens, qualifying adjectives such as "discretionary", "absolute" or "sovereign" should not be applied to that right because, far from being absolute or discretionary, it was governed by certain principles of international human rights law and by States' internal law. Generally speaking, domestic law permitted the expulsion of aliens only on certain specified grounds, which usually served the same purposes, such as the protection of public order or State security. Those grounds ought to be clarified rigorously. To that end, national laws would have to be compared in order to identify common solutions which might be said to acquire an international character.

67. International law prohibited the expulsion of aliens in some exceptional circumstances defined in international human rights conventions and in the case law of the judicial bodies or other organs set up under those conventions. All those exceptions would have to be examined individually in order to determine if they could be accepted as customary law, if they were rules coming under the heading of the progressive development of international law, or if some or all of them ought to be rejected.

68. Collective expulsions imposed by a strong State on a weaker State during an armed conflict were always illegal; any other interpretation would be dangerous and retrograde. The Special Rapporteur should also examine all the procedural steps preceding the execution of an expulsion order. In that connection, it would be useful to study States' internal law and international law, including that of the Council of Europe. Two issues of vital importance in that respect were the State's obligation to notify the alien concerned of its decision to expel him, and the right of that person to have a reasonable period of time within which to lodge an appeal against that decision. It was equally important to ensure that the execution of the decision to expel was carried out in a manner which was not inhumane, degrading or humiliating, since respect for

the dignity of the alien being expelled was indeed one of the standards guaranteed by international law.

69. The question of the right to expel aliens had to be treated in its entirety, following the Commission's usual approach of codification and progressive development. It was too early to say what form the final product should take but, bearing in mind the sensitive nature of the subject matter, a code of conduct might be more effective than a legally binding text.

70. Mr. KEMICHA said that, although every State had a sovereign right to expel from its territory aliens whose presence it deemed undesirable, that right was not and must not be absolute. The crux of the matter was, as the Special Rapporteur had stated in paragraph 5 of his report, how to reconcile the right to expel, which seemed inherent in State sovereignty, with the demands of international law and, in particular, the fundamental rules of human rights law. That consideration must serve as the starting point for the Commission's work in the years ahead.

71. The minimalist definition of "expulsion" proposed in paragraph 13 of the report, while clear and succinct, did not embrace the full complexity of an act which could have extremely serious consequences, particularly for the person expelled. The grounds given by a State for expulsion must be consonant with and limited by international law and the principles of respect for the rights of individuals. The rights related to expulsion comprised aliens' rights and the rights of their States of origin and raised the two crucial issues of the responsibility of States which had committed a wrongful act and the possible exercise of diplomatic protection by the alien's State of origin in the event of improper or illegal expulsion. The Commission would doubtless be able to apply the rules it had codified on State responsibility and diplomatic protection in its study of the expulsion of aliens. The methodology and work plan proposed were certainly useful at the current stage of the Commission's deliberations and it would also be helpful if the Secretariat were to prepare a documentary study of the subject.

The meeting rose at 12.55 p.m.

2851st MEETING

Thursday, 14 July 2005, at 10 a.m.

Chairperson: Mr. Djamchid MOMTAZ

Present: Mr. Addo, Mr. Brownlie, Mr. Candioti, Mr. Chee, Mr. Comissário Afonso, Mr. Daoudi, Mr. Dugard, Mr. Economides, Ms. Escarameia, Mr. Fomba, Mr. Gaja, Mr. Galicki, Mr. Kabasti, Mr. Kamto, Mr. Kateka, Mr. Kemicha, Mr. Kolodkin, Mr. Koskenniemi, Mr. Mansfield, Mr. Matheson, Mr. Pambou-Tchivounda, Mr. Sreenivasa Rao, Mr. Rodríguez Cedeño, Mr. Sepúlveda, Ms. Xue, Mr. Yamada.

Cooperation with other bodies (*continued*)

[Agenda item 11]

VISIT BY THE PRESIDENT OF THE INTERNATIONAL COURT OF JUSTICE

1. The PRESIDENT welcomed Judge Shi Jiuyong, President of the International Court of Justice, and invited him to address the Commission.

2. Mr. SHI (President of the International Court of Justice), noting that it was the third time he had addressed the Commission in his capacity as President of the International Court of Justice, recalled that the intensity of the work accomplished by the Court had been a recurrent theme of his statements. Over the past year, as in previous years, the activity of the Court had been particularly sustained. The Court had rendered one advisory opinion (para. 4 below) as well as final judgments in 10 cases (the judgments in the 8 cases concerning the *Legality of Use of Force* had been rendered simultaneously).[1] That made 11 decisions in one year. The Court had also held oral hearings in three cases. During the same period, one new case had been filed with the Court, by Romania versus Ukraine,[2] attesting to the Court's vitality and the continuing trust States placed in it. As a result of its efforts, the total number of cases on its docket, which had stood at 21 one year earlier, had dropped to 12. He could not but insist on how much had been accomplished since that not too distant time when there had been talk of a serious backlog of cases at the Court.

3. As in the previous year, he wished to brief the Commission on the judgments and other decisions rendered by the Court since his last visit; in view of their number, however, he would confine himself to some of the principal legal findings contained in each of those decisions, in the hope that such a selective overview would prove more interesting to the members of the Commission than a comprehensive presentation.

4. On 9 July 2004, exactly two days after his previous visit to the Commission, the Court had handed down its advisory opinion on the *Legal Consequences of the Construction of a Wall in the Occupied Palestinian Territory*. As the members of the Commission would remember, on 8 December 2003, the General Assembly had adopted resolution ES-10/14 in which it had requested the Court, pursuant to Article 65 of its Statute, to "urgently render an advisory opinion on the following question: [w]hat are the legal consequences arising from the construction of the wall being built by Israel, the occupying Power, in the Occupied Palestinian Territory, including in and around East Jerusalem, as described in the report of the Secretary-General [prepared pursuant to General Assembly

---

[1] In addition to the final judgments rendered on 15 December 2004 in the 8 cases concerning *Legality of Use of Force*, the ICJ also rendered a decision in *Certain Property* (*Liechtenstein* v. *Germany*) on 10 February 2005 (see paragraph 18 below) and in *Frontier Dispute (Benin/Niger)* (see paragraph 21 below).

[2] *Maritime Delimitation in the Black Sea* (*Romania* v. *Ukraine*), Application instituting proceedings, filed in the Registry of the Court on 16 September 2004, 2004 General List No. 132.

resolution ES-10/13 (A/ES-10/248)], considering the rules and principles of international law, including the Fourth Geneva Convention of 1949, and relevant Security Council and General Assembly resolutions?".

5. Before addressing the question posed by the General Assembly, the Court had considered whether it had jurisdiction to respond to the request and had examined the judicial propriety of exercising its jurisdiction in that instance. The Court had unanimously found that it had jurisdiction to give the advisory opinion and had decided, by 14 votes to 1, to accede to the request (para. 163.1–2 of the opinion).

6. The Court had then considered the legality of the construction of the wall before dealing with the legal consequences of its construction. It had found by 14 votes to 1 that "[t]he construction of the wall being built by Israel, the occupying Power, in the Occupied Palestinian Territory, including in and around East Jerusalem, and its associated regime, are contrary to international law" (*ibid.*, para. 163.3 A). With regard to the legal consequences of those violations, the Court had distinguished between the consequences for Israel, those for other States and those for the United Nations. Turning firstly to the consequences for Israel, the Court, by 14 votes to 1, had found that "Israel is under an obligation to terminate its breaches of international law" and that "it is under an obligation to cease forthwith the works of construction of the wall being built in the Occupied Palestinian Territory, including in and around East Jerusalem, to dismantle forthwith the structure therein situated, and to repeal or render ineffective forthwith all legislative and regulatory acts relating thereto" (*ibid.*, para. 163.3 B). The Court had further decided, again by 14 votes to 1, that "Israel is under an obligation to make reparation for all damage caused by the construction of the wall in the Occupied Palestinian Territory, including in and around East Jerusalem" (*ibid.*, para. 163.3 C).

7. In respect of the consequences for other States, the Court had found, by 13 votes to 2, that "[a]ll States are under an obligation not to recognize the illegal situation resulting from the construction of the wall and not to render aid or assistance in maintaining the situation created by such construction", and that "all States parties to the Fourth Geneva Convention relative to the Protection of Civilian Persons in Time of War of 12 August 1949 have in addition the obligation, while respecting the United Nations Charter and international law, to ensure compliance by Israel with international humanitarian law as embodied in that Convention" (*ibid.*, para. 163.3 D). Finally, with regard to the United Nations, the Court had found, by 14 votes to 1, that "[t]he United Nations, and especially the General Assembly and the Security Council, should consider what further action is required to bring to an end the illegal situation resulting from the construction of the wall and the associated regime, taking due account of the present Advisory Opinion" (*ibid.*, para. 163.3 E).

8. In order to render its advisory opinion, the Court had examined the principles of international law relating to the prohibition of the threat or use of force and the rules governing the acquisition and occupation of territory. It had also addressed the principle of self-determination and had considered the applicability of international humanitarian law and human rights law in the Occupied Palestinian Territory. In addition to reviewing those vital elements of international law, which were enshrined in numerous treaties, including the Charter of the United Nations, and customary law and reflected in various General Assembly resolutions, the Court had also recognized the need for the construction of the wall to be placed in a more general context. In particular, the Court had noted that Israel and Palestine were "under an obligation scrupulously to observe the rules of international humanitarian law", and it had expressed the view that "this tragic situation in the region can be brought to an end only through implementation in good faith of all relevant Security Council resolutions". The Court had also drawn the attention of the General Assembly to the "need for these efforts to be encouraged with a view to achieving as soon as possible, on the basis of international law, a negotiated solution to the outstanding problems and the establishment of a Palestinian State, existing side by side with Israel and its other neighbours, with peace and security for all in the region" (para. 162 of the opinion).

9. On 15 December 2004, the Court had rendered its judgments in the eight cases concerning the *Legality of Use of Force*. In each of those cases it had found unanimously that it had no jurisdiction to entertain the claims made by Serbia and Montenegro. On 29 April 1999, the Government of the Federal Republic of Yugoslavia (as from 4 February 2003, "Serbia and Montenegro") had seized the Court of 10 separate legal disputes against Belgium, Canada, France, Germany, Italy, the Netherlands, Portugal, Spain, the United Kingdom and the United States of America, alleging that those States had participated in the bombing of the territory of the Federal Republic of Yugoslavia in 1999 and in the training, arming, financing, equipping and supplying of the so-called "Kosovo Liberation Army". In its applications, the Government of the Federal Republic of Yugoslavia had contended that, by those acts, each of the 10 States concerned had violated "its international obligation banning the use of force against another State, the obligation not to intervene in the internal affairs of another State, the obligation not to violate the sovereignty of another State, the obligation to protect the civilian population and civilian objects in wartime, the obligation to protect the environment, the obligation relating to free navigation on international rivers, the obligation regarding fundamental human rights and freedoms, the obligation not to use prohibited weapons [and] the obligation not to deliberately inflict conditions of life calculated to cause the physical destruction of a national group" (see paragraphs 1–4 of the judgments rendered in these 10 cases).

10. Although a different basis for the Court's jurisdiction was invoked in each of the 10 cases, the applications relied mainly on Article 36, paragraph 2, of the Statute of the Court, article 38, paragraph 5, of the Rules of Court and article IX of the Convention on the Prevention and Punishment of the Crime of Genocide of 1948. By subsequent letters, the Agent of the Federal Republic of Yugoslavia had submitted a "Supplement to the Application", invoking a further basis for the Court's jurisdiction in

the cases against Belgium[3] and the Netherlands. Each of the 10 defendants had responded by raising preliminary objections relating to the Court's jurisdiction to entertain the case and to the admissibility of the application. Immediately after filing its application, the Federal Republic of Yugoslavia had also submitted a request for the indication of provisional measures pursuant to article 73 of the Rules of Court. By 10 orders dated 2 June 1999 the Court had rejected that request. The Court had further decided that the cases against Spain and the United States of America should be removed from the list for manifest lack of jurisdiction.

11. The most important legal findings in the eight cases essentially concerned the question of the access of Serbia and Montenegro to the Court and the interpretation of Article 35, paragraph 2, of the Statute of the Court.

12. On the first point, as the members of the Commission most certainly knew, the Court had often referred in its jurisprudence to "its freedom to select the ground upon which it will base its judgment" (*Application of the Convention of 1902 governing the Guardianship of Infants (Netherlands* v. *Sweden)*, p. 62). In particular, when the Court's jurisdiction was challenged on diverse grounds, it was free to base its decision on one or more grounds of its own choosing, in particular "the ground which in its judgment is more direct and conclusive".[4] However, in those instances the parties to the cases before the Court had been, without doubt, parties to the Statute of the Court, and the Court had thus been open to them under Article 35, paragraph 1, of the Statute. The situation had been different in the eight cases concerning the *Legality of Use of Force*. As the Court had pointed out in those proceedings, an objection had indeed been made regarding the right of the applicant to have access to the Court. The question whether Serbia and Montenegro was or was not a party to the Statute of the Court at the time of the institution of the proceedings had therefore been fundamental, for if it had not been a party, the Court would not be open to it under Article 35, paragraph 1, of the Statute; in that situation, subject to any application of paragraph 2 of that Article, Serbia and Montenegro could not have properly seized the Court, whatever title of jurisdiction it might have invoked, for the simple reason that it did not have the right to appear before the Court. Only if the answer to that question had been in the affirmative, would the Court have had to deal with issues relating to its jurisdiction as laid down in Articles 36 and 37 of its Statute.

13. The Court had noted in that respect that there was no doubt that Serbia and Montenegro was a State for the purpose of Article 34, paragraph 1, of the Statute. However, certain respondents had objected that, at the time of filing its application on 29 April 1999, that State had not met the conditions set down in Article 35 of the Statute, in particular that it had not been a Member of the United Nations and thus not a Party to the Statute of the Court pursuant to Article 93, paragraph 1, of the Charter. The Court had therefore had to assess what had been the status of Serbia and Montenegro in relation to the United Nations at the time it had filed its application.

14. After recapitulating the sequence of events relating to the legal position of the applicant State *vis-à-vis* the United Nations, the Court had concluded that the legal situation within the United Nations during the period 1992–2000 concerning the status of the Federal Republic of Yugoslavia, following the break-up of the Socialist Federal Republic of Yugoslavia, had remained ambiguous and open to different assessments. That had been due to the absence of an authoritative determination by the competent organs of the United Nations defining that status clearly.

15. The Court had considered, however, that that situation of uncertainty had ended with a new development in 2000. On 27 October of that year the Federal Republic of Yugoslavia had requested admission to membership of the United Nations, and it had been admitted on 1 November, by General Assembly resolution 55/12. Serbia and Montenegro had thus had the status of Member of the United Nations as from 1 November 2000. However its admission to the United Nations had not had, and could not have had, the effect of dating back to the time when the Socialist Federal Republic of Yugoslavia had broken up and disappeared. It had become clear that the *sui generis* position of the applicant could not have amounted to its membership of the Organization. In the view of the Court, the significance of that new development in 2000 was that it had clarified the hitherto amorphous legal situation concerning the status of the Federal Republic of Yugoslavia *vis-à-vis* the United Nations.

16. The Court had found that from the vantage point from which it currently viewed the legal situation, and in the light of the legal consequences of the development since 1 November 2000, Serbia and Montenegro was not a Member of the United Nations, and as such a State party to the Court's Statute at the time of filing its application. Since the applicant had not become a party to the Statute on any other basis, it followed that the Court was not open to it under Article 35, paragraph 1, of the Statute. The Court had then had to decide whether it could be open to the applicant under Article 35, paragraph 2, which stipulated:

> The conditions under which the Court shall be open to other states [i.e. States not parties to the Statute] shall, subject to the special provisions contained in treaties in force, be laid down by the Security Council, but in no case shall such conditions place the parties in a position of inequality before the Court.

17. The question, put simply, was to determine whether the Convention on the Prevention and Punishment of the Crime of Genocide could be considered as a "treaty in force" in the sense of Article 35, paragraph 2. The Court had started by noting that the words "treaty in force", in their natural and ordinary meaning, did not indicate at what date the treaties contemplated were to be in force. They could therefore be interpreted as referring either to treaties that had been in force at the time the Statute itself had come into force, or to those which had been in force at the date of the institution of proceedings in a case

[3] In his letter of 12 May 1999, the Agent of the Federal Republic of Yugoslavia invoked article 4 of the Convention of Conciliation, Judicial Settlement and Arbitration between the Kingdom of Yugoslavia and Belgium, signed at Belgrade on 25 March 1930 (League of Nations, *Treaty Series*, vol. CVI, No. 2455, p. 343).

[4] See, for example, *Certain Norwegian Loans*, Judgment of 6 July 1957, p. 25. See also, *inter alia*, the judgment of the Court rendered in 2004 in *Legality of Use of Force (Serbia and Montenegro* v. *Belgium)*, p. 298, para. 46.

in which such treaties had been invoked. The Court had pointed out that Article 35, paragraph 2, was intended to regulate access to the Court by States that were not parties to the Statute, and that it would have been inconsistent with the main thrust of the text to make it possible for States not parties to the Statute to obtain access to the Court simply by the conclusion of a special treaty, multilateral or bilateral, containing a provision to that effect. The Court had also found that the interpretation of Article 35, paragraph 2, whereby that paragraph was to be construed as referring to treaties in force at the time the Statute had come into force, was in fact reinforced by an examination of the *travaux préparatoires* of the text. The Court had thus concluded that, even assuming that the applicant had been a party to the Convention on the Prevention and Punishment of the Crime of Genocide at the relevant date, Article 35, paragraph 2, of the Statute did not provide it with a basis for access to the Court under Article IX of that Convention, since the Convention had only entered into force on 12 January 1951, after the entry into force of the Statute. Accordingly, the Court had not considered it necessary to decide whether Serbia and Montenegro had or had not been a party to that Convention on 29 April 1999, when the current proceedings had been instituted.

18. In February 2005, the Court had also concluded the proceedings between Liechtenstein and Germany in the case concerning *Certain Property (Liechtenstein* v. *Germany)* by finding that it had no jurisdiction to consider the application filed by Liechtenstein. The facts of the case were somewhat complicated, but he would endeavour to summarize them. In 1945 Czechoslovakia had confiscated certain properties belonging to Liechtenstein nationals, including Prince Franz Josef II of Liechtenstein, pursuant to the Beneš Decrees, which authorized the confiscation of "agricultural property", including buildings, installations and movable property pertaining thereto, of "all persons of German and Hungarian nationality, regardless of their citizenship".[5] A special regime with regard to German external assets and other property seized in connection with the Second World War had been created under the Convention on the Settlement of Matters Arising out of the War and the Occupation, signed at Bonn in 1952. In 1991, a painting by the Dutch master Pieter van Laer had been lent by a museum in Brno, Czechoslovakia, to a museum in Cologne, Germany, for an exhibition. The painting, which had been the property of the family of the reigning Prince of Liechtenstein since the eighteenth century, had been confiscated in 1945 by Czechoslovakia under the Beneš Decrees. Prince Hans-Adam II of Liechtenstein had then filed a lawsuit in the German courts in his personal capacity to have the painting returned to him as his property, but that petition had been dismissed on the grounds that, under article 3 of chapter six of the Convention on the Settlement of Matters Arising out of the War and the Occupation, no claim or action in connection with measures taken against German external assets in the aftermath of the Second World War was admissible in the German courts. A claim brought by Prince Hans-Adam II before the European Court of Human Rights concerning the decisions by the German courts had also been rejected (see *Prince Hans-Adam II of Liechtenstein* v. *Germany*). Liechtenstein had therefore brought an application to the Court concerning "decisions of Germany, in and after 1998, to treat certain property of Liechtenstein nationals as German assets having been 'seized for the purposes of reparation or restitution, or as a result of the state of war'— i.e. as a consequence of World War II—, without ensuring any compensation for the loss of that property to its owners, and to the detriment of Liechtenstein itself" (*Certain Property*, para. 1). As a basis for the Court's jurisdiction, the application had invoked article 1 of the European Convention for the Peaceful Settlement of Disputes. In response, Germany had raised six preliminary objections to the jurisdiction of the Court and to the admissibility of Liechtenstein's application (see paragraph 19 of the judgment). It was those preliminary objections that the Court had had to deal with.

19. Rejecting Germany's first objection, the Court had found that there existed a legal dispute between the parties, the subject of which was whether, by applying chapter six, article 3 of the Convention on the Settlement of Matters Arising out of the War and the Occupation to Liechtenstein property that had been confiscated by Czechoslovakia in 1945, Germany had been in breach of international obligations it owed to Liechtenstein and, if so, what was Germany's international responsibility (paras. 25–27).

20. Germany's second preliminary objection had required the Court to decide whether, in the light of the provisions of article 27 (*a*) of the European Convention for the Peaceful Settlement of Disputes, the dispute related to facts or situations that had arisen prior to 18 February 1980, the date on which the Convention had entered into force between Germany and Liechtenstein. The Court had noted that it was not contested that the dispute had been triggered by the decisions of the German courts in the aforementioned case. The critical issue, however, had not been the date when the dispute had arisen, but the date of the facts or situations in relation to which the dispute had arisen. In the Court's view, the dispute brought before it could have related to the events that had taken place in the 1990s only if, as Liechtenstein had argued, Germany had during that period either departed from a previous common position that the Convention had not applied to Liechtenstein property, or if the German courts, by applying their earlier case law under the Convention for the first time to Liechtenstein property, had applied that Convention "to a new situation" after the critical date. Having found that neither was the case, the Court had concluded that, "although those proceedings [had] been instituted by Liechtenstein as a result of decisions by the German courts concerning a painting by Pieter Van Laer, these events [had] their source in specific measures taken by Czechoslovakia in 1945, which [had] led to the confiscation of property owned by Liechtenstein nationals, including Prince Franz Josef II of Liechtenstein, as well as in the special regime created by the Settlement Convention", and that the source and real cause of the disputes had accordingly to be found in the Convention and the Beneš Decrees. In the light of the provisions of article 27 (*a*) of

[5] Decree No. 12 on "the Confiscation and Expeditious Redistribution of the Agricultural Property of Germans, Hungarians, and also Traitors and Enemies of the Czech and Slovak Nations", art. 1 (1) a) (Z. Beneš *et al.*, *Facing History: The evolution of Czech–German relations in the Czech provinces, 1848–1948*, Prague, Gallery, 2002, p. 317).

the European Convention for the Peaceful Settlement of Disputes, the Court had therefore upheld Germany's second preliminary objection, finding that it could not rule on Liechtenstein's claims on the merits (paras. 52–53).

21. Lastly, on 12 July 2005, a chamber of the Court had rendered its final judgment in the *Frontier Dispute (Benin/Niger)* case. On 3 May 2002, the Governments of Benin and the Niger had transmitted to the Court a copy of a special agreement whereby they had agreed to submit to a chamber of the Court a boundary dispute. Based on this special agreement of 15 June 2001, the parties had requested the Court to:

"(*a*) determine the course of the boundary between the Republic of Benin and the Republic of Niger in the River Niger sector;

"(*b*) specify which State owns each of the islands in the said river, and in particular Lété Island;

"(*c*) determine the course of the boundary between the two States in the River Mekrou sector" (para. 2 of the judgment).

22. The Court had unanimously decided to accede to the request of both parties that it should form a special chamber of five judges to deal with the case (para. 6).

23. In its judgment, the Chamber had first found that in the River Niger sector, neither Benin nor Niger could provide evidence of a legal title to support their claim as to the precise location of the boundary. It had subsequently found that, although it could be concluded on the basis of several French administrative documents that the course of the River Niger had constituted the intercolonial boundary between Niger and the colony of Dahomey (which had become Benin upon independence), those documents had not helped to determine the precise location of that boundary. The Chamber had therefore considered the *effectivités* invoked by the parties to determine the course of the frontier in the River Niger sector and to which of the two States each of the islands in the river belonged. The Chamber had emphasized in particular in that respect the importance of a letter, dated 3 July 1914, from the *commandant* of the *secteur* of Gaya (Niger) aimed among other things at "delimiting the territorial jurisdiction of the indigenous tribunals in the two colonies". The letter specified that the main navigable channel was "the river's main channel, not the widest channel, but the *only channel navigable at low water*" (emphasis in the original) in order to determine the colony to which each island belonged (para. 83). On the basis of the evidence before it, the Chamber had found that the terms of the *modus vivendi* between the local authorities established by the 1914 letter had in general been respected in subsequent years and that during that period the main navigable channel of the River Niger had been considered by both parties to be the boundary. As a result, administrative authority had been exercised by Niger over the islands to the left, including the island of Lété, and by Dahomey over the islands to the right of that line. The Chamber had noted, however, that on the basis of the same *modus vivendi*, three islands situated opposite the city of Gaya had been considered to fall under the jurisdiction of Dahomey, so that in that sector of the river the boundary had been regarded as passing to the left of those three islands. For all those reasons, the Chamber had concluded that:

the boundary between Benin and Niger follows the main navigable channel of the River Niger as it existed at the dates of independence, it being understood that, in the vicinity of the three islands opposite Gaya, the boundary passed to the left of those islands. Consequently, Benin has title to the islands situated between the boundary thus defined and the right bank of the river, and Niger has title to the islands between that boundary and the left bank of the river [para. 103].

The Chamber had then determined the precise location of the boundary line in the main navigable channel, namely the line of deepest soundings as it had existed at the dates of independence, by indicating the coordinates of 154 specific points positioned all along it. On that basis it had then determined to which of the parties each of the islands in the River Niger belonged, specifying that the determination in regard to the attribution of the islands had been without prejudice to any private law rights which might be held in respect of them. The Chamber had similarly found that the boundary on the bridges between Gaya and Malanville followed the course of the boundary in the river (para. 124).

24. As to the course of the boundary between the two States in the Mekrou River sector, the Chamber had found that, "at least from 1927 onwards, the competent administrative authorities [had] regarded the course of the Mekrou as the intercolonial boundary separating Dahomey from Niger, that those authorities [had] reflected that boundary in successive instruments promulgated by them after 1927", and that that had been the state of the law at the dates of independence in August 1960. The Chamber had thus found it "unnecessary to look for any *effectivités* in order to apply the *uti possidetis* principle, since *effectivités* [could] only be of interest in a case in order to complete or make good doubtful or absent legal titles, but [could] never prevail over titles with which they [were] at variance" (para. 141). With a view to determining the exact location in the River Mekrou of the boundary between Benin and the Niger, the Chamber had recalled that in the case concerning *Kasikili/Sedudu Island (Botswana/Namibia)* it had observed that:

[t]reaties or conventions which define boundaries in watercourses nowadays usually refer to the thalweg as the boundary when the watercourse is navigable and to the median line between the two banks when it is not, although it cannot be said that practice has been fully consistent (p. 1062, para. 24 of the judgment)

25. The Chamber had noted that, in the *Frontier Dispute (Benin/Niger)* case, "in view of the circumstances, including the fact that the river [was] not navigable, a boundary following the median line of the Mekrou would more satisfactorily meet the requirement of legal security inherent in the determination of an international boundary". It had therefore concluded that, in the River Mekrou sector, the boundary between Benin and the Niger was constituted by the median line of that river (para. 145).

26. Having concluded his overview of the decisions and advisory opinions rendered by the Court during the period under review, Mr. Shi said that the Court had also taken a number of other extremely varied decisions. Among other things, it had amended the procedure for promulgating amendments to the Rules of Court and its Practice Direction V, which set a four-month period for the presentation by a party of its observations and submissions on preliminary objections by clarifying that the period ran from the date of filing of the preliminary objections. The

Court had furthermore promulgated three new Practice Directions (Practice Directions X, XI and XII).[6] Practice Direction X enjoined the agents of the parties to attend as early as possible any meeting called by the President of the Court whenever a decision on a procedural issue needed to be made in a case. Practice Direction XI stated that in their oral pleadings on provisional measures, parties should limit themselves to what was relevant to the criteria for the indication of such measures. Lastly, Practice Direction XII established a procedure to be followed with regard to written statements and/or documents submitted by international non-governmental organizations in connection with advisory opinion cases.

27. The Court had been particularly active that year, and it intended to maintain that level of activity. The two cases concerning *Armed Activities on the Territory of the Congo (Democratic Republic of the Congo v. Uganda) and Armed Activities on the Territory of the Congo (New Application: 2002) (Democratic Republic of the Congo v. Rwanda)* were currently under deliberation. The Court had furthermore already announced that public hearings on the case concerning *Application of the Convention on the Prevention and Punishment of the Crime of Genocide* would start on 27 February 2006.

28. The coming months would bring many changes to the Court. On 11 February 2005, the former President, Judge Gilbert Guillaume, had resigned and had been replaced by Judge Ronny Abraham, newly elected from France. At the end of 2005 the General Assembly and the Security Council would hold further elections for five members of the Court. Four of the five members whose term was coming to an end had decided not to run for reelection: Judge Elaraby, Judge Kooijmans, Judge Rezek and Judge Vereshchetin.

29. The CHAIRPERSON thanked Mr. Shi for his presentation and invited members of the Commission to ask him questions.

30. Mr. BROWNLIE said he wished to know the opinion of the President of the Court on the practical value of oral arguments, as compared with written pleadings, in contentious cases.

31. Mr. SHI said that the Court attached great importance to the oral arguments of counsels to parties in all of its cases, since very often the parties presented new arguments which were not necessarily in their written pleadings. In some cases new points were stressed during oral arguments.

32. Mr. DUGARD noted that since July 2004, when the General Assembly had approved the Court's advisory opinion on the *Legal Consequences of the Construction of a Wall in the Occupied Palestinian Territory*, neither the Security Council nor the General Assembly had made any further mention of it. There was a real danger that that opinion was being rapidly forgotten, just like the one the Court had handed down on the Western Sahara. He therefore wondered whether the Court was concerned at the fact that the international community was doing so little in respect of that advisory opinion.

33. Mr. ECONOMIDES asked Mr. Shi whether obligations *erga omnes* were identical to or different from obligations of *jus cogens*.

34. Mr. PAMBOU-TCHIVOUNDA said that in its advisory opinion on the *Legal Consequences of the Construction of a Wall in the Occupied Palestinian Territory*, the Court had had no choice but to call on the parties concerned to apply the resolutions of the Security Council in good faith. He could not help but note, however, that the Security Council had adopted numerous resolutions on the matter which had rarely been applied in good faith.

35. In the cases concerning *Legality of Use of Force*, the Court had taken great pains to determine whether a treaty was or was not in force *vis-à-vis* a State that was or was not a party to the Court's Statute; however, he himself did not feel that the issue had merited so much attention.

36. Lastly, on 12 July 2005, when the Court had handed down its decision in the *Frontier Dispute (Benin/Niger)* case, it had had few options other than to base itself on the 1914 letter from the French colonial authorities. That letter had been destined for a historic fate, since in it, basing itself on the jurisdiction of customary tribunals, France had practically conferred competence for one side of the River Niger on one party and for the other side on another party. Developments in the situation up until the time of independence had ultimately confirmed that premature attribution of competence, and the Court had had little choice in the matter. Even though it had not expressly resolved the issue of *uti possidetis juris*, it had previously observed that that principle had some political merit in that it froze the situation, thereby preventing a number of acts previously adopted by the colonial powers from being questioned. Consequently the Court had not been obliged to give an opinion as to whether the *effectivités* should prevail over *uti possidetis juris* or vice versa, since the *effectivités* had been implicit in the 1914 letter from France. The realism of the Court's decision was thus noteworthy.

37. Mr. CANDIOTI asked whether the Court had ever considered travelling to the site of a dispute in order to obtain a better grasp of the context. He wished also to know what practical implications the decision had for the inhabitants of the islands involved.

38. Mr. KAMTO said that the Court's decisions were of incontestable value for peace among nations, hence the importance of their being precise. In that connection, the manner in which the Court had just decided the *Frontier Dispute (Benin/Niger)* case was to be commended: as the navigable channel selected as the boundary was determined by 154 points whose coordinates had been specified, the two parties would have no difficulty in implementing the judgment. That concern for precision had not, however, always driven the Court, a case in point being its judgment of 10 October 2002 in the case concerning the *Land and Maritime Boundary between Cameroon and Nigeria*, in which, for certain points on the boundary, the Court had merely made reference to watercourses without

[6] The Practice Directions are published in *I.C.J. Reports 2004–2005* and are available on the ICJ website (www.icj-cij.org).

specifying the methodology to be used or giving coordinates. As a result, it was difficult to implement the judgment on site, and no one doubted that if the Court had visited the site, it would have been more precise about certain points. One might then ask whether, in particularly complex cases, the Court ought not to contemplate visiting the sites or send experts there even if the parties made no such request, so that non-compliance with certain judgments did not discourage States from turning to the Court, thereby undermining the position it had acquired throughout its history on the basis of its body of well-grounded decisions.

39. Mr. DAOUDI asked whether the Court had any particular views on the reform of the United Nations, particularly the expansion of the Security Council, and whether it thought that the Council could continue to function with 15 members as it currently did, using the same methods of work.

40. Ms. ESCARAMEIA said that she wished to know whether the Court was concerned at the fact that the Security Council had not requested any advisory opinions of it and what its relations with other international courts were.

41. Mr. SHI (President of the International Court of Justice), replying to Mr. Dugard's question, said that the Court had been glad to see that the General Assembly had adopted with very few alterations the Court's advisory opinion on the *Legal Consequences of the Construction of a Wall in the Occupied Palestinian Territory*, and that it would be happy if the Security Council followed up on the General Assembly's resolution, but that the advisory opinions of the Court were not binding, by virtue of its functions.

42. As to *in situ* visits, he said that the Court had made such a visit only once, in the case concerning the *Gabčíkovo–Nagymaros Project (Hungary/Slovakia)*, in order to view the Danube River project at the invitation of the Governments concerned. It must be recalled that the disputes it had to resolve concerned very sensitive matters, and the parties might not agree on the advisability of such on-site visits. It was, however, a good suggestion that was worthy of consideration.

43. Concerning the effects of transfers of territory on local populations, the Court considered that the inhabitants' private rights should not be affected.

44. Once a judgment had been rendered, the Court had no other duties to fulfil. Since its jurisdiction was based on the consent of States, the parties normally implemented its decisions. If they did not, then Article 94 of the Charter of the United Nations, which stipulated that "[i]f any party to a case fails to perform the obligations incumbent upon it under a judgment rendered by the Court, the other party may have recourse to the Security Council", would apply. It was then for the Security Council to decide what measures should be adopted.

45. With regard to the relationship between the reform of the United Nations and the role of the Court, it should be noted that in his report entitled *In Larger Freedom: Towards Development, Security and Human Rights for All*, the Secretary-General of the United Nations had urged those States that had not yet done so to consider recognizing the compulsory jurisdiction of the Court—generally if possible or, failing that, at least in specific situations.[7] He had also urged United Nations bodies to make greater use of the Court's advisory powers.

46. Lastly, the ICJ had minimal relations with the international criminal courts because their jurisdictions were completely different: those courts adjudicated the criminal responsibility of individuals, whereas the ICJ was open only to Member States. Nevertheless, some type of cooperation could be useful, particularly with a view to resolving the worrisome problem of fragmentation of international law.

Expulsion of aliens (*continued*) (A/CN.4/554)

[Agenda item 7]

Preliminary report of the Special Rapporteur (*continued*)

47. Mr. DAOUDI said that paragraph 5 of the report had correctly identified the key problem posed by the topic, which was how States could reconcile the exercise of their sovereign right to expel with their international obligations, notably in the area of human rights. It was on that problem that the Commission must focus its work. The Special Rapporteur had rightly begun by defining the two fundamental terms upon which the study was based: "expulsion" and "alien". As an "alien" was defined as an individual who did not have the nationality of the State in which he found himself, any expulsion measure taken by a State in respect of its own nationals who were of a different ethnic, religious or racial origin from the majority of the population went beyond the scope of the subject. Such a measure would constitute a violation of fundamental human rights norms under the domestic legislation of the State and would be contrary to article 3 of the European Convention on Human Rights.

48. With regard to the cases mentioned in paragraph 10 of the report, namely that of Palestinians who had been forced to leave their country during and after the 1948 war and that of Palestinians and Syrians who had suffered the same fate following the Israeli occupation of the West Bank and the Golan Heights in 1967, they, too, exceeded the scope of the study. It should also be pointed out that any forced transfer of population constituted a war crime under the Geneva Conventions of 1949 and the first Additional Protocol thereto of 1977.

49. The notion of expulsion should be taken in a relatively broad sense: it should cover all cases in which the purpose of a measure was to force an alien to leave the territory of the State in which he found himself, regardless of the reason for his presence. Therefore, *refoulement* and non-admission were excluded from the scope of the topic.

50. In addition, the study of the legal regime of expulsion should take into consideration the status of the alien in the host State. In the case of migrant workers who had

[7] A/59/2005, para. 139.

entered the country without valid documents, the host State was exercising a sovereign right when it expelled them, but it was under an obligation to respect those individuals' fundamental rights. On the other hand, when an alien was legally present in the territory of a State or when his presence was governed by a bilateral or multilateral treaty, as was the case with refugees, the State's power of expulsion was much more limited, as was stipulated, for example, in article 32 of the Convention relating to the Status of Refugees.

51. In the event that the treaty norms governing the status of an alien in the territory of the expelling State were not respected or violations of human rights occurred, provision should be made for a State to be able to exercise diplomatic protection on behalf of its national and, possibly, for the expelling State to be held responsible.

52. Referring to the question raised by the Special Rapporteur in paragraph 30 of his report, he said that the purpose of the study should be to establish the legal regime for the expulsion of aliens. To be complete, such a regime must be based both on existing international rules and on rules which the Commission might propose in the context of the progressive development of international law. If the Commission succeeded in striking an acceptable balance between the sovereign right of States to expel aliens and States' obligations to ensure respect for the fundamental rights of those expelled, it ought to be possible to complete a set of draft articles on the subject.

53. Mr. Sreenivasa RAO said that it was essential to delimit the scope of the subject clearly. Accordingly, a distinction must be drawn between the expulsion of aliens and: (*a*) the non-admission of asylum-seekers; (*b*) internal displacement; (*c*) international displacement in times of armed conflict, following the creation of new States or after the dismemberment of a State or in the wake of natural disasters; and (*d*) refusal to admit aliens to the territory (*refoulement*).

54. Similarly, the topic should not address issues arising from the expulsion of illegal immigrants, other than those who stayed in the territory for long periods and lacked even a valid entry permit. In the latter case, any arbitrary exercise of the right of expulsion could give rise to issues of human rights and humanitarian rights.

55. He agreed with the Special Rapporteur that, in general, the study should avoid dealing with issues of immigration and emigration. Thus the grounds for refusal of entry into a territory referred to in paragraph 18 of the report should not be part of the study.

56. As noted in paragraph 20, the most difficult part of the exercise was to identify which of the many grounds for expelling aliens were admissible under international law and which were prohibited. The study should not, however, simply attempt to draw common denominators from national laws on the subject but should critically examine them with a view to promoting human rights and protecting human dignity. For example, the grounds listed in the draft work plan in annex I under "Contingent grounds debatable under international law" were highly questionable in an era of globalization and mixing populations, and it might be preferable to try to identify procedures applicable to all expulsion decisions rather than grounds for expulsion. Such procedures should be considered from the standpoint of due process, non-discriminatory access to justice for all persons threatened with expulsion, access to consular services or legal assistance, protection of personal property and investments, and respect for applicable international obligations.

57. Any act of expulsion was also subject to the principles of State responsibility and diplomatic protection. Moreover, the expulsion of migrant workers must be in keeping with the principles set out in the 1990 International Convention on the Protection of the Rights of All Migrant Workers and Members of their Families. The Commission should take the opportunity offered by the study to continue developing those standards, amending them to the extent necessary in the light of practice relating to the implementation of the Convention and evolving universal human rights norms. Collective expulsion, which was discussed in paragraph 24, was in principle prohibited under international law. At the very least, a clear presumption in favour of its prohibition must be established. With regard to methodology, there was good reason to develop a comprehensive legal regime drawing from different sources, including international treaties, human rights standards and general principles of international law, which could be derived from a comparative study of national legislation and practice.

58. In the light of the comments made by a number of members of the Commission, the draft work plan in annex I of the report might have to be revised. For example, population displacement, listed in part 1, section I.A.2, should deal only with international displacement and not internal displacement. The case of stateless persons deserved separate treatment and should not be dealt with as part of expulsion of aliens.

59. Lastly, the problem of the discrimination or persecution on account of race, religion, ethnic origin or political opinion that an expellee might face in the country to which he was returned must also be taken into account.

60. Mr. KATEKA drew attention to the definitions of the terms "alien" and "expulsion" in paragraphs 7 and 13 of the preliminary report and noted that "alien" did not cover internally displaced persons. The term should, however, cover stateless persons.

61. As for the term "expulsion", one member of the Commission had found the definition too narrow while for another it was too broad; he himself thought that the Commission should confine itself provisionally to the definition according to which expulsion was "a legal act in which a State compels an individual or group of individuals who are nationals of another State to leave its territory" (para. 13 of the report). The link between the physical crossing and its consequences could be looked at later, as the Special Rapporteur proposed.

62. The fundamental principle which should run through the topic was that under international law, a State had the right to expel aliens, provided that it did not do so arbitrarily. Thus, the study should help to harmonize the different

situations regarding the expulsion of aliens, which had led to varied national legislation and court decisions.

63. For example, there was the so-called "constructive expulsion", in which the person concerned was not the subject of a formal expulsion, yet the conditions in the host country made it impossible for him to stay. It would be interesting to have the Special Rapporteur comment on that type of expulsion in a future report. It would also be useful to give greater attention to situations in which the right of expulsion was exercised to the detriment of human rights.

64. The use of a double standard was also a problem. Developed countries regularly expelled so-called "economic refugees" to developing countries, but when developing countries expelled illegal aliens, they were accused of violating human rights. To cite an example, one African country had generously hosted hundreds of thousands of refugees, some of whom had settled there and refused to leave, even though the conditions in their country of origin had stabilized. Yet their expulsion had incurred protests from UNHCR, which had invoked the principle of *non-refoulement*. The Special Rapporteur should look into such cases in future reports.

65. As for methodology, the Special Rapporteur should deal with existing treaty rules on the question and then formulate basic principles which could guide States. State responsibility and diplomatic protection should be invoked whenever necessary, without repetition or duplication. The draft should also cover the right of return of expellees.

66. Mr. CHEE commended the Special Rapporteur for his concise and well-written preliminary report. He noted that although a State had the sovereign right to admit aliens and to expel them from its territory, that right was qualified by the right of the State to protect its nationals abroad and by international rules for the protection of human rights. He cited a number of court decisions granting compensation to expellees because the right to expel had not been exercised properly. For example, in the *Boffolo* case, the arbitrator had noted that the State possessed the general right of expulsion, but that "expulsion should only be resorted to in extreme instances and must be accomplished in a manner least injurious to the person affected" (p. 537 of the judgement). It should also be borne in mind that in resolution 40/144 of 13 December 1985 the United Nations General Assembly had adopted the Declaration on the Human Rights of Individuals Who are not Nationals of the Country in Which They Live, article 7 of which provided that, "except where compelling reasons of national security otherwise require, [an alien lawfully in the territory of a State shall] be allowed to submit the reasons why he or she should not be expelled".

67. Migrant workers were currently an important category of aliens, and it would therefore be helpful if the Special Rapporteur devoted more time to analysing the content of the International Convention on the Protection of the Rights of All Migrant Workers and Members of their Families.

68. Lastly, he sought clarification from the Special Rapporteur on a number of expressions used in the draft work plan and asked in particular what was meant by the term "extraordinary transfer" in part 1, section I.A.9.

The meeting rose at 1 p.m.

2852nd MEETING

Friday, 15 July 2005, at 10.05 a.m.

Chairperson: Mr. Djamchid MOMTAZ

Present: Mr. Addo, Mr. Al-Marri, Mr. Brownlie, Mr. Candioti, Mr. Chee, Mr. Comissário Afonso, Mr. Daoudi, Mr. Dugard, Mr. Economides, Ms. Escarameia, Mr. Fomba, Mr. Gaja, Mr. Galicki, Mr. Kabatsi, Mr. Kamto, Mr. Kateka, Mr. Kemicha, Mr. Kolodkin, Mr. Koskenniemi, Mr. Mansfield, Mr. Matheson, Mr. Pambou-Tchivounda, Mr. Sreenivasa Rao, Mr. Rodríguez Cedeño, Mr. Sepúlveda, Ms. Xue, Mr. Yamada.

Expulsion of aliens (*concluded*) (A/CN.4/554)

[Agenda item 7]

Preliminary report of the Special Rapporteur (*concluded*)

1. Mr. KABATSI thanked the Special Rapporteur for his extremely interesting and scholarly report (A/CN.4/554), which provided an overview of the topic and the legal issues pertaining to it, and congratulated him on his mastery and grasp of the subject.

2. Unfortunately strangers were sometimes mistrusted, envied for their industriousness and wealth and made scapegoats for all kinds of misfortunes. For that reason, throughout the ages and in all regions of the world, aliens had been and, sadly, still were being expelled. Admittedly a State was entitled, in exercise of its sovereignty, to exclude "undesirable" aliens from its territory in accordance with its authorities' decisions and through the operation of its internal law. Nevertheless the interplay between States and the dictates of globalization demanded the intermixing and interaction of peoples across borders. Rules attempting to introduce some order into that process existed in general customary international law, in treaties and in international agreements, as well as in State practice and internal laws. It was therefore the task of the Commission and the Special Rapporteur to identify carefully the rules from those sources, to develop them further where possible and to codify them with a view to improving their application.

3. The rules should clearly define the term "aliens" and choose the term, or terms, to be used to describe the process for excluding them, a task upon which the Special Rapporteur embarked in section II of the report. It might be wise to omit from the study aliens who wished

to enter the territory of a State but who were still outside its borders; expulsion following disputes over territory by different groups; and, possibly, aliens illegally present in a State.

4. Although clarification of the concepts involved in determining the scope of the notion of "expulsion of aliens" for the purpose of formulating a set of draft articles would require much time and effort, it would be a useful exercise. For the reasons set out in paragraph 13 of the report, it would be preferable to retain the term "expulsion". While it was correct to emphasize the right to expel, that right must not be abused and must be consistent with internal and international law, especially international human rights and humanitarian law. While State practice with regard to the grounds for expulsion was extremely varied, expelling States must abide by their own internal law and procedures and international law; otherwise they might incur international responsibility for their acts. Account must also be taken of the rights of other States, including the right to exercise diplomatic protection.

5. Existing treaty rules on the subject and other settled rules should not be taken up in the draft articles. The task should be limited to bridging any clearly identifiable gaps. The methodology proposed in the work plan in annex II of the report should be used as a tool to formulate general principles to fill those gaps. On the whole he therefore welcomed and supported the proposals contained in the preliminary report.

6. Mr. SEPÚLVEDA said that the report paved the way for the consideration of a subject of fundamental importance to the protection of human rights. Consideration of the topic would also offer an opportunity for the identification of general international legal standards pertaining to the expulsion of aliens, and for codification and progressive development of international law in that area. The Special Rapporteur had rightly noted that no final solutions yet existed which could be embodied in positive law. For his own part, he therefore wished to assist the process of formulating general rules by highlighting possible inconsistencies in the approaches proposed in the report.

7. It would seem that acknowledgement of an inherent sovereign right of the State to expel aliens ought to be a guiding principle of the report. The concept of the expulsion of aliens comprised various elements: such a measure must be a unilateral legal act; it constituted a coercive measure against a person or group of persons; it was an act inherent in State sovereignty; its application meant that a State obliged a person or group of persons to leave its territory; that person or group of persons had to be the national or nationals of another State; generally speaking, the grounds for expulsion must serve the purpose of protecting public order; international law recognized that any State had the discretionary power to expel aliens as an attribute of sovereignty; and, lastly, it was a principle of customary international law.

8. Yet those elements were at odds with other statements in the report, which affirmed, for example, that a State's right to expel aliens fell within the realm of international law. That argument appeared to contradict totally the principle of a State's sovereign power to expel aliens, an essential attribute of sovereignty which would be eroded if it were subjected to restrictions and limitations. The all-important question was to determine when a State was abusing the right to expel and specify the grounds warranting and legitimizing the expulsion of an alien. It was therefore necessary to identify the limits on sovereign powers and to establish the nature and scope of a general international legal regime deriving from treaties or custom, which was universally recognized, accepted and applied both in wartime and in peacetime. Such a regime would put an end to the ingenious justifications offered by States for arbitrary acts. The various grounds for expulsion listed in paragraph 19 of the report provided a broad range of arguments adduced by States for the adoption of a unilateral measure, whether or not justified, to protect their interests in certain circumstances.

9. The main challenge facing the Commission and the Special Rapporteur was to demonstrate that standards protecting fundamental human rights transcended State competence and that this new state of affairs had consequences for the law pertaining to the expulsion of aliens. As the Special Rapporteur had pointed out, it was necessary to decide which of the many grounds for expelling aliens were admissible under international law and which were to be prohibited.

10. The legal validity of the thesis that rights related to expulsion could derive either from the internal law of the expelling State or from international human rights law was disputable. The report asserted that the lawfulness of the expulsion depended on the measure's conformity with the expulsion procedures in force in the expelling State, and that this requirement could be regarded as an obligation under general international law, rather than as a treaty obligation or an obligation under domestic law alone. That hypothesis was then disposed of in paragraph 23 of the report with an argument that needed to be more solidly grounded, namely, that "[i]n the absence of a treaty, it might be reasonable to claim that the requirement [concerning respect for procedures] has a basis in customary law, or to consider it a general legal principle". Those conclusions ought to be studied in greater depth. It would be difficult to prove that all or a significant majority of States regulated expulsion procedures in their internal law. The international community still aspired to the principle of universal adherence to and applicability of international human rights treaties. It was probable that customary international law on the expulsion of aliens was still in the process of gestation.

11. As for expulsion regimes for migrant workers, it would be advisable to examine the mechanisms used by States to repatriate nationals who were illegally present in another State. Such repatriation could not be described as a unilateral act since it was based on bilateral agreements concerning readmission. Nor did it constitute a coercive measure because it involved the relocation of a person not lawfully present in the territory of a State of which it was not a national. The essence of such agreements was that the authorities of the State of origin would, at the formal request of the authorities of the requesting State, readmit to its territory the nationals of third States who had illegally entered the territory of the requesting State from the

territory of the requested State. Spain, for example, had recently entered into numerous agreements of that kind with European and African Governments and was on the verge of signing several more. The Special Rapporteur could investigate whether such repatriation agreements might be a useful legal method of alleviating the harshness of an expulsion process.

12. Lastly, it would be necessary to explore the possibility that the expelled person's State of nationality could resort to diplomatic protection by taking up the cause of one of its nationals. That possibility presupposed the existence of an injury suffered in consequence of an internationally wrongful act, and would certainly open up very attractive possibilities for defending basic human rights, but only where it could be ascertained that the expelling State had in fact committed a wrongful act. That too would be a valid criterion for the creation of an integrated international legal regime governing the expulsion of aliens in which a system of State responsibilities would play a role.

13. The Special Rapporteur's proposal, in paragraph 28 of his report, that national practice with regard to the expulsion of aliens should be compared in order to identify rules that the international community could be considered to hold in common and that were therefore codifiable as international legal norms would certainly require much effort, but it would be extremely useful.

14. Mr. KAMTO (Special Rapporteur), summing up the debate, thanked members of the Commission for their constructive, enlightening comments and clear, precise answers to the questions he had raised in his preliminary report, which, on the whole, had been well received. Mr. Koskenniemi had been the only member who had basically disagreed with the approach suggested, since he had contended that the Commission should first examine what interests were at stake in the expulsion of aliens as a social process and to what extent legislation, or the law, could supply appropriate responses, before going on to consider the scope and other aspects of the topic. Mr. Koskenniemi had held that the method of commencing with a study of the scope and general principles would be too remote from reality and that, on the contrary, the Commission should formulate norms which would help ordinary people. More specifically, he had expressed reservations about what the Special Rapporteur had regarded as the main problem, taking the view that the key issue was not how to reconcile the State's right to expel with that of the rights of the person expelled. He had been of the view that a State had no *a priori* right to expel and that such an approach would be too general in nature. He had felt that an examination of the four categories of restrictions on expulsion proposed by Mr. Gaja would result in a more practical approach, even if they were not the only possible restrictions.

15. In response to Mr. Koskenniemi's objections, he wished to draw attention to the fact that the historical background to the subject and the main socio-economic considerations related to expulsion had been dealt with in paragraphs 1 to 6 of the report. He did not intend to discuss those matters any further in future reports for, in keeping with the Commission's mandate and established practice, the topics on its programme of work must be studied in order to identify rules established by custom or relevant to the progressive development of international law. General considerations surrounding the topic merely provided an introduction to it and should not take up any more space than was necessary.

16. As for the approach he had proposed, any work plan was always general in nature, as its purpose was to outline categories covering a variety of situations. The latter were listed in part 1 of the work plan in annex I. He hoped that future reports would dispel any impression of lack of specificity which the preliminary report might have created.

17. Members of the Commission generally agreed on a number of points. First, the current title of the topic should be retained, although the contents of its two constituent elements, "expulsion" and "aliens", should be fleshed out. Second, the central problem identified at the end of paragraph 5 of the report, namely, how to reconcile the right to expel, which seemed inherent in State sovereignty, with the demands of international law, had been deemed apposite. The scope of application had to be carefully considered and the concept of expulsion delimited. Third, refusal of admission and, generally, immigration matters, should not be considered. Fourth, migratory movements and situations resulting from decolonization, the exercise of self-determination or occupation in the Middle East should likewise not be considered, judging from the reservations expressed by Mr. Dugard, Mr. Brownlie and Mr. Matheson and the historical insights provided by Mr. Daoudi. Fifth, the methodology proposed was generally acceptable. While some members, such as Mr. Sepúlveda, had expressed reservations, most agreed that as comprehensive a legal regime as possible should be elaborated, taking up, where necessary, existing treaty rules. Comparative and critical analyses of relevant national legislation should be used as sources. The case law of international and regional human rights bodies, for example, the Human Rights Committee, the European Court of Human Rights, the European Commission of Human Rights, the African Commission on Human and Peoples' Rights, the Inter-American Court of Human Rights, the Iran–United States Claims Tribunal and the Eritrea–Ethiopia Claims Commission, should be examined. Lastly, most speakers had endorsed the general thrust of the work plan, on the understanding that answers would be provided to the questions they had raised.

18. That, then, was the basis for agreement that had emerged from the debate. On the other hand, reservations had been expressed, *inter alia*, about the definition of expulsion of aliens. Mr. Gaja, supported by Mr. Mansfield, Ms. Escarameia and Mr. Fomba, had said that it should encompass situations in which an alien was compelled in practice, by a variety of manoeuvres, to leave an expelling State's territory. Mr. Fomba had gone on to say that expulsion could in some instances constitute a material or legal event of the State without necessarily taking the form of an official legal act. While he acknowledged that viewpoint, he did not think that the two approaches were mutually exclusive. The future definition would accordingly seek to cover both situations when expulsion took the form of a unilateral, official legal act and those in which it was a legal event.

19. The clarifications of the definition of "alien" requested would have a bearing on the scope of the project, the purpose of which was precisely to specify which categories of persons were covered by the draft. He could already affirm that they would include persons living in the territory of a State of which they were not nationals, a distinction being drawn between those lawfully and unlawfully present. In that connection, it would also be useful to take into account the situation of persons unlawfully present yet already living in an expelling State. In addition, the persons covered by the draft would include refugees, asylum-seekers, stateless persons and migrant workers.

20. It would be difficult, on the other hand, to include persons refused admission, as Ms. Xue had requested. Such persons, if they had already entered the territory of a State, were aliens unlawfully present, but if they had not yet crossed the border and completed immigration procedures, they remained persons requesting admission and, consequently, their situation did not fall within the scope of the topic. Ms. Xue was right in saying that a stateless person might be expelled to a country where he or she had already lived, and Mr. Sreenivasa Rao had suggested that such cases should be studied separately. He had taken due note of those views.

21. He did not intend completely to exclude from the future draft articles rules applicable to expulsion in the event of armed conflict, since international humanitarian law laid down specific rules in that regard. On the other hand, he intended to avoid entering into the complex issues of nationality that often arose following changes in territorial status, such as that which had arisen when Eritrea's accession to independence had resulted in some Ethiopians changing their nationality and being expelled as a result. Nevertheless, the situation of such persons as expelled persons would be addressed to see what international law offered in terms of solutions. The point was to deal with the alien *per se*, without entering into considerations relating to his or her individual nationality.

22. Mr. Chee had queried such concepts as "extrajudicial transfer" and "extraordinary transfer". He was absolutely right to be concerned about certain strange terms that were not necessarily well established in international law. His own objective was to clear away some of the dead wood surrounding the concept of expulsion, delimiting its scope and pruning away any ancillary notions that were not directly germane to the topic. The concepts to which Mr. Chee had referred were often borrowed from the language of political and diplomatic discourse or journalism, and had been mentioned in the work plan only with a view to their exclusion.

23. Some members of the Commission had pointed out that the work plan omitted a number of general principles applicable to expulsion. Mr. Gaja, Mr. Sreenivasa Rao and Mr. Rodríguez Cedeño had made specific suggestions in that regard. While the remarks were justified, the omission was intentional: most of the principles in question were to be listed in part 1, section II.B.2: "Principle of respect for fundamental human rights during expulsion proceedings". But those principles needed to be underscored. Accordingly, when revising the workplan, he would give greater emphasis to the principle that expulsion must be carried out in accordance with the law, meaning both procedural and substantive rules; the principle of non-discrimination; the principle that the expelled person had the right to choose the receiving State if more than one State agreed to receive him; and the principle that the investments and property of the expelled person must be safeguarded. Other rights, such as respect for privacy, family life and human dignity, would be examined in the context of respect for fundamental human rights during expulsion proceedings. The right of expelled persons to consular protection was an interesting issue and could be covered in the context of diplomatic protection through non-judicial means.

24. Some members of the Commission, among them Mr. Sepúlveda, appeared to have misunderstood what he had said about the right to expel. Mr. Economides had said that qualifiers such as "absolute" or "discretionary" should be avoided, but he himself had never used the word "absolute" in that sense. On the contrary, in paragraph 16 of his report he stated that the right to expel was not an absolute right of the State. He had indeed referred to "discretionary" rights, but all writers, without exception, did so. *Oppenheim's International Law*, to quote just one source, indicated that while a State had a broad discretion in exercising its right to expel an alien, its discretion was not absolute.[1]

25. Mr. Brownlie had undoubtedly been labouring under the same misapprehension when he had pointed to a contradiction between paragraph 16, which said that the State was bound to invoke the grounds for expulsion, and paragraph 15, which said that the right to expel was an attribute of the sovereignty of the State. He himself saw no contradiction there: an attribute of sovereignty was not an absolute right, and sovereign rights, in that domain as in others, were always exercised in accordance with international law.

26. Mr. Pambou-Tchivounda had claimed that the heading of part 2 of the work plan (annex I), "Expulsion regimes", did not reflect the concept of a regime. Yet if "legal regime" was taken to mean the set of rules applicable to a legal institution, covering both organs and standards, then part 2 would indeed deal with the legal regimes, in the plural, applicable to the various categories of aliens who had been or could be expelled. General rules were set out in part 1, and the subdivisions of part 2 referred, not to separate rules forming a single legal regime, but rather to separate categories of aliens subject to expulsion, with each category to be studied in terms of the specific rules applicable to it. There could be no unified regime for part 2, since the situations it covered were not uniform, but varied depending on whether they involved refugees, persons lawfully present in a country, stateless persons, etc.

27. The problem of justiciability of an expulsion act would be taken up in part 2, as would the relationship between the expelling State and third or transit States, a relationship which was covered by the specific expulsion

[1] See *Oppenheim's International Law*, vol. I, Peace, 9th edition, R. Y. Jennings and A. D. Watts (eds.), Harlow, Longman, 1992, pp. 940–941.

regimes of certain categories of persons such as refugees or asylum-seekers. Part 2 would also affirm the principle of the right of a State to expel any person unlawfully in its territory, on the grounds of unlawful presence alone: on that point he was fully in agreement with Mr. Matheson. Respect for expulsion procedures and for the rights of persons in the event of expulsion was of course an entirely different matter.

28. Conditions for expulsion would be covered in part 2. The distinction he had drawn between conditions set by international law, including international human rights law, and by the internal law of the expelling State, seemed to him to be well grounded. In the first instance, the State was bound by the *pacta sunt servanda* rule: it had undertaken and had also to respect a number of international obligations, relating to expulsion procedures and the substantive conditions applicable in that context. In the second instance, the State was bound by the rule of *tu patere legem quam ipse fecisti*: it had to comply with the legislation that it had itself enacted. If there was internal legislation setting out procedures for expulsion of aliens, the State that had freely adopted them had to respect them. In the first instance, failure to respect the rule could render the expulsion proceedings unlawful and entail the international responsibility of the expelling State, while in the second instance, non-respect rendered the expulsion proceedings unlawful and could lead to its annulment in domestic courts. To avert any ambiguity, it would doubtless be best to speak, even in the latter instance, of conditions for expulsion rather than of expulsion proceedings, since even domestic legislation might combine procedural and substantive rules. The 1987 decision of the Iran–United States Claims Tribunal in the *Yeager* v. *Islamic Republic of Iran* case clearly showed that the granting of a reasonable period of time for the expelled person to pack his or her belongings could be viewed both as a procedural rule and as a substantive rule.

29. Lastly, on part 3 of the work plan, "Legal consequences of expulsion", some members of the Commission seemed to have reservations about referring to diplomatic protection and the responsibility of the expelling State. There, too, there was apparently a misunderstanding. As he had indicated in paragraph 27, that would not involve studying again the relevant regimes, but rather, taking advantage of rules already developed in order to devise a complete legal regime for expulsion of aliens by examining the legal consequences of unlawful expulsion. As to the right to return, on which Mr. Dugard had raised questions, he himself did not see it in the context of the Palestinian–Israeli conflict, but simply as a right of an individual who had obtained the annulment of unlawful expulsion proceedings to return to the country from which he or she had been unlawfully expelled.

30. He wished in closing to request all members of the Commission to transmit to the Secretariat the legislation of their countries or others concerning expulsion of aliens. He would be particularly grateful to Mr. Kateka if he would be willing to draft a short paper and transmit any relevant documentation explaining the concept of "constructive expulsion", of which he had to confess ignorance. He would also be grateful if the Secretariat would prepare a study similar to the one it had produced on the effects of armed conflict on treaties but comprising a compilation of documents relating to expulsion of aliens, organized according to the work plan on which the Commission appeared to be broadly agreed. Such a study would facilitate his analytical work, on the basis of which he would then be able to draw consequences with a view to formulating the draft articles.

31. In conclusion, he undertook to make every effort to submit a first report on the topic to the Commission at its next session.

32. Mr. KOSKENNIEMI thanked the Special Rapporteur for his exhaustive overview of the debate and especially for responding to the concerns he himself had expressed. The Special Rapporteur had labelled those concerns "reservations", but he had not intended them as opposition of any kind, precisely because it was unclear to him what there was to oppose or support at the present stage of the work. What he wished to see was a historical and socio-economic overview of the topic, to be conducted at the outset of the codification process. He persisted in thinking that such an overview was necessary before the Commission could identify a legislative purpose for its work.

33. His concern that such historical or socio-economic studies should be carried out went beyond the topic of expulsion of aliens to a number of issues that the Commission was now dealing with or might take up in future. The topic of expulsion of aliens was fundamentally different from others that the Commission had handled successfully in the past. As an academic from a developed country, he had very limited knowledge of the factual circumstances surrounding expulsion of aliens, the different interests at stake and the motivations of particular actors. He sometimes read reports in the press about such events, which seemed very remote from his own experience. He had been moved by Mr. Fomba's account of encountering on an aeroplane a compatriot being expelled from a European country. While that was an isolated incident, it did indicate that legislation was necessary if the rule of law was to be upheld in such situations.

34. He therefore asked himself, as a public international lawyer, what attitude he should take towards the codification exercise. In the past, the Commission had dealt successfully with topics such as the law of treaties, diplomatic relations and State succession, immunity and responsibility. All of those were matters in which he was an expert, as were the other members of the Commission, and it was only right that they should be the ones to codify the law in such areas. In respect of expulsion of aliens, however, he did not feel at all like an expert: in fact, he felt very vulnerable to objections that his position was based on insufficient knowledge of the subject.

35. One could identify clusters of problems on which studies could be carried out. What, for example, was the geographical region in which expulsion of aliens occurred most often? What modalities, namely individual or mass expulsions, were the most problematic? What were the economic reasons for expulsion, the racial reasons—surely more dubious—or the security reasons? The Special Rapporteur dealt with those reasons as motivations. When

States engaged in suspect activities, they gave explanations of their motivations that put them in the best possible light. Beneath such acceptable motivations, however, there was often an underlying unacceptable reason for expulsion, for example, racism. One did not unearth that real reason until a socio-economic study had been done.

36. There were thus two ways to proceed in such an exercise: one was to identify a problem and try to solve it; the other, to identify a concept and try to clarify it. The Commission had very often chosen the latter option in its work on the topics he had mentioned earlier. However, expulsion of aliens was a different matter. There the focus was on a specific topical problem which needed to be resolved. The report's reference to the concept of the expulsion of aliens was thus frustrating, because he was not interested in the concept, but in the problem.

37. He was asking for a socio-economic study, not out of academic interest or because the subject of expulsion of aliens was especially intellectually stimulating, but because such a study would help the Commission to identify the purpose of the legislative effort. That might seem a daunting task. The members of the Commission were not economic or social experts, and he was not asking for a 500-page paper on the subject, replete with graphs and statistics. Rather, an overview should be produced of the most important problems and situations involving the expulsion of aliens that had arisen over the past 20 years, from which typical cases and interests could be identified. That was how Max Weber would have proceeded.

38. In sum, a novel approach was needed to address the subject, the core issue of which was different from that of earlier, more traditional topics of public international law which the Commission had dealt so successfully with in the past.

39. Mr. BROWNLIE said that despite the care that the Special Rapporteur had taken in responding to comments, he had failed to deal with three points. The first was the relationship between paragraphs 15 and 16. He himself continued to believe that they were contradictory, and it did not help to say that the right of expulsion should not be abused—that would apply to almost any topic which involved principles of some kind or another. It just happened that in the literature there was a tendency to say that, because it was a discretionary right, that right should not be abused.

40. Admittedly, the Special Rapporteur had not asserted that the right to expel was an absolute right, but one had to ask what was the polarity between discretion and its opposite. Discretionary power was also regulated by law, and thus there was no simplistic polarity between discretionary power on the one hand and discretion which was regulated by law on the other. The Commission would get itself into terrible trouble if it did not accept that in a general way, the State had discretionary power, albeit regulated by law and limited by other principles of international law.

41. Thus—and that was his second point—it was important to maintain the simple distinction between a right and the modalities for exercising it. There had been the usual erroneous focus on human rights matters. Human rights came into the picture in connection with modalities. Even if in principle a State exercised the right of expulsion on a lawful basis, certain modalities of human rights standards must be observed, but they were different. They were applicable, highly relevant and very important, but they were not central to the subject.

42. His third point, which in a sense overlapped with Mr. Koskenniemi's concerns, was that the problem was not what interests were concerned, because they were multiple. Some were human rights interests, because a State had a duty, not only under multilateral standard-setting human rights treaties, but also under customary international law, to maintain order on its territory so that it could protect its own people and visitors, who might include long-term migrant workers; indeed, visitors were a very complex group. Thus, it was not so much a matter of reviewing the socio-economic history, because that would vary from country to country and from region to region within a particular country. The subject was not "about" expulsion of aliens. Why should the Commission focus on a State which announced that it was going to expel aliens? Not many States bothered to expel aliens as an end in itself. Rather, the subject was the lawful control by a State of its territory in order to enforce its own municipal law and principles of international law. The expulsion of aliens in appropriate circumstances was a mode of exercising that control. The Special Rapporteur had disregarded that important focus. The expulsion of aliens was a useful label and the conventional term, but it did not provide a very good description. If he was right, denial of entry should not be excluded from the topic of expulsion, because it was part of the overall issue of appropriate and effective control by a State of conditions on its territory.

43. Ms. XUE said she doubted whether the physical crossing of a boundary by an alien should be a required criterion. If a State had an inherent right to expel aliens from its territory, that immediately touched upon the territorial scope of the State and the territorial scope of a sovereign right. All cases involving the expulsion of aliens actually had to do with the scope of State jurisdiction and control. The example given by Mr. Fomba illustrated that point. An alien did not have to be placed on board an aeroplane in the physical territory of the expelling State, but merely in an area that was under the expelling State's jurisdiction and control. If the Commission confined itself to the aspect of territory and disregarded the extent of jurisdiction and control, the study would fail to cover a number of cases.

44. No particular case could best be categorized under the broad heading of "expulsion of alien". Such cases could always be reduced to specific categories of issues such as illegal immigration, State actions against transboundary crimes, border control issues, migrant workers, refugees or asylum-seekers. Now that the Commission was attempting to draw up a comprehensive regime on the expulsion of aliens, it must ask what practical interests were involved. She was very impressed with Mr. Koskenniemi's eloquent remarks in that connection. The expulsion of aliens was not an isolated problem, but an everyday occurrence and a very topical issue. A balance must

be struck between a State's right to expel aliens and the need to protect the interests of individuals. The topic was very important: cases involving the expulsion of aliens affected the interests of many more individuals than did cases involving diplomatic protection.

45. The CHAIRPERSON, speaking as a member of the Commission, and taking up Ms. Xue's point that the subject went beyond territorial sovereignty alone, said that the expulsion of stowaways was another question which might be addressed; indeed, it had already been considered by the international community, and an international text had been adopted on the protection of the basic rights of such persons, who often did not have the nationality of the flag State whose authorities expelled them.

46. Mr. CHEE recalled that in the *Boffolo* case a crucial distinction had been made between the existence of a right and the manner of its application. Judge Hersch Lauterpacht, too, had stressed that an unjustifiable method of expulsion amounted to an abuse of rights.[2] In the *Yeager* v. *Islamic Republic of Iran* case the principle was the same: the manner of expulsion, in which the person had been given 30 minutes to pack his belongings, had been wrongful. Thus, wrongful manner of expulsion or abuse of expulsion had to be borne in mind in discussing the right to expel as one inherent in State sovereignty. With reference to the case law of the international tribunals, the doctrine of the publicists and international instruments, it may be held that it is customary that aliens who are legal residents may not be unjustly expelled from the country in which they reside.

47. The State has various grounds under which to exercise its right to expulsion. The Special Rapporteur concludes that the lawfulness of expulsion depends on two factors: (*a*) conformity with expulsion procedure in force in the expelling States and (*b*) respect for fundamental human rights. Goodwin-Gill suggests that there are substantive as well as procedural limitations on the power to expel aliens: State practice accepts that expulsion is justified: (*a*) for entry in breach of law; (*b*) for breaching the conditions of admission; (*c*) for involvement in criminal activities; and (*d*) in the light of political and security considerations.[3]

48. In paragraph 25 of his report, the Special Rapporteur deals with the case of migrant workers and refers to the International Convention on the Protection of the Rights of All Migrant Workers and Members of their Families. Today the most salient feature of the expulsion of aliens concerns aliens who are migrant workers everywhere in the world. The Special Rapporteur could have gone more in detail to help the Commission.

49. Mr. ECONOMIDES said he wanted to dispel a misunderstanding. His point that qualifying adjectives such as "absolute", "discretionary" or "sovereign" should not be used with "the right of expulsion" had not been meant as a criticism of the Special Rapporteur, but was a remark of a general nature addressed to all members of the Commission concerning future work on the topic. The right of expulsion was exercised in accordance with internal law, but the latter must not be contrary to international law, which governed the law of expulsion and which set conditions and limits for the exercise of all rights. The Commission should not talk of discretionary or absolute rights before considering those conditions and limits. If, at the end of its work, the Commission found there was a need for qualifiers for legal reasons, it could add them at that stage, but the qualifier "discretionary" was premature at the present juncture.

50. Mr. MANSFIELD said that the Special Rapporteur's approach was not at all incompatible with Mr. Koskenniemi's. If the Commission took Mr. Brownlie's conception of the subject, namely, the lawful control of a State over its territory, that included access not only of persons, but also of goods. If the Commission were to address the question of access of goods, it would be helpful to have an overview of the most recent problems with regard to the import of goods, such as the application of health regulations to exclude goods, difficulties in applying rules of origin for goods, and problems relating to the potential introduction of alien species. That would help to inform the Commission's work. Likewise, if the Secretariat could prepare a summary of the most pressing and controversial problems encountered in the past 20 years concerning the expulsion of aliens, that, too, would usefully inform the Special Rapporteur's work.

51. Mr. BROWNLIE said he was obviously not suggesting that the Commission should study special boundary regimes, demarcations, control of territory and other matters as subjects in their own right. Rather, it should look at the rationale of the subject. The expulsion of aliens was an important aspect of the problem of control, and the Commission was studying the expulsion of aliens against the background of what it was about, namely, the effective control of national territory for the purpose of maintaining the rule of law.

52. Ms. ESCARAMEIA commended Mr. Koskenniemi's eloquent remarks. Like Mr. Mansfield, she did not think there was any incompatibility between the two approaches. Any paper prepared by the Secretariat should analyse specific situations in which aliens had been expelled. That did not contradict Mr. Brownlie's remarks, because such situations were a consequence of the need for State control of its territory. She therefore endorsed Mr. Mansfield's proposal.

53. She also suggested that, as had been done in the case of other topics, the Commission should hear the views of experts in the field in order to gain an insight into the situation of persons who were expelled. She had in mind experts from IOM, UNHCR and OHCHR, as well as from non-governmental organizations active in the field. The scientific community had been very informative on the topic of aquifers, and there was also a precedent in the Commission's contacts with United Nations human rights treaty bodies on the topic of reservations to treaties.

54. Mr. KEMICHA, referring to Mr. Koskenniemi's moving testimony on how little he knew about the reality

[2] H. Lauterpacht, *The Function of Law in the International Community*, Oxford University Press, 1933, p. 289.

[3] G. S. Goodwin-Gill, *International Law and the Movement of Persons between States*, Oxford University Press, 1978, p. 307.

of expulsions and how isolated from that reality international legal experts were, pointed out that the incident described by Mr. Fomba was not exceptional: such incidents took place every day at European airports, in European aeroplanes and at European harbours. One need only open one's eyes and ears to take note of what was taking place.

55. Mr. Brownlie had stressed that a State had every right to enact and apply legislation for the protection of its territory, but nothing in the Special Rapporteur's preliminary report asserted the contrary. It went without saying that every State had legislation and safeguards to ensure that expulsions took place with due regard for internal law. As for the right of return, he referred to the recent case of a person who had successfully appealed against an expulsion order and had been allowed to return to France from Algeria. Such cases were referred to in paragraph 27 of the report. It was therefore unfair to maintain that the Special Rapporteur disregarded the basic right of the State to protect its territory and its citizens.

56. Mr. BROWNLIE said that if he was right in saying that the rationale for studying the subject was the effective control of State territory for reasons of international public order, then the Commission must decide whether it was logical to include the question of refusal of entry. Thus, there would be practical consequences if the Commission decided to confine the topic to expulsion of aliens, which was just one mechanism that could be used to characterize the problem of effective control of State territory in relation to the movement of foreigners. If he was correct, it would be logical to extend the subject to include refusal of entry.

57. Mr. Sreenivasa RAO, commenting on Ms. Escarameia's suggestion, said that at this early stage in its study of the topic it would be premature for the Commission to seek the views of experts on expulsion of aliens. It would be preferable to give the Special Rapporteur the opportunity to study the materials available and to inform the Commission on the outcome of his research in a subsequent report. The Commission was not a fact-finding body, and should be wary of setting a precedent that might not be in keeping with its specific mandate. While he endorsed the idea of greater flexibility and the need for the Commission's work to be of relevance to contemporary society, there were better ways of achieving those ends than by risking unnecessary exposure to the vagaries of public opinion.

58. Mr. KAMTO (Special Rapporteur), responding to the comments and suggestions made during the discussion, said that while he understood Mr. Koskenniemi's concern about the need for background studies to place the topic in its overall context, he also endorsed Mr. Sreenivasa Rao's comments with regard to the Commission's mandate and working methods. There was nothing to prevent him drawing on the material or advice of experts available on the subject, but there seemed no need to make a formal request for their input to the Commission at the present juncture. He was therefore in favour of Mr. Mansfield's suggestion that the Secretariat should be requested to prepare a brief overview of the situation, covering mainly the historical background but possibly also some socio-economic factors, in the form of an information document for members rather than as part of the Special Rapporteur's subsequent reports.

59. The Special Rapporteur took note of Mr. Brownlie's very valid point concerning the distinction between a right and the modalities for exercising it, which should help to settle the matter of whether the right of expulsion was indeed one inherent in State sovereignty. However, he took issue with the view that expulsion should be seen as part of the wider issue of the right of the State to control its territory, and that accordingly the question of non-admission should fall within the scope of the topic. Broadening the scope to such an extent would merely complicate matters by diluting the very concept the Commission was trying to define. Moreover, he found it difficult to reconcile the ideas of expulsion and non-admission, since someone who had not yet entered a territory could not be expelled from it. Even if one were to take up Mr. Brownlie's correct assertion that expulsion was one aspect of a State's right to exercise control over its territory, a distinction must be drawn between measures adopted by a State to that end by refusing entry to persons who did not meet certain conditions, and other measures governing persons already on its territory who might be subject to expulsion.

60. As for the question, raised by Ms. Xue, whether the concept of expulsion could be extended to include areas that were not territorial *stricto sensu* and thus cover situations where persons on board vessels or aircraft were refused entry into the territory of a State, he had already rejected such an approach in the preliminary report by referring to the *MV Tampa* case (para. 9), and he maintained his position on the matter. The concept of expulsion could not apply to persons until they had physically crossed the border and gone through the entry formalities of the State in question; consequently, refusal of entry and *refoulement* should not be dealt with. Although some members might feel that that would limit the scope of the topic unduly, such limitations were necessary; otherwise the Commission would make its task more difficult and the set of draft articles it produced would create more problems than it resolved. In any case, the Commission's task was to deal with the problem of expulsion in the context of international law, not with problems of immigration and admission that were clearly matters of internal policy.

61. He took note of Mr. Economides' clarification, but considered nonetheless that in the light of Mr. Brownlie's remarks on the distinction between a right and the modalities for exercising it, the term "discretionary" could be used without prejudice to the concept of expulsion. However, for the time being he would not press the matter, since he was certain it would come up again, given that the literature unanimously asserted that expulsion was a right inherent in State sovereignty, and consequently a discretionary one too.

Unilateral acts of states (A/CN.4/549 and Add.1, sect. C and A/CN.4/557)[4]

[Agenda item 5]

Eighth report of the Special Rapporteur

62. Mr. RODRÍGUEZ CEDEÑO (Special Rapporteur), introducing his eighth report on unilateral acts of States (A/CN.4/557), recalled that a Working Group, chaired by Mr. Pellet,[5] had been set up to analyse some of the examples of State practice contained in the seventh report,[6] with a view to their further consideration in the present report. He thanked all members of the Commission who had provided valuable input in that connection. Moreover, in its discussion of the topic during the fifty-ninth session of the General Assembly, the Sixth Committee had emphasized that as the next step the Commission must develop a clear definition of unilateral acts and formulate general rules applicable to all unilateral acts and declarations considered by the Special Rapporteur in the light of State practice with a view to promoting the stability and predictability of their mutual relations (A/CN.4/549, para. 75). The definition of unilateral acts must be sufficiently broad and flexible to give States room for manoeuvre in carrying out their political acts and must also include other types of conduct capable of producing legal effects. He hoped that task could be achieved during the current session.

63. Chapter I of the report provided detailed information on 11 examples of different types of acts to be considered on the basis of the guidelines agreed on by the Working Group at the previous session and listed in paragraph 12 of the report. The first example was the note dated 22 November 1952 from the Minister for Foreign Affairs of Colombia concerning the sovereignty of the Bolivarian Republic of Venezuela over the Los Monjes archipelago. It was of particular interest since it highlighted the diverging views of two different branches of State power: the Government of Colombia had accepted the validity of the note, whereas the Council of State of Colombia had nullified it.

64. The second example was the Declaration of the Minister for Foreign Affairs of Cuba concerning the supply of vaccines to the Eastern Republic of Uruguay. The case was of interest because the addressee had rejected the act in the sense it had been intended by Cuba—namely, as a donation—and had viewed it as a commercial transaction.

65. The third example was Jordan's waiver of claims to the West Bank territories, which differed from the earlier examples in that it had prompted reactions from other States, including the United States and France. It also raised the important issue of whether the person making the declaration on behalf of the State—the King of Jordan—had been competent to do so. Given that the Constitution of Jordan prohibited any act related to the transfer of territory, it would appear that the King had exceeded his authority, although that had not prevented the waiver from producing legal effects, since the transfer of the territory to the State of Palestine had actually taken place. The example illustrated the subsequent confirmation of an act formulated by a person not competent to do so under the domestic laws of the State in question.

66. The fourth example was the Egyptian declaration of 24 April 1957. The fifth example, of statements made by the Government of France concerning the suspension of nuclear tests in the South Pacific, was noteworthy because, although the statements had taken various forms, including a diplomatic note and a statement to the General Assembly, they constituted a single unilateral act (para. 72).

67. The sixth example was of two unilateral protests by the Russian Federation against Turkmenistan and Azerbaijan in relation to the status of the waters of the Caspian Sea, in the form of diplomatic notes. They had been sent directly to the addressees with the intent of producing specific legal effects: to prevent the acquisition or the formation of certain rights or claims by the two countries in question.

68. The seventh example, the statements made by nuclear-weapon States to the Security Council and the Conference on Disarmament, had already been touched on by the Commission. The statements were similar in content and their objective was to provide negative guarantees of the non-use of nuclear weapons. The eighth example was the Ihlen Declaration of 22 July 1919. The ninth example was the Truman Proclamation of 28 September 1945, which had been considered by the Commission in connection with the draft conventions on the law of the sea and by the ICJ in its judgment in the *North Sea Continental Shelf* case.

69. The interesting feature of the tenth example was that the act in question was addressed, not to a State but to an international organization, and consisted of various statements made by different authors or organs in Switzerland at different times on the subject of tax exemptions and privileges of the United Nations and its staff members. The last example concerned the conduct of Thailand and Cambodia with reference to the *Temple of Preah Vihear* case.

70. Chapter II set out the conclusions that could be drawn from the statements analysed. What was noticeable was their very varied nature in terms of subject matter, form, authors and addressees. The latter included specific States or those *in statu nascendi*, such as the Palestine Liberation Organization in 1988, staff of international organizations, groups of States or the international community in general. Similarly the consequences of unilateral acts were varied: in some cases they had resulted in international treaties, in others they had profoundly affected an important legal regime. In others again, the unilateral act had been intended to avoid undesirable effects that could result from silence. Generally speaking, it was difficult to draw any hard and fast conclusions regarding the evolution of unilateral acts over time.

71. He hoped that the examples contained in the report would serve as a basis for constructive discussion with a view to adopting a definition of unilateral acts of

[4] Reproduced in *Yearbook ... 2005*, vol. II (Part One).

[5] See *Yearbook ... 2004*, vol. II (Part Two), p. 96, paras. 245–247.

[6] *Ibid.*, vol. II (Part One), document A/CN.4/542.

States during the current session, on the basis of which certain rules or principles governing the matter could be identified.

The meeting rose at 1 p.m.

2853rd MEETING

Tuesday, 19 July 2005, at 10.05 a.m.

Chairperson: Mr. Djamchid MOMTAZ

Present: Mr. Addo, Mr. Al-Marri, Mr. Brownlie, Mr. Candioti, Mr. Chee, Mr. Commissário Afonso, Mr. Daoudi, Mr. Dugard, Mr. Economides, Ms. Escarameia, Mr. Fomba, Mr. Galicki, Mr. Kabatsi, Mr. Kamto, Mr. Kateka, Mr. Kemicha, Mr. Kolodkin, Mr. Koskenniemi, Mr. Mansfield, Mr. Matheson, Mr. Niehaus, Mr. Pambou-Tchivounda, Mr. Pellet, Mr. Sreenivasa Rao, Mr. Rodríguez Cedeño, Ms. Xue, Mr. Yamada.

Unilateral acts of states (*continued*) (A/CN.4/549 and Add.1, sect. C and A/CN.4/557)

[Agenda item 5]

EIGHTH REPORT OF THE SPECIAL RAPPORTEUR (*continued*)

1. Ms. ESCARAMEIA thanked the Special Rapporteur for his report but said she was disappointed that he had not devoted more time to the conclusions and that the report did not contain any proposals as to how work should proceed.

2. The topic of unilateral acts of States gave rise to two types of criticism. One, more radical, was that there was no such thing as a legally binding unilateral act of a State, because such an act involved only one party and thus could be modified or revoked at any time (inapplicability of the principle of *pacta sunt servanda*). However, the report had shown that that position was untenable, given international jurisprudence (namely, the *Legal Status of Eastern Greenland*, *Temple of Preah Vihear* and *Nuclear Tests* cases). In the *Nuclear Tests* case, the ICJ had clearly rejected the possibility of revocation of a unilateral act: "the unilateral undertaking resulting from these statements cannot be interpreted as having been made in implicit reliance on an arbitrary power of reconsideration" (para. 82 of the report). Then there were those who felt that the unilateral acts of States were so diverse that they could not be a source of international law. Although such acts differed considerably, the practice described in the report indicated that they had a number of common traits, which had been identified by the Working Group, on which the Commission could base its work.

3. Whereas the date, form and content of the act might not be so decisive, the author and its competence (*vis-à-vis* international law rather than domestic law) must be taken into consideration. In that connection, article 7 of the 1969 Vienna Convention on the Law of Treaties, although too restrictive, might offer some guidance, provided that competence was expanded to include other authors, including legislative bodies. Intent, context and circumstances were fundamental in determining whether an act produced legal effects. Once again the ICJ, in the *Nuclear Tests* case, had declared that "statements [...] must be held to constitute an engagement of the State, having regard to their intention and to the circumstances in which they were made" (para. 83 of the report). The addressees could also vary considerably, but they should always be subjects of international law. The reaction of addressees was particularly important when it consisted of action taken on the basis of the act in question or in reply to a specific request. The reactions of third parties could also help to determine whether a unilateral act was involved, as could the adoption of implementing instruments, whether by the author, the addressees or third parties.

4. As to how the Commission should proceed with its work, she did not think that the 1969 Vienna Convention was the best model; it should only be used as a reference, particularly for the competence of authors. Unilateral acts were in fact very different from treaties; they were acts by States which produced legal effects on their own. Thus the Commission should begin by agreeing on a definition, drafted in sufficiently broad terms to leave scope to manoeuvre: for example, "an act that originates in a State authority and produces international legal effects". It should then analyse case law and State practice to compile the list of factors (intent, circumstances, reactions of the addressees or third parties, etc.) that supported the presumption that a given act produced legal effects. In that connection, it would be very useful if the Secretariat could produce a paper similar to the excellent document on the effects of armed conflicts on treaties (A/CN.4/550 and Corr.1–2). Once the notion of unilateral act was established, the Commission might consider what cases did not fall under that category and then consider the consequences of unilateral acts, such as responsibility for their violation. For the time being, those objectives were sufficient, because the project was very ambitious. States would then have an idea of what they could or could not do and with what consequences.

5. Mr. PELLET said that he shared Ms. Escarameia's interest in the subject but did not think that the project was too ambitious. The aim was to tell States the extent to which they risked becoming trapped by their own declarations, i.e. their own commitments. States needed to know, for example, what statements they could make in the international arena without such statements being regarded as legal acts that could be used against them.

6. In essence, the report was based on the work of the Working Group. The practice described was more limited than in the previous report,[1] but more usable, although the acts addressed were perhaps not entirely representative. The report's conclusions were not developed to any great extent, but they constituted a starting point for further consideration. He noted several ambiguities (paras. 179 and 199) and some vagueness (paras. 183 and 186), in particular with regard to the Ihlen Declaration, about

[1] See 2852nd meeting, footnote 6.

which it was still unclear whether it was a declaration or an agreement (paras. 121–126); he hoped that the Special Rapporteur would express a definitive view on that point. In any case, the report provided sufficient support for a definition of a unilateral act. In 2006 the Special Rapporteur should propose one or more draft articles containing a definition for consideration and adoption by the Drafting Committee. The Commission also had sufficient material to move ahead on the questions of the capacity and competence of the authors of unilateral acts. However, it would seem quite premature to study informal conduct of States that might constitute unilateral acts, such as that of Thailand and Cambodia in the *Temple of Preah Vihear* case, but whose interference with unilateral acts as understood in the decision on the *Nuclear Tests* case obscured the problem rather than helping to clarify it, particularly as it was not even certain that it constituted an aspect of the topic.

7. Mr. KOSKENNIEMI said that there was a contradiction between Mr. Pellet's starting point and his conclusions. He personally was of the view that unilateral acts of States could not be codified and that all the work of the Commission on the topic confirmed that fact. If, however, one assumed, as Mr. Pellet did, that such codification would help to alert States to situations in which they risked being entrapped by an obligation they had not considered, two conclusions followed. One was that the Commission was dealing with a source of non-voluntary obligations. States sometimes found themselves bound in spite of themselves by obligations resulting from their past statements or acts. That in itself was not a problem, but on a purely practical level the Commission should perhaps ask States whether they would be prepared to accept a codifying convention in which they agreed to be bound irrespective of their will. The second and much more important point was that, if it was true that States were sometimes entrapped irrespective of their words, then the question arose of where such obligations emerged from.

8. Mr. PELLET suggested that the conditions in which a State might become "entrapped" by the unilateral declaration of their intentions should be spelled out; however, it seemed impossible to compile an exhaustive list of such conditions, and in fact that was not the Commission's role. The Commission could, however, indicate to States that they might be bound by certain behaviours, for example the principle of good faith, and that this could occur even in the absence of any agreement. It would therefore be more appropriate for the Commission to give guidance on what was meant by unilateral acts.

9. He was afraid that there was a misunderstanding between Mr. Koskenniemi and himself. When he had said that unilateral acts were a "trap of intent", he had not meant that States—in the context of the topic—could be bound against their will, but that once they had unilaterally made a public declaration of intent (otherwise than through a treaty), they were "trapped" by that declaration. Unilateral acts were clearly a part of voluntary law (as opposed to what some, following the thinking of Ago, called "spontaneous" law[2]). However, the problem lay in determining when the State became entrapped by its declaration of intent. As Ms. Escarameia had pointed out, Heads of State sometimes said things of little consequence, and in such cases there was no intent to be bound. The ICJ had itself made that observation, for example in its 1986 judgment in the *Frontier Dispute (Burkina Faso/Republic of Mali)* case, when it had found that there were no grounds for considering that the Malian Head of State had intended to be bound by his declaration, which had been political in nature and thus had not produced legal effects (para. 40 of the judgment).

10. Mr. Koskenniemi's conclusion also posed a problem: as soon as one acknowledged that the State could become entrapped—in his own view, intentionally, and in Mr. Koskenniemi's view, unintentionally—it was important to ascertain just when such entrapment occurred. Consequently, States needed draft articles that were as precise as possible so that they could know, for example, what the conditions were for making declarations of intent, who was entitled to make such a declaration, and above all—a matter that had not yet been elucidated—whether they could withdraw such a unilaterally expressed declaration. The Working Group had not been able to gather enough examples of practice to clarify the latter point, which would probably be a matter for the progressive development of international law.

11. He reiterated his conviction that the topic was useful and that it was in fact possible to prepare a set of draft articles that would be genuinely helpful to States.

12. Mr. BROWNLIE said he thought that the appropriate vehicle for the work under way should have been an expository study, a view shared by several Governments. He agreed with most of the points made by Mr. Koskenniemi. The subject, quite frankly, was non-existent: there was no such thing as a "unilateral act". The term was used in textbooks because it was a standard reference and people knew what it referred to. The whole point about unilateral acts was that they all occurred in context, and it was only in that context that the possibility of legal effects arose. There was a complete contrast, technically and culturally, between the law of treaties and unilateral acts. The law of treaties was a well-established matrix of law, and when a State concluded a treaty it usually knew what it was doing, which was not always the case with a unilateral act.

13. He greatly hoped that the Commission would not persist in elaborating draft articles or even a simple definition of unilateral acts. That would be a very protracted exercise, and as the members of the Commission would have difficulty agreeing, the definition would be incomplete and might create enormous confusion. Moreover, it would be said that the Commission had somehow tried to diminish the significance of estoppel, which had been set aside. What was important at the current stage was to preserve the positive elements of what had been done so far: the accumulation of State practice produced by the Special Rapporteur and the Working Group, and the demonstration of the risks. If the Commission continued the work within the same model, it would be tantamount to assuming that the topic was analogous to the law of treaties, which was not true.

[2] See R. Ago, "Positive law and international law", *AJIL*, vol. 51 (1957), pp. 717, 729 and 732. See also Daillier and Pellet, *op. cit.* (2839th meeting, footnote 10), p. 321.

14. Mr. PELLET said that there had never been any question of setting aside estoppel. It was simply that estoppel was not on the same level as a unilateral act, which could give rise to an estoppel. If one approached the topic as Mr. Brownlie did, it was indeed impossible to deal with. The problem was that the topic was not the conduct of States in the international arena but the unilateral acts of States, in other words, the unilateral expression of their intent at the international level. Legal acts certainly did exist and they had a definition, which was precisely the expression of intent. An expression of intent in the international arena could be either unilateral, which was the type that was of interest to the Commission, or bilateral or multilateral, taking the form of a treaty. What was irksome about the view taken by some members was that they were altering the topic in order to conclude that it was impossible to deal with.

15. Mr. CHEE said he was surprised to hear that one could say that unilateral acts did not exist as such when a number of distinguished authors, including Oppenheim, frequently referred to them. Moreover, the notion was found in private law, where the "quasi-contract" was similar to a unilateral act of intent.

16. Mr. BROWNLIE said that it was somewhat by way of provocation that he had stated that unilateral acts did not exist as such. What he had wanted to say was that the expression "unilateral acts" was used because it was convenient and one could immediately see what it meant, much as one could recognize a riot without actually understanding the legal definition and consequences of it. The phrase did not have any analytical basis, since, as the acts in question necessarily came under the scope of relations between States, they could not, strictly speaking, be "unilateral". He also wished to draw attention to a far more serious theoretical problem, namely the drawing of an analogy with the law of treaties, essentially bilateral ones, with which he simply did not agree.

17. Mr. KOSKENNIEMI said that the exchange that had just taken place between Mr. Pellet and Mr. Brownlie was a perfect illustration of the confusion surrounding the topic. When Mr. Pellet had accused Mr. Brownlie of reformulating the topic so as to focus on the conduct of States and in so doing to nullify it, he was basing himself on certain specific aspects of French doctrine, which enshrined the concept of "the legal act". For those who did not have a background in that doctrine, however, it was only natural that the topic should cover the conduct of States at the international level.

18. Mr. PELLET said that a concept should not be rejected just because it had been developed by French doctrine. That having been said, the origin of the topic lay not in French doctrine but with the ICJ, for instance in the *Legal Status of Eastern Greenland* case and, more clearly, in the *Nuclear Tests* cases.

19. The CHAIRPERSON, speaking in his personal capacity, said that the difficulty probably stemmed from the absence of specific criteria that would make it possible to ascertain a State's intent to undertake international commitments through a unilateral act.

20. Mr. KAMTO noted that the question of the existence or non-existence of unilateral acts had been the subject of debate in the Commission for some time and that the Commission needed to take a clear decision in the matter. Moreover, it was unusual that a concept so clearly established by the ICJ should be called into question because, although not infallible, the Court was generally considered to be a reliable source. At any rate, the legal act was a valid concept in all legal systems, regardless of ideology or culture.

21. He thanked the Special Rapporteur and the Working Group for having endeavoured to clarify matters by listing several categories of unilateral acts, and he endorsed the conclusions, notwithstanding their brevity, that the Special Rapporteur had tried to draw concerning all of them.

22. Turning to a question of terminology which he believed had substantive implications, he expressed concern that in paragraph 157 of the French version of the report, the Special Rapporteur referred to declarations that contained ("*qui contiennent*") unilateral acts. In fact, the point was to ascertain whether the declarations contained or constituted unilateral acts. If the declarations contained the act, that was a tautology and the form (*instrumentum*) might be sacrificed to the substance (*negotium*). However, the form was extremely important because it allowed for a distinction to be drawn between unilateral acts—normative statements that complied with rules of form—and forms of conduct. The Special Rapporteur had perhaps been a trifle careless in that area, since he said in paragraph 170 that

> [t]he first conclusion that can be drawn is that the form is relatively unimportant in determining whether we are dealing with a unilateral legal act of the type in which the Commission is interested—in other words, an act that can produce legal effects on its own without the need for its acceptance, or for any other reaction on the part of the addressee.

Even though he then went on to say that "it may still be considered that the formality of the act has a role to play in determining the intent of its author", he ought to have drawn the conclusion more clearly and stated whether the oral form of the act should be rejected or retained. In that connection, it was worth noting that the dissenting opinion of Judge Anzilotti in *Legal Status of Eastern Greenland*, cited in paragraph 126 of the report, was based on the very subjective view that the declaration was one part of an international agreement and not a unilateral act.

23. With regard to types of unilateral acts, he noted that in paragraph 180 of the report the Special Rapporteur addressed the issue of persons authorized to formulate unilateral acts and suggested that they were the persons authorized to represent the State as defined in the 1969 Vienna Convention. However, persons other than those identified in that Convention could bind a State through a unilateral act. In an earlier report the Special Rapporteur had referred to the Helms–Burton[3] and D'Amato-Kennedy Acts[4] (international trade legislation of the United States), the declarations of acceptance of the compulsory jurisdiction of the ICJ and national legislation

[3] See 2841st meeting, footnote 3.

[4] "Iran and Libya Sanctions Act of 1996", *ILM*, vol. 35, No. 5 (September 1996), p. 1274.

on the delimitation of maritime boundaries of States. He wondered whether the Special Rapporteur still intended to examine that type of act. Indeed, some legislative acts of national parliaments had all the characteristics of unilateral acts in the sense intended by the Commission. A good example was Israel's Revised Disengagement Plan of 25 October 2004, by which the Israeli Parliament had adopted the plan for Israel's unilateral withdrawal from the Gaza Strip, even though it confirmed earlier declarations by the Israeli Prime Minister. The Special Rapporteur might wish to examine that category of acts.

24. Another category of unilateral acts might be judicial decisions. There a distinction needed to be drawn between decisions of national courts that referred to an international legal instrument, such as the decisions of the United States courts in the *Breard*, *LaGrand* and *Avena* cases, and those that did not refer to such instruments, as in, for example, the cases concerning the Arrest Warrant of 11 April 2000 (*Democratic Republic of the Congo* v. *Belgium*) and *Certain Criminal Proceedings in France*. That might also be another avenue worth exploring. Where unilateral acts were concerned, the legislative and judicial bodies of States were perfectly capable of expressing the intent of the State at the international level.

25. Another interesting example was the statement made by the agent of Cameroon before the ICJ in the *Land and Maritime Boundary between Cameroon and Nigeria* case, according to which Cameroon, faithful to its tradition of hospitality, would afford protection to Nigerian nationals living in those parts of the territory concerned by the dispute. The Court had dealt with that statement in a questionable manner, and it had taken note of it in the operative part of its judgment (paras. 317 and 325 (V)(C)), with the result that Nigeria had been able to use it against Cameroon when the judgment was being enforced.

26. Lastly, as Ms. Escarameia had said, the Commission might also wish to consider statements made by future Heads of State or Government between the time they were elected and the time they took office. If such a statement was not refuted after the person concerned had taken office, then it must be considered to be a unilateral act. An example was to be found in the statement made by Mr. Zapatero before he became Prime Minister concerning the withdrawal of Spanish troops from Iraq, a statement that had indeed been confirmed after he had taken office. One might well ask whether such confirmation was necessary for the statement to produce the legal effects of a unilateral act when it had not been refuted after the individual in question had taken office. There was a grey area there at the very least that perhaps warranted the Special Rapporteur's attention.

Cooperation with other bodies (*continued*)*

[Agenda item 11]

Statement by the Observer from the Asian–African Legal Consultative Organization

27. The CHAIRPERSON welcomed Mr. Kamil, Secretary-General of the Asian–African Legal Consultative Organization (AALCO), and invited him to address the Commission.

28. Mr. KAMIL (Asian–African Legal Consultative Organization (AALCO)) said that his organization attached immense significance to its traditional ties with the Commission. One of the organization's primary functions, as envisaged in its statutes, was to examine questions under consideration in the Commission and to ensure that the views of its member States were placed before the Commission. AALCO had held its forty-fourth session at Nairobi, from 27 June to 1 July 2005, during which it had, as at previous sessions, considered an agenda item on the work of the Commission and had mandated him to bring to the attention of the Commission the views expressed by AALCO member States.

29. Concerning diplomatic protection, he said that the States members of AALCO had welcomed the progress achieved on the topic and had observed that the 19 draft articles adopted by the Commission on first reading represented a significant advance in the development of international law,[5] as they covered all aspects of diplomatic protection, an institution that had undergone vast changes over the years.

30. One delegate had observed that the 19 draft articles basically reflected the relevant rules of customary international law. While expressing satisfaction over the progress achieved, the delegate had expressed the hope that the Commission would continue its efforts to improve the draft articles, taking into account the comments offered by States, so as to ensure that the topic could be completed on schedule in 2006.

31. Observations had also been made on individual issues relating to the topic. One delegate had expressed reservations about extending diplomatic protection to stateless persons and refugees, as such a step departed from the traditional rule that only nationals could benefit from diplomatic protection. He had further observed that his delegation's reservations derived also from its reluctance to accept any definition of the term "refugee" that expanded the universally accepted definition set out in the 1951 Convention relating to the Status of Refugees, irrespective of the purpose for which the introduction of a new definition had been proposed.

32. Another delegate had agreed with the general thrust of the draft articles but had underlined that the application of the nationality principle raised a number of difficulties arising from multiple or dual nationality. He had thus supported retention of the traditional continuous nationality rule. One delegate had indicated that a State bore responsibility for injury to an alien caused by its own wrongful act or omission, and that diplomatic protection enabled the State of nationality of the injured persons to secure their protection and obtain reparation for the harm inflicted. He had observed that the 19 draft articles established several legal principles on the subject. The application of diplomatic protection to legal persons, as described in articles 9

* Resumed from the 2851st meeting.

[5] See *Yearbook ... 2004*, vol. II (Part Two), chap. IV, sect. C, pp. 18 *et seq.*

to 13 of the draft, set out a standard principle by virtue of which a corporation was protected by its State of nationality and not by the State of nationality of its shareholders. The State of nationality of the shareholders nevertheless had the right to exercise diplomatic protection, but only under specific conditions, as indicated in article 11. The delegate had been of the view that that draft article adequately balanced the interests of States and those of investors. With regard to the application of diplomatic protection to ships' crews, covered in article 19, the delegate had seconded the Commission's views that both the right of the State of nationality to exercise diplomatic protection and the right of the flag State to seek redress for the crew should be recognized, with priority being accorded to neither. His delegation was of the view that ships' crews should enjoy the maximum protection that international law could offer, especially since the threat of unilateral coercive acts at sea within the framework of Proliferation Security Initiatives and Regional Maritime Security Initiatives could endanger global stability.

33. Another delegate had been of the view that the right to exercise diplomatic protection was a right that accrued to the State as a subject of international law and not a right of individuals or corporations. He had supported the wording of article 10, which stipulated that it was the State that was entitled to exercise diplomatic protection on behalf of its nationals. The article conferred an entitlement upon the State without imposing any obligation upon it. It was the State which had discretion to decide how and when it would apply its right to exercise diplomatic protection on behalf of its nationals.

34. Turning to the topic "Reservations to treaties", he said that comments had been made on a number of specific issues. One delegate had held that the intention of both parties should be taken into account in determining the kind of treaty relationship that existed between the reserving State and the objecting State. Another delegate had observed that the Special Rapporteur's ninth report relating to the object and definition of objections[6] constituted a complement to the eighth report on the formulation of objections to reservations and interpretative declarations.[7] He had welcomed the adoption of five draft guidelines and the commentaries thereto, namely draft guidelines 2.3.5, 2.4.9, 2.4.10, 2.5.12 and 2.5.13.[8] With regard to draft guideline 2.6.1, he had supported the wording prepared by the Commission but preferred the deletion of the words in square brackets.

35. Another delegate had focused on two points: the definition of an objection and the question of which States or international organizations were entitled to formulate objections to a reservation. On the first point, he had observed that his delegation shared the view of the Special Rapporteur that a definition of objections was needed before the Commission could deliberate on their legal effects. Nevertheless, as had already been noted in the Commission, the definition could be revised, if necessary, when the effects of objections had been appropriately formulated. The term "objection" should be defined in the light of the established principles of international law, including the principle of the sovereignty of States. That principle, which formed the basis of the consensual framework defined by the 1969, 1978 and 1986 Vienna Conventions, ensured that States were bound to a treaty obligation only after they had expressed their consent to be bound and that no State could bind another against its will. His delegation believed that objections with "super maximum" effect had no place in international law. Such an effect, which would create a binding relationship between the author of the reservation and the objecting State in respect of the treaty in its entirety, including the provisions to which the reservation had been made, amounted to imposing treaty obligations on a State without its prior consent. It changed the Vienna regime on reservations to treaties and was not in conformity with the general practice of States. As the Commission had indicated in its report, the guidelines were intended to assist States in their practice and must in no way alter the relevant provisions of the Vienna Conventions.[9]

36. On the question of which States or international organizations were entitled to formulate objections, the delegate had been of the view that a reservation and an objection thereto created bilateral legal relations between the reserving State and the objecting State; accordingly, only parties to a treaty were entitled to formulate objections to reservations made to that treaty. That argument was also based on the principle that there should be a balance between the rights and obligations of the parties to a treaty. Signatory States did not have the right to formulate objections because they did not assume all the obligations flowing from the treaty. Moreover, the subject of reservations and objections thereto could vary widely, from substantive issues to purely procedural aspects of the treaty. Therefore, in that delegate's view, it did not seem legally appropriate to give a signatory the right to make objections to reservations when its overall obligation towards the parties to the treaty was limited to refraining from acts that would defeat the object and purpose of the treaty. At most, a signatory State could be entitled to formulate objections to reservations it deemed contrary to the object and purpose of the treaty.

37. Concerning unilateral acts of States, he recalled the Commission's request for comments from States on their practice in that area[10] and noted that one delegate had asked for more details and guidance from the Commission on the information it wished to gather, as the subject was very broad. Another delegate had agreed that the concept of a unilateral act had not been analysed rigorously enough; consequently, the first step should be to consider specific aspects of the topic thoroughly in order to get a picture of State practice and the applicable law. The term "unilateral acts" covered a wide range of legal norms and procedures used by States in conducting their international relations. In addition, in the absence of objective criteria, political acts must be distinguished from legal acts. The delegate had proposed that the Working Group

[6] See 2842nd meeting, footnote 12.

[7] *Ibid.*, footnote 11.

[8] *Yearbook ... 2004*, vol. II (Part Two), chap. IX, sect. C.2, p. 106, para. 295.

[9] *Ibid.*, chap. IX, p. 97, para 251.

[10] *Yearbook ... 2001*, vol. II (Part Two) and corrigendum, p. 19, para. 29 and p. 205, para. 254.

should undertake an in-depth study of the definition and classification of unilateral acts of States.

38. Turning to the topic of international liability for injurious consequences arising out of acts not prohibited by international law, he said that one delegate had observed that the report presented by the Special Rapporteur provided an in-depth analysis of the need to protect the interests of innocent victims of transboundary harm caused by hazardous activities.[11] The scope of the topic and the triggering mechanism should be the same as those relating to the prevention of transboundary harm. In a scheme covering either liability or allocation of loss, the primary liability should be that of the operator, as it was he who controlled the activity and therefore had a duty to redress the harm caused. The same delegate had further stated that the draft presented by the Special Rapporteur was not only innovative but also flexible and propounded a scheme that was without prejudice to the claims that might arise and to the applicable law and procedures. That flexibility was further strengthened by the Special Rapporteur's formulation of "principles" rather than "rules". That approach was to be welcomed, as some of the draft principles had been accepted only in certain sectors and most were in the nature of progressive development of international law.[12] In addition, the proposal advocating compensation for transboundary damage caused to the environment *per se* was not sufficiently supported by State practice to enable general principles to be derived, and it was difficult to quantify such damage in monetary terms or to establish *locus standi*, for example.

39. The same delegate had further observed that the need for technology transfers and capacity-building in developing countries had been recognized in various international instruments and that several multilateral legal instruments acknowledged that different standards should be applied to developing countries in matters of environmental protection. That delegate had stressed that that balancing factor ensured that environmental consensus was viewed as an essential part of the right of States to meet their development needs. The Special Rapporteur's report underscored the importance of that view and acknowledged that the choices made and approaches followed in the draft principles and their implementation might also be influenced by the stage of economic development of the countries concerned.

40. One delegate had supported the idea of prompt and adequate compensation embodied in principle 4. That principle rightly articulated the four prerequisites for guaranteeing such compensation: firstly, a liability regime must be adopted; secondly, such liability should not require proof of fault; thirdly, any conditions or limitations placed on such liability should not erode the requirement of prompt and adequate compensation; and, fourthly, the operator or other person or entity should take out insurance or establish bonds or other financial guarantees to cover compensation claims.

41. With regard to principle 6, the same delegate had been of the view that it was closely linked to principle 4: while principle 4 established States' obligation to provide prompt and adequate compensation, principle 6 indicated the measures that must be taken in order to give effect to principle 4 and to achieve its objective. Access to the domestic procedures that must be available in the event of transboundary damage should be similar to that enjoyed by nationals.

42. One delegate had stressed the complexity of the question of the responsibility of international organizations, observing that, unlike States, which shared certain basic qualities, international organizations varied widely in their structure, functions and competence. It was therefore difficult to formulate and apply a set of common norms that would cover all the entities termed "international organizations". The delegate had noted that, in the commentary to draft article 5, the criterion of "effective control" had been based largely on practice relating to peacekeeping forces.[13] He had said it was unclear whether that criterion could be applied to all situations covered by draft article 5.

43. As to the three questions put by the Special Rapporteur in his third report (A/CN.4/553), one delegate had suggested that a study of the topic should be based as far as possible on in-depth research into the practices followed by various international organizations, but that it should be confined to intergovernmental organizations. Moreover, the Commission should give more weight to the codification of international law than to its progressive development. The "effective control" criterion was an evolving rule that needed to be fleshed out in practice. Lastly, necessity should not be invoked by an international organization as a circumstance precluding wrongfulness.

44. One delegate had observed that some of the expressions used throughout the draft articles, such as "other acts" and "other entities", ought to be clarified.

45. With regard to the subject of the fragmentation of international law, one delegate had expressed the hope that the Study Group's work would have a positive effect on the application of international law and would help to elucidate the relationship of rules stemming from different branches of international law without weakening its basic principles.[14]

46. On the topic of shared natural resources, one delegate had emphasized the need to learn more about transboundary aquifers in general, about particular aquifer conditions and about State practice in the matter. His delegation had taken the view that specific agreements and arrangements were the best way to resolve questions relating to transboundary groundwaters or aquifer systems. On the question of the final form the draft text should take, he agreed with those delegates who had been in favour of a form that was as flexible as possible so as to permit the conclusion of arrangements tailored to individual circumstances.

[11] See *Yearbook ... 2004*, vol. II (Part One), document A/CN.4/540.

[12] For the draft principles and commentaries thereto adopted by the Commission on first reading, see *ibid.*, vol. II (Part Two), paras. 175–176.

[13] See 2839th session, footnote 16.

[14] For the report of the Study Group presented at the fifty-sixth session of the Commission, see *Yearbook ... 2004*, vol. II (Part Two), chap. X, sect. C, pp. 111–119, paras. 300–358.

Recalling that the Convention on the Law of the Non-navigational Uses of International Watercourses had failed to garner enough support to enter into force, he had advocated the adoption of guidelines which States could use when negotiating bilateral or regional agreements.

47. Another delegation had commented that the principle of States' sovereignty over their natural resources should not be overlooked. As the Commission was currently elaborating draft principles on the allocation of loss in case of transboundary harm arising out of hazardous activities and had already adopted draft articles on the responsibility of States for internationally wrongful acts,[15] there seemed to be no need for it to look into the issue of liability and responsibility as part of the topic under consideration. Lastly, the Commission should decide on the final form of the outcome of the topic after progress had been made on substantive matters.

48. Another delegation had pointed to the need to draw up an international legal instrument to guide the use, allocation, preservation and management of aquifers, bearing in mind the non-renewable nature of that resource. It would be useful to examine whether the principles of the Convention on the Law of the Non-navigational Uses of International Watercourses could be applied to non-renewable underground water resources, or whether transboundary aquifers should be governed by a regime akin to those of other natural resources, such as oil or natural gas. Given the sensitive nature of the topic, it would be useful to undertake a comprehensive study of State practice. Lastly, the delegate had suggested that the Commission's work on the subject should take the form of a framework document or guiding principles that would enable States to arrive at appropriate national and regional arrangements.

49. As to the future work of the Commission, one delegation had endorsed the two new topics chosen, namely the effects of armed conflicts on treaties and expulsion of aliens.

50. At its forty-fourth session, AALCO had considered not only the Commission's work but also: (*a*) the deportation of Palestinians and other Israeli practices; (*b*) the jurisdictional immunity of States and their property; (*c*) international terrorism; (*d*) cooperation against trafficking in women and children; (*e*) the International Criminal Court: recent developments; (*f*) an effective international legal instrument against corruption; (*g*) the WTO as a framework agreement and code of conduct for world trade; (*h*) expressions of folklore and its international protection; and (*i*) human rights and Islam. In addition, a special meeting had been devoted to environmental law and sustainable development.

51. In 2006, AALCO would be celebrating its golden jubilee. That celebration would coincide with the inauguration of the organization's permanent headquarters in New Delhi. To mark the occasion, all members of the Commission were invited to attend the forty-fifth session of AALCO. It was to be hoped that, as was customary, a meeting between the members of the Commission and AALCO could be organized after the meeting of AALCO legal advisers and that that meeting would provide an opportunity to intensify collaboration between both bodies.

52. The CHAIRPERSON, speaking on behalf of the Commission, thanked Mr. Kamil for his statement and his invitation.

53. Mr. Sreenivasa RAO thanked Mr. Kamil for his excellent report in which he had provided a very detailed account of the views of AALCO members on various aspects of the Commission's work. That constituted a much appreciated contribution of the African–Asian region to the development of international law. In that connection, he commended the efforts of the Secretary-General of AALCO to encourage French-speaking countries to join his organization.

54. He hoped that in the future AALCO would be able to mobilize the necessary resources for the establishment of working groups to study certain subjects of international law.

55. Mr. GALICKI thanked Mr. Kamil for his presentation and said that he was impressed by the very constructive attitude of AALCO members. Their observations on the form and substance of the questions they had addressed would be of great use in the Commission's work. Given the wide variety of topics considered by AALCO, it was to be hoped that the organization would be able to find the resources needed to establish working groups on topics of interest to both regions. He wished to know if AALCO was planning any initiatives to promote the ratification of regional conventions and treaties.

56. Ms. XUE said that she had found Mr. Kamil's report most interesting and that the comments made by AALCO members on the Commission's work were particularly timely and useful as the Commission prepared to embark on the last year of the current quinquennium.

57. She also drew attention to the publication of the Commission's yearbooks on CD-ROM. Since she knew how difficult it could be for law institutes and universities to obtain such information, she encouraged Mr. Kamil to purchase the CD-ROM in question, provided that doing so would not give rise to copyright problems.

58. Mr. KAMIL (Observer from AALCO), replying to Mr. Sreenivasa Rao, said that his efforts to persuade French-speaking countries to join his organization had not yet met with great success, but he was sure that they would ultimately be fruitful.

59. As for working groups, he was happy to be able to announce that the establishment of six such groups had been proposed at the previous session, a move that could only enhance the quality of the work of AALCO.

60. In response to Mr. Galicki's question, he said that AALCO was currently working on two conventions, one on trafficking in women and children and the other on the respective rights of the countries of origin and host countries of migrant workers.

[15] See 2838th session, footnote 5.

61. Lastly, he thanked the members of the Commission for their warm welcome and the interest they showed in the work of AALCO.

62. Mr. MIKULKA (Secretary to the Commission) said that the circulation of the Commission's yearbooks on CD-ROM still posed copyright problems, but it was hoped that all that documentation would be accessible on the Internet in the near future.

The meeting rose at 1.10 p.m.

2854th MEETING

Wednesday, 20 July 2005, at 10.05 a.m.

Chairperson: Mr. Djamchid MOMTAZ

Present: Mr. Addo, Mr. Al-Marri, Mr. Brownlie, Mr. Candioti, Mr. Chee, Mr. Comissário Afonso, Mr. Daoudi, Mr. Dugard, Mr. Economides, Ms. Escarameia, Mr. Fomba, Mr. Gaja, Mr. Galicki, Mr. Kabatsi, Mr. Kamto, Mr. Kateka, Mr. Kemicha, Mr. Kolodkin, Mr. Koskenniemi, Mr. Mansfield, Mr. Matheson, Mr. Niehaus, Mr. Pellet, Mr. Sreenivasa Rao, Mr. Rodríguez Cedeño, Mr. Sepúlveda, Ms. Xue, Mr. Yamada.

Unilateral acts of states (*continued*) (A/CN.4/549 and Add.1, sect. C and A/CN.4/557)

[Agenda item 5]

EIGHTH REPORT OF THE SPECIAL RAPPORTEUR (*continued*)

1. Mr. FOMBA thanked the Special Rapporteur for his eighth report on unilateral acts of States (A/CN.4/557), which would serve as a useful basis for the Commission's further work. Before commenting in detail on the report, he wished to provide information on the statement made by the Head of State of the Republic of Mali, in connection with the territorial dispute between Burkina Faso and Mali, considered by the ICJ as the case concerning the *Frontier Dispute (Burkina Faso/Republic of Mali)*, in a judgment dated 22 December 1986. He regretted that he had been unable to provide the promised input to the Working Group on the subject, owing to difficulties in obtaining the relevant documentation in his capital.

2. Following an armed conflict between the two countries, which had broken out on 14 December 1974, appeals had been launched for conciliation, notably by the President of the Organization of African Unity. In January 1975, the Organization's Mediation Commission had formed a Legal Sub-Commission whose role was to draw up an initial proposal for submission to the Mediation Commission comprising an outline solution. On 11 April 1975, the Head of State of Mali had made the following statement during an interview with Agence France-Presse:

> Mali extends over 1,240,000 square kilometres, and we cannot justify fighting for a scrap of territory 150 kilometres long. Even if the Organization of African Unity Commission decides objectively that the frontier line passes through Bamako, my Government will comply with the decision. (para. 36 of the judgment)

3. On 14 June 1975, the Legal Sub-Commission had presented its report to the Mediation Commission and had suggested that the parties should accept the implementation of the principle of the intangibility of colonial frontiers; the use for that purpose of texts and maps; and specific proposals for the frontier line. On 17 and 18 June 1975, the Mediation Commission had met with the two Heads of State, and had adopted a final communiqué whereby the two States undertook to bring their dispute to an end on the basis of the Mediation Commission's recommendations, and agreed to the establishment of a neutral technical committee to determine the location of certain villages, to reconnoitre the frontier, and to make proposals for its materialization to the Mediation Commission. On 10 July 1975, the Heads of State had met again, and in a joint declaration had welcomed the efforts made and the results achieved by the Mediation Commission and had affirmed their common intention to do their utmost to transcend the results, especially by facilitating the delimitation of the frontier between the two States in order to place the final seal on their reconciliation. The technical committee had been unable to fulfil its function, and despite further contacts between the parties, that was how matters had remained until the conclusion of the Special Agreement by which the case had been brought before the ICJ.

4. With regard to the legal positions of the two parties and areas of agreement, they had agreed in the first place that the Mediation Commission had not been a jurisdictional body and had lacked the power to take legally binding decisions. In the second place, they had agreed that the Mediation Commission had never actually completed its work, since it had not formally taken note of the reports of its subcommissions, and had submitted no definitive overall solution for consideration by the parties in the context of its mediating functions.

5. As for areas of disagreement, Burkina Faso had argued that there had been acquiescence by Mali in the solutions outlined in that context, on three grounds. First, the final communiqué of 27 December 1974 setting up the Mediation Commission must be considered as a genuine international agreement binding upon the States parties. Second, while admitting that the Mediation Commission had not been empowered to render binding decisions, Burkina Faso had alleged that the report of the Legal Sub-Commission, endorsed by the summit meeting of Heads of State in June 1975, had become binding for Mali because it had proclaimed itself already bound by the report which might have been made by the Mediation Commission, by virtue of the declaration made by the President of Mali on 11 April 1975. Third, Burkina Faso had also argued that the effect of the final communiqué of 18 June 1975, which had emanated from the enlarged Mediation Commission, and had also been an international agreement which the parties were bound to observe, had been to reinforce Mali's obligations in the matter.

6. Mali had challenged that interpretation of the statement of its President on two counts. First, the Mediation Commission would have to have had a power of decision, which had not legally been the case. Second, it claimed that its President's comments had merely been a witticism of the kind regularly uttered at press conferences which had implied no more than that Mali had been anxious to consider the Mediation Commission's recommendations with good will and in good faith. Mali had also challenged Burkina Faso's interpretation of the final communiqué of 18 June 1975 on three grounds. First, the Mediation Commission had not, strictly speaking, made any recommendation. Second, the Heads of State had not accepted any predetermined line; on the contrary, in entrusting a neutral technical committee with the task of determining the position of certain villages, reconnoitring the frontier and making proposals to the Mediation Commission for its materialization, they had instructed that committee to produce new proposals, which in Mali's opinion indicated that the proposals of the subcommissions had not been final.

7. The Court's position had been that the statement of 11 April 1975 had not been made during negotiations or talks between the two parties. At most, it had taken the form of a unilateral act by the Government of Mali. Such declarations concerning legal or factual situations might indeed have the effect of creating legal obligations for the State on whose behalf they were made, but it all depended on the intention of the State in question. In the case in point there had been nothing to hinder the parties from manifesting an intention to accept the binding character of the conclusions of the Organization of African Unity Mediation Commission by the normal method: a formal agreement on the basis of reciprocity. Since no agreement of that kind had been concluded between the parties, the Chamber of the Court had found that there were no grounds to interpret the declaration made by Mali's Head of State as a unilateral act with legal implications (para. 40 of the judgment).

8. In conclusion, he noted, first, that even if the statement was considered merely a witticism, it could not be denied that it raised the substantive issue of good will and good faith. Second, it should be borne in mind that in Mali there was a long-established cultural tradition of keeping one's word, which was considered a sacred obligation. Third, the statement was a perfect illustration of the risk of a State being entrapped by its own words, referred to by Mr. Pellet at the previous meeting. Lastly, it would have been useful to have had an opportunity to analyse the statement on the basis of the criteria identified by the Mediation Commission.

9. Turning to the report, Mr. Fomba said that the examples of State practice analysed were sufficiently representative and that the Special Rapporteur's conclusions would help to establish some basic principles. Concerning the form of the examples analysed, the Special Rapporteur had drawn two basic conclusions: first, that the examples took a wide variety of forms; second, that the form was relatively unimportant in determining whether one was dealing with a unilateral legal act of the type in which the Commission was interested, namely, one which produced legal effects on its own. However, there seemed to be some contradiction between the statement in paragraph 170 of the report that the formality of the act had a role to play in determining the intent of its author, and the statement in the same paragraph that the form could have an impact insofar as the statement might be considered to produce legal effects. The most important conclusion to be drawn was that the variety in form established a principle based on respect for the sovereignty, will and freedom of expression of States.

10. On the criterion of authorship, the Special Rapporteur noted that the authors of the acts were exclusively States; hence, it would seem advisable to establish the principle of the exclusive right of States to formulate unilateral acts, pending later consideration of the case of international organizations.

11. The addressees of such acts were also varied, with different possible combinations, which might give rise to specific problems depending on the type of addressee concerned. The instrumental consequence would be to enshrine the principle of diversity of addressees in any future legal regime for unilateral acts. He endorsed the analogy drawn by the Special Rapporteur in paragraph 172 of the report concerning the possibility of transferring the provision relating to the capacity of the State to conclude treaties, contained in article 6 of the 1969 Vienna Convention, to any legal regime on unilateral acts that might be established.

12. As indicated in paragraph 175 of the report, not all of the acts examined had a single origin; some were compound, which was important when interpreting their contents and the subjective factors associated with the consent of the State formulating the acts to be bound by them. The instrumental consequence would be to enshrine that diversity, as in the law of treaties, along with the principles of sovereignty and of unity of representation and expression of will and consent of the State.

13. On the question of who was competent to represent and to commit the State by formulating unilateral acts, the Special Rapporteur referred in paragraph 180 of the report to the Vienna treaty regime and rightly reaffirmed the capacity of the Head of State or Government and the Minister for Foreign Affairs in such matters. As for the issue raised in paragraph 181, he was in favour of the application of the 1969 Vienna Convention, *mutatis mutandis*, taking into account the specific characteristics of unilateral acts and hence the possibility of including other persons authorized to formulate them.

14. With regard to the criterion of context, the Special Rapporteur noted in paragraph 182 that almost all of the acts in question were connected in some way with negotiations on a specific issue. That underscored their importance, along with or in relation to conventions, in the peaceful settlement of disputes between States.

15. In terms of how to qualify the acts, some were clearly unilateral, while others might be considered differently, as illustrated in paragraphs 183–188 of the report. The question was to what extent the results of the analysis would help to systematically identify the nature of such acts or types of conduct.

16. In paragraph 189, the Special Rapporteur drew attention to some of the most difficult aspects of the topic: the validity of the act, its possible invalidation and the capacity and competence of the author. A comparative analysis of articles 6, 7, 26, 27 and 46 of the 1969 Vienna Convention would be useful in relation to the question of the hierarchy and distribution of competences between international and internal law in formulating and implementing international State commitments.

17. Another important question was how to determine the moment at which an act produced legal effects. According to paragraph 194 of the report, in the cases considered it seemed difficult to determine that moment, although the situation was not always very clear, as was borne out by the *Nuclear Tests* decisions.

18. As far as modification or revocation were concerned, in paragraph 198 the Special Rapporteur noted that on the whole the content of the acts examined had been maintained; however, that should not be interpreted as prejudging the issue of the right to modify or revoke such acts in future.

19. With regard to the conduct of a State that did not constitute a unilateral act *stricto sensu*, in paragraph 203 the Special Rapporteur noted that such conduct might produce relevant legal effects, based on the findings of the ICJ in the *Temple of Preah Vihear* case. However, that was a separate issue and must be treated as such.

20. On the subject of estoppel, silence and acquiescence, in paragraphs 204 and 205 the Special Rapporteur recalled the extremely close relationship between the various forms of State conduct and gave a good description of the mechanism of the legal scope of silence.

21. Lastly, he endorsed the conclusions set out in paragraphs 207 and 208 of the report.

22. Mr. CANDIOTI thanked the Special Rapporteur for his eighth report, and the Working Group for its valuable contribution to the study of the topic. He welcomed the compilation of examples of State practice provided in the report, especially given the scant response thus far by States to the Commission's repeated requests for information on the matter. The report provided a further opportunity to establish what forms of State conduct produced legal effects, *inter alia*, with a view to warning States about the risks of engaging in certain unilateral acts or types of conduct at the international level.

23. In paragraphs 168 *et seq.* of the report the Special Rapporteur highlighted the importance of determining whether the examples of unilateral acts of a State produced legal effects at the international level on their own and, if so, exactly what such effects were. He suggested that the conclusions might form the basis of a document to be prepared by the Working Group for submission to the sixty-first session of the United Nations General Assembly in 2006, reflecting a measure of consensus on the Commission's study of the topic since 1996. Such a document might be along the lines of the Commission's preliminary conclusions on reservations to treaties adopted at its forty-ninth session and submitted to the General Assembly in 1997.[1]

24. In his view there were sufficient objective grounds for consensus among the members of the Commission to enable such preliminary conclusions to be drafted. He rejected the persistent assertion by certain members that unilateral acts of States did not exist. For centuries, international maritime law had recognized States' entitlement to determine unilaterally the extent of its territorial sea, conduct which must be qualified as a unilateral act that produced legal effects. Moreover, over the years the Commission had successfully dealt in the context of treaty law with certain legal acts, such as reservations, objections and denunciation, which could also be seen as unilateral acts that produced legal effects and were regulated and recognized by international law. Many of the members of the Commission and other eminent jurists exercised their profession at the ICJ, where their work was often predicated on a unilateral act—that of the acceptance of the optional clause recognizing the binding jurisdiction of the Court under article 36 of the Court's Statute. No State was obliged to accept that clause; acceptance thereof was a unilateral act in its form, content and nature, which had substantial legal consequences. Any denial of the existence of unilateral acts was therefore not borne out by the facts.

25. The discussion had possibly generated a basis for an objective consensus on some general conclusions which it might be wise to enunciate at that stage in order to structure the Commission's work, even if it might subsequently prove necessary to narrow down the study of the phenomena constituting lawful unilateral acts producing legal effects.

26. It might first be concluded that international law attributed legal effects to certain types of lawful act or conduct of States without the need for any reaction on the part of another subject of international law. Another conclusion might explain that, as shown by the examples offered by the Special Rapporteur, such unilateral conduct could consist in acts through which the State expressly manifested its will, or in other types of conduct by the State which had legal effects. The tacit acceptance of reservations under the 1969 Vienna Convention was an example of conduct of that kind. Silence and acquiescence were also recognized and regulated by international law. The absence of a manifestation of will at the time at which an act entailing legal consequences took place had frequently been recognized in international case law.

27. A third conclusion could convey the idea that unilateral acts of States might be in written or unwritten form and comprise one or more actions or omissions. A further conclusion might be that the legal effects of the unilateral act or unilateral conduct of a State could consist in a State's acceptance of an international obligation, the preservation or affirmation of a right, the waiver of a right by that State or the recognition of a right of another subject of international law. The State could perform all those acts of itself, without another State's assistance and irrespective of another State's will.

[1] *Yearbook ... 1997*, vol. II (Part Two), pp. 56–57, para. 157.

28. A fifth conclusion could be that, given the great variety of lawful unilateral conduct by States which might produce legal effects, the characterization of conduct by a State as a unilateral legal act would, in each case, depend crucially on the specific circumstances in which that conduct had taken place. For that reason, it would be advisable to follow Ms. Escarameia's proposal to provide a list of examples of the main factors and circumstances which had to be borne in mind for the purposes of characterizing that unilateral conduct as an act capable of producing legal effects.

29. One last conclusion might be that, in accordance with the principle of good faith and in the interests of international stability, security and cooperation, States must maintain a position which was compatible and consistent with their unilateral legal acts, honour the obligations they might have assumed by virtue of those acts, and respect the trust and legitimate expectations created thereby.

30. After 10 years of debate, the time had come for the Commission to present some results to the General Assembly. A set of general preliminary conclusions along the lines of those Mr. Candioti had just suggested would help to decide what direction the treatment of the topic should take in the future.

31. Mr. BROWNLIE said that, while he agreed with many of Mr. Candioti's suggestions regarding the Commission's possible approach to the topic in the future, he had raised a canard in asserting that many of his colleagues denied the existence of unilateral acts. He himself was the author of a textbook which since 1966 had contained a chapter on such acts.[2]

32. The phrase "unilateral acts" was a useful way of referring succinctly to the subject matter and that was why it had been included in the Commission's agenda in that form. It was not, however, a very helpful analytical model because, obviously, although a unilateral act was a necessary threshold, it was not sufficient; a State could not create relations with other States off its own bat. States' freedom of action was subject to the rights of other States. Obligations could not be imposed on other States by a unilateral act. A unilateral act was therefore a mechanism triggering the possibility that, in the right context, that act might have legal consequences for other States. No act was ever, strictly speaking, unilateral, otherwise it would have no legal effect; it would be a non-entity. That was what he meant when he said that unilateral acts, as such, did not exist.

33. The whole culture of unilateral acts was politically and qualitatively very different from that of treaties. With a few rare exceptions, when a treaty was concluded, a State knew that it had made a treaty in a political and legal milieu in which that instrument would be readily recognized. Problems of interpretation might arise but, by and large, the act had taken place within a recognized legal milieu. In the case of unilateral acts, with the possible exception of forms of renunciation, no such milieu existed. It was therefore not surprising that States had not provided examples of State practice, because until some third-party determining body dealt with the regulation and recognition of the putative unilateral act, it was unclear whether it existed or not. Hence the examples given involved *ex post facto* validation of unilateral acts: until the third-party authority took such action, the unilateral act went unrecognized. The subject matter was completely different from that of the law of treaties. If the Commission confused the two, it would not contribute to the progressive development of international law.

34. Mr. PELLET observed that the debate seemed to be going round in circles. Mr. Brownlie was mistaken on two important points: first, it was not true that States could not impose obligations on other States by means of unilateral acts. Mr. Candioti had provided the excellent example of the determination of the extent of the territorial sea. Those were unilateral acts in accordance with international law and they produced effects applicable to all States, even though, in order for them to do so, special authorization was required. Nevertheless, in the absence of such authorization, States could themselves enter into an obligation *vis-à-vis* other specified States or the international community as a whole, as had been confirmed by the judgments in the *Nuclear Tests* case and the *Frontier Dispute (Burkina Faso/Mali)* case to which Mr. Fomba had referred. That obligation was a legal effect, whatever Mr. Brownlie might say. Hence unilateral acts existed and produced effects.

35. Second, Mr. Brownlie had contradicted himself by saying that the topic did not lend itself to codification although he regarded unilateral acts of States as a threshold. The fundamental purpose of discussing the subject was to decide how to determine that threshold and at what point in time the unilateral conduct of a State bound that State and imposed obligations on it and, possibly, on other States. The subject existed, if only because it was necessary to try to find that threshold.

36. Mr. CANDIOTI said he wished to make it clear that he had never implied that unilateral acts should be equated with the law of treaties. On the contrary, it would be completely wrong to try to use the law of treaties as the basis for establishing rules on unilateral acts. Nor did he believe that the law of treaties was the sole branch of international law in existence, or that a unilateral act produced legal effects only when it was recognized by another subject of international law. Customary international law and the general principles of international law indeed attributed legal effects to some kinds of unilateral conduct.

37. Mr. BROWNLIE explained that his previous statement had not applied to everything that Mr. Candioti had said, but only to his analysis of what was meant by the affirmation that unilateral acts did not exist. In response to Mr. Pellet's reference to the law of the sea and a State's ability to bind other States by extending its territorial sea or creating a new economic zone, he wished to point out that a State could not adopt measures of that nature unilaterally, since such action was subject to international law. The judgment in the *Nottebohm* case had drawn an important analogy with the territorial sea in the context of nationality law. Similarly, the *Fisheries (United Kingdom* v. *Norway)* case had established that it was possible to extend the territorial sea only subject to and in keeping

[2] Brownlie, *op. cit.* (2846th meeting, footnote 8).

with the conditions of general international law (p. 143 of the judgment).

38. The CHAIRPERSON, speaking as a member of the Commission, drew attention to the fact that the content of treaties, like that of unilateral acts, had to be in accordance with international law, for example with *jus cogens*.

39. Mr. KOSKENNIEMI, responding to Mr. Pellet's comments on the circular nature of the debate, said that he personally felt it was moving forward. He agreed with Mr. Brownlie that unilateral acts did exist in some sense, and emphasized that he himself had never asserted that unilateral acts did not exist. It was therefore legitimate for lawyers to discuss them. He would, however, hesitate to go so far as to assert that they were a kind of legal institution.

40. While all the members of the Commission seemed now to agree that unilateral acts did exist, they were unable to agree on the existence of a threshold making it possible to identify in international legal reality and in the behaviour of States those types of conduct which constituted unilateral acts. In some sense it was possible to say that a threshold existed. It was constituted by good faith, equity and reasonableness, which were covered in German jurisprudence by the term *Vertrauensschutz* (the protection of legitimate expectations).

41. Why, then, was it not possible to codify that threshold? The threshold in the law of treaties had been codified, but when it came to unilateral acts such a process would necessarily involve using language that was completely indeterminate and open-ended. If the Commission wished to describe the situation with regard to the Ihlen Declaration and the *Nuclear Tests* and *Temple of Preah Vihear* cases in terms of a threshold, the result would be a threshold that was so open-ended as to be useless.

42. The point was not that there was no such thing as unilateral acts, or that they were impossible to codify, but that such action would be inadvisable, because that category of acts was not defined in a way that lent itself to such predetermination. That was probably what Mr. Brownlie had meant when he had held that unilateral acts were identified *ex post facto* by courts. When Mr. Ihlen had made his unfortunate declaration, he had not been formulating an act, he had been saying something off the top of his head, but later on, when the dispute arose, his words had been interpreted in such a way that Norway could no longer retract the declaration. Nonetheless, when Mr. Ihlen had uttered those words, there had been no predetermined threshold. That they were regarded as a unilateral act was an *ex post facto* construction of a court.

43. Mr. CHEE recalled that the *Fisheries (United Kingdom* v. *Norway)* case had involved a crucial issue, as the use of the straight baseline method had led to a substantial expansion of the territorial sea into an area where British fishermen had been operating, so that their vital interests were at stake. Nevertheless the Court had ruled in favour of Norway's practice, *inter alia* on the grounds that the United Kingdom had not entered a protest and that the practice had long been tolerated by the international community. He therefore considered that the wider implications of the case should be borne in mind, namely, that the Court had upheld a unilateral act (p. 139 of the judgment).

44. Mr. PELLET welcomed the newly enlightened position adopted by Mr. Koskenniemi and said that the very purposes of discussing unilateral acts were to prevent a situation where the determination of a threshold occurred *ex post facto* in a haphazard fashion and also to provide States and courts with guidance as to when persons such as Mr. Ihlen were likely to be entrapped by their words, which would subsequently be treated as an expression of a State's will. He was personally not convinced that a unilateral act could be determined only *ex post facto*. That was the current situation only because international law as yet provided no other mechanisms. The solution was therefore to codify the case law in the matter.

45. He was puzzled by Mr. Brownlie's understanding of the term "unilateral". It did not mean "autonomous". It meant that one State or one side took an initiative. That did not signify that such action did not come within the realm of international law. Clearly unilateral acts produced legal effects because there was a rule of international law allowing them to do so. As the Chairperson had pointed out, the same was true of treaties in accordance with the principle of customary international law that *pacta sunt servanda*, under which treaties were binding. Similarly there was a rule that *acta sunt servanda*, even if the conditions applying to such acts were harder to grasp.

46. He failed to follow the Chairperson's reasoning when he had said that treaties must comply with *jus cogens*. That was a question of content, whereas the Commission was considering the basis for unilateral acts. Unilateral acts must certainly comply with *jus cogens*, but the key issue was why they were binding. The reason was that there was a rule or rules, for example, those of the law of the sea, which made them binding in the same way as treaties; that was known as a rule of authorization.

47. Mr. KAMTO said that the longer the debate progressed, the more confused it became. While he welcomed the fact that some members of the Commission had come round to recognizing the existence of unilateral acts, they seemed to have done so only in order to prove that they could not be codified. The existence of unilateral acts had, however, been sufficiently demonstrated. It was time to structure the Commission's work by distinguishing in international law between unilateral acts validated by authorization and autonomous unilateral acts where the State formulated the act without the authorization conferred by another international legal act. When a State determined the external limits of its territorial sea, it did so upon the authorization of a treaty or convention. On the other hand, the Ihlen Declaration was an example of an act which had not been solicited by the other party, yet which had been made by the representative of a State. It was a unilateral declaration not based on any other international legal act making that declaration possible.

48. On the basis of that distinction, it might be possible to say that, in the first case, the issue raised was one of validity. If one act depended on another, it would be necessary to ascertain the validity of the second act

in the light of the first and of general international law. Had the act been formulated in accordance with the rules or criteria laid down by the act authorizing it? Were the effects it produced consonant with that act or with general international law?

49. In the second case, it seemed that the issue turned on whether it was a legal act and on its validity. In order to reply to those questions, it was necessary to define the criteria for legality of the act, and that was what the Special Rapporteur was trying to do. Had the act been formulated by a person with the capacity to do so under international law? Had that person formulated the act with the intention to bind the State? Had he expressed the will of the State? Once those questions had been answered and it had been ascertained that the act in question might indeed be a legal act, the next issue was whether it was valid under international law by virtue of respecting other principles of international law, whether general or specific to the area in which the unilateral act had been formulated. Of course, there were many other criteria, such as the addressee of the act, but if the Commission's work could be structured along the lines he had suggested, perhaps more rapid progress could be made in its deliberations.

50. Mr. BROWNLIE said that Mr. Chee had drawn a conclusion which was not borne out by the *Fisheries (United Kingdom* v. *Norway)* case. The United Kingdom, as applicant State, had asked for a declaratory judgment as to whether the Norwegian State baseline system was or was not in accordance with general international law. The Court had found that it was indeed valid in accordance with the principles of general international law. Judge Hackworth had been the only member of the Court to hold, in a separate opinion, that the system's compliance with international law depended on British recognition (p. 144 of the judgment).

51. While he greatly appreciated Mr. Kamto's analysis of the question, it was built on the metaphor of a threshold. In fact, what he had said earlier was that an original unilateral act—a trigger mechanism—was a necessary but not a sufficient element. The main question was, what were the sufficient elements producing a legal result, in other words an act which was not only necessary, but sufficient. There were a huge variety of such elements. International law did not require a particular form and great uncertainty prevailed. If the Commission tried to legislate in that sphere, it could make matters worse.

52. Ms. ESCARAMEIA said it had become clear, particularly from the latest comments by Mr. Brownlie, that the issue was whether a unilateral act produced legal effects of itself, or whether it was simply a trigger mechanism. Reactions by third parties were necessary before one could determine that legal effects had been produced. It would then be the trigger mechanism, in addition to the reactions of third parties, that produced legal effects, something that would become apparent only *ex post facto*, and probably only in a decision by a court.

53. It was true, as Mr. Brownlie had pointed out, that treaties sometimes predetermined what the reactions of States would be: on the extent of a territorial sea, for example, or the exploitation of an exclusive economic zone. On the other hand, case law revealed that whenever courts dealt with a unilateral act, the date they assigned to it was not the date on which the legal effects had been produced, but rather the date on which the act had been formulated. Accordingly, in the practice of the courts, a legal act existed whenever a State expressed its will unilaterally. The next step was to find out what factors conferred the status of a unilateral act on the expressed will of the State. That was what the Commission was attempting to do. Some members thought it would be useful to look at how treaties predetermined such factors, while others thought that approach a waste of time.

54. Ms. XUE said that although the topic of unilateral acts of States had been on the Commission's agenda for some time, the current discussion showed that it was still debating the very basic issue of whether the topic was necessary or suitable for codification. Doubts had been expressed as to whether unilateral acts existed as a legal institution or concept in the international legal order. While it might be true that, unlike the situation with treaties, diplomatic protection or State responsibility, the concept of unilateral acts of States did not clearly connote a legal context, that did not mean that there was no need for a meaningful legal study of the concept.

55. As State practice, court decisions and arbitral awards had demonstrated time and time again, under certain circumstances some unilateral acts of States were seen as having produced binding effects, both on the acting State itself and, in some cases, on other States as well. As they were taken by the acting State itself, such acts could not be regarded as involuntary. On the other hand, their consequences might result in a situation where the acting State was bound by its own acts. Such consequences might be anticipated by the acting State or might take it by surprise. Hence the belief that it was necessary to spell out the conditions under which binding effects might be produced in order to avoid such surprises and make State relations more stable and predictable. If a State did not intend to produce binding effects, it should avoid certain acts or take action to prevent such legal effects from being produced. Against that background, the present study was useful.

56. Of course, a policy consideration was also involved. As the Special Rapporteur pointed out in paragraph 3 of his report, during the discussions in the Sixth Committee Member States had emphasized that "[t]he Commission should offer a clear definition of unilateral acts of States capable of producing legal effects, with sufficient flexibility to leave States a timely margin for manoeuvre in order to be able to carry out their political acts". As Mr. Brownlie had remarked, the effects of unilateral acts were *ex post facto*: sometimes they were intended by States but often they were not. In the latter situation, the question arose to what extent States should be given a "timely margin" for political manoeuvre. In that sense, every State's interests were at stake.

57. While unilateral acts had so far been deemed to produce legal effects, thus involving the assumption of legal obligations, the cases presented in the report revealed another type of situation, in which the effects produced were not legal but were nonetheless binding on the acting

State. Commitments by nuclear-weapon States not to use nuclear weapons against non-nuclear-weapon States, for example, were undertaken intentionally without legal effects. They were political in nature and made as part of an agreement in the context of the Nuclear Non-Proliferation Treaty process. The Commission might opt to exclude that type of case from the scope of its study, targeting only those with legal effects, but such a policy direction might miss the objective that the Commission was aiming at. After all, the whole issue of unilateral acts was about good faith and predictability based thereon.

58. Concerning the form, she shared the doubts expressed by some members over the Special Rapporteur's conclusion that the form was relatively unimportant in determining whether the unilateral act was one that could produce legal effects on its own without the need for its acceptance or for any other reaction on the part of the addressee. The *Nuclear Tests* case adduced in support of that conclusion was neither conclusive nor exhaustive. Other cases could be found in which the binding effects of the unilateral act of a State might depend on the response of the addressee. Since the analysis of unilateral acts was mostly contextual and circumstantial, the form for carrying out such acts and the relations between the author and addressee could vary considerably from case to case, proving decisive in some cases but not in others for determining the binding effects of the acts concerned. Of 11 cases outlined in the report, three—those of Colombia (paras. 13–35), Jordan (paras. 44–54) and the Truman Proclamation (paras. 127–137)—involved domestic legal procedure, but the relevant practice pointed in three different directions. While it was impossible to say which was normal and which was exceptional, one thing was clear: political circumstances played a decisive role regarding the effects of the acts in each case. Thus, the Commission was faced with contextual uncertainty.

59. As to the second conclusion drawn by the Special Rapporteur, namely, that the authors of unilateral acts were States, she said that by the very nature of the topic, it was acts of States and not of other entities that were being considered. It was somewhat surprising that it had taken the Commission so long to reach that conclusion. Her concern was not with the conclusion itself but rather with the analysis that followed, which gave the general impression that the Special Rapporteur's approach was still very much affected by treaty regimes (para. 171 *et seq.*). The core issue with unilateral acts was whether an obligation or binding effects were created, not to whom such an obligation could and should be owed, although that issue was not totally irrelevant.

60. In short, the study of unilateral acts could provide useful guidance for States in conducting their foreign relations. In considering the issues involved, the Commission must not lose sight of the political context within which legal rules operated. As to the next step to be taken, she understood the reservations expressed concerning the Special Rapporteur's proposal that the Commission should consider some of the draft articles separately from the study of practice, and thought that the suggestion made by Mr. Candioti regarding the preparation of a set of general preliminary conclusions deserved serious consideration.

Reservations to treaties (*continued*)* (A/CN.4/549 and Add.1, sect. D, A/CN.4/558 and Corr.1 and Add.1 [and Corr.1]–2, and A/CN.4/L.665)

[Agenda item 6]

Tenth report of the Special Rapporteur

61. Mr. PELLET (Special Rapporteur), introducing his tenth report on reservations to treaties (A/CN.4/558 and Corr.1 and Add.1 [and Corr.1]–2), said he owed the Commission both explanations and apologies. The document before the Commission constituted only a portion of his tenth report, and it had initially been intended to form an even smaller portion. Brimming with good intentions, he had planned to submit a report with three separate components: an introduction which, in the usual way, would have summed up the reception given to the previous report and recent developments concerning reservations to treaties; a first part, which would have dispatched once and for all the problem of formulation, in other words how to define the form and procedure for objections to and acceptance of reservations; and a second part, on the validity of reservations.

62. He had launched into the work with vigor, beginning with the formulation of objections, a logical extension of his previous two reports devoted wholly or partly to the definition of objections. A new development had intervened, however: in the context of an article-by-article commentary on the 1969 Vienna Convention undertaken by the Université Libre de Bruxelles, he had had to give priority to a major academic work involving commentaries on several articles dealing with reservations. He had commented in particular on article 19 of the 1969 Vienna Convention and of the 1986 Vienna Convention on the Law of Treaties between States and International Organizations or between International Organizations, which dealt with the validity of reservations, the very problem to which he had proposed to devote the second part of his tenth report.

63. The Commission was not a university, and he could hardly serve it up a warmed-up version of his commentary on article 19 in lieu of a report. He had accordingly chosen to adapt those commentaries, an exercise that had proved more time-consuming than he had expected. He had finally had to admit that he would be unable to respect the ambitious deadline he had set himself and had had to choose between completing his work on the formulation and acceptance of objections and leaving for happier times the more interesting question of validity of reservations, or giving priority to the validity of reservations, with the danger that nothing would be ready in time.

64. He had gambled on the second course of action, but had lost his bet: not only had he been unable to finish either the introduction or the first part of his report, but he had also left the submission of the second part until too late, with the result that only sections A and B had been translated into all working languages of the Commission. He was informed by the Secretariat that section D would not become available in all languages until after the end of the session. Even though the Secretariat had adopted

* Resumed from the 2842nd meeting.

the laudable policy of furnishing documents in their original language—in the present case, French—in advance of their issuance in all other languages, it would obviously be impossible to discuss the report in its entirety at the current session, for while English was a working language for nearly all members of the Commission, the same was not true of the native language of Molière, Georges Scelle and Paul Reuter.

65. All that was by way of explanation and apology for the rather abrupt opening of the document before the Commission, which had originally been intended as the concluding part of a much longer report. The Commission would nevertheless have grist for its mill.

66. In sections A and B now before the Commission, he had first sought to defend the expression "validity of reservations" before addressing, in section A, the principle derived from the chapeau of article 19 of the 1969 and 1986 Vienna Conventions, namely, presumption of validity of reservations, and going on to discuss the problems raised by the express or implicit prohibition of reservations, covered in subparagraphs (*a*) and (*b*) of that article.

67. Section C of his report related to the absolutely crucial requirement of compatibility of reservations with the object and purpose of the treaty, as called for in article 19 (*c*). That also provided an opportunity for an in-depth discussion of several difficult issues, including the validity or invalidity of reservations relating to the application of internal law, vague and general reservations, and reservations relating to provisions embodying customary rules or setting forth rules of *jus cogens*. In section D of his report, he addressed such questions as how to determine the validity of reservations and the consequences thereof; who was able to assess that validity; and what were the consequences of a reservation that, once formulated, was found to be invalid.

68. Returning to sections A and B and to the sometimes disputed phrase that he had chosen as the title, namely, "Validity of reservations", he recalled that in view of the difficulties raised by the expression, he had proposed that the Commission should request the views of States in the Sixth Committee on the matter. The Commission had done so,[3] but as was often the case, the results of that consultation were not particularly illuminating for two reasons.

69. First, the responses from States had shown that they were nearly evenly split between those that had doubts about the word "validity" and those that accepted it. Second, delegates had taken advantage of the opportunity to review the entire legal regime for reservations (A/CN.4/549, paras. 101–112), an exercise that was not without interest but went beyond the confines of the work which, to his mind, consisted in finding the most neutral formulation, one which prejudged in no way, or as little as possible, the legal regime to be applicable to reservations or to the various categories thereof, should the Commission resign itself to the fact that several categories existed.

70. That was precisely why the words "validity/invalidity" and "valid/invalid" were infinitely more acceptable than their rivals, "admissibility/inadmissibility", "permissibility/impermissibility" and "opposability/non-opposability". The reason he sought to revert to the terminology he had initially used, namely, "validity", was that it was entirely neutral, whereas the three rival expressions had strong doctrinal connotations and were thus unnecessarily assertive.

71. The great doctrinal battle on the question of reservations pitted the proponents of permissibility, who thought a reservation could be intrinsically invalid by being contrary to the object or purpose of the treaty, against the advocates of opposability, for whom the reservations regime was governed in its entirety by the reactions of other States. One could speak of the objective and subjective schools. It thus seemed obvious that in using one or the other of those expressions, the Commission would be taking a position in favour of one or the other of those schools, a state of affairs that was not terminologically necessary, since a more neutral term, "validity", existed. There was some truth in the arguments for its equivalents, although neither did justice to the complex reality of the legal regime of reservations.

72. Sir Derek Bowett, the undisputed leader of the "permissibility" school, had urged the Commission to use that terminology. For his own part, however, he was not sure that the Commission had been right in following Bowett's lead and adopting the term "permissible" to describe reservations that raised no problems in terms of validity and the term "impermissible" for those that did (see paragraphs 4–5 of the report). A reservation could be valid or invalid on grounds of permissibility but also for other reasons, and it did not seem wise for the Commission to tie its own hands by resorting to doctrinally partisan terminology.

73. "Permissible" was translated into French as "*licite*" and "impermissible" as "*illicite*", or rather, vice versa, since the Special Rapporteur's working language was most emphatically French. The terminology was equally unsatisfactory in French, however. First, because there was a big difference between "permissible", which was most accurately rendered in French as "*recevable*", and "*licite*", which corresponded to "lawful" in English, as opposed to "wrongful". Second, the terminology, which hinged on the permissibility of reservations, was misleading. The Commission had realized as much when Mr. Tomka had very rightly pointed out that the terminology had an unfortunate tendency to hark back to the topic of responsibility of States. It was not reasonable to affirm that a reservation not valid for reasons of form or substance, whether of permissibility or of opposability, entailed the responsibility of the State or international organization that had formulated it, and in any event it was totally unreasonable to suggest that such was always the case. There was in any event absolutely no precedent to that effect, and if some writers, albeit very few, had sometimes contended that an impermissible reservation engaged the responsibility of its author, that singular notion had, to his knowledge, never been maintained by any State in any specific case. The worst fate that could befall a reservation was for it to be null and void, impermissible or not opposable—but it

[3] See *Yearbook ... 2004*, vol. II (Part Two), paras. 33–37.

could not engage the responsibility of its author. If there was a dispute in that regard, it was about legality, but certainly not about responsibility.

74. For want of anything better, he returned to the very neutral idea that some reservations were valid, and others not, regardless of the cause or effects of that validity or invalidity. That, then, was the title of that part of his report, and it was for that reason too that he suggested that the Commission stick to that terminology in its future work and adopt it in the cases left open in 2002, which concerned the draft guidelines already adopted, namely 1.6 and 2.1.8, in which the words "impermissible" and "impermissibility" were used.[4] The Commission should revert to the much more neutral terms "validity" and "non-validity". That did not mean that there were no "impermissible" or "permissible" reservations, but that in the context of article 19 it was unduly partisan to speak of permissibility or admissibility.

75. Section A of his tenth report ("Presumption of validity of reservations") called to mind the principle stemming from the chapeau of article 19 of the 1969 and 1986 Vienna Conventions, pursuant to which a State or an international organization could formulate a reservation, which, as the Commission had explained in its commentary of 1962 and 1966, amounted to "the general principle that the formulation of reservations is permitted". That principle was clearly at odds with the proposals made by the special rapporteurs who had preceded Sir Humphrey Waldock, and with past practice,[5] at any rate according to the 1951 advisory opinion of the ICJ on Reservations to the Convention on Genocide. However, the entire structure of article 19 showed that the presumption of validity of reservations was far from absolute, and the power to formulate a reservation was obviously not unlimited. In the first place, it was limited in time, since a reservation could be formulated only when signing a treaty or when definitively expressing consent to be bound by it. Furthermore, by its nature a treaty could require that a reservation be unanimously accepted, failing which the reservation would, as clearly specified in article 20, paragraph 2, have been formulated, but not "made" or "established". Moreover, States could in any event limit the power to formulate reservations in the treaty itself, a possibility envisaged in article 19, subparagraphs (*a*) and (*b*), but those paragraphs did not cover all instances of treaty limitations on the power to formulate reservations, and in any case, it clearly emerged from article 19, subparagraph (*c*), that a reservation incompatible with the object and purpose of the treaty could not be formulated.

76. Admittedly, States had the power to formulate reservations, but that was not an absolute right; moreover, that power concerned the formulation of reservations, and the word "formulation", which appeared in the very title of article 19, had not been chosen by chance. It stressed what a State could do as author of a reservation, but as Waldock and the Commission had rightly pointed out, that did not mean that the reservation would be "made", i.e. that it would actually produce the effects intended by its author. For that to be the case, it was necessary—to cite a phrase which was fundamental yet too often disregarded and which appeared in article 21, paragraph 1, of the 1969 and 1986 Vienna Conventions—for the reservation to be "established with regard to another party in accordance with articles 19, 20 and 23". In other words, compliance with article 19 was one of the conditions for a reservation to be made or established, so that the reservation could produce its effects, but it was not the sole condition, and it therefore seemed that neither the permissibility school, which focused on article 19 to the exclusion of all other considerations, nor the opposability school, which was interested solely in article 20 and the reaction of other States, provided a complete and faithful account of the legal regime of reservations in all its enormous complexity.

77. The conditions posed in article 19 were necessary for establishing a reservation, but they were not sufficient. They were, nonetheless, at the start of the chain which enabled the reservation to produce the effects that its authors expected, and thus the elements of article 19 were essential to the validity of reservations. In the presence of a reservation, the first thing to be done was obviously to ask whether the reservation passed the test of article 19 before proceeding any further.

78. That said, the freedom to formulate reservations was the basic principle. Other relevant considerations merely qualified the principle, which was that States could formulate reservations. He thus asked in paragraph 16 whether it might be useful to make the principle of the presumption of the validity of reservations the subject of a separate draft guideline, because that presumption was one of the fundamental guides of the regime of reservations as a whole. However, he had decided not to, less for reasons of substance than of method. As he explained in paragraphs 17 and 18, isolating the chapeau of article 19 of the 1969 and 1986 Vienna Conventions would have had the serious disadvantage of splitting article 19 over two or more separate draft guidelines. It was preferable to avoid taking such a step so as to keep the Guide to Practice user-friendly. As had been done many times in the past—and he had cited most of the relevant examples in that regard in footnote 39 in paragraph 17—it would be better to reproduce article 19 of the 1986 Vienna Convention in its entirety in a single draft guideline 3.1 (para. 20 of the report). As usual, he preferred to use the 1986 Vienna Convention, because it was more complete than the 1969 Vienna Convention, since it included international organizations.

79. It was no secret that the mere reproduction of article 19 in draft guideline 3.1 was not ideal, for a reason which he set out in paragraph 19 of the report. Article 19 was poorly drafted in that it merely repeated what had been stated in article 2, paragraph 1 (*d*), of the 1969 and 1986 Vienna Conventions and which he had used in the definition of reservation in draft guideline 1.1, because those three provisions (article 2, paragraph 1 (*d*), article 19 and guideline 1.1) specified in a not entirely complete fashion the cases or moments in which a reservation could be formulated. As it was already in the definition it did not have to be repeated when speaking of the

[4] See *Yearbook ... 1999*, vol. II (Part Two), p. 126, and *Yearbook ... 2002*, vol. II (Part Two), p. 45, respectively.

[5] See *Yearbook ... 1962*, vol. II, document A/5209, pp. 175–181, and *Yearbook ... 1966*, vol. II, document A/6309/Rev.1, pp. 202–209.

conditions of validity of reservations. However, the methodological flaw in the Vienna Conventions was not a sufficient reason to correct them, which might unnecessarily confuse the users of the Guide to Practice. It would be vastly preferable to reproduce the entire text of article 19 in draft guideline 3.1. It was better to repeat oneself than to contradict oneself.

80. In sections B and C of the report, it had seemed legitimate to distinguish between article 19, subparagraphs (*a*) and (*b*), on the one hand, and subparagraph (*c*), on the other, even though in section D, in which he spoke of the determination of validity, he had thought it necessary to bring together the three cases again in connection with the determination of the validity of reservations and the consequences of said determination, since nothing whatsoever in article 19 itself or in articles 20 to 23 suggested that it was necessary to distinguish reservations prohibited by the treaty or reservations contrary to the object and purpose of the treaty with regard to the applicable legal regime. That was the subject of section D.

81. In section C, he planned to give lengthy consideration to the very difficult question of the compatibility of a reservation with the object and purpose of the treaty, and section B was devoted to reservations prohibited by the treaty, either expressly or implicitly, which corresponded to article 19, subparagraphs (*a*) and (*b*), of the Vienna Conventions. Those cases were simpler than the ones considered under subparagraph (*c*), albeit not perhaps as simple as his predecessor Paul Reuter had claimed.[6]

82. While he would spare the Commission the detailed description of the *travaux préparatoires* for those provisions contained in paragraphs 23, 24, 31 and 35–37 of the report, a reading of those paragraphs showed that the matter was not as simple as it might seem and that the two cases addressed in article 19, subparagraphs (*a*) and (*b*), did not take by any means all possible cases into account. The starting point was that the Commission was in the presence of treaties which contained reservation clauses—that was the joint chapeau of article 19, subparagraphs (*a*) and (*b*). Subparagraph (*a*) covered the case in which the treaty prohibited the reservation, but that could in reality result from two categories of reservation clauses which were actually rather different. A treaty containing a reservation clause could prohibit all reservations, or only certain reservations. In the situation in which the reservation clause prohibited all reservations, for example in the Rome Statute of the International Criminal Court, the United Nations Convention on the Law of the Sea or the 1989 Basel Convention on the control of transboundary movements of hazardous wastes and their disposal, matters were simple, but only relatively so, since it was still necessary to decide whether or not a unilateral declaration constituted a reservation, because a unilateral declaration was still possible in principle and even expressly provided for, as in the United Nations Convention on the Law of the Sea. However, in the first place that was a problem of the definition of reservation, and not of validity *stricto sensu*, and in the second place, if the declaration was a reservation and not a simple interpretative declaration, then clearly the reservation could not be formulated, and if it was formulated, it was not valid. He would discuss later on, in section D, what that word meant, because it was not sufficient to say that a reservation was not valid; it was also necessary to understand what exactly that meant.

83. That being said, treaties that simply prohibited all reservations were rather rare. More often, the prohibition was partial and concerned only certain reservations. But such cases must in turn be divided into at least two further subcategories. For example, a treaty might prohibit reservations to specific provisions of the treaty, which were usually referred to by their article or paragraph number. He cited examples in paragraph 29 of the report. However—and that was a much more complicated situation—sometimes the prohibition did not concern specified provisions but categories of reservations, some clearly defined, others less so.

84. The first thing that the Commission should do was to indicate that the three above-mentioned cases were covered by article 19, subparagraph (*a*). That would be a useful clarification, all the more so because the *travaux préparatoires* of article 19 had shown just how much uncertainty had persisted on that point, as was shown by the comments of a number of former members of the Commission, who had considered that only some cases of prohibition were covered, while others were not. In his own view, the provision covered all cases of prohibition, even though it did not always automatically have the same effect. Thus, that was what he proposed to do in draft guideline 3.1.1, which should not pose major problems, because it merely specified what was meant by "prohibited reservation".

85. However, it was important to state clearly, although probably not in the text of the draft guidelines, but instead in the commentary, that all the cases covered in article 19, subparagraph (*a*), of the Vienna Conventions concerned express prohibitions only and not, despite what had been written, implicit prohibitions. It could be seen from the *travaux préparatoires* that Waldock and the Commission had clearly ruled out the idea that certain treaties excluded reservations by their very nature, even though a special regime had been retained for two particular categories of treaties, namely treaties concluded between a limited number of parties and the constituent instruments of international organizations, but in those two cases, those distinctions had been allowed under article 20 and not at all under article 19. The Commission had rightly decided not to consider that certain multilateral treaties excluded reservations by their very nature. Article 20 had distinguished particular categories of treaties because it was a problem of opposability and not of permissibility.

86. On the other hand, article 19 did make reference to a form of implicit prohibition of reservations, but that did not have to do with the nature of treaties, but with an *a contrario* reasoning when a treaty allowed only specified reservations. That implicit prohibition was the subject of article 19, subparagraph (*b*). However, logical

[6] See P. Reuter, "Solidarité et divisibilité des engagements conventionnels" *in* Y. Dinstein (ed.), *International Law at a Time of Perplexity: Essays in Honour of Shabtai Rosenne*, Dordrecht, Nijhoff, 1989, p. 625; also reproduced in P. Reuter, *Le développement de l'ordre juridique international: Écrits de droit international*, Paris, Economica, 1995, p. 363.

as the idea underlying subparagraph (*b*) might be, the prohibition which it envisaged was rather complex and assumed, as he had pointed out in paragraph 34 of his report, that three conditions had been fulfilled: the treaty must permit the formulation of reservations; the reservations permitted must be "specified"; and it must be specified that "only" those reservations "may be made". Actually, those three conditions were so restrictive, especially the latter two, that they were rarely fulfilled. The third condition had been inserted by the Drafting Committee of the United Nations Conference on the Law of Treaties following an amendment proposed by Poland which had certainly been less innocuous than it had seemed, because it had reversed the presumption made by the Commission, whose draft had quite logically accepted that, if certain reservations were permitted by the treaty, then others should be regarded *a contrario* as prohibited.[7] However, the tendency in the mid– and late–1960s had been to accept reservations liberally, and he had no intention of asking the Commission to go back on the Polish amendment, which had been incorporated in the Vienna Conventions, although he personally thought it most regrettable. The Commission should, however, specify whether a reservation which was neither expressly permitted nor implicitly prohibited must observe the criterion of compatibility with the object and purpose of the treaty. He had no doubt that the answer to that question must be in the affirmative, but he would return to the question when he introduced section C to the tenth report. The same applied when the other condition imposed by subparagraph (*b*) was not fulfilled, namely, when the reservations permitted were not specified. The word "specified" might seem innocuous, and the reader might think that the Commission had had in mind specified reservations in the same way that it might have said that the treaty must permit "certain" reservations or "specific" reservations. It must be said that no decisive argument to the contrary could be derived from the *travaux préparatoires*. However, in the *English Channel* case, a dispute between France and the United Kingdom concerning the continental shelf, the Arbitral Tribunal, in its award of 30 June 1977, had interpreted article 12 of the Geneva Convention on the Continental Shelf, which permitted the parties to make reservations to all the provisions of the Convention other than articles 1 to 3 inclusive, as not entailing the obligation for the other parties to accept them, because they were not "specified". It also followed that reservations formulated by virtue of an unspecified reservation clause, i.e. which did not specify what reservations were permitted, were unquestionably subject to the test of compatibility with the object and purpose of the treaty.

87. For all those reasons, it was very important for the Commission to attempt to define in draft guideline 3.1.2 what was meant by "specified reservations". That was no easy task. He had tried to do so, seeking to avoid being either too lax—the word "specified" must mean something—or excessively strict, because subparagraph (*b*) must not be deprived of all practical effect by too narrow a definition of "specified reservation". If the definition was too strict, it would be tantamount to likening the notion to "negotiated reservations", i.e. those whose content was provided for in advance by the treaty following negotiations between parties. The expression "negotiated reservations", as had been seen during the consideration of his fifth report,[8] had a very specific meaning, and he did not think that the definition of the expression "specified reservation" should be limited to such an extent. The definition which he proposed in paragraph 49 struck an acceptable balance between those two pitfalls, but it went without saying that any definition could be improved, and to that end, he hoped that the Commission would agree to refer draft guideline 3.1.2 together with draft guidelines 3.1 and 3.1.1 to the Drafting Committee.

88. He had two remarks to make in closing. First, he urged members to read the document entitled "The practice of human rights treaty bodies with respect to reservations to international human rights treaties".[9] It was regrettable that its very useful appendices were in English only. He would discuss the document in greater detail at a later stage, time permitting, but wished to point out that, at the end of paragraph 30, the human rights secretariat had ascribed to him an opinion which was not his and which he did not think he had ever voiced, at any rate in the form indicated.

89. Second, the Commission had met with members of the Committee against Torture, the Committee on Economic, Social and Cultural Rights, the Human Rights Committee, the Committee on the Elimination of Racial Discrimination, the Committee on the Rights of the Child and, on two occasions, the Sub-Commission on the Promotion and Protection of Human Rights, to discuss the question of reservations. Those meetings had been very interesting and instructive. For budgetary and scheduling reasons the Commission had not been able to have direct contact with members of the Committee on the Elimination of Discrimination against Women, which was unfortunate, since that body had been among the most active in the area of reservations. The time had come to organize a seminar or a one- or two-day joint study meeting, of a more formal and systematic nature than in the past, with the human rights treaty bodies, to focus on the subject of reservations to human rights treaties. He had been calling for such a meeting for several years and hoped that it would be possible to hold one in 2006; the treaty bodies had also endorsed the idea. The Commission could then review its preliminary conclusions of 1997,[10] to which Mr. Candioti had referred. It would be for the Planning Group to discuss the necessary arrangements.

90. The CHAIRPERSON said that the Commission had taken note of the Special Rapporteur's proposal regarding a meeting with the human rights treaty bodies.

The meeting rose at 1 p.m.

[7] *Official Records of the United Nations Conference on the Law of Treaties, First session, Vienna, 26 March–24 May 1968, Summary records of the plenary meetings and of the meetings of the Committee of the Whole* (United Nations publication, Sales No. E.68.V.7), document A/CONF.39/11, 70th meeting, p. 415, para. 16. See also, *ibid.*, First and second sessions, Vienna, 26 March–24 May 1968 and 9 April–22 May 1969, *Documents of the Conference* (United Nations publication, Sales No. E.70.V.5), document A/CONF.39/14, p. 134.

[8] *Yearbook ... 2000*, vol. II (Part One), document A/CN.4/508 and Add.1–4, pp. 174–175, paras. 164–165 and 169–170.

[9] HRI/MC/2005/5.

[10] See footnote 1 above.

2855th MEETING

Thursday, 21 July 2005, at 10.05 a.m.

Chairperson: Mr. Djamchid MOMTAZ

Present: Mr. Addo, Mr. Al-Marri, Mr. Candioti, Mr. Chee, Mr. Comissário Afonso, Mr. Daoudi, Mr. Dugard, Mr. Economides, Ms. Escarameia, Mr. Fomba, Mr. Gaja, Mr. Galicki, Mr. Kabasti, Mr. Kamto, Mr. Kateka, Mr. Kemicha, Mr. Kolodkin, Mr. Koskenniemi, Mr. Mansfield, Mr. Matheson, Mr. Melescanu, Mr. Niehaus, Mr. Pellet, Mr. Sreenivasa Rao, Mr. Rodríguez Cedeño, Mr. Sepúlveda, Ms. Xue, Mr. Yamada.

Unilateral acts of states (*continued*) (A/CN.4549, sect. C, and A/CN.4/557)

[Agenda item 5]

EIGHTH REPORT OF THE SPECIAL RAPPORTEUR (*concluded*)

1. Mr. ECONOMIDES, deploring the fact that the Commission was still deadlocked notwithstanding the tireless efforts of the Special Rapporteur and the Working Group, said that, in his view, that situation was due to the fact that the Commission had thus far been unable to define the unilateral acts which formed the subject of its deliberations. To date it had concerned itself with any unilateral act that might produce legal effects at the international level, a sweeping category that made the subject impossible to handle, for any unilateral act could produce various types of legal effects. In order to break that deadlock, the Commission must focus its deliberations on autonomous unilateral acts creating positive or negative international legal obligations on the part of the State that was the author of the act *vis-à-vis* another State, several States, other subjects of international law or the international community as a whole. Conversely, it should not look at non-autonomous, or dependent, unilateral acts that fell within the framework of the execution of a treaty, the application of a custom or the implementation of an international organization's decision. Those acts which, as Mr. Kamto had said, were predicated on the authorization of an existing norm of international law, were already regulated: those falling within the realm of treaties by the 1969 Vienna Convention, those in the realm of customary law by customary law itself and those relating to the decisions of international organizations by the organization's constituent instrument.

2. The Commission must therefore give some structure to its work if it was to progress. It must turn its attention, at least initially, to unilateral acts of States as a source of international law that gave rise to obligations in the same way as treaties, customs and binding institutional acts. The criterion that must be used was the notion of an international legal obligation and not that of international legal effects. Yet unilateral acts as a source of legal obligations had already been defined by the ICJ in the *Nuclear Tests* and *Frontier Dispute (Burkina Faso/ Republic of Mali)* cases.

3. Every effort must be made to adopt on first reading at the current session a restrictive definition of unilateral acts as a source of international law, and to transmit that definition to the Sixth Committee. That would constitute a substantial step forward and would greatly facilitate work at the next session.

4. Mr. MATHESON thanked the Special Rapporteur for having considered in his report several important instances of State practice of direct relevance to the topic. That was precisely the kind of material the Commission needed in order to understand the complexities of the law concerning unilateral acts. Of course, Mr. Pellet was also to be congratulated for his role in organizing that effort.

5. As several members had already noted, the most obvious conclusion to be drawn from the examples cited in the report was that unilateral acts differed widely in form, substance, language, purpose and effect. Everything therefore depended on the specific circumstances of each particular case. Accordingly, it would be very difficult to create coherent rules applying to all types of unilateral acts.

6. Another obvious conclusion was that the intent of the State that was the author of the act was of overriding importance: an act's consequences differed depending on whether the State in question intended it to have legal consequences or to be purely political in character. For example, it was clear that the nuclear-weapon States that had given other States assurances in 1995[1] had not intended to make any legal commitments, and other States had seemed to understand that quite well. Consequently those assurances were not legally binding. In contrast, the States in the other cases cited in the report manifestly intended their statements to produce legal effects. Thus the defining factor of intention should figure prominently in whatever final form the Commission's work took.

7. It had been suggested that the form of unilateral statements was of little relevance when judging their legal effects. That was not necessarily correct, as several examples had demonstrated. The 1945 Truman Proclamation (paras. 127–137 of the report), the 1952 Colombian note (paras. 13–35), the 1988 Jordanian statement (paras. 44–54) and the 1994 Russian protest (paras. 84–105) had all indicated by their form that their authors intended them to have legal effects and that others could reasonably rely on that fact. In contrast, the form and language of the assurances given by nuclear-weapon States in 1995 had been deliberately chosen to make it clear that they were political rather than legal in character, and that was how they had been understood by others.

8. Different views had been expressed on the degree to which the legal effects of a unilateral statement depended on the reactions of other States. Once again, it seemed difficult to draw a general conclusion. In some cases the reactions of other States might be of marginal importance, whereas in other cases they might be quite important. For

---

[1] See the declarations of the Russian Federation (S/1995/261), the United Kingdom (S/1995/262), the United States (S/1995/263), France (S/1995/264) and China (S/1995/265) on the security assurances given to non-nuclear-weapon States parties to the Treaty on the Non-Proliferation of Nuclear Weapons.

example, the 1988 Jordanian statement had probably been effective in waiving Jordan's claim to the West Bank without the need for acquiescence by others, but its effect in promoting Palestinian claims to that territory had presumably depended to a substantial degree on the reactions of other States.

9. In the light of those difficulties, he thought that, rather than drafting articles that set forth rules governing unilateral acts, the Commission ought to produce a concise expository study or report that might give useful guidance to States, as Mr. Candioti had suggested. It should not so much focus on reaching a definitive set of conclusions, which would be neither possible nor desirable, as review various factors that determined whether or not unilateral acts had legal effects. Those factors would in essence be those identified by the Working Group at the previous session[2] for the purpose of the case studies that had been carried out.

10. In any event, the Commission should complete the project at the next session, at least in a preliminary form, and thus add it to the list of its accomplishments of the current quinquennium. If it persisted in its pursuit of articles, rules and definitions, it would reach the end of the quinquennium without any coherent results on the topic and with little prospect for any in the near future, and it would have wasted its own time and the Special Rapporteur's efforts.

11. Mr. DAOUDI said that the Special Rapporteur's eighth report confirmed that the subject lent itself to codification. Indeed, an analysis of the cases selected by the Working Group on the basis of the method it had chosen showed that it was possible to draw conclusions that could serve as a basis for draft articles on various aspects of the question. The Commission's method was deductive rather than inductive: it began with an analysis of State practice in the area of unilateral acts and ended up with the establishment of common denominators that constituted the principles of unilateral legal acts in international public law.

12. While no one disputed the particular features that distinguished unilateral legal acts from international treaties or denied the differences in their respective legal regimes, those differences did not preclude the use of the 1969 Vienna Convention as a reference framework.

13. In paragraph 170 of his report the Special Rapporteur noted that "form is relatively unimportant in determining whether we are dealing with a unilateral act of the type in which the Commission is interested", a statement which highlighted the difference between a unilateral act and an international treaty. The latter's distinguishing features, at least as established in the 1969 Vienna Convention, were that it was a written act concluded in accordance with a specified procedure. Thus in a treaty it was possible to determine States' rights and obligations with greater certainty, whereas a unilateral act—which could take the form of a simple verbal statement, one or more written documents or even conduct—could create uncertainty as to its author's intention to undertake an international commitment.

14. In that context the 1969 Vienna Convention, while neither denying their existence nor disputing their importance, was silent on verbal agreements, which did not possess the formal aspect of an international treaty yet posed the problem of proving their existence in the same way that an unwritten unilateral act did.

15. What was important to pinpoint in the case of both unilateral legal acts and verbal agreements was the intent to undertake a commitment, the form they might take and all the circumstances surrounding their formulation, with the understanding that the absence of a criterion concerning form had no bearing whatsoever on intent.

16. In paragraphs 171 and 172 of his report, the Special Rapporteur limited the scope of the study to unilateral acts formulated by States and concluded that any State was endowed with the capacity to commit itself at the international level through unilateral acts, since international law did not contain any rules forbidding States to express their intention to commit themselves unilaterally, while exercise of that right meant that any unilateral manifestation of a State's intention to assume an obligation *vis-à-vis* other subjects of international law produced legal effects. The Special Rapporteur was therefore correct in suggesting that article 6 of the 1969 Vienna Convention could be transferred and applied to the capacity of States to formulate unilateral legal acts.

17. The competence of State organs to commit the State through unilateral acts and the conformity of their conduct with the domestic legal order were sensitive subjects. Prudence dictated that the pertinent rules of the 1969 Vienna Convention should be applied to them, bearing in mind that the problem of unconstitutionality raised different issues in the case of treaties.

18. By its very nature a unilateral legal act produced effects from the time of its formulation by its author, since it did not have to be accepted by the addressee. The Special Rapporteur seemed to confirm that thesis in paragraphs 195 and 196 of his report, but it would be worthwhile ascertaining that the same held true for those unilateral acts dealt with in earlier reports that had not been analysed in the eighth report.[3]

19. The opinions expressed by Commission members regarding the possibility of codifying the topic of unilateral acts revealed an ongoing lack of agreement that was impeding the debate's progress. While no member disputed the existence of unilateral acts, some were highly sceptical about the success of the undertaking. Yet if the Commission's deliberations should prove fruitless, States could do as they pleased. Codification of the topic would ensure the security of international legal relations,

[2] See *Yearbook ... 2004*, vol. II (Part Two), p. 96, para. 247.

[3] See *Yearbook ... 1998*, vol. II (Part One), document A/CN.4/486; *Yearbook ... 1999*, vol. II (Part One), document A/CN.4/500 and Add.1; *Yearbook ... 2000*, vol. II (Part One), document A/CN.4/505 ; *Yearbook ... 2001*, vol. II (Part One), document A/CN.4/519; *Yearbook ... 2002*, vol. II (Part One), document A/CN.4/525 and Add.1–2; *Yearbook ... 2003*, vol. II (Part One), document A/CN.4/534 ; and *Yearbook ... 2004*, vol. II (Part One), document A/CN.4/542 [and Corr.2–3].

for States needed to know what acts could produce legal effects and obligate them to other subjects of international law. Whatever form the Commission's final document took, it would have the merit of preventing States from finding themselves unintentionally bound by unilateral acts.

20. The Commission must stop procrastinating and adopt a constructive attitude. The time had come for the Special Rapporteur to propose draft articles on the capacity of States to formulate unilateral acts, the competence of State organs and other aspects of the topic.

21. Mr. ECONOMIDES said that for mainly political reasons it would be difficult to begin work by considering the capacity of a State and by defining unilateral acts. First of all, States' confidence had to be built; to that end the Commission should begin by looking at the conditions that had to be met in order for them to be bound. The priority subject must therefore be the State's intention to assume legal obligations by means of a unilateral act. Naturally for a State to commit itself the act in question must be extremely clear, unambiguous and indisputable. If there was any doubt as to the State's intention, the method of restrictive interpretation should be employed to protect its interests.

22. The second issue to consider was the revocability of the act. He believed that any unilateral act could be freely revoked by its author, save for two exceptions: when the unilateral act itself stipulated that it could not be revoked and when, after the addressee had accepted it, the unilateral act became a conventional act, which was then governed by the law of treaties.

23. Mr. Sreenivasa RAO said that unilateral acts were of crucial importance to international relations because States' ministries of foreign affairs had frequent recourse to them. That explained why the subject was of interest not only to the academic community, but also to practitioners of international law and to Governments themselves. Similarly, when ministers met they often issued joint statements; when natural disasters occurred offers of assistance were made; and States made offers to promote the objectives of international organizations, for example in the field of peacekeeping operations. Most of the time, however, written agreements were signed, and so such declarations or offers could not be treated as part of the topic.

24. The report under consideration also provided numerous examples of protest notes which purported to preserve rights, at least in the context of competing claims, and prevent the other party from consolidating its claims.

25. From the outset, the Special Rapporteur had emphasized the "autonomy" of unilateral acts, a term borrowed from the "French school". An autonomous unilateral act was one that did not impose obligations on other States or oblige them to perform certain acts for it to come fully into effect, and whose effects were not contingent upon certain factors.

26. The numerous examples given in the report under consideration were very useful, and the Commission must be grateful to the members who had supplied them and to the Chairperson of the Working Group and its members for having provided a framework for examining that information. Ms. Escarameia had noted that the Special Rapporteur could have devoted more space to the examination of those examples and the conclusions that could be drawn from them. Although that was true, after seven years of deliberations, it was incumbent upon the members of the Commission to make their contribution to the study undertaken by the Special Rapporteur. The time had come to end doctrinal debates and to establish a modest framework based on the results of the work done since the topic had first been placed on the agenda; such a framework should be set out in a statement addressed to the Sixth Committee of the General Assembly, as Mr. Candioti had suggested. The Commission must collaborate in the drafting of a document setting out the following conclusions, which could be drawn from the examples of unilateral acts cited in the Special Rapporteur's eighth report and in previous reports.

27. Unilateral acts were highly diverse in nature and it was hard to categorize them. The study must focus on autonomous acts, or "legal acts", to echo a term from French doctrine, which could have legal effects without requiring any action on the part of other States. That definition included the recognition of States or Governments, unconditional offers of aid or assistance, renunciation of claims or titles to territory, undertakings to abstain from particular action or the renunciation of rights established under international law. Such acts produced legal effects when performed by persons with suitable authorization to formulate them, the notion of authorization being very important in that regard. The study could also cover unilateral acts that were not strictly autonomous, but which gave rise to international rights and obligations, such as unilateral acts which created rights and obligations when they were associated with subsequent unilateral acts of a similar nature. No matter whether they were fully or partially autonomous acts, their validity and legal effects, as well as the international commitment they entailed, would depend upon several factors, to wit the authority of the agent, the latter's authorization or presumed authorization, the form and content of the statement, the nature of the act, its objective, specified conditions, its context, the reaction of addressee States or States directly affected, and international obligations stemming from the imperative norms involved. Of course, not all of these factors would be relevant in every case.

28. The CHAIRPERSON, speaking in his personal capacity, said that he wished to make two comments. First, he believed that it would be better to speak of India's offer, rather than its commitment, not to develop nuclear weapons. So long as the addressee States had not accepted that offer, India was free to withdraw it. On the other hand, once that offer had been accepted, it would become irrevocable.

29. As far as the Truman Proclamation was concerned, he did not think that a unilateral act could create *ipso facto*, *ab initio*, rights for the author State. The Truman Proclamation had not encountered any opposition, and a number of States had even incorporated provisions from the Proclamation in their national legislation, which had

not been the case with acts such as those by which Chile and Peru had created territorial seas with a breadth of 200 nautical miles,[4] a move that had prompted objections from the States concerned.

30. Mr. PELLET said that he wished to make a terminological clarification with regard to expressions currently used in French legal theory. Firstly, it should be pointed out that, on the one hand, acts could be either autonomous or non-autonomous, while on the other, they could be either "*autonormateur*" or "*hétéronormateur*".

31. Acts that were autonomous had no pre-existing specific legal basis of any kind. For example, when Truman had made his proclamations in 1945, no rule of international law authorized the United States to claim a fishing area or a continental shelf. Similarly, when France had suspended its atmospheric nuclear tests in 1973, it had done so autonomously. Conversely, when a State set the breadth of its territorial sea at 12 nautical miles, that was not an autonomous act, since a rule of international law provided that States might act unilaterally in that respect.

32. If the character of an act was "*autonormateur*", that simply meant that the author of the act imposed obligations on itself: for example, a State that undertook not to conduct nuclear tests did not impose any obligation on other States. An act that was "*hétéronormateur*", meanwhile, imposed or purported to impose obligations on other States. That was the case of acts whereby States set the breadth of their territorial sea at 12 nautical miles.

33. Returning to the example of India's commitment, which the Chairperson had described as an offer, he considered that in order for that to be the case, the commitment in question would have had to be conditional. If India had pledged not to resort to nuclear weapons provided that Canada supplied it with the technology it needed, that would have been an offer. But if India had merely stated that it was foregoing nuclear weapons without further clarification, it would have undertaken a commitment and, in its disappointment that Canada had not granted it the anticipated benefits, had reneged on that commitment.

34. It was not certain that the act in question was an offer, nor was it certain that a State could go back on a statement. Consequently as Chairperson of the Working Group, he wished to request Mr. Sreenivasa Rao to conduct a brief study of the Indian commitment. Such a study would usefully complement the examples the Commission already had with regard to a fundamental issue, that of the revocability of unilateral acts.

35. In conclusion, he was pleased to see signs of a consensus emerging around Mr. Candioti's proposal. Personally he was prepared to accept that the Commission, while reserving the possibility of undertaking a more precise codification, should for the time being endeavour to adopt preliminary conclusions. Although he was in favour of the method proposed by Mr. Candioti, he was much less convinced by the examples cited, since they were a mixture of unilateral acts proper and acts that fell within the realm of State conduct, which raised a quite different set of issues.

36. Mr. CANDIOTI recalled that he had criticized the use of the term "autonomous" in the context of the study on unilateral acts in the past, as it could only generate more confusion. In his view, the Truman Proclamation and the French statements on nuclear tests were not autonomous acts because they were based on rules of law, and particularly on the principle of State sovereignty. He was therefore opposed to the use of the term "autonomous", since it would only cloud the debate.

37. Mr. CHEE said that the term "autonomous" was not to be found in English doctrine. He wished to note first of all that the text of the 1945 Truman Proclamation clearly indicated that the United States had rights *ab initio*. It also used the term "opportunism". To his way of thinking, those two factors had helped to expand the concept of the continental shelf. It should be recalled that in 1945 no other country had had the necessary capacity to exploit the continental shelf. Subsequently other declarations had been added to the Truman Proclamation which had ultimately crystallized and given rise to the law of the sea.

38. Mr. ECONOMIDES, replying to Mr. Candioti, said that the term "autonomous" had to do with the basis of the action, the legal justification for the act, which could lie in a treaty, customary law or a request by an international organization. Any acts for which such a legal justification existed were not autonomous. Conversely, if the State formulated an act in order to assume a legal obligation on the basis of nothing more than its will, then that act was autonomous.

39. Mr. DUGARD said that, like earlier reports, the eighth report on unilateral acts of States provided evidence of the difficulties inherent in the topic but also of the topic's importance. The Special Rapporteur had examined, with the help of several colleagues, certain unilateral acts that had received the attention of international tribunals, Governments and scholars. The studies carried out had to do with the nature and consequences of unilateral acts, the prescribed form of such acts, the persons who were authorized to make them and the Vienna regime. Some authors even described unilateral acts as a new source of international law.

40. He drew attention, by way of example, to the recent case brought before the ICJ by the Democratic Republic of the Congo against Rwanda (*Armed Activities on the Territory of the Congo (New Application: 2002)*). The Democratic Republic of the Congo had argued that the ICJ had jurisdiction by virtue of the Convention on the Prevention and Punishment of the Crime of Genocide. Rwanda had indicated that it had formulated a reservation in that regard, to which the Democratic Republic of the Congo had replied that the Rwandan Minister for Foreign Affairs had announced that his country intended to withdraw that reservation. That example showed that unilateral acts were an established part of international law and that they could not be ignored. It might be difficult to

[4] For the Chilean Presidential Declaration of 23 June 1947 and the Peruvian Presidential Decree of 1 August 1947, see *Laws and Regulations on the Regime of the High Seas*, vol. I (ST/LEG/SER.B/1) (United Nations publication, Sales No.: 1951.V.2), pp. 6 and 16, respectively.

codify them, but the Commission should at least engage in the progressive development of international law. It must do so because States needed guidance on the subject.

41. The debate that had been taking place between several members of the Commission had focused more on the function of the Commission than on unilateral acts. In that connection, he disagreed profoundly with Mr. Brownlie's position on the matter. Unilateral acts were an important subject, and if the Commission admitted failure it would have been derelict in its duty. Nevertheless, he did not think it would be possible to complete the work on the topic by 2006, as Mr. Candioti had proposed. The Commission should not only seek a definition of unilateral acts, but should also look into the possible consequences of such acts.

42. Mr. KATEKA said that he found it puzzling that the Commission was still debating the existence of unilateral acts. Irreconcilable philosophical and ideological differences separated Commission members on the issues of the definition and scope of unilateral acts. The debate at the previous meeting and even at the current meeting had revealed that certain members saw the notion of autonomy as being the foundation of the study, while others denied the very existence of such a concept. The question of capacity to formulate and revoke unilateral acts and the constitutional procedures involved had also given rise to controversy, as had the question of the threshold or trigger mechanism.

43. At that rate it was likely that the Commission would spend the next 10 years on the topic. The Commission would therefore be wise to accept Mr. Candioti's proposal.

44. In his most recent report, in which he had considered 11 cases on the basis of the Working Group's guidelines, the Special Rapporteur had endeavoured to differentiate between unilateral acts of a legal nature and unilateral acts that did not produce legal effects, although the distinction was still dubious.

45. For example, with regard to the Colombian note of 22 November 1952, the Special Rapporteur wrote that it had produced effects from the time it had been formulated and then, in the same paragraph, said that it had not produced effects until the addressee, Venezuela, had received it. Under a third scenario the note had begun to produce effects only after the addressee had acknowledged receipt. In his view, the case involved a typical exchange of notes that had amounted to the conclusion of a bilateral agreement between Colombia and Venezuela. Similarly, he did not see how the exchanges of notes between Cuba and Uruguay concerning the supply of vaccines advanced the study of unilateral acts. On the other hand, Jordan's waiver of any territorial claims to the West Bank was of legal interest and should be considered in greater detail. That was the case also with the Egyptian declaration of 24 April 1957 concerning the Convention between Austria-Hungary, France, Germany, Great Britain, Italy, the Netherlands, Russia, Spain and Turkey respecting the Free Navigation of the Suez Canal (Constantinople Convention) that sought to guarantee free use of the Suez Maritime Canal. He had in fact been surprised to learn that that declaration had been published in the United Nations *Treaty Series*.[5] Unilateral acts should not be registered or published by the United Nations because they were not treaties in the sense of Article 102 of the Charter of the United Nations.

46. The commentary by the Special Rapporteur concerning the Egyptian declaration led him to note that a multilateral treaty could not be abrogated by a party that purported to replace it with a unilateral declaration. A party to a multilateral treaty could certainly withdraw from the treaty, but the unilateral annulment of a treaty by one party would render the principles of the law of treaties, such as good faith and *pact sunt servanda*, meaningless.

47. As for examples of the so-called "security guarantees" given by nuclear-weapon States to non-nuclear-weapon States, the Special Rapporteur had already considered them in his second report; they were acts that had propaganda value and were thus political statements that had no legal content.[6]

48. The Ihlen Declaration and the Truman Proclamation were unilateral acts in the strict sense of the term. The Truman Proclamation in particular had had a major impact on the development of the law of the sea. The Special Rapporteur should look at those examples more closely and also at the conduct of Thailand and Cambodia in the *Temple of Preah Vihar* case.

49. In conclusion, he said that the Commission should try to adopt general principles on unilateral acts of States that could guide States and should complete its work on the topic in 2006.

50. Mr. CHEE said that the topic of unilateral acts of States had been with the Commission for a long time, and it was time for the Commission to wind up its work on the subject and adopt guidelines or a convention.

51. It had come to be generally accepted that unilateral acts were a source of international obligations additional to the other sources under general international law set out in article 38 of the Statute of the ICJ. Unilateral acts had been the subject of several detailed studies. Éric Suy, for instance, had classified them in five categories: (*a*) protest; (*b*) notification; (*c*) promise; (*d*) renunciation; and (*e*) recognition.[7] Jennings-Watts had put them in four categories: (*a*) declaration; (*b*) notification; (*c*) protest; and (*d*) renunciation or waiver,[8] as had Cassese, who had classified them as: (*a*) protest; (*b*) renunciation; (*c*) notification; and (*d*) promise.[9] Jennings-Watts also provided another definition of unilateral acts: "Acts performed by

[5] United Nations, *Treaty Series*, vol. 265, No. 3821, p. 299.

[6] See *Yearbook ...1999*, vol. II (Part One), document A/CN.4/500 and Add.1, para. 23, footnote 11. See also the seventh report of the Special Rapporteur, *Yearbook ... 2004*, vol. II (Part One), document A/CN.4/542 [and Corr.2–3], paras. 34–47.

[7] E. Suy, *Les acts juridiques unilatéraux en droit international public*, Paris, Librairie générale de droit et de jurisprudence, 1962.

[8] *Oppenheim's International Law* (see 2852nd meeting, footnote 1), p. 1188.

[9] A. Cassese, *International Law*, Oxford University Press, 2001, p. 150.

a single State, which nevertheless have effects upon the legal position of other States particularly, but not exclusively in their relation with the actor State." Jennings-Watts had gone on to state that:

[t]here are other kinds of unilateral acts, however, which are treated separately. These include: recognition, the conferment of nationality, certain acts in relation to conclusion of treaties such as signature, accession, approval, and ratification, as well as the making of reservations. It may also be noted that a unilateral act may take the form of state conduct, and need not be in the form of or be accompanied by any written document.[10]

52. Georg Schwarzenberger had catalogued three types of unilateral acts: (*a*) those that produced legal effects in accordance with their intent; (*b*) those that produced legal effects contrary to their intent; and (*c*) those that were irrelevant from the standpoint of international law. He had also described six categories: recognition, reservation, notification, acquiescence, renunciation and protest. He had concluded his study by observing that unilateral acts had come to be governed by the *ius aequum* rule and, in particular, by rules that underlined the principle of good faith.[11]

53. Wilfried Fiedler classified unilateral acts in six categories: recognition, protest, renunciation, notification, acquiescence and revocation.[12] The Special Rapporteur defined a unilateral act as "an act that can produce legal effects on its own without the need for its acceptance, or for any other reaction on the part of the addressee" (para. 170), a definition that was somewhat similar to Jennings-Watts's. The Commission might wish to apply that formula while dealing with other types of unilateral acts on an exceptional basis. In addition, the conduct of States should be combined with unilateral acts, as they were frequently interrelated where the producing of legal effects was concerned.

54. With reference to the debate in which he and Mr. Brownlie had engaged concerning the *Fisheries* case (*United Kingdom* v. *Norway*), he said that a passage of the judgment showed the obvious acquiescence of the United Kingdom to Norway's act with regard to the use of baselines:

Norway has been in a position to argue without any contradiction that neither the promulgation of her delimitation Decrees in 1869 and in 1889, nor their application, gave rise to any opposition on the part of foreign States. […] The general toleration of foreign States with regard to the Norwegian practice is an unchallenged fact. For a period of more than sixty years the United Kingdom Government itself in no way contested it. [p. 138 of the judgment]

55. Mr. MANSFIELD said that he had not been optimistic about the direction of the Commission's work on unilateral acts; however, in the light of the current debate he had begun to believe that it could conclude its work on the topic after all. The cases that the Special Rapporteur and the Working Group had studied were very useful. In particular, they were very different and provided clear illustrations of the essential point of the topic, which was that unilateral acts could produce legal effects and bind a State even though that may not have been its intention. That raised two policy considerations: on the one hand, it was desirable that States should continue to make political statements or carry out actions that contributed to international peace and security without being concerned that they might be legally bound; on the other hand, it was important that they should not make statements or undertake actions on which other States might reasonably rely unless they did so in good faith and lived up to their statements and actions.

56. As Mr. Candioti had rightly stressed the day before, there was no point in attempting to reach agreement on definitions or rules that were comparable to those of the 1969 Vienna Convention. Instead, the Commission should seek to draw up, on the basis of the cases studied, some reasonably broad guidelines that would set out for States the factors that determined whether or not a unilateral act might produce legal effects. That seemed to be a sound and useful objective for the coming quinquennium.

57. The CHAIRPERSON invited the Special Rapporteur to summarize the debate and present his conclusions thereon.

58. Mr. RODRÍGUEZ CEDEÑO (Special Rapporteur) thanked the members of the Commission for their valuable comments on his eighth report on unilateral acts of States. He noted first of all that everyone was in agreement that such acts did exist, even if they were difficult to identify and certain cases were not worth codifying. Not all acts bound a State legally; a number of elements made it possible to determine whether a unilateral act produced legal effects, particularly the competence and capacity of the author, the author's intention, the context, circumstances, the reaction of the addressee or a third party, subsequent conduct of the State and so forth. A unilateral act could be involuntary; it had been seen, for example, in the *Nuclear Tests* case that even though France had believed its declarations to be non-binding, the ICJ had held that the Government had assumed an obligation in formulating them and was obliged to conduct itself accordingly.

59. Certain unilateral acts, such as reservations or interpretative declarations, fell within the realm of treaties and were already governed by the law of treaties. They were therefore excluded from the work of the Commission. Unilateral acts were distinguished from conventional acts in that they produced legal effects from the time they were formulated and not from a time decided by the parties. One member of the Commission had recommended that declarations of acceptance of jurisdiction should also be considered, along with domestic legislation and case law.

60. The Commission's task was thus to define the elements that characterized unilateral acts capable of producing legal effects and, as a first step, to come up

---

[10] *Oppenheim's International Law* (see 2852nd meeting, footnote 1), p. 1188.

[11] G. Schwarzenberger, *International Law: International Law as Applied by International Courts and Tribunals*, vol. I, London, Stevens and Sons, 1957, p. 548–550.

[12] W. Fiedler, "Unilateral acts in international law", *in* R. Bernhardt (ed.), *Encyclopedia of Public International Law*, vol. IV, Amsterdam, Elsevier, 2000, pp. 1018–1022.

with a definition of such acts. That question had given rise to a number of controversies ever since work on the topic had begun in 1997, and some common ground would have to be found. Likewise, some members felt that the conduct of States must be included, while others thought that it had nothing to do with the topic. Yet State conduct could not be overlooked entirely, since it produced indisputable legal effects that were often similar to those of unilateral acts. In any event, the Commission's definition should not be too precise. The definition proposed by one member seemed to be sufficiently flexible: "an act emanating from the authority of a State that produces legal effects in international law" (2853rd meeting, above, para. 4).

61. It appeared from the debate that the 1969 Vienna Convention could not be transposed to unilateral acts but could serve as a useful reference, particularly in establishing the competence of the authors of unilateral acts, provided, of course, that the relevant criteria were expanded.

62. With regard to his eighth report, he had voluntarily limited his conclusions, as it had seemed to him preferable for the Commission to draw its own conclusions at the close of the debate. In addition, as some members appeared to have found a contradiction as to the irrelevance of form in identifying a unilateral act, he wished to note that he himself drew a distinction between form and formalism: a statement delivered before the General Assembly of the United Nations, for example, was surely not comparable to a press statement.

63. In conclusion, he proposed that work should continue within the Working Group with a view to drawing up the outlines of a new report. In 2006 the Commission should be in a position to submit a document containing preliminary conclusions, or rather general guidelines that would allow States to determine when and how they might become legally bound by the formulation of an act, and what the consequences under international law would be.

64. Mr. Sreenivasa RAO said that any examples he gave in his earlier statement were referred to only by way of raising some underlying issues and not for opening up any discussion on their merits.

65. The CHAIRPERSON thanked the Special Rapporteur for his summary. He believed that the Commission should continue its work on unilateral acts of States and suggested that the Working Group, chaired by Mr. Pellet, should consider the elements that would be discussed during the debate.

It was so decided.

The meeting rose at 1.05 p.m.

2856th MEETING

Friday, 22 July 2005, at 10.05 a.m.

Chairperson: Mr. Djamchid MOMTAZ

Present: Mr. Addo, Mr. Al-Marri, Mr. Candioti, Mr. Chee, Mr. Comissário Afonso, Mr. Daoudi, Mr. Dugard, Mr. Economides, Ms. Escarameia, Mr. Fomba, Mr. Gaja, Mr. Galicki, Mr. Kabatsi, Mr. Kamto, Mr. Kateka, Mr. Kemicha, Mr. Kolodkin, Mr. Koskenniemi, Mr. Mansfield, Mr. Matheson, Mr. Niehaus, Mr. Pambou-Tchivounda, Mr. Pellet, Mr. Sreenivasa Rao, Mr. Rodríguez Cedeño, Mr. Sepúlveda, Ms. Xue, Mr. Yamada.

Reservations to treaties (*continued*)* (A/CN.4/549 and Add.1, sect. D, A/CN.4/558 and Corr.1 and Add.1 [and Corr.1]–2, and A/CN.4/L.665)

[Agenda item 6]

TENTH REPORT OF THE SPECIAL RAPPORTEUR (*continued*)

1. The CHAIRPERSON invited the members of the Commission to comment on sections A and B of the Special Rapporteur's tenth report on reservations to treaties.

2. Mr. GAJA said that the tenth report on reservations to treaties was a remarkable work which covered an important area of the topic of reservations. Mr. Pellet's analysis was in many respects more far-reaching than any that could be found in the extensive literature on the question.

3. On the problem of terminology, he had no objection to the choice of terms proposed. In French, the term "*invalide*" (invalid) clearly indicated that a reservation did not have the necessary character to achieve the result intended by the State that formulated it, namely, as stated in article 2, paragraph 1 (*d*), of the 1969 Vienna Convention on the Law of Treaties, "to exclude or to modify the legal effect of certain provisions of the treaty in their application to [the reserving] State". However, it must be made clear that if the fact that a reservation was invalid prevented the reservation from producing the effects intended by the State formulating it, that invalidity also affected the ratification or equivalent act that the reservation accompanied, which in principle should then also be regarded as invalid. Only in exceptional cases could just the invalid reservation be regarded as null and void. If that point was not highlighted, the term "invalid" might suggest that the reservation could be disregarded and that the treaty was accepted *in toto*, which was probably not what the Special Rapporteur had in mind.

4. With regard to draft guideline 3.1 (para. 20 of the report), his preference would be to indicate only those conditions for validity which had to do with the content of reservations. There was little point in reproducing the entire text of article 19 of the 1969 Vienna Convention in the draft. Article 19 also dealt with the moment at which a reservation could be formulated, which, as the Special

* Resumed from the 2854th meeting.

Rapporteur had pointed out, was superfluous, as that matter was already covered in the definition in article 2, paragraph 1 (*d*). However, the repetition in the 1969 Vienna Convention was to some extent justified, whereas it was less so in the draft guidelines, because in the Convention, article 19 was the first article to address the question of reservations, the section on reservations having begun at that point. Thus, it was perhaps useful to recall that there was a temporal problem. In contrast, draft guideline 3.1 was preceded by a whole part concerning procedure, which dealt with the temporal problem in detail, and it therefore seemed rather strange to reopen the temporal question at that point in the draft.

5. Turning to draft guideline 3.1.1 (para. 32), he noted that the title contained the word "expressly", which was not found in article 19 (*a*) of the 1969 Vienna Convention. It was probably unusual for a treaty to implicitly prohibit the formulation of a reservation in cases other than those considered in article 19 (*b*). However, the existence of other implicit prohibitions could not be categorically ruled out. Thus, the implicit prohibition in subparagraph (*b*) was not the only one, and some cases might also arise under subparagraph (*a*). To cite one example, the Charter of the United Nations did not have any provisions on reservations, but there was an implicit prohibition in Article 4, which required that States seeking admission should accept the obligations contained in the Charter. That indicated that total acceptance was required and thus that reservations could not be formulated. Draft guideline 3.1.1 should therefore not confine itself to making provision for express prohibitions but should also include implicit prohibitions not covered in subparagraph (*b*).

6. On a drafting matter, the words "prohibiting reservations to specified provisions" in draft guideline 3.1.1 could be misconstrued as suggesting that a prohibition concerning specified provisions invalidated all reservations. That was clearly not what the Special Rapporteur had had in mind. The reservation in question was not prohibited unless it was in the list of such prohibited reservations. Needless to say, the fact that a provision of a treaty prohibited reservations to specified provisions did not mean that all reservations to the treaty were prohibited.

7. On draft guideline 3.1.2 (para. 49), noting that article 19 (*b*) referred to the case in which a treaty "provides that only specified reservations, which do not include the reservation in question, may be made", he said that the word "only" was vital, because it meant that a valid reservation could not be made with regard to any other part of the treaty. It was a problem of interpretation of treaties to see whether that exclusive element was or was not present. In respect of a treaty which provided that only specified reservations could be made, it was necessary to decide whether a reservation which had been formulated could be included among the sole valid specified reservations, or whether, on the contrary, it could not and thus was implicitly (or indirectly) prohibited. To that end, one would have to determine the category of reservations which the treaty considered to be the only valid reservations. In draft guideline 3.1.2, the definition of the words "specified reservations" in article 19, subparagraph (*b*), was accompanied by additional elements which were not essential and should be deleted. He did not think that the proposed definition was supported by the arbitral ruling in the *English Channel* case. The Arbitral Tribunal had pointed out that article 12 of the Convention on the Continental Shelf, which allowed reservations to articles other than articles 1 to 3, did not make it possible "to contest the right of the French Republic to be a party to the Convention on the basis of reservations the making of which is authorized by that Article". Thus, the validity in principle of the French reservation, which had concerned article 6 of the same Convention, had not been at issue. The Arbitral Tribunal had then ruled out the possibility that the French reservation could be regarded as accepted in advance, emphasizing that "[o]nly if the Article had authorised the making of specific reservations could parties to the Convention be understood as having accepted a particular reservation in advance".

8. Those statements seemed to suggest a distinction between, on the one hand, the question whether the treaty excluded or allowed a reservation, and, on the other, the question of the acceptance of a valid reservation. In principle, a reservation to article 6 was valid, and it had to be decided whether any subsequent acceptance was necessary, because article 20 of the 1969 Vienna Convention provided that it was sufficient for the reservation to be authorized by the treaty. It was only with regard to the latter effect that, according to the Arbitral Tribunal, the content of the reservation must be identified in the treaty in a sufficiently specific manner. In other words, if the treaty had stated that any reservation could be made with regard to the delimitation of the continental shelf, it would be a reservation already allowed for in all its details, and a State which formulated it would merely be doing what was expressly and specifically authorized in the treaty; there would therefore be no need to accept the reservation later, because acceptance was already provided for in the treaty. If a more general reservation was allowed, it would have to be ascertained whether it was compatible with the object and purpose of the treaty and whether it had been accepted by the relevant contracting State. By contrast, under article 19 (*b*), a general indication was sufficient to establish that the reservation was specified and therefore in principle valid.

9. Mr. KAMTO said that in paragraph 2 of his tenth report, the Special Rapporteur explained why he had decided to revert to the notion of "validity" in preference to the term "permissibility" ("*licéité*"), a term which was of relevance in the area of State responsibility but hardly appropriate in connection with reservations. According to the Special Rapporteur, the expression "validity of reservations" described "the intellectual operation consisting in determining whether a unilateral statement made by a State or an international organization and purporting to exclude or modify the legal effect of certain provisions of the treaty in their application to that State or organization [was] capable of producing the effects attached in principle to the formulation of a reservation". It was the last part of the sentence that posed problems. If that definition was accepted, the question of validity would be assessed in terms of the power or capacity of the act to produce legal effects. Such an approach took account of only one aspect of the notion of validity, with consequences for the title of draft guideline 3.1 (para. 16). It was generally agreed that validity was the quality of those elements of a legal

system, whether legal acts or legal events, that fulfilled all the conditions relating to form and content necessary for them to produce legal effects therein. It followed from that definition of validity that the conformity of an act with those conditions made it possible to decide whether it was valid or invalid. Thus, if the Commission focused solely on the capacity to produce legal effects, it would lose sight of the conditions relating to form and content.

10. In its judgment in the *Fisheries* case (*United Kingdom* v. *Norway*), the ICJ had stressed that "[a]lthough it is true that the act of delimitation is necessarily a unilateral act, because only the coastal State is competent to undertake it, the validity of the delimitation with regard to other States depends upon international law" (p. 132 of the judgment). He took that passage, and also the definition of validity to which he had just referred, to mean that a State was free to formulate a reservation, but must comply with the conditions relating to form (e.g. capacity to formulate, time of formulation) and content (e.g. compatibility with the object and purpose of the treaty, absence of conflict with a rule of *jus cogens*) which enabled it to produce legal effects. Draft guideline 3.1 had to do with the freedom to formulate reservations, not with the presumption of validity, and the title "Presumption of validity of reservations" did not reflect its content. The alternative title "Freedom to formulate a reservation" should be the one retained.

11. Furthermore, if one accepted the Special Rapporteur's line of reasoning, the amendment to draft guideline 1.6 proposed in footnote 16 to paragraph 8 was incomplete, because it would also be necessary to delete the words "and effects": if validity was the capacity of the reservation to produce legal effects, it would be tautological to say "without prejudice to the validity and effects", because validity was precisely the capacity to produce such effects.

12. Mr. Sreenivasa RAO paid tribute to the Special Rapporteur for his tenth report, which contained an extraordinary wealth of information and detail. The task of making sense out of the obvious sometimes demanded extraordinary communication skills.

13. The Special Rapporteur was clearly in favour of States' freely expressing limitations, conditions and individual situations by way of reservations when becoming parties to a treaty. He himself also endorsed that approach, because in a diverse world it was important for as many States as possible to become parties to treaties and, as long as their basic object and purpose were promoted, States must be allowed some flexibility in that regard. That policy was at the core of the concept and institution of reservations.

14. Turning to details, he thought it a good idea to reproduce article 19 of the 1969 Vienna Convention and to indicate the parameters within which it could be used by States. On the terminology, he would go along with the proposals by the Special Rapporteur, who had rightly suggested reverting to the term "validity", as long as its meaning was set out clearly and did not prejudice the issue of the rival claims of the permissibility school and the opposability school. Validity was certainly a neutral term.

15. There were good grounds for concluding that reservations expressly permitted other categories of reservations that were implicitly excluded. However, that point should be made clear in the draft guidelines. He also endorsed the Special Rapporteur's point that reservations neither expressly permitted nor implicitly prohibited must be compatible with the object and purpose of the treaty, and looked forward to further information in that regard.

16. In response to a comment by Mr. Kabatsi, he concluded by saying that over the years the subject matter had been so thoroughly researched and so many conclusions had been drawn that the complexity of the process was not necessarily obvious to those unaware of the background. For that reason the report would be of great value to all those with an especial interest in the technicalities of treaty-making. The Special Rapporteur's careful sifting of the material had unravelled many knots that in other hands would have proved inextricable.

17. The CHAIRPERSON invited Mr. Pellet to introduce section C of his tenth report on reservations incompatible with the object and purpose of the treaty.

18. Mr. PELLET (Special Rapporteur) said it was regrettable that the beginning of his report had elicited statements from only three members. He was grateful to those members, but preferred to respond to them at a later stage. He had taken particular note of the issues raised by Mr. Gaja, some aspects of which were not absolutely clear. Admittedly, sections A and B of his report did not make for very exciting reading, but he would have thought, given the amount of information it contained, that it warranted fuller discussion. He was tempted to interpret the silence of the other members as unanimous approval, but feared that would be too good to be true. He therefore hoped that section C of his report would arouse greater interest and lead to a constructive exchange of views.

19. The task of a special rapporteur was a thankless one, particularly where such a dry and technically difficult subject was concerned, but when the general reaction to his work was a polite silence he sometimes felt rather frustrated. He always appreciated any constructive criticism: indeed, the main merit of the Commission lay in the collective approach it took to its work, and while a special rapporteur must not allow himself simply to bend with the prevailing wind, the debate should nonetheless point the way forward. He could quite easily take a wrong turn, and the draft guidelines he was proposing could be improved upon both in their form and substance. It was his responsibility as Special Rapporteur to provide members with the factual and legal materials necessary to stimulate discussion. However, he was not infallible, and could change his views, sometimes radically, in the light of the Commission's debates, as had happened recently in connection with the definition of objections.

20. Turning to section D, he said that it dealt with the validity of reservations, a concept he had explained at length during his presentation of sections A and B of his report (see 2854th meeting, above). Members' comments on those sections made him think that perhaps his definition of the validity of reservations was somewhat too restrictive, and that he had not made it sufficiently clear

that validity applied both to the form and substance of reservations. He would, however, revert to that matter at a later stage.

21. Issues relating to validity were essentially governed by article 19 of the 1969 and 1986 Vienna Conventions, according to which reservations might be formulated, not made, under two conditions. First, the reservation that the State intended to formulate must not be expressly prohibited (art. 19 (*a*)), or implicitly prohibited (art. 19 (*b*)) by the treaty, and in that connection he took note of Mr. Gaja's comment that subparagraph (*a*) might also cover some cases of implicit prohibition. Such issues were dealt with under paragraphs 22 to 49 of the report.

22. Second, subparagraph (*c*) provided that in cases not falling under subparagraphs (*a*) and (*b*), the reservation must be compatible with the object and purpose of the treaty. Section C of his report focused on that fundamental condition, which was an essential element of the "flexible system" stemming from the ICJ advisory opinion of 1951 on *Reservations to the Convention on Genocide* (p. 24 of the advisory opinion) and the 1969 Vienna Convention. By virtue of that clarification, the "right" of States to make reservations was balanced by the requirement, not to preserve "the integrity" of the treaty—it being argued that reservations undermined that integrity—but rather to preserve the core contents or raison d'être of the treaty. It was worth noting that the criterion of compatibility with the object and purpose of the treaty applied to the formulation of reservations but not to that of objections, which was contrary to the position taken by the ICJ in its advisory opinion of 1951 (p. 24 of the advisory opinion) and to the view of States, which often felt it necessary to justify their objections to the reservation on grounds of its incompatibility with the object and purpose of the treaty. Article 20 of the 1969 Vienna Convention made no such requirement: States could object to a treaty for whatever reason they pleased, and, on careful reflection, their justification that the reservation was not compatible with the object and purpose of the treaty was often seen to be unconvincing.

23. Mr. Sreenivasa Rao seemed to be under the impression that he was in favour of States entering reservations. He had no strong views on the matter. Reservations were a fact of international life, a necessary evil that allowed States to become parties to treaties, and that option should not be foreclosed. On the other hand, he attached great importance to the concept of the object and purpose of the treaty, which was the decisive factor in preventing States from voiding treaties of their substance. Subparagraph (*c*) of article 19 of the 1969 Vienna Convention was therefore an essential provision that prevented States from abusing reservations as a means of stating their will at the international level. It set forth a rule that was now regarded as a customary norm to be taken into account by all States and international organizations irrespective of whether they were parties to the Vienna Conventions. However, it was a customary norm and not a peremptory norm—if States so wished they could indeed authorize reservations that voided treaties of their substance. Moreover, a cursory reading of article 20, paragraphs 2 and 3, made it clear that the framers of the Vienna Conventions had not had that in mind, and that the principle of compatibility with the object and purpose of the treaty did not apply in practice to treaties with limited participation or to the constituent acts of international organizations, since those provisions reintroduced the concept of unanimity. Moreover, if the treaty expressly prohibited certain reservations, it was pointless to ask whether they might be compatible with the object and purpose of the treaty—they were prohibited, and that was all.

24. The same was true when a specified reservation was authorized (he was not persuaded by Mr. Gaja's argument in that regard (paras. 7–8 above)): in their collective wisdom, the parties had decided that a specified reservation could be made irrespective of whether it was compatible with the object and purpose of the treaty, and even if that was an exception to subparagraph (*c*), it was quite acceptable because the latter was not a peremptory norm.

25. He then turned to two other cases, which he had already examined under section B, that were also covered by article 19, subparagraphs (*a*) and (*b*), of the 1969 and 1986 Vienna Conventions, where the question of whether reservations permitted *a priori* under the treaty were subject to the test of compatibility outlined in subparagraph (*c*) was not resolved directly by the Vienna Conventions. The first case was that of reservations that were implicitly authorized because they were not expressly prohibited; the second was that of reservations that were expressly authorized but not specified in the terms he had endeavoured to explain in draft guideline 3.1.2. In both those cases, where what was authorized was somewhat vague, it seemed that a State or an international organization could formulate a reservation only where it did not leave the treaty devoid of substance, in other words, where it was not contrary to the object and purpose of the treaty.

26. With regard to reservations that were implicitly authorized because they were not prohibited under article 19 (*a*) of the 1969 and 1986 Vienna Conventions, Sir Humphrey Waldock had very sensibly observed, as Special Rapporteur on the law of treaties in 1962, that it might not be unreasonable to regard compatibility with the object and purpose as still an implied limitation on the making of other reservations.[1] To his knowledge, there were no precedents to illustrate that point, but there seemed to be no reason to treat reservations that were implicitly authorized any differently from those that were expressly authorized but not specified. With regard to the latter, Sir Humphrey Waldock's rational inference was substantiated on two grounds. One was based on the *travaux préparatoires* for article 19 (*b*), of the 1969 Vienna Convention. The current wording of the provision was the result of a Polish amendment adopted by the United Nations Conference on the Law of Treaties, which provided for the insertion of the word "only" before "specified reservations".[2] Its adoption had required a consequential amendment to subparagraph (*c*): in place of the original text which had reserved the application of the compatibility crite-

[1] *Yearbook ... 1962*, vol. II, document A/CN.4/144, commentary to article 17, pp. 65–66, para. (10).

[2] See *Official Records of the United Nations Conference on the Law of Treaties...*, document A/CONF.39/11 (2854th meeting above, footnote 7), p. 415, para. 16. See also document A/CONF.39/14 (*ibid.*), p. 134.

rion to treaties that contained no provisions regarding reservations, the Conference had adopted the current text whereby the criterion concerning compatibility with the object and the purpose of the treaty was extended to all cases not falling under subparagraphs (*a*) and (*b*).[3] In the light of that amendment, subparagraph (*b*) clearly referred to specified reservations only, and in other cases subparagraph (*c*) applied. Therefore, authorized reservations that were not specified were clearly subject to the compatibility criterion. The second ground was the 1977 ruling of the Arbitral Tribunal in the *English Channel* case.

27. Since the problem arose in the same terms in the two situations mentioned (implicitly authorized reservations; reservations expressly authorized but not specified), it would probably make sense for it to be the subject of a single draft guideline 3.1.3/3.1.4, whose text was reproduced in paragraph 70 of the report. Nevertheless, given that the first of the cases he had mentioned referred implicitly to subparagraph (*a*), whereas the second referred to subparagraph (*b*), his preference would be for the adoption of two separate draft guidelines (3.1.3 and 3.1.4 respectively) to clarify matters for the users of the Guide to Practice.

28. Having thus clarified the applicability of the criterion of the reservation's compatibility with the object and purpose of the treaty, he wished to turn to the most sensitive issue not only of his tenth report, but of the entire legal regime of reservations and, perhaps, of the law of treaties as a whole, namely the definition of the concept of the object and purpose of a treaty. He saw that issue in very broad terms, since he had linked a question which was central to the law of treaties to others which could have been separated from it. While such a course of action might have simplified matters, a distinction of that nature would have been artificial. He had therefore cast his net wide in order to gain as general an idea as possible of an issue which was central both to the law on reservations to treaties and to the law of treaties itself.

29. Article 19 of the 1969 Vienna Convention on the Law of Treaties was by no means the only provision of the Vienna Conventions to have recourse to the notion of the object and purpose of the treaty; there were six others, which he mentioned in footnote 169 to paragraph 77 of the report. It did not seem possible to claim that the words "object and purpose of the treaty" contained in those other six provisions differed in meaning from the same expression as it appeared in the context of article 19 (*c*). When presenting the draft text of what was to become article 19 to the Commission in 1962, Sir Humphrey Waldock had expressly relied on the expression, which the Commission had already included in what was to become article 31 of the Vienna Convention, in order to justify its inclusion in article 19 (*c*). That clearly showed that the term "object and purpose of a treaty" had the same meaning throughout the 1969 Vienna Convention. That said, none of the seven provisions employing that enigmatic expression shed any particular light on its meaning, and article 19 certainly did not do so. Legal writers were unanimous in emphasizing the term's subjectivity, which had already been denounced in the joint dissenting opinion which Vice-President Guerrero and Judges McNair, Read and Hsu Mo had appended to the 1951 advisory opinion on *Reservations to the Convention on Genocide*.

30. Admittedly, it was inevitable that the subjective view of the interpreter would strongly influence any appreciation of a reservation's compatibility with the object and purpose of a treaty. That was why, in section D of his tenth report, the Special Rapporteur devoted much space to a discussion of the question of competence, which was of great significance when it came to determining the validity of a reservation and, more specifically, to assessing its compatibility with the object and purpose of the treaty. It was vital to know who could express an opinion on that matter, because that body would have to make a subjective assessment of the object and purpose of the treaty, since there was no magic formula for determining them.

31. That reference to the subjectivity of the notion was not, however, sufficient reason for holding the concept up to obloquy. It was not the first time—nor would it be the last—that an eminently legal notion had appealed to the subjective view of the body interpreting and giving effect to it. What was more subjective than the notion of "public morals"? Not only was it subjective, it evolved with time. Obviously, the public morals of the past were not those of the modern world. Yet national courts adapted to such notions and managed to draw a distinction between what was or was not contrary to public morals. The notions of "reasonableness" and "good faith" which were all-pervasive and omnipresent in international law and which had very real consequences, or of "proportionality", "necessity" or "abuse of a right" could not be defined in an objective manner either, but they were legal notions nonetheless. They permeated States' foreign legal policy and Government action. They were constantly present in the minds of the legal advisers of Governments and international organizations. They constituted the basis of numerous rulings by international courts and arbitral awards, which were certainly accepted as the law by the parties to whom those rulings or awards were addressed. The same was true of pornography, for which the usual criterion was "I know it when I see it". Although in some borderline cases something that one person might define as pornographic might appear erotic to another, on the whole any person of good faith would arrive at an identical or very similar conclusion, in any case (and this was the important factor) in a given cultural context. Given that legal norms were meant to be interpreted in a special context and did not belong to some Platonic heaven of ideas, the object and purpose of a treaty were no different from public morals or pornography in that, in a specific international context, interpreters acting in good faith ought to find it relatively easy to agree subjectively or intuitively on what constituted the object and purpose of a treaty.

32. He provided some examples in paragraphs 93 and 94. But, not unsurprisingly, he had found few examples of precedents, because States naturally refrained from formulating reservations which would be manifestly incompatible with the object and purpose of a treaty. For example, although a number of reservations had been formulated to the Convention on the Prevention and Punishment of the Crime of Genocide of 1948, it would never

[3] See *Official Records of the United Nations Conference on the Law of Treaties...*, document A/CONF.39/11 (2854th meeting above, footnote 7), p. 415, para. 17.

occur to a State to ratify that Convention while reserving the right to commit genocide, since that would plainly conflict with the Convention's object and purpose. Admittedly the intolerable colonial clause (article XII of the Convention) did raise some problems in that respect, but that was another matter.

33. Even though the subjectivity of the notion of the object and purpose of a treaty was not a dramatic problem in itself and although in most cases, the problem could be avoided by simply interpreting that notion in good faith, it would be useful to try to guide the subjective view of the body interpreting the term by endeavouring to define it and the means of giving effect to it. That was what he had striven to do in paragraphs 79 to 85 on the basis of case law and legal doctrine, but the result would definitely not satisfy those enamoured of certainty. No matter what the French school of legal doctrine might suggest, it would be futile to try to distinguish between the two terms "object" and "purpose", for the reasons he had explained in paragraphs 82 and 83. They were one and the same notion and not a combination of two concepts. His task might have been simpler if he had been able to break them down into two elements, as that would have afforded the prospect of an objective analysis. He had, however, been unable to do so and he failed to see why French legal writers insisted on separating the concepts of the object and the purpose of a treaty. The rather disappointing result he had produced after racking his brains was set out in draft guideline 3.1.5 in paragraph 89, and read: "For the purpose of assessing the validity of reservations, the object and purpose of the treaty means the essential provisions of the treaty, which constitute its *raison d'être*".

34. He recognized that that wording constituted a very general guideline, but in view of international practice and precedents and the literature, he did not honestly believe it was possible to go much further. He would nevertheless be open to suggestions from members on ways of adding to the draft guideline, since he was deeply convinced that law was not about providing magic solutions or confining the interpreter within rigid formulae. Such a process decidedly required more "*esprit de finesse*" than "*esprit de géométrie*". His proposal for draft guideline 3.1.5 was certainly better than nothing because, if the Commission agreed with him, users would henceforth know that a reservation could not void a treaty of its substance. Thus the guideline would somewhat strengthen the meaning of the expression the "object and purpose of a treaty".

35. Moreover, the disadvantages which the general and very vague character of draft guideline 3.1.5 (para. 89 of the report) might present were limited in two ways. First, the vague nature of the draft text was offset by the method of determining the object and purpose of a treaty which he suggested in draft guideline 3.1.6 (para. 91), which was prompted by, but was not an exact copy of, the method of interpreting treaties set forth in articles 31 and 32 of the 1969 and 1986 Vienna Conventions, for the precedents he had analysed in his report did indeed deal with the question of interpretation and hence the question of the determination of the object and purpose of a treaty.

36. The only really knotty problem in that connection was whether the time chosen was that when the treaty was concluded, or that when the attempt was made to identify its object and purpose. That was a question of interpretation which was often described as a choice between the method of a fixed or mobile point of reference, to which he had alluded, perhaps all too briefly, in paragraphs 83 and 86. Like Sir Gerald Fitzmaurice, he was inclined to the idea that law evolved, that there was no inherent object or purpose and that it might therefore be necessary to bear in mind the subsequent practice of the parties in order to determine the object and purpose of the treaty. As there might be pros and cons to that approach, he had left the expression "and the subsequent practice of parties" in square brackets in draft guideline 3.1.6 and he would be grateful to receive the views of the other members of the Commission on that matter.

37. The second factor mitigating the disadvantages of the very general definition of the notion "object and purpose of the treaty" related to the large number of guidelines he was proposing for adoption in paragraphs 93 to 146 of the report on "Application of the criterion". On reflection, that title might be rather ambiguous and inaccurate because in proposing the draft guidelines he had tried to analyse the problems raised by particular kinds of reservations. A detailed study of the object and purpose of the treaty would make it possible to break the subject matter down into a number of subsidiary questions which would facilitate the quest for an answer to the main issue.

38. In fact it was not so much a matter of describing the methods of applying the criterion of the object and purpose of a treaty as of attempting to give States, courts and interpreters generally some guidelines as to the conduct to be followed in the main circumstances in which the problem of the validity of reservations arose. In that connection, he would commence his introduction of paragraphs 83 *et seq.* with four general preliminary comments. First, he had certainly not thought of all the possible cases; although the Guide to Practice had attempted to be fairly detailed on the whole, it was not the purpose of a codification text to cover absolutely every conceivable case. While he had endeavoured not to omit anything vital, he would supplement draft guidelines 3.1.7 (para. 115) to 3.1.13 (para. 99) if other members of the Commission were to suggest additional situations that arose with relative frequency. The more reasonable hypotheses were covered, the more the Commission's clients, in other words, States and international organizations as well as their legal services and international courts, would appreciate the assistance which the Guide tried to offer.

39. Secondly, there would always be some situations which were not covered and, in those cases, it would be necessary to refer only to draft guidelines 3.1.5 (para. 89) and 3.1.6 (para. 91), even if that meant proceeding by analogy with the situations envisaged in the subsequent guidelines.

40. Thirdly, the six or seven situations considered in paragraphs 96 to 146 were fairly heterogeneous. The first two concerned reservations to particular kinds of treaties or clauses: reservations to dispute settlement clauses and to clauses on the monitoring of the application of treaties, or reservations to general human rights treaties. The next two categories covered reservations which were

problematic on account of their content, namely, those relating to the application of internal law on the one hand, and vague or general reservations on the other. The last two headings pertained to reservations to "androgynous" treaty provisions, in that they were provisions embodied in a treaty but which enunciated customary rules or *jus cogens* norms.

41. Admittedly his method had not been very Cartesian, but his aim had been to take a useful rather than a highly theoretical or abstract approach. He had pondered the difficulties which States would really face when assessing the validity of reservations, both those they wished to formulate themselves and those formulated by their peers. He had then tried to outline positive solutions based on practice or, failing that, on the literature, or, failing even that, by attempting to think as logically as possible.

42. Of course, it could happen that a particular reservation could fall under several of the headings envisaged. For example, a reservation to a general human rights treaty, such as the 1966 International Covenant on Economic, Social and Cultural Rights and the 1966 International Covenant on Civil and Political Rights or regional human rights conventions, might affect a customary law rule or an imperative norm and purport to preserve the application of internal law. Obviously, in such cases, it would be necessary to combine the rules he had outlined.

43. The order he had followed in his report was not the one he proposed to follow for the numbering of the draft guidelines. In the report, he proceeded from specific to general considerations, whereas he suggested proceeding in the reverse order for the draft guidelines. In the remainder of his presentation, he would follow the order of his report. The numbering of the draft guidelines was not completely arbitrary or haphazard, but was fairly logical.

44. Turning to the different categories of reservations and the specific issues raised by them, he recalled that reservations to dispute settlement clauses or clauses concerning the monitoring of the application of a treaty formulated by the former "Eastern bloc" countries had given rise to a major debate leading to the adoption of the flexible system. The General Assembly had seized the ICJ in the matter of those countries' reservations to article IX of the 1948 Convention on the Prevention and Punishment of the Crime of Genocide, which provided that disputes relating to the interpretation or application of the Convention must be submitted to the ICJ. In response thereto, the Court had rendered its advisory opinion of 28 May 1951, which was justifiably famous, despite the fact that it was of an abstract nature and did not deal with the specific question which had prompted the request for an opinion.

45. Against the background of the cold war, Western writers, including Sir Gerald Fitzmaurice, at the time Special Rapporteur of the Commission on the law of treaties, had affirmed that such reservations were contrary to the object and purpose of the Convention on the Prevention and Punishment of the Crime of Genocide. That position had been rejected by the ICJ in its orders of 1999 in two cases concerning *Legality of Use of Force*, namely those of *Yugoslavia* v. *Spain* and *Yugoslavia* v. *United States of America*. More recently, in its order of 2002 in the case concerning *Armed Activities on the Territory of the Congo*, the ICJ had clearly stated that "whereas the reservation does not bear on the substance of the law, but only on the Court's jurisdiction [...] it therefore does not appear contrary to the object and purpose of the Convention" (p. 246 of the judgment).

46. Human rights bodies had apparently adopted a different stance. That held good for the Human Rights Committee in its General Comment No. 24[4] and in its decision on Communication No. 845/1999, *Kennedy* v. *Trinidad and Tobago*, and for the European Court of Human Rights in the *Loizidou* v. *Turkey* case. Both bodies had maintained that monitoring rules constituted guarantees for securing the rights set forth in the treaties and were thus essential to the object and purpose of the treaty in question.

47. It might appear hard to reconcile those two relatively firm stances. It was not, however, impossible, and he had tried to do this in paragraph 99 of the report, which contained draft guideline 3.1.13 stating the principle that, in keeping with the case law of the ICJ, "A reservation to a treaty clause concerning dispute settlement or the monitoring of the implementation of the treaty is not, in itself, incompatible with the object and purpose of the treaty". He had however indicated that the position would be different if the provision to which the reservation related was the *raison d'être* of the treaty or if "[t]he reservation [had] the effect of excluding the author from a dispute settlement or treaty implementation monitoring mechanism with respect to a treaty provision that the author [had] previously accepted, if the very purpose of the treaty or protocol [was] to put such a mechanism into effect".

48. Quite apart from reservations concerning monitoring mechanisms, reservations to general human rights treaties posed other problems that gave rise to the liveliest controversy. The Commission had considered the subject at length when, in 1997, after examining his second report,[5] it adopted its preliminary conclusions on multilateral normative treaties, including human rights treaties.[6] Given that it was hoped that, in 2006, it would be possible to hold a seminar with human rights bodies in order to consider the issue, he had briefly returned to the question in his tenth report and had merely pondered whether it was necessary to contend that a reservation to one of the rights guaranteed by general human rights treaties, in other words the two Covenants of 1966, the three main general conventions and other comprehensive human rights instruments, was in principle or by its very nature incompatible with the object and purpose of those treaties. It would seem, on a reading of certain passages of General Comment No. 24 of the Human Rights Committee, that such might well be the case. Yet a perusal of the whole text would lead to a more qualified conclusion, since in practice two things were clear: first, that States formulated many reservations to provisions guaranteeing a specific right in general treaties; secondly, that other States did not systematically object to such reservations.

[4] *Official Records of the General Assembly, Fiftieth session, Supplement No. 40* (A/50/40), volume I, annex V, p. 119.

[5] *Yearbook ... 1996*, vol. II (Part One), documents A/CN.4/477 and Add.1 and A/CN.4/478.

[6] See 2854th meeting, footnote 1. *Yearbook ...1997*, vol. II (Part Two), chap. V, sect. B and C, pp. 44–58.

49. Since the relevant practice was unclear and ambiguous, it would be wise to spare the feelings of "human rights-ists", within the bounds of reason, by adopting a fairly flexible draft guideline. The one he proposed as draft guideline 3.1.12 in paragraph 102 of the report simply indicated that to assess the compatibility of a reservation to a general human rights treaty with the object and purpose of such a treaty, "account should be taken of the indivisibility of the rights set out therein, the importance that the right which [was] the subject of the reservation [had] within the general architecture of the treaty, and the seriousness of the impact the reservation [had] upon it". To his mind, that meant that a reservation concerning a fundamental right was incompatible with the object and purpose of a general human rights treaty, but that not all the rights safeguarded in such treaties necessarily constituted fundamental rights, and that even in the case of fundamental rights, one could not reasonably exclude the possibility of reservations targeting particular or marginal aspects of the implementation of such rights.

50. Another question that frequently arose in the area of human rights, and not only there, was whether a State could formulate a reservation to safeguard the application of its internal law. Reading the objections he reproduced in paragraph 103, one might think that the reply could only be in the affirmative. Objecting States sometimes adduced what was allegedly a general principle prohibiting States from invoking their internal law as justification for refusing to apply a treaty. In his opinion, that begged the question. True, article 27 of the 1969 and 1986 Vienna Conventions provided that a State or international organization could not invoke the provisions of its internal law as justification for its failure to perform a treaty. But—and it was a huge but—that presupposed that the provision that the State or organization failed to apply was already applicable to it. The problem, however, arose at an earlier stage: could a State prevent a provision from applying to it by making a reservation thereto and, for that purpose, could it invoke its internal law? The question was not whether a State could refuse an obligation incumbent upon it, but whether it could refuse to accept that obligation in the first place. It was thus an entirely different situation from the one covered by article 27 of the 1969 Vienna Convention, and in that sense, the States whose objections he cited in paragraph 103 were seriously mistaken in their reasoning.

51. If the question was put properly, the response would have to be much more finely nuanced than it usually was. First, there was a general presumption of the validity of reservations. Second, States were not obliged to justify their reservations, although it would be useful if they did, and perhaps the Guide to Practice should include a recommendation to that effect, even though it was not a legal obligation. It would be absurd to consider that a reservation with no explanation accompanying it was valid, whereas the same reservation was invalid if it was ascribed to the difficulties its author faced on account of its existing internal law. Third, in practice, it was most often considerations of internal law that led States to formulate reservations. The only reservations authorized by as emblematic a treaty as the European Convention on Human Rights were precisely those that were justified by the requirements of the internal law in force at the time the State ratified that Convention.

52. It therefore seemed to him impossible to affirm categorically that as a matter of principle a State could not formulate a reservation in order to preserve the integrity of its internal law. In so doing, however, the State must not undermine the object and purpose of the treaty. Internal law or no internal law, it had to respect the general precepts set out in draft guidelines 3.1.5 and 3.1.6. That might seem self-evident, but it could benefit from being spelled out, which was precisely what he did in draft guideline 3.1.11, contained in paragraph 106 of his report.

53. The problem of reservations prompted by the desire of their author to preserve the application of its internal law was often confused with that of vague and general reservations, but was in fact an entirely different matter. What was unacceptable was not that a State should invoke its internal law to justify a reservation, but that it should try to seek shelter behind its internal law in general, without further specification, in order to claim that its provisions took precedence over those of the treaty. The invalidity of such a reservation was attributable, not to the invocation of internal law, but rather to the fact that it was impossible for other States to assess the true scope of the reservation and, in particular, its compatibility with the object and purpose of the treaty. Indeed, the reason for the reservation's invalidity did not necessarily derive from the fact that the State invoked its national law; it could also derive from the fact that the reservation was formulated in a general and vague manner or invoked national policies of the State in question. Whenever it was impossible to understand the effective scope of a reservation, that reservation was invalid.

54. By not permitting other parties to assess the scope of its reservation, the reserving State rendered the entire reservations mechanism inoperative and deprived the other contracting parties of the possibility of reacting that must be available to them under article 20 of the 1969 Vienna Convention. As he indicated in paragraph 109 of his report, it was not the reference to internal law in itself that was the problem but rather the frequent vagueness and generality of the reservations, which made it impossible for the other States parties to take a position concerning them. As the Human Rights Committee had indicated in its General Comment No. 24, reservations must be specific and transparent, so that the Committee, those under the jurisdiction of the reserving State and the other States parties might be clear as to what obligations of human rights compliance had or had not been undertaken. Reservations could thus not be general, but must refer to a particular provision of the convention in question and indicate in precise terms its scope in relation thereto. As the European Commission of Human Rights had stated, a reservation was of a general nature when it was worded in such a way that it did not allow its scope to be determined. The European Court of Human Rights had taken a similar position in the famous *Belilos* case.

55. It therefore seemed legitimate to propose a draft guideline 3.1.7, to read: "A reservation worded in vague, general language which does not allow its scope to be determined is incompatible with the object and purpose of the treaty" (para. 115 of the report).

56. In paragraphs 110 and 111 he gave several examples of reservations to which that provision seemed relevant and which had been the subject of objection for that reason. Some reservations entailed the invocation by States of their constitutions or internal law with no explanation of the effect of those provisions on the treaty; some of those based on Islamic sharia did not cite specific provisions of the treaty and failed to indicate why sharia prohibited the application of the treaty in question. Other types of reservation were that of the Holy See to the Convention on the rights of the child, which it had ratified on the understanding that the application of the Convention should be compatible in practice with the particular nature of the Vatican City State and the sources of its objective law, and that of the United States, which had reserved the general right to have its Constitution prevail over the Convention on the Prevention and Punishment of the Crime of Genocide. In such cases, the States or other entities confined themselves to saying that they could not apply the convention because it was contrary to its constitution or, in the case of the Holy See, to the "sources of its objective law", and it was absolutely impossible to know what precise provision of the convention was the object of the reservation and what the scope of the reservation was. Other States were thus unable to react. Such reservations, it must be clearly indicated in the Guide to Practice, were unacceptable—not on grounds of ideology, but because of the mechanism for reservations.

57. The issues addressed in paragraphs 116 *et seq.* were of a different type. There, it was not the reservations as such that were questionable, but rather the provisions to which they related, either because those provisions embodied customary rules or because they set forth norms of *jus cogens* or rules defined in the treaty itself as non-derogable. At first sight, one might think the three categories of problems were similar, and when he had started to write his report, that had been his working hypothesis. Upon reflection, however, he now thought that each case should be analysed and treated differently.

58. First, an analysis of reservations to provisions embodying customary rules must begin with the 1969 judgment of the ICJ in the *North Sea Continental Shelf* case. However, it was the judgment itself that must be considered, as writers on the subject had frequently misunderstood what the Court had been trying to say. His brief analysis of the issue could be found in paragraphs 117 to 119 of his report. Essentially, the Court said three important things in its judgment. First, it had said that article 12, on reservations, of the 1958 Convention on the Continental Shelf indicated that in prohibiting reservations to certain provisions and not to others, the negotiators had presumably considered that those provisions on which reservations were not prohibited did not have the force of customary rules. Second, the Court had found that it was possible to formulate a reservation to a provision embodying a customary rule (paras. 64–65 of the judgment). Although that could only be deduced *a contrario* from some of the phraseology in the judgment, there seemed to be no doubt whatsoever on that point. It was perhaps precisely because the deduction had to be made *a contrario* that writers often committed errors of interpretation.

59. Third, the Court had recalled that even if such a reservation was made, the customary rule continued to apply to the reserving State, on the basis not of treaty law but of custom. As the Court said,

> speaking generally, it is a characteristic of purely conventional rules and obligations that, in regard to them, some faculty of making unilateral reservations may, within certain limits, be admitted;—whereas this cannot be so in the case of general or customary law rules and obligations which, by their very nature, must have equal force for all members of the international community, and cannot therefore be the subject of any right of unilateral exclusion exercisable at will by any one of them in its own favour. (para. 63 of the judgment)

60. If that was so, despite a minority of doctrinal opinions to the contrary and despite the sometimes slightly ambiguous nature of the relevant practice, one might ask what a State or international organization could achieve by formulating a reservation to a conventional rule, since in any event, the substance of the rule remained opposable in the form of custom. The answer was that it achieved the not very laudable purpose—States not needing to be laudable but simply compliant with international law—of avoiding the consequences of "conventionalization" of the rule. When a treaty contained a provision on compulsory dispute settlement, for example, by making a reservation to one of those substantive provisions, the author prevented the judge designated by the treaty from hearing disputes relating to possible breaches of the rule in question. In addition, such a reservation provided an opportunity for a "persistent objector" to manifest the persistence of its objection. That was certainly true of treaties that reflected customary rules but even so were not codification treaties.

61. What, then, of treaties whose very purpose was to standardize the application of customary law? As he indicated in paragraphs 124 and 125 of his report, it did not seem appropriate to prohibit *ipso facto* any and all reservations to any provision whatsoever of a codification convention, if only because all the rules therein did not necessarily reflect a rule that had been customary in nature at the time of its adoption. Indeed, the so-called "codification conventions" set out customary rules and simultaneously engaged in progressive development of international law. At what level of codification or progressive development would it no longer be possible to formulate reservations? Such a question was impossible to answer.

62. In any event, practice was clear and indisputable: States often formulated reservations to codification conventions—in fact most reservations were in respect of such conventions—and other parties did not systematically object. When they did, it was only occasionally on the grounds that it was impossible to formulate reservations to such conventions. That being the case, and in conformity with the 1969 judgment of the ICJ, which it had repeated in its famous 1984 dictum in the case concerning *Military and Paramilitary Activities in and against Nicaragua*,

> [t]he fact that the above-mentioned principles [of general and customary international law], recognized as such, have been codified or embodied in multilateral conventions does not mean that they cease to exist and to apply as principles of customary law, even as regards countries that are parties to such conventions. (para. 73 of the judgment)

63. It was those two fundamental principles that he sought to enunciate in draft guideline 3.1.8 (para. 129 of the report). First, the customary nature of a norm set forth in a treaty provision did not in itself constitute an obstacle to the formulation of a reservation to that provision; but second, a reservation to a treaty provision which set forth a customary norm did not affect the binding nature of the customary norm in question in relations between the reserving State or international organization and other States or international organizations which were bound by that norm. He was convinced that those principles applied in all areas, irrespective of the object of the treaty in question. They applied in particular in respect of human rights, even though the Human Rights Committee had seemed to dispute that fact in its famous but sometimes debatable General Comment No. 24. The Human Rights Committee was certainly right in considering that the formulation of a reservation to the International Covenant on Civil and Political Rights did not release the reserving State from the obligation not to engage in slavery or not to subject human beings to cruel, inhuman or degrading treatment. In any event, however, the State was subject to those obligations under the rules of customary law. In addition, and perhaps most importantly, virtually all—and probably all—the obligations cited by the Human Rights Committee to illustrate its thesis were not only customary but also peremptory in nature.[7]

64. The situation was different with reservations to provisions setting forth norms of *jus cogens* as opposed to provisions simply embodying customary rules. Whereas a reservation to the latter type of treaty provisions could be envisaged, even if its effects were limited, the same was not true of a reservation to a provision setting forth a peremptory norm. The difference was not self-evident and even if it could be sensed intuitively, it was difficult to explain. He had had first to set aside explanations given by a number of authors, often very eminent ones, which, upon reflection, had turned out to be unconvincing. The Human Rights Committee and others postulated that one could not make a reservation to a provision setting out a peremptory norm, but justified that categorical assertion only with the very vague affirmation that reservations that offended peremptory norms would not be compatible with the object and purpose of the treaty. It seemed to him, nevertheless, that some further explanation was called for.

65. One could maintain that, as in the case of reservations to a provision embodying a customary rule, reservations to a peremptory norm left intact the obligation to respect the norm itself, with all the consequences that that entailed, independently of the treaty. The difference resided in the fact that customary rules were of benefit to society, whereas peremptory rules were indispensable to society. As a result, reservations to peremptory norms would be prohibited only if one acknowledged that *jus cogens* produced its effects outside the realm of the law of treaties and of the strict confines of articles 53 and 64 of the 1969 and 1986 Vienna Conventions. He was deeply convinced of that, but had not seen the need to demonstrate it in his report, since that would have involved going into the whole theory of *jus cogens*. In that regard, he could, however, cite no less an authority than the Chairperson of the Commission, who at a previous meeting, speaking of unilateral acts of States, had said that States must respect the peremptory norms of general international law (2854th meeting, above, para. 38). If that was so, and he had no doubt whatsoever that it was, then reservations must also respect such rules. They constituted a particularly common example of unilateral acts. Accordingly, any reservation that sought to avoid the application of a peremptory rule was contrary to that rule and must be considered null and void.

66. The invalidity of reservations to treaty provisions setting out peremptory norms must be seen as deriving not from the fact that they were contrary to the object and purpose of the treaty but, *mutatis mutandis*, from the principle set forth in article 53 of the 1969 Vienna Convention, namely, that a unilateral act was void if, at the time of its formulation, it conflicted with a peremptory norm of general international law. On the basis of that remark, he thought that draft guideline 3.1.9 on reservations to provisions setting forth a rule of *jus cogens* could very simply read: "A State or an international organization may not formulate a reservation to a treaty provision which sets forth a peremptory norm of general international law" (para. 146 of the report).

67. Turning to the seventh and last category of problems, that of reservations to non-derogable provisions in a treaty, he said the problem generally related to the human rights treaties which often, if not always, contained provisions which the parties undertook not to suspend, irrespective of the circumstances. There again, one might assume that the problem was similar to that of reservations to provisions setting forth peremptory norms, and that had indeed been his initial impression. In statistical terms it was true, since very often norms were non-derogable because they set out principles of *jus cogens*. The correlation was not always automatic, however, as the Human Rights Committee had stressed, in both General Comment No. 24 and in General Comment No. 29 (2001).[8] The Human Rights Committee had acknowledged that, in contrast to reservations to provisions setting out a peremptory norm, reservations to provisions that were non-derogable but not *jus cogens* were possible under the usual conditions, namely, of not being incompatible with the object and purpose of a treaty. That had also been the position of the Inter-American Court of Human Rights in its 1983 advisory opinion on *Restrictions to the Death Penalty*.

68. One had to acknowledge, therefore, that where a non-derogable rule was not peremptory, a reservation could be formulated with respect to it, as long as it related only to certain limited aspects concerning the implementation of the right in question. On the other hand, if a reservation to such a provision was to void it of its substance, it would have to be considered as being incompatible with the object and purpose of the treaty, in accordance with draft guidelines 3.1.5 and 3.1.6. It was those complex and nuanced principles that he had sought to enunciate in draft guideline 3.1.10 (para. 146).

[7] See footnote 4 above.

[8] *Official Records of the General Assembly, Fifty-sixth session, Supplement No. 40* (A/56/40), volume I, annex VI, p. 202.

69. It had been his original intention to provide a brief overview of section D of his report, which addressed two questions relevant to the entire exercise: first, who could assess the validity of reservations, and in particular, their compatibility or non-compatibility with the object and purpose of a treaty; and second, the consequences of their possible non-validity. As that section was currently available in French only, he would refrain from introducing it at the present juncture; however, he reserved the right to change his mind if, during the discussion, it appeared necessary to make a few clarifications in order better to convey the underlying logic that had guided him in his inquiry into the fundamental characteristics of the validity of reservations to treaties.

The meeting rose at 1 p.m.

2857th MEETING

Tuesday, 26 July 2005, at 10.05 a.m.

Chairperson: Mr. Djamchid MOMTAZ

Present: Mr. Addo, Mr. Candioti, Mr. Chee, Mr. Comissário Afonso, Mr. Daoudi, Mr. Dugard, Mr. Economides, Ms. Escarameia, Mr. Fomba, Mr. Gaja, Mr. Galicki, Mr. Kabatsi, Mr. Kamto, Mr. Kateka, Mr. Kemicha, Mr. Kolodkin, Mr. Koskenniemi, Mr. Mansfield, Mr. Matheson, Mr. Niehaus, Mr. Opertti Badan, Mr. Pambou-Tchivounda, Mr. Pellet, Mr. Sreenivasa Rao, Mr. Rodríguez Cedeño, Ms. Xue, Mr. Yamada.

Reservations to treaties (*continued*) (A/CN.4/549 and Add.1, sect D, A/CN.4/558 and Corr.1 and Add.1 [and Corr.1]–2, and A/CN.4/L.665)

[Agenda item 6]

TENTH REPORT OF THE SPECIAL RAPPORTEUR (*continued*)

1. The CHAIRPERSON invited the members of the Commission to continue their consideration of the tenth report on reservations to treaties (A/CN.4/558 and Corr.1 and Add.1 [and Corr.1]–2) submitted by the Special Rapporteur.

2. Mr. KOLODKIN commended the Special Rapporteur, whose well-thought-out tenth report had provided him with great intellectual satisfaction, even if he did not always agree with its author. The report called for comments, first of all, on the terms and concepts of permissibility/admissibility and validity of reservations. Reading the document was in fact a stimulating intellectual effort in which a comparison of the various language versions revealed that the terms had different meanings in different languages. For example, in paragraph 5 of his report the Special Rapporteur wrote that the word "validity" was fairly neutral in comparison with the word "permissibility"; yet, in Russian at least, the word "validity" was not entirely neutral. It referred specifically to legal consequences. To be legally valid meant to entail legal consequences, to be in force, and to be invalid meant the opposite.

3. He agreed with those members of the Commission and States in the Sixth Committee of the General Assembly who objected to the use of the word "inadmissible". The word carried above all the connotation of responsibility, yet introducing the notion of responsibility in the context of the formulation of reservations was a doomed enterprise. The word currently used to qualify reservations in the English text of the draft guidelines, namely "permissible", seemed perfectly appropriate. Most representatives in the Sixth Committee had said that they preferred the words "permissible/impermissible" (A/CN.4/549, para. 103). In draft guideline 1.6, the word "permissibility" referred to the stage of formulation of reservations,[1] and in draft guideline 2.1.8, the word "impermissible" applied to the attributes of the depositary.[2] It should be noted in that connection that the depositary did not as a general rule have the right to express an opinion, either on the validity or non-validity of reservations, or on their permissibility or impermissibility. The depository must remain neutral.[3]

4. He would further note that the idea advanced in paragraph 8 of the report, namely that the words "admissible" and "inadmissible" should be replaced by the words "valid" and "invalid" in draft guidelines 1.6 and 2.1.8, did not apply to the Russian and English texts, since the words used there were not "admissible" and "inadmissible" and their equivalents, but "permissible" and "impermissible". On the whole, it would appear that an act or a document was generally characterized as valid or invalid only *a posteriori*. Such judgements were made on the basis of criteria applicable only once the act had been completed or the document adopted. That value judgement applied to the existence or absence of legal consequences of the act or document in question and not to the process of its execution or formulation. In that connection, paragraph 103 of the topical summary of the discussion held in the Sixth Committee (A/CN.4/549) set out several arguments against the use of the word "validity" to qualify reservations. If one ultimately had to use the terms and concepts of "validity" and "invalidity" in connection with reservations, it would be best to do so only in assessing the legal consequences of reservations formulated, rather than for making a judgement about those that possessed the right to formulate them, in particular States or courts. It was precisely in that sense that the provisions in the 1969 Vienna Convention concerning the validity of international agreements appeared to have been elaborated.

5. Secondly, the concept of presumption of validity of reservations described in the report was not very convincing. The Special Rapporteur based his arguments on article 19 of the 1969 and 1986 Vienna Conventions, but that article, common to both Conventions, seemed merely to

---

[1] See *Yearbook ... 1999*, vol. II (Part Two), p. 126, para. (4) of the commentary.

[2] See *Yearbook ... 2002*, vol. II (Part Two), pp. 45–46, paras. (3)–(6) of the commentary.

[3] *Ibid.*

reinforce the right of States and international organizations to formulate reservations, while making it subject to certain conditions. He agreed with the Special Rapporteur that it was, more properly speaking, a "right to 'formulate' reservations" than a "right to reservations", a matter covered in paragraphs 12 and 13 of the report. Even if one replaced permissibility with validity, it was still not very clear why the notion of presumption of validity of reservations was being introduced, and the Special Rapporteur might need to provide further justification for doing so. Draft guideline 3.1 as proposed in paragraphs 16 and 20 of his report reproduced the provisions of article 19 of the Vienna Conventions, confirming that the text referred simply to the right to formulate reservations and to the corresponding restrictions. In his view, to entitle the provision "Presumption of validity of reservations" (para. 16) would be to go too far, and the word "freedom" (para. 20) should be replaced by the word "right", since that was actually what was meant. It was precisely the right to formulate reservations, subject to certain conditions, that constituted the essence of the Vienna regime. He questioned whether it was necessary to introduce a new concept, "presumption". Surely it was sufficient to enunciate and define the right, and not the "freedom", to formulate reservations.

6. In that regard, and thirdly, the question of language had once again to be addressed. Perhaps the word "*faculté*" had several meanings in French, including "right", but paragraphs 12 and 13 of the report contained the word "*droit*" ("right"), whereas the title of draft guideline 3.1 employed the word "*faculté*" ("freedom"). In the English version of paragraphs 12 and 13, the word "right" was used, whereas in the title of draft guideline 3.1, one found the word "freedom". In Russian, the word used in the title of draft guideline 3.1 ("*sposobnost*") referred not so much to the right or prerogative with which the subject of the phrase was endowed as to the subject itself, something that did not conform to the thrust of draft guideline 3.1 as currently proposed. That was why, since it was in fact a right that was at issue, it would be more accurate to use the word "*pravo*" ("right") in Russian. As to the proposal in paragraph 20 of the report concerning draft guideline 3.1, the task could be entrusted to the Drafting Committee.

7. The question of the "validity", or more precisely the "invalidity", of reservations should be considered in conjunction with that of the legal consequences of invalid reservations. The crux of the matter was whether or not invalid reservations could be dissociated from the expression by a State of its consent to be bound by a treaty to which reservations had been formulated; basically, that was the question raised in paragraph 53 of the report. Thus it must be determined what happened when a State expressed its consent to be bound by a treaty to which a reservation that appeared to be invalid had been formulated. Did the treaty remain in force or not? What was its legal effect during the period when an objection to the reservation could still be formulated? The whole question of validity of reservations and whether it was appropriate to use the concept of validity in the draft guidelines must be considered from the standpoint of the consequences arising from the characterization of reservations as invalid.

8. Fourthly, he agreed with the Special Rapporteur that article 19 (*a*) of the 1969 and 1986 Vienna Conventions related solely to reservations whose formulation in respect of a treaty was expressly prohibited. Moreover, as was rightly pointed out in paragraph 26 of the report, that interpretation "is the only one compatible with the great liberalism that pervades all the provisions of the Convention that deal with reservations". He therefore supported draft guideline 3.1.1.

9. Fifthly and lastly, the arguments put forward by the Special Rapporteur in paragraphs 45 to 49 of his report seemed entirely logical and well founded, hence the potential usefulness of draft guideline 3.1.2, "Definition of specified reservations", proposed in paragraph 49.

10. Mr. PAMBOU-TCHIVOUNDA joined all previous speakers in expressing satisfaction with the work done by the Special Rapporteur. As he had done with definitions and elaboration techniques, the Special Rapporteur had remained faithful to the methodology adopted by the Commission when the topic of reservations to treaties had been included in the programme of work: in keeping with the expectations of States, the Guide to Practice must refrain from challenging the rules codified in the Vienna Conventions, its purpose being to explicate those rules in order to fill in any areas on which they were silent. That methodological standard, adopted once again by the Special Rapporteur and applied to examining the problems underlying conditions of validity and effects of reservations, had its drawbacks, namely that it might hold back the process of progressive development. It must thus be used with caution.

11. The Special Rapporteur's tenth report elicited comments primarily on two points: the question of validity and the typological analysis of reservations.

12. The question of validity had been addressed in previous reports, but the Special Rapporteur had been quite right to highlight it once again, as it was to some extent the foundation that ensured that the building under construction was solid. Yet however pertinent it might be, the concept of validity was by no means a kind of intellectual operation to determine whether a reservation was capable of producing the effects sought by its author. That procedural operation was external to or independent of validity. Validity was a feature inherent in the reservation itself, signalled by its concordance with, or at least correspondence to, a standard of reference. Validity fulfilled a need for consistency *vis-à-vis* the legal system set up by that standard of reference, in the present instance the Vienna Conventions. It derived from an assessment made by the author of a reservation or a determination made by a third party. Validity could be presumed from an assessment made by the author of a reservation, but it could also be deduced after the reservation had been formulated, based on acceptance by other States parties to the treaty community or a third party, for example a judge or arbitrator. However, "objecting" States also had a role to play in the determination of validity or invalidity.

13. As a concept, validity had to comprise just three variables in order to be operational. The first was the standard of reference, which was the whole range of

premises offered by international law itself. In the present instance, the standard of reference was the Vienna Conventions. The second variable was the factual situation, namely the reservation formulated by a State or international organization. The third and last variable was either the objections formulated by other parties to the treaty, which could in fact relate to the validity of the reservation, or an assessment by a third party, judge or arbitrator of the reservation's conformity or lack thereof with the standard of reference.

14. The concept of validity gave rise to three sets of comments. First, the validity of reservations was not fundamentally a linguistic issue: rather, it tapped into a problem of substance, namely whether the situations contemplated in article 19, subparagraphs (*a*), (*b*) and (*c*) of the 1969 Vienna Convention, which set out conditions limiting *ratione materiae* the freedom to formulate reservations, were interrelated or, conversely, distinct in terms of their scope. That was a major problem, and it arose in particular with regard to specified reservations, permitted reservations, and even implicitly prohibited reservations in terms of their performance on the test of compatibility with the object and purpose of the treaty.

15. Second, the dual controversy that pitted the partisans of validity against those of admissibility on the one hand and the proponents of permissibility against those of opposability on the other was not in itself decisive in determining the legal regime of reservations. One of the fundamental requirements for a legal act to be legal was validity. The concepts of validity and admissibility were thus in a relationship of exact equivalence. The concept of opposability, meanwhile, had more of a causal relationship to the concept of validity, since it was its conformity, or assumed conformity, with the conditions set by article 19 of the 1969 Vienna Convention that made a reservation opposable against those that had accepted it. Thus he fully endorsed the Special Rapporteur's choice of the more neutral option (see paragraphs 5 and 8 of the report).

16. Turning to his third set of comments, Mr. Pambou-Tchivounda remarked first of all that the Special Rapporteur had written that "[t]he principle of freedom to formulate reservations undoubtedly constitutes a key element of the Vienna regime" (para. 16). He himself was in favour of devoting a draft guideline to that principle, although he questioned the advisability of elevating the freedom in question to the level of a principle (para. 17). Draft guideline 3.1 was intended as the point of departure for all the guidelines in which the problems inherent in validity were to be addressed—problems of competence, but also of form and substance. Moreover, if it was accepted that third parties (from an objecting State to a declaring third party) were involved in the determination of validity, then there must be draft guidelines on that subject. He wondered whether moving all the draft guidelines on objections to the third part of the Guide to Practice might be appropriate; he himself was not sure.

17. The second point on which he wished to comment had to do with the Special Rapporteur's typological analysis of reservations. The Special Rapporteur deserved praise for his effort to clarify the limitations *ratione materiae* on the freedom to formulate reservations, and particularly for his success in underpinning certain theoretical categories of reservations with examples of international practice. While such practice was abundant, however, it varied in significance, and that raised questions about the relevance of the categories outlined. Unless practice was taken into account, some categories of reservations bordered on mere intellectual constructs. Such was the case, *inter alia*, with implicitly prohibited reservations, whose very existence might be questioned and which were defined, one might say *a contrario*, in relation to permitted reservations (paras. 34–39). It could be concluded that whereas authorization, specified or conditional, was conducive to determination, a concept with which it was identified, that was not always the case, particularly when the authorization was of a general nature. One had to wonder, then, how reservations that were by definition indeterminate because they were not subject to any limitations *ratione materiae* could be categorized as "specified".

18. In fact the Special Rapporteur had not lost sight of that phenomenon, for he wrote in paragraph 44 of his report that "a general authorization of reservations itself does not necessarily resolve all the problems. In particular, it leaves unanswered the question of whether the other Parties may still object to reservations and whether these expressly authorized reservations are subject to the test of compatibility with the object and purpose of the treaty". He himself would answer those two questions in the affirmative—in the first case, because the capacity to object was preserved, given that the Vienna regime imposed no limitations on it, and in the second case, because submitting such reservations to the compatibility test was inevitable, given that that was a requirement implicit in the resolution's very validity. The Special Rapporteur confirmed as much in paragraph 46 of his report by stating that "reservations which are not 'specified' must pass the test of compatibility with the object and purpose of the treaty".

19. In conclusion, Mr. Pambou-Tchivounda said that such typological analysis, the relevance of which was entirely relative, had served as the foundation for only two draft guidelines, 3.1.1 (para. 32) and 3.1.2 (para. 49). However, the two provisions were quite consistent with the situations contemplated in article 19, subparagraphs (*a*) and (*b*), of the 1969 Vienna Convention, which, according to Paul Reuter, constituted "very simple cases".[4] There was perhaps no reason to complicate them.

20. Mr. KABATSI said that he had understood Mr. Pambou-Tchivounda to say that the draft guidelines were intended to fill in the gaps that existed in the Vienna regime. He himself was not so sure that that was the objective of the draft guidelines, since any addition to the Vienna regime would be tantamount to a modification of that regime. Moreover, he was not convinced that the Special Rapporteur had been engaged in such an enterprise throughout his various reports. Clarification from Mr. Pambou-Tchivounda would be appreciated.

21. Mr. PAMBOU-TCHIVOUNDA said he thought he had spoken of areas on which the Vienna Convention "was silent", which was not the same thing as "gaps". He had likewise suggested that the methodological standards

[4] Reuter, *loc. cit.* (2854th meeting, footnote 6).

used might hamper progress. What he had meant was that the definition of reservations given by the Special Rapporteur combined certain elements of the 1969, 1978 and 1986 Vienna Conventions. However, that combined reading was not by any means a rethinking of the Vienna regime, even though draft guideline 3.1.2 contained what might be a first step towards progressive development.

22. Ms. ESCARAMEIA commended the Special Rapporteur on his tenth report, which was well researched and incisive. The Commission's lengthy disquisitions on terminology, on the other hand, were not always very helpful. She herself would favour using the word "permissible" in the English text, especially with reference to the formulation of reservations, because it was the most neutral term. The word "admissible" was not appropriate because it implied certain consequences. The Special Rapporteur said that he had chosen the word that seemed to him to be the most neutral, "validity", but it seemed to her that that word also implied that the act in question had certain consequences. At the same time, she did not favour replacing the word "validity" in the draft guidelines that had already been adopted, for the reasons given by Mr. Kolodkin.

23. With regard to the presumption of validity of reservations, she said that she, like other members of the Commission, had the impression that the Special Rapporteur had taken the formulation of reservations as being synonymous with reservations themselves. Article 19 of the Vienna Convention set out the general principle of the permissibility of formulating reservations, however, not that of the validity of reservations, and the two concepts must not be confused. She endorsed draft guideline 3.1 (para. 20), which corresponded to article 19 of the Vienna Convention, and agreed with the change of title, which had the merit of reflecting the process rather than the outcome.

24. As to prohibited reservations, she pointed out that in addition to reservations that were expressly prohibited there were reservations that could not be made because of the nature of the treaty. She was thinking in particular of the constituent instruments of international organizations: a State could hardly become a member of an organization while formulating reservations to the competence of its fundamental organs or its general mandate. In any event, the concepts of the "nature of the treaty" and the "object and purpose of the treaty" were very similar. Moreover, such a distinction would be necessary only if the Commission decided to create separate regimes for reservations under article 19, subparagraph (*a*), and those under article 19, subparagraph (*c*), of the 1969 Vienna Convention.

25. She endorsed draft guideline 3.1.1 (para. 32), even though it was not easy to distinguish among the various categories. Draft guideline 3.1.2 (para. 49) seemed more problematic, however. She did not understand what was meant by the phrase "and which meet conditions specified by the treaty". The wording was unclear; it would be preferable to say that only reservations that were permitted could be formulated. That provision should therefore be redrafted, particularly since some members had seen in it a development of the Vienna regime.

26. She expressed surprise that no other member of the Commission had referred to the seminar proposed by the Special Rapporteur (see 2854th meeting, above, para. 89). It was an excellent idea, and she supported it wholeheartedly. The seminar should bring together representatives of human rights treaty monitoring bodies and of the Sub-Commission on the Promotion and Protection of Human Rights; ideally, representatives of the Committee on the Elimination of Discrimination against Women should also take part, since the Convention on the Elimination of All Forms of Discrimination against Women was one of the instruments that had drawn the greatest number of reservations. It would therefore be a good idea if at least the Chairperson of that Committee could participate in the seminar. The work should focus on the tenth report on reservations to treaties, the final working paper prepared in 2004 by Ms. Françoise Hampson, a member of the Sub-Commission,[5] and General Comment No. 24 of the Human Rights Committee.[6] The seminar should last at least two days in order to permit a serious exchange of ideas.

27. Mr. MANSFIELD commended the Special Rapporteur for his thoughtful analysis of the question of reservations to treaties. He found the commentary to be more useful than the draft guidelines themselves in understanding article 19. Like the Special Rapporteur, he thought that it was not possible to separate the freedom to formulate a reservation from the exceptions to that principle and that it was therefore necessary to reproduce article 19 in its entirety. Mr. Gaja had nevertheless been right to draw attention to the fact that article 19 (*a*) did not speak of "expressly" prohibited reservations.

28. In relation to draft guideline 3.1.1, he pointed out that there was another type of reservation clause which the report did not discuss, namely one that prohibited all reservations other than those specifically permitted (for example, by other articles of the treaty). The Special Rapporteur would presumably regard such a clause as one that prohibited reservations to specified provisions rather than one that prohibited certain categories of reservation. On draft guideline 3.1.2, as Ms. Escarameia had suggested, the drafting needed to be made less elliptical.

29. As the Special Rapporteur stated in his conclusion in paragraph 52, the consideration of the effects of a reservation formulated in spite of a prohibition within the meaning of article 19 (*c*) should not be separated from that of the consequences of a reservation that was contrary to the object and purpose of the treaty. He saw no reason why the draft guidelines should not be referred to the Drafting Committee, and he supported the aforementioned proposal regarding a seminar.

30. Mr. FOMBA welcomed the report on reservations to treaties, a highly technical topic that had to be addressed from the standpoint of both the theoretician and the practitioner. Concerning the choice of terminology, he agreed that the word "validity" had the merit of being neutral

[5] E/CN.4/Sub.2/2004/42. See also the first working paper presented by Ms. Hampson (E/CN.4/Sub.2/1999/28 and Corr.1) and the "Reservation Charts" in document E/CN.4/Sub.2/2002/34.

[6] See 2856th meeting, footnote 4.

and of prejudging neither the Commission's stance on the opposability/permissibility dispute nor the effects of the formulation of a reservation contrary to the provisions of article 19. The presumption of validity of reservations flowed from the general principle that their formulation must be permitted, but the freedom to formulate was limited *ratione temporis*, *ratione materiae* and *ratione personae*. Thus one could not speak of a "right to reservations"; the introductory wording in article 19 accorded States only the right (the freedom) to "formulate" reservations. One might then ask what the difference was between the "right to reservations" and the "right to formulate reservations".

31. The principle of freedom to formulate reservations was a key element of the Vienna regime, and it should be the subject of a draft guideline reproducing article 19 in its entirety so as not to separate the principle from the exceptions to it. The Special Rapporteur proposed to deal separately with the three conditions for validity of reservations set out in article 19, taking up, on the one hand, the propositions posited in subparagraphs (*a*) and (*b*) and, on the other, those contemplated in subparagraph (*c*). That was perfectly logical. He seemed to have hesitated between "Freedom to formulate reservations" and "Presumption of validity of reservations" (para. 16 of the report) for the title of the draft guideline before finally choosing the first option, which established an implicit connection between the concepts of formulation and validity. If, on the other hand, it was felt that the connection should be made explicit, then it would be better to speak of the "Freedom to formulate a valid reservation" or of the "Formulation and validity of a reservation". Since those alternatives were likely to create difficulties, however, the Special Rapporteur's proposal seemed acceptable.

32. The Special Rapporteur rightly noted that the cases contemplated in subparagraphs (*a*) and (*b*) were not as simple as they appeared; aside from the fact that not all possibilities were explicitly covered, problems might arise as to the exact scope of a clause prohibiting reservations and the effects of a reservation formulated despite such a prohibition.

33. Regarding the scope of clauses prohibiting reservations, he noted that a distinction was drawn between express prohibition, contemplated in subparagraph (*a*), and implicit prohibition, contemplated in subparagraph (*b*). Where the prohibition was clear and, in particular, where it was general, no problem arose (except that of deciding whether or not a statement constituted a reservation). The prohibition could, however, be ambiguous or partial. Subparagraph (*a*) should be assumed to cover three cases: clauses prohibiting all reservations, clauses prohibiting reservations to specified provisions and clauses prohibiting certain categories of reservations. There was no harm in spelling that out, and that was precisely the purpose of draft guideline 3.1.1.

34. Where implicit prohibitions were concerned, the question arose as to whether there should be a draft guideline concerning the scope of subparagraph (*b*). The Special Rapporteur proposed to define the phrase "specified reservations" in that subparagraph chiefly in order to reconcile the various and contradictory theories about how it should be construed: that was the purpose of draft guideline 3.1.2 (para. 49). One could go along with his argument that "specified reservations" must relate to specific provisions and also fulfil certain conditions specified in the treaty, without going so far as to require that their content should be predetermined; moreover, one might well ask whether such a provision would ultimately do away with all interpretative difficulties.

35. Mr. MATHESON welcomed the excellent report by the Special Rapporteur, the basic thrust of which seemed to be that reservations were a valid means of encouraging the widest possible participation in treaties. That principle should be the basis for the Commission's treatment of the topic.

36. The choice of the words "valid/invalid" was satisfactory, at least in English, but if there were terminological difficulties with respect to the other languages, then those difficulties should be further explored. Draft guideline 3.1 was also satisfactory: although it might appear in a sense superfluous, it provided a useful framework for the guidelines that followed. Draft guideline 3.1.1 (para. 32) required some adjustment, as Mr. Gaja had suggested. It should be made clear in particular that when a treaty prohibited reservations to specified provisions, then only reservations to those provisions were expressly prohibited and, likewise, that when a treaty prohibited certain categories of reservations, then only reservations falling into those categories were expressly prohibited. He had doubts about the idea of including additional categories. Draft guideline 3.1.1 should deal exclusively with express prohibitions, which it did as currently worded.

37. On the other hand, he was not certain that draft guideline 3.1.2 was actually necessary. The definition therein was not clear: one might ask whether it applied where a treaty authorized a certain category of reservations but did not refer to specific provisions; moreover, the English text said literally that "specified" reservations were only those that met conditions "specified" by the treaty. Those matters needed clarification before a decision to retain the draft guideline was made.

38. Mr. PELLET drew attention to a translation problem with the definition in draft guideline 3.1.2. The English text did indeed speak of "specified reservations" that had to meet "specified" conditions, whereas the French original used two different terms: reservations that were "*déterminées*" ("specific") which needed to meet conditions that were "*spécifiées*" ("specified"). The Drafting Committee could surely solve the problem.

39. Mr. CANDIOTI said that he, too, welcomed the excellent report on reservations to treaties. Concerning the use of the word "validity", he thought that the problem was more a conceptual one than a terminological one, but that it must be resolved without delay in order to prevent even more confusion later on. In his view, article 19 referred only to one aspect of the validity of a reservation; in fact, it did not use the words "valid", "invalid" or "null" at all, but spoke only of prohibited reservations and those that could be made. The concept of "admissibility" seemed more appropriate, since a reservation that was permitted or accepted was not necessarily valid. It went without saying that prohibition entailed invalidity, but a

reservation acquired validity from many other factors, such as its formulation by a competent organ, having a specific object, having been made within the time allotted, having been formulated in writing, and so forth. It would thus be inaccurate to give a chapter that ultimately dealt only with prohibited and authorized reservations the title "Validity of reservations".

40. Similarly, in the title of draft guideline 3.1 (para. 20), it would be preferable to avoid the word "freedom", whose meaning was too broad, and to speak instead of "prohibited and authorized reservations". On the whole, however, the text of the draft guidelines was acceptable and could be referred to the Drafting Committee, with the additional comments made by members of the Commission, in particular by Mr. Gaja.

41. Mr. Sreenivasa RAO said it was fairly self-evident that if a treaty prohibited reservations to specific articles, *a contrario* it authorized reservations to others. On the other hand, in seeking to determine what was implicitly prohibited or authorized by using criteria such as the nature of the treaty or the obligations that had to be performed or accepted by the parties or monitoring bodies established, one might be stretching the boundaries of interpretation to the point of excessive subjectivity. The intention of the parties upon becoming parties to the treaty was not necessarily clear. Indeed, that mystery must be preserved in order to leave States a certain margin of manoeuvre. Accordingly, implicit prohibitions or authorizations should be limited to situations that could logically and reasonably be deduced from the intention of the parties at the time they concluded the treaty.

42. Mr. GAJA said that section C of the Special Rapporteur's tenth report represented a major contribution to the study of the problem of reservations. Nevertheless, it raised a number of difficulties. According to article 19 (*c*) of the 1969 Vienna Convention, the criterion of incompatibility of a reservation with the object and purpose of a treaty entered into play only in cases when a reservation was not prohibited under subparagraphs (*a*) and (*b*) of that article. The reservations concerned were thus those that were not prohibited, either explicitly or implicitly, by the treaty. Draft guideline 3.1.4 proposed by the Special Rapporteur aimed to make it clear that the question of compatibility did not arise if a reservation had specifically been authorized by the treaty (para. 69). If, on the other hand, the authorization was only general, or if the treaty contained no provisions relating to reservations, then the reservation was subject to the test of compatibility with the object and purpose of the treaty. If that was indeed what was meant, then it should be expressed more clearly. The phrase "[w]here the treaty authorizes certain reservations without specifying them" was infelicitous (para. 69). It would be better to speak of cases where a reservation was not specifically authorized by the treaty.

43. The Special Rapporteur went on to undertake the colossal task of listing certain criteria for determining the object and purpose of the treaty. Those two pivotal concepts were notoriously not defined in the 1969 Vienna Convention. In order to define the object and purpose of the treaty, draft guideline 3.1.5 referred to the "essential provisions of the treaty, which constitute its *raison d'être*" (para. 89), something that was hardly instructive. If in order to speak of a material breach of a treaty (Vienna Convention, art. 60) one used that definition—proposed, it was true, solely "[f]or the purpose of assessing the validity of reservations"—the wording that resulted would be clearly inappropriate. According to article 60, paragraph 3 (*b*), of the Vienna Convention, a material breach of a treaty consisted in "the violation of a provision essential to the accomplishment of the object or purpose of the treaty". Transposing the proposed definition, one would arrive at the following wording: "the violation of a provision essential to the accomplishment of the essential provisions of the treaty". If the objective was to define the concepts of object and purpose, it should be done in a manner that was useful, not only for reservations, but also for the law of treaties in general. Still, nothing indicated that the Commission must elaborate such a definition.

44. As to the method advanced for determining the object and purpose of a treaty, the fact that draft guideline 3.1.6 was based on articles 31 and 32 of the Vienna Convention had the disadvantage of leaving aside the very important role that those two concepts played in the interpretation of treaties (para. 91). There again, it would be better to avoid setting out a general rule in a draft guideline.

45. The most substantial part of the report, paragraphs 93 *et seq.*, was aimed at what the Special Rapporteur called the "application of the criterion", in other words, determining whether a reservation was compatible with the object and purpose of the treaty. The question could hardly be resolved using a general, rigid criterion, since compatibility depended on the content of the reservation. A reservation could be aimed at a minor modification of a given provision, in which case it might still be compatible, even if the provision in question was fundamental to the accomplishment of the object and purpose of the treaty.

46. In his view, it would be better to apply more generally the relatively flexible wording in the second part of draft guideline 3.1.12 concerning reservations to general human rights treaties, according to which the compatibility of a reservation with the object and purpose of a treaty depended, among other things, on "the importance that the right which is the subject of the reservation has within the general architecture of the treaty, and the seriousness of the impact the reservation has upon it" (para. 102). It would be prudent to stop there. In order to assess the seriousness of the reservation's impact, it was obviously necessary to know the scope of the reservation. If the reservation was "worded in vague, general language", as indicated in draft guideline 3.1.7, it might be incompatible with the object and purpose, but was not necessarily so (para. 115). It would thus be advantageous to adopt a different perspective, that of procedure. One could then ask whether a reservation worded in vague, general language "purports to exclude or to modify the legal effect of certain provisions of the treaty in their application" to the reserving State, according to the definition set out in article 2, paragraph 1 (*d*) of the 1969 Vienna Convention.

47. He agreed that a reservation could not be deemed to be prohibited solely on the grounds that it purported to safeguard the application of certain rules of domestic law

or related to a provision embodying a rule of customary law. Draft guideline 3.1.8 was useful in that it highlighted the need to distinguish between the lawfulness of a State's conduct in respect of customary law, on the one hand, and acceptance of a treaty obligation parallel to customary law, on the other (para. 129). In contrast to what was asserted by the Human Rights Committee in its famous General Comment No. 24, the relevant portion of which was cited in footnote 298 to paragraph 122 of the report, a State that formulated a reservation to a provision of a treaty that dealt with torture was not reserving the right to practise torture. It simply wished to avoid adding a treaty obligation to an obligation flowing from customary law or *jus cogens*. It was understandable that such a reservation might be puzzling and ultimately incompatible with the object and purpose of the treaty, but one could not say in general that all reservations to a provision corresponding to a rule of customary law were automatically invalid.

48. Similar reasoning should be brought to bear in order to prevent a reservation to a provision corresponding to a rule of *jus cogens* from being automatically qualified as invalid. A State making such a reservation was not trying to preserve the right to violate such a rule, much less asserting some obligation to do so. The prohibition of reservations to provisions setting forth a rule of *jus cogens* (draft guideline 3.1.9) should be categorical only if, by modifying the legal effect of such a provision, the reserving State purported to introduce a rule contrary to *jus cogens* (para. 146). Such would be the case if a State formulated a reservation to a treaty providing for the right of intervention by which it affirmed that such intervention could, where necessary, involve the use of force. As the Special Rapporteur pointed out, the invalidity of the reservation would then flow from article 53 of the 1969 Vienna Convention rather than from its incompatibility with the object and purpose of the treaty.

49. Even if it might be difficult for the Commission to enunciate certain rules in the form of draft guidelines, the extremely rich analysis of practice and the numerous observations contained in the Special Rapporteur's tenth report would surely serve as reference points for any future discussion on the compatibility of a reservation with the object and purpose of a treaty.

The meeting rose at 1 p.m.

2858th MEETING

Wednesday, 27 July 2005, at 10.05 a.m.

Chairperson: Mr. Djamchid MOMTAZ

Present: Mr. Addo, Mr. Candioti, Mr. Chee, Mr. Comissário Afonso, Mr. Dugard, Mr. Economides, Ms. Escarameia, Mr. Fomba, Mr. Gaja, Mr. Galicki, Mr. Kabatsi, Mr. Kateka, Mr. Kemicha, Mr. Kolodkin, Mr. Koskenniemi, Mr. Mansfield, Mr. Matheson, Mr. Niehaus, Mr. Opertti Badan, Mr. Pambou-Tchivounda, Mr. Pellet, Mr. Sreenivasa Rao, Mr. Rodríguez Cedeño, Ms. Xue, Mr. Yamada.

Reservations to treaties (*continued*) (A/CN.4/549 and Add.1, sect. D, A/CN.4/558 and Corr.1 and Add.1 [and Corr.1]–2, and A/CN.4/L.665)

[Agenda item 6]

TENTH REPORT OF THE SPECIAL RAPPORTEUR (*continued*)

1. Ms. ESCARAMEIA said that the tenth report was an extraordinary feat of scholarship, particularly in view of the short period of time in which it had been prepared. The report went to the heart of the issue, and for that reason merited far more time for debate than had been accorded to it in the Commission's programme of work.

2. Referring to section C, she said that codification was indeed feasible in the area of reservations incompatible with the object and purpose of the treaty: indeed, States in the Sixth Committee had been eagerly waiting for the Commission to address precisely that issue. Nor did she share the Special Rapporteur's view that the 1969 and 1986 Vienna Conventions set forth a liberal regime concerning reservations: on the contrary, she found the regime to be extremely strict.

3. In the interests of providing clear guidance to readers, draft guidelines 3.1.3 (para. 63 of the report) and 3.1.4 (para. 69) should not be combined in a single draft guideline 3.1.3/3.1.4 (para. 70). She endorsed their contents and was in favour of their referral to the Drafting Committee. On the concept of the object and purpose of the treaty, which was the centrepiece of the study, she would have liked to see a more extensive analysis of the two distinct terms "object" and "purpose". In her view, the object was the essential content of the treaty, and the purpose was the objective pursued. Any reservation that went against one or another should not be permitted. The two often went hand in hand, and in draft guideline 3.1.5 (para. 89) they were subsumed in the phrase "*raison d'être*". The draft guideline indicated that the yardstick against which the validity of reservations was to be measured was "the essential provisions of the treaty, which constitute its *raison d'être*", but that seemed an unduly high threshold. A reservation could go against a single provision which, in itself, was not a "*raison d'être*" of the treaty, but the effect of the reservation would nevertheless be extremely damaging. She would prefer the final phrase of the draft guideline to refer instead to essential provisions concerning the contents of the treaty and the objectives sought thereby.

4. Turning to draft guideline 3.1.6, she endorsed the Special Rapporteur's use of the interpretative techniques referred to in the Vienna Conventions but did not understand why some of those techniques had been omitted (para. 91). Why, for example, was no mention made of the related agreements and instruments referred to in article 31, paragraph 2, of the Vienna Conventions? Why the reluctance to use subsequent agreements and the subsequent practice of the parties, as provided for in article 31, paragraph 3 (*b*), of those Conventions? Reservations could be made not only at the time of ratification, but also at the time of accession, when subsequent practice of the parties was already available.

5. The debate on application of the criterion of object and purpose had been particularly interesting, but far more time was needed to do justice to the subject. For that reason she welcomed the proposal for a joint seminar with treaty monitoring bodies. On reservations to dispute settlement clauses and clauses concerning the monitoring of the implementation of a treaty, she considered that the threshold was once again too high. It was too much to require that the provision to which the reservation was made should be the "*raison d'être*" of the treaty: it might be only one of the essential provisions. In draft guideline 3.1.13, subparagraph (i), therefore, she would replace the words "constitutes the raison d'être" with "constitutes an essential provision" (para. 99 of the report).

6. In draft guideline 3.1.12 on reservations to general human rights treaties, the Special Rapporteur focused on rights embodied in such treaties, but a reservation could also be made to a provision that did not enunciate a right (para. 102). Many essential provisions had to do with such issues as the implementation of rights and the way they were modified. Provisions on non-discrimination were a case in point. She would therefore replace the word "right" with "provision" in draft guideline 3.1.12.

7. Reservations relating to the application of domestic law often met with negative reactions, not on the grounds that they concerned domestic law, but because they were framed in vague and general terms. Yet when States invoked domestic law to justify a reservation, that reservation was necessarily vague and general. States were not required to refer to any specific provision, and they cited domestic law generally precisely so that their reservation could remain vague and they could retain some degree of control. Draft guideline 3.1.11, as currently worded, did not cover that point. It seemed to refer to the whole of domestic law when it spoke of "preserv[ing] the integrity of its domestic law" (para. 106 of the report). A more precise formulation was required, indicating that reservations could be accepted if they were made with reference to a specific provision of domestic law. She also found it odd to speak of the domestic law of international organizations and would prefer the phrase "internal rules", which had been used in the topic of responsibility of international organizations.

8. Draft guideline 3.1.7 referred to vague, general language which did not allow the scope of the reservation to be determined (para. 115 of the report). But various actors might be called upon to make that determination: other States, treaty monitoring bodies or courts, for instance. The problem was not that the scope could not be determined, but rather, that it might be determined differently by different actors.

9. She had some difficulty with the Special Rapporteur's reasoning on reservations to provisions embodying customary norms. He appeared to be saying that customary law continued to apply between the reserving State and the other parties to the treaty, but not as a treaty norm, because States might wish to exclude supervision by monitoring or other mechanisms provided for in the treaty. It seemed to her, however, that it should be made clearer in draft guideline 3.1.8 that customary law always applied between the reserving State and other parties because of its nature as customary law, not by virtue of the treaty (para. 129 of the report).

10. She strongly endorsed draft guideline 3.1.9 on "Reservations to provisions setting forth a rule of *jus cogens*" and was in favour of referring it to the Drafting Committee (para. 146). On draft guideline 3.1.10, if a treaty considered a right to be non-derogable, then it was certainly an essential part of the treaty and a reservation that went against it would go against the object and purpose of the treaty (*ibid.*). However, reservations could also be made, not with respect to a right, but regarding some aspect of the relevant regime. That should be made clearer in the draft guideline.

11. To sum up, she thought that draft guidelines 3.1.3, 3.1.4 and 3.1.9 could be referred to the Drafting Committee, but that a working group was needed to give further consideration to the remaining draft guidelines proposed. Some additional categories could be considered, for example, reservations to provisions on implementation of treaties in domestic law.

12. Mr. KOSKENNIEMI said that the report was comprehensive, well argued and balanced, a real *tour de force*, but also paradoxical. Precisely because it was exhaustive and balanced, it demonstrated the impossibility of achieving the goals it set itself. He fully subscribed to the Special Rapporteur's statement in paragraph 91 of his report that the object and purpose of the treaty was to be ascertained in good faith, in accordance with the techniques laid down in articles 31 and 32 of the 1969 and 1986 Vienna Conventions. Yet once the object and purpose test was defined as a task of treaty interpretation, one had to conclude that, as was the case with treaty interpretation in general, it could not be controlled by pre-established rules or definitions.

13. Interpretation, as countless textbooks had pointed out, was an art and not a science. It could not be captured in methods, rules, techniques or illustrations. Any attempt to do so would automatically lead to a vicious circle in which ambiguous or open-ended words were replaced by other, equally open-ended words. The Special Rapporteur was undoubtedly right when, in paragraph 77, he said that the object and purpose of the treaty referred to the "essence" or the "mission" of the treaty. But what, in turn, did those notions mean? New expressions, "*raison d'être*" and "fundamental core", emerged in paragraph 89 of the report. Those expressions were apt, but infected with the same uncertainty that attended the meaning of "object and purpose".

14. He was not saying that the exercise of seeking synonyms for "object and purpose" was wholly pointless. On the contrary, it needed to be carried out—and the Special Rapporteur had done so, quite brilliantly—in order to demonstrate that the use of open-ended language was not a mistake by the drafters or an inadvertency that could be corrected by replacing one set of words by another. No: the problems lay deeper, in the nature of treaty interpretation and the role of treaties in the international legal system as transformers of State party intent into formal obligations. Treaties expressed intent: their point was the point that States wished to give them, and where States themselves did not spell out what they intended as the

mission of the treaty, their intent could not be replaced by speculation on the part of interpreters or the Commission about what that intent might be.

15. That was evident from the 1951 advisory opinion of the ICJ on *Reservations to the Convention on Genocide*. The problem the Court had faced was how to limit the subjectivity involved in a fully consensual treaty system that threatened to create chaos by allowing every State to make whatever reservation it wished to the Convention on the Prevention and Punishment of the Crime of Genocide, and every State to object to every reservation that was made, for any reason whatsoever. Such subjectivity, indeed politicization, of the Convention would have wholly undermined its mission. The Court had needed to find a foothold or standard other than the intent of States for determining which reservations might and might not be held to be valid. It had accordingly opted for the object and purpose test: a reservation was invalid if it was contrary to the object and purpose of the treaty. A non-subjective standard had thus been created against which reservations could be assessed.

16. That, of course, had not been the end of the matter. When the Court had gone on to ask itself what the object and purpose of the Convention actually was, it had only been able to say that that was for each State party to decide and that each State party exercised the right to do so individually and from its own standpoint. That led back to where one had started: the meaning and applicability of the objective standard was determined by reference to what States subjectively wanted it to mean. In seeking to escape from the anarchy of unlimited reservations, the ICJ had fallen into the anarchy of unlimited interpretations. The same structure was repeated again and again in treaty law, from *jus cogens* to the operation of *rebus sic stantibus*. On the one hand, there must be a standard other than the will of the party that determined what the parties could legitimately will; on the other hand, what that standard was and how it should be applied could be determined only by recourse to the will of the parties. Such was the liberal voluntarism of international law.

17. The Special Rapporteur himself recognized as much: in paragraph 91 he modestly suggested that while the various alternatives proposed to the "object and purpose" test would not resolve all problems, they could certainly contribute to a solution if they were "applied in good faith and with a little common sense". That might perhaps be the case, though not in a manner that was immediately obvious. The new words did not solve the interpretation problem, but the experience of an endless accumulation of new words might, with "good faith" and "a little common sense", lead the interpreter to a sound assessment of what might seem acceptable for any given audience. In the end, everything depended on good faith and common sense, and nothing on a particular set of words, methods or rules. He agreed with Mr. Gaja that no definition of the object and purpose test seemed necessary.

18. The bulk of the report, paragraphs 93 to 146, aimed to go beyond purely linguistic considerations, pinpointing typical cases of contested reservations in order to draw conclusions from them. That effort gave an excellent overview of the state of play with regard to the formulation of reservations and objections thereto by reference to three types of cases: first, specific types of treaty provisions; second, specific types of reservations; and, third, specific types of treaties, namely human rights treaties.

19. Regarding the first category, the Special Rapporteur suggested that there were some types of treaty provisions to which, judging from the object and purpose test, reservations would sometimes, perhaps always, be inappropriate. He had singled out three: dispute settlement and implementation provisions; provisions embodying customary rules; and provisions setting forth *jus cogens* or other non-derogable rules.

20. While a reservation to the first category of provisions might be contrary to the object and purpose of the treaty, why should that particular category be singled out? There might be other types of provisions—even institutional provisions—regarding, for example, the funding of common activities or the establishment of panels or technical cooperation committees, which might be equally or more relevant for some of the parties to a treaty. On the other hand, provisions on dispute settlement were often included in a treaty as part of the legal formalities, but were of little interest to the signatories. What was of interest to the parties to treaties on economic cooperation, development assistance or technology transfer were the substantive provisions, rather than provisions on dispute settlement and implementation. He saw no reason to single out such provisions from among the many that might be deemed essential to the mission of the treaty. Indeed, he suspected that highlighting the importance of such clauses reflected an unwarranted bias in favour of legal activities, one that might not be widely shared outside the Commission. It was impossible to know in advance which provisions of a treaty were crucial to its object and purpose. As the advisory opinion on *Reservations to the Convention on Genocide* had revealed, that had to be assessed by individual States from their own standpoint, and there was little reason to suppose that dispute settlement and implementation provisions would be given pride of place.

21. Mr. Koskenniemi's second objection to the singling out of specific provisions was that very often a treaty simply had no single object and purpose at all. States entered into treaties, especially multilateral ones, with differing hopes and expectations, and with differing views on what was essential. In the case of the United Nations Convention on the Law of the Sea, some States had become parties because they were keen on its provisions on navigation, others because of its maritime delimitation aspects, and others because of the rules on deep seabed mining or technology transfer. That was precisely why the Convention permitted only specified reservations.

22. But what of similar instruments that had no such provisions? Most multilateral treaties emerged as a *quid pro quo*. They had, not a single object and purpose, but a cluster of purposes that emerged out of a process involving a trade-off between conflicting considerations. In an environmental treaty that provided for financial assistance for developing countries, for example, it was the provisions on environmental protection that reflected its object and purpose from the perspective of environmental groups, whereas for the developing States the object and

purpose was the provision of funding or technology transfer. States often became parties to multilateral treaties in situations where only a part of the treaty concerned them, but concerned them vitally.

23. Thus, it was not possible to ascertain which provisions of a treaty reflected its object and purpose and should therefore not be subject to reservations, without some knowledge of the *travaux préparatoires* and the expectations and policies that had led States to subscribe to the treaty, and those provisions might and did in the case of many "trade-off" treaties differ for different States. Any unilateral, *a priori* determination that one provision could not be the subject of a reservation while another could was simply illegitimate interference in the balance created by the trade-off that the treaty represented.

24. On treaties embodying custom or *jus cogens*, he endorsed Mr. Gaja's point that not every reservation to such a treaty was a prelude to a breach of the relevant custom or *jus cogens* rule.

25. Human rights treaties were the most controversial group, the one in which the interplay of reservations and objections had been the most intensive. However, like Mr. Gaja, he was doubtful about the value of singling them out, for two reasons. First, it was not clear what constituted a human rights treaty. When the European Economic Community had been set up in the 1950s, for example, its object and purpose had been to establish a customs union. Some time in the 1970s or 1980s, however, the Court of Justice of the European Communities had decided to re-interpret the four freedoms in the Treaty of Rome as establishing fundamental rights. Such rights had now become an integral part of the European Union's treaty framework. Was the Treaty establishing the European Economic Community therefore a human rights treaty, although initially it had not been thought of in those terms? The designation of particular treaties as human rights treaties was not only arbitrary but also limited the degree to which any treaty provision conferring rights or benefits on individuals might be classified as a human rights treaty provision. The Commission's own draft articles on diplomatic protection were a case in point.[1]

26. What justified the separate treatment of reservations to human rights treaties was the fact that the idea of the treaty as a trade-off was almost totally inapplicable in such cases. What lent an objection to such reservations its cogency was not so much the fact that a human rights treaty was involved, as the fact that such a treaty was conceived by the parties as a common undertaking for a single purpose. However, other treaties—on environmental protection, protection of a natural resource, development assistance, social welfare, labour rights and the movement of individuals, to name but a few—were also conceived as common undertakings. Furthermore, there was no reason to suppose that human rights treaties might not sometimes be the result of conflicting considerations, bargains and expectations. One could not rule out the possibility that accession to a human rights treaty was premised, not on its human rights provisions, but upon the desire to obtain some (usually economic) benefit, provision of which was made conditional on accession to the treaty in question. Why should a State not be allowed to invoke the object and purpose criterion to object to a reservation made to such a provision? Why should a benefit that one party wished to receive from the treaty be immune to challenge, while benefits received by another party were open to challenge?

27. In the final analysis, the assessment of the object and purpose remained dependent on such considerations. That did not mean it was impossible to imagine treaties in which all parties were genuinely motivated by a common undertaking, and in such cases a reservation to a provision that was essential to the realization of that undertaking must not be shielded from the challenge that it was contrary to the object and purpose of the treaty. Treaties involving a common undertaking were not limited to the human rights field—a field that could not be delimited by any clear criterion, since any international arrangement involving benefits (bilateral investment treaties, for example) could be described as having to do with protection of the private rights of the beneficiaries.

28. On the face of it, to regard reservations relating to domestic law and vague and general reservations as being always contrary to the object and purpose of the treaty seemed reasonable. Mr. Koskenniemi had a nagging doubt, however, that one perceived them as objectionable only where they reflected one of the two criteria he had identified as relevant, namely, that they undermined either the very basis on which a State had entered into an agreement, or else the common undertaking that the treaty had been intended to establish. A vague reservation to an incidental provision was surely not against the object and purpose of the treaty. He could therefore not see the point of singling out vagueness or non-specific references to domestic law as decisive criteria, irrespective of their effect on the common undertaking or the expectations of the parties.

29. While the Special Rapporteur's tenth report was one of the best he had encountered in his time on the Commission, its special value lay—as he had already noted—in the way it undermined its own conclusions. Guiding the Commission through a dense thicket of arguments and considerations in an effort to pin down the meaning of "object and purpose", it had highlighted the nature of that assessment as treaty interpretation. In so doing, however, it had shown that no general rules or methods could have an authority independent of an assessment of the nature of the common understanding that the treaty was intended to serve or the expectations of the parties. Object and purpose were what they were, as assessed by a reading of the treaty and an attempt to understand what the parties might have wished to achieve by it.

30. That effort had led the Special Rapporteur to highlight certain typical cases. His analyses were relevant and illustrative, but they demonstrated not so much the relevance of his classifications as the impossibility of making such classifications without tackling the underlying rationales that affected, and should affect, the conclusion and interpretation of treaties. Those rationales were, in his own view, twofold. First, a party should not be allowed to opt out of a treaty that involved what he had called

[1] See 2844th meeting, footnote 1.

"a common undertaking", whether in the field of human rights, the economy, environmental protection, technical cooperation or elsewhere. Anything less would seem lacking in good faith. Second, a party should not be able to frustrate the legitimate expectations of another party by making a reservation to a provision that had been the condition of that party's joining the treaty in the first place. Again, that seemed called for by the same criterion of good faith. Beyond those two considerations, he submitted that all the Commission could provide, and all the Special Rapporteur had provided, was a set of illustrations of how those two considerations came into play. Without an express mention of those rationales, however, the illustrations would remain incomprehensible, and doubt would remain as to where their authority as examples lay.

31. For all those reasons, he did not think that the illustrations were needed in the guidelines. All that could be said was that "object and purpose" was what it was, and the interpreter must turn to the Special Rapporteur's report to understand that it was impossible to give clear criteria and guidance for its determination.

32. Mr. FOMBA noted that paragraph 61 of the report stated that the aim of the Guide to Practice was "to provide States with coherent answers to all questions which they [might] have in the area of reservations". That statement should dispel some groundless fears which had been expressed. The purpose of the Guide to Practice was to facilitate the process of formulation, interpretation and implementation of reservations which were an important instrument in international legal life. That was what the Special Rapporteur had sought to do, particularly in the tenth report, and, all things considered, the undertaking had been very successful.

33. With regard to draft guideline 3.1.3 (para. 63 of the report), it was logical and important to specify that reservations which were implicitly permitted must be compatible with the treaty's object and purpose. As for draft guideline 3.1.4 (para. 69), on non-specified reservations authorized by the treaty, the reasoning in paragraphs 65 and 68 was well founded, namely, that such reservations must be subject to the same general conditions as reservations to treaties which did not contain specific clauses and that their validity should be assessed in the light of their compatibility with the object and purpose of the treaty. Thus, the spirit and letter of the draft guideline were acceptable.

34. On the joint draft guideline 3.1.3/3.1.4 (para. 70), it was his view that, given the nature and purpose of the Guide to Practice, and for the reasons adduced by the Special Rapporteur in paragraph 71, two separate draft guidelines would be preferable. As to draft guideline 3.1.5 ("Definition of the object and purpose of the treaty"), subject to any difficulties which might exist on the interpretation of the phrases "essential provisions" and "*raison d'être*", the wording seemed to be a step in the right direction (para. 89).

35. Draft guidelines 3.1.5 and 3.1.6 (para. 91) read in combination provided a general—albeit not ideal—definition of the object and purpose and explained how it was to be determined. In his view, it was legitimate to transpose the principles set forth in the Vienna Conventions. With regard to the reference in square brackets to the subsequent practice of the parties, all factors, criteria and parameters that might be relevant should be taken into account, including practice. That approach was justified by the words "where appropriate".

36. Draft guideline 3.1.13 established the principle of the presumption of compatibility, together with two clearly relevant exceptions, and, again, seemed to be on the right track (para. 99). Draft guideline 3.1.12 ("Reservations to general human rights treaties") concerned a difficult subject which posed problems of approach and interpretation (para. 102). However, for lack of a better solution, and given that the wording was sufficiently flexible to leave scope for interpretation, it was acceptable.

37. With regard to draft guideline 3.1.11, what was important was that the State or international organization formulating the reservation should not use its domestic law as a pretext for evading a new international obligation (para. 106). On the "proper law" of international organizations, he agreed with the parallel drawn with the domestic law of States. The Special Rapporteur was right to stress that domestic law must be at the service of international law, and not vice versa, that national rules were "merely facts" with regard to international law (para. 105), and that the very object of a treaty could be to lead States to modify them. Interestingly, the media had recently reported on a case involving Germany and the European Union, in which Germany had argued that domestic law was applicable, whereas the European Union had contended that Germany must bring its domestic legislation into line with European Union law.

38. Draft guideline 3.1.7 ("Vague, general reservations") relied on the practice of the European Court and the European Commission of Human Rights (para. 115). Its underlying idea was that when a reservation was couched in terms too vague for it to be possible to determine their meaning and scope, there was a presumption of incompatibility with the object and purpose of the treaty, always supposing that the assessment of the object and purpose did not pose difficulties of the same nature. Subject to that observation, he endorsed the draft guideline.

39. With regard to draft guideline 3.1.8, he agreed that there was no watertight separation between treaty sources and customary sources of international law (para. 129); rather, there was a dialectical link between those two categories. A convention could contain customary norms, which by their very nature had the particular virtue of linking all States, whether or not they were parties to the treaty. It therefore seemed appropriate to draw attention to two fundamental principles: first, the customary nature of the rule set forth in a treaty provision did not in itself constitute an obstacle to the formulation of a reservation; second, such a reservation must not call into question the binding nature of the rule in question in relations between the reserving State or international organization and other States or international organizations, whether or not they were parties to the treaty.

40. Lastly, draft guideline 3.1.10 had its place in the Guide to Practice (para. 146), given that the category of

non-derogable rights was well established in international human rights law, and in view of the importance of non-derogable rights and the need to preserve their legal effect.

41. In closing, he said he was in favour of referring the draft guidelines to the Drafting Committee, which should take into account the main areas of disagreement that had emerged in the debate. However, he would not object if the majority favoured setting up a working group on the topic, with a clear mandate.

42. Mr. Sreenivasa RAO congratulated the Special Rapporteur on his extraordinary effort to go to the heart of the problem and provide the best possible guidance to decision makers and practitioners. The fact that so little time was available to debate what was already a complex topic had made the Commission's task even more difficult.

43. The problem of definition discussed in paragraph 84 was at the heart of the issue. Despite close consideration of various options, it had to be concluded that it would be difficult to pinpoint the full meaning and scope of what exactly constituted the object and purpose of a treaty. It had been, and would remain, an enigma, one to which the guidelines, useful as they were, would not provide a definitive solution.

44. Draft guideline 3.1.5 on the definition of the object and purpose of the treaty was reasonable (para. 89), but it was not always easy to decide what was essential and what was not. It could even be argued that non-essential provisions sometimes became essential, because they helped to give effect to or implement essential provisions. In such cases, an absurd situation might arise in which the entire text could be said to be the object and purpose of the treaty and no reservations would be permitted. The solution lay in identifying, not the letter, but the spirit of the treaty provisions.

45. In paragraph 2 of draft guideline 3.1.6, on the determination of the object and purpose of the treaty, the words in square brackets should be omitted and the matter dealt with in the commentary, in the interests of ensuring a clear and readily comprehensible text (para. 91).

46. Draft guideline 3.1.12, on reservations to general human rights treaties, posed a host of problems, and the Special Rapporteur could probably have done little more than simply citing the importance that the right which was the subject of reservations had within the general architecture of a treaty and the seriousness of the impact of a reservation upon it as criteria for assessing the validity of a particular reservation (para. 102). However, those criteria were very general, and he wondered whether, in practice, anything other than the context and specific situations would be of much help in coming to any conclusions on the validity of such a reservation.

47. As to draft guidelines 3.1.11, on domestic law, and 3.1.7, on vague, general reservations, it simply bore noting that once again context was the ultimate guide, and that each party to the treaty must enable its object and purpose to be achieved in good faith and should desist from such reservations as they themselves knew to be contrary thereto. In the event of conflicting views, dispute settlement procedures would of course be available.

48. He had no problem with the Special Rapporteur's observations on customary law. The distinction between customary law incorporated in a treaty provision and reservations made to it would not absolve the party from any rights or obligations otherwise stemming from treaty law. He thus endorsed draft guideline 3.1.8.

49. With regard to draft guideline 3.1.9, on *jus cogens*, his initial reaction was to say that no guideline was needed: it was a matter of general law that no treaty could be concluded which was in violation of *jus cogens*; likewise, any provision of the treaty or reservation to it which was in violation of *jus cogens* was *ipso facto* rendered inoperable by virtue of that very concept. It could also be claimed that *jus cogens* principles were of a higher order, in which case the Commission should not link them to a discussion of reservations. While he personally could live without draft guideline 3.1.9, he would be prepared to defer to the majority view if other members thought differently.

50. Mr. KEMICHA paid tribute to the Special Rapporteur for his tenth report, which constituted the cornerstone of the draft Guide to Practice, proposing no fewer than 14 draft guidelines. The Special Rapporteur's discussion of terminological points was most convincing, as was his decision to revert to the term "validity", which had the virtue of being neutral and did not prejudice the Commission's replies to a number of unresolved questions. Having noted that the validity of reservations should be studied in the light of article 19 of the Vienna Conventions (para. 9), the Special Rapporteur wisely reproduced article 19 of the 1986 Vienna Convention in draft guideline 3.1 (para. 20).

51. Although he could follow the reasoning which had led the Special Rapporteur to his proposed definition of specified reservations in draft guideline 3.1.2 (para. 49), he found the actual wording somewhat ambiguous, and in particular the phrase "reservations that are expressly authorized by the treaty to specific provisions". The Special Rapporteur's explanation in paragraph 49 that "reservations that are specified [...] must, on the one hand, relate to specific provisions and, on the other, fulfil certain conditions specified in the treaty" was clearer.

52. The section of the tenth report on reservations incompatible with the object and purpose of the treaty was extraordinarily rich, and constituted, along with the draft guidelines contained therein, a major contribution to the work of the Commission. As the Special Rapporteur rightly pointed out in paragraph 55 of the report, the concept of the object and purpose of the treaty was "the pivot between the need to preserve the nature of the treaty and the desire to facilitate accession to multilateral treaties by the greatest possible number of States". Furthermore, although that criterion now reflected a rule of customary law that was unchallenged, its contents remained vague and there was still some uncertainty as to the consequences of the incompatibility of a reservation therewith.

53. Draft guideline 3.1.3 was clearly of the utmost importance (para. 63), in that it set up a last barrier which protected the treaty from the ingenuity of States that wished to make certain reservations to evade an obligation set forth in a treaty to which they felt the need to accede. As to the question posed by the Special Rapporteur in paragraph 71, it seemed preferable, for the sake of clarity, to have two separate draft guidelines, rather than combining draft guidelines 3.1.3 and 3.1.4 into a single guideline.

54. In paragraphs 72 to 88 the Special Rapporteur conceded the essentially subjective nature of the concept of the object and purpose of the treaty, before singling out the key notion of the treaty's *raison d'être* in the very concise draft guideline 3.1.5 (para. 89). Draft guideline 3.1.6 transposed the principles of interpretation contained in articles 31 and 32 of the Vienna Conventions. While those principles certainly had their place in the Guide to Practice, the bracketed reference to the subsequent practice of the parties should probably be consigned to the commentary (para. 91).

55. Draft guidelines 3.1.7 to 3.1.13 covered the problems that might arise concerning the compatibility with the object and the purpose of the treaty of six categories of reservations listed in paragraph 95. Draft guideline 3.1.13 showed that reservations to treaty clauses concerning dispute settlement or the monitoring of the implementation of the treaty were not in themselves incompatible with the object and purpose of the treaty except under the two conditions specified in subparagraphs (i) and (ii) (para. 99).

56. Some authors held that the reservations regime was wholly incompatible with human rights treaties. In draft guideline 3.1.12, the Special Rapporteur had adopted a more moderate approach, but some might feel that such phrases as "the general architecture of the treaty" and "the seriousness of the impact" were still too vague and did not afford such human rights treaties sufficient protection (para. 102).

57. Reservations relating to the application of domestic law were also complex, and one might be tempted to apply the regime provided for under article 27 of the 1969 and 1986 Vienna Conventions. In paragraph 105 the Special Rapporteur rejected that approach in favour of one that was less categorical, albeit expressed in rather ambiguous terms. Moreover, the syntax of draft guideline 3.1.11, in which a restriction was followed by a double negative, made it rather difficult to read (para. 106).

58. As indicated in draft guideline 3.1.7, vague, general reservations were incompatible with the purpose and object of the treaty (para. 115). When a reservation was of unlimited scope and undefined character, other States would be unable to determine to what extent the reserving State accepted its obligations under the treaty.

59. In connection with draft guideline 3.1.8, the Special Rapporteur's convincing analysis of the judgment of the ICJ in the *North Sea Continental Shelf* case led him to suggest that the customary nature of the rule set forth in a treaty provision did not in itself constitute an obstacle to the formulation of a reservation to that provision (paras. 128–129).

60. Draft guideline 3.1.9 made it clear that no reservations to provisions setting forth a rule of *jus cogens* were permitted (para. 146). It would be useful to indicate in the commentary that the prohibition did not result from article 19 (*c*) of the 1969 Vienna Convention but, *mutatis mutandis*, from the principle set out in article 53 of that Convention. The Special Rapporteur was right to treat reservations to provisions relating to non-derogable rights in a separate draft guideline 3.1.10 (*ibid.*).

61. In conclusion, he said that the fact that his comments on the report had been more descriptive than critical reflected the high quality and thoroughness of the Special Rapporteur's brilliant discussion and analysis of the issues. He therefore recommended that the draft guidelines should be referred to the Drafting Committee forthwith.

62. Mr. ECONOMIDES said that the decision taken to draw up a separate list of those members who wished to comment on the beginning of Mr. Pellet's report effectively penalized those members, as they had not been allowed to make their statements until the very end of the debate, although some of them had asked to be placed on the list of speakers several days previously.

63. The CHAIRPERSON said that the decision to have separate lists had been taken at the request of the Special Rapporteur and endorsed by the Commission as a whole.

64. Mr. PELLET (Special Rapporteur) said that Mr. Economides and other members were not being penalized; indeed, it was better to speak towards the end of a debate, having heard the views of others. He would certainly pay equal attention to all comments in his summary, irrespective of when they had been made.

65. On what he regarded as a more serious matter, he noted that, once upon a time, the Special Rapporteurs' proposals had been discussed one by one. The recent fashion for dealing with everything at the same time did not allow for any real debate to take place. That was why he had proposed that, at the very least, the first sections of his report, which dealt with very different issues, should be discussed separately. He found it regrettable that so many members had wished to comment on the beginning of the report together.

66. Mr. ECONOMIDES thanked Mr. Pellet for his masterly presentation of his tenth report on reservations to treaties. The section of the report concerning incompatibility with the object and purpose of the treaty was undoubtedly the best study of the doctrine in international law currently available. He wished to preface his comments on the report as a whole with two general remarks. First, the Special Rapporteur had not done enough to pave the way for the progressive development of law, nor had he drawn all the requisite conclusions concerning the codification of existing law. Second, there was also the problem of objections to reservations. Admittedly, the report made several references to the fact that States rarely objected to reservations. Nonetheless, it was

his experience that an absence of objections was usually attributable to political rather than legal considerations. It would therefore be mistaken to use the absence of objections as a criterion.

67. Turning to specific comments on the report in its entirety, he said that a decision on whether to use the term "validity" or "permissibility" should be deferred, pending consideration of the legal effects of reservations that were not compatible with treaty law. In the meantime, he could agree to the provisional use of the term "validity", a concept that Mr. Pambou-Tchivounda had analysed in great depth.

68. Secondly, it was not appropriate for the Commission to take a stance on the international responsibility of States that formulated impermissible reservations. That question should be taken up on the basis of the topic on responsibility of States for internationally wrongful acts.[2] He therefore did not endorse the views expressed in paragraphs 6 and 7 of the report.

69. Like the Special Rapporteur, he preferred the second version of draft guideline 3.1 (para. 20), which reproduced the full text of article 19 of the 1986 Vienna Convention. As to the title, neither "Freedom to formulate a reservation" nor "Presumption of validity of reservations" seemed appropriate (para. 16). Perhaps "Limits on the formulation of reservations" would be more apt, particularly since the word "limits" was used in the 1951 advisory opinion of the ICJ and its judgment in the *North Sea Continental Shelf* case, cited in paragraphs 55 and 117 of the report respectively. The term "limits" was also more in keeping with the considerable circumspection regarding the whole question of reservations that could be inferred from a close reading of article 19.

70. With regard to draft guideline 3.1.1 (para. 32), he had only some minor editing amendments to suggest that could be taken up in the Drafting Committee, which might also consider simplifying the wording of draft guideline 3.1.2 (para. 49). However, an additional draft guideline, on the subject of implicitly prohibited reservations, was also required, to expand on article 19 (*b*) of the Vienna Convention and other treaty provisions, including the Charter of the United Nations, as mentioned by Mr. Gaja.

71. He had greater difficulty with draft guidelines 3.1.3 and 3.1.4 (paras. 63, 69 and 70), firstly because of the Special Rapporteur's interpretation of article 19 (*b*), namely that, "*a contrario*, if a reservation [did] not fall within the scope of subparagraph (*b*) (because it [was] not specified), it [was] subject to the test of compatibility with the object and purpose of the treaty" (para. 66). He considered that such a reservation was, quite simply, implicitly prohibited by subparagraph (*b*). Secondly, any reservation permitted by a treaty, whether specified, not clearly specified or not specified at all, could not in principle be considered as incompatible with the object and purpose of the treaty. For those reasons he proposed that draft guideline 3.1.3/3.1.4 should be amended to read: "When the treaty does not prohibit reservations, expressly or implicitly, or when it makes no mention of reservations, a reservation may be formulated by a State or an international organization only if it is compatible with the object and purpose of the treaty."

72. He was not in favour of the idea of dispensing with draft guidelines 3.1.5 and 3.1.6 (paras. 89 and 91). The Drafting Committee could undoubtedly improve upon the current wording, and in an area where total uncertainty reigned, it would be preferable to have some guidelines on the definition and determination of the object and purpose of the treaty than none at all.

73. Draft guideline 3.1.13 was too strict (para. 99), far more restrictive than the rule set forth in article 19 (*c*). It was possible that in some treaties such clauses could be essential provisions within the meaning of draft guideline 3.1.5. It should either be broadened in scope or else deleted so as to rely solely on the general rule. However, it would be ill-advised for the Commission to open the floodgates to reservations concerning dispute settlement.

74. Draft guideline 3.1.12 needed to be recast to include a real presumption against such reservations and allow them only in limited, exceptional circumstances when they were of secondary importance within the overall architecture of the treaty (para. 102).

75. Draft guideline 3.1.11 (para. 106) added nothing to the general rule set forth in article 19 (*c*) and should be reformulated along the lines of the amendment submitted by Peru at the Vienna Conference to the effect that the reservation must not render the treaty inoperative by making its application subject, in a general and indeterminate manner, to national law (see paragraph 109 of the report). The draft guideline thus amended could be usefully supplemented by the finding of the European Commission of Human Rights in the *Temeltasch* v. *Switzerland* case that "[a] reservation is of a general nature [...] when it is worded in such a way that its scope cannot be defined" (para. 84 of the decision, p. 149). Draft guidelines 3.1.7 (para. 115) and 3.1.11 might be combined in some way, given the obvious similarities between them.

76. He was in favour of reversing the rule reflected in draft guideline 3.1.8, paragraph 1 (para. 129): the customary nature of a norm set forth in a treaty provision should constitute an obstacle to the formulation of a reservation to that provision. There were several arguments in favour of that rule, most of them put forward by the Special Rapporteur. Mention might also be made in the report of the fact that the rule belonged to the field of the progressive development of the law rather than of its codification. He also noted that the theory of a "persistent objector" (para. 120) no longer had any currency in modern international law.

77. He fully endorsed draft guideline 3.1.9 (para. 146). Any reservation, irrespective of its importance, must be rejected *in toto* if it related to a rule of *jus cogens*, for reasons of international public order. Lastly, draft guideline 3.1.10 (*ibid.*) should be dealt with in the same way as draft guideline 3.1.12 (para. 102). Such

[2] See *Yearbook ... 2002*, vol. II (Part Two), par. (7) of the commentary on draft guideline 2.1.8, p. 46. See also article 1 of the draft articles on State responsibility for internationally wrongful acts, *Yearbook ... 2001*, vol. II (Part Two) and corrigendum, p. 32, paras. 76–77.

reservations should be permitted only in exceptional circumstances, when they were of secondary importance within the overall architecture of the treaty.

78. Ms. XUE said that the tenth report on reservations to treaties was of high intellectual quality, logically cogent, well researched and thoroughly analysed. The fairly large part of the report devoted to the history of the Commission's work on relevant provisions relating to reservations in the 1969 Vienna Convention helped to put the topic into perspective.

79. With regard to the terminology used, she noted that in Chinese the words for "permissibility" and "admissibility" had more neutral connotations than "validity", which went closer to the substance of the matter. She therefore had no difficulty in accepting the Special Rapporteur's choice of words. Given that the first part of the report was intended to examine the conditions for the validity of reservations to treaties, it was appropriate to begin the third part of the Guide to Practice by reproducing the entire text of article 19 of the 1986 Vienna Convention in draft guideline 3.1. Since that was the substantive part of the restatement of the law on reservations, it was important to reaffirm the freedom or right of States to formulate reservations to treaties and, at the same time, the need to preserve the unity of treaty regimes.

80. Draft guideline 3.1.1 set out the three types of reservations expressly prohibited by the treaty (para. 32). The first case was clear-cut; and the second, too, posed no problem. In theory, Fitzmaurice might be right in saying in his first report on the law of treaties that "[i]n those cases where the treaty itself permits certain specific reservations, or a class of reservations, to be made, there is a presumption that any other reservations are excluded and cannot be accepted"[3] (cited in para. 35 of the report). In treaty practice, if the terms of the treaty were sufficiently clear to restrict reservations to a certain provision or provisions, they would be unlikely to give rise to any dispute between the contracting parties. However, there could be difficulties if the terms of the relevant provision were ambiguous or too general. The third case also gave rise to no difficulty in principle. She shared the views of some members that the current wording of draft guideline 3.1.1 differed from that of the Vienna Convention, article 19 (*a*) and (*b*). Subparagraph (*a*) referred to a categorical prohibition of all types of reservations to a treaty, whereas subparagraph (*b*) allowed reservations to be formulated on two conditions, namely: where the treaty provided that specified reservations could be made and that reservations could be made only to those specified provisions. Draft guideline 3.1.1 failed to make the second condition clear.

81. While in principle she had no difficulty with draft guideline 3.1.2, two minor points required clarification (para. 49). First, the term "authorized" might be appropriate in article 19 (*b*) of the Vienna Conventions, since the reservation was specifically permitted under the treaty provision. Under subparagraph (*c*), the situation was rather more subtle. As long as the reservation was not incompatible with the object and purpose of the treaty, it was not prohibited. However, could it then be considered as being "authorized", or should one simply say that it was "conditionally permitted"? The accuracy of the term "authorized" was questionable, for, as the title of draft guideline 3.1 indicated, the freedom of States to formulate reservations was not conferred, but inherent, and could be restricted only by law.

82. Second, in response to queries concerning the phrase "which meet conditions specified by the treaty", the Special Rapporteur had explained that there was an inconsistency between the French and English texts (see 2857th meeting, above, paras. 37–38). However, despite his clarification, she considered the phrase still implied that for each specified reservation there were always conditions attached, which was not true of many treaties. Since those points were mainly of a drafting nature, she recommended that the three draft guidelines should be referred to the Drafting Committee.

83. The issues raised in section C were far more substantial and substantive. However, since the Commission had received the English version of the document only a few days previously, she would simply make a few general comments. Given the importance of that part of the report to the study as a whole, it should be given further consideration in plenary session.

84. As noted in paragraph 55 of the report, the issue of compatibility with the object and purpose of the treaty was "the pivot between the need to preserve the nature of the treaty and the desire to facilitate accession to multilateral treaties by the greatest possible number of States". The question how to define the criterion of compatibility required not only legal perception, but also political wisdom, as Mr. Sreenivasa Rao had pointed out.

85. She endorsed the statement in draft guideline 3.1.3 to the effect that reservations were permitted to treaty provisions other than those to which reservations were specifically prohibited by the treaty, as long as they were compatible with the object and purpose thereof (para. 63). Both draft guideline 3.1.4 (para. 69) and the alternative draft guideline 3.1.3/3.1.4 (para. 70) proposed seemed unnecessary and would tend to obscure the meaning of article 19 (*c*) of the Vienna Convention, by appearing to address a separate category of reservations.

86. Apparently there was a logical connection between the two guidelines 3.1.5 and 3.1.6 relating to the object and purpose of the treaty, but the current draft provided neither a workable definition of the concept, nor objective elements permitting its determination. Draft guideline 3.1.5 stated that "the object and purpose of the treaty means the essential provisions of the treaty..." (para. 89). The notion "essential" was not a standard term found in treaty law or legal terminology. If it was to "constitute its *raison d'être*", it could be said that all the treaty's provisions, except its final clauses, might be deemed "essential provisions". That interpretation would render the argument less meaningful. Likewise, in draft guideline 3.1.6, if the essential provisions indicated the object and purpose of the treaty, those provisions should be examined before anything else in determining the object and purpose. Instead, draft guideline 3.1.6 stated

[3] *Yearbook ... 1956*, vol. II, document A/CN.4/101, p. 115.

that the object and purpose must be interpreted in the light of the context, which included ordinary meaning, the preamble, annexes and the preparatory work of the treaty, as well as the subsequent practice of States (para. 91). That approach was questionable. In saying that, she did not wish to imply that the rules on treaty interpretation could not be taken into account in determining the object and purpose of a treaty; on the contrary, they were highly relevant in that context. The problem was that, if the object and purpose of a treaty could be determined by applying interpretation rules, it was unclear why there was any need for a definition of the concept in the first place. Moreover, if interpretation rules could facilitate the determination of the object and purpose, why was no direct reference made to those rules, rather than applying them in a fragmentary fashion? Thirdly, technically speaking, some of the elements to which reference was made in the draft guideline might not be needed in order to determine the object and purpose; for example, in the phrase "subsequent practice of the parties", the word "subsequent" covered the period of time between the date at which the State concerned had become a party and the time the problem arose. That term might have some bearing on the interpretation of the provisions of a treaty, but it should not be of any relevance in the event of a reservation, since reservations should be made only at the beginning of the implementation of the treaty and when there was a need for determination of its object and purpose. Of course, the Special Rapporteur was right in saying that it was by no means easy to put together in a single formula all the elements that had to be taken into account.

87. In the section on the application of the criterion (paras. 93–146), it was unclear why the Special Rapporteur had singled out two categories of treaties—namely, dispute settlement and human rights treaties—for which he had provided separate guidelines. Both categories could be examined within the general framework of rules on reservations. The fact that more reservations tended to be made to such treaties did not signify that they presented a special or different type of legal issue which could not be handled by existing treaty law. When assessing the compatibility of reservations to a human rights treaty with the treaty's object and purpose, the Special Rapporteur had focused on three elements: the indivisibility of the rights set out therein, the importance of the right within the general architecture of the treaty, and the seriousness of the reservation's impact. Those criteria might perhaps be equally applicable to other treaties. The subsequent guidelines, on reservations relating to the application of domestic law, vague and general reservations and reservations relating to provisions embodying customary norms, and setting forth rules of *jus cogens* or non-derogable rights, would inevitably concern both types of treaties. It was really not necessary to formulate separate guidelines for them.

88. The Special Rapporteur categorically rejected reservations formulated in vague and general terms. But the notion of what constituted a vague or general reservation was itself vague and susceptible to subjective assessment. The draft guideline [3.1.7] therefore required further consideration (para. 115).

89. She endorsed draft guideline 3.1.11 on reservations relating to the application of domestic law, which indicated that such reservations should be compatible with the object and purpose of the treaty (para. 106). More thought should, perhaps, be given to the relationship between international obligations and domestic law.

90. The last two categories of reservations to provisions relating to customary norms, *jus cogens* and non-derogable rights and duties, were more complicated, since they involved broader legal issues such as relations between sources of law and the general principles of treaty law, for instance articles 43 and 53 of the 1969 Vienna Convention. Hence those draft guidelines [3.1.9 and 3.1.10] also required further examination and study (para. 146).

91. In sum, the tenth report offered a considerable intellectual challenge, and one to which more time needed to be devoted in plenary session.

92. Mr. YAMADA said that, regrettably, he had not been able to devote the requisite time to studying the first three sections of the tenth report on reservations to treaties. To comment on them without fully digesting the wealth of material they contained would not do justice to them. He therefore wished to defer his observations until the fifty-eighth session.

93. Progress must, however, be made on the draft text. He had no problems with the substance of draft guidelines 3.1, 3.1.1, 3.1.2, 3.1.3 and 3.1.4, which he had been able to review briefly. He hoped that the Commission would decide to refer those five guidelines to the Drafting Committee for consideration during the first week of the fifty-eighth session.

94. Mr. PELLET (Special Rapporteur), responding to Mr. Yamada's statement, said that, in his own opinion, reference to the Drafting Committee of the five draft guidelines mentioned would be a good compromise solution. It would be wise for the Commission to refer some guidelines to the Drafting Committee for many reasons, not least that it would facilitate the Commission's work at its next session. While he could understand the dissatisfaction of colleagues who felt that they had not had enough time to study the text and express their views on it, there was nothing to prevent the Commission from reopening the debate in 2006, provided that he had an opportunity to present the preliminary conclusions he had drawn from the deliberations thus far at the Commission's 2859th meeting.

95. While he agreed that it was not a realistic proposition to refer all the draft guidelines to the Drafting Committee, he strongly supported Mr. Yamada's suggestion that the five draft guidelines he had mentioned should be referred to it. There would, however, be no point in referring draft guideline 3.1.2 to the Drafting Committee without draft guidelines 3.1.1 and 3.1.4.

96. Mr. CHEE said that he required more time to study the end of the tenth report and reserved the right to speak on it in due course. His comments were therefore confined to the beginning.

97. The Special Rapporteur's reports were always challenging and offered a chance to learn more about the subject of reservations to treaties. The tenth report went to the heart of the reservations regime. However, like a number of previous speakers, he was unsure whether the use of the term "validity of reservations" was felicitous—a doubt that had been shared in 1993 by the delegation of the United Kingdom to the Sixth Committee, whose views were quoted *in extenso* by the Special Rapporteur in paragraph 4 of his report. It therefore seemed that the use of the term "validity" was inappropriate, since it denoted acceptance of the reservation by the parties. Moreover, the title of article 19 of the 1969 Vienna Convention referred to the "formulation of reservations", not to the "validity of reservations".

98. He supported draft guidelines 3.1, which simply reflected the content of article 19 of the Vienna Convention (para. 20); 3.1.1, in the light of the explanation set out in paragraph 33; and 3.1.2 (para. 49), which went somewhat further towards elucidating the meaning of article 19 (*b*) of the Vienna Convention. All three draft guidelines could be referred to the Drafting Committee.

99. Mr. RODRÍGUEZ CEDEÑO said that the term "validity" was not the most appropriate term in the context of reservations. "Validity" referred essentially to the conditions in which an authorized reservation was formulated. Some of those conditions were of a formal nature (such as those laid down in the Vienna Conventions, in article 19, relating to time of formulation, and in article 23, relating to procedure). For those reasons, draft guideline 3.1 was acceptable and the title "Freedom to formulate a reservation" was the correct one.

100. The Special Rapporteur had tackled the question of the object and purpose of a treaty very thoroughly and in great depth. He had endeavoured to provide a definition and the means of determining that object and purpose. Like other speakers, he personally believed that the two terms were complementary and together constituted one sole criterion to which reference was made in a number of provisions of the Vienna Conventions, such as articles 18, 31, 41, 58 and 60.

101. Draft guideline 3.1.5 defined the concept in terms of its relationship with the essential provisions of the treaty, which constituted its *raison d'être* (para. 89). It was vital to try to provide a definition and the reference to essential provisions was important, even if it was difficult to ascertain which provisions were essential and what the *raison d'être* was.

102. Draft guideline 3.1.6, concerning the determination of the object and purpose of the treaty, brought together the appropriate rules on interpretation and included a bracketed reference to the subsequent practice of States (para. 91). The object and purpose of a treaty could well evolve over time, but such practice had to be widespread, accepted by all States parties and clear enough to show exactly what evolution had taken place.

103. Turning to draft guideline 3.1.13, on reservations to clauses concerning dispute settlement and the monitoring of the implementation of the treaty (para. 99), he maintained that the two types of clauses were quite different; one dealt with potential disputes arising from the interpretation and implementation of a treaty, the other with monitoring States parties' compliance with, or respect for, the treaty. The mechanisms involved were also dissimilar. Reservations to a dispute settlement mechanism were not incompatible *per se* with the object and purpose of the treaty, but in some cases it might appear that they were if those mechanisms could be considered as essential provisions of the treaty. For example, the Agreement establishing the International Fund for Agricultural Development contained an arbitration clause (art. 11, sect. 2) whose inclusion had been opposed by some States, including his own.[4] Its proponents had defended its inclusion on the grounds that the nature of the Fund, an international financial institution, called for the inclusion of dispute settlement machinery capable of adopting final and binding decisions which would completely resolve any disputes that might arise. Opponents had insisted that it was necessary to include an express provision permitting reservations in relation to that mechanism. It was therefore obvious that dispute settlement mechanisms could sometimes be closely linked to the object and purpose of the treaty and could thus be essential provisions. The text of the draft guideline could perhaps be improved by making it clear that not all such reservations were necessarily incompatible with the object and purpose of the treaty. Given the difference between the two mechanisms, it might even be possible to split the guideline into two separate guidelines.

104. As for reservations relating to the application of domestic law, such reservations could be formulated only when fundamental norms of domestic law were at stake. For constitutional reasons, for example, those invoked by the Bolivarian Republic of Venezuela in the case of International Fund for Agricultural Development, a State might be unable to accept recourse to an international arbitration mechanism and might formulate a reservation. Such a reservation might, however, be impermissible because it related to an essential provision of the treaty. Draft guideline 3.1.11 needed to be read in conjunction with draft guideline 3.1.13, because both situations could arise simultaneously.

105. In concluding, he said he was in favour of referring the draft guidelines to the Drafting Committee.

106. Mr. MANSFIELD said he did not intend to comment on section C until section D became available in English. It was not yet possible to give the issues under discussion the serious reflection they deserved. In view of the brief time allocated to the discussion of the topic at the current session, he would have to defer his observations until the Commission's next session.

107. He was, however, very pleased that the Commission was finally arriving at the core of the subject, which was of real practical significance. He greatly appreciated the excellent and scholarly basis for the Commission's consideration of the topic that the Special Rapporteur had provided. Even on a preliminary reading of section C, one could not but be impressed by the quality and quantity of the information and analysis it contained, and he looked forward to debating it further, along with the

[4] United Nations, *Treaty Series*, vol. 1059, No. 16041, p. 323.

closely related matters covered in section D, in plenary session and in a working group. While he did not yet have a considered view on the issues, his preliminary reading led him to share some of the concerns raised by Mr. Gaja, Mr. Koskenniemi and others about the main guidelines proposed in the document. While he in no way questioned the value of the report, he felt that the Commission would have to give very careful consideration to the really quite fundamental underlying issues before referring any of the proposed guidelines other than the first two [3.1 and 3.1.1] to the Drafting Committee.

108. Mr. KOLODKIN said that, like many other members of the Commission who had spoken before him, he would very much have liked to extend the debate on section C in plenary. The subject matter really deserved more thorough analysis and he did not wish to limit his comments to a few sporadic remarks. He would welcome an opportunity to go over the very interesting material thoroughly and to comment on all aspects of it. The best time to do so would be at the Commission's fifty-eighth session in 2006.

109. The CHAIRPERSON noted that a number of members of the Commission had expressed the wish to have more time to digest the contents of section C of the report. He therefore suggested that the Special Rapporteur should sum up the debate thus far at the next plenary meeting. A decision could then be taken on whether to pursue the discussion of the report at the fifty-eighth session.

It was so agreed.

The meeting rose at 1.05 p.m.

2859th MEETING

Thursday, 28 July 2005, at 10.05 a.m.

Chairperson: Mr. Djamchid MOMTAZ

Present: Mr. Addo, Mr. Candioti, Mr. Chee, Mr. Comissário Afonso, Mr. Dugard, Mr. Economides, Ms. Escarameia, Mr. Fomba, Mr. Gaja, Mr. Galicki, Mr. Kabatsi, Mr. Kateka, Mr. Kemicha, Mr. Kolodkin, Mr. Koskenniemi, Mr. Mansfield, Mr. Matheson, Mr. Niehaus, Mr. Opertti Badan, Mr. Pambou-Tchivounda, Mr. Pellet, Mr. Sreenivasa Rao, Mr. Rodríguez Cedeño, Mr. Yamada.

Reservations to treaties (*concluded*) (A/CN.4/549 and Add.1, sect. D, A/CN.4/558 and Corr.1 and Add.1 [and Corr.1]–2, and A/CN.4/L.665)

[Agenda item 6]

TENTH REPORT OF THE SPECIAL RAPPORTEUR (*concluded*)

1. The CHAIRPERSON invited the Special Rapporteur to sum up the Commission's discussion on reservations to treaties.

2. Mr. PELLET (Special Rapporteur) thanked all the members of the Commission who had taken part in the discussion, first, because it was always enjoyable to hear compliments, guilty pleasure that it was; members had not been stingy with them and he was grateful for that. There was always something soporific in opening tributes, however, as if one was anaesthetizing the patient the better to operate, sometimes even removing the vital organs and confining the invalid to a wheelchair for life. He had sometimes had that feeling while listening to Commission members, because with the exception of the first five draft guidelines, total evisceration was apparently indicated. To cite the most extreme views expressed, some speakers thought that draft guidelines 3.1.5 and 3.1.6 had to be excluded because they were too general, focusing instead on those that followed, while others felt it was in fact draft guidelines 3.1.7 to 3.1.13 that were superfluous. Those extreme views were minority opinions, however, and before giving a detailed account of the debate and outlining his conclusions, he wished to explain why he did not share them.

3. It was certainly not because he thought he was always right: in the past, he had acknowledged that some of his draft guidelines should be given the axe, and he was still very open to constructive criticism. As a matter of fact, he intended to demonstrate the extent to which certain constructive suggestions seemed to him promising. Nevertheless, some members of the Commission seemed at times to lose sight of the very purpose of the exercise. As Mr. Fomba had pointed out at an earlier meeting in connection with paragraph 61 of the report, it was not a matter of elaborating an abstract doctrinal construct, but of helping States and international organizations to determine what their conduct should be in relation to reservations while staying on the "straight and narrow" of the 1969 Vienna Convention and trying to find realistic solutions that were reasonably coherent and as widely acceptable as possible.

4. That, to him, was a first stab at a response to the brilliant doctrinal exposé made the day before by Mr. Koskenniemi, a highly stimulating intellectual exercise that was nevertheless, to his mind, brilliantly useless. As was often the case with the "new school of criticism", the analysis that Mr. Koskenniemi had undertaken had brilliantly deconstructed not the report before the Commission but the entire set of draft guidelines he had proposed, without offering any alternative solution. In the end he himself had had to turn those criticisms to positive advantage. Furthermore, there was a major contradiction in Mr. Koskenniemi's remarks: after completing his "demolition", he had concluded, against all expectations, that what he called the interpreters, meaning diplomats, arbitrators or judges, would be obliged in future to use the report as a reference. That showed that it was extremely useful for States to be guided by something, obviously not in the precise terms he himself had proposed, but at least along the lines he had endeavoured to indicate. And the voice of the Commission, which made itself heard through the guidelines it adopted after collectively evaluating them and through the commentary it attached to those guidelines, was surely more authoritative than his voice alone.

5. The brief statement by Mr. Mansfield at the previous meeting called for the same response. It might be true that the report and, even more so, the commentary to the guidelines were more useful than the guidelines themselves, but it was still necessary to anchor the commentary somewhere. The Commission was not writing a doctrinal work on reservations. As it had decided back in 1996, it was drafting a guide to practice consisting of guidelines accompanied by commentary.[1] The guidelines were in a sense the anchor, the introduction, the indispensable underpinnings of the commentary, and there could be no commentary without something to comment upon.

6. Turning to another category of general remarks, he observed that the material in the parts of the report that the Commission had begun to consider was without doubt quite difficult, as many members had pointed out, and thus gave rise to controversy. It was natural, then, that members should express opposing viewpoints, even if they had nearly always done so in moderate terms. Some had reproached him for being too timid (he had codified only a little, and certainly not progressively developed), whereas others felt he had been too audacious, if only in having suggested that general human rights treaties raised particular problems and warranted special attention. He understood both points of view, and after extensive consultation of the literature on reservations and the *travaux préparatoires* of the Vienna Conventions, he felt that he could furnish additional arguments to both camps. However, his extensive consultation of the literature had taught him that the juridical truth of the matter was certainly more in flux and less definite than either side would like it to be. The 1969 Vienna Convention seemed to lean towards broad tolerance, rather than encouragement, of reservations. The famous Polish amendment he had mentioned when introducing his report revealed as much.[2] Even if one claimed to have a more "progressive" outlook, meaning a more restrictive view of the validity of reservations, that juridical reality had to be considered. As for the conservatives, who argued for broad freedom in the matter of reservations, he hoped they would be good enough to understand that the Vienna Convention did leave the door open to change and that, short of engaging in a rear-guard action, the Commission must, while respecting the Convention, show itself to be attentive to the aspirations of civil society, especially in the area of human rights, which were being relayed by a number of States and reflected in certain practices that must be taken into account. He had written his report and drafted the 14 draft guidelines, which were reproduced in the first three sections, bearing precisely that moderate viewpoint and concern for the "happy medium" in mind, and he would remain faithful to that philosophy when he responded in greater detail to the proposals made. That did not necessarily mean that he was wedded to the draft texts he had proposed, however, as he had profited from many constructive criticisms.

7. He attached great importance to the question of validity, which had rightly been described as going well beyond a mere terminological problem. In the end it was not just a discordance between the French and English texts, even though it could more easily be dealt with in the latter language. Speakers had taken a variety of stances on the issue. A majority, including Mr. Gaja, Mr. Kamto (who had made some very interesting points), Mr. Sreenivasa Rao, Mr. Pambou-Tchivounda (who had also made interesting points), Mr. Mansfield, Mr. Fomba, Mr. Matheson, Mr. Kemicha, Mr. Economides and Ms. Xue, had rallied, or in some cases resigned themselves, to the views expressed in paragraphs 2 to 8 of the report, leaving aside Mr. Economides's problem with permissibility. That notwithstanding, and taking into account certain comments from the majority camp which acknowledged that his own wish to refer to validity of reservations was justified, he had again changed his mind to some degree on that point. First of all, he was not prepared to accept the argument of authorities put forward by Mr. Chee: however great his respect for the British legal counsel and Sir Derek Bowett, it was not enough for those eminent practitioners to say something for them always to be right; he had examined their viewpoints at length in his report (paras. 4–7) and had nothing to alter in what he had written. Nor was he particularly receptive to the position taken by Mr. Economides and perhaps by Mr. Pambou-Tchivounda, who advocated a "hurry up and wait" approach, for he did not think that the effects of reservations had to be known before one could determine validity. The question of validity arose by definition at an earlier stage, as Mr. Kamto and Mr. Pambou-Tchivounda had pointed out. A legal text that was invalid could not produce the effects that its author expected of it. In that regard, Mr. Pambou-Tchivounda was wrong to equate validity and permissibility, the latter term harking back to the law of responsibility. The main reason he had been led to moderate the position he had taken in his report, and which had been emphasized in particular by Mr. Kamto, Mr. Fomba, Mr. Candioti and Mr. Rodríguez Cedeño, was that validity was not solely a question of substance but also of form. According to Salmon's *Dictionnaire de droit international public*, validity was that quality of elements of a legal order that met the formal or substantive requirements for producing legal effects.[3] More succinctly, *Black's Law Dictionary* defined validity as that which was "legally sufficient".[4] It would therefore be necessary either to amend the title of chapter III of the Guide to Practice in order to cover only the substantive or material validity of reservations, or to adopt a draft guideline 3 recalling that a reservation was valid only if it fulfilled the formal and substantive requirements imposed by the Vienna Conventions and set out in the Guide to Practice. It was the latter solution that had won him over for the time being. The option seemed to him to be linked to the wording of the chapeau of a provision that he saw as fundamental to the law of reservations, namely article 21, paragraph 1, of the Vienna Convention, according to which a reservation was established with regard to another party in accordance with article 19, which referred to substantive requirements, article 20, referring to requirements for enforceability, and article 23, referring to procedural requirements; however, the guidelines reflecting and deriving from that provision would not be submitted until later.

[1] *Yearbook ... 1996*, vol. II (Part Two), pp. 79–80, paras. 105 and 112.

[2] See 2854th meeting, footnote 7.

[3] *Dictionnaire de droit international public*, J. Salmon, Brussels, Bruylant, 2001, p. 1126.

[4] *Black's Law Dictionary*, B. Garner (ed.), 8th ed., St. Paul (Minn.), West Group, 2004, p. 1586.

8. The fact remained that, for the time being, he had reached the following conclusions: first, and in French only, the word "*validité*" referred, in respect of reservations, to the procedural requirements in article 23 of the 1969 Vienna Convention, as explicated in chapter II of the Guide to Practice, and to the substantive requirements in article 19. A reservation that did not meet all those requirements was not "*valide*". Secondly, the conditions set out in article 19, which were to be reproduced in draft guideline 3.1, related solely to the substantive requirements of validity. Thirdly, the machinery in article 20 governed the enforceability of a reservation, not its validity.

9. As to the Arabic, Chinese, Spanish and Russian texts, he would leave to the members who spoke those languages the task of proposing the most appropriate solutions in each, bearing in mind his report and the discussions it had engendered. He had taken due note of the comments by Mr. Kolodkin and Ms. Xue concerning the translation into Russian and Chinese of the French word "*validité*". As for the English language, it had a convenient word, "permissible", and like Mr. Kolodkin, he thought that it pinpointed the content of article 19. Yet when one came back to the French, a problem arose, since the equivalent of "permissible" simply did not exist. The sole translation that appeared to suit, for lack of anything better, was "*permis*", it being understood that he was still unable to come up with an unmodified noun that could be used in French to designate the substantive, or material, validity of a reservation. He nevertheless proposed to retain in French and English the phrase "*Validité des réserves*" ("Validity of reservations") as the title of the third part of the Guide to Practice, with the proviso, and that was his second point, that it would later be stipulated that that expression covered requirements of both procedure and substance, even if only the requirements of substance were to be elaborated in that part, since those of form and procedure were covered in the second part.

10. Thirdly, in draft guideline 1.6, "*licéité*" in the French text and "permissibility" in the English would be replaced by "*validité*" and "validity". While Mr. Kamto was intellectually correct in pointing out that the impact of invalidity was to prevent a legal instrument from producing effects, he himself thought that that observation, however valid in itself, should not affect the wording of draft guideline 1.6, which did not link validity and effects but merely indicated that the definitions in the first part of the Guide to Practice were without prejudice either to the validity—not permissibility, since both substance and procedure were involved—or to the effects of the unilateral statements defined in the Guide. To his mind, that formulation was neutral and should be retained.

11. Fourthly, in draft guideline 2.1.8, on procedure in case of manifestly [impermissible] reservations, the penultimate word having been left in square brackets, a reference to invalidity should be incorporated. Perhaps the draft guideline could be entitled "Procedure in case of reservations manifestly lacking in validity", with paragraph 1 to read: "Where, in the opinion of the depositary, a reservation is manifestly lacking in validity, the depositary shall draw the attention of the author of the reservation to what, in the depositary's view, constitutes such lack of validity." As a drafting problem was involved, the draft guideline could be sent back to the Drafting Committee on the understanding that it was not a matter of reopening an issue that had already been decided, since the Commission would have decided to reconsider the question.[5] The commentary to draft guidelines 1.6 and 2.1.8 would have to be modified accordingly.

12. Fifthly, that line of reasoning raised questions about the title to be given to draft guideline 3.1. To reassure those who, like Mr. Kamto, Mr. Kolodkin and Mr. Pambou-Tchivounda, had concerns in that regard, he recalled that he had abandoned the idea of having a separate draft guideline on the freedom to formulate a reservation or presumption of validity of reservations: paragraphs 17 and 18 of the report said as much. There was thus no reason to pursue the matter further. On the other hand, he agreed with those who had criticized the title he had proposed, "Freedom to formulate reservations" (para. 20), since it emphasized only part of the question at hand, even though, as Ms. Xue had pointed out, it was an important part. Mr. Rodríguez Cedeño had proposed that the title should be "Formulation of reservations", which had the great advantage of being the title of article 19 of the Vienna Conventions, the wording of which draft guideline 3.1 simply reproduced. He did not think that that solution could be adopted, however, since the word "formulation" had already been used, specifically in the title of draft guideline 2.1.3, and to his mind that choice of wording should not be revisited. The word "formulation" referred much more to form and procedure than to the substantive requirements that were nevertheless the essence of article 19. Although he was not radically opposed to the idea, he thought that Mr. Kolodkin's proposal, which had been supported by Ms. Escarameia and Ms. Xue, to give draft guideline 3.1 the title "Right to formulate a reservation" was somewhat problematic. The same held true for Mr. Economides' proposal of "Limitations on the formulation of reservations". Mr. Fomba had proposed "Formulation and validity", and for the same reasons he was not enthusiastic about the idea of using the term "formulation" in the title. It would surely be better to go with the proposal by Mr. Kolodkin and Mr. Candioti to say in English "Permissible reservations", with the French equivalent to be "*Réserves permises*" or "*Validité matérielle des réserves*". Still, that was a drafting problem, and no one appeared to oppose the referral of draft guideline 3.1 to the Drafting Committee. Mr. Gaja had given an entirely convincing reason for eliminating the reference to the time when a reservation might be made, but unless he himself was mistaken, that proposal had not been supported by other members of the Commission. Still, if the Commission considered that the third part of the Guide, and certainly draft guideline 3.1, applied solely to the material validity of reservations, then the proposal was not without merit and the Drafting Committee should consider it.

13. There had been no fundamental objection to the referral of draft guideline 3.1.1 to the Drafting Committee, although once again it had been Mr. Gaja who had released two hares and set other members of the

[5] *Yearbook ... 2002*, vol. II (Part Two), chap. IV, sect. C.2, p. 46, para. (7) of the commentary.

Commission running after them. Mr. Gaja had remarked, as had Mr. Mansfield, Mr. Matheson, Mr. Candioti and Ms. Xue after him, that the text was poorly drafted and that it should be made clear that the reservations covered had to fall within the categories specified in the final two indents. On that point, he thought Mr. Gaja was right. However, he was a bit less persuaded by Mr. Gaja's second "hare", even though Mr. Sreenivasa Rao, Ms. Escarameia, Mr. Mansfield and Mr. Economides had espoused his line of reasoning. According to those speakers, the possibility that reservations could be implicitly prohibited must also be mentioned, either in draft guideline 3.1.1 or in a separate text. The speakers had given only one example, however, that of the Charter of the United Nations, and he, for his part, could not see why it should be so obvious that a State could not formulate a reservation to a secondary provision of the Charter of the United Nations since it would be accepted by the Organization's competent organs. Aside from that, he, like Mr. Matheson, was far from enthusiastic about the proposition. First, it was clearly excluded by the *travaux préparatoires*, and he thought that the members of the Commission at that time had had good reason for excluding it, as he stated in his report. In addition, in relation to the Charter of the United Nations and probably also to the other treaties which might be thought implicitly to exclude reservations, namely the constituent instruments of international organizations, the requirement of acceptance by the Organization's competent organ set out in article 20, paragraph 3, of the Vienna Convention afforded perfectly adequate safeguards. Lastly, and especially, he was convinced that the problem lay not in subparagraphs (*a*) and (*b*) of article 19, but in subparagraph (*c*): if a reservation was implicitly prohibited, it was because it was contrary to the object and purpose of the treaty. If one assumed that there could be treaties which by their nature actually prohibited reservations, it was on account of their object and purpose, and there was no need to insert a provision on that point in the draft guideline. Nevertheless, he saw no reason why the Drafting Committee should not consider the matter, and if the Commission requested him to, he was prepared to write a note setting out the arguments for and against, although at the present stage he saw precious few arguments in favour of the proposition.

14. Draft guideline 3.1.2 (para. 49) seemed also to have been accepted insofar as the principle was concerned, and nothing seemed to prevent its referral to the Drafting Committee. Several members had nevertheless drawn attention to problems with the wording. The problem with "specified" in the English text had already been mentioned (2857th meeting, above, paras. 37–38). It might be worthwhile to clarify the phrase "and which meet conditions specified by the treaty", but it would be unfortunate to delete it, since, in his view, the reference to "specific provisions" was not in itself sufficient to enable one to speak of "specified reservations"; that would compromise the careful balance that had been achieved in the provision, which was all the more indispensable in that the concept of "specified reservations" did indeed have major practical effects.

15. Draft guidelines 3.1.3 and 3.1.4 had met with general approval, again with some suggestions regarding drafting. Those of Mr. Economides surely merited discussion. Thus both draft guidelines could also be sent to the Drafting Committee, especially as it would be unfortunate to consider them separately from draft guideline 3.1.2.

16. The wording of draft guidelines 3.1.5 and 3.1.6 could be improved, and some of the suggestions made to that end were extremely useful. Contrary to the views of some, however, it was essential to try to define the concept of object and purpose, since it was fundamental to the law of reservations and to the law of treaties in general. Another problem that arose in connection with the two draft guidelines was that of the interpreter, in other words the person or organ that determined whether or not a reservation was compatible with the object and purpose of the treaty. In fact, five draft guidelines dealt with competence to assess the validity of reservations and an additional five, of even greater importance, covered the consequences of non-validity of a reservation.

17. With regard to draft guidelines 3.1.7 to 3.1.13, he emphasized that he had not chosen the categories of reservations used as "illustrations" randomly, but had done so on the basis of the principle that the main function of the Guide to Practice was to help States determine their position on a problem relating to reservations. He had therefore focused on the most challenging and frequently encountered problems. One could add other categories, but no credible proposals had been made so far. It had been rightly pointed out that a single treaty could have several objects and purposes, and that its provisions could fall into several of the categories identified. All that needed to be done, then, was to take the various applicable guidelines as a basis and to apply them together, although nothing prevented each situation from being codified separately. He wished to point out that draft guideline 3.1.12 related not to reservations to human rights treaties, and even less so to reservations to human rights provisions, but only to reservations to general human rights treaties, a particular category of human rights treaty that seemed perfectly unambiguous.

18. Lastly, concerning the proposal for consultation with human rights bodies (the six treaty-monitoring bodies and the Sub-Commission on the Promotion and Protection of Human Rights), he said it would be fairly difficult, although not impossible, to find a common date, probably towards mid-May 2006, and that it would undoubtedly be necessary to finance the travel of members of the treaty bodies that were not meeting in Geneva at that time. Any suggestions on that matter would be welcome.

19. Mr. KOSKENNIEMI said that he always tried to offer constructive criticism, in other words criticism that contained a specific proposal, because negative criticism was sterile. He wished to return briefly to the point he had made, namely that the categories proposed in the section C of the report on reservations to treaties were useful but inadequate. They were at once too comprehensive since they covered reservations that the Commission did not wish to address, such as vague and general reservations to secondary provisions, and incomplete, as they left out other important reservations such as reservations to human rights treaties. That was why it seemed appropriate to provide explanations with the categories to guide future users of the guidelines. In particular, it should be made

clear that a reservation was incompatible with the object and purpose of a treaty if it went against what the parties expected of the treaty when they became parties or if the reservation went against the common undertaking that the treaty expressed.

20. Mr. PELLET (Special Rapporteur), speaking on a point of order, said that the discussion could not be reopened at the present stage.

21. Mr. CHEE, referring to the possibility mentioned by the Special Rapporteur of formulating reservations to the Charter of the United Nations, noted that Article 108 of the Charter related to amendments, not reservations.

22. Concerning "validity", he wished to recall that Part V, section 2, of the Vienna Conventions was entitled "Invalidity of treaties", as opposed to "validity". The Special Rapporteur described the word "validity" as neutral, but according to the dictionary, a word that was neutral must be so from all standpoints. In the interests of averting confusion, he intended to bring the subject up again at the next session.

23. The CHAIRPERSON recalled that the Special Rapporteur had proposed that draft guidelines 3.1, 3.1.1, 3.1.2, 3.1.3, 3.1.4, 3.1.6 and 3.1.8 should be referred to the Drafting Committee.

24. Mr. GAJA said he had understood that only the first five of those draft guidelines were to be referred to the Drafting Committee, since there were still a number of problems with the other two (3.1.6 and 3.1.8).

25. Mr. MATHESON agreed with Mr. Gaja, stressing that, in his opinion, draft guidelines 3.1.6 and 3.1.8 should be considered at the next session in plenary meeting.

26. Mr. PELLET (Special Rapporteur) explained that he had not intended to refer those two draft guidelines to the Drafting Committee; his proposal had related only to draft guidelines 1.6 and 2.1.8 (see paragraph 10 above) as well as to draft guidelines 3.1 and 3.1.1 to 3.1.4.

27. The CHAIRPERSON suggested that draft guidelines 1.6, 2.1.8, 3.1, 3.1.1, 3.1.2, 3.1.3 and 3.1.4 should be referred to the Drafting Committee, on the understanding that the discussion on the other draft guidelines would be continued at the fifty-eighth session.

It was so decided.

Unilateral acts of states (*concluded*)* (A/CN.4/557 and A/CN.4/549 and Add.1, sect. C)

[Agenda item 5]

Report of the Working Group

28. The CHAIRPERSON invited Mr. Pellet, as Chairperson of the Working Group on Unilateral acts of States, to make a presentation on its work.

29. Mr. PELLET said that the Working Group had held four meetings in 2005. The first three meetings had been given over to an analysis of specific cases according to the grid established the previous year and to the conclusions to be drawn from them; the final meeting had covered preliminary or general conclusions, or "proposals" (no decision had been taken regarding the future document's title), that would reflect the outcome of the Commission's nine years of work on the topic.

30. An initial exchange of views had uncovered common ground on which a consensus might emerge. Members of the Working Group had generally agreed on the "format" and form of the document. On substance, they appeared to agree on the need to proceed from the principle that the unilateral conduct of States could produce legal effects, however they might be manifested, but that one could differentiate between unilateral conduct and unilateral acts *stricto sensu*. In its report on the work of its fifty-fifth session the Commission had drawn a clear distinction between unilateral conduct and unilateral acts and had decided to give priority to the latter, defined as "a statement expressing the will or consent by which [a] State purports to create obligations or other legal effects under international law".[6]

31. The Working Group had also considered questions relating to the diversity of unilateral acts and their effects, the importance of the surrounding circumstances in assessing their nature and effects, their relationship to other commitments under international law undertaken by their authors, and the conditions for their revision and revocation.

Programmes, procedures and working methods of the Commission and its documentation (A/CN.4/L.675 and Corr.1)

[Agenda item 10]

Report of the Planning Group

32. Mr. PAMBOU-TCHIVOUNDA (Chairperson of the Planning Group), introducing the report of the Planning Group (A/CN.4/L.675 and Corr.1), said that during its four meetings the Planning Group had considered, among other things, cost-saving measures, the documentation of the Commission, an interim report by the Working Group on the long-term programme of work, and the date and place of the fifty-eighth session of the Commission.

33. Pursuant to paragraph 8 of General Assembly resolution 59/41 of 2 December 2004 and in the light of the Commission's programme of work, the Planning Group had considered the question of cost-saving measures, and on its recommendation the Commission had reduced the duration of the second part of the current session by one week.

34. Having also considered the question of the Commission's documentation and the timely submission of reports by the Special Rapporteurs, the Planning Group

* Resumed from the discussion at the 2855th meeting.

[6] *Yearbook ... 2003*, vol. II (Part Two), *Recommendation 1*, p. 57, para. 306.

had recalled that if the dates originally indicated were not observed, the timely availability of reports might be jeopardized, which could have adverse consequences for the Commission's work. The Group had formulated a recommendation on that subject in paragraph 4 of its report.

35. The Chairperson of the Working Group on the long-term programme of work had reported orally to the Planning Group. The Working Group would submit its final report in written form to the Commission at its fifty-eighth session, in 2006. The Working Group was open to the consideration of any topic that might seem relevant, especially as the Commission urgently needed to include new topics on its agenda. Any member having a proposal should submit it to the Working Group in the form of a short preliminary report.

36. The Planning Group had recalled that at its fifty-sixth session, the Commission had decided to include in the agenda of its current session the topic "Obligation to extradite or prosecute (*aut dedere aut judicare*)", which had already been included in the Commission's long-term programme of work.[7]

37. The Planning Group recommended that the views expressed in the Commission's report on the work of its fifty-sixth session with regard to honoraria for members of the Commission should be reaffirmed in full in the report on the work of its fifty-seventh session.[8]

38. Lastly, the Planning Group had taken note of a proposal that the Planning Group to be established at the fifty-eighth session should consider as a priority question the Commission's methods of work and rules of procedure with a view to enhancing the its effectiveness and transparency.

39. Mr. ECONOMIDES, who had been the author of that proposal, said that it would be more accurate to say "The Planning Group had given a favourable reception to a proposal…". In fact, the exact wording of his proposal had been "…relating to the establishment of a working group which, with the assistance of the secretariat, would examine the Commission's methods, rules and practices in order to enhance its effectiveness and transparency". He suggested that his proposal should be transmitted to the Sixth Committee to show that the members of the Commission were sensitive to the climate of reform prevailing throughout the United Nations and because it would be interesting to know what the Sixth Committee thought about the proposal.

40. The CHAIRPERSON said that a decision on the proposal would be taken when the Commission's report was considered in the General Assembly.

41. Mr. KABATSI said that he fully endorsed the idea of trying to improve the Commission's working methods but thought that that was perhaps an internal matter for the Commission alone and that it might not be appropriate at the present stage to transmit it to the Sixth Committee.

[7] *Yearbook ... 2004*, vol. II (Part Two), chap. XI, p. 120, paras. 362–363, and annex.

[8] *Ibid.*, pp. 120–121, para. 369.

42. Ms. ESCARAMEIA pointed out that the Commission was in the process of adopting the report of the Planning Group, not its own report to the General Assembly. She endorsed Mr. Economides's comment about the way paragraph 8 was currently worded and suggested that the proposal he had just made should be adopted, or else that the phrase should be amended to read: "The Planning Group took note of a proposal … and recommended that it should be considered as a priority question by the Planning Group…".

43. Mr. YAMADA, supported by Mr. PELLET, said that the fact that the plenary Commission was endeavouring to amend a report already adopted by the Planning Group was not irregular.

44. The CHAIRPERSON explained that the plenary Commission was merely taking note of the report of the Planning Group and that the questions and recommendations contained therein would be considered when the Commission's report was considered in the General Assembly.

45. Ms. ESCARAMEIA said that the Planning Group had never seen paragraph 8 of the report in its current form.

46. Mr. PAMBOU-TCHIVOUNDA (Chairperson of the Planning Group) confirmed that that was the case.

47. Mr. ECONOMIDES said that the plenary Commission could not be deemed to be correcting the text in question since he himself had made no written proposal. On the other hand, there had been an exchange of views, and his proposal had met with no objection.

48. Mr. PAMBOU-TCHIVOUNDA (Chairperson of the Planning Group) said that he could ask the Planning Group to include in paragraph 8 of its report a reference to the consensus that had emerged concerning Mr. Economides's proposal.

49. Mr. PELLET said that it was totally unrealistic to ask the Planning Group to amend its own report. It was true that the proposal had been adopted by consensus, but that was true of most of the decisions or recommendations adopted by the Group. There was no need to spell that out, especially as "consensus" simply referred to the absence of objection, not to an enthusiastic unanimity.

50. Mr. CHEE fully endorsed the comments by Ms. Escarameia and Mr. Economides.

51. Mr. KEMICHA, who had been a member of the Planning Group, confirmed that the reaction to Mr. Economides's proposal had been closer to a favourable response than to the simple act of taking note. While he acknowledged that it was unusual for the plenary to amend a report of that nature, he saw no reason why the members of the Group, almost all of whom were present, could not take the opportunity to meet with Mr. Pambou-Tchivounda as their Chairperson and amend their report.

52. Mr. MATHESON proposed that the plenary Commission should simply invite the Chairperson of the

Planning Group to amend the report of the Group to better reflect the agreement reached orally.

53. Mr. PAMBOU-TCHIVOUNDA (Chairperson of the Planning Group) proposed that the idea that a favourable reception had been given to the proposal made by Mr. Economides should be incorporated in paragraph 8 of the Group's report, after the words "took note".

54. Mr. MATHESON said that he would prefer the wording suggested by Ms. Escarameia. It was not correct to say that the Group had given a favourable reception to Mr. Economides' proposal, since it had not considered it in detail. On the other hand, the Group had endorsed the idea that the proposal should be considered as a priority question at the fifty-eighth session.

55. The CHAIRPERSON said that if he heard no objection, he would take it that the Commission wished to take note of the report of the Planning Group, as amended by Ms. Escarameia.

It was so decided.

Fragmentation of international law: difficulties arising from the diversification and expansion of international law (A/CN.4/549 and Add.1, sect. E, and A/CN.4/L.676 and Corr.1)[9]

[Agenda item 9]

56. The CHAIRPERSON invited Mr. Koskenniemi to introduce his briefing note on the work of the Study Group on Fragmentation of international law.

57. Mr. KOSKENNIEMI (Chairperson of the Study Group on Fragmentation of international law: Difficulties arising from the diversification and expansion of international law) explained that his briefing note was an informal document whose sole purpose was to promote an exchange of views between members of the Commission who had participated in the Study Group and those who had not. The document was thus intended primarily to provide information.

58. He recalled that when the Study Group had been established, great confusion had reigned as to what it was supposed to do.[10] While the Commission regularly set up working groups or drafting committees, the format of the Study Group was entirely new. In 2004 the Study Group's objective had been decided on and endorsed by the Commission as well as by many representatives of States in the Sixth Committee. As the outcome of its work, the Study Group was to prepare a collective document on fragmentation consisting of two parts. One would be a relatively large analytical study of conflicts and the overlap between rules of international law, composed on the basis of the outlines and studies submitted by individual members of the Study Group during 2003–2005. The other part would consist of a condensed set of approximately 40 conclusions, guidelines or principles (the Commission had not yet decided which) emerging from the studies and the discussions in the Study Group and designed to help in thinking about and dealing with the issue of fragmentation in legal practice.[11] The objective was to provide guidance for lawyers, judges, arbitrators and members of international committees in resolving problems created by conflicts or overlap between the various rules in the different systems of international law. A draft of both documents would be submitted in 2006 to the Commission, which still had to determine the form in which it would adopt them. He suggested that the Commission might wish to take note of the substantive study and endorse the conclusions.

59. Turning to the basic approach, he said that the Study Group had focused on the substantive aspects of fragmentation, leaving aside institutional considerations such as conflict of jurisdiction of particular bodies. It had looked at the relevant issues from the standpoint of the 1969 Vienna Convention, an approach that seemed justified in view of the Commission's special relationship with the Vienna Convention and regime. It was therefore necessary to determine what resources were available under the Vienna Convention for the resolution of actual or potential conflicts between norms applicable in the same circumstances.

60. The Study Group had concentrated on the following five types of approaches to the resolution of conflict of norms in international law:

(*a*) the function and scope of the *lex specialis* rule and the question of "self-contained regimes" (a study he himself had carried out);

(*b*) the interpretation of treaties in the light of "any relevant rules of international law applicable in the relations between the parties" (article 31, paragraph 3 (*c*), of the Vienna Convention) (study by Mr. Mansfield);

(*c*) the application of successive treaties relating to the same subject matter (article 30 of the Vienna Convention) (study by Mr. Melescanu);

(*d*) the modification of multilateral treaties between certain of the parties only (article 41 of the Vienna Convention) (study by Mr. Daoudi); and

(*e*) hierarchy in international law: *jus cogens*, obligations *erga omnes* and Article 103 of the Charter of the United Nations (study by Mr. Galicki).

On each of the five topics, the Study Group had received a report by one of its members. It had held extensive substantive discussions on items (*a*), (*b*) and (*e*) and preliminary debates on items (*c*) and (*d*).

61. The Study Group had endorsed the principle of *lex specialis* but had stressed that the special law did not necessarily make the general law inapplicable, but merely set it aside provisionally. It should also be noted that the concepts of "special law" and "general law" were interdependent and had to be understood in relation to one

[9] Reproduced in *Yearbook ... 2005*, vol. II (Part Two), chap. XI, sect. C.

[10] *Yearbook ... 2002*, vol. II (Part Two), chap. IX, p. 97, para. 493.

[11] See *Yearbook ... 2004*, vol. II (Part Two), chap. X, pp. 111–112, para. 302.

another. In practice, treaties often acted as *lex specialis* in relation to customary law and general principles. The Study Group had analysed "self-contained regimes" and had concluded that no treaty was isolated from others, from customary law or from general principles, and that therefore no regime was entirely "self-contained". The term had been seen as a misnomer, since no set of rules was completely isolated from general international law. In that connection, the Study Group had also discussed cases in which general law filled in gaps or lacunae in special regimes.

62. With regard to article 30 of the 1969 Vienna Convention, the Study Group had found that the principle that subsequent treaties overrode previous ones was generally unproblematic, apart from the case where the parties to the later treaty were not identical to the parties to the former treaty. The mere conclusion of a treaty incompatible with an earlier treaty was not a breach of international law. Article 30 did not address the issue of validity but only that of priority.

63. With regard to article 31, paragraph 3 (*c*), of the Vienna Convention, the Study Group had stressed the need to operationalize that provision, which had been generating considerable interest but had not often been applied in the past. The "other obligations" to be taken into account in the interpretation of a treaty included not only other treaties, but also customary law and general legal principles. The Study Group had also discussed whether the parties to the treaty to be interpreted needed also to be parties to the "other obligations". It had also reviewed the question of intertemporality, in other words whether the obligations used in the interpretation of a treaty needed to have already been in force at the time the treaty had been concluded. The Study Group had endorsed certain conclusions on that subject.

64. In its consideration of article 41 of the 1969 Vienna Convention, the Study Group had highlighted the fact that that provision was aimed at reconciling the need to preserve the integrity of the treaty as originally concluded, with the need to take into account or to agree to the taking into account of modifications subsequently introduced under an *inter se* agreement. The Study Group had emphasized that *inter se* agreements raised questions similar to those raised by *lex specialis* and that the impermissibility of a modification might follow from the *pacta tertiis* rule or the fact that the modifying agreement might otherwise undermine the original treaty.

65. With regard to the question of hierarchy in international law, the Study Group had agreed that there was no general hierarchy of sources. The three notions (*jus cogens*, obligations *erga omnes* and Article 103 of the Charter) also operated largely independently of each other. Only *jus cogens* and Article 103 of the Charter had to do properly with normative hierarchy. Obligations *erga omnes* had to do with the scope of application of the relevant norms. The Study Group had decided that the understanding of *jus cogens* and *erga omnes* norms adopted under the draft on State responsibility must be followed. It had also decided that it was not its task to identify specific rules under either of the two categories but to highlight how they might be used as "conflict rules" in order to deal with fragmentation. The issue of normative hierarchy governed the permissibility of particular agreements as *leges specialis*, as subsequent agreements or as *inter se* modifications of multilateral treaties.

66. In conclusion, he said that the Study Group had tried to avoid taking fixed positions. Its study of practice showed that conflicts and overlap between various rules of international law had always existed and had been resolved by applying a variety of techniques. The objective must thus be to show practitioners of the law that the difficult problems they faced were not new ones and that courts had already overcome them successfully in the past.

67. The CHAIRPERSON thanked Mr. Koskenniemi and announced that volume XXIV of the Reports of International Arbitral Awards had just been issued.[12]

The meeting rose at 12.55 p.m.

2860th MEETING

Friday, 29 July 2005, at 10.05 a.m.

Chairperson: Mr. Djamchid MOMTAZ

Present: Mr. Addo, Mr. Candioti, Mr. Chee, Mr. Comissário Afonso, Mr. Dugard, Mr. Economides, Ms. Escarameia, Mr. Fomba, Mr. Gaja, Mr. Galicki, Mr. Kabatsi, Mr. Kateka, Mr. Kemicha, Mr. Kolodkin, Mr. Koskenniemi, Mr. Mansfield, Mr. Matheson, Mr. Niehaus, Mr. Opertti Badan, Mr. Pambou-Tchivounda, Mr. Pellet, Mr. Sreenivasa Rao, Mr. Rodríguez Cedeño, Mr. Yamada.

Cooperation with other bodies (*concluded*)*

[Agenda item 11]

VISIT BY REPRESENTATIVES OF THE COUNCIL OF EUROPE

1. The CHAIRPERSON welcomed Mr. de Vel, Director-General of Legal Affairs of the Council of Europe and Mr. Benítez, Deputy Head of the Public Law Department of the Directorate General of Legal Affairs of the Council of Europe and invited Mr. de Vel to address the Commission.

2. Mr. de VEL (Council of Europe) said it was an honour to attend a meeting of the Commission in order to inform it of developments at the Council of Europe since the Commission's previous session. Such meetings had become a welcome tradition.

3. The Council's political life over the past year had been marked by the Third Summit of Heads of State

* Resumed from the discussion at the 2853rd meeting.

[12] United Nations publication (Sales No.: E. F. 04.V.18), July 2005, 380 pages.

and Government of the Member States of the Council of Europe, which had been held in Warsaw, on 16 and 17 May 2005, at the invitation of the Polish Government. The two previous summits, held in Vienna in 1993 and in Strasbourg in 1997, had lent decisive impetus to the integration of the European continent. The Third Summit had taken place against a background of a Europe undergoing substantial changes and had endeavoured to define the Council's place in the European and international institutional landscape, with a view to giving it a precise political mandate for the years to come. The Summit had culminated in the adoption of the Warsaw Declaration,[1] in which the Heads of State and Government of the member States had emphasized that further progress in building a Europe without dividing lines must continue to be based on the common values embodied in the Statute of the Council of Europe: democracy, human rights and the rule of law. They had noted that Europe was guided by a political philosophy of inclusion and complementarity and by a common commitment to multilateralism based on international law. They had defined the Council's core objective as that of preserving and promoting human rights, democracy and the rule of law.

4. The Heads of State and Government had committed themselves to enhancing the role of the Council of Europe as an effective mechanism of pan-European cooperation, while at the same time strengthening and streamlining the Council's activities, structures and working methods in order to ensure that it played its due role in a changing Europe. They had also expressed their determination to ensure the complementarity of the Council of Europe and the other organizations involved in building a democratic and secure Europe by creating a new framework for enhanced cooperation with them. To that end, they had instructed the Prime Minister of Luxembourg, Mr. Jean-Claude Juncker, to prepare, in his personal capacity, a report on relations between the Council of Europe and the European Union, on the basis of the decisions adopted at the Summit and taking into account the importance of the human dimension in building Europe. In that connection, a memorandum of understanding was due to be signed in the near future between the Council of Europe and the European Union in order to define relations between the two institutions. In the Warsaw Declaration, the Heads of State and Government had also undertaken to foster cooperation between the Council of Europe and the United Nations and to achieve the Millennium Development Goals[2] in Europe. They had likewise adopted an Action Plan.

5. Both the Action Plan and the Warsaw Declaration had alluded to the most appropriate means of guaranteeing the long-term effectiveness of the Convention for the Protection of Human Rights and Fundamental Freedoms. That was why a "group of wise persons" would be established to consider the issue of the long-term effectiveness of the Convention's control mechanism, including the initial effects of Protocol No. 14 to the Convention. That group had been asked to submit proposals going beyond the measures already taken, while preserving the basic philosophy underlying the Convention.

6. As members would recall, the previous year, he had informed the Commission of the adoption of Protocol No. 14, amending the control system of the Convention, with a view to reducing the Court's backlog of cases. That Protocol had now been signed by 31 States and ratified by 13. In addition, Protocol No. 12 to the Convention, which was aimed at combating discrimination, had entered into force in April 2005. The Warsaw Declaration and Action Plan plainly attached particular importance to the activities of the Directorate General of Legal Affairs.

7. During the past year, the Directorate General of Legal Affairs had devoted much effort to measures to counter terrorism. The recent bomb attacks in London and Egypt unfortunately proved that it must pursue its action tirelessly. Since November 2001 his Directorate General had striven to make a practical contribution in that field by turning to good account the added value the Council could provide. Its activities were aimed at strengthening legal action against terrorism and its sources of financing, and at safeguarding fundamental values. The Council's rich legal heritage made it possible to preserve essential values which, more than ever before, had to be reconciled and not treated as incompatible, namely, respect for human rights and effective measures to combat terrorism. The Council of Europe was particularly well placed to meet that challenge: it had more than 50 years' experience in promoting and defending human rights and fighting crime, as was evidenced by its pioneering international legal achievements such as the European Convention on Extradition (1957), the European Convention on Mutual Assistance in Criminal Matters (1959), the European Convention on the suppression of terrorism (1977), the Convention on laundering, search, seizure and confiscation of the proceeds from crime (1990) and the Convention on cybercrime (2001). The 1977 European Convention on the suppression of terrorism was the one and only European convention to deal specifically with terrorism. In the 1970s it had marked a breakthrough, for it had made it possible to depoliticize certain terrorist crimes and offences with a view to extraditing those suspected of perpetrating them.

8. The first fruits of the implementation of the action plan against terrorism adopted by the Committee of Ministers in the wake of the events of 11 September 2001, the Protocol amending the European Convention on the Suppression of Terrorism, which had been opened for signature in May 2003, had gathered 26 signatures and 18 ratifications. All the current 44 States parties to the 1977 Convention had to become parties to the Protocol before the latter could enter into force. The Council was therefore making a considerable effort to ensure that outcome as soon as possible.

9. A number of priority fields of action identified in 2001 had led to the drafting of several international standard-setting instruments, which had been adopted in the first half of 2005. They included, first and foremost, the Council of Europe Convention on the Prevention of Terrorism which was designed to bridge gaps in legislation and secure international action to combat terrorism

[1] Council of Europe, document CM(2005)79 final, 17 May 2005. For the Action Plan adopted at the Summit, see document CM(2005)80 final, 17 May 2005.

[2] See the United Nations Millennium Declaration, adopted by the General Assembly in its resolution 55/2 of 8 September 2000.

by a variety of means. Various types of conduct likely to lead to the commission of acts of terrorism, such as public provocation to commit a terrorist offence, recruitment for terrorism and training for terrorism, had been classified as criminal offences. The tragic events in London and Sharm el-Sheikh had revealed the extent of those challenges. Cooperation to prevent terrorism had also been strengthened at both the national and international levels.

10. Another new Council of Europe Convention, on Laundering, Search, Seizure and Confiscation of the Proceeds from Crime and on the Financing of Terrorism, took account of recent developments, in particular the recommendations of the Financial Action Task Force on Money Laundering concerning measures to combat the financing of terrorism in accordance with Security Council resolution 1373 (2001) of 28 September 2001. In that sphere, the Council had a leading-edge instrument, the Select Committee of Experts on the Evaluation of Anti-Money Laundering Measures and the Financing of Terrorism (MONEYVAL Committee), which assessed, at the regional level, member States' action to prevent and suppress money laundering and the financing of terrorism in keeping with the methods advocated by the Financial Action Task Force on Money Laundering. The Committee comprised Council of Europe member States which were not members of the Task Force.

11. Both the Council of Europe Convention on the Prevention of Terrorism and the Council of Europe Convention on Laundering, Search, Seizure and Confiscation of the Proceeds from Crime and on the Financing of Terrorism had been opened for signature at the Third Summit of Heads of State and Government and, despite the fact that they had been adopted by the Committee of Ministers just two weeks before the Summit, they had already gathered 19 and 13 signatures respectively. They had to be ratified by six States parties in order to enter into force. Moreover, they were open, subject to certain conditions, to States not members of the Council of Europe.

12. In the field of soft law, the Committee of Ministers had recently adopted three recommendations to member States' Governments concerning special investigation techniques in relation to serious crimes including acts of terrorism, the protection of witnesses and collaborators of justice, and identity and travel documents and the fight against terrorism, which would doubtless prove their worth in the coming months.

13. Other international standards, specifically designed to protect human rights, had been formulated in addition to those new instruments. In July 2002, the Committee of Ministers had adopted a first series of Guidelines on human rights and the fight against terrorism, which had been the first international legal text on the matter.[3] The guidelines laid down 17 principles which set limits that States must observe in combating terrorism and which had been drawn from international texts and the case law of the European Court of Human Rights. That legal text had recently been supplemented by a further series of Guidelines on the Protection of Victims of Terrorist Acts, adopted by the Committee of Ministers in March 2005.[4] They complemented an earlier achievement by the Council in that sphere in the shape of the European Convention on the compensation of victims of violent crimes of 24 November 1983. Furthermore, existing Committee of Ministers recommendations on assistance to victims and the prevention of victimization were being revised. Action had likewise been taken to tackle the root causes of terrorism through the promotion of intercultural and interreligious dialogue.

14. A third convention opened for signature at the Third Summit of Heads of State and Government was the Council of Europe Convention on Action against Trafficking in Human Beings, which had already been signed by 15 States. Its purpose was to prevent and combat trafficking in human beings, whether national or transnational and whether or not connected with organized crime. Its principal added value lay in its focus on the rights of individuals, the attention it paid to the protection of victims and its independent monitoring mechanism guaranteeing parties' respect for the provisions of the Convention.

15. In the Group of States against Corruption (GRECO), the Council of Europe possessed an integrated and fully operational monitoring system which might serve as a model for worldwide action to stamp out corruption. A number of bodies were examining the idea of a follow-up to the United Nations Convention against Corruption. If that idea were accepted, it would be necessary to examine how to coordinate that follow-up with other monitoring processes and systems in order to avoid duplication and the overlapping of activities and guarantee that the various monitoring procedures reinforced one another. That was all the more important since follow-up was often a heavy burden on the countries concerned and, at least in Europe, there were signs of monitoring fatigue which should not be treated lightly.

16. GRECO was continuing the evaluation of its 39 members, including one non-member State, the United States, using methods which had proved their worth. It was about to complete its second round of evaluations (2003–2006) on the proceeds of corruption, corruption in public administration and the use of legal persons to shield corruption offences. The first round (2000–2002) had been concerned with the independence and specialization of anti-corruption bodies and immunities from investigation and prosecution in corruption cases. At its plenary meeting in June 2005, GRECO had decided to devote its third evaluation round to transparency in the funding of political parties, and to the incrimination of offences provided for in the Criminal Law Convention on Corruption.

17. Fighting cybercrime was another key area of the Council of Europe's action. His Directorate General was pushing for the widest possible ratification of the Convention on cybercrime, which had entered into force on 1 July 2004, and its Additional Protocol concerning the criminalization of acts of a racist or xenophobic nature

[3] Committee of Ministers, 804th meeting, document CM/Del/Dec(2002)804, appendix 3; annexed to the "Letter dated 1 August 2002 from the Permanent Representative of Luxembourg to the United Nations addressed to the Secretary-General" (A/57/313).

[4] Committee of Ministers, 917th meeting, document CM/Del/Dec(2005)917, appendix 2.

committed through computer systems required only one more ratification in order to enter into force. That event should occur in the very near future, once France, which had just ratified both the Convention and the Protocol, deposited its instrument of ratification. Both Council of Europe instruments were open to non-member States of the Council of Europe, since their ambit was intended to extend far beyond the continent of Europe, as had been noted at the Eleventh United Nations Congress on Crime Prevention and Criminal Justice held in Bangkok on 18–25 April 2005.[5] The Council of Europe would be convening a conference in Madrid later in the year to encourage the accession of Latin American countries to the Convention on cybercrime.

18. The Action Plan adopted by the Third Summit of Heads of State and Government reflected their agreement on another very important objective, that of ending the sexual exploitation of children and drafting legal instruments for that purpose. At a conference jointly organized by the Council of Europe and UNICEF in Ljubljana on 8 and 9 July 2005 to review, for Europe and Central Asia, the Yokohama (2001) commitments on the sexual exploitation of children, the relevant working party had recommended the drafting of a new convention. It was essential to coordinate work in that sphere with the United Nations, especially with regard to the follow-up to the Optional Protocol to the Convention on the Rights of the Child on the sale of children, child prostitution and child pornography.

19. In response to a request from the European ministers of justice and in keeping with the Action Plan agreed at Warsaw, the Directorate General of Legal Affairs was in the process of finalizing updated European Prison Rules paying due heed to technological, legal and social advances since 1987, when the last version had been issued.[6] They were expected to be adopted by the Committee of Ministers before the end of the year.

20. It was also important to mention the Additional Protocol to the Convention on Human Rights and Biomedicine concerning Biomedical Research, which had been opened for signature in January 2005, because it supplemented the Convention for the Protection of Human Rights and Dignity of the Human Being with regard to the Application of Biology and Medicine (Convention on Human Rights and Biomedicine), which was still the only international treaty on the subject. Further standard-setting work would be done in that sphere with the drafting of an additional protocol to the Convention on genetic testing and the preparation of a draft instrument on stored human biological materials (biobanks).

21. The law of nationality was an important area of concern of both the Council of Europe and the Commission. The Council had just drawn up a draft protocol on the avoidance of statelessness in relation to State succession. In June 2005 it had been referred to the Parliamentary Assembly for opinion, and it should be adopted before the end of the year. That protocol supplemented the 1997 European Convention on Nationality, in particular its chapter on State succession and nationality. It had been drafted in response to a Committee of Ministers recommendation to member States in 1999 on the avoidance and reduction of statelessness[7] and it was based on a number of countries' recent practical experience in respect of State succession and statelessness. It also took account of the Convention on the reduction of statelessness, the Declaration on the consequences of State succession for the nationality of natural persons[8] prepared by the European Commission for Democracy through Law (Venice Commission), and, last but not least, the International Law Commission's own draft articles on nationality of natural persons in relation to the succession of States.[9] In that connection, he wished to thank Mr. Galicki and Mr. Mikulka, Secretary to the Commission, for their invaluable contribution to the Council's text.

22. He welcomed the excellent cooperation which had grown up between the Committee of Legal Advisers on Public International Law (CAHDI) and the Commission and the constant participation of Commission members in the CAHDI meetings. CAHDI was rounding off the Pilot Project of the Council of Europe on State Practice Regarding State Immunities with the preparation of an analytical report of State practice. The General Assembly's adoption of the United Nations Convention on Jurisdictional Immunities of States and their Property, a landmark event, far from reducing the relevance of the Council's activity, had highlighted the fact that it would facilitate the implementation of the Convention at national level.

23. Reservations to international treaties was another of the main topics of CAHDI, one in which it functioned as a European Observatory. Over the years, its activities in that respect had broadened and extended into the field of reservations to international treaties against terrorism, irrespective whether or not an objection could be entered to such reservations. CAHDI had made a list of "possibly problematic" reservations of that nature and, at its recommendation, the Committee of Ministers, through the good offices of the Secretary-General, had initiated a dialogue among reserving States, including non-members of the Council of Europe, with a view to persuading them to withdraw those reservations. Hence it had supplemented its approach to individual States with a collective *démarche*.

24. Another area on which CAHDI had been focusing since 2004 and which had aroused much public interest was that of United Nations sanctions. CAHDI was studying their implementation at national level and the repercussions they could have on respect for human rights. The topic would be discussed at the thirtieth meeting of CAHDI in September 2005, when the Committee would receive several special guests, including a member of the Court of Justice of the European Communities. It would

[5] See the Report of the Eleventh United Nations Congress on Crime Prevention and Criminal Justice (A/CONF.203/18), chap. I, Bangkok Declaration (para. 16), and chap. VI, para. 338.

[6] Recommendation No. R (87) 3, 12 February 1987, 404th meeting of the Ministers' Deputies.

[7] Recommendation No. R (99) 18, 15 September 1999, 679th meeting of the Ministers' Deputies.

[8] Adopted at the 28th Plenary meeting, Venice, 13–14 September 1996 (document CDL-NAT(1996)007Rev).

[9] *Yearbook ... 1999*, vol. II (Part Two), chap. IV, sect. E, p. 21, para. 47. Also annexed to General Assembly resolution 55/153 of 12 December 2000.

also examine the latest report of the International Committee of the Red Cross on customary international humanitarian law[10] and, would, as usual, consider the outcome of the annual session of the Commission. He looked forward to the participation of Mr. Koskenniemi in that meeting.

25. In the field of constitutional and electoral law, the Council's Venice Commission had recently adopted some important opinions on constitutional reform in Armenia, on draft amendments to the electoral codes of Armenia and Azerbaijan, on the compatibility of Italy's Gasparri Law and Frattini Law with the standards of the Council of Europe in the field of freedom of expression and media pluralism, on the Russian Federal Law on the Prosecutor's Office and on the amendments to the Ukrainian Constitution adopted on 8 December 2004. It was also assisting the Constitutional Commission of Kyrgyzstan with constitutional reform, and had signed an agreement with the United Nations Interim Administration Mission in Kosovo (UNMIK) on the application in Kosovo of the Framework Convention for the Protection of National Minorities and the European Convention for the prevention of torture and inhuman or degrading treatment or punishment.

26. It could thus be seen that the action of the Council of Europe was aimed at promoting the building of a Europe without dividing lines, based on the common values embodied in the Statute of the Council of Europe: democracy, human rights and the rule of law.

27. Mr. KOLODKIN said that the work of the Council of Europe in the legal sphere was a valuable source of practice against which the efforts of the Commission in the areas of codification and progressive development of international law could be measured. Mr. de Vel had touched on the relations between the Council and the European Union, noting that a memorandum of understanding was about to be signed. In the Commission's consideration of the fragmentation of international law, the interplay between the Council's conventions and European Union law had come to the fore. Just the day before, introducing his briefing note, Mr. Koskenniemi had mentioned that the Study Group on Fragmentation had discussed "disconnection clauses" (see 2859th meeting, above, paras. 60–61).

28. The three conventions opened for signature at the Third Summit of Heads of State and Government of the Council of Europe contained such clauses: he cited in particular article 52, paragraph 4, of the Council of Europe Convention on Laundering, Search, Seizure and Confiscation of the Proceeds from Crime and on the Financing of Terrorism. There had been heated discussions on those clauses in the final stages of the Council's work, and not all member States were entirely satisfied with the outcome. The interplay between Council of Europe conventions and European Union law thus remained a burning issue.

29. He would like to know Mr. de Vel's views on "disconnection clauses", which he personally considered to be a misnomer: it would be better to refer to "connection clauses". How should the search for formulas and instruments to promote appropriate relations between the Council's legal texts and European Union law be pursued?

30. Mr. GALICKI endorsed that question. Having participated in the elaboration of the Council of Europe Convention on the Prevention of Terrorism, he was well aware of the difficulties experienced in drafting the final version of the "disconnection clauses". The clauses differed from convention to convention, and he would be interested to know what Mr. de Vel thought about that sort of differentiation. The final versions of the clauses incorporated into the three most recent conventions were much milder than the original texts, their most extreme elements having been eliminated.

31. He would also like to know Mr. de Vel's views regarding the participation of the European Union, separately from that of member States, in the conventions concluded under the auspices of the Council of Europe. Some States that were not members of the European Union feared that such dual representation might be contrary to the principle of equality of parties to conventions. Lastly, did Mr. de Vel think that further legal steps could be undertaken by the Council of Europe against terrorism? Two possibilities came to mind. The first was a comprehensive convention against terrorism, something that might be envisaged as an extension of the step-by-step approach the Council had taken in the long struggle against terrorism. The second was the conclusion of an additional protocol to the European Convention on Human Rights to deal with a new human right: the right to be protected against terrorism. The repeated violent terrorist attacks that were directed against States but primarily affected individuals gave every reason to entertain such a radical possibility.

32. Mr. ECONOMIDES said that the Council of Europe, as an eminently juridical body that dealt with international law, had much in common with the Commission. He endorsed the question already raised about disconnection clauses. Most of the conventions that contained such clauses were conventions adopted by the Council of Europe. That was understandable, because members of the European Community occupied a dominant place among members of the Council of Europe. Disconnection clauses necessarily caused fragmentation, since when they were applied, all members of the European Community disconnected themselves from the convention, ceased to apply it and applied Community law, although the hierarchical relationship between that law and the conventions was not clear. The question was whether such fragmentation was good or bad. He considered that it was good when it helped to strengthen, clarify and develop international law, and bad when it weakened international law or created obstacles to or restrictions on its application. He therefore suspected that disconnection clauses were a threat to international law and, even though it was too soon to assess their effects, their very existence was a matter of concern. He would like to know Mr. de Vel's views on the matter.

33. Mr. PAMBOU-TCHIVOUNDA said he had a broad issue and a very specific question to raise on the subject of terrorism. Freedom was under attack in democratic

[10] J.-M. Henckaerts, "Study on customary international humanitarian law: A contribution to the understanding and respect for the rule of law in armed conflict", *International Review of the Red Cross*, vol. 87, No. 857 (March 2005), pp. 175–212.

societies. Democracy was a valued commodity on the international political market, and both the established Western democracies and the emerging or transitional democracies elsewhere were faced with a challenge to its underlying precepts, particularly freedom. The challenge was particularly acute for European democracies, which seemed to need to rethink both the content and the goals of freedom while at the same time assessing its limitations in the light both of Europe's involvement in the movement towards globalization and the search for a balance between security and freedom. Hence the broad question he wished to raise was whether the Council of Europe's handling of terrorism was diverting it from the mission assigned to it by the founding fathers in 1949 and 1950. If that was so—and he believed it was—then was it appropriate for European and, by extension, other democracies to move in that direction, or was it a rash venture?

34. His specific question related to the Guidelines adopted in 2002 and 2005 by the Committee of Ministers, a practice that had apparently been found useful. Mr. de Vel had referred to the Guidelines as "legal texts" (para. 13 above), and he wondered what that meant and whether an assessment had yet been made of the success with which the two sets of Guidelines had been applied.

35. Ms. ESCARAMEIA noted that there had been intensive debate in academic and other circles on the relationship between the application of international humanitarian law and the protection of human rights in situations of war. Had the Council of Europe discussed the issue, either within CAHDI or in another forum? Mr. de Vel had mentioned that a list of reservations that were deemed problematic was to be drawn up, and she would like to know whether the list cited specific reservations, or identified types of reservations to the Council of Europe's conventions that should be prohibited.

36. Mr. de VEL (Council of Europe), replying first to the questions about disconnection clauses, said that they were actually called "transparency clauses" by the Council and that the term "disconnection clauses" emanated from the European Commission in Brussels. Such clauses now figured in eight conventions, the first usage having been in 1989 in the European Convention on Transfrontier Television. In response to Mr. Galicki's question about the differing versions of the clauses, he said that whenever such a clause was included in a convention, it was discussed with the European Commission's legal services with a view to adapting it to the content of the convention concerned. Obviously, when a convention enunciated fundamental rights, it was difficult to insert a disconnection clause, and when a convention envisaged a monitoring system, the disconnection clauses had to be drafted accordingly.

37. The discussion had become heated during the run-up to the Third Summit of Heads of State and Government because three major conventions—on the prevention of terrorism, against trafficking in human beings and on money laundering and the financing of terrorism—had been ready for adoption by the Committee of Ministers. The European Commission had referred to the need to insert disconnection clauses in those conventions, but they had not been accepted by the Committee of Ministers. There had been major differences of opinion among Council member States and even among member States of the European Union. Protracted negotiations had ensued, but in the end, thanks to the good offices of the President-in-Office of the Council, Mr. Juncker of Luxembourg, the clauses had been softened and the three conventions had been accompanied by an explanatory statement by the President of the Council and by the European Commission.

38. One could ask, as had Mr. Economides, whether fragmentation was a good or a bad thing. It was too soon to speak of bad fragmentation, since the members of the European Union continued to apply the Council of Europe conventions. He could confirm that there had been no problems with the implementation of the clauses; however, member States had to remain vigilant. The Council was following very closely the discussion of the matter in certain international bodies such as UNESCO and UNCITRAL, where, in contrast to the situation in the Council of Europe, European countries were not in the political majority. The Council was also considering the issue in the context of the memorandum of understanding that was to be concluded between the European Union and the Council of Europe, the report of the Prime Minister of Luxembourg, Mr. Juncker, and the evolving situation in other institutions.

39. The Council had been active in the struggle against terrorism for nearly 30 years, and it could certainly not be said that that struggle was not part of its mission. Since the 1970s, the time of the Rote Armee Fraktion, the Red Brigades and the troubles in Northern Ireland, the European Court of Human Rights had handed down numerous decisions in cases concerning terrorism because it understood very well that foremost among human rights was the right to life. As to whether a protocol to the European Convention on Human Rights enshrining the right to protection against terrorism could be adopted, serious consideration must be given to the matter, but in his view, that right was already covered by the right to life, enshrined both in the Convention and in the extensive case law of the European Court of Human Rights.

40. As to other activities in the struggle against terrorism, the Council was continuing to compile the profiles that were submitted voluntarily by member States and the European Union. Attempts had been made to conclude a comprehensive convention against terrorism at the regional level, but States had not wished to obstruct the efforts under way in the United Nations to elaborate a convention which would incorporate a definition of terrorism. Especially since the events in London and Egypt, and with the renewed determination of many States to resume the exercise and try to arrive at a definition, now was not the time for action on that front by the Council of Europe. In his personal view, only if efforts in the United Nations failed could the Council revert to the issue.

41. With regard to the question by Mr. Pambou-Tchivounda, guidelines were a rather recent development in Council of Europe practice. Two types of Council of Europe legal instruments existed: recommendations of the Committee of Ministers to member States (soft law), and binding conventions, agreements or treaties. In

addition, two guidelines existed which the Committee of Ministers had termed "legal documents" and which were also of considerable political importance. The first time that guidelines had been taken into account had been in connection with the Protocol to the 1977 European Convention on the suppression of terrorism, which had been drawn up in parallel with the Guidelines on human rights and the fight against terrorism. Likewise, the Guidelines on the Protection of Victims of Terrorist Acts had been elaborated in parallel with the draft convention on the prevention of terrorism, which contained provisions on victims. Close consideration would be given to those Guidelines when revising the recommendation of the Committee of Ministers on assistance to victims and the prevention of victimization.

42. The Directorate General of Human Rights had already begun an informal appraisal of the application of the Guidelines on human rights and the fight against terrorism; however, the Guidelines on the Protection of Victims of Terrorist Acts were too recent. In sum, although the concept of guidelines was rather new, the guidelines seemed useful in areas in which it was not possible to produce recommendations or treaties.

43. With regard to Ms. Escarameia's question on human rights in situations of war, he noted in that connection that Protocol No. 6 to the European Convention on Human Rights prohibited the death penalty, even in cases of conflict or in times of war.

44. Mr. BENÍTEZ (Council of Europe) said that human rights in times of war and international humanitarian law were subjects which were regularly on the CAHDI agenda. The next meeting of CAHDI, in September 2005, would focus specifically on the relationship between human rights law and international humanitarian law, and on the recent report on customary international humanitarian law prepared under the auspices of the ICRC.

45. On the question of reservations, he said that in the late 1990s CAHDI had begun a general consideration of objections to inadmissible reservations to international law, drawing up what had later become a Committee of Ministers recommendation on model objection clauses to inadmissible reservations, so that there was a standard clause that member States of the Council of Europe and a number of observer States could use in reacting to inadmissible reservations.[11]

46. CAHDI functioned as an observatory for reservations to international treaties, in particular for outstanding reservations, i.e. those for which the deadline for introducing an objection had not yet passed. Normally, a list was drawn up jointly by the presidency and the secretariat and submitted to the members of CAHDI, who could then point to problems with some of those reservations, following which they either entered into a dialogue with the reserving State and reported to CAHDI on the outcome, or, if the outcome was not satisfactory, announced their intention to lodge an objection and called upon all Council of Europe member States to do likewise, for greater effect.

[11] Recommendation No. R (99) 13, of 18 May 1999.

47. On the question of reservations to anti-terrorism treaties, for the first time CAHDI was considering non-outstanding reservations, i.e. those for which deadlines for objections had passed. Those were specific reservations by member States or non-member States of the Council of Europe with regard to Council of Europe or other conventions. CAHDI had drawn up the list in September 2004 and forwarded it to the Committee of Ministers, proposing that the Secretary-General, on the instructions of the Committee of Ministers, write to the ministers for foreign affairs of the reserving States asking them to consider withdrawing their reservations. It was the first time that the Council of Europe had adopted such a *démarche*. It had already received a number of replies to the Secretary-General's letter, which had been brought to the attention of CAHDI, and at its March 2005 meeting CAHDI had begun to revise the list in the light of developments. That action was specific to the area of counter-terrorism and was also closely related to Security Council resolution 1373 (2001).

48. Mr. CHEE said that the Commission had recently met with the ICRC and had learned about the very competent and extensive work being done on the subject of customary international humanitarian law. He therefore wondered whether work being undertaken by the Council of Europe on the same topic was not an unnecessary duplication.

49. Mr. BENÍTEZ (Council of Europe) stressed that CAHDI was not undertaking a new study. One of the authors of the ICRC study on customary international humanitarian law would attend the next CAHDI meeting to discuss the ICRC report and its findings. Thus, the Council of Europe was simply holding an exchange of views with one of the authors of the ICRC study to see to what extent it reflected the relevant positions of States.

50. The CHAIRPERSON thanked Mr. de Vel and Mr. Benítez for their information concerning the activities of the Council of Europe, and for the interest they had shown in the work of the Commission.

Organization of work of the session (*continued*)*

[Agenda item 1]

51. The CHAIRPERSON announced that the Commission would suspend the meeting in order officially to close the International Law Seminar.

The meeting was suspended at 11.20 a.m. and resumed at 12.15 p.m.

Fragmentation of international law: difficulties arising from the diversification and expansion of international law (*continued*) (A/CN.4/549 and Add.1, sect. E and A/CN.4/L.676 and Corr.1)

[Agenda item 9]

52. The CHAIRPERSON invited members of the Commission to comment on the briefing note on fragmentation

* Resumed from the discussion of the 2848th meeting.

of international law: difficulties arising from the diversification and expansion of international law, introduced by the Chairperson of the Study Group, Mr. Koskenniemi, at the previous meeting.

53. Mr. PAMBOU-TCHIVOUNDA said that the well-prepared briefing note and the oral introduction had confirmed his evaluation of the topic, about which information had previously been available only sporadically. The information now provided was of an extraordinary intellectual and methodological quality, whether it concerned the hierarchy of rules in international law, interpretation or the application of successive treaties. He expressed his appreciation to Mr. Koskenniemi and thanked the members of the Commission who had worked on the various aspects of the subject of fragmentation. The information to be made available at the next session would provide more grist to the Commission's mill.

54. Mr. ECONOMIDES said that all the questions that had been or were being taken up by the Study Group were of considerable theoretical and practical interest, dealing with difficult issues on which there was little guidance in textbooks on international law. The contribution of the Study Group was thus considerable. However, the purpose of such a group was not only to produce theoretical studies, but also to formulate specific recommendations for practitioners on all the difficult problems posed for the application of international law.

55. There was good fragmentation and bad. The goal of the Commission should be to encourage good fragmentation, which specified, developed and strengthened rules of law and facilitated their application, whereas bad fragmentation was the very opposite and consisted of practices, rules and institutions which aimed to introduce exceptions to or derogations from the rules and thereby undermined international law.

56. In that connection, he referred again to the question of the disconnection clauses which the European Union and its member States attempted to insert in international conventions which they concluded and which he regarded as an example of bad fragmentation. One such disconnection clause, which was found in a number of Council of Europe treaties, read: "In their mutual relations, parties which are members of the European Community shall apply Community rules and shall not therefore apply the rules arising from this Convention except insofar as there is no Community rule governing the particular subject concerned." That clause was applied automatically and was even mandatory. If the European Community had any rules relating to the treaty, it no longer applied the treaty, but Community law. However, in its relations with other parties to the treaty, the Community would continue to apply the treaty. Thus, the disconnection clause was a flagrant case of fragmentation, because when the Community had rules which were parallel to the rules of another convention, the member States of the Community opted out of the international treaty regime in the context of their relations with each other and ceased to apply it. Such clauses clearly conflicted with the basic rules of international law and in particular with the law of treaties. They challenged the principle that a treaty took precedence over the internal law of States and international organizations. Nor were they in keeping with the fundamental principle of *pacta sunt servanda*, and they were hardly compatible with the principle of reciprocity which constituted the basis of the law of treaties. By creating a regime customized for certain States, the disconnection clause undermined the principle of equality between States, and in particular the right of the contracting parties to juridical equality. Although it was somewhat premature to decide whether the disconnection clause was legal, its effects on international treaty law were already alarming, and he agreed with Mr. de Vel that, although there had not yet been any problems with the clause in practice, extreme vigilance was called for.

57. Mr. PELLET said he would be less intrepid than Mr. Economides in pronouncing on what was good and what was bad. Fragmentation was a fact, and the function of the Commission's study was to help States find their way through situations in which a problem of fragmentation arose. Jurists should not hand out praise and blame. International law must meet the needs of its users.

58. Fortunately, that also seemed to be the intention of the Study Group, although he was somewhat puzzled about the relative weight to be attributed to the general study and the specific conclusions which the Study Group proposed to provide for States. He hoped that the 150-page analytical study announced by the Chairperson of the Study Group in his briefing note would not be too general. Personally he would have preferred the presentation to be linked to the condensed set of 40 conclusions, because that was more in keeping with the mission of the Commission than a study which, even if interesting from the point of view of doctrine and the result of a collective effort, might not be closely coordinated with the condensed proposals or guidelines, which, in his view, would be the most useful outcome of the study.

59. On the whole, the Study Group had produced a substantial and interesting piece of work. He welcomed the indicative list of cases in which fragmentation posed problems. One of the most intriguing areas of fragmentation was that of reservations to treaties. It would be interesting to see how the Study Group thought that the subject matter tied in with the topic of reservations to treaties, as, numerically speaking, reservations probably constituted the largest group of examples of fragmentation of international law.

60. Turning to more specific comments, he said that both the draft report of the Study Group and the briefing note contained fairly vague references to "general principles of international law", which had been translated in the French versions as "*les principes généraux du droit international*". He recalled that there was a clear distinction for French speakers between "*les principes généraux du droit international*" and "*les principes généraux de droit reconnus par les nations civilisées*", the latter being those covered by article 38 of the Statute of the ICJ. He suggested that both the briefing note and the draft report should be carefully revised to make it quite clear which of the two the Study Group had in mind.

61. Secondly, he disagreed with the Study Group's unduly restrictive and conservative view of the evolutive

interpretation of treaties. He believed that the law should evolve in line with the needs of international society; when the context changed, a treaty could no longer be interpreted as having frozen the law at a given point in time, irrespective of the intentions of its framers.

62. Thirdly, he welcomed the distinction drawn in the briefing note between *jus cogens* and obligations *erga omnes*—the former relating to the normative hierarchy, the latter to the scope of application of norms—particularly since not even the ICJ had always been consistent in that regard. If the Commission, with all its authority, were to do no more than stress that point, that alone would have made work of the Study Group worthwhile.

63. Fourthly, he questioned the appropriateness of the title of Mr. Galicki's study, namely, "Hierarchy in international law". What was at issue was a hierarchy in the sources or norms of international law. There was a hierarchy of norms, albeit in embryonic form, based on the notion of *jus cogens*. Otherwise, there were a number of devices such as *lex specialis* and *lex posterior* which helped to choose between norms that were apparently incompatible. That, however, was not a question of hierarchy, but one of deciding which norms should be applied.

64. In conclusion, he said that, while he had not participated in the work of the Study Group, he hoped that the study of the topic would result in specific information or recommendation for States, such as were expected of the Commission.

65. Mr. GALICKI, responding to Mr. Pellet's concerns regarding the title of his study, drew attention to the paragraph of the study which explained that although "Hierarchy in international law" was the title agreed upon by the Commission, the Study Group was dealing with norms with a special status under international law, with the different relationships between them, or even with obligations deriving from them.

66. Mr. Sreenivasa RAO said that, despite his initial reservations regarding the usefulness of the topic, he had benefited greatly from his participation in the Study Group. The Group's detailed analysis would indeed help practitioners and scholars to take a broader view of the somewhat unorganized development of international law and its application in disparate contexts. While he shared the concerns expressed by Mr. Economides and Mr. Pellet regarding the potentially very broad scope of the topic and the possible difficulties of such a study, the preliminary conclusions drawn and the summary of the discussions thus far had persuaded him that the Study Group was following the right methodological approach and in so doing would produce results that would be of real use to practitioners. It was clear that the Study Group had much work to do in the coming year and that some of the issues it had raised, including self-contained regimes and hierarchy, required further clarification. Another issue taken up by the Study Group that was not reflected in the summary of the discussions was regionalism, a topical issue on which very useful work had been done.

67. Mr. OPERTTI BADAN said he was satisfied with the methodical analysis being conducted by the Study Group. The valuable input it would provide for legal experts in foreign ministries and international organizations was in itself justification for the study of the topic. The *ratione materiae* approach adopted consisting of the study of five broad themes was a good basis for the subsequent analysis. The risks of the proliferation of norms were felt not only by the international community as a whole, but also at the regional level, where efforts were under way on the codification of regional and subregional laws. The Commission could make a valuable contribution in that area. The differing dispute settlement mechanisms available under the auspices of the WTO and the regional integration organizations offered an obvious example of the fragmentation of the law and constituted a potential source of conflict. He hoped that the Study Group's work would result in a set of guidelines or recommendations which, although not binding in nature, would be of practical use.

68. Lastly, he endorsed the Study Group's view of international law as a system of interrelated norms. Mr. Pellet had referred to reservations as a prime example of fragmentation of law. The links between that topic and the present topic should be explored so as to provide practical guidance to legal experts and practitioners on how to deal with the threat posed by the proliferation of norms.

69. Mr. KOSKENNIEMI (Chairperson of the Study Group) said that although the debate on the fragmentation of international law would be continued at a subsequent meeting, he would respond immediately to a few of the points raised. On the point raised by Mr. Economides, it was generally recognized that the fragmentation of law was a many-sided phenomenon, and there was broad agreement among the members of the Study Group that it was not befitting for them to identify developments as good or bad. On the other hand, it was clear that the Commission must be able to produce information for experts in the Sixth Committee and in relevant institutions so that they could draw their own conclusions on the matter. It was his intention to provide a very clear description of practice relating to disconnection clauses.

70. He endorsed Mr. Pellet's comment concerning the looseness of the terminology used with regard to general principles of law; he understood that distinctions needed to be made and would revise the text accordingly.

71. There were several references in the documents before the Commission to evolutive interpretation, and in its final submission the Study Group would have to address the extent to which interpretation should take into account developments subsequent to the conclusion of treaties. It was necessary to strike a balance between the conflicting considerations of stability and change—a task traditionally dealt with by the courts. The Study Group had no magic formula to identify where the line should be drawn, but it could assist by providing examples of practice.

72. He noted Mr. Opertti Badan's satisfaction with the Study Group's fundamental approach to its work whereby international law was viewed as a system of rules that operated in relation to other rules. In concluding, he said that any further input from members, even on very specific points relating to the five studies conducted, would

be of great assistance to participants in the forthcoming meeting of the Study Group.

The meeting rose at 1.05 p.m.

2861st MEETING

Tuesday, 2 August 2005, at 10.05 a.m.

Chairperson: Mr. Djamchid MOMTAZ

Present: Mr. Addo, Mr. Al-Baharna, Mr. Al-Marri, Mr. Brownlie, Mr. Candioti, Mr. Chee, Mr. Comissário Afonso, Mr. Dugard, Mr. Economides, Ms. Escarameia, Mr. Fomba, Mr. Gaja, Mr. Galicki, Mr. Kabatsi, Mr. Kateka, Mr. Kolodkin, Mr. Koskenniemi, Mr. Mansfield, Mr. Matheson, Mr. Niehaus, Mr. Pambou-Tchivounda, Mr. Pellet, Mr. Sreenivasa Rao, Mr. Rodríguez Cedeño, Mr. Yamada.

Draft report of the International Law Commission on the work of its fifty-seventh session

1. The CHAIRPERSON invited the Rapporteur of the Commission to introduce the draft report of the Commission on the work of its fifty-seventh session.

2. Mr. NIEHAUS (Rapporteur) said that the draft report was divided into 12 chapters: chapter I contained the introduction, chapter II provided a brief summary of the work of the Commission at its fifty-seventh session and chapter III dealt with specific issues on which comments from Governments would be of particular interest to the Commission. Chapters IV to XI dealt with the substantive topics considered by the Commission at the current session, while chapter XII concerned other decisions.

CHAPTER IV. ***Shared natural resources* (A/CN.4/L.667)**

3. The CHAIRPERSON invited the members of the Commission to consider chapter IV of the draft report of the Commission (A/CN.4/L.667).

A. Introduction

Paragraphs 1 and 2

Paragraphs 1 and 2 were adopted.

Section A was adopted.

B. Consideration of the topic at the present session

Paragraph 3

4. Ms. ESCARAMEIA asked why the presentation on the joint management of the Geneva aquifer system was not mentioned in the paragraph. Had it not been an informal technical presentation?

5. The CHAIRPERSON said that that question had been raised in the Working Group.

6. Mr. CANDIOTI said that the final sentence of the paragraph should be completed by inserting figure 11 in the blank space.

7. Mr. GAJA asked whether the report of the Working Group on Shared Natural Resources would be included in the Commission's report or whether it was only mentioned by way of reference.

8. Mr. YAMADA (Special Rapporteur) said that the Chairperson of the Working Group, Mr. Candioti, would give a presentation the following day in plenary meeting that ought to be mentioned; perhaps the paragraph should be set aside, as it would have to be redrafted.

9. The CHAIRPERSON said that a sentence would be added to that effect.

10. Mr. MANSFIELD said that the chapter should reflect the fact that the Working Group had worked tirelessly, had reached agreement on several draft articles and was continuing its work. It was not enough to say that the Working Group had held 11 meetings.

11. The CHAIRPERSON replied that it would be preferable to have the Working Group's report in hand before adding a sentence or paragraph that would reflect those concerns.

Paragraph 3, as amended, was adopted.

Paragraphs 4 to 11

Paragraphs 4 to 11 were adopted.

Paragraph 12

12. Mr. PELLET said that it had been his understanding that the principle of reasonable utilization applied to non-recharging aquifers and asked whether the first sentence did not contain a mistake.

13. Mr. YAMADA (Special Rapporteur) said that the sentence summarized the introduction to his report in which the application of the principle of reasonable utilization had been considered in respect of two categories, namely recharging and non-recharging aquifers. He recalled that under the 1997 Watercourses Convention the principle of sustainable utilization applied to surface waters but not to groundwaters.

14. Mr. MANSFIELD said that he, too, thought that the wording of the first sentence did not reflect the content of the two draft articles and proposed that it should be amended to read: "Paragraph 2, on reasonable utilization (i.e. sustainable utilization), was divided into subparagraphs (*a*) and (*b*) to reflect the practical application of this principle in different circumstances of a recharging and a non-recharging aquifer."

Paragraph 12, as amended, was adopted.

Paragraphs 13 to 17

Paragraphs 13 to 17 were adopted.

Paragraph 18

15. Mr. ECONOMIDES proposed that the word "politically" should be replaced by a more neutral term, such as "generally".

Paragraph 18, as amended, was adopted.

Paragraphs 19 to 21

Paragraphs 19 to 21 were adopted.

Paragraph 22

16. Ms. ESCARAMEIA drew attention to the first sentence and proposed that the words "reliance on" should be replaced with the words "reference to" and that the word "other" should be deleted from the English version, which appeared to be in contradiction with the word "generally". Ms. ESCARAMEIA proposed that in the interest of balance a new sentence should be added after the third sentence, which would read: "Some members considered that the present topic was substantially different from that of watercourses and that therefore the 1997 Convention should not be taken as a guide."

17. Mr. MANSFIELD proposed that the words "largely non-renewable nature and" in the third sentence should be deleted, since some aquifers were renewable.

Paragraph 22, as amended, was adopted.

Paragraph 23

Paragraph 23 was adopted.

Paragraph 24

18. Mr. PAMBOU-TCHIVOUNDA said that he failed to grasp the meaning of the phrase "there was a contextual role for the principle in the draft articles".

19. The CHAIRPERSON suggested that the words "a contextual" should be replaced by the word "any".

Paragraph 24, as amended, was adopted.

Paragraphs 25 to 27

Paragraphs 25 to 27 were adopted.

Paragraph 28

20. Mr. GAJA thought that the word "conducive" in the second sentence, the meaning of which was not clear, should be replaced and that the final sentence should be deleted, as it appeared to contradict what preceded.

21. The CHAIRPERSON suggested that the word "conducive" should be amended to "helpful" and that the final sentence should be deleted.

Paragraph 28, as amended, was adopted.

Paragraph 29

Paragraph 29 was adopted.

Paragraphs 30 and 31

22. Mr. GAJA proposed that the word "third" should be deleted from the first sentence of paragraph 30 as well as from paragraphs 31 and 74 of the English text.

Paragraphs 30 and 31, as amended, were adopted.

Paragraphs 32 to 37

Paragraphs 32 to 37 were adopted.

Paragraph 38

23. Ms. ESCARAMEIA proposed the insertion of a phrase that would read "'recharge and discharge zones' in the territories of third States in draft article 13, paragraph (3)," after the phrase "in draft article 7 *et al.*".

Paragraph 38, as amended, was adopted.

Paragraph 39

Paragraph 39 was adopted.

Paragraph 40

24. Mr. PELLET proposed that the phrase "an equal opportunity of participation", the meaning of which was unclear, should be amended to read "for participation on flexible terms".

Paragraph 40, as amended, was adopted.

Paragraph 41

Paragraph 41 was adopted.

Paragraph 42

25. Ms. ESCARAMEIA proposed that the following sentence should be inserted after the first sentence: "Some members thought, however, that the expression 'consider harmonizing' was too weak and needed to be replaced."

Paragraph 42, as amended, was adopted.

Paragraph 43

26. Mr. PELLET said that the second time the term "*projet d'article*" appeared in the first sentence of the French text it ought to be rendered in the plural. That error occurred frequently in both the French and English texts, and he urged the Secretariat to review the entire text.

Paragraph 43 was adopted.

Paragraph 44

27. Mr. GAJA proposed that the second sentence should be broken into two sentences: the phrase "to the extent that it presupposed that" in that sentence should be replaced by the word "if" and the words "in which case" should be replaced by "according to some members". The newly formed sentences would thus read: "Such a proposition would only be valid if all States which shared an aquifer were parties to the 1997 Convention. According to some members, it would be reasonable to contemplate … ".

28. Mr. PAMBOU-TCHIVOUNDA said that he did not understand what was meant by the phrase "*tant sur le plan juridique que sur celui des principes*" ("legally and policy-wise") in the French version of the last sentence of the paragraph and asked whether they referred to methodological rather than legal principles.

29. The CHAIRPERSON asked whether it might be possible simply to delete the words "legally and policy-wise".

30. Mr. PELLET said that the problem was one of translation and proposed replacing the words "*des principes*" in the French text with "*de l'opportunité*".

31. Mr. MANSFIELD said that during the debate legal reasons and general policy reasons had been advanced specifically with regard to the vulnerability of watercourses to pollution; he admitted, however, that the word "policy-wise" was odd.

32. Mr. BROWNLIE said that the words "legally and as a matter of policy" would be preferable.

Paragraph 44, as amended by Mr. Gaja and Mr. Brownlie, was adopted.

Paragraph 45

33. Mr. MANSFIELD proposed that the reference to the framework instrument should be deleted and that the first sentence should be reworded to read: "Although attention was drawn to article 311 (2) of the United Nations Convention on the Law of the Sea, some members doubted that that article could serve as a precedent for paragraph 2."

Paragraph 45, as amended, was adopted.

Paragraphs 46 to 48

Paragraphs 46 to 48 were adopted.

Paragraph 49

34. Mr. PELLET said he found the penultimate sentence to be incomprehensible and proposed replacing it with a sentence that would read: "It was suggested that one of the factors to be taken into account in subparagraph (*c*) was the importance of drinking water."

Paragraph 49, as amended, was adopted.

Paragraph 50

35. Mr. PELLET noted that in the last sentence of the French version the words "*autres que l'État de l'aquifère*" should read "*autres que les États de l'aquifère*".

36. Ms. ESCARAMEIA said that the phrase "since the effects on groundwaters may take years before they are detectable" should be added to the seventh sentence.

37. The CHAIRPERSON suggested that the Commission should adopt paragraph 50 with the amendments proposed by Mr. Pellet and Ms. Escarameia.

Paragraph 50, as amended, was adopted.

Paragraph 51

Paragraph 51 was adopted.

Paragraph 52

38. Mr. MANSFIELD pointed out that the word "operate" in the first sentence of the English text should read "cooperate".

Paragraph 52 was adopted with a minor drafting change.

Paragraphs 53 to 55

Paragraphs 53 to 55 were adopted.

Paragraph 56

39. Ms. ESCARAMEIA said that the second sentence seemed to contradict the first and proposed replacing "for example" with "however".

Paragraph 56, as amended, was adopted.

Paragraph 57

40. Mr. GAJA proposed that the beginning of the last sentence, which read "Such States benefit highly from aquifers, and", should be deleted and that the words "no legal basis" in that sentence should be amended to read "any legal basis".

Paragraph 57, as amended, was adopted.

Paragraph 58

41. Mr. GAJA proposed that the word "of precaution" should be added after the word "principle" in the first sentence.

42. Ms. ESCARAMEIA said that the last sentence did not reflect her statement in plenary and asked that it should be reworded to read: "The principle was well recognized as a principle of international environmental law and needed to be stressed in the draft articles."

43. The CHAIRPERSON suggested that the Commission should adopt the paragraph as amended by Mr. Gaja and Ms. Escarameia.

Paragraph 58, as amended, was adopted.

Paragraph 59

44. Mr. PELLET said that he would like to settle once and for all the question of when the term "draft article" should be written with an "s", as doing so could change the meaning. He himself thought that it should be written without an "s" when reference was being made to a single draft article and with an "s" when the reference was to several draft articles or the draft articles as a whole; the problem was particularly in evidence in paragraph 59: was the Commission talking about the objectives of the draft articles as a whole or of draft article 14? The second hypothesis would appear to be the correct one, and if that was the case, then the final "s" must be deleted.

45. Mr. YAMADA (Special Rapporteur) said that the reference in paragraph 59 was solely to draft article 14, and that the term "draft articles" should read "the draft article".

46. The CHAIRPERSON suggested that the Commission should adopt paragraph 59 as amended.

Paragraph 59, as amended, was adopted.

Paragraphs 60 to 66

Paragraphs 60 to 66 were adopted.

47. Mr. GALICKI said that the references to the subject matter of individual draft articles in all the paragraphs that had just been adopted should be standardized in the English version; either "on" should be used in every case or it should be deleted throughout.

48. The CHAIRPERSON said that Mr. Galicki's proposal would be transmitted to the Secretariat.

Paragraphs 67 and 68

Paragraphs 67 and 68 were adopted.

Paragraph 69

49. Mr. PELLET said that the phrase "in accordance with the General Assembly mandate" in the fourth sentence was ambiguous and proposed that it should be amended to read "in accordance with the mandate given to it by the General Assembly".

Paragraph 69, as amended, was adopted.

Paragraphs 70 to 75

Paragraphs 70 to 75 were adopted.

Paragraph 76

50. Mr. PELLET said that the Commission should clarify what was meant by the term "administrative organization" in the first sentence.

51. Mr. Sreenivasa RAO suggested that the text should instead read "institutional mechanisms and management of transboundary aquifers".

52. Mr. PAMBOU-TCHIVOUNDA wondered whether the use of the term "*rivières*" in the second sentence of the French text was deliberate or whether the term used ought to be "*fleuves*".

53. The CHAIRPERSON suggested replacing the word "*rivières*" in the French text with "*cours d'eau*"; the word "rivers" in the English text would thus become "watercourses".

54. Mr. CANDIOTI proposed that the name of the organization appearing in the second sentence should be corrected in the English version to read "Franco-Swiss Genevese Aquifer Authority."

55. The CHAIRPERSON suggested that the Commission should adopt the paragraph with the amendments proposed by Mr. Pellet, Mr. Sreenivasa Rao, Mr. Pambou-Tchivounda, himself and Mr. Candioti.

Paragraph 76, as amended, was adopted.

Paragraph 77

Paragraph 77 was adopted.

Section B, as amended, was adopted.

Chapter IV of the draft report, as amended, was adopted.

CHAPTER V. *Effects of armed conflicts on treaties* (A/CN.4/L.668)

56. The CHAIRPERSON invited the members of the Commission to consider chapter V of the draft report, on effects of armed conflicts on treaties (A/CN.4/L.668).

A. Introduction

Paragraphs 1 and 2

Paragraphs 1 and 2 were adopted.

Section A was adopted.

B. Consideration of the topic at the present session

Paragraphs 3 to 4

Paragraphs 3 to 4 were adopted.

Paragraph 6

57. Mr. GAJA observed that the manner in which chapter V was presented was unusual but seemed to constitute an interesting innovation. Some problems of a chronological order were nevertheless apparent: for example, in paragraph 25, concerning article 1, reference was made to a proposal that had been made at a later time, in the context of article 10. The Special Rapporteur's conclusions should therefore be grouped together at the end of the report, or else amendments should be made to a number of paragraphs.

58. Mr. PELLET said he thought that the new format was an excellent initiative on the part of the Special Rapporteur, and he disagreed with Mr. Gaja that the Special Rapporteur's conclusions should be placed at the end of the chapter. He thought that the chapter should be left as it stood, subject to a few changes to correct chronology where necessary.

59. Mr. ECONOMIDES said that there was a considerable disparity between various chapters of the draft report. While the chapter on shared natural resources was excellent, the chapter under consideration did not adequately reflect the positions taken by members. He himself had been unable to find any trace of his statements, and he wondered what criteria the Secretariat had used in summarizing the debate. That led to the more general question of working methods and transparency.

60. The CHAIRPERSON said that Commission members, and Mr. Economides in particular, were entirely free, as the various paragraphs were considered, to request that a sentence should be added to reflect the views they had expressed.

61. Mr. BROWNLIE (Special Rapporteur) said that the problem of determining the extent to which members' views should be reflected in a report such as the one before the Commission was not a new one.

62. Mr. GAJA, referring to the new format used in chapter V, said he wished that the Commission would adopt a standard format.

Paragraph 6 was adopted.

Paragraph 7

63. Mr. PELLET said that the word "*justifiable*" in the French text should read "*justiciable*".

Paragraph 7 was adopted, with a minor drafting change to the French version.

Paragraphs 8 and 9

Paragraphs 8 and 9 were adopted.

Paragraph 10

64. Ms. ESCARAMEIA proposed that the word "extremely" should be inserted before the word "helpful" in the second sentence, as the Secretariat memorandum had indeed been very helpful.

Paragraph 10, as amended, was adopted.

Paragraph 11

Paragraph 11 was adopted.

65. Mr. ECONOMIDES said that the question that had dominated the debate was barely mentioned in the summary; accordingly, he proposed that a new paragraph 11 *bis* should be added after paragraph 11, which would read:

> Several members observed that the draft articles should be compatible with the purposes and principles of the United Nations. In particular, they should take into account the unlawful character of the use of force in international relations and above all of the fundamental distinction between aggression on the one hand and individual or collective self-defence or the use of force in the context of the collective security of the United Nations on the other.

66. The CHAIRPERSON said it was his understanding that the Commission wished to adopt the new paragraph 11 *bis* proposed by Mr. Economides.

It was so decided.

Paragraph 12

67. Mr. GAJA proposed that the last sentence of paragraph 12 should be reworded to read: "The importance of municipal case law was borne out by the Secretariat memorandum which referred to a number of such decisions."

Paragraph 12, as amended, was adopted.

Paragraphs 13 to 18

Paragraphs 13 to 18 were adopted.

Paragraphs 20 and 21

Paragraphs 20 and 21 were adopted.

Paragraph 22

68. Mr. GAJA proposed that the first sentence and the word "accordingly" in the second sentence should be deleted, and that the last sentence should be reworded to read: "Some members said that they favoured including treaties which had not entered into force, while others maintained that only treaties in force at the time of the conflict should be covered by the draft articles."

Paragraph 22, as amended, was adopted.

Paragraphs 23 to 31

Paragraphs 23 to 31 were adopted.

Paragraph 32

69. Ms. ESCARAMEIA, supported by Mr. GAJA, proposed that the final clause of the first sentence, beginning with the word "although", should be deleted.

70. Mr. PELLET said that the words "the scope of" should be inserted after the word "limit" in the third sentence.

Paragraph 32, as amended, was adopted.

Paragraphs 33 to 36

Paragraphs 33 to 36 were adopted.

Paragraph 37

71. Mr. MANSFIELD proposed that the word "as" in the first sentence should be replaced by "from".

Paragraph 37, as amended, was adopted.

Paragraph 38

72. Mr. ECONOMIDES said that the last sentence made little sense as currently worded. He proposed that the words "in the context of draft article 3" should be added at the end of that sentence.

Paragraph 38, as amended, was adopted.

Paragraphs 39 and 40

Paragraphs 39 and 40 were adopted.

Paragraph 41

73. Mr. GALICKI said that the phrase "war was the polar opposite" should be amended to read "that war was the polar opposite", to make it consistent with the other numbered clauses in that paragraph.

Paragraph 41, as amended, was adopted.

Paragraph 42

Paragraph 42 was adopted.

Paragraph 43

74. Mr. PELLET said he found the last sentence of paragraph 43 to be extremely weak; the problem could be solved by replacing the words "could also play a role" with the words "was essential".

75. Mr. BROWNLIE (Special Rapporteur) said that a clear distinction must be made—and it was that distinction that he had had in mind when he had submitted his original, deliberately provocative, version of article 10—between making the ban on the use of force and the lawfulness or unlawfulness of a particular armed conflict a condition for applying the draft articles, which he opposed, and preserving the question of the legal effect of such lawfulness or unlawfulness. It would in fact be most upsetting to arrive at a solution in which, so long as the lawfulness or unlawfulness had not been authoritatively assessed, the draft articles would simply not apply.

76. Mr. PELLET said that, as some members of the Commission considered that to be a key element, it should be reflected in the report. Similarly, he proposed that the words "a plausible" in the penultimate sentence of the paragraph should be replaced by the words "an important".

77. Mr. ECONOMIDES, supporting Mr. Pellet, said that the equality of the belligerents was acceptable only in the context of international humanitarian law. In all other areas there could be no equality, since aggression could not produce legal effects.

78. The CHAIRPERSON pointed out that the last sentence of the paragraph reflected what some members had said during the debate. It was not an affirmation but a position. If Mr. Brownlie felt it necessary to do so, he could include an explanation to that effect in his conclusions.

79. Mr. Sreenivasa RAO said that he endorsed the Chairperson's suggestion. It was important to mention all the positions taken by Commission members, provided that it was done proportionately.

80. The CHAIRPERSON suggested that the Commission should adopt paragraph 43 as amended by Mr. Pellet.

Paragraph 43, as amended, was adopted.

Paragraph 44

81. Mr. ECONOMIDES proposed that the words "vague and subjective" in the first sentence should be replaced with the words "vague, subjective or non-existent". He further proposed adding the phrase "at least insofar as treaties concluded after the Second World War were concerned" at the end of the second sentence.

82. Ms. ESCARAMEIA said that she could support Mr. Economides' first proposal; she believed that the report should make clear that one of the criteria that could be used was the type of treaty and its compatibility with situations of armed conflict.

83. Mr. GAJA said that Mr. Economides' second proposal tended to narrow the scope of the sentence. He did not think that such precision was really necessary, but he would not object to its inclusion.

84. Mr. KOSKENNIEMI said that he agreed with Mr. Gaja and proposed that a new sentence should be added after the second sentence, to read: "When concluding a treaty, States rarely reflect on the effect any possible armed conflict might have on it."

85. Mr. PELLET said that he was prepared to accept Mr. Koskenniemi's proposal, although it did not mean the same thing as Mr. Economides' second proposal. In his view, both amendments should be accepted. Ms. Escarameia's proposal was substantively correct, but that clarification should be made in paragraph 45 rather than in paragraph 44.

86. The CHAIRPERSON suggested that the Commission should adopt paragraph 44 as amended by Mr. Economides and Mr. Koskenniemi.

Paragraph 44, as amended, was adopted.

Paragraphs 45 to 52

Paragraphs 45 to 52 were adopted.

Paragraph 53

87. Mr. MATHESON said that a sentence should be added at the end of the paragraph that would read: "The Special Rapporteur agreed that the principle enunciated in the Legality of the Threat or Use of Nuclear Weapons advisory opinion should be appropriately reflected."

Paragraph 53, as amended, was adopted.

Paragraph 54

Paragraph 54 was adopted.

Paragraph 55

88. Mr. ECONOMIDES proposed that the phrase "others expressed some doubts" should be amended to read "doubts were expressed as to the provision's compatibility with contemporary international law".

Paragraph 55, as amended, was adopted.

Paragraph 56

Paragraph 56 was adopted.

Paragraph 57

89. Mr. PELLET said that the word "*préserver*" in the second sentence of the French text should be replaced with the word "*présumer*".

Paragraph 57 was adopted with a minor drafting change to the French version.

Paragraphs 58 to 73

Paragraphs 58 to 73 were adopted.

Paragraph 74

90. Mr. PELLET said that the word "*article*" in the last sentence of the French text should be in the plural.

Paragraph 74 was adopted with a minor drafting change to the French version.

Paragraph 75

91. Mr. ECONOMIDES said that since articles 7, 8 and 9 of Resolution II/1985 of the Institute of International Law were cited in the paragraph, the text of those articles should be provided in a footnote, in order to facilitate comparison.

92. In addition, he wondered what was meant by the adjective "different" in the second sentence of the paragraph. He proposed that a new sentence should be added at the end of the paragraph, to read: "It was noted that only treaties incompatible with the exercise of the right to self-defence should be suspended or abrogated."

93. The CHAIRPERSON suggested that the word "different" should be replaced by the word "conflicting".

94. Mr. BROWNLIE said that he did not recall that that position had been expressed during the debate.

95. Mr. ECONOMIDES said that he himself had upheld that position, and he insisted that the sentence he had proposed should be included in the text.

96. The CHAIRPERSON, speaking in his personal capacity, recalled that one of the articles of the Institute of International Law dealt with that very aspect of the question. He suggested that the Commission should adopt paragraph 75 as amended by Mr. Economides.

Paragraph 75, as amended, was adopted.

Paragraphs 76 and 77

Paragraphs 76 and 77 were adopted.

97. The CHAIRPERSON announced that the Commission would conclude its consideration of document A/CN.4/L.668 at its next meeting.

The meeting rose at 1.10 p.m.

2862nd MEETING

Tuesday, 2 August 2005, at 3.10 p.m.

Chairperson: Mr. Djamchid MOMTAZ

Present: Mr. Addo, Mr. Brownlie, Mr. Candioti, Mr. Chee, Mr. Comissário Afonso, Mr. Dugard, Mr. Economides, Mr. Escarameia, Mr. Fomba, Mr. Gaja, Mr. Galicki, Mr. Kabatsi, Mr. Kateka, Mr. Kolodkin, Mr. Koskenniemi, Mr. Mansfield, Mr. Matheson, Mr. Niehaus, Mr. Pellet, Mr. Sreenivasa Rao, Mr. Rodríguez Cedeño, Mr. Yamada.

Draft report of the Commission on the work of its fifty-seventh session (*continued*)

Chapter V. *Effects of armed conflicts on treaties* (*continued*) (A/CN.4/L.668)

B. Consideration of the topic at the present session (*continued*)

Paragraph 78

1. Mr. PELLET sought clarification regarding the last sentence, which read: "At the same time, he pointed out that such proviso would not solve the problems of legal causation, i.e. it was not clear to what extent the States concerned could rely on it as a basis for suspending treaties unless there existed some causal connection necessitating suspension or termination."

2. Mr. BROWNLIE (Special Rapporteur) said that the last sentence concerned the problem of *ipso facto* termination, which was supposed to have been clarified by his ill-fated version of draft article 10. As he had repeatedly explained, apparently to no avail, the intent of the draft article was to raise an intellectual problem, not to prove that he did not accept the post–1945 version of the use of force. The issue at stake was *ipso facto* suspension or termination and the principle stated in article 3 based on one of the more important parts of the Institute of International Law's resolution II/1985, according to which there was no *ipso facto* effect. The *ipso facto* effect problem was two-pronged. First there was causation: there had to be some factual basis for suggesting that armed conflict affected the treaty. Second, there was a need to distinguish between a proviso making it clear that the contents of the Commission's draft would not have any effect on the provisions of the Charter of the United Nations relating to the use or threat of force, and the situation in which the principles relating to the use of force—the substantive principles—were brought into play to deal with the question of the legal validity of the use of force concerned. That did not come under the topic under consideration, which explained his reaction during the previous meeting when the Chairperson had accepted a statement that represented the view of only one member of the Commission. Some members of the Sixth Committee would be justifiably concerned if the Commission embarked en passant on a codification of the legal principles relating to the use of force by States.

3. The CHAIRPERSON asked the Special Rapporteur whether he could propose alternative wording to meet Mr. Pellet's concern.

4. Mr. BROWNLIE (Special Rapporteur) said that the current wording was perfectly clear to him: it simply meant that there had to be a legal basis on the facts for asserting the suspension or termination of the treaty concerned. He would need some time to reflect on a formulation that would be as clear to others.

5. The CHAIRPERSON suggested that consideration of paragraph 78 should be deferred.

It was so agreed.

6. Mr. BROWNLIE (Special Rapporteur) said that in the light of amendments made during the previous meeting and the resulting shift in emphasis in the original summary of the debate produced by the Secretariat, the Special Rapporteur's concluding remarks set out in paragraph 78 needed to be expanded on somewhat. He suggested the addition of a sentence that would not in any way prejudice the views of the Commission as a whole, to read: "The Special Rapporteur stated that it was not his intention to examine the question of the validity or voidability of treaties in terms of the Charter provisions relating to the use or threat of force."

7. The CHAIRPERSON suggested that the additional sentence should form a new paragraph 78 *bis*.

It was so agreed.

Paragraph 78 bis *was adopted.*

Paragraph 79

Paragraph 79 was adopted.

Paragraph 80

8. Mr. ECONOMIDES questioned the appropriateness of the assertion that general support existed in the Commission for draft articles 11 to 14, given that some members had not had the opportunity to express their views on them.

9. Mr. GAJA recalled that the problem had arisen because the Commission had not discussed the draft article by article. He suggested the deletion of the words "in the Commission" to meet Mr. Economides' concern.

Paragraph 80, as amended, was adopted.

Paragraphs 81 and 82

Paragraphs 81 and 82 were adopted.

10. Following a procedural discussion on the reference to a questionnaire in paragraphs 5, 15 and 19, the CHAIRPERSON suggested that the Commission should revert to those paragraphs in the context of its consideration of chapter III of the draft report.

It was so agreed.

CHAPTER VI. *Responsibility of international organizations* (A/CN.4/L.669 and Add.1)

A. Introduction (A/CN.4/L.669 and Add.1)

Paragraphs 1 and 2

Paragraphs 1 and 2 were adopted.

Paragraph 3

11. Mr. GAJA (Special Rapporteur) drew attention to the fact that articles 1 to 7 had been adopted after consideration of the first and second reports and that a further nine articles had been adopted since then. He therefore proposed that the last sentence of the paragraph should read "The Commission provisionally adopted articles 1 to 7."

Paragraph 3, as amended, was adopted.

Section A, as amended, was adopted.

B. Consideration of the topic at the present session

12. Mr. PELLET, raising a general problem, said that the text of paragraphs 4 to 9 had been drafted in the customary manner, so as to reflect only the views of the Special Rapporteur, and not those of other members of the Commission. It was not therefore an accurate account of the debate on the topic. That situation was most unsatisfactory; the views of the Special Rapporteur were already well known, since they were contained in his report. For that reason, thought should be given to providing a more balanced report in the future. To that end, it would be necessary to decide whether to record merely that the Commission had adopted the draft articles in question and to reflect members' views in the commentary without giving any particular emphasis to the position of the Special Rapporteur, or whether to make a summary of all the views expressed. He himself was in favour of the latter solution, although he was aware that it would place an extra burden on the Secretariat.

13. Mr. GAJA (Special Rapporteur) said that he would be very much in favour of the report containing some trace of the views expressed by other members of the Commission. The draft report had merely followed previous practice. When draft articles were adopted on the basis of a report presented the same year, it was standard practice not to give any indication of members' opinions, which would be reflected to some extent in the commentaries to the articles. It would probably be better to change that practice in the future. In order for the Sixth Committee to have more information, it would also be useful to include in the report the wording of the articles originally presented to the Commission, because the latter's documents were not widely circulated. As they stood, only paragraphs 8 and 9 contained a very brief summary of his views, and they did not give undue emphasis to his position.

14. The CHAIRPERSON asked whether the problem could be resolved by deleting paragraphs 8 and 9.

15. Mr. PELLET said that paragraphs 8 and 9 were superfluous and not counterbalanced by a conspectus of other members' views. In the future, there would be

nothing to prevent the text of each draft article as proposed by the Special Rapporteur from being placed in a footnote, to enable the reader to compare the original text and the final version adopted by the Commission.

16. Mr. KOSKENNIEMI said that deletion of paragraphs 8 and 9 would diminish the clarity of the whole chapter, since the paragraphs in question set out the Special Rapporteur's views in a summarized version that was useful to the reader. Although he had some sympathy for Mr. Pellet's position, he believed that, in the case in point, deletion of those two paragraphs would lead to a loss of intelligibility.

17. Mr. Sreenivasa RAO said he had never understood why, when draft articles were adopted, the report contained only the commentary and not members' views. A very complicated set of draft articles had been proposed, a highly complex discussion had ensued, but the General Assembly would see only the commentary to the draft articles as they had been adopted. It would have no idea of the permutations and combinations of the arguments which had been debated and which had resulted in the set of articles as they now stood.

18. Mr. GAJA (Special Rapporteur) said that the solution lay in adding material to the report rather than removing it. In the future, consideration should therefore be given to providing a fuller report. He did not insist on the retention of paragraphs 8 and 9. However, if the Commission considered that they were useful in that they helped to explain the draft articles, then they should be retained.

19. The CHAIRPERSON said he took it that the Commission wished to retain paragraphs 8 and 9.

It was so agreed.

Paragraphs 4 to 8

Paragraphs 4 to 8 were adopted.

Paragraph 9

20. Mr. GAJA (Special Rapporteur) suggested that the penultimate sentence should be amended to read: "They involved compliance with acts of international organizations by their members. Such acts may be binding decisions or non-binding recommendations or authorizations."

Paragraph 9, as amended, was adopted.

Paragraphs 10 to 13

Paragraphs 10 to 13 were adopted.

Section B, as amended, was adopted.

C. Text of the draft articles on responsibility of international organizations provisionally adopted so far by the Commission (A/CN.4/L.669/Add.1)

1. TEXT OF THE DRAFT ARTICLES

Paragraph 11

Paragraph 11 was adopted.

2. TEXT OF THE DRAFT ARTICLES WITH COMMENTARIES THERETO

Paragraph 12

Paragraph 12 was adopted.

Commentary to chapter III (Breach of an international obligation)

Paragraphs (1) to (3)

Paragraphs (1) to (3) were adopted.

The general commentary to chapter III was adopted.

Commentary to article 8 (Existence of a breach of an international obligation)

Paragraphs (1) to (4)

Paragraphs (1) to (4) were adopted.

Paragraph (5)

21. Mr. PELLET said that a major problem arose in respect of paragraph (5) of the commentary to article 8 and footnote 26, because the last sentence of the paragraph created the impression that there were only three views regarding the legal nature of the rules of international organizations whereas, in fact, there were four strands of opinion. The first, most radical, stance was that the internal law of an organization did not form part of international law. A number of authors, including Cahier, Barberis and Bernhardt, took that view. Conversely, footnote 26 put forward the thesis that the rules of international organizations were part of international law, a theory supported by Decleva, Balladore Pallieri and others. He failed to see why that opinion, which was quite tenable, was mentioned only in a footnote rather than being included among the theoretical positions enumerated in the body of the commentary. Moreover, the "exception" referred to was an exception only according to the second view, which was not cited. He therefore proposed inserting a new sentence after the marker to footnote 26, encapsulating the idea that other authors contended that the internal law of international organizations was part of international law. A new footnote 26 *bis* would consist of the second part of original footnote 26 starting with the words "The theory that the 'rules of the organization' …". The body of the commentary would then continue more or less as in the original, with a few consequential amendments, but justice would have been done to all the positions adopted by legal writers and the commentary would contain a logical sentence concerning international organizations that had achieved a high degree of integration—an allusion to the European Union.

22. Mr. GAJA (Special Rapporteur) said he had no objection to Mr. Pellet's proposal. Nevertheless, the structure of the text did not justify giving equal emphasis to all four positions. The assumption underlying paragraph (4) of the commentary was that the rules of international organizations formed part of international law, whereas paragraph (5) stated that some authors had raised objections to that position in the case of certain organizations or of particular rules of certain organizations. It would perhaps be preferable to state the majority view of Commission members and refer to the fact that some authors had held that all the rules of international organizations were

part of international law. The second part of footnote 26 could then be added and the remainder of the text could be retained as it stood.

23. After a discussion in which Mr. Pellet, Mr. Gaja (Special Rapporteur) and Mr. Economides participated, Mr. MANSFIELD suggested that, after the second sentence, a new sentence should be added, to read: "Many consider that the rules of treaty-based organizations are governed by international law." The text would continue: "Some authors have held that ..." and the remainder of paragraph (5) could be retained without further amendment.

24. After further contributions from Mr. PELLET and Mr. ECONOMIDES, Mr. GAJA (Special Rapporteur) proposed the following amendments to paragraph (5) of the commentary to article 8: in the second sentence, the words "to some extent" would be deleted. A new sentence would be added after the second sentence, to read: "Many consider that the rules of treaty-based organizations are part of international law." A footnote would be added, comprising the portion of footnote 26 from the phrase "The theory that" to the end of that footnote. In the sentence beginning with the words "Another view", the words "an exception should be made with regard to" should be deleted and the words "are a special case" appended at the end of the sentence.

25. Mr. PELLET said that, in the French version of the final sentence, the words "*une troisième opinion*" should be replaced by "*une autre opinion encore*".

Paragraph (5), as amended, was adopted.

Paragraph (6)

26. Mr. MATHESON said he had doubts about the final sentence. It was not true that "most, if not all" obligations arising from the rules of an organization fell within the category of obligations under international law. At best, one could say that "some" obligations fell within that category. Moreover, the entire paragraph deliberately avoided making a judgement as to how much of that category of internal rules fell within international law. He proposed that the sentence be deleted.

Paragraph (6), as amended, was adopted.

Paragraphs (7) to (9)

Paragraphs (7) to (9) were adopted.

Paragraph (10)

27. Mr. PELLET said he disliked the paragraph and wished it to be deleted. If, however, the Special Rapporteur felt strongly that it should be retained, he should at least include a reference to draft article 16, which he personally regarded as highly exceptionable. The idea expressed in paragraph (10) was premature, it impinged too strongly on the domain of responsibility of States, and in any event, such a remark could apply to nearly every provision in the draft.

28. Mr. GAJA (Special Rapporteur) said it was true that the remark could apply to many other provisions. Indeed, if a reference was to be inserted, it should be not solely to article 16. The point being established related to the attribution of responsibility to international organizations, not to member States or to States in general, as that was governed by the rules established in the draft articles on responsibility of States for internationally wrongful acts. At its next session, the Commission would take up the question of the subsidiary responsibility that member States or other States might incur in the event of the responsibility of an international organization arising; that, however, was an entirely different matter.

29. He remained convinced that somewhere in the draft the idea must be conveyed that the references to responsibility of international organizations were without prejudice to the entirely separate question whether member States or other States also incurred responsibility. He was willing to locate the content of paragraph (10) elsewhere, perhaps at the end of the general commentary to chapter III: it would then become a new paragraph (4) of that section of chapter III.

30. Mr. ECONOMIDES said that the question covered in paragraph (10) was of such importance that it should be the subject of a separate article in the draft itself, not simply relegated to the commentary. A "without prejudice" clause should be inserted, indicating that when an international organization incurred responsibility, that was without prejudice to the responsibility of member States under the articles on responsibility of States. Such a provision would apply to the entire draft on responsibility of international organizations.

31. Mr. GAJA (Special Rapporteur) drew attention to the "without prejudice" clause in article 16. Although it referred to the responsibility of a State or international organization which committed an act, it could perhaps be redrafted in more general terms. He feared, however, that that might create the false impression that the Commission had settled the problems of State responsibility while dealing with responsibility of international organizations. On reflection, he felt that it would not be a good idea to relocate paragraph (10) at the end of the general commentary to chapter III, and that perhaps it would be best to delete it after all.

32. Mr. KOLODKIN said he would prefer to retain the paragraph but to transpose it to the commentary to article 16.

33. Mr. PELLET said that he, too, had been thinking along those lines, but that attention would have to be paid to how the paragraph fitted in with the commentary to article 16: one could not simply do a "cut and paste" job.

34. Mr. GAJA (Special Rapporteur) explained that article 16 was a "without prejudice" clause relating solely to chapter IV, in other words, to cases when an international organization incurred responsibility in connection with the act of a State or of another international organization. Paragraph (10) of the commentary to chapter III, article 8, stated something quite different: that where there was wrongful conduct on the part of an international organization, it might incur responsibility, but that did not mean that there was no parallel responsibility on the part of

member States. That was not a new idea, but one that had been discussed for several years.

35. Mr. MANSFIELD reverted to the Special Rapporteur's earlier idea of relocating paragraph (10), with the addition of a suitable introductory phrase, so as to form paragraph (4) of the general commentary to chapter III. That would mean that the idea would be present in one's mind throughout a reading of chapter III.

36. Mr. Sreenivasa RAO said that a statement like that in paragraph (10) must be included somewhere in the commentary. An international organization was an entity governed by the rules of its constituent instrument. Member States played roles in the decision-making process, some more actively than others, but all the decisions adopted by the organization entailed common responsibility. Some, like himself, had tried to argue that the draft articles should go beyond that façade so that members that had effectively participated in the adoption of a wrongful decision were not absolved simply because they were members of the organization. That view must be represented somewhere, and it would be represented if the final phrase of paragraph (10), following the words "incur responsibility", was deleted.

37. Mr. PELLET said that he was very opposed to the Special Rapporteur's proposal because if it was endorsed, it would not be possible to understand how paragraph (10) related to article 16. There was absolutely no reason to separate the idea in paragraph (10) from that in article 16, even if it was explained that it was different, in which case the entire paragraph would have to be recast to say that it was also true for article 16. Although he did not like the idea, the advantage of Mr. Kolodkin's proposal was that at least the two were linked. The Special Rapporteur would then need to decide whether to say "*en outre*" (moreover) or "*en particulier*" (in particular) so as to show how it tied in with article 16.

38. The CHAIRPERSON suggested that further discussion of where to locate the idea contained in paragraph (10) of the commentary to article 8 should be postponed until the Commission came to consider the commentary to article 16.

It was so agreed.

Commentary to article 9 (International obligation in force for an international organization)

Commentary to article 10 (Extension in time of the breach of an international obligation)

Commentary to article 11 (Breach consisting of a composite act)

The commentaries to articles 9, 10 and 11 were adopted with a minor editing amendment.

Commentary to chapter IV (Responsibility of an international organization in connection with the act of a State or another international organization)

Paragraphs (1) to (4)

Paragraphs (1) to (4) were adopted.

Paragraph (5)

39. Mr. GAJA (Special Rapporteur) said that the reference to the *Bosphorus* case should be corrected, because the issue was no longer before the European Court of Human Rights; thus, the sentence should state that the issue "was also before the European Court of Human Rights …".

40. Mr. PELLET said that paragraph (5) was too long and should be subdivided into five paragraphs numbered (5) to (9).

41. He was very hostile to the assertion in the last paragraph, which began with the words "For the purposes of the present Chapter, it seems preferable at the current stage …". The justification given in that same paragraph that such a rule would run counter to the general rule on attribution of conduct to States expressed in article 4 of the draft articles on the responsibility of States for internationally wrongful acts was not convincing.[1] All the draft articles on the responsibility of States were without prejudice to what happened when an international organization was concerned. Article 57 of the draft articles on State responsibility was extremely broad, because it provided that "[t]hese articles are without prejudice to any question of the responsibility under international law of an international organization, or of any State for the conduct of an international organization".[2] He had been very opposed to the Special Rapporteur's position on that matter in his report. It would mean taking a position which was the contrary of what was set out in the draft articles on State responsibility on the grounds that it ran counter to what was expressed in article 4, but it was not intellectually acceptable to say that when an international organization was concerned, no position would be taken. That was simply passing the buck, since it was asserted that a position had already been taken on the question in the draft articles on State responsibility, whereas attempts made to address such questions during the work on the draft articles on State responsibility had been countered with the argument that international organizations were not to be covered. He was very concerned by the justification given in the last sentence, and before making any proposal, he wanted to hear the Special Rapporteur's opinion on it. The matter augured ill for the future, because if, whenever a position was taken which was not identical with the one in the draft articles on State responsibility, the Commission were to say that it ran counter to the draft articles on State responsibility, the draft articles on responsibility of international organizations would be completely "smothered" by the draft articles on State responsibility, something which should not be allowed to happen.

42. Mr. GAJA (Special Rapporteur) said that that debate had come up a number of times in the past. The position of the Commission of the European Union was that when a member State acted in implementing a decision or other binding act of the European Communities, that act was

[1] *Yearbook … 2001*, vol. II (Part Two) and corrigendum, p. 40.

[2] *Ibid.*, p. 141.

to be attributed to the international organization. In his view, that ran counter to article 4 of the draft articles on State responsibility which was based on the assumption that the act of a State organ would be attributed to that State unless that State organ was put at the disposal of an international organization. Article 57 on State responsibility did not go so far as to say that there could be an exception to the rules of attribution in the sense that what was considered to be an act of a State under those articles suddenly became an act of an international organization. The judgement in the *Bosphorus* case bore out his point of view: although a number of member States had argued that they had been acting on behalf of the European Community and that the act concerned had been committed not by Ireland, but by the organization, the judges of the Grand Chamber of the European Court of Human Rights had unanimously ruled that the conduct must be attributed to the member State, even if that member State had used no discretion in implementing a given regulation. When he had drafted the text, a judgement on the merits in the *Bosphorus* case had still been pending and, not wanting to anticipate that ruling, he had left room for possible exceptions. Thus, the sentence beginning with the words "For the purpose of the present chapter …" was probably too cautious, since the judgement in the *Bosphorus* case had clearly shown that an act of a State was involved, and not an act of the European Community, even though in acting the State had implemented a regulation of the European Community.

43. Various judgements of the European Court of Human Rights supported his view that an act of an organ of a State was an act of a State, not an act of an international organization. His suggestion, therefore, would be to delete the last sentence of the last paragraph, although the penultimate sentence could perhaps also be altered to make it more assertive.

44. With regard to the numbering of paragraph (5), he proposed that only two new paragraphs should be created: a new paragraph (6) would begin with the words "A different view …", and a new paragraph (7) with "The issue …".

45. The CHAIRPERSON said he took it that the Commission wished to endorse Mr. Gaja's proposal to delete the last sentence of paragraph (5) and to instruct the Secretariat to adjust the numbering of the paragraphs.

It was so decided.

Paragraph (5), as amended and renumbered, was adopted.

The general commentary to chapter IV, as amended, was adopted.

46. Mr. PELLET said that the Special Rapporteur had been too quick to claim victory by citing the *Bosphorus* case. The decisions of the European Court of Human Rights were not always entirely convincing. Moreover, the WTO panel had arrived at the opposite conclusion. Thus, he did not concede defeat; Mr. Gaja's interpretation remained debatable.

Commentary to article 12 (Aid or assistance in the commission of an internationally wrongful act)

The commentary to article 12 was adopted with a minor editing amendment suggested by the Chairperson.

Commentary to article 13 (Direction and control exercised over the commission of an internationally wrongful act)

Paragraph (1)

Paragraph (1) was adopted.

Paragraph (2)

47. Ms. ESCARAMEIA said she gathered that paragraph (2) had been included in response to one of her earlier remarks. She had proposed that the title should read, not "Direction and control …", but "Direction and/or control …". She was aware that the current wording was in keeping with the formulation in the draft articles on State responsibility, but it had not been explained why "and" was appropriate whereas "or" was not. Paragraph (2) itself cited the example of one body (NATO) which was responsible only for the direction of the international peacekeeping force in Kosovo (KFOR) and of another (the United Nations) responsible only for its control. It had been her understanding that some of her concerns would be reflected in the commentary, and she had therefore expected a statement to the effect that "direction and control" meant the same thing as "direction or control", which she would not find entirely logical but could accept, since it would have clarified the situation and would have practical implications. The point of paragraph (2) seemed to be that although "direction" and "control" were separated, a joint exercise was probably envisaged. The commentary should specify that "direction and control" meant "direction or control", particularly because the fourth line before the end of paragraph (3) also referred to "direction or control". She asked the Special Rapporteur to clarify the matter.

48. Mr. GAJA (Special Rapporteur) said that the wording "direction and control" was found in the draft articles on State responsibility, and the approach adopted with regard to international organizations should be no different. There had been extensive discussions on the question when the draft articles on State responsibility had been produced, and he did not see any justification for saying that direction and control were the same thing or that one of the two was sufficient. The somewhat odd example was due to the dearth of practice. Although he had made every effort to reflect the views of the entire Commission in the commentary, it could not be all-inclusive. It had been his understanding that most members of the Commission had been in favour of retaining the wording used in the draft articles on State responsibility.

49. The CHAIRPERSON said he took it that the Commission wished to adopt paragraph (2) as it stood.

Paragraph (2) was adopted.

Paragraphs (3) and (4)

Paragraphs (3) and (4) were adopted.

The commentary to article 13 was adopted.

Commentary to article 14 (Coercion of a State or another international organization)

Paragraphs (1) to (3)

Paragraphs (1) to (3) were adopted.

The commentary to article 14 was adopted.

Commentary to article 15 (Decisions, recommendations and authorizations addressed to member States and international organizations)

Paragraph (1)

50. Mr. MATHESON said that the language in the last part of the first sentence was not entirely clear with respect to the relationship between the two elements described in the sentence. It could be clarified by replacing the words "thereby circumventing" with "and that would circumvent".

Paragraph (1), as amended, was adopted.

Paragraphs (2) to (5)

Paragraphs (2) to (5) were adopted.

Paragraph (6)

51. Mr. PELLET wondered whether, as paragraph (6) was very abstract, it could not be illustrated with a reference to the *Matthews* v. *United Kingdom* case, in which, as he interpreted it, the Court had found against the United Kingdom, not for implementing the Act concerning the Election of the Representatives of the European Parliament by Direct Universal Suffrage, but for doing so in a way which did not necessarily result from the position of the European Community. The inclusion of such an example would enrich the commentary.

52. Mr. GAJA (Special Rapporteur) said he was not persuaded by the proposal to refer to the *Matthews* case. Although the United Kingdom had in fact implemented an act in a particular way, that act had been an international agreement, not an act of the European Community. It was an act which had modified the treaty by opening up the possibility of elections by universal suffrage. A better example might be the *Cantoni* v. *France* case, although there had been no breach, and from that point of view the *Matthews* case would have been more convincing. He would review the various cases to see whether he could find a better example in time for the following day's meeting.

53. The CHAIRPERSON suggested that, in view of the Special Rapporteur's remarks, further discussion of paragraph (6) should be postponed until the next plenary meeting.

It was so agreed.

The meeting rose at 5.55 p.m.

2863rd MEETING

Wednesday, 3 August 2005, at 10.05 a.m.

Chairperson: Mr. Djamchid MOMTAZ

Present: Mr. Addo, Mr. Al-Baharna, Mr. Al-Marri, Mr. Brownlie, Mr. Candioti, Mr. Chee, Mr. Comissário Afonso, Mr. Dugard, Mr. Economides, Ms. Escarameia, Mr. Fomba, Mr. Gaja, Mr. Galicki, Mr. Kabatsi, Mr. Kateka, Mr. Kolodkin, Mr. Koskenniemi, Mr. Mansfield, Mr. Matheson, Mr. Niehaus, Mr. Pambou-Tchivounda, Mr. Pellet, Mr. Sreenivasa Rao, Mr. Rodríguez Cedeño, Mr. Yamada.

Shared natural resources (*concluded*) (A/CN.4/549 and Add.1, sect. B, A/CN.4/551 and Corr.1 and Add.1, A/CN.4/555 and Add.1)

[Agenda item 4]

Report of the Working Group

1. The CHAIRPERSON invited the Chairperson of the Working Group on Shared natural resources to introduce the report of the Working Group.

2. Mr. CANDIOTI (Chairperson of the Working Group on Shared natural resources), introducing the report of the Working Group (A/CN.4/L.681 and Corr.1), said that during the 11 meetings which the Working Group held from 19 May to 28 July 2005 the Working Group considered the draft articles submitted by the Special Rapporteur in the annex to his third report (A/CN.4/551 and Corr.1 and Add.1) with a view to the possible submission of a revised text that would take into account the debate on the topic in the Commission. The Working Group had had the benefit of the advice and briefings of experts on groundwaters from UNESCO and the International Association of Hydrogeologists, and had had a briefing by the Franco-Swiss Genevese Aquifer Authority on 12 July 2005. All that had facilitated the work of the Working Group.

3. Eight draft articles, which the Working Group had reviewed in the course of its work, were contained in the annex to the report.

4. With regard to form, the Working Group had essentially agreed with the approach proposed by the Special Rapporteur that the focus should be on the substance without prejudice as to the final form. Thus reference was made to "draft articles" wherever "Convention" appeared in the text presented by the Special Rapporteur. The question of the final form was, of course, an important matter, and some members had expressed a wish for the Working Group to address it at some particular point. It was to be hoped that such an opportunity would be afforded if the Commission decided to reconvene the Working Group in 2006. The Working Group had not completed its work, and proposed, in paragraph 6 of its report, that the Commission consider reconvening it during the first part of its fifty-eighth session. The Working Group was mindful

of the busy work schedule that was anticipated for the next year, but it nevertheless hoped that the Commission would be able to complete its first reading of the draft articles in 2006.

5. Consistent with the Commission's practice, the Working Group had not dealt with final clauses. It had also employed footnotes or square brackets as appropriate to denote points that might require resolution, further consideration or clarification at a later stage or elaboration in the commentary. The article numbers appearing in square brackets corresponded to those in the Special Rapporteur's third report. The Working Group had also agreed to organize the draft articles in such a way that the general principles applicable would appear in the earlier chapters. Accordingly, the articles that had appeared as draft articles 3 and 4 in the Special Rapporteur's third report, concerning bilateral and regional arrangements and the relationship between the draft articles and other conventions and international agreements, respectively, would be addressed, together with their placement, at a later stage.

6. The Working Group had also considered whether it would be necessary to structure the draft articles by setting out obligations that applied to all States generally, obligations of aquifer States and obligations of aquifer States *vis-à-vis* third States. Recently it had been focusing on the obligations of aquifer States and would revert to related issues at a later stage.

7. Turning to the substance of the draft text, he said that draft articles 1 and 2 were essentially the same as those proposed by the Special Rapporteur. The additional reference to "underground" to describe a geological formation in the definition of the term "aquifer" was meant to underscore the fact that aquifers were found on the subsurface. A number of footnotes or square brackets reflected issues that might require further consideration by the Commission or elaboration in the commentary, including points which the Working Group thought could best be dealt with in the commentary rather than in the texts of draft articles.

8. During the Commission's debates some members had made comments about the principles of territorial sovereignty and permanent sovereignty over natural resources. Draft article 3, on sovereignty of aquifer States, sought to reflect a convergence of views on the way the issue should be addressed in the context of the draft articles. It simply reflected the proposition that an aquifer State had sovereignty over the portion of a transboundary aquifer or aquifer system located within its territorial jurisdiction. It was clearly understood that sovereignty was not absolute. As noted in the footnote, the second sentence would have to be reviewed after consideration of the draft articles as a whole.

9. Draft article 4, on equitable and reasonable utilization, took a different approach from that taken by the Special Rapporteur. It did not provide different standards for determining reasonable utilization between a recharging and a non-recharging aquifer. The distinction between the two types of aquifer was maintained, but the same minimum standard of reasonable utilization applied to both. The aim was thus to maximize the long-term benefits derived from the use of the water contained in the aquifer or aquifer system, and to that end the States concerned should establish an overall plan for utilization, taking into account present and future needs and alternative water resources. In addition, there was a need in the case of recharging aquifers to maintain the continued effective functioning of the aquifer or aquifer system, in which case utilization levels should not be such as to prevent such functioning. That did not imply that the level of utilization must necessarily be limited to the level of recharge. That point would be explained in the commentary, as would such other notions as "long-term benefits" and "agreed lifespan of the aquifer or aquifer system", which were contained in an earlier draft by the Special Rapporteur.

10. In both paragraphs of draft article 4, the phrase "in their respective territories" had been deleted to take into account the peculiarities of transboundary aquifers. Paragraph 3 had also been deleted, as it had been felt that the question of cooperation could be dealt with elsewhere.

11. The factors to be taken into account in determining equitable and reasonable utilization were contained in draft article 5, which had largely been kept in the form proposed by the Special Rapporteur. Certain points such as the replacement of "natural conditions" with "natural characteristics" in paragraph 1 (*a*) and the elements relating to viability and costs in paragraph 1 (*h*), would be elaborated in greater detail in the commentary. Moreover, the Working Group had considered it necessary to include the place of the aquifer or aquifer system in the related ecosystem as a relevant factor for reasonable utilization, which could be a germane consideration in arid regions. However, that subparagraph remained in brackets, in view of the different meanings attached to the term "ecosystem" within the scientific community, and the Special Rapporteur would seek further clarification on that point, taking also into account draft article 12, on protection and preservation of ecosystems. Some members had felt that that factor would be a useful corollary to the obligation set out in that draft article.

12. The Working Group had also discussed the special consideration to be given to drinking water and other vital human needs. That was why a reference to vital human needs, which had initially been reflected in draft article 11, on the relationship between different kinds of utilization, in the Special Rapporteur's third report, had been added to the end of paragraph 2 of draft article 5.

13. Draft article 6, which dealt with the obligation not to cause harm to other aquifer States, addressed the question of harm arising from utilization or from activities other than utilization and the question of the elimination and mitigation of significant harm despite the exercise of due diligence. The Working Group had agreed to consider addressing in a separate article compensation in circumstances where harm resulted despite efforts to eliminate or mitigate it. It was clearly understood that the concept of significant harm was a relative one, and that the matter would be adequately dealt with in the commentary.

14. There was no major change of substance in draft article 7, on the obligation to cooperate. While the Working Group had agreed to proceed on the basis of existing precedents, including the 1997 Watercourses Convention,

questions had been raised as to whether the principles of sovereign equality and territorial integrity could be better reflected elsewhere than in a provision on cooperation. That matter might be reconsidered at a later stage. The principle of sustainable development had been included as a general principle that ought to be taken into account as well. It must be distinguished from the principle of sustainable utilization in the context of draft article 4. The Working Group had decided to speak of "equitable and reasonable" utilization rather than simply "reasonable" utilization, as had been done in the original text.

15. Paragraph 2 of draft article 7 had been simply streamlined, and some of the elements contained in the Special Rapporteur's draft would be reflected in the commentary.

16. The changes made to draft article 8 were of a drafting nature. It was understood that some of the scientific terms would be clarified in the commentary.

17. He concluded by thanking all members of the Working Group and the Special Rapporteur and said he hoped that the Working Group would complete its work in 2006. He recommended that the Commission take note of the report of the Working Group and said that the Commission would take up the question of reconvening the Working Group at its fifty-eighth session.

18. The CHAIRPERSON thanked the members of the Working Group on Shared natural resources and suggested that the Commission should take note of the report of the Working Group and add to chapter IV of the draft report of the Commission (A/CN.4/L.667) a new paragraph 3 *bis* that would read:

> At its 2863rd meeting, held on 3 August 2005, the Commission took note of the report of the Working Group. It welcomed the significant progress made by the Working Group, which had considered and amended eight draft articles. It took note of the proposal by the Working Group to reconvene the Group at its session in 2006 so that it could complete its work.

New paragraph 3 bis *was adopted.*

Draft report of the Commission on the work at its fifty-seventh session (*continued*)

Chapter VI. *Responsibility of international organizations* (*concluded*) (A/CN.4/L.669 and Add.1)

19. The CHAIRPERSON invited the members of the Commission to resume consideration of chapter VI, section C, of the draft report of the Commission, on responsibility of international organizations.

C. Text of the draft articles on responsibility of international organizations provisionally adopted so far by the Commission

2. Text of the draft articles with commentaries thereto *(concluded)*

Commentary to draft article 15 (Decisions, recommendations and authorizations addressed to member States and international organizations)

New paragraph (5 *bis*)

20. Mr. GAJA (Special Rapporteur) proposed that a new paragraph (5 *bis*) should be inserted before paragraph 6; the new paragraph would read:

> A member State or international organization may be given discretion with regard to implementation of a binding decision adopted by an international organization. In its judgement on the merits in *Bosphorus Hava Yollari Turizm ve Ticaret AS* v. *Ireland*, the European Court of Human Rights considered conduct that member States of the European Community take when implementing binding EC acts and observed:
>
>> "… a State would be fully responsible under the Convention [for the Protection of Human Rights and Fundamental Freedoms] for all acts falling outside its strict international legal obligations … numerous Convention cases … confirm this. Each case (in particular, the Cantoni judgement, p. 1626 at paragraph 26) concerned a review by this Court of the exercise of State discretion for which EC law provided".

21. A footnote would refer to the paragraph from which the quotation was taken.

22. The CHAIRPERSON thanked the Special Rapporteur and suggested that the Commission adopt new paragraph (5 *bis*) of the commentary to draft article 15.

New paragraph (*5* bis) *was adopted.*

Paragraph (6)

23. Mr. PELLET said that the correct expression in French was "*décision obligatoire*" and not "*décision contraignante*".

Paragraph 6 was adopted with a drafting change in the French version.

Paragraphs (7) to (12)

Paragraphs (7) to (12) were adopted.

The commentary to draft article 15 was adopted.

Commentary to draft article 16 (Effect of this chapter)

The commentary to draft 16 was adopted.

Commentary to draft article 8 (Existence of a breach of an international obligation) (*continued*)

Paragraph (10) (*concluded*)

24. The CHAIRPERSON invited members to resume consideration of paragraph (10) of the commentary to draft article 8.

25. Mr. GAJA (Special Rapporteur) said that the proposal made by Mr. Kolodkin and Mr. Pellet at the previous meeting to include the text of paragraph (10) in the commentary to draft article 16 risked creating confusion. Draft article 16 had a specific purpose, since it concerned a specific chapter, whereas paragraph (10) contained a general statement. He preferred the other proposal, which was to introduce a final clause in the draft articles that would clarify matters.

It was so decided.

26. Mr. PELLET welcomed the proposal by the Special Rapporteur but said that he reserved his position with regard to the substance of the matter; under the circumstances, he questioned whether draft article 16, to which he continued to object, was really useful.

Section C, as amended, was adopted.

Chapter VI, as amended, was adopted.

CHAPTER VII. ***Diplomatic protection*** **(A/CN.4/L.670)**

27. The CHAIRPERSON invited the members of the Commission to begin consideration of chapter VII of the draft report of the Commission on diplomatic protection.

A. Introduction

Paragraphs 1 to 17

Paragraphs 1 to 17 were adopted.

Paragraph 18

28. Mr. GAJA proposed that the second sentence should state, even if it was already implicit, that the commentary had been adopted at the same time as the draft articles; that could be done by adding the words "and the commentaries thereto" after the word "articles" in the first sentence.

Paragraph 18, as amended, was adopted.

Section A, as amended, was adopted.

B. Consideration of the topic at the present session

Paragraphs 19 to 22

Paragraphs 19 to 22 were adopted.

Paragraph 23

29. Mr. GAJA proposed that the order of the last two sentences of the paragraph should be reversed for the sake of logic, as the cases mentioned in the last sentence in fact illustrated what was said in what was currently the antepenultimate sentence.

Paragraph 23, as amended, was adopted.

Paragraphs 24 to 34

Paragraphs 24 to 34 were adopted.

Paragraph 35

30. Mr. PELLET said that the last clause of the last sentence was unacceptable, since the progressive development of law was as much a statutory function of the Commission as was codification. He wished to know the Special Rapporteur's views on the matter.

31. Mr. DUGARD (Special Rapporteur) endorsed the view expressed by Mr. Pellet and proposed that the clause in question should be deleted.

32. Mr. BROWNLIE said that the deletion notwithstanding, the sentence still seemed somewhat out of context. He therefore proposed that it should be deleted entirely.

33. Mr. PELLET objected to such a deletion, since the sentence explained why the Commission had decided to retain the *Mavrommatis* principle. Accordingly, he proposed that the latter portion of the sentence, beginning with the words "and the Commission had sought" should be replaced with the words "and for this reason it has been retained".

Paragraph 35, as amended, was adopted.

Section B, as amended, was adopted.

Chapter VII, as amended, was adopted.

CHAPTER VIII. ***Expulsion of aliens*** **(A/CN.4/L.674)**

34. The CHAIRPERSON invited the Commission to begin its consideration of chapter VIII of the report, on expulsion of aliens.

A. Introduction

Paragraphs 1 to 2

Paragraphs 1 to 2 were adopted.

B. Consideration of the topic at the present session

Paragraph 4

35. Mr. GAJA proposed that the words "applicable to international law" in the penultimate sentence should be deleted.

It was so decided.

36. Mr. PAMBOU-TCHIVOUNDA said that he did not like the word "genuine" in the third sentence, which seemed to imply that there were questions of international law that were "not genuine". He proposed that the phrase in question should be amended to read "important questions of international law".

Paragraph 4, as amended, was adopted.

Paragraphs 5 to 10

Paragraphs 5 to 10 were adopted.

Paragraph 11

37. Mr. KOSKENNIEMI said that it was his view that was reflected in paragraph 11, and his comments had been somewhat distorted. He therefore proposed that, in order for the view he had expressed to be stated correctly, the word "typical" should be deleted from the second sentence, the words "the social process" in the same sentence should be replaced with the words "typical cases" and, in the final sentence, the word "significance" should be replaced with the words "intended direction".

Paragraph 11, as amended, was adopted.

Paragraphs 12 to 18

Paragraphs 12 to 18 were adopted.

Paragraph 19

38. Mr. RODRÍGUEZ CEDEÑO proposed that the words "political asylum-seekers" in the second sentence should be replaced with the words "political refugees" and that the words "asylum-seekers and" should be inserted following the comma immediately after the first set of parentheses. He also believed that the Caracas Convention, mentioned in the paragraph, was in fact the Inter-American Convention of 1954.

39. The CHAIRPERSON said that the title would be checked.

40. Mr. PAMBOU-TCHIVOUNDA said that he did not like the word "viability" in the last sentence.

41. Mr. PELLET said that the whole last sentence was absurd because it stated something that was self-evident: it was obviously impossible to define the term "alien" without raising questions of nationality. He therefore proposed that the sentence should be deleted.

Paragraph 19, as amended, was adopted.

Paragraphs 20 and 21

Paragraphs 20 and 21 were adopted.

Paragraph 22

42. Mr. Sreenivasa RAO said that the word "could" in the fifth sentence should be amended to "would".

It was so decided.

43. Mr. RODRÍGUEZ CEDEÑO said that the portion of the paragraph from the fourth sentence on should be placed under heading (*c*), which dealt specifically with the right to expel.

Paragraph 22, as amended, was adopted.

Paragraph 23

Paragraph 23 was adopted.

Paragraph 24

44. Mr. GAJA said that the suggestion mentioned in the first sentence of paragraph 24 was his, and it had been somewhat distorted. He proposed that the beginning of that sentence should be reworded to read: "It was further suggested that the study should consider a set of issues".

Paragraph 24, as amended, was adopted.

Paragraph 25

45. Mr. RODRÍGUEZ CEDEÑO said that it had been stressed throughout the debate that expulsion procedures should be official or formal so that the persons concerned would have a remedy available. Accordingly, he proposed that a new sentence should be inserted after the first sentence of paragraph 25 that would read: "It was noted that the act of expulsion must be formal in order for the person concerned to be afforded an opportunity to appeal."

46. Mr. MATHESON said that that was just an opinion. He therefore proposed rewording Mr. Rodríguez Cedeño's proposed new sentence to read: "It was suggested that the act of expulsion … ".

Paragraph 25, as amended, was adopted.

Paragraph 26

Paragraph 26 was adopted.

Paragraph 27

47. Mr. PAMBOU-TCHIVOUNDA proposed that the words "*faisaient l'objet*" in the second sentence of the French text should be replaced with the word "*relevaient*".

Paragraph 27 was adopted with a minor drafting change to the French version.

Paragraph 28

48. Ms. ESCARAMEIA noted that the Special Rapporteur had said that the Commission ought to prepare draft articles on the topic. She therefore proposed that the word "covering" in the second sentence should be replaced with "drafting articles on".

Paragraph 28, as amended, was adopted.

Paragraph 29

Paragraph 29 was adopted.

Paragraph 30

49. Mr. PELLET proposed that the words "arising from" in the final sentence should be replaced with the words "pertaining to".

Paragraph 30, as amended, was adopted.

Paragraph 31

50. Mr. PELLET said he was appalled at the idea that the Commission would not consider questions of refusal of admission, movements of population or situations of decolonization or self-determination, nor the position of the occupied territories in the Middle East. He felt that the very point of the topic had been done away with, and he wished to know just what the Commission was

going to talk about if it was not going to consider any of those questions.

51. The CHAIRPERSON pointed out that the text reflected the conclusions of the Special Rapporteur and that they could not be amended in his absence.

Paragraph 31 was adopted.

Paragraph 32

52. Mr. GAJA said that he was not sure what the second sentence meant; it was unfortunate that the Special Rapporteur was not present to clarify it. He proposed that the words "both the case" should be replaced with the words "all cases" and that the remainder of the sentence should be deleted.

53. Mr. BROWNLIE proposed replacing the words "of a legal nature" with "with legal consequences".

54. Mr. PELLET said he thought Mr. Brownlie's proposal distorted the Special Rapporteur's meaning, since an expulsion could take place without a formal act and still have legal consequences. The French text was in fact correct, although the word "formal" might be added to modify "unilateral act" for the sake of clarity.

55. Mr. BROWNLIE proposed that the word "legal" should be deleted from the expression "unilateral legal act" in the second sentence, since the word had been incorrectly used twice in that sentence.

56. Mr. MATHESON said he did not think that a distinction was being drawn between acts that had legal consequences and those that did not, but between formal and informal acts. He therefore proposed either ending the first sentence after the phrase "the taking of a formal act", or adding "and also include informal acts" after that phrase.

57. Mr. GAJA proposed replacing the words "both the case" with "this case"; the words "and also informal acts" could be added, and the rest of the sentence would be deleted.

58. Mr. MANSFIELD said that he could accept either Mr. Matheson's first proposal or the insertion of the words "formal and informal cases of expulsion" after the word "both" in the second sentence, with the remainder of the sentence deleted.

59. Mr. PELLET proposed that the words "unilateral legal act" should be amended to read "formal unilateral acts" and the words "of an act" to read "of a conduct", since the fundamental idea was to contrast a formal unilateral act with conduct.

60. Mr. CANDIOTI concurred with Mr. Pellet and endorsed Mr. Matheson's proposal to end the sentence after the words "formal act" and to amend the words "not to require" to read "not necessarily to require".

61. Mr. PAMBOU-TCHIVOUNDA asked whether the amendments being proposed for adoption also concerned the French text, which did not appear to pose any problem; if they did, he wished to have the words "in all cases" added after the word "necessarily", since that word did not seem sufficiently explicit in the light of the original version.

Paragraph 32, as amended, was adopted.

Paragraph 33

Paragraph 33 was adopted.

Section B, as amended, was adopted.

Chapter VIII as a whole, as amended, was adopted.

Chapter V. Effects of armed conflicts on treaties (*continued*) (A/CN.4/L.668)

B. Consideration of the topic at the present session (*continued*)

62. The CHAIRPERSON invited the Commission to return to paragraph 78 of chapter V of the draft report (A/CN.4/L.668), on effects of armed conflicts on treaties, and said that Mr. Brownlie had proposed a new sentence to replace the last sentence of the paragraph, to read: " It could not be presumed that the States concerned could rely on such a proviso unless the legal conditions existed necessitating suspension or termination."

Paragraph 78, as amended, was adopted.

Chapter IX. Unilateral acts of states (A/CN.4/L.672 and Add.1–2)

63. The CHAIRPERSON invited the members of the Commission to consider chapter IX of the draft report of the Commission on unilateral acts of States (A/CN.4/L.672 and Add.1 and 2).

A. Introduction (A/CN.4/L.672)

Paragraphs 1 to 19

Paragraphs 1 to 19 were adopted.

Section A was adopted.

B. Consideration of the topic at the present session (A/CN.4/L.672/Add.1)

Paragraphs 1 to 6

Paragraphs 1 to 6 were adopted.

Paragraph 7

64. Ms. ESCARAMEIA said that she did not understand what was meant in the second and third sentences, in particular the phrase "ramifications of certain acts".

65. Mr. RODRÍGUEZ CEDEÑO (Special Rapporteur) proposed the deletion of the second sentence.

66. Mr. PELLET endorsed that proposal and added that he did not understand what was meant by the first sentence, either.

67. Mr. ECONOMIDES found the beginning of the first sentence awkward, particularly the words "lead to

international treaties", and proposed deleting the entire sentence.

68. The CHAIRPERSON suggested that paragraph 7 as a whole should be deleted.

Paragraph 7 was deleted.

Paragraphs 8 and 9

Paragraphs 8 and 9 were adopted.

Paragraph 10

69. Ms. ESCARAMEIA proposed that the words "if necessary" should be deleted.

Paragraph 10, as amended, was adopted.

Paragraph 11

70. Ms. ESCARAMEIA proposed that the words "for some members" should be added before the words "the diversity of effects" in the first sentence in order to reflect that there had been a variety of opinions expressed; she further proposed inserting, at the end of that sentence, a new sentence that would read: "Some others, however, thought that it was possible to establish such a regime." Turning to the antepenultimate sentence, she said that the reason some members had found article 7 of the 1969 Vienna Convention too restrictive was not just because they thought that legislative and judicial acts should be included, but because the circle of persons mentioned in that article might be too restrictive. She therefore proposed that the words "cases of declarations of other members of the executive, as well as" should be inserted after the word "studying".

71. Mr. PELLET drew attention to numerous problems in the French version and proposed a number of amendments: in the fourth sentence, the words "*afin de procéder à*" should be replaced by "*d'*"; in the fifth sentence, the word "*champ*" should be replaced by the word "*cercle*"; and in the sixth sentence, the words "*d'actes unilatéraux ... du comportement*" should be replaced by "*entre actes unilatéraux ... d'une part et des comportements d'autre part*" and the words "*relevant de*" by the words "*relatives à*".

Paragraph 11, as amended, was adopted.

Paragraphs 12 and 13

Paragraphs 12 and 13 were adopted.

Paragraph 14

72. Mr. PELLET drew attention to the French text and proposed that the words "*étude comparative des*" should be replaced by the words "*comparaison avec les*".

Paragraph 14 was adopted with a minor drafting change to the French version.

Paragraph 15

73. Mr. PELLET said that it would be safer and more accurate to amend the phrase "unanimously accepted" to read "accepted by consensus". He also proposed replacing the word "then" in the final sentence with the word "also".

Paragraph 15, as amended, was adopted.

Paragraphs 16 and 17

Paragraphs 16 and 17 were adopted.

Paragraph 18

74. Mr. GAJA proposed that the word "exploratory" in the fourth sentence should be amended to read "expository".

75. Mr. PELLET pointed out that the word "expositif" did not exist in French and would have to be replaced.

76. Mr. ECONOMIDES proposed that the words "*une étude expositive*" in the French text should be amended to read "*un exposé*".

Paragraph 18, as amended, was adopted.

Paragraph 19

Paragraph 19 was adopted.

Paragraph 20

77. Mr. Sreenivasa RAO said that he did not understand the last sentence of the paragraph.

78. Mr. PELLET agreed that the sentence did not make sense and said that the preceding sentence was not much better. In addition, it would be better in the French text to speak of "*licéité*" rather than "*légalité*", and he proposed that the final sentence should be deleted.

Paragraph 20, as amended, was adopted.

Paragraph 21

Paragraph 21 was adopted.

Paragraph 22

79. Mr. PELLET proposed that the words "according to some members" should be inserted before the words "in any event".

Paragraph 22, as amended, was adopted.

Paragraph 23

80. Mr. PELLET proposed that the first part of the first sentence should be amended to read: "It was also pointed out that, besides States' intentions and the conditions, the authority, the capacity or competence of the author and the deciding factors … ". He also requested that the word "*expectation*" in the last sentence of the French version should be replaced with the word "*expectative*".

81. Mr. GAJA proposed that the beginning of the last sentence should be reworded to read: "If such acts were

not accepted by other States and did not raise any legitimate expectations for those States … ".

82. Mr. Sreenivasa RAO said that he could accept the correction proposed by Mr. Pellet, although the English text did not seem to pose any problem. With regard to the second sentence, he proposed that the latter portion should be reworded to read "or treated as a basis for valid legal engagements by other States".

83. The CHAIRPERSON suggested that the Commission should adopt paragraph 23 as amended by Mr. Sreenivasa Rao.

Paragraph 23, as amended, was adopted.

Paragraph 24

84. Mr. BROWNLIE said that he did not understand what the first sentence meant. He found it impossible to believe that a legal act could have no antecedent in either customary or treaty law.

85. Mr. PELLET said that the meaning was not much clearer in the French version. He proposed the following wording for the first sentence: "Several members remarked that the only unilateral acts *par excellence* that ought to be considered were autonomous acts, namely acts that had no specific antecedent in customary or treaty law." In his view, the problem that arose in the English text had to do with the use of the term "antecedent", which should perhaps be replaced by "basis" or "habilitation".

86. Mr. BROWNLIE said that he still did not understand what was meant by an autonomous act.

87. Mr. PELLET said that Mr. Brownlie was complaining about the substance of the problem. However, many members had supported that position, and it must therefore be mentioned in the report.

88. Ms. ESCARAMEIA said that the term "basis" might give the impression that such acts had no legal justification. She proposed the following wording: "or acts that were not already governed by treaties or a specific rule of treaty law".

89. Mr. CANDIOTI proposed replacing the words "several members" with "some members". He also wanted the report to contain a few words about the position of those who, like himself, thought that, in legal terms, there was no such thing as an autonomous act.

90. Mr. ECONOMIDES recalled that he had been among the "several" or "some" members who had defended that argument and that he had linked the question of the autonomy of acts with that of sources of law. He proposed that the second part of the first sentence should be reworded to read: "valid as a source of international law and not those that derived from customary or treaty law".

91. Mr. PELLET said that Mr. Brownlie's criticism was directed at the substance rather than at the form. However, the position was one that had been supported by several members, and it must therefore be reflected in the report. He could accept the wording proposed by Mr. Economides, even though he did not entirely agree with him. He nevertheless proposed that the phrase in question should read "… those deriving from a treaty authorization". He added that, in proposing the wording "that had no specific antecedent", he had intentionally sought to refer back to the very rules that Ms. Escarameia had mentioned.

92. Mr. BROWNLIE said that he preferred Mr. Economides' wording, even though he still found that view outrageous.

93. Mr. CHEE said that if experts could not understand the paragraph, it was hard to imagine how mere mortals would be able to do so. To him the paragraph was incomprehensible, and he still did not understand what was meant by "auto-normativity" and "hetero-normativity".

94. Mr. Sreenivasa RAO said that he had no objection to the wording proposed by Mr. Economides and suggested that a few words should be added at the end of the paragraph to reflect Mr. Brownlie's position.

95. The CHAIRPERSON suggested that the Commission should adopt the paragraph as amended by Mr. Pellet, Mr. Candioti and Mr. Economides.

Paragraph 24, as amended, was adopted.

The meeting rose at 1 p.m.

2864th MEETING

Wednesday, 3 August 2005, at 3.05 p.m.

Chairperson: Mr. Djamchid MOMTAZ

Present: Mr. Addo, Mr. Al-Baharna, Mr. Brownlie, Mr. Candioti, Mr. Chee, Mr. Comissário Afonso, Mr. Dugard, Mr. Economides, Ms. Escarameia, Mr. Fomba, Mr. Gaja, Mr. Galicki, Mr. Kabatsi, Mr. Kateka, Mr. Kolodkin, Mr. Koskenniemi, Mr. Mansfield, Mr. Matheson, Mr. Pambou-Tchivounda, Mr. Pellet, Mr. Yamada.

Fragmentation of international law: difficulties arising from the diversification and expansion of international law (*concluded*)* (A/CN.4/L.676 and Corr.1, and A/CN.4/549, sect. E)

[Agenda item 9]

1. Mr. CHEE said he had taken the floor to endorse the conclusions reached by Mr. Koskenniemi and Professor Päivi Leino in an article which had appeared in the Leiden Journal of International Law in 2002 under the title "Fragmentation of international law? Postmodern anxieties"[1],

---

* Resumed from the discussions at the 2860th meeting.

[1] Vol. 15, No. 3 (2002), pp. 553–579.

in which the authors discussed the effects of the proliferation of international courts. In the article they noted that two judges of the ICJ, Judge Schwebel and Judge Guillaume, had expressed their concern that such a development might affect the unity of international law, by leading to conflicts between the Court's judgments and those of other international tribunals, such as the International Criminal Tribunal for the former Yugoslavia, the International Criminal Court and WTO panels.

2. However, institutional fragmentation need not affect the continuity and unity of international law. In *The Development of International Law by the International Court*, Judge Hersch Lauterpacht had pointed out that the ICJ, by its nature as a court of law, would continue to play its role through the practice of referrals to the Court, notwithstanding the provisions of article 59 of its Statute, and that, pursuant to article 38, paragraph 1 (*d*), of the Statute, the Court was also to apply judicial decisions as subsidiary means for the determination of rules of law.[2] The weight of past decisions of international courts and awards of international arbitral tribunals would constitute a bulwark of international jurisprudence in the future.

3. Mr. ECONOMIDES, speaking on a point of clarification, said he had several times been criticized for distinguishing between "good" and "bad" fragmentation. All rules of international law, whether customary, conventional or institutional, other than rules of *jus cogens*, to which *lex specialis* did not apply, could be fragmented. Such fragmentation could, in his view, be positive in cases where it strengthened an international rule, or negative, in cases where it weakened that rule.

4. Mr. KOSKENNIEMI (Chairperson of the Study Group) said that it was perhaps unnecessary to draw conclusions at the present juncture. The Bureau had thought it useful to set aside the present meeting for discussion of the topic of fragmentation, as the last opportunity at the present session for members to provide input to the study to be produced by the Study Group. As the study would be rather substantial and lengthy, and as it would not be possible for the Commission to discuss it in its entirety at the next session, he had wanted to give members a chance to address some of its aspects at the current session.

5. Members appeared broadly to have endorsed the work of the Study Group and the direction it had taken. The five studies referred to in his briefing note had not been the subject of any detailed debate; indeed, it had not been his intention to hold such a debate at the present stage.

6. As Chairperson of the Study Group, he was pleased that it would be possible to continue the preparation of the substantive study and the conclusions in the period between the two sessions, on the basis of work done to date. The necessary documents would be available at the beginning of the fifty-eighth session for perusal and comment by members, so that conclusions could be adopted as early as possible.

7. There being no need for any detailed reflection on what had after all been a rather short debate, he proposed that the meeting should be suspended to enable the Study Group to convene and spend the remainder of the meeting dealing with other matters on its agenda.

8. The CHAIRPERSON said he took it that Mr. Koskenniemi's proposal was acceptable to the Commission.

It was so agreed.

The meeting rose at 3.20 p.m.

2865th MEETING

Thursday, 4 August 2005, at 10.05 a.m.

Chairperson: Mr. Djamchid MOMTAZ

Present: Mr. Addo, Mr. Al-Baharna, Mr. Al-Marri, Mr. Brownlie, Mr. Candioti, Mr. Chee, Mr. Comissário Afonso, Mr. Dugard, Mr. Economides, Ms. Escarameia, Mr. Fomba, Mr. Gaja, Mr. Galicki, Mr. Kabatsi, Mr. Kateka, Mr. Kolodkin, Mr. Koskenniemi, Mr. Mansfield, Mr. Matheson, Mr. Niehaus, Mr. Pambou-Tchivounda, Mr. Pellet, Mr. Sreenivasa Rao, Mr. Rodríguez Cedeño, Mr. Yamada.

Draft report of the International Law Commission on the work of its fifty-seventh session (*continued*)*

Chapter IX. ***Unilateral acts of states*** **(*concluded*)* (A/CN.4/L.672 and Add.1–2)**

B. Consideration of the topic at the present session (A/CN.4/L.672/Add.1)

1. The CHAIRPERSON invited the members of the Commission to resume consideration of chapter IX of the draft report of the Commission, on unilateral acts of States.

Paragraph 25

2. Mr. PELLET proposed adding to the word "identify" in the second sentence the phrase "the legal regime applicable to" and, in the last line, amending the word "freedoms" to read "freedom of action".

Paragraph 25, as amended, was adopted.

Paragraph 26

3. Mr. RODRÍGUEZ CEDEÑO (Special Rapporteur) drew attention to the first sentence and proposed that the word "political" should be deleted and that the word "legal" should be inserted before the word "obligations".

4. Mr. PAMBOU-TCHIVOUNDA proposed that the words "enter into obligations" in the first sentence should be replaced with "undertake commitments", which would make the word "legal" unnecessary, and that the words "and their legal regime" should be added at the end of the last sentence.

[2] London, Stevens and Sons, 1958.

* Resumed from the discussions at the 2863rd meeting.

5. Mr. RODRÍGUEZ CEDEÑO (Special Rapporteur) insisted that the word "legal" was important, as it made it clear that the provision did not apply to all acts. As to the second sentence, he saw no reason to add the words "and their legal regime", since there was a reference to that effect in the preceding paragraph; paragraph 26 dealt only with identification.

6. Mr. PELLET noted that, in the light of the amendment that had been made to paragraph 25, the word "freedoms" in the first sentence should be amended to read "freedom to act".

7. The CHAIRPERSON suggested that the Commission should adopt the paragraph with the first sentence amended to read: "When taking States' freedom to act into consideration, it went without saying that there were acts by which States did not intend to enter into legal obligations" and with the words "and of their regime" added at the end of the paragraph.

Paragraph 26, as amended, was adopted.

Paragraph 27

8. Mr. ECONOMIDES noted that the two sentences were contradictory and proposed that the words "most often" should be inserted before the word "resulted" in the first sentence and that the second sentence should be redrafted to read: "In fact, the 'bilateralization' of an act could in some cases have nothing to do with treaty relations."

9. Mr. PELLET said that the words "most often" reflected a statistical position that changed the meaning; he proposed that the word "resulted" should be replaced with the words "could result".

10. Mr. BROWNLIE endorsed Mr. Pellet's proposal, although he did not think it would be enough to resolve the contradiction that had been pointed out.

11. Mr. RODRÍGUEZ CEDEÑO (Special Rapporteur) explained that the fact that a relationship became bilateral did not necessarily mean that it derived from a conventional act, even if the State acquired rights arising from its acceptance of the obligation; consequently, a distinction must be made between "bilateralization" and the conventional nature of an act. He proposed that the paragraph should be amended to read: "The fact that the formulation of a unilateral act established a relationship with another State or States did not mean that the act was necessarily a conventional act."

12. Mr. PAMBOU-TCHIVOUNDA proposed that the second sentence should be amended to read: "However, such 'bilateralization' of a unilateral act was not always of a conventional nature": that would highlight the difference between the two sentences.

13. Mr. GALICKI, speaking on a point of order, recalled that the conclusions were those of the Special Rapporteur, and that only he was authorized to make substantive changes.

14. Mr. BROWNLIE, supported by Mr. ECONOMIDES and Mr. CHEE, endorsed the proposal made by the Special Rapporteur.

Paragraph 27, as amended by Mr. Rodríguez Cedeño, was adopted.

Paragraph 28

15. Mr. PELLET proposed that the word "*possible*" should be replaced with the words "*préférable*" in the French version.

Paragraph 28 was adopted, with a minor drafting change to the French version.

Paragraph 29

Paragraph 29 was adopted.

Paragraph 30

16. Mr. PELLET said that the examples given in parentheses were poorly chosen, as it was important to make a distinction between obligations on the one hand and renunciation and recognition on the other. He therefore proposed that the word "obligations" should be replaced by "promises".

Paragraph 30, as amended, was adopted.

Paragraph 31

17. Mr. PELLET proposed that the word "Conventions" should be amended to "Convention" and, in the French text, the words "*au vu de*" amended to "*étant donné*".

Paragraph 31, as amended, was adopted.

Paragraphs 32 to 34

Paragraphs 32 to 34 were adopted.

18. The CHAIRPERSON invited the Commission to consider document A/CN.4/L.672/Add.2.

Paragraph 1

19. Mr. BROWNLIE asked why the composition of the Working Group was not shown in the report.

20. The CHAIRPERSON explained that the Working Group was open-ended and that there was thus no reason to list the names of those who had participated in its work.

Paragraph 1 was adopted.

Paragraphs 2 to 4

Paragraphs 2 to 4 were adopted.

Paragraph 5

21. Mr. GAJA proposed that the words "was likely to" in the first sentence should be replaced with the word "could". He also proposed that the phrase "whatever form they might take" should be deleted or reworded, and that the second part of the sentence should be amended to read

"it was possible, although often difficult in practice, to draw a distinction between unilateral conduct and unilateral acts *stricto sensu*".

22. Mr. ECONOMIDES said that he could accept Mr. Gaja's amendments in principle; however, the way in which he had reworded the second part of the first sentence introduced a substantive change. In his view, what was important was to indicate that such a distinction was possible.

23. Mr. MANSFIELD recalled that he had been one of those who had found it very difficult to make such a distinction in practice. He proposed that vaguer wording should be adopted, with the second part of the sentence reworded to read: "it would attempt to produce provisional conclusions in relation to unilateral acts *stricto sensu*". However, the wording proposed by Mr. Gaja was entirely acceptable.

24. Mr. PELLET said that the wording proposed by Mr. Mansfield had the merit of not distorting the content of the Working Group's efforts.

25. Mr. RODRÍGUEZ CEDEÑO (Special Rapporteur) said that he would prepare draft conclusions which the Working Group could consider.

Paragraph 5, as amended, was adopted.

Paragraph 6

26. Mr. PAMBOU-TCHIVOUNDA pointed out that the paragraph referred to "these principles", when no principles had been mentioned earlier.

27. The CHAIRPERSON suggested that the word "these" should be deleted and that the word "can" should be amended to "could".

28. Mr. ECONOMIDES, returning to the question of the distinction between unilateral conduct and unilateral acts *stricto sensu*, said that he saw a way out of the Commission's deadlock. Priority should be given to unilateral acts *stricto sensu*, while indicating that the principles in question would have to do with unilateral acts.

29. The CHAIRPERSON noted that the report was that of the Working Group, and the Commission would have to limit itself to what had actually been said during the Group's debates.

30. Mr. PELLET said that ambiguity was sometimes a good thing. The Commission should be careful not to be too categorical, for while the Working Group had agreed to focus on formal acts, they should not be given priority. His preference would be to accept Mr. Mansfield's proposal, for the wording proposed by Mr. Economides was too "strong", to his way of thinking.

31. Mr. MATHESON said that Mr. Pambou-Tchivounda had been right to question the use of the word "principles". Paragraph 5 contained references to question and conclusions, but said nothing about principles. It would therefore be better to use one of those terms.

32. Mr. CHEE agreed with Mr. Pambou-Tchivounda and said that it was necessary to specify which principles were meant.

33. Mr. PELLET said that the Working Group had spoken of applicable principles and provisional conclusions. He proposed that the words "as necessary" should be inserted after the words "Special Rapporteur".

34. The CHAIRPERSON suggested that the words "these principles" should be replaced with "provisional conclusions".

It was so agreed.

Paragraph 6, as amended, was adopted.

Section B, as amended, was adopted.

Chapter IX of the report of the Commission as a whole was adopted, as amended.

CHAPTER X. *Reservations to treaties* (A/CN.4/L.671 and Add.1–2 and Corr.1)

35. The CHAIRPERSON invited the Commission to consider chapter X of the draft report of the Commission (A/CN.4/L.671).

A. Introduction

Paragraphs 1 to 10 were adopted.

Section A was adopted.

C. Text of draft guidelines on reservations to treaties provisionally adopted so far by the Commission

Paragraph 11

Paragraph 11 was adopted.

36. The CHAIRPERSON invited the Commission to consider document A/CN.4/L.671/Add.2.

Guideline 2.6 (Formulation of objections to reservations)

Paragraphs (1) and (2)

Paragraphs (1) and (2) of the commentary were adopted.

Guideline 2.6.1 (Definition of objections to reservations)

Paragraphs (1) to (9) of the commentary were adopted.

Paragraph (10)

37. Mr. GAJA said that the second part of the first sentence was awkward and should be amended. He therefore proposed that it should read: "which envisages that the author of the objection may indicate whether it opposes the entry into force of the treaty between it and the author of the reservation".

Paragraph (10), as amended, was adopted.

Paragraph (11)

Paragraph (11) was adopted.

Paragraph (12)

38. Mr. PELLET (Special Rapporteur) said that the title of the study by Pierre-Henri Imbert, cited in a footnote, should be rendered in full by inserting the words "*du 30 juin 1977*" after the words "*décision arbitrale*".

Paragraph (12) was adopted, with the above-mentioned minor drafting change in the French version.

Paragraphs (13) and (14)

Paragraphs (13) and (14) were adopted.

Paragraph (15)

39. Mr. GAJA proposed that the word "reservations" in the clause in the text immediately following the footnote marker should be replaced with the word "statements".

Paragraph (15), as amended, was adopted.

Paragraphs (16) to (18)

Paragraphs (16) to (18) were adopted.

Paragraph (19)

40. Mr. GAJA proposed that the words "other reactions, of the same type" in the first sentence should be amended to read "reactions of the type mentioned above".

Paragraph (19), as amended, was adopted.

Paragraphs (20) to (22)

Paragraphs (20) to (22) were adopted.

Paragraph (23)

41. Mr. GAJA proposed that the words "to be associated" should be replaced with the words "to enter treaty relations" and that the words "exclusion of treaty relations" should be replaced with "effect of the reservation".

Paragraph (23), as amended, was adopted.

Paragraph (24)

Paragraph (24) was adopted.

Paragraph (25)

42. Mr. ECONOMIDES noted that the Special Rapporteur reserved the position of the Commission with regard to the validity of objections producing a "super-maximum" effect; it should also reserve its position on the validity of objections producing an intermediate effect. Accordingly, he proposed that the beginning of the paragraph should be amended to read: "The Commission is aware that the validity of the objections mentioned in paragraphs 23 and 24 has sometimes been questioned".

43. Mr. PELLET (Special Rapporteur) said that he would prefer to retain the first sentence as drafted and replace the words "this 'super-maximum' effect" in the second sentence with "such intermediate or 'super-maximum' effects".

44. Mr. MATHESON proposed that the word "sometimes" should be deleted from the first sentence and that the final sentence of the first footnote should be moved to the end of the paragraph.

Paragraph (25), as amended, was adopted.

Paragraph (26)

45. Mr. GAJA proposed that the word "not" should be inserted after the words "and even" in the second sentence.

Paragraph (26), as amended, was adopted.

Paragraph (27)

Paragraph (27) was adopted.

Guideline 2.6.2 (Definition of objections to the late formulation or widening of the scope of a reservation)

Paragraphs (1) to (4)

Paragraphs (1) to (4) were adopted.

Section C, as amended, was adopted.

CHAPTER XI. *Fragmentation of international law: difficulties arising from the diversification and expansion of international law* (A/CN.4/ L.676 and Corr.1 and A/CN.4/L.677)

46. The CHAIRPERSON invited the Commission to consider document A/CN.4/L.677.

A. Introduction

B. Consideration of the topic at the present session

Paragraphs 1 to 6

Paragraphs 1 to 6 were adopted.

Sections A and B were adopted.

C. Report of the Study Group (A/CN.4/676 and Corr.1)

47. Mr. ECONOMIDES said that he would like to be mentioned by name in paragraph 23 of the report of the Study Group on Fragmentation of international law, which contained a reference to "one of its members", so that no one would think that he had wished to remain anonymous.

48. Mr. MIKULKA (Secretary to the Commission) said that as the document was an informal one, it was not the practice of the Commission to mention individuals by name; however, he saw no problem in doing so if that was the wish of the Study Group.

49. Mr. KOSKENNIEMI (Chairperson of the Study Group) said that he had no set opinion on the matter.

50. The CHAIRPERSON said that Mr. Economides would be referred to by name in paragraph 23 of the report of the Study Group.

51. The CHAIRPERSON said that it was his understanding that the Commission wished to take note of the report of the Study Group on Fragmentation of international law (A/CN.4/L.676 and Corr.1).

It was so decided.

Section C, as amended, was adopted.

Chapter XI of the draft report of the Commission as a whole, as amended, was adopted.

CHAPTER XII. *Other decisions and conclusions of the Commission* (A/CN.4/L.678)

A. Programme, procedures and working methods of the Commission and its documentation [paras. 1–8]

B. Date and place of the fifty-eighth session of the Commission [para. 9]

Paragraphs 1 to 9

Paragraphs 1 to 9 were adopted.

Sections A and B were adopted.

C. Cooperation with other bodies

Paragraph 10

52. Ms. ESCARAMEIA proposed that Ms. Villalta Vizcaya's title should be indicated, as had been done in the case of the other visitors mentioned in the report.

Paragraph 10, as amended, was adopted.

Paragraphs 11 and 12

Paragraphs 11 and 12 were adopted.

Paragraph 13

53. Ms. ESCARAMEIA proposed that Mr. Guy de Vel's title should be indicated.

Paragraph 13, as amended, was adopted.

Paragraph 14

54. Mr. BROWNLIE said that the word "of" should be inserted before the word "responsibility".

Paragraph 14, as amended, was adopted.

Paragraph 15

Paragraph 15 was adopted.

55. Mr. PELLET proposed that a new paragraph 15 *bis* should be inserted indicating that on 4 August 2005 an informal exchange of views on issues of mutual interest, and in particular on the topic "Reservations to treaties", had been held between the members of the Commission and the members of the Sub-Commission on the Promotion and Protection of Human Rights.

New paragraph 15 bis *was adopted.*

Paragraph 16

Paragraph 16 was adopted.

Paragraph 17

56. The CHAIRPERSON said he would take it that the Commission wished to adopt paragraph 17 with the text completed to read: "Moreover, at its 2865th meeting, on 4 August 2005, the Commission requested Mr. Brownlie, Special Rapporteur on the topic 'Effects of armed conflicts on treaties', to attend the sixtieth session of the General Assembly under the terms of paragraph 5 of General Assembly resolution 44/35."

Paragraph 17, as amended, was adopted.

Paragraphs 18 to 30

Paragraphs 18 to 30 were adopted.

Section C, as amended, was adopted.

Chapter XII of the draft report of the Commission as a whole was adopted.

CHAPTER I. *Introduction* (A/CN.4/L.673)

57. The CHAIRPERSON invited the Commission to consider chapter I of the draft report of the Commission (A/CN.4/L.673).

Paragraphs 1 to 11

Paragraphs 1 to 11 were adopted.

Chapter I as a whole was adopted.

Chapter II. *Summary of the work of the Commission at its fifty-seventh session* (A/CN.4/L.679)

58. The CHAIRPERSON invited the Commission to consider chapter II of the draft report of the Commission

Paragraph 1

59. Mr. GAJA said that a sentence should be added at the end of the paragraph to indicate what the Working Group had actually done during the session.

60. The CHAIRPERSON said that the Commission secretariat would attend to the matter.

Paragraph 1 was adopted.

Paragraph 2

61. Mr. PELLET said that the last sentence of the paragraph was not consistent with the facts: the Commission had not approved the Special Rapporteur's proposal to prepare a questionnaire for circulation to Member States.

62. Mr. BROWNLIE (Special Rapporteur on the topic of Effects of armed conflicts on treaties) said that it was not a questionnaire that was involved, but a written request for information; he believed that the problem was one of translation.

63. The CHAIRPERSON said that the French and Spanish versions would be aligned with the English text.

Paragraph 2 was adopted.

Paragraph 3

64. Mr. PELLET said that the words "and the commentaries thereto" should be inserted after the words "nine draft articles" and also after the words "two draft guidelines" in paragraph 7.

Paragraph 3, as amended, was adopted.

Paragraphs 4 to 6

Paragraphs 4 to 6 were adopted.

Paragraph 7

65. Mr. PELLET said that the words "part of" should be inserted after the word "considered" in the first sentence.

Paragraph 7, as amended, was adopted.

Paragraph 8

66. Mr. KOSKENNIEMI (Chairperson of the Study Group on Fragmentation of international law) said that the words "preliminary reports" in the second sentence should be replaced with the words "final report" and that a full stop should be inserted after the words "conflict rules" in the same sentence. The following sentence should be amended to begin: "The Study Group also received the final report on the Study concerning the modification ...". In addition, he proposed that a sentence should be added at the end of the paragraph, which would read: "The Study Group decided to submit a consolidated study and a set of conclusions, guidelines or principles to the fifty-eighth session of the Commission (2006)."

67. Mr. GAJA asked whether it was wise to announce so categorically what the Study Group intended to do the following year.

68. Mr. MANSFIELD, addressing Mr. Gaja's comment, suggested that the wording proposed by Mr. Koskenniemi should be reworded to read: "The Study Group considered that it would be in a position to submit a consolidated study ...".

Paragraph 8, as amended, was adopted.

Paragraph 9

Paragraph 9 was adopted.

Paragraph 10

69. Mr. ECONOMIDES said that for the sake of clarity the words "of the Council of Europe" should be inserted after the words "Public International Law".

Paragraph 10, as amended, was adopted.

Paragraphs 11 and 12

Paragraphs 11 and 12 were adopted.

Chapter II as a whole was adopted, as amended.

The meeting rose at 1.05 p.m.

2866th MEETING

Friday, 5 August 2005, at 10.05 a.m.

Chairperson: Mr. Djamchid MOMTAZ

Present: Mr. Addo, Mr. Al-Baharna, Mr. Al-Marri, Mr. Brownlie, Mr. Candioti, Mr. Chee, Mr. Comissário Afonso, Mr. Dugard, Mr. Economides, Ms. Escarameia, Mr. Fomba, Mr. Gaja, Mr. Galicki, Mr. Kateka, Mr. Kolodkin, Mr. Koskenniemi, Mr. Mansfield, Mr. Matheson, Mr. Niehaus, Mr. Pambou-Tchivounda, Mr. Pellet, Mr. Sreenivasa Rao, Mr. Yamada.

Draft report of the Commission on the work of its fifty-seventh session (*concluded*)

Chapter X. ***Reservations to treaties* (*concluded*) (A/CN.4/L.671 and Add.1–2 and Corr.1)**

1. The CHAIRPERSON invited the Commission to resume its consideration of chapter X of the draft report and drew attention in that connection to the portion of the chapter contained in document A/CN.4/L.671/Add.1.

B. Consideration of the topic at the current session

Paragraphs 1 to 7

Paragraphs 1 to 7 were adopted.

1. Introduction by the Special Rapporteur of his tenth report

Paragraphs 8 to 10

Paragraphs 8 to 10 were adopted.

Paragraph 11

2. Mr. PAMBOU-TCHIVOUNDA drew attention to the French text and said that the words "*Se tournant vers*" in the first sentence should be modified.

Paragraph 11 was adopted.

Paragraphs 12 to 14

Paragraphs 12 to 14 were adopted.

Paragraph 15

3. Mr. GAJA said that the words “permissibility/impermissibility” in the English text should be replaced by “lawfulness/unlawfulness”.

4. Mr. PELLET (Special Rapporteur) said that in the draft guideline, the French word “*licéité*” had been translated as “permissibility”. It would therefore be preferable to reword the beginning of the English text to read: “Furthermore, the French terms ‘*licéité/illicéité*’ could be misleading.”

5. Mr. GAJA said that his preference had been for the terms “lawfulness/unlawfulness” because responsibility was linked not to an impermissible act but to an unlawful one; however, if Mr. Pellet insisted on retaining the words “permissibility/ impermissibility” in the English text, the French words “*licéité/illicéité*” could be added in square brackets.

6. Mr. PELLET (Special Rapporteur) said that he did not insist on retaining the phrase “the terms ‘permissibility/impermissibility’”; on the contrary, he proposed replacing it by “the French terms ‘*licéité/illicéité*’”. For the sake of clarity, it should perhaps even read “Furthermore, the French terms ‘*licéité/illicéité*’, which are translated in the English text as ‘permissibility/impermissibility’ could be misleading.”

Paragraph 15, as amended, was adopted.

Paragraph 16

Paragraph 16 was adopted.

Paragraph 17

7. Mr. GAJA said that the word “*faculté*” in the second sentence of the French text should be rendered in the English text as “freedom” and not “power”.

Paragraph 17, as amended, was adopted.

Paragraph 18

Paragraph 18 was adopted.

Paragraph 19

8. Mr. GAJA said that, as in paragraph 17, the word “*faculté*” should again be translated as “freedom” and not “power”. He also proposed inserting the word “himself” after “asked” in the first sentence of the English text in order to bring it into line with the French text.

9. Mr. BROWNLIE proposed replacing the word “asked” by “considered”.

Paragraph 19, as amended, was adopted.

Paragraph 20

Paragraph 20 was adopted.

Paragraph 21

10. Mr. GAJA said that the word “since” in the penultimate sentence of the English text was an incorrect rendering of the French text and should be replaced by the word “although”.

Paragraph 21, as amended, was adopted.

Paragraphs 22 to 28

Paragraphs 22 to 28 were adopted.

Paragraph 29

11. Mr. GAJA pointed out that the word “text” in the final sentence should read “test”. In addition, the end of that sentence, beginning with the phrase “the same was true of a specified reservation”, was unclear. He proposed replacing the semicolon after the words “the object and purpose of the treaty” with a full stop, deleting the words “the same was true of a specified reservation” and starting a new sentence, which would read: “As they were expressly authorized by the treaty, specified reservations were automatically valid and were not subject to the test of compatibility with the object and purpose of the treaty.”

12. Mr. PELLET (Special Rapporteur) said that he did not see the point of Mr. Gaja’s proposal. In his view, both the French text and the English translation faithfully reflected what he had said.

13. Mr. GAJA assured the Special Rapporteur that his intention was not to make a substantive change in the text but merely to propose clearer wording.

Paragraph 29, as amended, was adopted.

Paragraphs 30 to 32

Paragraphs 30 to 32 were adopted.

Paragraph 33

14. Mr. GAJA suggested deleting the word “nevertheless”, which did not make sense in the context.

15. Mr. PAMBOU-TCHIVOUNDA, referring to the second sentence, said that it might be inconsistent to speak of a “notion” on the one hand and “concepts” on the other.

16. Mr. PELLET (Special Rapporteur) said that in his view the two terms were synonymous; the phrase should be left as it stood.

Paragraph 33, as amended, was adopted.

Paragraphs 34 to 37

Paragraphs 34 to 37 were adopted.

Paragraph 38

17. Mr. PAMBOU-TCHIVOUNDA drew attention to the French text and proposed replacing the words “*Se tournant*” in the first sentence with “*En ce qui concerne.*”

Paragraph 38, as amended, was adopted.

Paragraph 39

Paragraph 39 was adopted.

Paragraph 40

18. Mr. PAMBOU-TCHIVOUNDA said that in the footnote to paragraph 40 of the French text, the word "*traits*" should be replaced by "*traités*".

Paragraph 40, as amended, was adopted.

Paragraph 41

19. Mr. GAJA said that the word "affirmative" in the second sentence of the English text should be replaced by "categorical", to bring it into line with the French text.

Paragraph 41, as amended, was adopted.

Paragraph 42

Paragraph 42 was adopted.

Paragraph 43

20. The CHAIRPERSON said that the word "*objections*" in the third sentence of the French text should be replaced by "*réserves*".

21. Mr. GAJA said that, in order to make the English text consistent with the amended French text the words "also objected" in the third sentence should be replaced by "made reservations". On a purely editorial matter, he said that the word "to" after "embodying" in the first sentence should be deleted.

22. In order to make the second sentence more understandable, he proposed rewording it to read "States made reservations to such provisions chiefly in order to avoid the consequences of 'conventionalization' of the customary rule."

Paragraph 43, as amended, was adopted.

Paragraphs 44 to 46

Paragraphs 44 to 46 were adopted.

2. Summary of the debate

Paragraph 47

Paragraph 47 was adopted.

Paragraph 48

23. Mr. ECONOMIDES said that the statement made in the last sentence was premature, since the Commission had not yet considered the consequences of invalidity; moreover, he had doubts as to the statement's accuracy. If the last sentence was retained, a further sentence should be added to indicate the existence of an opposing view.

24. Mr. GAJA suggested deleting the last sentence, which was not clear in the context. To make the second sentence more understandable, he proposed redrafting it after the word "reservation" to read "generally affected the ratification of the treaty itself, which would also be invalid".

25. Mr. CANDIOTI said that it was not clear whether the term "invalidity" referred to ratification or to the treaty. Deleting the word "itself" might dispel the ambiguity.

26. Mr. PELLET (Special Rapporteur) said that the French text was acceptable as it stood.

27. Mr. GAJA said that while the French text was clear, it was somewhat weak and should therefore be amended along the lines of the text he had proposed for the English text.

28. Mr. MANSFIELD said that the proposition in the second sentence could be succinctly stated: "At the same time, the invalidity of a reservation generally invalidated the ratification of the treaty itself."

Paragraph 48, as amended, was adopted.

Paragraph 49

29. Mr. GAJA said that the word "achievement" at the end of the third sentence was unclear, and he proposed replacing it with "completion".

Paragraph 49, as amended, was adopted.

Paragraph 50

30. Mr. GAJA said that the spelling of the Latin word "ratione" should be corrected in the English text. On a more substantive point, the word "power" should be replaced by "freedom", as elsewhere in the text.

Paragraph 50, as amended, was adopted.

Paragraph 51

31. Mr. PAMBOU-TCHIVOUNDA said that the words "de la pratique" should be inserted after the word "Guide" in the French text.

Paragraph 51 was adopted, with a drafting change to the French version.

Paragraphs 52 to 57

Paragraphs 52 to 57 were adopted.

Paragraph 58

32. Mr. GAJA again requested correction of the spelling of the word "ratione" in the English text and suggested that the word "text" in the third sentence should be replaced by "draft guidelines" for the sake of clarity.

33. Ms. ESCARAMEIA suggested the inclusion of a new sentence that would read: "It was pointed out that article 19 of the Vienna Conventions established, at the most, a presumption of freedom to formulate reservations, which was substantively different from the presumption of validity of reservations."

Paragraph 58, as amended, was adopted.

Paragraph 59

34. Mr. ECONOMIDES said that a sentence should be inserted at the end of the paragraph to reflect his own contribution to the debate. Such a sentence might read: "Another opinion held that the title that best corresponded to the content of article 19 was 'Limitations on the formulation of reservations'".

35. Mr. PELLET (Special Rapporteur) said that while he had no problem with that proposal, it sounded a bit odd to speak of limitations on formulation. It would be preferable to say "Limitations on the freedom to formulate reservations".

36. Mr. PAMBOU-TCHIVOUNDA said that he could accept the amendment proposed by Mr. Economides but suggested replacing the phrase "best corresponded" with "might best correspond" to make the statement less categorical.

Paragraph 59, as amended, was adopted.

Paragraph 60

37. Mr. GAJA said that the words "their very nature" in the second sentence should be replaced by "implication". The sentence should end after the words "United Nations".

38. Mr. MATHESON suggested that a new sentence should be inserted at the end of the paragraph to reflect what he had said during the debate. It would read: "Others took the view that this guideline should be limited to express prohibitions."

39. Mr. ECONOMIDES said that in the fourth sentence the words "and vice versa" should be deleted.

Paragraph 60, as amended, was adopted.

Paragraph 61

Paragraph 61 was adopted.

Paragraph 62

40. Ms. ESCARAMEIA said that in the final sentence the words "part of the" should be inserted between "last" and "sentence".

41. Mr. GAJA said that the words "the Commission" in the first sentence should be replaced by "according to article 19, subparagraph (*b*), of the Vienna Convention, one".

42. Mr. PELLET said that the French text made no reference to the Commission.

43. Mr. GAJA agreed that the French text accurately reflected the view he had expressed in the debate; however, there would be no harm in inserting the reference to article 19, subparagraph (*b*), in the French text as well.

Paragraph 62, as amended, was adopted.

Paragraph 63

Paragraph 63 was adopted.

Paragraph 64

44. Mr. GAJA suggested the insertion of the word "also" before "expressly".

Paragraph 64, as amended, was adopted.

Paragraphs 65 to 68

Paragraphs 65 to 68 were adopted.

Paragraph 69

45. Ms. ESCARAMEIA proposed the insertion of a new second sentence to reflect comments that she had made, which would read: "This term was also seen by others as very restrictive, leading to the result that only very few reservations would actually be prohibited."

46. Mr. GAJA said that, in the final sentence, the words "two terms" should be replaced by "terms 'object' and 'purpose'". The sentence should be split into two after the word "separated". The words "in fact" should be deleted, and the words "the opposite" replaced by "vice versa".

Paragraph 69, as amended, was adopted.

Paragraphs 70 to 72

Paragraphs 70 to 72 were adopted.

Paragraph 73

47. Mr. KOSKENNIEMI said that the entire paragraph, which reflected a comment he had made, should be replaced by the following sentence: "It was pointed out that it might be useful to make express the rationales that the Special Rapporteur's examples sought to illustrate, namely cases where the reservation undermined either the legitimate expectations of the parties or the nature of the treaty as a common undertaking."

48. Mr. PELLET (Special Rapporteur) said that he had no objection to the content of Mr. Koskenniemi's proposal but suggested that the drafting should be improved.

Paragraph 73, as amended, was adopted.

Paragraph 74

49. Mr. GAJA said that the paragraph gave an entirely false impression of the view he had expressed during the debate. Accordingly, the words "said nothing about the important role of" should be amended to read "gave an important role to".

Paragraph 74, as amended, was adopted.

Paragraph 75

Paragraph 75 was adopted.

Paragraph 76

50. Mr. GAJA said that, in the first sentence, the words "the question covered in" should be inserted after "approach" and the words "sought to" replaced by "could be said to intend to".

51. Mr. PELLET (Special Rapporteur) said that in the French text the word "*et*" should be inserted between "*vagues*" and "*généraux*".

Paragraph 76, as amended, was adopted.

Paragraph 77

Paragraph 77 was adopted.

Paragraph 78

52. Mr. ECONOMIDES, supported by Ms. ESCARAMEIA, suggested that the paragraph should be broken into two. The first paragraph would consist of a single sentence, as did paragraph 77 and would read: "Several members supported draft guideline 3.1.9". The actual view reflected in the remainder of paragraph 78 should form a new paragraph, which would immediately follow.

Paragraph 78, as amended, was adopted.

Paragraphs 79 to 82

Paragraphs 79 to 82 were adopted.

Paragraph 83

53. Mr. MATHESON suggested the insertion of a phrase at the end of the paragraph, to read: "and in the meantime reserved their position with respect to the issues raised by this section of the report".

Paragraph 83, as amended, was adopted.

3. Conclusions of the Special Rapporteur

Paragraph 84

Paragraph 84 was adopted.

Paragraph 85

54. Mr. PELLET (Special Rapporteur) drew attention to the second sentence and suggested the deletion of the word "still" and the phrase "which was through the solid corpus that was the Guide to Practice".

Paragraph 85, as amended, was adopted.

Paragraphs 86 to 88

Paragraphs 86 to 88 were adopted.

Paragraph 89

55. Mr. PELLET suggested that the words "on the fact" should be inserted after the word "agreed".

Paragraph 89, as amended, was adopted.

Paragraph 90

Paragraph 90 was adopted.

Paragraph 91

56. Mr. MATHESON drew attention to a typographical error in the English numbering of the draft guidelines.

Paragraph 91 was adopted, with a drafting change to the English version.

Paragraphs 92 to 93

Paragraphs 92 to 93 were adopted.

Section B as a whole, as amended, was adopted.

Chapter X as a whole, as amended, was adopted.

Chapter III. ***Specific issues on which comments would be of particular interest to the Commission*** **(A/CN.4/L.680)**

Shared natural resources

Paragraph 1

Paragraph 1 was adopted.

Effects of armed conflicts on treaties

Paragraph 2

57. Mr. ECONOMIDES suggested that an additional question should be included to reflect an issue that had been discussed extensively by the Commission: "Can the topic be addressed without taking into account the Charter of the United Nations and, in particular, the distinction between the use of force and self-defence?"

58. Ms. ESCARAMEIA said that there were in fact two points on which there had been much discussion that were not reflected in the list of questions. The first was the point raised by Mr. Economides, although she would have preferred the question to read: "What are the consequences for the topic of compliance or non-compliance with the rules of the Charter of the United Nations on the use of force?"

59. The second point concerned the criterion for distinguishing between different regimes in the light of the emphasis placed by the Special Rapporteur on the intention of the parties to a treaty. She therefore suggested that a second question should be added to the list, which would read: "What would be the best criterion for distinguishing between different regimes of effects on treaties in the case of armed conflict?"

60. The CHAIRPERSON questioned whether all points raised during the Commission's debate needed to be reflected in the list of questions addressed to Governments represented on the Sixth Committee.

61. Mr. BROWNLIE (Special Rapporteur) said that the list of questions had been distributed some time previously and he would have expected members to propose any amendments to it before the current meeting. He was very surprised by the Commission's continued obsession with

the relevance of the provisions of the Charter on the use of force, particularly since it had been made clear when the topic had originally been formulated that it would not involve a codification of those principles. If a question along the lines suggested by Mr. Economides should be addressed to the Sixth Committee, it would undoubtedly prompt a negative reaction.

62. Furthermore, the Secretariat had considered that it was premature to transmit the very detailed list of questions he had drawn up to Governments. It had therefore prepared the simplified list of questions based on his first report (A/CN.4/552), on the understanding that more substantive questions would be formulated the following year when the Commission embarked on its first reading of the draft articles. It might have been more appropriate to entitle his first report a "preliminary report". At the present juncture, the intent was to obtain information on State practice, which, together with the Commission's comments on the topic during the current session, would form the basis of his second report.

63. Mr. PELLET said that the discussion under way raised a matter of principle, since the list of questions did not fully reflect the Commission's debate on the topic. Moreover, while the list might well have been distributed in advance, the Commission had not had an opportunity to discuss it. He agreed with Ms. Escarameia that the two key issues that had given rise to some controversy were not included in the list. The first had to do with the consequences for the topic of compliance with the provisions of the Charter of the United Nations concerning the prohibition of the use of force, and despite the Special Rapporteur's assurances some members were still confused by the absence of any reference to that question in the first report. The second issue concerned the intention of the parties, a concept on which the first report was essentially based. He had considerable reservations regarding that approach, a feeling shared by several other members, and it was therefore only logical that those two issues should be referred to the Sixth Committee.

64. He supported the basic thrust of Mr. Economides' proposal, although perhaps not the wording, and suggested that the new question should most logically be placed at the top of the list as subparagraph (*a*). He also endorsed the intent of Ms. Escarameia's second proposal, but suggested that the question should read: "Should the intention expressed by the parties to a treaty be the criterion on which the draft article should be based?" Lastly, he questioned the need for the word "comprehensively" in subparagraph (*b*).

65. Mr. KOSKENNIEMI said that paragraph 2 posed a problem of principle as well as a more practical one. The problem of principle lay in the fact that the Commission was still in the early stages of its consideration of the topic, and the usefulness of seeking the views of Governments on issues that might eventually be resolved through further discussion was questionable. The question of the relevance of the provisions of the Charter of the Untied Nations relating to the use of force was still open, and he doubted that Governments would be able to propose any useful solutions.

66. Turning to the more practical problem of the wording of the proposed new questions, he said that there could be no doubt that Governments would say that the provisions relating to the use of force must be taken into account; the question was to what extent. Similarly, Governments would feel duty-bound to reply that treaties should be interpreted and applied according to the intention of the parties, yet the members of the Commission knew that the intentions of individual parties could be conflicting or difficult to determine. For those reasons he believed that questions formulated in the manner proposed would not, practically speaking, lead the Commission any further forward in its work.

67. Mr. BROWNLIE (Special Rapporteur) shared Mr. Koskenniemi's view. The purpose of the list of questions was to elicit more information on State practice, which was significantly lacking. The questions being discussed at the current meeting would be better asked after the Commission had completed a first reading of the draft articles. The questions drawn up by the Secretariat were fairly simple and would not do any harm, and he would not object to including an additional question concerning the intention of the parties, although he thought it might be premature to do so. However, it would be most inappropriate for the Commission to seek the views of Governments on the relevance of the provisions of the Charter of the United Nations. The Commission knew full well that the Charter of the United Nations was relevant, and it was not true that he had overlooked it in his report: draft article 10 concerned the use of force, and he had already explained why he had drafted the article as he had, although the members of the Commission seemed to have ignored what he had said on that point.

68. Mr. Sreenivasa RAO said that he was confused by the thrust of the debate. The Commission usually yielded to the better judgement of the Special Rapporteurs where lists of issues were concerned. In the case at hand, members who considered that their views on some of the more difficult issues were not reflected should be reassured by the fact that the summary of the debate on the topic in the Commission's report would be available to the Sixth Committee and circulated to relevant Government departments. As the Special Rapporteur had pointed out, the first report should be viewed as a preliminary report, and it would be redrafted in the light of the debate in the Commission and input from the Sixth Committee. He therefore recommended that the Commission should retain the list of questions drawn up by the Secretariat, although he would not object if any member felt strongly that further questions should be added.

69. Mr. PELLET said that the list of questions was not to his liking. The first report on the effects of armed conflicts on treaties was very general in scope and covered a wide range of issues, but the Commission's discussion had focused on only a few of them, in particular on two basic issues: the question of intent and the relevance of the provisions of the Charter of the United Nations relating to the use of force. The list of questions in the document prepared by the Secretariat could be misleading, since it addressed issues that were essentially of secondary importance and disregarded those on which the Commission was divided. There were two possible courses

of action. If the Commission decided to retain the list of questions, he would insist on the inclusion of the two additional questions proposed. Alternatively, the list of questions could be deleted and the Commission could simply request Governments to provide information on State practice. He was in favour of the latter course of action, given that the Commission was in the preliminary stages of its consideration of the topic and would not wish to have ideas imposed on it by Governments.

70. The CHAIRPERSON said that it was important not to confuse the work of the Commission with that of the Sixth Committee.

71. Mr. BROWNLIE (Special Rapporteur) endorsed Mr. Pellet's proposal, which would be in line with the Commission's general approach that reports should be based on State practice. For the time being the Commission should simply request from Governments information on State practice, then, after a first reading of the draft articles, it could seek their views on more substantive questions of principle.

72. Ms. ESCARAMEIA said that she knew from her many years' experience as a representative of a small Southern European country in the Sixth Committee that questions regarding specific issues on which comments would be of particular interest to the Commission were of fundamental importance to small- and medium-sized countries because such States lacked the human resources of larger States and were thus unable to prepare general analyses of a topic for presentation in the General Assembly. They could, however, express their opinions during the Sixth Committee's debates by focusing on specific points raised in chapter III of the Commission's report.

73. However, she agreed that the questions in paragraph 2 should be asked at a subsequent stage in the Commission's consideration of the topic. The questions that ought to be put immediately should be of a fundamental nature and designed to permit the establishment of a framework for further work on the topic. It was vital to ascertain State practice in the matter. Indeed, that had been the whole purpose of the questionnaire proposed by the Special Rapporteur. However, if the Commission asked a very general question, only two or three countries would respond and the Commission would not really know what the real opinion of the majority of States was. For that reason it would be a pity to delete questions (*a*), (*b*), (*c*) and (*d*), as they might have yielded very useful information.

74. Although the Commission was a body of experts, it was also a subsidiary organ of the General Assembly. It should not therefore allow a project to move in a direction entirely different to that desired by the Assembly. She had been encouraged by what she had believed to be the Special Rapporteur's plan to investigate whether the intention of the parties constituted a good criterion for distinguishing between different regimes in respect of the effects of armed conflicts on treaties. She failed to understand why a question relating to the relevance of compliance with the provisions of the Charter of the United Nations relating to the use of armed force should be problematic. She would therefore be in favour of retaining all four questions and of adding two more framed in the wording deemed most appropriate by the Commission.

75. The CHAIRPERSON noted that a full account of the discussion of the points on which members' opinions had diverged was faithfully reflected in the summary records, which were available for perusal by the members of the Sixth Committee.

76. Mr. MATHESON agreed entirely with Mr. Pellet's suggestion and said that, while he had no doubt that the questions were quite important and that the Commission would ultimately have to address them, it was premature to put them to Governments at the current stage. In some cases Governments were not yet in a position to understand what the context and alternatives were. Moreover, the Commission would probably resolve some issues and define others more clearly within the coming year. Thus if the Commission sought States' views on the substance of the issues raised when it returned to those points at its next session, the queries would make more sense. What was important at the current stage was to identify State practice.

77. Mr. ECONOMIDES, responding to Mr. Pellet's criticism of the way he had formulated his question, explained that the underlying reason for the wording he had chosen was the fact that the report had completely ignored the Charter and had thus placed aggressor States and States defending their legitimate interests on the same footing. That situation was completely unacceptable in the twenty-first century. He had tried to phrase his question in the clearest and most direct manner possible.

78. He fully agreed with Mr. Pellet that the only issue of central importance was that of State practice. Since the latter was virtually inexistent in many countries, the question should be supplemented with the words "or any other useful information on the subject". He likewise concurred with Mr. Matheson that it was premature to convey the Commission's point of view to the Sixth Committee, since Commission members' opinions were still too divided on the subject. For that reason, questions (*a*) to (*d*) could be deleted.

79. The CHAIRPERSON said he took it that the Commission wished to adopt paragraph 2 as amended by Mr. Pellet and Mr. Economides.

It was so agreed.

Paragraph 2, as amended, was adopted.

Responsibility of international organizations

Paragraph 3

Paragraph 3 was adopted with minor drafting changes.

Expulsion of aliens

Paragraph 4

80. Mr. PELLET drew attention to question (*d*) and asked whether the Commission wished to consider the collective expulsion of aliens in general, or whether it

wished to deal with collective expulsion only in the context of armed conflict. In his opinion, two separate questions ought to be asked: should the Commission deal with collective expulsion of aliens and, if so, ought it also to consider such expulsion in the context of armed conflict?

81. The CHAIRPERSON agreed that it would be wise to reformulate question (*d*) along the lines suggested by Mr. Pellet.

82. Mr. PELLET said that he wondered whether paragraph 4 (*d*) was not even wider in scope and whether the Commission ought to consider all forms of expulsion of aliens during armed conflicts, rather than confining its attention to collective expulsion. It might be wise to have one question asking whether the Commission should also consider the subject of expulsion in the event of armed conflict and to add the question he had formulated earlier as a new question (*e*).

83. The CHAIRPERSON said that the real question was whether, in the event of armed conflict, the rule that had existed in the past—namely that all citizens and nationals of a belligerent State could be expelled—still applied.

84. Mr. PELLET said that the issue to which the Chairperson had referred did arise; however, he had the impression that the Commission was pondering whether it should consider expulsion during an armed conflict in general. That was a query that should be put to the General Assembly. Naturally he believed that the Commission should consider that question, because the problem of expulsion, whether individual or collective, arose mainly in the context of armed conflicts.

85. Ms. ESCARAMEIA said that two issues that had been considered during the debate had been combined in question (*d*). There had been no doubt as to whether or not the Commission should deal with collective expulsion. The discussion had first turned on the matter of whether or not collective expulsion was legal and had then centred on collective expulsion in the context of armed conflict. While those were two separate questions, the first had not been controversial, as all members had agreed that the Commission should deal with collective expulsion. The only controversy had concerned expulsion during an armed conflict.

86. Mr. MATHESON asked whether it would be possible to treat the topic in the same way it had approached the topic of the effects of armed conflicts on treaties. Once again, the Commission had just embarked on its study of the matter; it did not yet know what the scope of the topic would be and it had not defined the issues. He questioned whether it was useful at that preliminary stage to ask the General Assembly a series of detailed questions. He therefore proposed that paragraph 4 should be deleted and that only the request for information contained in paragraph 5 should be retained.

87. Mr. AL-BAHARNA and Mr. CHEE endorsed that proposal.

88. Ms. ESCARAMEIA reiterated the concerns she had expressed with regard to the deletion of questions in paragraph 2.

Paragraph 4 was deleted.

Paragraph 5

89. Mr. PELLET proposed the deletion of the words "through the Secretariat", as member States should be able to provide information by all available channels, including the Sixth Committee.

Paragraph 5, as amended, was adopted.

Unilateral acts of States

Paragraph 6

Paragraph 6 was adopted with some minor editorial changes.

Reservations to treaties

Paragraph 7

Paragraph 7 was adopted.

Chapter III as a whole, as amended, was adopted.

Chapter V. *Effects of armed conflicts on treaties* (*concluded*)* (A/CN.4/L.668)

Paragraphs 5 and 19

90. The CHAIRPERSON drew attention to paragraphs 5 and 19 of document A/CN.4/L.668 and said that the word "questionnaire" in those paragraphs should be replaced with the phrase "a note requesting information".

Paragraphs 5 and 19, as amended, were adopted.

Section B, as amended, was adopted.

Chapter V as a whole, as amended, was adopted.

The report of the International Law Commission on the work of its fifty-seventh session as a whole, as amended, was adopted.

CLOSURE OF THE SESSION

91. After the customary exchange of courtesies, the CHAIRPERSON declared the fifty-seventh session of the International Law Commission closed.

The meeting rose at 12.35 p.m.

* Resumed from the discussion at the 2863rd meeting.